Midwest Studies in Philosophy
Volume VIII

MIDWEST STUDIES IN PHILOSOPHY

EDITED BY PETER A. FRENCH, THEODORE E. UEHLING, JR., HOWARD K. WETTSTEIN

Many papers in MIDWEST STUDIES IN PHILOSOPHY are invited and previously unpublished. The editors will consider unsolicited manuscripts that are received by January of the year preceding the appearance of a volume. All manuscripts must be pertinent to the topic area of the volume for which they are submitted. Address manuscripts to MIDWEST STUDIES IN PHILOSOPHY, University of Minnesota, Morris; Morris, MN 56267, or Trinity University, San Antonio, TX 78284, or University of Notre Dame, Notre Dame, IN 46566.

The articles in MIDWEST STUDIES IN PHILOSOPHY are indexed in THE PHILOS-OPHER'S INDEX.

Forthcoming Volumes

Previously Published Volumes

Midwest Studies
in
Philosophy
Volume
VIII
Contemporary Perspectives
on the
History of Philosophy

Editors
PETER A. FRENCH
Trinity University
THEODORE E. UEHLING, JR.
University of Minnesota, Morris
HOWARD K. WETTSTEIN
*University of Notre Dame
and Stanford University*

University of Minnesota Press • Minneapolis

Published by the University of Minnesota Press,
2037 University Avenue Southeast, Minneapolis, MN 55414
Printed in the United States of America

Library of Congress Cataloging in Publication Data
Main entry under title:

Contemporary perspectives on the history of philosophy.

(Midwest studies in philosophy; v. 8)
1. Philosophy — History — Addresses, essays, lectures.
I. French, Peter A. II. Uehling, Theodore Edward.
III. Wettstein, Howard K. IV. Series.
B73.C66 1983   109   83-5408
ISBN 0-8166-1207-2
ISBN 0-8166-1212-9 (pbk.)

The University of Minnesota
is an equal-opportunity
educator and employer.

This volume is dedicated to
the memory of
MORRIS WEITZ

Midwest Studies in Philosophy
Volume VIII
Contemporary Perspectives
on the History of Philosophy

Midwest Studies in Philosophy
Volume VIII

The First Stage
of the Idea of Mathematics:
Pythagoreans, Plato, Aristotle

PETER H. NIDDITCH

1. INTRODUCTION

1.1. The sense to be carried by the frame 'the idea of' in the title of this paper resembles the sense that frame has in Collingwood's use, in *The Idea of History* (and elsewhere). Collingwood's practice, though with a different terminology, had a long line of precursors, including Whewell's in his *Philosophy of Discovery: Chapters Historical and Critical*. Collingwood painted incisive portraits of a select succession of historical conceptions, i.e., of historiographies of historic moment; but his depictions were not passive replicas, for though he aimed at exhibiting the distinctive traits of his subjects, he vigorously engaged in revealing their deficiencies as perceived from his own perspectival center.

The term 'idea', then, in the frame-phrase 'the idea of', in the context of philosophical history, may be employed for a notion considered extensionally and intensionally in conjunction, or even in combination, in critico-historical chapters (note the order within the epithet): extensionally, in reference to reflective articulations of the notion in question in their historical sequence and connection, and intensionally, in reference to the nature of that notion as conceived and critically utilized by the commentator from his or her own methodical and regulative viewpoint.

1.2. The treatment here of the initial, ancient phase of the idea of mathematics is selective and abbreviative in several ways. (i) It is restricted to so-called pure mathematics (arithmetic, geometry, etc.) and so far as possible disregards mathematical physics and other fields of so-called applied mathematics. Work on the idea of applied mathematics in antiquity would be a different inquiry. (ii) I do not claim to be covering all the features of the mathematical philosophies[1] of the Pythagoreans, Plato, and Aristotle, nor, consequently, do I claim to be providing a fully balanced account of these philosophies. On the other hand, broad notice of their major preoccupations and characteristics is an objective, within the limits of a concise, philosophically motivated consideration. (iii) The themes I air are relatively few, chosen out of a much more varied range of possibilities. I concentrate on issues of certain basic epistemological, logical, and ontological kinds concerning knowledge, truth, and existence, and their organizations.

Greek mathematical philosophy from its beginnings to Aristotle has exerted a great influence and attracted a lively philosophical interest down through the ages; yet, strangely, it has been attended to in an overwhelmingly piecemeal way. Overall scrutinies of it are a rarity, and, so far as I know them, they are largely intruded by rehearsals of the story of early Greek mathematics as such, with the representation of mathematical details hardly, if at all, relevant to philosophical history.[2] At any rate, I confine my synopsis more or less to a straight and narrow philosophical path. In the course of looking at the Hellenic philosophies of mathematics I want to bring out, not merely incidentally, what I see as significant continuity.

1.3. A silhouette of one face of the view regulating my pursuit of the present topic shadows forth the following features.[3]

(a) Mathematics is taken to be in general (arithmetic may be a peculiar exception) a symbolic, ratiocinative, and manifold field of discourse and thought to which there are no fixed conceptual bounds; it is a potential infinity of discursive conceptual structures, many of which themselves involve the nonfinite.

(b) That discourse is regarded as being free throughout from realist and constativist presuppositions and implications concerning knowledge, truth, and existence, and their organizations. It engages with conceptibles, not reals: with conceivable relationships concerning thought-objects (*objectiva in anima*).[4]

(c) All of it, however, is in principle applicable, through interpretations either internal to mathematics itself (e.g., algebra or calculus to geometry) or external to it (e.g., algebra or calculus to physics).

To illustrate (b) plus (c): the calculus is applicable to geometry and to physics, but these facts neither presuppose nor imply any actual existence of numbers, whether the so-called reals or the so-called hyperreals,[5] nor of operations on or relations between them. Of course, I am here not pretending to defend my antirealist and anticonstativist view, but only enunciating it so that the reader can better understand what philosophically motivates my criticisms of the ancients in what follows.

(d) The regions of mathematical discourse are characteristically founded, in logical procedure, on postulates, i.e., axioms or axiomatic definitions; these are devised to be economically capable of coping both with precise resolution of intriguing particular problems and with the need for a synthesis of associated results in a region.

(e) The mathematician's avowal and enunciation of an array of postulates constitutes a postulatory speech act, which is a performative utterance and act. This affords a quite different reason for the absence of truth-value from postulatory assertions than that which is given by a formalist. I concur with the latter in addition with respect to *what* is postulated for some regions of mathematics, e.g., the theory of abstract groups.

(f) A specification of the illocutionary force[6] of a postulatory speech act makes emphatic use of the notions of *demand* and *commitment*: to postulate P is to demand P and to commit oneself to the logical deployment of P in the relevant region. This demand and commitment by a mathematician are motivated by purposes of research and proof that interest him or her as a communicating member of the mathematical community.

2. PYTHAGOREANS

2.1. Aristotle's assertion[7] that the Pythagoreans were the first to advance mathematics is controversial and is much controverted nowadays. Although he did not say it, what could be said more securely about them, as an adjustment of his remark, is that they were the first to advance a philosophy of mathematics. Hence, I begin with them. Some of the other early Greek philosophers—e.g., Anaximander, Parmenides, Zeno, Anaxagoras, and the Atomists—propounded doctrines or arguments that might be interpreted as contributions to a philosophical way of thought about mathematicals, such as infinity, plurality, and magnitude; but it is not apparent that any of the early thinkers besides the Pythagoreans took a systematic philosophical interest in mathematical concepts, proffering an ontological and epistemological theory about mathematicals as a whole.

2.2. The scrappy and, predominantly, secondary (or still further removed) evidence concerning the doctrines of Pythagoras and of Pythagoreans has generated numerous and conflicting assessments and explications swirling in a dark sky filled largely with clouds of unknowing. The scholarly storms and stresses have been especially heavy since the mid-nineteenth century, concurrently with the expanding spirit of philological criticism and of philological self-assurance. I will take it for granted (i) that Aristotle's testimony[8] regarding the Pythagoreans yields reliable information when used cautiously and with discretion; (ii) that the contents of certain doxographical fragments ascribed to Philolaus or to Archytas[9] are an authentic reflection of Pythagorean tenets from ca. 430 B.C. until Plato's time (when I make use of Philolaus fragment 11, commonly deemed to be dubious or spurious,[10] I mention it by name; the arguments against its authenticity have not persuaded me of its unreliability); and (iii) that, on the basis of various other sources,[11] Pythagorean thought and teachings in that period included both some elementary algorithmic number theory, e.g., how to determine the greatest common divisor of two integers, and the recognition of some incommensurable magnitudes, such as the length of the diagonal of a square whose sides have "unit" length.

2.3. Accordingly, the following are among the chief philosophico-mathematical presuppositions or affirmations of the Pythagoreans.

(*a*) Numbers are the fundamental natures, causes,[12] and invariants of all bodies and modes. Unlike any one or more of the sorts of matter entertained by other Pre-Socratics as being the sources of things, the Pythagoreans reckoned that numbers, embodied in patterns, afford a precise, everywhere applicable, and adequate account of individuals of any sort; they implicitly denied that, e.g., water or fire could fulfill this requirement.

(*b*) Whatever is real is countable. As Locke expressed it later for his own part,

"Number applies it self to Men, Angels, Actions, Thoughts, every thing that either doth exist, or can be imagined."[13] For the Pythagoreans, not only was whatever is real countable, it is also gradable. In regard to anything real, a definite numerical degree is involved, even if such definiteness is (somehow) conjoined with indefiniteness. As Plato expressed it later for his own part:

> Our forefathers . . . passed on this tradition, that those things which are from time to time said to be are made up of one and many, with a determinant and indeterminacy inherent in them. Since this is how things are constituted we should always posit a single form in respect to every one and search for it—we shall find one there—and if we are successful, then after the one we should look for two, if there are two, or otherwise for three or whatever number is; each of these ones should be treated in the same way, until one can see of the original one not only that it is one, a plurality, and an indefinite number, but also its precise quantity.[14]

Whether (a) and (b) were clearly distinguished is uncertain; they may have been confounded with one another or, dimly, supposed to be mutually implicative.

(c) The physical world throughout displays orderliness and harmony. (Indeed, astronomical bodies literally produce a musical harmony: "the whole heaven [is] a musical scale and a number," and "the movement of the stars produces harmony, the sounds which they make being in accord."[15]) These properties are the outcome of numerical factors and regularities.

(d) Numbers have no separate existence of their own; they are all numbers of real things. As Mill expressed it later for his own part, "All numbers must be numbers of something; there are no such things as numbers in the abstract."[16]

(e) The integers greater than one are composed of equal and comparable units. Such a (concept of) number is called "mathematical" by Aristotle; in contradistinction to, in particular, the Platonic view according to which each member of the number sequence is a unique Idea composed of units specific to itself, different numbers being uncombinable as are likewise their respective units, "in *mathematical* number no one unit is in any way different from another . . . *mathematical* number is counted thus—after 1, 2 (which consists of another 1 besides the former 1), and 3 (which consists of another 1 besides these two), and the other numbers similarly."[17]

(f) Although the Pythagoreans posited and deployed a theory of "mathematical" numbers in the sense of "mathematical" elucidated in (e), numbers for them did not consist of abstract units but of *monads*—units having spatial magnitude.[18] The Pythagoreans maintained on this basis a *geometrical* arithmetic; by this means they sought to explain the configuration of all things.[19]

(g) Numbers are not a mere plurality, nor are they as a plurality the ultimate principles, for these must be (i) at most very few and (ii) opposites. What underlay their belief centered on (i) is, presumably, the assumption of a certain simplicity at the root of reality. Their belief, in common with many other Greek thinkers, centered on (ii) turned, perhaps, on the assumption, first, that all sorts of things, including numbers, are penetrated by a contrasting diversity in the form of a polar duality and, second, that, on the model of human reproduction, only such a polar duality has generative power. Aristotle reports that the Pythagoreans "consider that number is the principle both as matter for things and as forming both their modifications and their permanent states, and hold that the elements of number are the even and the odd, and that of these the latter is limited, and the former unlimited; and that the One proceeds from both of these (for it is both even and odd), and number from the One."[20] Two polar dualities are adduced here: the limited and the unlimited and the odd and the even. It will be suitable to approach these and their relationship via a consideration of the doctrine that number proceeds from the one, i.e., 1. For the Pythagoreans, the number sequence runs (1), 2, 3, 4, . . . ; 1 is not fully on a par with 2, 3, 4, etc., but is rather their immediate source. These divide into two types, the odd numbers and the even numbers. Members of each type were represented by geometrical patterns, possibly along the following lines for odd and even, respectively:[21]

The odd numbers 3, 5, 7, . . . and the even numbers 2, 4, 6, . . . were regarded as steming from 1 alone: every number is a compound solely of 1s. The notion that 1 is both even and odd might, in a rational reconstruction, have been arrived at and warranted by an application of the rule: If c is the sole elementary constituent of ϕ and of ψs, then c must be ϕ and ψ. This is a sibling of a more familiar causality rule: a property of an effect must be a property of the cause.

In the preceding dot diagrams, the geometrical shape representing the odd numbers as it is expanded remains a square, but the geometrical shape of the diagram representing the even numbers as it is expanded undergoes infinite variation as an oblong (3:2 ≠ 4:3 ≠ 5:4 ≠ . . .). It seems that in some such way the Pythagoreans perceived the odd and the even to be kinds, respectively, of the limited and the unlimited, this pair of opposites comprising their ultimate and most pervasive principle: "Nature in the cosmos was constructed out of unlimited and limiting factors, as was the whole cosmos and all things in it."[22]

(b) The whole of mathematics is, or is reducible to, arithmetic, which concerns primarily the positive integers but also secondarily their ratios. This arithmetic, however, has geometrical aspects.

(i) Certain operations on and relations between arithmetical quantities, e.g., the determination of the greatest common divisor of two integers, can be computed by rule: there are definite constructive numerical procedures (algorithms).

(j) Some magnitudes are irrational, i.e., incapable of reduction to an integer or a ratio of integers; e.g., the length of the diagonal of a square with a side of "unit" length is irrational, and the magnitude of the diagonal's length and that of the side's length are incommensurable.

(*k*) The Pythagoreans developed an arithmological epistemology conformable with their numerical ontology. (Wrongly, many scholars have bypassed or barely glanced at this conception.) From the outset, starting with Pythagoras himself, they laid special emphasis on mathematico-theoretical learning as a vital method for becoming "wise" and free. Thus, Pythagoras was early on described as a "polymath" and as one engaged in scientific inquiry. The Pythagoreans of the fifth century supposed that the natures and causes of things, as mathematical, are within human grasp: they can be exactly thought, understood, and expressed by human beings, though not by all human beings in the ordinary course of life. Exact wisdom, and the spiritual detachment that accompanies it, are attainable only by those who are specially gifted and purified, practicing the requisite detachment: for the Pythagoreans "life is like a festival; just as some come to the festival to compete, some to ply their trade, but the *best* people come as spectators, so in life the slavish men go hunting for fame or gain, the philosophers for the truth."[23] (There is evidently a resonance of this in Plato's *Republic*.) *Proof* in the discipline of mathematics also had a general significance for them.[24]

The epistemological side of the Pythagorean philosophy of mathematics is clearly attested by fragments ascribed to Philolaus;[25] it was a major key for them. "Actually, everything that can be known has a number; for it is impossible to grasp anything with the mind or to recognise it without this [number]"; "it would be impossible for any existing thing to be even recognised by us if there did not exist the basic Being of the things from which the universe was composed, [namely] both the Limiting and the Non-Limited"; and more fully in fr. 11:

> [Without] the power of the decad . . . all things are unlimited, obscure, and indiscernible. For the nature of number is the cause of recognition, able to give guidance and teaching to every man in what is puzzling and unknown. For none of existing things would be clear to anyone, unless there existed number and its essence. But in fact number, fitting all things into the soul through sense-perception, makes them recognisable and comparable with one another . . . .[26]

(*l*) The Pythagoreans matched truth with, and wholly dissociated falsehood from, number. "Falsehood can in no way breathe on number; for falsehood is inimical and hostile to its nature, whereas truth is related to and in close natural union with the race of number" (Philolaus, fr. 11).

2.4. Why did the Pythagoreans produce a philosophy that gives a predominant role to the mathematical? Aristotle, in a sketch of his metaphysical predecessors, asserts that the Pythagoreans' study of mathematics itself was the genetic ground of their philosophical principles. Citing no *reasons* on their behalf, he says that "the so-called Pythagoreans, who were the first to take up mathematics, not only advanced this study, but also *having been brought up in it* they thought its principles were the principles of all things."[27] This version of events is singular in suggesting that the Pythagoreans began their school as mathematicians only and that it was afterward, and solely because mathematics was their frame of intellectual interest, that they turned to philosophizing, in which (he proceeds to elucidate) they fundamentally and universally mathematicized — more precisely, arithmetized — the nature of things. A modern historian, keeping to Aristotle's track but with a modern readiness to use a more flamboyant vocabulary, might put it this way: the Pythagoreans, who at first engaged in the study of mathematics, were carried away by their successes in it and enthusiasm for it into supposing it to be *the* universal science.

Aristotle's *causal* answer to the "why" question is too simple and one-sided. Like smoke, it obscures from view and even chokes off an inquiry into the intended considerations likely to have been compelling in the minds of the Pythagoreans. Evidence of the grounds conceived — maybe no better than partially or blurrily, and far from articulatedly — by the early philosophical thinkers as warranting their respective doctrines is, notoriously, mutilated and scarce. This general shortfall holds also for the Pythagoreans. Nevertheless, some definite and coherent indications survive of what served as rational support for the Pythagoreans' mathematicism.

Three branches of this rational support may be singled out of the historically more ramified complex. First, discoveries, some of them then recent, had been made of the remarkable and exciting applicability of mathematics to natural or manufactured systems/collections/items/modes, e.g., in astronomical predictions, in the correlation of numerical ratios with the principal intervals of the musical scale (a discovery attributed to Pythagoras himself),[28] in the determination of distances by triangulation, and in the exact construction of the Egyptian pyramids. Second, at a more mundane level, there was the widespread recognition, established in the thought, language, and practice of humankind, of quantitative aspects of common things and the knowledge of how to count them or how to calculate some dimension of them. Aristotle, in a part of the *Metaphysics* other than the one cited at the beginning of this section, comes close to acknowledging this broader background to the formation of Pythagoreanism: "Again, the Pythagoreans, *because* they saw many attributes of numbers belonging to sensible bodies, supposed real things to be numbers — not separable numbers, however, but numbers of which real things consist. But why? Because the attributes of numbers are present in a musical scale and in the heavens and in many other things."[29] Third, their cherishing mathematics was rationally self-supporting, for it was the supreme rational science through its proofs.[30]

2.5. The Pythagoreans scored a crucially original success in bringing mathematics into distinct and fundamental intellectual prominence. Other early Greek philosophers concentrated on qualitative conceptions, focusing mostly on certain natural sorts (e.g., water and air) or on abstracts from any natural types (e.g., Anaximander's Infinite and Parmenides' Being) and on quasi-passionate or quasi-intellectual cosmic agencies (e.g., Love or Reason). They did not pursue a positive and systematic reckoning with the numerical or the figured.

Further, mathematical methods had been largely, in Greek states no less than in Mesopotamia and Egypt, motivated by practical needs — agricultural, astronomico-religious, commercial, constructional, geographical, and medical. These methods had lacked any overt degree of theoretical organization or allure; still less had they received any philosophical conceptualization. The Pythagoreans initiated the latter and made considerable contributions to the new development of mathematics as an abstract and liberal, as well as applicable, science. Perhaps, indeed, they were the founders of mathematics as an abstract, liberal science, which is what Proclus attributed to them in the person of Pythagoras: "Pythagoras transformed this study into the form of a liberal education, examining its principles from the beginning and tracking down the theorems immaterially (*aulōs*) and intellectually."[31] Perhaps it was as such founders of "pure mathematics" that Aristotle had them in mind when he remarked, in the historical introduction to the *Metaphysics*, that the Pythagoreans "were the first to take up mathematics"; this possibility is strengthened by the fact that Aristotle's own conception of mathematics was as an abstract, theoretical science.

The intellectual prominence of mathematics that the Pythagoreans originated and promoted survived throughout subsequent antiquity; and even when not under their banner, yet it was under their radiating influence—via Plato and Aristotle[32]—that it increasingly regained that status from the thirteenth century (when it was heralded anew by Roger Bacon)[33] until its full restoration in the seventeenth century and after.

2.6. A solid basis for the Pythagoreans' historic success lay in their idea of the pervasively mathematical character of reality; through this idea they rough-hewed the foundation stone of the later towering achievements of mathematical physics/astronomy. Correspondingly, they pioneered the powerful methodological policy according to which one understands a species or a rhythm of fact if, and only if, one grasps it in appropriate quantitative terms. The seed of their mathematicism developed in its maturity into a threefold faith "justified" by many works. The first strand of the faith is that mathematics's vitality depends on its renewing itself by seeking an ever more comprehensive description of nature in mathematical terms, thereby drawing on the inherently mathematical sources of nature and that in the absence of such physical contacts mathematics degenerates into idle symbolism. The second is that the adequate and clear expression of physical conceptions requires the use of appropriate mathematical language, with its precision and abstractness and with its ratiocinative—and so precisely predictive—power. The third strand is that physical conceptions, when formulated in an appropriate mathematical way, exhibit a beautiful economy matching nature's own.

2.7. Unlike some of the Pythagoreans' other teaching, e.g., that on the transmigration of souls, their philosophemes regarding numbers were no frenzied folly and no crude relic of animistic or contagious-magical modes of thought. On the contrary: they made a decided intellectual advance and became the ancestors of many gifted intellectual offspring. Those philosophemes were not wholly sweetness and light, however. Besides having various other deficiencies and defects, the mathematical philosophy of the Pythagoreans has a disturbing vagary at its metaphysical core, just where it might seem, to an antirealist concerning abstract objects, to be solid and stable. This vagary occurs at the place—the central fire[34] of the system—where the Pythagoreans posited the inherence of numbers in things; the vapors of this realism concerning mathematical objects were inhaled and assimilated by the mathematical philosophies of Plato and Aristotle.

2.8. Most of the Pythagoreans' doctrines are lacking in clear and distinct ideas and in clear and distinct logical concatenation. Consider, for example, their proposition that numbers are the fundamental natures and causes of the bodies and modes in the cosmos. The Pythagorean adoption of mathematical-type notions and standards by reason of their exactitude and plenitude is markedly at odds with their proposition's vagueness and inadequacy. *How* numbers are responsible for the *properties* of bodies (e.g., their mass, texture, color) and for such modes as justice, reason, and opportunity (examples cited by Aristotle) is left obscure (see p. 14 below, however). This obscurity also surrounds the way in which numbers were thought to be responsible for *change*, including motion and animate development. The Pythagorean analysis of bodies into geometrico-arithmetical figures does not by itself have the capacity to explain change and nonextensional properties, and the invocation of geometrico-arithmetical *transformations* of one figure into another, as a kind of quantitative stereochemistry, brings with it the objection that it requires *principles* of transformation and that these principles must lie beyond the static — because purely mathematical — concepts of their ontology.

Aristotle goes further in criticizing the Pythagorean assertion that bodies are composed of numbers. In his characteristically concise and adversative style he says:

> [T]hat bodies should be composed of numbers, and that this should be mathematical number, is impossible. For it is not true to speak of indivisible spatial magnitudes; and however much there might be magnitudes of this sort, units at least have not magnitude; and how can a magnitude be composed of indivisibles? But mathematical number, at least, consists of abstract units, while these thinkers identify number with real things; at any rate they apply their propositions to bodies as if they consisted of those numbers.[35]

Aristotle here is pinpointing two objections: first, that bodies essentially possess spatial magnitude, which cannot be accounted for on the basis of numerical units, for these have no magnitude; second, that there is a categorial confusion in the Pythagoreans' identifying mathematical numbers, which are essentially abstract, with physical realities as such.

As already indicated, the Pythagoreans did not suppose number to be the absolutely fundamental ontological source of the quantitative; it stemmed from two "principles" or "elements,"[36] each consisting of a pair of contraries, namely, the limit and the unlimited, and the odd and the even. It is the principle constituted by the limit and the unlimit that is the absolutely fundamental ontological source of the quantitative, and of number specifically. Now, the sequence (1), 2, 3, 4, . . . ,[37] which was recognized by the Pythagoreans, is an infinite sequence; it is a case, perhaps the paradigm case, of the effect of the unlimited. Concurrently, each item in that infinite sequence is finite; this is a case, perhaps the paradigm case, of the effect of the limit. The principle of the limit and the unlimited is, however, an unsatisfactory way of accounting for the infinite sequence of positive integers, because it cannot by itself determine the actual progression, which is in terms of a unit increase at each step after the initial one. In other words, the law governing that sequence is not covered, or at any rate is not precisely covered, by the principle of the limit and the unlimited.[38] An analogous defect occurs in the Pythagoreans' notion of the odd and the even as the "elements" of number, i.e., of 2, 3, 4, etc.; because although, obviously, the items in this sequence are odd or even, exclusively and exhaustively, the mentioned notion cannot by itself account for the *alternation* of odd and even numbers or for the successive unit increases in the actual progression. What is missing is the logical equivalent of: $2 = 1 + 1$, $3 = 2 + 1$; $4 = 3 + 1$; etc.

2.9. I will say a little about three further coordinates of the Pythagorean position before I recur to what I called the "disturbing vagary at its metaphysical core."

First, with respect to the thesis that "the movement of the stars produces harmony, the sounds which they make being in accord" cited in 2.3(c): this, taken prosaically, has long since been found empirically wanting. Critics from antiquity onward have noted the absence of relevant evidence supporting the claim, e.g., the fact (conceded by the Pythagoreans) that one does not hear any musical sounds attributable to celestial causes (this unawareness they ingeniously explained as being due to the continuous presence of the sound, with no contrasting silence); and they have noted observational facts incompatible with the Pythagorean astronomy or musical theory.[39] Therefore, in the prosaic sense the claim is a fantasy (not to say, Fantasia). Doubtless it is more precious when interpreted figuratively, but this lies beyond my present province.

Second, with respect to the tenet that arithmetic, in geometrical form, is the reduction base of mathematics. This tenet is implied by the overt Pythagorean ideas about number. If their tenet were correct, all affirmations in mathematics should be reducible to affirmations in their arithmetic. Stretching the sense of "their arithmetic" as generously and sympathetically as possible, it still turns out that almost all mathematics is irreducible to theirs; this applies not only to later developments, e.g., in algebra and analysis, but also to already existing mathematical results. The concepts of elementary plane geometry, as established in the fourth and fifth centuries B.C., are irreducible to ones in Pythagorean arithmetic; 'angle' and 'area' are examples. According to tradition, the Pythagoreans themselves were discomforted by the realization that their kind of arithmetic could not cope with irrational magnitudes, whose "existence" had recently been discovered—ironically, by one of their own members:[40] thus, the square root of 2 cannot be expressed in terms of a regular and "rational" pattern of positive whole numbers in an exact and terminating way, so that here the limit and harmony are overruled by the unlimited and disorder.

Third, with respect to the Pythagorean (or, at least, Philolausian) theory of knowledge: the theory's insistence on number being the cause of all grasp, perception, recognition, distinction, and comparison is understandable, given their numerical ontology whereby the characters, structure, and stability of things are a function of embodied number; but the dubiousness of this ontology proportionately threatens the tenability of their epistemology. Besides, the very plurality of cognitive terms used by them prompts an additional critical reflection: they failed to provide a philosophy of mind, conformable with their numerical ontology, that signals how the cognitive states and processes between which they discriminated are possible and have their distinctive natures.

2.10. The Pythagoreans' naturalistic conception[41] of mathematical entities and truths is unsatisfactory for the following reasons, among others. (i) Their conception would make mathematics a natural science, such as physics; whereas mathematics, including arithmetic, is not an empirical science, either in its subject matter or in its method of determining its assertibles. Patently, mathematical entities and mathematical "facts," in general (I leave aside the Pythagorean doctrine of monads in order to avoid begging the question), e.g., in algebra, analysis, and topology, are not given to us through sense perception; and the mathematician's demonstrations stand or fall not by reference to the outcome of empirical verification/falsification, but by reference to his postulates and the rules of a deductive logic. The Pythagoreans' treatment of mathematics as physics is the naive origin of the persistent view of mathematics as a body of "truths." (ii) Their conception counterproductively debars the imaginative construction and pursuit of abstract types of possibility in mathematics; yet, it is this imagination that seeds the harvest of mathematics. (iii) The Pythagoreans' view would require that the mathematician's use of language be descriptive/constative; on the contrary, his use, in general, is nondescriptive/nonconstative, for typically his language is symbolical, geared to an abstract type of possibility rather than to depicting a definite actuality. (iv) Their conception does not make clear, if indeed it allows at all, a distinction, which it is important to be able to make firmly, between, e.g., *the* number 10 and this or that particular cluster of ten things. By the Pythagoreans' ontology, "the number 10" can hardly be other than a(ny) decadal case. (For them, "the number 10 is thought to be perfect and to comprise the whole nature of numbers":[42] $10 = 1 + 2 + 3 + 4$.) (v) Although the Pythagoreans recognized the significance of proof in mathematics, they contributed little, if anything, to the theory of proof; and the "a priori" status of mathematical assertibles was not within their grasp. It was the Academy and the Lyceum that first philosophically deliberated on and articulated a methodology of mathematics.

3. PLATO

3.1. "Let us not fail to notice, however, that there is a difference between arguments from and those to the first principles. For Plato, too, was right in raising this question and asking, as he used to do, 'are we on the way from or to the first principles?' "[43] Plato's mathematical philosophy is an *ascent to* the first principles: to the first principles of mathematics, and, cognately, of everything. Plato's clambering climb to the first principles in his mathematical philosophy tallies, in its direction, with Russell's characterization of mathematical philosophy.

> The more familiar direction [in the study of mathematics] is constructive, towards gradually increasing complexity: from integers to fractions, real numbers, complex numbers; from addition and multiplication to differentiation and integration, and on to higher mathematics. The other direction, which is less familiar, proceeds, by analysing, to greater and greater abstractness and

logical simplicity; instead of asking what can be defined and deduced from what is assumed to begin with, we ask instead what more general ideas and principles can be found, in terms of which what was our starting-point can be defined or deduced. It is the fact of pursuing this opposite direction that characterises mathematical philosophy as opposed to ordinary mathematics.[44]

There is, nonetheless, a difference between Russell and Plato in this connection, which the common term 'principles' obfuscates. Stated simply it is this: Plato's mathematical philosophy is wider than Russell's constitutive characterization, inasmuch as it, unlike Russell's, includes a broad epistemological concern.

3.2. Before I turn to an outline of some of the leading topics of Plato's mathematical philosophy, I should draw attention to two of its traits. Each is a tension, or a self-conflict. And each is already apparent in Pythagoreanism. On the one hand, the Pythagoreans wanted to pinpoint the arithmetical constitution of bodies and modes, to show how, in a definite, physical way, a body or mode is actually "nothing but" a figured arrangement. This makes their mathematicism as concrete as possible: a body or mode *is* a complex of monads. On the other hand, the Pythagoreans were concerned about emphasizing the mathematical structures and regularities of things, rather than about claiming the identity (without any remainder) of the things with those mathematical aspects. Thus, they did not (I think) hold that musical concords are nothing but such and such numerical ratios, still less that the concords *are* series of monads; their conviction was that underlying the concords, acknowledged as sounds, lay definite mathematical structures and regularities. Take another example: justice. It is probable that the Pythagoreans numbered justice as four; they did so, perhaps, because justice was regarded as involving two parties and the proportionate distribution of two parts between them.[45] But this is not an identification of justice with four, either monadically or by way of maintaining that four and justice are identical; their idea was that justice has a four-term structure. Similarly, there is a tension, or a self-conflict, in Plato's mathematical philosophy, especially (but not only) in his Unwritten Doctrine that the Ideas are numbers.[46] This doctrine runs in two directions, one of these being toward the sheer identification of the Ideas with — as nothing but — numbers, while the other direction is toward a number-type basis of the structures and regularities of the Ideas.

The other tension, or self-conflict, common to Pythagorean and Platonic mathematical philosophy concerns the scope of the One. Trends toward dualism and infinitistic pluralism are quite marked in Pythagoreanism, which tended also to maximize the role of the One: "The One is the beginning of everything," "Harmony is a *Unity* of many mixed (elements), and an agreement between disagreeing (elements)."[47] Similarly, Plato was continually driven from pillar to post as between one and many. Each property and kind of the changing, sensible things amidst which we live and move, have, actually or potentially, many instances among these things (ourselves included); he found it necessary to posit an Idea, as the appropriate unity, accounting for each such instantial multiplicity of property or kind.[48] Nevertheless, Plato's quest for unity of this Ideal sort is, in his Dialogues, constrained and qualified by his equal acceptance of the plurality of the Ideal sorts: there are really irreducible differences; and, consequently, the Ideal, intelligible realm cannot be assimilated without comprehending the relationships of its different members. This issue is tackled in, e.g., *Republic* (in connection with the Idea of the Good), *Phaedrus*, and *Sophist*. His reality becomes layered. The study of what the scholastics called "transcendental" terms, viz., 'being', 'thing', 'something', 'one', 'true', and 'good',[49] was thus initiated. In seeking to determine the colligations and separations, the classifications and divisions, of Ideas, Plato found himself in difficulties with the status of One. He was disposed, and he was opposed, to a Parmenidean position, in the sense of the adoption of the absolute ontological primacy of the One. He may well have sensed the need for an ultimate, all-embracing unity of reality. Also, oneness is the most basic transcendental, if only because the transcendentals and the Ideas are each of them one,[50] as he supposed; whereas nothing else had for him that basic universal applicability. This disposition led him, in his Unwritten Doctrines, to allot a unique status to the One as the principle/origin of being. At the same time, he was steadily opposed to a Parmenidean position. Despite the attractiveness of a single principle/origin of reality, his reality is not uniform but inherently differentiated and layered: he is a thoroughgoing Ideal pluralist, who argued in the *Parmenides* that the One is not completely self-subsistent/coherent;[51] and he is a pluralist concerning numbers. Plato's ambivalence concerning the One ran deep (and it ran long, through Neoplatonism and beyond), and the crosscurrent was not (I think) caused at all by his failure to discriminate the different connotations of the term 'one'. (The term 'the one' (*to hen*) "can mean (1) Unity or Oneness in general; (2) the unity of anything that has unity or is one thing; (3) that which has unity, anything that is one; (4) the one thing we are speaking of, as opposed to 'other ones,' and so on."[52])

3.3. At first, and even at second, sight, Plato's Dialogues give expression to a somewhat changing mathematical philosophy, which, however, in none of its phases, appears to be the same as the mathematical philosophy of his Unwritten Doctrines. It therefore has to be considered in a doubly divided way, one division attending to differences within the Dialogues, the other to differences between the Dialogues and the Unwritten Doctrines evidence. Despite the various differences, what is usually taken for granted as most characteristic of Platonism is indeed prevalent throughout all that is known of Plato's thought in the philosophy of mathematics: his realist and constativist assumptions about mathematics and mathematicals.

Some commentators have held that Plato adhered to the Unwritten Doctrines, with its arithmetization of the Ideas, as a programmatic project and/or an esoteric theory concurrently with his production of at least the middle, as well as the later, Dialogues.[53] This is contrary to the usual view (with which I am inclined to agree) that the Unwritten Doctrines belong to Plato's older age only, say from his sixties. Interesting as the question of choice between these two hypotheses is, I will here proceed in neutral detachment from both of them, in the absence of decisive enough reasons for choosing either. That I begin next with the Dialogues on their own, before discussing the Unwritten Doctrines, is to be taken as a procedural order, with procedural precedence to the philosopher's own writings.

3.4. Although the Dialogues I will consider expressly are not the only ones, they include most of the most important, for studying Plato's philosophy of mathematics; they date from the earlier part of the middle, to the final, period of his production as an author.[54] In accordance with this chronology, I begin with *Meno*, whose bearing on the philosophy of mathematics is exceptional among the Dialogues in being almost exclusively epistemological and methodological.

(*a*) *Recollection*. A slave-boy—a prototype of ignorance—comes to recognize, through questions but (supposedly) without any information being conveyed to him by (the character) Socrates, what the correct answer is to the problem: Given a square each of whose sides is two feet long, what is the length of each side of a square having twice the area of the given square? (Answer: the length of the diagonal of the given square.) The process and success of the boy's discovery is proffered as illustration and confirmation of the prior suggestion that Socrates had heard from priests and priestesses and from many divinely inspired poets that the human soul is immortal and undergoes reincarnations and so it "has seen all things both here and in the other world, [and] has learned everything that is."[55] Sliding down the rainbow of Plato's rhetoric to a plainer level of discourse, one may say that Plato was projecting the notion that the attainment of conscious mathematical—more generally, a priori—knowledge is explicable only on the basis of direct learning previously. The person must have latently possessed the relevant knowledge; his excogitation in response to suitable questioning resuscitates that latent knowledge into consciousness. His latent possession originated in an acquaintance, in a preceding state of life, with whatever is involved in that knowledge.

Thus Plato, at a stroke, brought some major epistemological problems to the fore about the nature and genesis of a priori and, specifically, of mathematical knowledge. Unfortunately, the answers hovering on the surface of *Meno* are feeble fledglings that cannot get off the ground. What Plato tells us is itself, on the one hand, very problematical about soul and immortality and reincarnation, etc., and, on the other hand, very vague about "seen" and "all things" and "the other world" when he says of the soul that it "has seen all things both here and in the other world." He has failed to indicate the nature of the things relevant to the slave-boy's regained geometrical knowledge, e.g., whether they are objects or facts, and of what sorts. Nor has Plato catered for the evident difficulty that the slave-boy, at the terminus of the inquiry, has apparently no remembrance of the occasion or acquaintance originating his knowledge.[56]

Lurking inchoately at the back of Plato's mind was the presumption, powerful in the rationalist breed of philosophies, that what is knowable and what is necessarily[57] or essentially the case coincide. Something like this presumption motivated and afforded warrant for his epistemological optimism, although it came to be modified later when Plato conjoined with it a sharply hierarchical view of humankind, whereby only a select number of people have the firm[58] native ability to gain an intelligence of truth and reality.

(*b*) *Characteristics of mathematical knowledge*. Plato presupposed that mathematics is a matter of strict knowledge. All strict knowledge, for him, involves what exists eternally and independently of us; in later Dialogues, he held that whatever is known is abstract (*noētos*, "intellectual," i.e., "falling within the province of" *nous*, was how he later expressed this status). In *Meno* he emphasized what is characteristic of strict knowledge in contrasting this with "true" or "right" opinions. "[I]t is not, I am sure, a mere guess to say that right opinion and knowledge are different. There are few things that I should claim to know, but that at least is among them, whatever else is."[59] What is the difference? True opinions

> run away from a man's mind, so they are not worth much until you *tether* them by working out the reason [*aitias logismō*]. This process, my dear Meno, is recollection. . . . Once they are tied down, they become knowledge, and are stable. . . . What distinguishes one from the other is the *tether* [*desmos*].[60]

According to a stock modern analysis or defining set of conditions, "*A* knows that *p*" means (i) *A* believes that *p*, (ii) *A* can "justify" his belief, and (iii) *p* is true. This modern definition, making 'knowledge' equal 'justified true belief,' is similar to Plato's conception, whereby knowledge is true belief (or opinion) topped up by a justification, "the tether." One might extrapolate from his remarks and infer that, thinking of mathematical knowledge, he took the tether to be like a mathematical demonstration and that what he called "working out the reason," i.e., the excogitation of a rationale, was at least analogus to the mathematician's requirement and practice of a rationally demonstrative procedure in support of affirmed theorems. I would add that Plato, in assuming the truth condition for mathematical as for other knowledge, did not begin to discriminate between mathematical and any other sort of truth; for him, mathematical truth and its reality are on a par with all other truth and reality. Like the rest of the Greeks, Plato had no notion of mathematics as the disciplined exploration of *imaginative* possibilities or schemata. Mathematics was for him essentially "realistic," much as his conception of art was mimetic.

(*c*) *Ideas?* An insistent doctrine of the middle Dialogues in general is that the things known are ontologically altogether different from and superior to the things believed or opined: the objects of knowledge are Ideal realities, whereas the objects of belief or opinion are changeful vanities. In *Meno*, on the contrary, the different veridical cognitive states are not correlated with different objects; those states are differentiated only by virtue of the presence or absence of "the tether." This fits in with the fact that the Dialogue never mentions the term 'Idea' and says nothing implying the theory of Ideas. This is not to deny that, being wise after the event, one can discern a few green shoots from which the nascent theory will bud forth. Those[61] who have found the theory of Ideas in *Meno* have read the theory into it by working backward from *Phaedo* and *Phaedrus*, where the doctrine of recollection is indeed linked explicitly to an ontology of transcendent Ideas. Unlike these and other Dialogues written after *Meno*, in this Dialogue the objects of cognition are, it seems, unconfinedly heterogeneous, within "this world" and "the realm of Hades"; not until later did Plato ascribe a purely celestial[62] location for the knowable—the Ideas. In *Meno*, then, Plato left undetermined and unrestricted the ontological status of cognitive objects, including those of mathematics.

(*d*) *System*. He contributed to the furtherance of the notion, which he perhaps borrowed from and surely thought applicable to mathematics, that knowledge is systematically interconnected. "[W]hen a man has recalled a single piece of knowledge . . . there is no reason why he should not find out all the rest . . . ."[63] This obviously has specially forceful relevance to mathematical knowledge, whose ingredient theses in this or that setup are organized maximally under logical conditions and constraints. (I use the term 'theses' to designate axioms and theorems of a deductive system.[64]) Plato's was an incipient epistemological step toward the development of a methodology of axiomatic mathematics.

(*e*) *Hypotheses*. Many gallons of scholarly ink have been used up in controversy over the precise meaning of the passage in *Meno* that cites an example of geometers' use of "hypothesis" and proceeds to investigate the ethical problem in hand (viz., Is virtue teachable?) by an appropriate hypothesis (viz., Virtue is knowledge), used presumably in a way parallel to the geometrical one. Plato subjected geometers' reasoning and their use of hypotheses to a very serious critique in *Republic* (see pp. 21–22 below); to understand and assess this critique requires a grasp of what he meant there by the term 'hypothesis'. If its sense in *Meno* were about the same as it is in *Republic* or if geometers' use of hypothesis were the topic of separate philosophical comment in *Meno*, then I should need to dwell on the mentioned passage. But they are not and so I do not. Two clarifications are nonetheless called for. First, the geometrical problem in the *Meno* passage is (disregarding alternative interpretations), "whether it is possible for [a given] area to be inscribed as a triangle in a given circle"; the hypothesis, stated very obscurely, is, however, plainly ad hoc; it is not a postulate fixedly adopted and available for a whole body of geometry. Second, the hypothesis has the form: if such and such conditions are satisfied, then the result is so and so; while, if they are not, "the result is different."[65] Plato's standpoint in the *Republic*, where, in his high dialectical mood, he contended that mathematicians cannot attain consummate knowledge of ultimate reality, would have made him judge that geometrical hypothesis wanting, with its pervasive conditionality: he was there aiming at warrantably unconditioned knowledge.

3.5. *Phaedo* is the middle Dialogue in which Plato gave the theory of Ideas its first trenchant and rounded expression. The theory comprised both an ontology of *what is*, as eternal universals, paradigms, and prime causes; and an epistemology of these entities, deemed to be the sole (and the soul's) "truth," accessible only to pure thought (although the latter processes may, in some matters, be initially prompted by the senses[66]).

In this setting, various arithmetical notions are explained.[67] (i) Plato referred to the whole positive integer series. He switched back and forth, sometimes in a few lines, between number terms and Idea-of-number terms, e.g., from "threeness"/"Idea of three" to "three" and reversely; I surmise that this arose from his taking it for granted that his doctrine of Ideas as applied to numbers would be immediately read into his simpler phraseology, in a context containing the slightly more elaborate Ideas phraseology concerning numbers. He specifically mentioned the Ideas of 1, 2, 3, and 5. He probably meant to convey, then, not only that there are Ideas of all the positive integers, but also that all these integers are Ideas. (ii) He mentioned certain positive fractions, e.g., ½; but he did not intimate how he conceived of their ontological status, particularly in relation to Ideas of integers. (iii) He recognized overtly that, for example, in addition a plurality of the same number may be dealt with, e.g., in adding two 1s; he did not elucidate how, despite the uniqueness of each Idea, this is possible. (iv) He remarked the distinction between identity and partitive attribution; "3 is odd" is true as a partitive attribution but false as an identity. (v) The Ideas of the odd and the even are cited. He declared them to be opposites but pointed out that this relationship does not imply that cases of them are opposites, although such cases do exclude the relevantly opposite attribute; e.g., 2 and 3 are not opposites, yet 2 excludes the odd and 3 excludes the even.

Equality is a fundamental concept in and for mathematics. Plato treated it at some length in *Phaedo* as a general relation.[68] He argued that there is an Idea of equality: for when we think, in sense-experience, of one item being equal to another, e.g., a log to a log, we have to acknowledge that the apparent equalities are variable, relative, and deficient, not holding, utterly, permanently, and under all conditions; hence, we must, implicitly, be cognizant and make use of the paradigmatic Idea of equality. Further, since this paradigmatic notion cannot have been learned in this life, our present knowledge of equality must have come by recollection from a prebirth state of the soul. Similarly, we knew before birth into this life all the other Ideas, of the larger, the smaller, the just, the beautiful, etc.—and of one(ness), two(ness), and so on.[69]

Of course, a modern critic is liable to be repelled by what will strike him as Plato's naivety in invoking reincarnation and recollection to explain our possession and use of certain concepts and to presuppose, contrary to Plato, that humankind has a lively capacity for the original formation and the adaptive use of such concepts in the ordinary course of mortal life. And he is liable to be disappointed by what will strike him as the verbal and vacuous elucidation of mathematical notions by the theory of Ideas: according to the theory, (i) one must not say "that ten is greater than eight by two, and that this is the reason for its exceeding" but rather "that it's by numerousness, and because of numerousness"—which cannot explain the specific differences between, say, ten and eight, and ten and seven; and (ii) one must not say "that when one is added to one, the addition is the reason for their coming to be two . . . ; you [must] own no other reason for their coming to be two, save participation in twoness."[70] It looks as though Plato in this part of his garden has planted the flower beds with weeds.

3.6. *Republic* is the climactic Dialogue of Plato's middle period; it brought together and developed in a fresh perspective more or less all the themes of its predecessors. Its curving paths intersect many topics of mathematical philosophy. I will comment on three of the most important intersections.

(a) *Mathematics and Truth*. Plato used a concept of propositional truth and attached value to such truth.[71] But his explication of it, so far as he gave one, was in terms of the theory of—nonpropositional—Ideas. He conceived of truth principally as the totality of the "intelligible" entities that eternally are and that are the objects of our knowledge through pure thought.

We must accept as agreed this trait of the philosophical nature, that it is ever enamoured of the kind of knowledge which reveals to them something of that essence which is eternal, and is not wandering between the two poles of generation and decay. And, further, that their desire is for the whole of it. . . .

[Arithmetic] really seems to be indispensible for us, since it plainly compels the soul to employ pure thought with a view to *truth* itself.

What we have to consider is whether the greater and more advanced part of [mathematics] tends to facilitate the apprehension of the idea of good. That tendency, we affirm, is to be found in all studies that force the soul to turn its vision round to the region where dwells the most blessed part of reality . . . to contemplate essence.

[T]he real object of the entire study [sc. of geometry] is pure knowledge . . . [i.e.] the knowledge of that which always is. . . . Then, my good friend, it would tend to draw the soul to *truth*, and would be productive of a philosophic attitude of mind.[72]

Plato, then, viewed truth and knowledge as principally objectual. Mathematical truth and knowledge, correspondingly, were in the main geared by him to the Ideas. So far as he regarded those as being propositional, it was in a subsidiary way, and he did not investigate or state how the propositional is related to and, especially, founded on the objectual. This relative lack of interest in the propositional aspects stemmed from his reliance on an intellectual-visual model of reality and knowledge/understanding; thus, significantly, the highest philosophical activity—that of the dialectician —is *synoptical*.[73] In the event, he mistook the importance, scope, and role of the evident in mathematics; and his lofty metaphysical orientation resulted in his misinterpreting the character of specifically mathematical "truth."

(b) *Mathematicals: Ideas or Intermediates?* Aristotle tells us[74] that besides sensible things and Ideas, Plato says that there are the mathematicals (*ta mathēmatika*, "the objects of mathematics"); they are between (*metaxu*) those two, being different from Ideas in that each Idea is unique whereas each mathematical is plural and different from sensible things in that the mathematicals are eternal and unchangeable while (it is implied) sensible things are neither. Some scholars[75] have espied this Platonic doctrine in *Republic*. Their interpretation is an erroneous inference from two undeniable data. In one place in this Dialogue mention is made of units (in the plural) in "the numbers themselves," i.e., the Ideas of numbers; these units are spoken of as being absolutely equal and indivisible, in contrast with sensible unit(ie)s that are inherently diverse and divisible.[76] So, the interpreter's reasoning runs, Plato must have intended these ideal but plural units to occupy an intermediate position between the ideal and unique entities that are the Ideas and the plural entities that are sensible and similarly in respect of all other types of mathematical entity. There is a flimsy basis here for attributing this doctrine to Plato's "intention." The argument assumes that Plato realized an important distinction that he did not state, viz., between an Idea and an intelligible, ideal non-Idea, or that, if he did not realize it,

this distinction has to be drawn and applied unless he is to be convicted of inco-
herence/inconsistency. I discern too little evidence for the former of these alternatives. And the conclusion of the argument seems to me excessively generalized,
jumping from units to all types of mathematical entity. The second undeniable
datum is that Plato in *Republic* marked a difference between the mathematician's
intellection (*dianoia*) and that of the dialectician (*nous* or *noēsis*), and that he maintained that the mathematician's is intermediate (*metaxu*) between the dialectician's,
on the one hand, and belief related to the sensible, changeful world, on the other
hand.[77] In the light of Plato's analogies between ontic strata and cognitive grades,
the interpreter infers that for Plato the objects of mathematical cognition must be
intermediate between the objects of dialectical cognition and the objects of belief.
The fallacy committed in reaching this conclusion comes from assuming that Plato's
analogies are, first, to be taken to the foot of the letter and, second, to be given
more weight than Plato's own clear indications contrary to the conclusion, in particular that the objects of mathematical cognition are not intermediates but Ideas;
e.g., numbers, the square, and the diagonal are referred to in terms of Ideas.[78]

Besides and beyond his appeal to the odd bit of text, the 'intermediates' proponent has two connected reasons to advance. One is that the Ideas are paradigmatic
properties and not ideal things possessing such properties; e.g., circularity, square-
ness, and twoness and not the circle, the square, and the number two. But mathematics is about these things and not about the properties. Therefore, mathematicals
cannot be Ideas; of course, they are not sensibles either—they are between (*metaxu*)
the two strata. The other reason is that theses or proofs in mathematics often refer
to a plurality of mathematical entities of a single kind; '4 × 3 = 12' invokes a plur-
rality of 3s (and of 1s), a theorem about congruent triangles invokes a plurality of
triangles, and so on. However, although these may be good reasons for what Plato
ought to have claimed in *Republic*, the text shows no evidence that he wished to
claim in it the intermediate status of mathematicals—on the contrary. This verdict
does not debar that, especially, the second of these reasons may have influenced
Plato toward embracing the intermediate doctrine in his oral teaching.

(*c*) *A Twofold Critique of Mathematics*. Plato's commendation of mathematics
as propaedeutic to the philosophical encounter with truth/reality has been reported
in (*a*) above. Nevertheless, he went on, in a crucial passage of *Republic*, to fault and
delimit the mathematician's quest for knowledge on two grounds. The mathematician poses his postulates as though they were absolute, when they are as knowledge
still unjustified assumptions, the justification necessitating an ascent above the confined pediment of mathematics. The second criticism is that the mathematician, in-
escapably, proceeds by using sensible models; thus, the geometer uses diagrams or
solid figures and the arithmetician uses "numbers attached to visible and tangible
bodies."[79] For Plato, then, the mathematician's method to science is doubly defective.
What prevents its practitioner from attaining complete knowledge of truth/reality is
that the methodical constitution of mathematics is not properly supported or ori-
entated. Even though the mathematician's mind is on the exemplary Ideas, he or
she keeps standing on the soil of sensible things.

Plato's attitude toward the mathematician was that the latter's knowledge is not self-supporting and cannot be left hanging in the air; nor can it be suitably grounded on empirical insights, for these are altogether too weak and unsteady a basis. Further, Plato rejected the conception of mathematics as simply the working out *consistently* (*homologoumenōs*) of its supposedly *evident* postulates ("hypotheses,"[80] i.e., axioms or axiomatic definitions); the alleged obviousness of the postulates (including that of the very existence of their subject matter) and of the immanent logic of the mathematician was unsatisfactory, philosophically speaking, because it relied on mere presumption or on sensible prompting and guidance. Plato insisted that mathematical knowledge required apposite vindication; for him that meant a complete ascent and descent, using Dialectic, through the realm of the impersonal Ideas, with all hypotheses being surmounted at the summit of the ascent when the thinker "by thought itself" apprehends "the starting-point of all," viz., "the nature of the good itself," which is the supreme "confirmation."[81] Plato's objectually realist, and his constativist-veridicalist, presuppositions led him away and astray from the consistency conception of mathematics into the Dialectical labyrinth of his own making, where he was swallowed up by the Minotaur of his ambitious obscurity.

A continual factor of this obscurity was his failure to distinguish between the objectual and the propositional, to employ appropriately and clearly each of the two sides of this distinction, and to indicate how they are interrelated. He occasionally dropped hints of the relevance of the propositional: the mathematicians are only "dreaming about being, but the clear waking vision of it is impossible for them as long as they leave the assumptions which they employ undisturbed and cannot give any *account* (*logos*) of them."[82] But since he demanded that the account should be in terms of the Ideas, especially of the "starting-point" (*archē*) of all" that is the (nature of the) Idea of the good, it is hard to discern in *Republic* a coherent explanation of the foundations of mathematical knowledge.

3.7. *Philebus* illustrates the continuing importance, into his later period, that Plato attached to mathematical matters, partly the influence of Pythagoreanism, as in its deployment of the notion of the limit and the unlimited (cf. p. 6 above).[83] In this Dialogue Plato drew, and followed up for epistemological and other purposes, a contrast between two kinds of arithmetic (and likewise of other branches of mathematics), viz., the "popular" and the "philosophical"; in the former one calculates with unequal units, e.g., two armies or two oxen (each of which may be of different size), whereas the philosophical arithmeticians proceed "on the postulate that none of the myriad units under discussion is in any way different from any of the others" —and analogously in regard to, e.g., practical mensuration versus philosophical geometry. Philosophical mathematics is superior to the popular most notably in its "precision."[84] Plato graded the ordinary arts and sciences according to their degree of such precision. He ranked Dialectic, though, even higher than philosophical mathematics, for it alone being "concerned with the final truth [to on], the real nature of things and unchanging reality is the most genuine [*alēthestatos*] knowledge"; it has "as its province the clearest, most precise, and true [*alēthestatos*] subject-matter," on which thought and intelligence are engaged.[85] This Dialogue tells us (i) that mathematical objects and truths are "intelligible," objective, unchangingly existent, and exact; (ii) that no truly mathematical objects or perfect instances of mathematical truths exist in the sensible world; and (iii) that there is a science, Dialectic, superior even to mathematics in its concern with truth/reality in all its comprehensiveness. None of this, any more than what was said in *Republic*, can rightly be read as implying that mathematicals are intermediate between sensibles and Ideas. Plato has, again, failed to clarify the relationship between mathematical truths and mathematical entities and to justify his existential assumptions about them.

3.8. Before I leave Plato's writings, reference should be made to his (if genuine) Seventh Letter. Every real being, he wrote, is knowable, and there are four relevant things distinct from it: (1) its name, e.g., "circle," though this is arbitrary and variable; (2) its definition, e.g., in the case of circle, "the figure whose extremities are everywhere equally distant from its centre," and this too is not fixed inasmuch as it is composed of items of language that are arbitrary and variable; (3) an image, e.g., a so-called circle that we draw or erase; and (4) knowledge of the being, e.g., of (a) circle: "In the fourth place are knowledge (*epistēmē*), reason (*nous*), and right opinion (which are in our minds, not in words or bodily shapes and therefore must be taken together as something distinct both from the circle itself and from the three things previously mentioned). . . . The same thing is true of straight-lined as well as of circular figures; of colour; of the good, the beautiful, the just . . . ." And he added that "every circle that we make or draw in common life is full of characteristics that contradict the [real being itself], for it everywhere touches a straight line, while the circle itself, we say, has in it not the slightest element belonging to a contrary nature."[86] No doctrine of the intermediate status of mathematicals can be detected in this letter; indeed, they are absolutely on a par with the real beings—the Ideas—that are the good, the beautiful, the just, and so on.

3.9. The most convenient focal place for studying Plato's Unwritten Doctrines is Aristotle's *Metaphysics*, Book A, Chapter 6. There, Aristotle cited no oral or written sources, did not allude to this distinction, and gave no hint that Plato's philosophy underwent a change (though *Metaphysics*, Book M, Chapter 4, recognizes such a development) or that it was at all different orally from what it was in the Dialogues. It looks as though all of Aristotle's remarks in A6 were intended to apply to Plato's oral teaching. Aristotle makes the following statements.

(*a*) The philosophy of Plato in most respects followed the philosophy of the "Italians," i.e., the Pythagoreans (Aristotle might just possibly have meant to include Parmenides, also). Plato said that the many things exist by "participation" in the appropriate Idea; this is only a difference in terminology, however, from the Pythagoreans' saying that things exist by "imitation" of numbers. (This "imitation" is an expression of the doctrine that things are numerically structured, as against being nothing but numbers. See p. 14 above.) Aristotle's comparison clearly implies that for Plato the Ideas are, in some sense, numbers. This is an Unwritten Doctrine.

(*b*) Plato held that, besides the sensible things and the Ideas, there are the objects of mathematics, which occupy an intermediate position. (See pp. 20–21 above.)

I have argued that this Platonic view was not propounded in the Dialogues or Epistles. Aristotle's account does not answer the question: Did Plato maintain that there are mathematical Ideas on top of the mathematical intermediates, viz., one such Idea for each, many alike among the intermediates? The answer is yes and no: yes in that there are *some* mathematical Ideas, viz., Ideal numbers; no in that there is not an Idea for *each* sort of intermediates (e.g., there is no Idea of the circle, according to the Unwritten Doctrines, unlike in the original form of the theory of Ideas).[87]

(c) For Plato, "the Ideas [are] the causes of all other things," i.e., "the Numbers [= the Ideal numbers] are the causes of the reality of other things":[88] *all* the Ideas are Ideal numbers. This, I surmise, is why Aristotle did not deal with the question raised in (b): a general negative answer was implied by the doctrine he reported, that all the Ideas are Ideal numbers; so, more specifically, there were no geometrical Ideas in Plato's Unwritten Doctrines.

(d) Plato diverged from the Pythagoreans in two major respects, despite the resemblance described in (a). First, he introduced the Ideas. Second, it "is his view that the Numbers exist apart from sensible things, while they say that the things themselves are numbers, and do not place the objects of mathematics between Ideas and sensible things."[89]

(e) Plato accepted that the Ideal numbers are not self-sufficient/self-explanatory. They derive from two elements/principles: one is limiting—it is "essential reality, the One"; the other is the unlimited—it is the principle of plurality involving the endless alternation of the lesser and greater, e.g., the Number 3 is less than the Number 4 but is greater than the Number 2.[90]

On these points (d) and (e), Plato's thought is Pythagoreanism etherealized.

4. ARISTOTLE

4.1 Plato's ontology gave pride of place to supersensible entities—primarily those universal in character—existing in their own right, although sensible particulars have merely a cavernous or shadowy subexistence. Aristotle came to be scornful of all this. He argued against Plato's transcendentalism in favor of his own metaphysical priority ascribed to individual sensible substances. (I leave aside his theology, with its strained adoption of the reality of sheer form, perfect and partless—and living.) Aristotle's philosophy of mathematics[91] was shaped by his critical preoccupation with Platonism, no less than by his constructive need to show how mathematicals have only a dependent reality, i.e., dependent on individual sensible substances and on our processes of abstraction and reason.

I will skim the rooftops of certain terraces of Aristotle's ontology and methodology of mathematics: in his rejection of Plato's doctrines of intermediates and of numbers; his conception of mathematics in terms of the axiomatic method; his ontology of mathematicals generally and of geometricals, numbers, and infinity severally; and, associated with this ontology, his proposal of abstraction as the fundamental procedure of mathematical concept of formation.

4.2. Plato's doctrine of mathematicals as purely intelligible entities existing in a layer of reality between Ideas and sensible things was unacceptable to Aristotle, basically because the very idea of the separate existence of abstract entities savored of nonsense to him. He sublimated his distaste in a series of arguments, including the following:[92] (i) The doctrine presupposed the reality of Ideas (distinct from the mathematical intermediates). He dismissed them because, inter alia, they are superfluous duplications of features of the world of our sense-perception and action, can have no causal efficacy, and are inherently useless and unknowable principles, which cannot be coherently defined nor consistently circumscribed. (ii) The doctrine of intermediates, with its commitment to the separate existence of mathematical objects, was repugnant to Aristotle because of its absurd reduplicative consequences, as he thought them. (1) According to the doctrine, the mathematician's study is aimed not at sensible solids (e.g., pyramids) but at special — perfect and nonsensible — mathematical solids (e.g., tetrahedra) and likewise not at sensible but at mathematical planes and lines supposed over and above sensible planes and lines. Those mathematical solids also contain mathematical planes and lines. There must, therefore (by consistency in appealing to what has priority, "for incomposites are prior to compounds"), be further mathematical planes and lines distinct from those in the initial mathematical solids. And each range of the so far mentioned mathematical planes must contain distinct ranges of mathematical lines, additional to the initial set of mathematical lines. "The accumulation becomes absurd. . . . With which of these [mathematical planes and lines], then, will the mathematical sciences deal?" Analogous difficulties of reduplication arise, he alleged, in regard to numbers. (2) If mathematical intermediates are required to be the objects of mathematics, then there should also, by parity of reasoning, be appropriate sorts of intermediates to be the objects of other sciences; so, for biology, there would have to be "intermediate" animals apart from ordinary animals: a reduction to the absurd. (iii) Neither, e.g., lines nor numbers have any primary existence as substances, forms, or material substrata in Aristotle's senses of these terms; since, accordingly, mathematicals have only a subsidiary mode of existence, they cannot exist in their own right as the doctrine of intermediates demands.

Aristotle's irritation with Plato's theory of Ideas in its various versions spurred him to adduce a collection of criticisms against the theory of Ideal numbers, each composed of units specific to it (see 2.3 (e) above).[93] (i) In mathematics a number may derive, as a sum or product, from a plurality of numbers; but how can one Idea come from a plurality of Ideas? (ii) Plato was unable to explain how the unitary character of each of his Ideas is possible if these are composed of units. (iii) The relationship between an Ideal number (e.g., Three) and the correlative mathematical number (e.g., three[s]) — the latter being the object(s) of the mathematician's study — was left obscure. (iv) Plato was unable to explain how the two fives in the Ideal number Ten differ from the five units in the Ideal number Five. More generally, Aristotle charged to catch Plato on the horns of dilemma. Either all the units are alike or (as Plato had supposed) they are unlike specifically. (1) If all the units are alike, then the Ideas, i.e., Ideal numbers, would be related as parts to wholes; e.g., Three would be a part of Four and of all succeeding Ideal numbers. This result is incompatible with Plato's conception of Ideas as each having a completely distinct and self-subsistent reality (subject to its dependence on the One). (2) If the units are unlike except for those that combine to constitute a particular Ideal number, then some differentiating attribute(s) must occur among them; but this is incompatible with Plato's conception of units as absolutely qualityless indivisibles. (v) "Further, the units in 2 must each come from a prior 2; but this is impossible."[94] There are difficulties and differences of interpretation about this. I take the thrust of Aristotle's point to be that Plato's account of the nature of 2 involves him in presupposing something binary and that his account is, therefore, vitiated either by its circularity or by its entailing an infinite regress.

4.3. It may not have been long after Aristotle's matured rejection of Plato's doctrines of transcendent or separately existing abstract entities before he drafted his *Posterior Analytics*, in which he propounded a systematic methodology of scientific knowledge and understanding. 'Demonstration' was his kernel idea. He placed mathematics, even focally, within the scope of this methodology, as is revealed by his many mathematical references and illustrations (alongside many nonmathematical ones). Plato and the Academy had discussed "hypotheses" and definitions as starting-points of mathematical reasoning. And the need of proof in mathematics was already recognized, and the practice of proof in mathematics well established, by this time. With these developments and discussions behind him, Aristotle pioneered the elaborated philosophical formulation of the axiomatic method. Not that his version was clear-cut; it was misty and disorderly. Neither was it specific to mathematical science; it was meant to be applicable to all fields of scientific intelligence.

For Aristotle, each science has its special subject matter in the form of a domain or kind of elements; e.g., arithmetic has numbers and geometry has magnitudes. A mathematical science is an organization of knowledge of reasoned facts; this is the most exact knowledge. It is an enclosed body of demonstrations concerning its subject matter; demonstrations across domains, e.g., a demonstration of something geometrical by arithmetic, are debarred. Further, each mathematical science inherently requires the presence of two mutually exclusive sorts of truth, viz., principles (i.e., indemonstrable truths) and demonstrable truths; the former sort provides a finite basis of the latter. The principles of science, e.g., geometry, fall into three classes: basic existential truths about its domain, definitions concerning types in its domain, and basic truths having common applicability in the sciences (such as: "If equals are taken from equals, the remainders are equal"). Knowledge of the truth of principles is obtained by, above all, the exercise of the intellect's power of "intuitive reasons" (*nous*). Knowledge of demonstrable truths in a science is obtained by valid syllogistic reasoning relying ultimately on indemonstrable truths as premises.

Aristotle's appeal to his syllogisms in this connection was an unfortunate—and needless—restriction; it is a notorious fact that, in general, mathematical proofs cannot be satisfactorily molded into syllogistic patterns. He also laid down conditions—at least some of which are needlessly restrictive—of a proposition's being a principle in a mathematical science: it had to be true, primitive, universal, necessary, and explanatory. Thus, for instance, principles must be really true because (he claimed) we cannot "understand" (*epistasthai*), i.e., understandingly know, what is not the case; and he emphasized that we come to understand something not by mere deduction along valid lines but only by demonstration, i.e., deduction from true premises. Aristotle's methodology of mathematics was pervaded by his epistemological interests.

4.4. For Aristotle, mathematicals cannot exist apart from sensible substances. Two prospective possibilities are that mathematicals are themselves sensible substances or that they are one of the factors—form or matter—of Aristotelian substances. He denied that mathematicals have any such status.

> How can lines be substances? Neither as a form or shape, as the soul perhaps is, nor as matter, like the solid; for we have no experience of anything that can be put together out of planes or lines or points, while if these had been a sort of material substance, we should have observed things which could be put together out of them.[95]

He maintained, then, that mathematical objects neither are unchanging and eternal realities over and above sensible ones, nor are they sensible substances, nor are they the form or the matter of such substances. On the other hand, he took it for granted that mathematical assertions and knowledge are of real truths, at bottom on the same footing as the truths of physics and of metaphysics (the other two theoretical sciences, in his classification) and that mathematicals have an external reality whose basis lies in individual sensible substances.

> Obviously, physical bodies contain surfaces and volumes, lines, and points, and these are the subject-matter of mathematics [sc. geometry]. . . . The mathematician . . . does not treat of [figures] as the limits of a physical body; nor does he consider the attributes indicated as the attributes of such bodies. That is why he separates them; for in thought they are separable from motion, and it makes no difference, nor does any falsity result, if they are separated. . . . Geometry investigates physical lines but not *qua* physical.[96]

In this way, in terms of how the mathematician considers given attributes of the sensible, Aristotle specified what is distinctive of mathematical objects. He did, in fact, distinguish two types of mathematical objects, the universal and the individual, e.g., the universal circle and individual circles; and he paid attention to the "formula" (as he called it), i.e., the essential/defining conditions, relating primarily to the former.[97] However, he did not explicitly and carefully pursue the difference between the universal and the individual among mathematical objects when he concentrated on mathematical philosophy in the last two books of his *Metaphysics*.

All "[theoretical-]scientific knowledge is judgement about things that are universal and necessary."[98] Also, the theoretical sciences "omit the question whether the genus with which they deal exists or does not exist, because it belongs to the same kind of thinking to show *what* it is and *that* it is"[99]—a doubly questionable proclamation, which he applied to mathematicals by saying that the issue was "not *whether* they exist but *how* they exist."[100] What is peculiar to mathematics among the theoretical sciences is that, first, its objects have no real separate existence, and, second, these objects exist qua mathematical only by mental transformation and separation of movable, concrete substances into immovable, abstract entities through a process of considering the movable, concrete substances in abstraction from their physical makeup and features; the mathematician treats the sensible substances as though they were stripped of all their sensible components and attributes, e.g., their hardness and softness, heat and cold, etc., and he investigates the resulting abstractions.[101]

The mathematician may use a similar process of abstraction in regard to representations, such as geometrical diagrams. Aristotle's thought was this: the geometer has to draw a triangle with a determinate size, but he can and may disregard the fact that the size is determinate.[102]

4.5. Quantity is the immediately relevant category of mathematicals.[103] " 'Quantum' means that which is divisible into two or more constituent parts each of which is by nature a 'one' and a 'this'." A quantum is a 'plurality' if it is numerable and a 'magnitude' if it is measurable. Geometry is the science of magnitudes. Characteristic of a magnitude is that it is divisible into continuous parts, whereas a plurality is discrete. Mere continuous magnitude is pure extension; in one dimension it is length, in two dimensions breadth, and in three dimensions depth. If limited, length is a line, breadth a plane, and depth a solid.[104] A point has no extension; it is that which has position and is indivisible (a numerical unit has only the latter property) or is a division and limit of a line.[105]

Aristotle's conception of specifically geometrical objects is somewhat hazy through its invoking the notion of 'intelligible matter' without clearly explaining it. For him, as a rule, genus and matter are both correlated with potentiality; accordingly, those are in some cases equated.[106] A genus is a possibility of different determinate species: their commonality is their generic matter. And an individual in its actual concreteness must have a formal and a material component; the latter alone is only a possibility of individuality. Given the abstraction process already described, the matter of, e.g., an individual circle cannot be sensible; it is "intelligible matter." This is the ground—accessible to thought—common to all plane figures, whatever they are specifically. An individual circle is a composite of this intelligible matter together with the form/essence of circle. Circle itself, as a universal, is a species of the genus, plane.[107]

Aristotle's ontology of arithmetical objects, viz., one and the integers designating plurality, was intended to be mainly analogous to that of geometrical objects, but with the contrasts I have indicated above. One of the defects of his analyses of number was his repeated failure to keep distinct the notions of, e.g., (1) a mathematical number itself, (2) (i) the occurrence or (ii) the use of such numbers in arithmetical sums or products, (3) numbered aggregates of physical, etc., things, and (4) the process of numbering such an aggregate. Typical is his mixed remark that "a number, whatever number it is, is always a number of certain things, either of parts of fire or earth or of units";[108] also typical is his remark that "the one is the beginning of the knowable regarding each class. But the one is not the same in all classes. For here it is a quarter-tone, and there it is the vowel . . . ."[109]

4.6. Unlike the Aristotelian views presented in §§4.2, 4.4, and 4.5, which are in his *Metaphysics* (even if partly elsewhere in his works, too), his major discussion of infinity took place in *Physics*.[110] He dwelt on the physical bearings of the notion: on whether and, if so, in what sense, e.g., an infinite body is possible or time is infinite. He concurrently touched on the question of mathematical infinity. Besides, his treatment of physical infinity when conjoined with his theory of abstraction would be liable to have consequences for mathematical infinity.

Aristotle argued at length, deploying his special ideas of space and place, that there is no body that is actually infinite. However, he linked this with a denial that it means that the infinite does not exist in any way, for the unqualified nonexistence of the infinite would lead to such impossible consequences, he held, as time having a beginning and an end, as a magnitude not being divisible into magnitudes, and as number not being infinite. Are time, magnitude, and number, then, actual infinites? And if they are not actual infinites, how *are* they infinites at all? He did not supply all the requisite explanatory and justificatory details of his answers, and some of the details he gave are by no means convincing. His directing ideas are, nonetheless, straightforward enough. He maintained that neither time, magnitude, nor number has an independent—substantial—reality; none of them is a 'this', a complete, self-subsistent entity. In the substantial sense of "is," none *is* an actual infinite. On the other hand: "Generally the infinite has this mode of existence: one thing is always being taken after another, and each thing that is taken is always finite, but always different."[111] Time is infinite in being an unending process of coming to be and passing away; its ingredients are transient; they do not all exist to compose a single infinite state. A magnitude, i.e., a continuous quantum, is infinite in being infinitely divisible; continuity cannot be reduced to discreteness. "The number of times a magnitude can be bisected is infinite. Hence this infinite is potential, never actual: the number of parts that can be taken always surpasses any assigned number."[112] A magnitude is fixed; it does not lose its parts (like time) or grow (like number). Whereas in dividing a magnitude there is no terminus in the direction of smallness, in counting/adding number (positive integers) there is no terminus in the direction of largeness: "in the direction of largeness it is always possible to *think* of a larger number."[113] Finally, Aristotle offered the following characterization of infinity; its conceptive character is emphatic: "a quantity is infinite if it is such that we can always take a part outside what has been already taken."[114]

4.7. The philosophical development concerning mathematics from the Pythagoreans to Plato and thence to Aristotle might be proposed, albeit as a *jeu d'esprit*, as a pellucid example of a so-called Hegelian triad. Mathematicals were at first thought to be real as physical constituents or structures wholly embedded in sensible things. Plato moved to an antithesis of this, thinking mathematicals to be real as immovable, immaterial entities existing quite separately from sensible things. Aristotle's position was an ingenious synthesis in which he managed to combine a physicalism derived from the Pythagoreans with an abstractionism derived from Plato. He maintained their shared assumption of an external realism; he kept to the Pythagoreans' confinement of all mathematicals to an existence as aspects of sensible things, while he, stressfully, accommodated to this confinement an insistence, learned from Plato's orientation, on the ideality—the abstractness and perfection—of all mathematicals.

Aristotle took over from these predecessors two other assumptions about mathematics. One is the constativist and veridicalist nature of mathematical thought/ discourse. The second is the intelligibility of mathematicals. For him, it may be suggested, this feature was allied to the fact that mathematical concepts are an outcome of a certain kind of mental activity and attention by us; he made mathematical concepts our internalized constructions.[115] This was indeed an advance. But it still had this drawback, that it presupposed the priority and the limitations imposed by the sensible world as the matrix of mathematical concept formation.

Notes

1. In my usage the term 'mathematical philosophy' has the forefront sense of 'philosophy of mathematics'; in appropriate cases, it can also carry '(a) philosophy with a mathematical content or style' as a background sense. Cf. §3.1.

2. G. Milhaud, *Les Philosophes-géomètres de la Grèce* (Paris, 1900) (pre-Socratics and Plato only), and E. A. Maziarz and T. Greenwood, *Greek Mathematical Philosophy* (New York: Alcan Ungar, 1968), are cases in point.

3. Cf. my "Preface to the Grammar of Postulates," *Aristotelian Society Supplement*, Vol. LIII (1979), pp. 1–21.

4. For the Latin phrase, see Ockham, *Philosophical Writings*, ed. P. Boehner (London: Nelson, 1957), p. 41.

5. On the system of hyperreal numbers, cf. J. M. Henle and E. M. Kleinberg, *Infinitesimal Calculus* (Cambridge, Mass., and London: M.I.T. Press, 1979), and H. J. Keisler, *Elementary Calculus* (Boston: Prindle, Weber and Schmidt, 1976).

6. The term 'illocutionary force' originates on p. 100 (cf. pp. 98–99) of J. L. Austin, *How to Do Things with Words*, 2nd ed. rev., ed. J. O. Urmson and M. Sbisà, with index by P. H. Nidditch (Oxford: Oxford University Press, 1980).

7. *Metaphysics*, A5, 985b23–24, following trans. by W. D. Ross. (A translator's name is cited in these notes only on the first relevant occasion.)

8. In *Metaphysics, Physics, On the Heavens*, and elsewhere; see W. T. Organ, *An Index to Aristotle* (Princeton, N.J.: Princeton University Press, 1949), s.v. Pythagoreans.

9. Translated in K. Freeman, *Ancilla to the Pre-Socratic Philosophers* (Oxford: Blackwell, 1947). Cf. H. Thesleff, *An Introduction to the Pythagorean Writings of the Hellenistic Age* (Åbo: Acta Academiae Aboensis, 1961), and *The Pythagorean Texts of the Hellenistic Period* (Åbo: Acta Academiae Aboensis, 1965).

10. E.g., by E. Frank, *Plato und die sogenannten Pythagoreer* (Halle: Niemeyer, 1923), pp. 313–15, footnote, and W. Burkert, *Love and Science in Ancient Pythagoreanism*, trans. E. L. Minars (Cambridge: Harvard University Press, 1972), pp. 273–75. Cf. n.25.

11. Cf. Burkert, *op. cit.*, pp. 401ff.: B. L. van der Waerden, "Die Arithmetik der Pythagoreer," *Math. Annalen*, Vol. 120 (1947–49), pp. 127–53, 676–700; B. L. van der Waerden, *Science Awakening*, trans. A. Dresden (Groningen, Noordhoff, 1954), per index s.vv. "Pythagoras," "Pythagoreans;" W. R. Knorr, *The Evolution of the Euclidean Elements* (Dordrecht and Boston: Reidel, 1975).

12. "Natures": Aristotle, *Metaphysics*, A5, 985b34; "causes"; A6, 987b24–25, and A8, 990a19–20.

13. *Essay Concerning Human Understanding*, ed. P. H. Nidditch (Oxford: Oxford University Press, 1975), II.xvi.1: 205(8–10). My cross-quotations are meant to be taken as implying a substantial similarity, not an identity, of doctrine.

14. *Philebus*, 16c-d, trans. J. Gosling (Oxford: Oxford University Press, 1975).

15. Aristotle, *Metaphysics*, A5, 986a2-3; Aristotle, *On the Heavens*, ii.9, 290b12-14, trans. T. L. Heath, *Aristarchus of Samos* (Oxford: Oxford University Press, 1913), p. 105.

16. *System of Logic*, II.vi.2. J. Klein, *Greek Mathematical Thought and the Origin of Algebra*, trans. E. Brann (Cambridge, Mass., and London: M.I.T. Press, 1968), Part I, stresses the 'number of' sense of *arithmos*. Cf. p. 28 below.

17. *Metaphysics*, M6, 1080a22-33. Italics in quotations are mine unless the contrary is noted.

18. *Metaphysics*, M6, 1080b16-21; M8, 1083b8-19.

19. My term 'configuration' covers the Pythagorean doctrine that solid bodies are formed of planes, planes of lines, and lines of monadic points. Relevant details are given in, e.g., W. K. C. Guthrie, *History of Greek Philosophy* (Cambridge: Cambridge University Press, 1962), Vol. 1, pp. 259ff.

20. *Metaphysics*, A5, 986a15-21.

21. Cf. W. D. Ross, *Aristotle's Physics* (Oxford: Oxford University Press, 1936), pp. 542-45.

22. Philolaus, fr. 1, trans. Guthrie, *op. cit.*, p. 330.

23. Diogenes Laertius, viii.8, trans. G. S. Kirk and J. E. Raven, *The Presocratic Philosophers* (Cambridge: Cambridge University Press, 1957), p. 228. Cf. Aristotle, *Protrepticus*, fr. 11.

24. Cf. Iamblichus, *Comm. math. sc.*, 25: "The Pythagoreans, having devoted themselves to mathematics, and admiring the rigour of its arguments, because it alone of the studies men undertake contains proofs . . . ," trans. J. Barnes, *The Presocratic Philosophers* (London: Routledge, 1979), Vol. 2, p. 78. The text is given in Burkert, *op. cit.*, p. 50, n.112, who argues that it is derived from a now lost work by Aristotle, *On the Pythagoreans*. Archytas, fr. 4, links proof primarily with arithmetic, which is therefore superior to geometry.

25. The stock criticisms of the fragments' authenticity, which stem mainly from Bywater and Frank and are conveniently adduced by Kirk and Raven (*op. cit.*, pp. 308-11), are poorly reasoned, as was recognized by Guthrie (*op. cit.*, pp. 331-32). Cf. G. de Santillana and W. Pitts, "Philolaus in Limbo," *Isis*, Vol. 42 (1951), pp. 112-20.

26. Philolaus, frs. 4, 6, 11, trans. Freeman, *op. cit.*

27. *Metaphysics*, A5, 985b23-26.

28. See Burkert, *op. cit.*, pp. 369ff.

29. *Metaphysics*, N3, 1090b20-25.

30. Cf. Philolaus (Diels-Kranz) A29, and n.24 above. A. Szabò, *The Beginnings of Greek Mathematics* (Dordrecht and Boston: Reidel, 1978) is interesting but is one-sided in stressing the role of dialectic in the rise of the deductive method.

31. I. Thomas, *Greek Mathematical Works* (London and Cambridge, Mass.: Harvard University Press, 1939), Vol. 1, pp. 148-49.

32. Aristotle treated quantity as an important category; mathematics has an important place in his scheme of the sciences; and in his *Posterior Analytics* it has, in some respects, a prototypical role among the sciences.

33. See, e.g., A. C. Crombie, *Robert Grosseteste* (Oxford: Oxford University Press, 1953), pp. 110ff., 139ff.

34. Cf. Aristotle, *On the Heavens*, 293a21-22.

35. *Metaphysics*, M8, 1083b11-19.

36. Aristotle uses both terms in his exposition in *Metaphysics*, A5, 986a.

37. Of course, the Pythagoreans had no cognizance of zero or of negative integers.

38. "Harmony" as the agency of the combination of the limit and the unlimited in the universe is too general and indefinite (cf. Philolaus, fr. 6) to provide a means of defense against the criticism made in the paper.

39. Cf. Aristotle, *On the Heavens*, ii.9.

40. Cf. the Euclid scholium quoted in Thomas, *op. cit.*, (in n.31), pp. 214-17.

41. Cf. Aristotle, *Metaphysics*, A8, 989b33-34.

42. Aristotle, *Metaphysics*, A5, 986a8-9.

43. Aristotle, *Nicomachean Ethics*, 1095a32-33.

44. *Introduction to Mathematical Philosophy* (London: Allen and Unwin, 1919), p. 1.

45. Cf. Aristotle, *Nicomachean Ethics*, 1131a20ff.

46. Cf., e.g., Aristotle, *On the Soul*, 404b24–25, and the Aristotelian references in W. D. Ross, *Plato's Theory of Ideas* (Oxford: Oxford University Press, 1951), p. 216 n. The term 'Unwritten Doctrines' comes from Aristotle, *Physics*, 209b15. A compendium of translations of source passages on the Unwritten Doctrines is in J. N. Findlay, *Plato: The Written and Unwritten Doctrines* (London: Routledge, 1974), Appendix I.

47. Philolaus, frs. 8, 10, trans. Freeman. The Parmenidean One should be kept in mind as a part of the background to Pythagoreans and Plato on One.

48. Cf., e.g., *Republic*, 507b, 596a; *Parmenides*, 130a-d.

49. Cf. G. Leff, *William of Ockham* (Manchester: Manchester University Press, 1975), pp. 164ff. Sameness and Difference are among the important higher-level kinds or Ideas in some later Dialogues. 'Number' is a "transcendental" at *Sophist*, 238a-c.

50. Cf., e.g., *Republic*, 476a2–4.

51. *Parmenides*, 137aff.

52. F. M. Cornford, *Plato and Parmenides* (London: Routledge, 1939), p. 111. Locke, *Essay*, II.xvi.1, 2, slides from one to another of "one," "unity," and "unit."

53. Findlay, *op. cit.*, is the fullest committed presentation in English. Guthrie, *History of Greek Philosophy* (Cambridge: Cambridge University Press, 1978), Vol. 5, Chapter 8, contains references to the relevant literature —and a sharp critique.

54. I follow the chronology in J. B. Skemp, *Plato* (Oxford: Oxford University Press, 1976), pp. 13ff., 52ff. Ross, *Plato's Theory of Ideas*, p. 10, dates *Meno* earlier, to before Plato's first Sicilian visit, 389–388 B.C.

55. *Meno*, 81a-d, trans. Guthrie (Harmondsworth: Penguin Books, 1956). On "the other world" (the realm of Hades), cf. *Phaedo*, 68a-b; and note "Hades *under* the earth" at *Republic*, 596c.

56. 'Recollection' is hardly re-collection: the slave-boy does not remember the original acquaintance or occasion.

57. Cf., e.g., *Republic*, 458d.

58. Cf. *Republic*, 491.

59. *Meno*, 90b.

60. *Meno*, 90a.

61. E.g., J. A. Stewart, *Plato's Doctrine of Ideas* (Oxford: Oxford University Press, 1909), p. 28. (The word *eidos* at *Meno*, 72c, does not mean "Idea.")

62. Cf., e.g., *Phaedo*, 109e; *Republic*, 500c; *Phaedrus*, 247c.

63. *Meno*. 81d.

64. This sense of 'thesis' was introduced by Leśniewski and made well known by Łukasiewicz. Cf. Łukasiewicz in S. McCall, ed., *Polish Logic, 1920–1939* (Oxford: Oxford University Press, 1967), p. 44 n.

65. *Meno*, 86e–87a. On the whole matter, see R. S. Bluck, *Plato's Meno* (Cambridge: Cambridge University Press, 1961), pp. 75ff., 321 ff., 441ff.; and R. Robinson, *Plato's Earlier Dialectic*, 2nd ed. (Oxford: Oxford University Press, 1953), Chapter 8.

66. *Phaedo*, 65c-e, 74a–75b, etc.

67. See especially *Phaedo*, 101c, 104–5, and the commentary *ad locc.* in D. Gallop's translation (Oxford: Oxford University Press, 1975). (Gallop's criticism of Vlastos, on p. 186, is [I think] partly wrong.)

68. *Phaedo*, 74a–75b.

69. *Phaedo*, 75c, 104a, 105c.

70. *Phaedo*, 101b, c, trans. Gallop. My objection about specific differences at the end of (i) is made *pace* Cook Wilson, Ross, Gallop, et al.

71. *Republic*, e.g., 382bff., 389b-c, 485c; cf., e.g., *Timaeus*, 29c. I use 'proposition' in a broad sense, to contrast with 'objectual'.

72. *Republic*, 485b, 526a-b, 526d-e (cf. 508–9), 527a-b, trans. P. Shorey (Cambridge, Mass., and London: Harvard University Press, 1935). Cf. *Sophist*, 238a.

73. *Republic*, 531d, 537c.

74. *Metaphysics*, A6, 987b14–17.

75. E.g., J. Adam, *The Republic of Plato* (Cambridge: Cambridge University Press, 1902), Vol. 2, pp. 115 n., 159ff.; A. Wedberg, *Plato's Philosophy of Mathematics* (Stockholm: Almquist and Wiksell, 1955), p. 124; J. A. Brentlinger, "The Divided Line and Plato's Theory of Intermediates,'" *Phronesis*, Vol. 8 (1963), pp. 146–66. (Brentlinger's interpretation of *Rep.*, 534a, which he regards as decisively showing that the objects of *dianoia* and *noēsis* are on different ontological levels, is [I think] unfounded.)

76. *Republic*, 526a; cf. *Philebus*, 56d-e.

77. *Republic*, 511; cf. 533–34.

78. *Republic*, 510d, 525d-e.

79. *Republic*, 510a–511b, 525d.

80. *Republic*, 510–11.

81. *Republic*, 511, 532, 533.

82. *Republic*, 533b-c.

83. In *Timaeus* (somewhat earlier among the later Dialogues than *Philebus*), numbers, proportions, and shapes play prominent roles cosmologically. The influence of Pythagoreanism on this is apparent.

84. *Philebus*, 55d–57e, trans. Gosling.

85. *Philebus*, 58a–59d.

86. Seventh Letter, 342–43, trans. G. R. Morrow, *Plato's Epistles* (Indianapolis and New York: Bobbs Merrill, 1962).

87. Aristotle, *Metaphysics*, M4, discusses what it claims was the original form of Plato's theory of Ideas.

88. Aristotle, *Metaphysics*, A6, 987b18–25, Ross's trans. adapted; see also N2, 1090a4–6, and frag. 4 (Ross). Cf. Ross, *Plato's Theory of Ideas*, Chapter 15.

89. Aristotle, *Metaphysics*, A6, 987b27–29, Ross's trans. adapted.

90. Cf. p. 12 above. For elucidations of Plato's principles of generation of numbers, see Ross, *Plato's Theory of Ideas*, pp. 182ff.; and J. Annas, *Aristotle's Metaphysics, Books M and N* (Oxford: Oxford University Press, 1976), pp. 42ff.

91. Useful sources and references include: Aristotle, *Metaphysics*, Books Δ, E, Z, K, M, and N; T. Heath, *Mathematics in Aristotle* (Oxford: Oxford University Press, 1949); J. Barnes, *Aristotle's Posterior Analytics* (Oxford: Oxford University Press, 1975), with bibliography.

92. I select from *Metaphysics*, M2, 1076b11–1077a36.

93. I select from *Metaphysics*, A9 and M6–8.

94. *Metaphysics*, A9, 991b31–992a1.

95. *Metaphysics*, M2, 1077a32–36.

96. Aristotle, *Physics*, ii.2, 193b24–194a12, trans. R. P. Hardie and R. K. Gaye (Oxford: Oxford University Press, 1930).

97. *Metaphysics*, Z10, 11.

98. Aristotle, *Nicomachean Ethics*, vi.6, 1140b31–32, trans. Ross.

99. *Metaphysics*, E1, 1025b16–18.

100. *Metaphysics*, M1, 1076a36–37.

101. See *Metaphysics*, Z11, 1036a11–1036b3, 27–28, and K3, 1061a28–35.

102. Aristotle, *On Memory*, 450a1–8.

103. Cf. the notes on Chapter 6 of Aristotle's *Categories* in J. L. Ackrill's edition (Oxford: Oxford University Press, 1963).

104. *Metaphysics*, Δ13, 1020a7ff.

105. *Metaphysics*, Δ6, 1016b24ff., and K2, 1060b10ff.

106. Cf. A. C. Lloyd, *Form and Universal in Aristotle* (Liverpool: Cairns, 1981), pp. 32ff.

107. Cf. *Metaphysics*, Δ28, Z10, 11.

108. *Metaphysics*, N5, 1092b19-20.

109. *Metaphysics*, Δ6, 1016b20ff.; Aristotle's whole chapter is a valuable discussion of uses of 'one'.

110. Book III, Chapters 4-8. Valuable discussions are in Ross's editions, pp. 48ff., and in J. Hintikka, *Time and Modality* (Oxford: Oxford University Press, 1973), Chapter 6 (though its main purport is [I think] mistaken).

111. *Physics*, iii.6, 206a27-29.

112. *Physics*, iii.7, 207b10-13.

113. *Physics*, iii.7, 207b10.

114. *Physics*, iii.6, 207a7-8.

115. Aristotle, *On the Soul*, iii.4-7, is relevant in this connection.

Plato on Not-Being: Some Interpretations of the ΣΥΜΠΛΟΚΗ ΕΙΔΩΝ (259E) and Their Relation to Parmenides' Problem

FRANCIS JEFFERY PELLETIER

INTRODUCTION

W e have witnessed," says Mourelatos (1979: p. 3), "in the 'sixties and 'seventies, in English language scholarship, that rarest of phenomena in the study of ancient philosophy, the emergence of a consensus." This interpretation is so agreed upon that "one may even speak of a standard Anglo-American interpretation of Parmenides." One of the presentations counted by Mourelatos as standard, indeed one of the paradigms, is that of Furth (1968). According to this interpretation, Parmenides' infamous ontological views follow as corollaries from his implicit views about language and meaning. I will briefly present this Parmenidean view about language, but I will not here try to justify the attribution (for these sorts of arguments see Furth, 1968; Mourelatos, 1979; and Pelletier, forthcoming).

In this paper, I am interested in the Platonic response to Parmenides, especially the response that occurs in the middle portion of the *Sophist* (249–265). Since I am going to evaluate this as a response to the "standard interpretation" of Parmenides, it is clear that I owe a justification for my belief that Plato understood his opponent to be our "standard Parmenides." This issue, too, I will avoid here (further discussion can be found in Pelletier, forthcoming, which discusses the "Parmenidean" arguments of *Sophist* 237–241, *Theaetetus*, 188–189, and *Cratylus* 429–430, with an eye toward showing that Plato was aware of these types of argument.)

In the middle portion of the *Sophist* itself, Plato states that his opponents cannot overcome his position because he has made allowance for a *symplokē eidōn tōn allōn* ('interweaving of the forms with one another') and that it is this *symplokē eidōn* that makes all discourse possible. Presumably, then, Plato views his opponents —in particular "Father Parmenides"—as producing unsound arguments that would have the effect of making discourse impossible. As we will see, the argument attributed to the standard Parmenides does exactly that. Thus, one can use the standard interpretation to bolster one's account of Plato's refutation and also use facts about Plato's refutation to bolster one's belief in the standard interpretation of Parmenides.

It seems that one way to clarify the details of the interpretation of Parmenides is to investigate the *symplokē eidōn* of the *Sophist*. Unfortunately, Plato's position is also open to a variety of interpretations and cannot be convincingly elucidated in the absence of a precise account of what Parmenides' argument was. One, therefore, wishes to set up all the possible interpretations of Parmenides and all the interpretations of the *symplokē eidōn* and then to inspect these lists to discover which *pairs* of Parmenidean/Platonic interpretations mesh the best. This, it seems to me, would provide the best evidence possible that one had finally gotten both Plato and Parmenides right. I will not attempt that Herculean task. Rather, I will state *one* interpretation of Parmenides, Furth's, and ask which of the many ways to understand Plato's position best accords with that interpretation of Parmenides.

Let us start then with what I will call Parmenides' Problem. The premises are:

1. Either a declarative sentence is true or it is not true, but it is not both.
2. (a) The meaning of a sentence is the fact to which it refers.
   (b) The meaning of a singular term (or a predicate) is the object(s) to which it refers.
3. Whatever ("really") is, can meaningfully be stated by true sentences.
4. There are no "negative facts."

The first conclusion, that there is at most one meaningful sentence, can be reached in a number of ways. Furth (1968) gives one way, Mourelatos (1979) another. Here, without any of the intermediate details, is another.

1. S_1 and S_2 have distinct meanings if and only if there is a true and meaningful sentence S_3 that claims that S_1 and S_2 have different meanings (from premise 3).
2. S_3 is true if and only if $\ulcorner S_1$ does not mean the same as $S_2 \urcorner$.
3. $\ulcorner S_1$ does not mean the same as $S_2 \urcorner$ is either false or meaningless (from premises 1 and 4, plus a hidden application of premise 2).
4. S_3 is not true (from premises 2 and 3).
5. S_1 and S_2 do not have distinct meanings (from premises 1 and 4).
6. But S_1 and S_2 were chosen at random from the true sentences, and so every true sentence means what any other one does.

It is clear that such an argument effectively does away with the possibility of meaningful discourse, and it is an argument such as this that I think Plato wishes to prove unsound. Given this preliminary linguistic conclusion, the ontological conclusions for which Parmenides is infamous follow from repeated applications of premise 3. (If there were motion, then some sentence such as 'A thing is at one time at some place and at another time not there' would be true. But in light of premise 4 it cannot be. For details see Furth 1968.)

It seems to me (as it has to many others before me) that Plato's resolution of this paradoxical position is the construction of a "philosopher's language"—a language that accurately mirrors reality and in which Parmenides' Problem would not arise. It is almost as though Plato had granted that Parmenides' Problem *seems* to arise for natural language, but this appearance is due to the fact that natural language embodies certain "shorthand" abbreviations that do not truly correspond to reality.

One feature the philosopher's language will have is what may be called the naming principle: every general term will name something, which something is the meaning of the term. This would seem to be an endorsement of premise 2b of Parmenides' Problem, and, indeed, I think this is the proper way to look at the matter. The difference between Parmenides and Plato is in what Plato takes the general terms of the philosopher's language to name. For him, it is the forms. With just this sketch of the philosopher's language, we can see that certain things we were automatically forbidden to say (by the Parmenidean argument) are now permitted. 'Unicorns have one horn' is no longer ruled out on the grounds that there are no unicorns, so there is no meaning to 'unicorns' (via premise 2b), hence no meaning to any sentence containing 'unicorns'. Perhaps the sentence is still meaningless but at least not on these grounds.

Plato's altering of the force of premise 2b to talk about the Forms suggests that we change premise 2a in a similar manner: The meaning of $\ulcorner \alpha$ is $\phi \urcorner$ is the fact *about the Forms* to which it refers. But just *saying* this will not solve any of the problems that are involved in, say, the sentence 'Bachelors are not mothers'. If this sentence is to have any meaning (according to the new reading of premise 2a), there must be some fact about the Forms, of bachelors not being mothers. In light of premise 4, what meaning can we attach to this? Are we to say that there are negative facts in the world of Forms? If Plato still holds his earlier "orthodox" views about the relationship between Forms and the physical world, then there will also be negative facts in the physical world, since the world of Forms is "mirrored" (imperfectly) into the physical world. On the other hand, we could follow up recent discussions about "Pauline Predication"[1] and claim that 'Bachelors are not mothers' is somehow an expression to the effect 'All instances of the form Bachelor are not mothers'. We still have the problem—what could this mean but some negative fact? It is clear that a satisfactory answer to this will depend on some reasonable account of Plato's discussion of 'Not-Being' at 257–258.

I want to explain how I am going to proceed. I claim that Plato denied premise 2a and, furthermore, that he replaced it with a different analysis of the meaning of such sentences. The commentators have attributed (at times unwittingly) to Plato a number of different analyses, and I want to adjudicate among them. My criteria are these: (a) the analyses attributed to him must, in fact, not still involve Plato in Parmenides' Problem, and (b) the analysis must also account for Plato's claim that any discourse we can have owes its existence to the interweaving of the Forms with one another. If these two conditions are satisfied, then we will (c) look to the general philosophical acceptability of this analysis and (d) judge its textual plausibiltiy.

I broadly classify interpretations of Plato into four camps. The first group, the "nonstarters," either take Plato to be doing something different from answering Parmenides and these accounts cannot be converted into such an answer, or else they *say* they are showing how Plato answered Parmenides but they have a very strange understanding of Parmenides. (This is so because it is clear that the answer they supply on Plato's behalf would be scoffed at by Parmenides.) Among these nonstarters I include three groups consisting of A: Peck (1952, 1962) and Xenakis (1959); B: Hackforth (1945) and Robinson (1950); and C: Lee$_1$ (1972) and Frede$_1$ (1967).[2] These writers will be discussed below, at least in enough detail for me to indicate why I think they should be classified as nonstarters.

The second group, the "correspondence theorists," are those who make the claim that for every sentence of natural language Plato has some specific sentence of the philosopher's language that "corresponds" to it (and is to be taken as what the natural language statement "really means" and "really asserts about reality"). These theorists advocate, in effect, the replacement of premise 2a by something else. In particular, they want to show that Plato had a translation (into the philosopher's language) of the troublesome negative sentences and that this translation shows how Parmenides' Problem is to be avoided.[3] I detect thirteen correspondence theorists:

I. Cornford$_1$	VIII. Wiggins$_1$
II. Ross, Allan	IX. Wiggins$_2$
III. Hamlyn	X. Philip, Ackrill$_1$, Kostman
IV. Schipper, Bluck	XI. Sayre
V. Moravcsik, Runciman	XII. Frede$_2$
VI. Owen, Lewis$_1$	XIII. Lorenz and Mittelstrass$_1$
VII. Cornford$_2$	

The third group, the "backdrop theorists," take interweaving to be something "behind" language in general. That is, they do not view Plato as giving a determinate sentence of the philosopher's language to replace (say) the ordinary negations, but rather they view Plato to be claiming that there exists some reality or other that gives a "ground" for the meaningfulness of statements in general. These "grounds" might be viewed as the *presuppositions* of language — what must happen in order for there to be language at all. Here I will discuss Lorenz and Mittelstrass$_2$, Lee$_2$, and Lewis$_2$.

The fourth group I call "mixed theorists." Their theories have both a correspondence component and a backdrop component. These theories hold Plato both to be giving some reality that is a "ground" or presupposition for language in general and to be giving a specific sentence of the philosopher's language that corresponds to any chosen ordinary statement. These theorists might profitably be viewed as saying (with respect to some particular sentence) *what part* of the "ground" or backdrop is responsible for *that* sentence's meaning what it does. Here, Ackrill$_2$ might point to Ackrill$_1$ and Frede$_3$ might point to Frede$_2$.

NONSTARTERS

I have three different kinds of nonstarters in mind. The first kind think that Plato is doing something entirely different than I think. Peck (1952, 1962) and Xenakis (1959) do not believe that in the *Sophist* Plato is talking about any theory of Forms, whether it be his theory or anyone else's; although I think this wrong, it would take us too far afield to consider the idea in detail. (Peck thinks that the whole *megista genē* section is "dialectical" and that Plato is only answering the sophists by pointing out relationships among those concepts that they themselves will admit exist and by showing where their theories lead. Xenakis denies that the *Sophist* is about the Forms at all rather than about the conceptual framework of language. Of course, the way I am treating the matter the two overlap, but Xenakis denies that we should understand any of this to be about Forms and then draw conclusions about language or to understand it to be about language and then draw conclusions about Forms; rather, we should just understand it to be about rules for language *simpliciter*.)

The second group of nonstarters I wish to exclude from the general discussion, on textual grounds. Hackforth (1945) and Robinson (1950) both take Plato to be talking about *words* when he says *eidē*, and never about Forms, once the section starting at 259 has begun. In fact, they take these words to be akin to proper names. Therefore, the "interweaving of the Forms with one another" becomes "the interweaving of words with one another," which becomes (Robinson 1950: p. 11) "Each sentence is a compound of one noun and one verb. It asserts that this thing signified by its noun has the attribute signified by its verb." The problem with taking this view is that it affords no link between all the earlier work on the *megista genē* (which both Hackforth and Robinson admit is about the Forms) and the present work supposedly on words and sentences. At 259e there begins a self-contained discussion, they say, on the Being of speech that is independent of 251 through 258 on the relations of Forms with one another. The *symplokē eidōn* at 259e is translated as "interweaving of parts of speech" by them in looking forward to the *symplokē* mentioned at 262c6 and d4. Lorenz and Mittelstrass (1966b) claim that this forward looking is not sound since there was an occurrence of *symplokē* earlier at 240c, where it *clearly* signals a combination of something other than parts of speech.[4] I would not wish to decide the issue merely on this basis, but it does add to the overall difficulty in attributing this sort of strategy to Plato. Further, the translation of *eidē* here as "parts of speech" means that the distinction carefully drawn at 261a1–2 between *eidē* on the one hand and *grammata* ('letters') and *onomata* ('words' or 'names') on the other is empty wordplay. And this is not the best thing to attribute to Plato.[5]

The third group of nonstarters is to be ruled out on philosophic grounds. I insist that Plato did not invent "negative" Forms; that is, the mere addition of a negative prefix to a predicate does not directly generate a name for some Form. For instance, Plato would not answer Parmenides' objections to 'John is not a cat' simply by saying that its meaning is that John partakes of the Form Non-Cat. However the analysis of negation comes out in the end, it is nothing so simple as that. If the analysis given by the standard interpretation of Parmenides' argument is anything nearly correct, such a gratuitous addition of Forms would merely amount to Plato's replying to Parmenides: "Of course we can make negative predications—you see, there are these Forms . . . ." Parmenides would scoff at such a suggestion. It does not get to the root of Parmenides' Problem, as Plato himself saw; the whole program of the *Sophist* is aimed in a different direction — that of convincing Father Parmenides on his own grounds. Furthermore, *Politicus* 262 explicitly states that there are not necessarily Forms corresponding to a simple negation. (Also, see the Aristotelean comments on Plato: *Metaphysics* 990b13–14, 1079a9–10; Alexander's commentary [*in Meta.* 80, 15–81, 7] in which he quotes from *Peri Ideon*.[6])

Both Lee$_1$ (vide, inter alia, 1967: p. 275) and Frede$_1$ (1967: pp. 92–94) embrace the notion of a "negative" Form. Frede, however, gives an account of negative predication that does not presuppose them; this account will be considered in the next section. Lee$_1$ makes such Forms essential, however. They are "derived" and "intensional" — the Form Otherness, when directed to the Form X, yields the "sense" of "not-X." Thus, these negative Forms are not part of the basic ontology of Forms but are "intentionally constructed" out of the basic, positive ones with the aid of the Form Otherness. Lee$_1$ (1972: p. 292) makes a considerable point about claiming that such Forms are "definite."

> What 'x is not brown' says is that x (which is) partakes of a certain Part of Otherness (a Part which fully and securely *is* . . .); it says that x partakes of that Part of Otherness whose "name" is "(the) not-brown" and whose determinate nature consists in Otherness-precisely-than-brown.

No doubt most commentators would want to hold something like this as a *part* of their view, but Lee$_1$ (1972: pp. 293, 295) wants it to be *all* of his view.

> . . . it is no part at all of the sense of the negating proposition that it should refer to any (much less all) particular entities or predicates other than the negated predicate. . . . [The negating statement simply] says that the subject's partaking lies outside of the predicate negated . . . just that it lies outside-that-predicate. . . . The determinate sense of 'x is not brown' thus lies precisely, but lies entirely, in its saying that brown is what x is not. What the statement will signify — and all that it signifies, on Plato's analysis — is that the subject does not partake of *that* predicate.

(This position is in some ways similar to Schema I below, but, in view of the differences between Lee$_1$ and the holders of Schema I, it is perhaps best to separate them.) Given this statement of Lee's and the Parmenidean argument of above, it is difficult to see how Lee$_1$ can believe that such an account could possibly "vindicate the sense of negative expressions by showing that the understanding of any negative statement involves the apprehension only of 'existent,' positive, determinate contents" (1972: p. 291), for it does not remove the difficulty that Parmenides finds with Not-Being.[7]

CORRESPONDENCE THEORISTS

A correspondence theorist is one who is going to show how sentences of ordinary language are to be translated into the philosopher's language so as to exhibit reality correctly. To do this, the theorists must offer us some uniform translation procedure. For example, ordinary sentences such as 'Theaetetus is sitting' might be said to translate into 'Theaetetus partakes of (the form) Sitting' or 'Theaetetus partakes of (the form) Sitting, which blends with (the form) Being.' These latter sentences, being part of the philosopher's language, mean whatever (fact) they name or describe (or, alternatively, name the fact that they mean). Correspondence theorists thus deny the simple naming principle for ordinary language; instead, they translate the ordinary statement into a philosophic one and apply the naming principle to it. One way to put this is: correspondence theorists find Plato assigning meanings to ordinary sentences that are not "on their sleeves." I will adopt the convention that such theorists are attributing to Plato the view that the ordinary sentence *means* what is named by its philosophic translation. Thus, 'Theaetetus is sitting' *means* (according to some correspondence theorists) the fact of the referent of 'Theaetetus' (viz., Theaetetus) partaking of the referent of 'sitting' (viz., the form Sitting).

For simplicity of exposition, I will use quasi quotes; phrases like 'Ref (ϕ)' are to mean "whatever the referent of ϕ is." In the schemata to be given below as explications of what various commentators have attributed to Plato, I intend the terms to be understood in a nontechnical way. Plato uses *metexein, koinonia, summeixis*, and other terms in what I think is a fixed pattern;[8] here, however, I rather indiscriminately followed several authors at once and generally use 'partakes of' as a relation between individuals and forms, 'belongs to' as a way of saying the converse of 'partakes of', and 'blends' (for the most part) as indicating *some* relation holding among forms.[9] I use 'blends with the Different from' in a specific manner, indicating "is not identical to"; when I want this phrase to mean something else (e.g., "is incompatible with"), I use a formulation explicitly invoking the notion of an incompatibility range (see Schemata IX, X, and XI).

Cornford (1935) sometimes (pp. 300–301) holds a position like Schema I; that is, he claims that Plato could refute Parmenides' difficulties about Not-Being if he were merely to recognize that he needs to give separate sorts of translations for positive and negative sentences.

Schema I (Cornford$_1$, 1935: pp. 300–301):

2a$_1$. The meaning of $\ulcorner\alpha$ is $\bar\phi\urcorner$ is the fact of Ref (α) partaking of Ref (ϕ).

2a$_2$. The meaning of $\ulcorner\alpha$ is not $\bar\phi\urcorner$ is the fact of Ref (α) not partaking of Ref. (ϕ).

Immediately, however, we see that this does not solve the problem. Consider 'Theaetetus is not flying': Under the proposed analysis, this would have as its meaning the fact of flying not belonging to Theaetetus; but by premise 4 this purported fact does not exist, so the sentence has no meaning, etc. Thus, we can reject Cornford's account of negation as well as his account of the "interweaving of the Forms," since they do not adequately show that Plato has solved the problem he set for himself. Furthermore, Schema I does not account for the statement at 259e5–6 in which "the interweaving of the forms with one another" is claimed to be necessary for the possibility of discourse. On this point, Ross (1951: p. 115) claims that it was an "overstatement," i.e., that it is false; and Cornford (1935) simply does not translate *allelōn* ("with one another") and claims (p. 314) that the sentence at 259e5–6 means that every sentence mentions at least one form-name. Such moves violate our Principles of Charity of Interpretation and should, therefore, be rejected. Such readings of 259e5-6 have been attacked by many people, and I will not repeat their criticisms; we should note, however, that even if there were no other reason, we should be justified in rejecting this interpretation of interweaving because it does not supply us with an account of how to solve Parmenides' Problem. (I might mention that Cornford does not always hold Schema I; I will give another schema to which he sometimes resorts later.)

There is another way along the same lines to make sense out of the "interweaving of the forms with one another" in these sentences in which the subject is a proper name. This can be done without resorting to Cornford's mistranslation of "with one another." Ross (1951: pp. 115-16) says, "In sentence 'Theaetetus is not flying' Theaetetus exists and Flying (the Form or universal of flying) exists, so in saying the sentence we are not asserting of him something that does not exist, but simply something that does not belong to him." And Allan (1954: p. 285) says:

> [A true statement] describes things as they are; i.e., its components must (a) stand for real entities and (b) in their relation to one another, depict the relation between those entities. . . . In the false statement, the terms will likewise stand for entities — that is why it is significant — but they will represent them as related in a way which does not correspond to the facts.

It thus seems that such commentators are attributing the following schema to Plato.

Schema II (Ross, Allan):

   2a$_1$. The meaning of $\ulcorner\alpha$ is $\phi\urcorner$ is the fact that Ref (α) partakes of Ref (ϕ) and of Ref (ϕ) existing (and Ref [α] existing?).

   2a$_2$. The meaning of $\ulcorner\alpha$ is not $\phi\urcorner$ is the fact that Ref (α) does not partake of Ref (ϕ) and of Ref (ϕ) existing (and Ref [α] existing?).

I said that such a view makes some sense of the interweaving of forms with one another since the philosopher's sentence will contain reference to two forms: Being and Ref (ϕ). Whether such a relation between Being and Ref (ϕ) should be said to be "interweaving" in Plato's sense of the word is another question, one that I will defer until later. It is sufficient for us to notice that the proposed (2a$_2$) still has not helped us solve Parmenides' Problem, for the problem will now rearise in the philospher's language. Thus, Schema II must be rejected, in accordance with the Principles of Charity of Interpretation, from being Plato's account.

In their anxiety to satisfy the apparent requirement that each sentence of the philosopher's language somehow mention at least two form-names, a number of authors have resorted to supposing the existence of forms that are nowhere mentioned by Plato. One such method of finding enough forms to perform an interweaving in sentences (apparently) about particulars is to look "behind" the subject-term, e.g., behind 'Theaetetus'. According to the view of Hamlyn (1955), there are no names except those for forms in the philosopher's language. What appears to be a proper name of a physical particular is actually a mark of what Hamlyn calls a "characteristic," and this is a form that applies to exactly one single entity. Therefore, the "inter-weaving" behind the sentence 'Theaetetus is sitting' is that between the (unique) form indicated by 'Theaetetus' and the form Sitting. The recommendation for meaning is:

Schema III (Hamlyn):

2a$_1$. The meaning of ⌐α is φ⌐ is the fact that A blends with Ref (φ).

2a$_2$. The meaning of ⌐α is not φ⌐ is the fact that A does not blend with Ref (φ), where A is the Form or "characteristic" of Ref (α).

Such an account cannot stand up under scrutiny of Plato's use of proper names in the Sophist, and, hence, it is already implausible as an account of the Sophist. In 263, the name 'Theaetetus' is explained as being "about the Theaetetus with whom [the Stranger] is talking now"; this is distinguished from those things that hold of him. The only place I have never found Plato to be talking of the unique character of a particular is Theaetetus 209, but even then there is no hint that Plato is talking about the Forms as opposed to some person's concept of the particular. (Some claims about proper names being akin to predicates are made in the Cratylus, but I will not discuss them now. See Schema XII.) Furthermore, such a view cannot possibly account for negative predication in the manner needed, for consider 'Theaetetus is not Flying': this sentence asserts (according to Hamlyn) that the Form of Theaetetus does not include anything of flying, i.e., Theaetetus' Form does not blend with the Form Flying. But, as we can immediately see, this does not solve Parmenides' Problem.

No one that I know of has explicitly taken up Hamlyn's Characteristic-Form theory (although Turnbull's [1964] interpretation has something like it), but it has suggested various emendations to some. Schipper, for instance, holds that there are no true individuals at all. What 'Theaetetus' refers to is precisely the set of Forms that can truly be said to characterize Theaetetus. Thus, there are no individuals who partake of some unique Form, but rather there are sets of Forms corresponding to each proper name. Schipper (1964: p. 44) makes the point that particulars exist only by dint of the Forms that characterize them. In Forms in Plato's Later Dialogues (1965: p. 40), she says:

> Though the name 'Theaetetus' may be the grammatical subject of statements about him, the experienced Theaetetus is not a substantial subject existing in-dependently of forms, about whom forms are predicated. . . . Theaetetus may be spoken of, not as an existing object beyond the forms, but as described by the interrelated forms. Logos is about them, only.

Bluck's (1957) view is similar but does not include the notion that individuals exist only by dint of their characterizing Forms. He starts with 262c9-d6, which is taken to give a syntactical definition of meaningful sentences. ("Sounds uttered signify nothing until you combine verbs with names. The moment you do that the simplest combination becomes a statement. . . . It gets you somewhere by weaving together verbs with names.") It is we who interweave words together to make a sentence, and (he says) it is therefore we who interweave the appropriate Forms; 259e5-6 now becomes (p. 182) "that in any statement we make we are in fact weaving Forms together, either correctly or incorrectly, and that only so is discourse possible." But now what will "incorrectly weaving the Forms" come to? And how will that become a solution to Parmenides' Problem? The Forms involved in the sentence 'Theaetetus is sitting' when we utter it are all the Forms Theaetetus partakes of plus the Form(s) that "this-individual-sitting-here" partakes of. Thus, in weaving together 'Theaetetus' with 'sitting' we are also weaving together 'this particular man with such and such properties' and 'this-individual-sitting-here', and, therefore, we are weaving together the Forms Man, etc. (all of Theaetetus' properties) and the Form Sitting. And when we utter 'Theaetetus is Flying', we interweave the words and so interweave the Forms, but there is not an individual-flying-here, and so we have a false sentence. I doubt that this is going to solve any of the problems raised earlier on in the text about falsity, but here I will just note that, even though his focus is on falsity rather than on negative sentences, Bluck commits himself to the view embodied in Schema IV (for true sentences). For, since the meaningfulness of sentences in general is taken to be syntactically defined and since 'Theaetetus is not flying' satisfies that criterion, the relationships among the forms *behind* this sentence must be just those behind any meaningful sentence, and that is just whether or not the Forms holding of the subject are blended with that indicated by the predicate. These views may be represented by Schema IV; version (i) is Schipper's (1964: p. 42), and version (ii) is Bluck's (1957).

Schema IV (i—Schipper, ii—Bluck):

2a$_1$. The meaning of $\ulcorner\alpha$ is $\bar{\phi}\urcorner$ is that Ref (ϕ_1), Ref (ϕ_2), Ref (ϕ_3), . . . blend with Ref (ϕ).

2a$_2$. The meaning of $\ulcorner\alpha$ is not $\bar{\phi}\urcorner$ is that Ref (ϕ_1), Ref (ϕ_2), Ref (ϕ_3), . . . do not blend with Ref (ϕ).

  i. Ref (α) = Ref (ϕ_1), Ref (ϕ_2), Ref (ϕ_3), ...

  ii. $\phi_1, \phi_2, \phi_3,$ . . . are all the predicates truly applicable to Ref (α).

Schipper's view clearly contradicts Plato's use of proper names at 263, where Theaetetus is distinguished from the things that are true of him, and what is being talked about by 'Theaetetus' is exactly the entity before the stranger and nothing else. Against both Schipper's view and Bluck's view, we can point out that it does not solve Parmenides' Problem and thus cannot be a correct analysis of 'Not-Being'; even though it can give *some* sense to the "interweaving of forms with one another," it just does not give the *right* sense. (This can also be seen by noting that the analysis of positive sentences makes them be *necessarily true*, if they are true. In 'Theaetetus is sitting', Sitting is presumably one of the Forms that Theaetetus partakes of [or is defined in terms of]. Thus, the proposed semantical theory gives no account of the difference to be found in 'man is man' and 'man is good', a difference Plato clearly believes his account to cover, 251.)

Another place to look for forms that Plato does not mention is the copula. Moravcsik (1960) and Runciman (1965), for example, suppose that there is a Form corresponding to the copula and one corresponding to the negative-copula; these

Moravcsik calls "Relational Being" and "the negative counterpart of Relational Being," and he gives what amounts to Schema V (Moravcsik, 1960: p. 127; Runciman, 1965: pp. 107–13).

Schema V (Moravcsik, Runciman):

   2a$_1$. The meaning of $\ulcorner\alpha$ is $\bar{\phi}\urcorner$ is that Ref (α) blends with Relational Being with respect to Ref (ϕ).

   2a$_2$. The meaning of $\ulcorner\alpha$ is not $\bar{\phi}\urcorner$ is that Ref (α) blends with the negative counterpart of Relational Being with respect to Ref (ϕ).

We should first notice that Schema V *does* provide a solution to Parmenides' Problem since the meaning of a "negative sentence" is no longer a "negative fact" but rather "something positive," viz., Ref (ϕ)'s blending with the negative counterpart of Relational Being. But there are difficulties with this solution. First, we should look at some textual difficulties. I said that Moravcsik merely invented these Forms. He points to 255d3–8, where it is said of Being that it participates in two *eidē*, *to kath' auto* and *to pros allo*, and he says that these two Forms, when combined with Being, are represented by the copula and its negative counterpart (p. 125). Now, in order for Moravcsik's interpretation to go through, *to kath' auto* and *to pros allo* must be understood as two-place relations. But this is impossible when we consider what use these concepts are put to in the text; viz., 'is' is said to have two uses: a *to kath' auto* use (an example of which is 'motion is') and a *to pros allo* use (an example of which is 'motion is the same [as itself]' or 'man is a learner'). Further, even if Plato did understand Forms as sometimes being two-place relations, there is no evidence that he ever took them to be Forms "behind" the copula, for if he did it would be strange that he did not directly state this (it being a rather important point).[10]

Furthermore, there is a serious philosophical objection to this purported solution. If we are to take seriously the rationale behind the attempt to give a justification for the meaning of predicative statements in terms of some ontological counterpart, we find that we will have to have something that works like glue in holding the reality together, similar to the way the copula works as a "syntactical glue" in holding sentences together. Usually, Plato is considered to have held that the ontological glue was "blending" or "partaking" (and Aristotle so takes it while demanding a further explanation). Moravcsik takes the glue to be "blends with . . . respect to . . . ." Now consider negative sentences; could there be any such glue between Theaetetus and Flying? Obviously not, since the point of the denial of Flying's blending with something with respect to Theaetetus is merely a denial of there being any "ontological glue" here. Therefore, the proposed Schema V certainly could not satisfy anyone; and, following our Principles of Charity of Interpretation, this is good grounds for denying that Plato held it.

Another thing to notice about Schema V is that it does not *justify* itself. We are told that the interweaving of the Forms underlies rational discourse; when asked how, we are told that (a) for statements of identity (or nonidentity), the Form Sameness (or Difference) interweaves with Relational Being and (b) for statements of positive (or negative) prediction, Relational Being (or its negative counterpart) interweaves with the Form indicated by the predicate. In what sense can this be said to explain how sentences have meaning? There is no plausibility to it other than that it does make the "interweaving of the Forms" claim seem true. The explanation given by Moravcsik (1960: p. 127) is simply: ". . . the meaning of any statement involves an attribute and a connector, and this is surely the essential point that Plato makes." But surely it is *not* the essential point. Plato is trying to overcome a logical problem presented by Parmenides. It is not enough to say in response that the problem is indeed a problem and what it shows is that we need to add more Forms to our ontology so that we can give negative statements meaning. What *would* be enough would be to show that on the basis of already accepted Forms, and certain plausible relations between them, we can account for the meaningfulness of negative statements exactly as we do for the positive statements that we accept.

Finally, the Moravcsik/Runciman interpretation of Plato's view does not explain truth and falsity of sentences. One of the things we are supposed to be able to do by means of an inspection of a sentence in the philosopher's language is to see why a sentence is true (or why it *can* be true). One should be able to inspect the sentence and say, "I see what reality this sentence is asserting." But consider the true sentence 'John is not a dog'. According to the Runciman/Moravcsik interpretation, the only reason we can give for this sentence being true is that the Form Dog is blending with the negative counterpart of Relational Being to John. Certainly this is not a very convincing reason—it strikes one as being merely a repetition of the original (if he understands it at all).[11]

I view Schemata I through V as exercises in futility. Somehow we all know (but I will not try to tell you how we know it) that the analysis of negation should bring in the form The Different. The most simpleminded way to bring it in is Owen's (1970: pp. 232, 237–38) and Lewis's (1976: pp. 104–5, 108).[12]

Schema VI (Owen, Lewis$_1$):

2a$_1$. The meaning of $\ulcorner \alpha$ is $\overline{\phi} \urcorner$ is that Ref (α) partakes of Ref (ϕ).

2a$_2$. The meaning of $\ulcorner \alpha$ is not $\overline{\phi} \urcorner$ is that Ref (ϕ_1), Ref (ϕ_2), Ref (ϕ_3), . . . blend with the Different with respect to Ref (ϕ), where Ref (ϕ_1), Ref (ϕ_2), Ref (ϕ_3), . . . are all the forms Ref (α) partakes of.

Although Schema VI solves Parmenides' Problem by assigning a "positive fact" as the meaning of ordinary negative sentences, it seems to me wrong for the following three reasons. First, it does not account for the apparent force of the *symplokē* at 259E, viz., that each sentence mention at least two forms (because 2a$_1$ only mentions one form). There are various ways that Owen and Lewis$_1$ could take around this objection, so perhaps it is not all that important. (They could say that the doctrine of vowel-forms does the requisite blending or that Plato was trying to stop Parmenides' Problem from even getting going and for that we need the interweaving of 2a$_2$.) Second, we should note that Plato is explicitly drawing some analogy between the *ontological* "Not-Being" and the *sentential* "Not-Being" (i.e., falsity). Under Owen's view, this analogy becomes this: in order to determine the falsity of

'Theaetetus is flying', we have to find out *all* the predicates that hold of Theaetetus in order to show that Flying is not one of them. It is not sufficient merely to find out that he is sitting, for according to Owen's analysis one cannot infer from this that he is not flying. Rather, to show he is not flying we must examine every predicate and show that it is not identical to flying. As Owen himself remarks, this makes falsifying statements an interminable business (p. 238 fn.). Owen finds no difficulty here, but this clearly shows that the analogy has broken down and, hence, that his analysis of the ontological "Not-Being" is incorrect. Third, and most telling, although singular affirmative statements are, according to this analysis, synthetic (the notion of "partaking" being somehow synthetic), we find that true singular negative statements are all analytically true. For, under Owen's analysis of "blends with the Different with respect to," two forms do so exactly in case they are not identical; therefore, whether or not Ref (ϕ_1), Ref (ϕ_2), Ref (ϕ_3), . . . are identical with Ref (ϕ) (in our singular negative statement) is a matter already settled by our semantics (i.e., by statements about how many, and what kinds of, Forms there are) and, thus, is logically necessary. Surely, whether it is true or false that Theaetetus is not standing is not a matter for our semantics to decide upon.

One way around the objections that Schema VI makes falsification "an interminable business" and makes singular negative sentences analytic (if they are true) is to adopt a view sometimes held by Cornford.

Schema VII (Cornford$_2$ [1935: pp. 314–15]):

2a$_1$. The meaning of $\ulcorner\alpha$ is $\phi\urcorner$ is that Ref (α) partakes of Ref (ϕ).

2a$_2$. The meaning of $\ulcorner\alpha$ is not $\phi\urcorner$ is that Ref (α) partakes of some form F, which blends with the Different with respect to Ref (ϕ),

where "blends with the Form Different with respect to X" is to be understood as not being identical with X.[13] Cornford's explanation of "Not-Being" when he is discussing falsity (pp. 314–15) exactly fits this schema. He is still committed, by dint of 2a$_1$ not mentioning two forms, to understand (per impossible) 'interweaving of Forms with one another' as 'at least one Form', but at least it does not commit him to other difficulties found in Schema I (which he otherwise advocates).

There are some difficulties with this kind of account because it does not assign the correct properties to negation. For example, this account makes contradictory sentences true. Suppose Socrates is a white man; 'Socrates is a man' is true by 2a$_2$, and, since White blends with the Different from Man (i.e., they are not identical), it follows that 'Socrates is not a man' is also true. As Wiggins (1970: pp. 293–94) notes, this account cannot be correct for another reason. Simple difference between Ref (ϕ_1) and Ref (ϕ_2) cannot suffice to make them exclude one another. Theaetetus' having some quality distinct from flying can hardly in itself rule out the possibility that Theaetetus flies. He would have a distinct quality even if he were flying.[14]

We can avoid at least some of the difficulties raised in connection with the Owen/Lewis$_1$ and Cornford$_2$ views by reimporting a Form behind the copula a la Moravcsik (but not one for the "negative copula") and always mentioning that the subject is partaking of these Forms (as is not done by Owen). The following is one of the accounts given by Wiggins (1970: pp. 288–90, 294).

Schema VIII (Wiggins$_1$):

2a$_1$. The meaning of $\ulcorner\alpha$ is $\bar\phi\urcorner$ is that Ref (α) partakes of Being with respect to Ref (ϕ).

2a$_2$. The meaning of $\ulcorner\alpha$ is not $\bar\phi\urcorner$ is that for all forms F, if Ref (α) partakes of Being with respect to F, then F blends with the Different with respect to Ref (ϕ).

Schema VIII, unlike Schemata VI and VII, satisfies the criterion that each sentence mention an interweaving of the Forms (here, the Form Being and at least one other Form). Second, again unlike Schema VI, the meaning of negative sentences is not such that they are logically true or false,[15] nor does it make contradictory sentences true. Furthermore, we might note that this account actually does solve Parmenides' Problem since the meaning of a negative sentence is now some "positive fact."

What can be said against it? Well, first, it still makes falsification of sentences "an interminable business." Wiggins (1970: p. 301) is sensitive to this sort of objection and wishes that Plato had replaced it by Schema IX.

Schema IX (Wiggins$_2$):

2a$_1$. The meaning of $\ulcorner\alpha$ is $\bar\phi\urcorner$ is that Ref (α) partakes of Being with respect to Ref (ϕ).

2a$_2$. The meaning of $\ulcorner\alpha$ is not $\bar\phi\urcorner$ is that there is a form F such that F belongs to the same incompatibility range as Ref (ϕ) and Ref (α) partakes of Being with respect to F,

where "belongs to the same incompatibility range as" is taken to imply that nothing can be characterized by two predicates in the same range at the same time. (The existential quantifier in [2a$_2$] makes the procedure terminate.) However, Wiggins just does not believe that Plato makes this move, even though all his examples (not-large, etc.) are consistent with it.[16] I think it quite clear that Schema IX is preferable to Schema VIII on philosophical grounds, and, as I've tried to show in Pelletier (1975), there is no legitimate textual reason to prefer one over the other. We, therefore, should apply the Principles of Charity of Interpretation and attribute Schema IX to Plato (at least provisionally, pending investigation of any other interpretations or considerations).

Yet, there are some problems with Schema IX that seem to me to show the desirability of finding some other account. When I discussed Moravcsik, I pointed to two difficulties in understanding there to be Forms corresponding to the copula and the "negative copula." The first was that a distinction between "positive Relational Being" and "negative Relational Being" could not be gleaned from the text; i.e., that *to kath' auto* did not mean "positive Relational Being" since it corresponded to a "complete" use of 'is', not a two-place relation. The second objection was of a more philosophical nature: it seemed to involve a misconstrual of the point of constructing a philosopher's language. It made *all* the words of a sentence be names and, hence, made the sentence be a list. What is needed is some kind of "ontological glue" to hold the "ontological building blocks" together, with the "ontological glue" corresponding to the "syntactic glue" (provided by 'is' and the like in ordinary discourse) that holds the "syntactic building blocks" (the *onomata* and the *rhemata*) together.

Here Wiggins is not making Moravcsik's distinction between kinds of "Relational Being" (he, in fact, agrees that these must be "complete" and not relative); rather, he is pointing to *to pros allo* (Moravcsik's "negative Relational Being") as needing to be understood as "being with respect to something else" and then is glossing this as "the Form Being blending with some other Form." All this seems quite unobjectionable until he applies this distinction to particular sentences by parsing 'Theaetetus is a man' into 'Theaetetus partakes of the Form Man' and then claiming that this is merely a contraction of 'Theaetetus partakes of the Form Being blended with the Form Man'. Wiggins's argument is, therefore, vulnerable to the second of the objections to Moravcsik. Either Wiggins is claiming (on Plato's behalf) (a) that we have to look "behind" the copula to find a Form, (b) that Theaetetus is partaking of "some special version of the Form Being, namely the Man version," or (c) that 'partaking of F' is always equivalent to 'partaking of Being blended with F'.

I cannot see that Plato ever said any of these things, although I do not take this as decisive against Schema IX. It is certainly true that Being is a vowel-form and hence "runs through all forms," but it is far from clear that this is equivalent to (c) of the last paragraph. It is also true that, when Plato discusses "the Different" (another vowel-form), he claims that "running through them all" gives rise to "parts of the Different" (257C-D), but I still do not see that this implies (b). Furthermore, such a view merely pushes various philosophical problems one step further back. Since 'is' is our "syntactic glue," if the ontology-sentence analogy is to hold up, we will not want to assign 'is' a "building-block" ontological role but rather a "glue" role. In Wiggins's account, we had to invent another glue, viz., "partaking" glue, a glue that does not correspond to any syntactical element.[17] For these sorts of reasons, I think we should look for another interpretation.

To avoid the sort of objections described in the preceding paragraphs, one might consider simply dropping the reference to Being in the formulations of ($2a_1$) and ($2a_2$). This would result in the sort of view held by Philip (1968: p. 319) and Kostman (1973). (I also call it Ackrill$_1$, although Ackrill is not a correspondence theorist but rather a mixed theorist. I attribute it to him merely because he might be willing to point to that part of reality indicated by the schema if he were asked "what portion of the backdrop makes *this* sentence true?")

Schema X (Philip, Kostman, Ackrill$_1$):

$2a_1$. The meaning of $\ulcorner \alpha$ is $\phi \urcorner$ is that Ref (α) partakes of Ref (ϕ).

$2a_2$. The meaning of $\ulcorner \alpha$ is not $\phi \urcorner$ is that there is a form F such that F belongs to the same incompatibility range as Ref (ϕ) and Ref (α) partakes of F.

This schema does not involve us in the difficulties associated with assigning to 'is' some entity that plays a "building-block" role rather than a "glue" role, but it fails at making sense of the "interweaving of the Forms with one another." On this point

Philip (1968: p. 231) gives the following peculiar comment: "[This doctrine of blending] puts a stop to eristical discussions. . . . To argue in the eristical way is quite barbarous and would put an end to philosophical discourse, which comes to pass 'through the mutual (or two-way) weaving together of kinds.'" Presumably then, ordinary discourse is not affected by the "Parmenidean denial of not-being, [whereby] identity is denied, difference is ignored, and opposite predicates are attached without regard to the principles [of blending]." This is clearly a misunderstanding of Parmenides. On the other hand, if Philip does not mean this but rather means something along the lines I have been indicating all along, he is indeed unable to account for the interweaving, for *not* every sentence specifically illustrates an interweaving of Forms. Kostman's (1973) view of the matter is considerably better thought out but, so far as I see, still has this unfortunate consequence: it cannot account for the interweaving of the forms with one another. If one is a correspondence theorist, the interweaving must be indicated in every sentence, and Schema X just does not do the job. (Of course, the backdrop portion of the mixed theory of Ackrill is not subject to this criticism. It is a hallmark of such theories that *not* every individual sentence must indicate a specific interweaving; only the backdrop must.)

Sayre (1969: p. 210) offers an account that has the advantages of ($2a_2$) of Schema X but explicitly embraces an interweaving for its ($2a_1$). (Actually, his account is not quite like the one I give here as Schema XI; he has negative forms. But his explanation of negative forms in footnote 89 on p. 210 and the discussion on pp. 195–96, especially in footnote 68, seems to make it clear that he would allow this paraphrasing away of negative forms.)

Schema XI (Sayre, 1969: p. 210):

$2a_1$. The meaning of ⌜α is ϕ⌝ is that every form Ref (α) partakes of is compatible with Ref (ϕ).

$2a_2$. The meaning of ⌜α is not ϕ⌝ is that there is a form F such that F belongs to the same incompatibility range as Ref (ϕ) and Ref (α) partakes of F.

I wish to reject this schema even though it has all the advantages of Schema X and none of the disadvantages (viz., the disadvantage of not being able to account for the *symplokē* requirement). One reason for casting a wary eye on it is that it makes "truification" an interminable business: we have to look to every one of the properties of Ref (α) in order to decide whether it is in fact ϕ. This seems a little too much. One can directly observe that Theaetetus is sitting without having to know or even to take cognizance of any other property of Theaetetus. I think it safe to say that Plato nowhere discusses any such necessity; neither does it seem "to constitute a likely and reasonable interpretation of Plato's own distressing brief discussion," as Sayre (1969: p. 211) would have it.

It simply looks (so far) as though we will have to face the fact that there is insufficient interweaving happening to account for the *symplokē* requirement.

Frede (1967) advocates a different sort of view. Instead of locating the difference "behind" the predicate (or copula), he finds it "behind" the subject.[18]

Schema XII (Frede₂):

2a₁. The meaning of $\ulcorner \alpha$ is $\bar{\phi}\urcorner$ is that Ref (α) partakes of Being in relation to Ref (ϕ).

2a₂. The meaning of $\ulcorner \alpha$ is not $\bar{\phi}\urcorner$ is that for all x, if x partakes of Being in relation to Ref (ϕ), then x is different from Ref (α).

Frede recommends this (2a₂) over the (2a₂) of Schemata VI through XI because his specifically illustrates Not-Being as a difference from Ref (α), not simply as something different from something that applied to Ref (α) (as Schemata VI through XI would seem to have it). Frede claims that this is decisive (p. 79), but in the spirit of Keyt we can say that at best this is an indicator. Such a move on Frede's part requires understanding 257b10-c3 in a particular way. It reads: ". . . what we get by placing 'not' before a term indicates something other (*tōn allōn ti*) than the following words; or rather, from the things indicated by the words pronounced after the negation." The qualifying clause admits of at best two interpretations, that corresponding to Frede's interpretation—where the "things indicated" are the (physical) entities falling under the negated concept—and the Owen-Wiggins-Lewis-Philip-Kostman-Cornford interpretation—where the "things indicated" are the Forms corresponding to the predicate. Now, both interpretations can make sense of Not-Being as a particular kind of difference: Frede as "difference from the subject" or alternatively "difference from what falls under the predicate which was negated," and the opposition theorists as "difference from the predicate which was negated." I fail to see how the first alternative is so clearly Plato's meaning that the second alternative can be decisively ruled out.[19]

One point in favor of (2a₂) in all of Schemata VI through XI is that they give a clear-cut understanding to "interweaving of the forms with one another" in negative predications. All the Forms blend with the Different in relation to one another, thereby making discourse possible. The weakness of VI and X is that their (2a₁) does not illustrate an interweaving. A weakness of Schemata VII through IX seems to me also to lie in (2a₁), where interweaving amounts only to the Form Being blended with the Form corresponding to the predicate. In Schema XII, (2a₁) is the same as it was in Schemata VII through IX; furthermore, here (2a₂) reduces even the interweaving for negative sentences to this same weak thing. The only interweaving in (2a₂) is exactly that of (2a₁): the Form Being with the Form corresponding to the predicate when unnegated. The difference between its (2a₁) and its (2a₂) is merely in which subjects partake of this blending. It is hard to see why such a "weak" type of interweaving should be so important as to "make all discourse possible." Frede, too, notices a difference between these two notions of interweaving. On p. 43 (1967), he gives them as:

1. The interweaving between predicate-forms[20] and the Form of Being.
2. The interweaving between the forms which are mentioned in the sentence.

The first kind of interweaving, says Frede, is presupposed by all sentences. The predicate must always have an associated Form that exists. The second type of interweaving, he continues, is not presupposed by all sentences, e.g., not by 'Theaetetus flies'; thus, Plato must have been thinking of only the first type when he insisted that all discourse is due to such interweaving.

Let us first note the similarity between this and the explanation given by advocates of Schemata I and II. Recall Ross (1951: pp. 115–16): "In the sentence 'Theaetetus is not flying' . . . the Form or universal of flying exists, so in saying the sentence we are not asserting of him something that does not belong to him." Now, Ross's position has been refuted already by many people, one of whom is Frede (1967: p. 80), who says that any interpretation that identifies the meaning of 'is not' with that of 'is different from' will not be able to find an adequate analysis of negative predication, but only of negative identity claims. The interweaving presupposed by the ($2a_2$) of Schemata I and II, on the one hand, and Schema XII, on the other, are identical; thus, Schemata I and II are no more susceptible to Frede's criticism than his own Schema XII is.

The distinction Frede makes between, on the one hand, the interweaving of the predicate-form and the form of Being and, on the other hand, an interweaving between forms named in the sentence, and his claim that not every sentence illustrates the latter, seem to me to make his final and official position one of a backdrop or mixed theorist. Enough people (e.g., Keyt and Lewis) have, however, interpreted him as a correspondence theorist to make it worthwhile to explore the possibility of attributing Schema XII to Plato and comparing its virtues and defects with those of Schemata VI through XI.

I can see two other rather serious philosophical difficulties with Schema XII that should make us chary of attributing it to Plato. First, let us notice that according to ($2a_2$) of Schema XII, if neither Socrates nor Theaetetus flies, then 'Socrates does not fly' and 'Theaetetus does not fly' have the same meaning. This is because of ($2a_2$)'s reference to the class of flying objects, which will be the same in the two cases. Second, and again against the consequent of ($2a_2$), Frede (1967: p. 78) has paraphrased this consequent as 'x is not y' means '(x is different from z) and (z is y)', where 'z' stands for the class of things that fall under y or else the Form y itself. Thus, some sense must first have been made of (say) 'Theaetetus differs from the members of the class of flying things' before 'Theaetetus is not flying' can be understood in the way Frede gives as his ($2a_2$). Now, I think it fair to say that Plato nowhere in the *megista genē* section discusses difference between individuals or between an individual and a class. Frede's evidence for this is 257c1–3, where 'the not x' could be taken to denote the class of things that are not large. But, as I mentioned above, this is not the only interpretation possible. And, though it is not so forced here to read this in Frede's manner, so reading it lends itself to reading other areas in the same way where it is truly implausible (e.g., 256e7 [see Frede, 1967: p. 80] and 257b3–4 [see Frede, 1967: pp. 83–84]). Furthermore, as Wiggins points out (1970: pp. 299–300), such a view will inevitably lead to contradiction because it presupposes the well-definedness of the complement of every class. We can bring this criticism down to a more Platonic level by wondering how it is that Plato thinks (as he would have to if he accepted the present view) he can identify an individual well enough to be able to distinguish it from others when he has no identifying characteristics or properties to help him. Given that, for example, in 'Theaetetus is not flying', we have absolutely no characterizing properties with which to pick out Theaetetus, how is it that we can ever know that the consequent of $(2a_2)$ is satisfied? —as we are able since we can (according to Plato) understand the original negative predication. Such considerations show the implausibility of attributing to Plato any interpretation in which 'is different' holds between physical objects.[21]

Lorenz and Mittelstrass (1966b) are backdrop theorists. Like all such theorists, they believe that language is given legitimacy in virtue of some preexistent blending that occurs among the forms. They are, however, quite certain that for any specific sentence they can indicate some blending. In this sense, they can (for the time being) be classified as correspondence theorists.[22] In order to make each sentence indicate specifically an interweaving, they claim that we must understand what we call proper names as examples of a Kind: that to an individual must be specified a characteristic Kind under which the individual falls. They say that the word 'Theaetetus' refers to the man Theaetetus and that the word has sense only insofar as one knows a priori that Theaetetus is a man. They give the following schema.

Schema XIII (Lorenz and Mittelstrass$_1$):

2a$_1$. The meaning of $\ulcorner\alpha$ is $\bar\phi\urcorner$ is that Ref (Aα) blends with Ref (ϕ).

2a$_2$. The meaning of $\ulcorner\alpha$ is not $\bar\phi\urcorner$ is that Ref (Aα) blends with some form F in the same incompatibility range as Ref (ϕ).

where by 'A' we are to understand something analogous to "the *man* Theaetetus" (if 'Theaetetus' were substituted for α), "blends with" means "is compatible with," and "blending with the Different from" means "is incompatible with." It is the "A part" of 'Aα' that does the blending with Ref (ϕ), and so it is somehow "Man blends with Sitting" that gives the "ground" for the meaning of 'Theaetetus is sitting'—but not the *sufficient* grounds. For that, say Lorenz and Mittelstrass, we need to add the "necessarily true" 'Theaetetus is a man'.

There seem to me to be several difficulties with Schema XIII. First, even if it *is* necessarily true that Theaetetus is a man, the blending of the Form Sitting with the Form Man will not be a sufficient "ground" for the *truth* of 'Theaetetus is sitting', for he could be standing while he is still a man and while the Eleatic Stranger (who is also necessarily a man) is sitting. Thus, the supposedly sufficient "grounds" are satisfied, although the sentence is false. Lorenz and Mittelstrass$_1$ want to separate the truth and falsity issue from the meaningfulness issue, but can they? If the sentence were 'Theaetetus is flying', the meaning should include that the Form Man was blending with the Form Flying. But this does not happen. What we want to say, therefore, is that the sentence is *false*; however, Lorenz and Mittelstrass$_1$ must say that it is *meaningless*. The relationship between truth and falsity, on the one hand, and the meaning of positive and negative predications, on the other, is clearly this: a sentence is false just in case its negation is true. Thus, if we are to account for the truth or falsity of sentences, we will first have to assign a definite meaning to them. It cannot be sufficient in affirmative sentences to use "compatible" as Lorenz and

Mittelstrass$_1$ do in (2a$_1$), for this will give rise to precisely the same problem that allowing 'blends with the Different' to mean 'nonidentical' in (2a$_2$) of Schema VII (Cornford$_2$) did.[23]

A second difficulty, of course, is their assertion that one is unable to understand a proper name unless one can fit it under a characteristic Kind. Two questions arise: Does Plato hold such a doctrine? And can any sense be made out of it? To the first, the authors refer to the *Cratylus*, where such a proper name as 'Hermogenes' supposedly occurs clearly as a predicate. I do not propose to discuss that issue here,[24] but I think we can see that, even if Plato did hold that silly position then, he no longer holds it in the *Sophist*. He gives the example of the proper name 'Theaetetus' as being of the one who is here before me now, and not necessarily as being characterized as a man. Further, Plato is fairly clear on the distinction between *onoma* and *rhema* so that an *onoma* names an entity to which we will then attribute some *rhema*. But, if Lorenz and Mittelstrass$_1$ are right, Plato is horribly confused, since there are no *onomata* but rather everything is (at least in part) a *rhema*. And this clearly contradicts Plato's present use of the terms. (Compare the criticisms above of Schema IV.) Thus, it seems clear that Plato did not hold this view in the *Sophist*. Furthermore, the whole view seems incoherent. Why was 'Man' picked out for Theaetetus? Perhaps Lorenz and Mittelstrass have some view about "essential properties"—something that I think no one has ever attributed to Plato, something that is acknowledged to be new with Aristotle. In a confusing footnote (p. 138), they say that the Form Wise or perhaps the Form Philosopher might be used for Socrates. If so, it would be tautologous to say that Socrates is wise or that he is a philosopher, and surely that will not do. Why did we not use the Form Sitting in talking about the sitting Theaetetus? Obviously, Lorenz and Mittelstrass$_1$ do not hold anything like Aristotle's doctrine of essential properties nor anything like *anyone* has ever held (an essential property of X must at least be a property of X that X always has, and their examples of 'philosopher' and 'wise' do not fit this). We should not saddle Plato with an indefensible theory that in any case does not appear in the text under consideration. For similar remarks, see Guthrie (1978: p. 161) and Sayre (1969: p. 209, fn. 87).

SOME CONCLUSIONS ABOUT CORRESPONDENCE THEORIES

What then should be our conclusions concerning correspondence theories? That is, if we were to grant that Plato's thought here is to be explicated as his use of the philosopher's language in the way called for by a correspondence theory, which of Schemata I through XIII should he be viewed as holding? I think that, if we continue to view the *Sophist* as a refutation of Parmenides' Problem in the form presented by the standard interpretation, we can apply Principles of Charity of Interpretation to come up with an answer. Reasons have been adduced along the way, but perhaps we should here adjudicate among them.

First, it seems clear, we should rule out Schemata I through IV on the grounds that they do not solve Parmenides' Problem (this alongside any textual problems one may find with them). The other schemata all give some solution to Parmenides' Problem, and so we must look to other features of these schemata to determine whether Plato is to be credited with them. Schema V is to be ruled out, I think, for various reasons. For one thing, there is *some* textual difficulty in attributing to Plato a "negative counterpart of *to pros allo*." Also, on philosophical grounds, there are the problems involved with finding a "connector form" (this "negative counterpart") for sentences concerned with *denying* that there is any connection (e.g., particular negatives) and those problems concerned with introducing forms that the "opposition" would not recognize. Schema VI makes all true negative sentences necessarily true and makes the determination of the falsity of false affirmative sentences "an interminable business." For these reasons, it should be rejected if a better account is available. (We might also note in passing that, according to Schema VI, not every sentence explicitly mentions an interweaving of two forms. For a correspondence theorist, this failure amounts to an inability to account for the *symplokē eidōn*. I will return to this issue shortly.) Schema VII is inadequate because it assigns the wrong properties to 'not'. (And it, too, cannot account for the *symplokē eidōn*.) Schema VIII is inadequate because it, too, makes falsification "an interminable business." It furthermore assigns to 'is' an ontological correlate, the form Being, thereby leaving us with no syntactical correlate to the "ontological glue" of partaking of. I find this quite a serious problem; so serious that in discussing Schema IX (which I found to have only this one drawback) I recommended against it in favor of Schema X even though Schema X is unable to account for the *symplokē eidōn*. Identifying the role of "building blocks" versus "glue" both in syntax and in ontology is crucial to a proper understanding of the point of the philosopher's language. I find that commentators who assume that the form Being will turn the trick for *symplokē eidōn* just have not thought enough about the whole point of a "correspondence theory of language/ontology," or else they would realize that this move effectively undercuts the whole project. (More on this point in the "mixed theories" section below.) I found Schema XI inferior to Schema X even though it *could* account for the *symplokē* requirement and even though X and XI had the same account of negative predication. Its fault was making the meaning of a positive sentence intolerably difficult. Schema XII makes 'α is not φ' and 'β is not φ' mean the same, even if Ref(α) and Ref(β) are distinct. It furthermore guarantees inconsistency because it assumes the well-definedness of the complement of every class and thereby commits Plato to thinking he can identify "all members of the class of nonflying objects" in the complete absence of any other identifying features. Therefore, I reject Schema XII. Schema XIII would attribute to Plato some (incoherent) doctrine of essential properties; it furthermore confuses falsity with meaninglessness and (if taken strictly as a correspondence theory) confuses truth with presupposition-satisfaction.

In sum, then, the best of the correspondence theories is seen to be Schema X, in spite of its inability to explain the *symplokē*. We have still, however, to consider backdrop theorists and the whole question of whether Plato is to be considered a correspondence theorist or a backdrop theorist.

BACKDROP THEORISTS

Officially, I have characterized (Platonic) backdrop theorists as those who believe that the world of forms exhibits some particular interweavings that give legitimacy to language but that these interweavings are not to be correlated in any one-to-one way with individual sentences as demanded by the correspondence theorists. In fact, though, different commentators have taken this route for different reasons. One reason to take it would be if one wanted to be a correspondent theorist but felt that $(2a_1)$ did not mention enough forms to perform a *symplokē*, for instance, Schema VII or Schema X. And then such a commentator might point to the backdrop to show that, nonetheless, the predicate-form blended with Being (for example) and, hence, the *symplokē* requirement is satisfied.[25] The other sort of justification for a backdrop theory is the view that the backdrop gives us *preconditions* for the use of language. Behind *no* sentence should we look for a particular *symplokē eidōn*. Rather, we should view the relationships among the Forms as general presuppositions for the possibility of a language at all. There must be concepts available for us so that we can use them in comparing two things and other concepts available so that we can distinguish things in order for us to carry on discourse. $Ackrill_2$ (1955) officially views the role of the Forms and their interconnections as providing us with just that; the general words in language that refer to the Forms that "pick up" these interconnections guarantee meaningful discourse. The "interweaving of Forms" is in a way antecedent to language, and, thus, we need not force ourselves to look at each sentence to find some interwoven Forms lurking about. In a similar vein, Lorenz and $Mittelstrass_2$ (1966b) view the interweaving behind (say) singular affirmative sentences in which the subject is a man as being given legitimacy by the form Man I-participating[26] in the predicate form. This is a *presupposition* of the sentence in this sense: if the sentence is true, then this participation must happen. But it is unclear what Lorenz and $Mittelstrass_2$ attribute to Plato in case the requisite participation does not hold—whether the sentence is simply false, necessarily false, or meaningless or "the issue of truth and falsity does not arise." Finally, there are the views of Lee_2 and $Lewis_2$ who hold that

> Plato is little concerned either with the truth-conditions of a negative sentence, or with supplying the details that will give a materially adequate account of such sentences. Instead, he is concerned almost exclusively with stating what is needed if we are to understand a negative predicate, and if it is to have a determinate meaning (Lewis, 1976: p. 105).

The idea here is that Plato will construct enough of the backdrop ("say what is needed if . . . [a negative predicate] is to have a determinate sense") that the details of "a materially adequate account" of negative sentences could be straightforwardly formulated.

    The first two kinds of backdrop theories mentioned in the last paragraph—those in which a *symplokē eidōn* is achieved by virtue of Being interweaving with the predicate-form but in which the determinate meaning of a sentence can be given a la $(2a_1)$ and $(2a_2)$ and those in which the *symplokē eidōn* is more pervasive than this and yet the determinate meaning of a sentence is still to be accounted for by a ($2a_1$) and ($2a_2$)—type of correspondence—are more profitably viewed as *mixed theories* and will be treated in the next section.

Let us deal here with the other two theories, which are properly called "backdrop theories." We should spend some time trying to decide whether any of these theories can form an answer to Parmenides' Problem.[27] The question we must ask is how these theories propose to deal with the troublesome negative sentences. It is rather difficult to deal with backdrop theorists here, since they could all have a very complex backdrop in mind—one complex enough to embrace a large number of the interweavings mentioned by our correspondence theorists. Thus, Ackrill, for example, might not only believe that there is the sort of interweaving mentioned explicitly in Schema X but also that there is interweaving of Being with every form and also the interweaving mentioned explicitly in Schema VI.[28] When the theory has so many possible kinds of interweavings that could be worked into it, it is difficult to know exactly where to criticize it. For this reason, we will attribute to the theories under consideration only the minimal interweavings that are mentioned by their authors and act as though the theory denied any further interweavings. Possibly this is unfair to some of the theorists, but at least it will have the effect of forcing such theorists to be more explicit in their account of the *symplokē eidōn*.

The backdrop theory of Lorenz and Mittelstrass$_2$ does not, it seems to me, show either how the philosopher's language can be said to exhibit reality or how Parmenides' Problem is to be solved. According to premise 3 of Parmenides' Problem, if some state of affairs exists in the world, some true sentence can express it. And, by premise 2, this true sentence will exhibit the meaning of that sentence. In a god-school—those antimaterialist philosophers (including Plato) opposed to the "giants" of 248—this will amount to showing the relations among particulars and forms and among the forms. The fault with the Lorenz-Mittelstrass$_2$ backdrop is that it does not give sufficient structure to do this. Consider again 'Theaetetus is sitting'. The relevant part of the backdrop has Theaetetus partaking of Man and Man I-participating with Sitting. But, far from giving the *meaning* of the original sentence, this backdrop does not even get sufficient truth-conditions (since the sentence could be false and the backdrop occur anyway). What needs to be added to their account is that it is the Theaetetus "part" of the form Man that blends with Sitting.[29]

The views of Lee$_2$ and Lewis$_2$ can be similarly criticized. Lewis does not really hold the view expressed in Schema VI; indeed, he thinks that any such "particularization" drastically overinterprets the text and that Plato should not be seen as trying to formulate any such account that might be "materially adequate." According to Lewis$_2$, it is an inappropriate criticism of an interpretation of Plato here to point out that its account of negation will not work; rather, he says, Plato is only trying to give "a definite sense" to negative sentences and is not trying to give their truth-conditions. However, according to the standard interpretation of Parmenides' Problem, the two cannot be separated. According to that formulation, it is required that any successful counterproposal be able to specify precisely the "fact described by the negative sentence." This simply amounts to giving the truth-conditions for a negative sentence.

It appears that the ploy taken by Lorenz and Mittelstrass$_2$, by Lewis$_2$, and by Lee$_2$ of understanding the backdrop to give necessary conditions for the meaningfulness of sentences (i.e., for the *possibility* of their being either true or false) cannot serve as a solution to Parmenides' Problem. Such a backdrop simply does not touch upon the heart of the difficulty as stated in the problem. What is further required is precisely what these writers deny: a statement of the precise configuration of "reality" that gives meaning to the troublesome sentences. Without this, Parmenides' Problem continues undiminished in force in precisely its original form.[30]

MIXED THEORIES

The upshot of the preceding discussion would seem to indicate that backdrop theories are doomed as accounts of an adequate response to Parmenides' Problem, since, if a backdrop theory does give "a precise characterization of reality" for every sentence, it is no longer a backdrop theory but instead is a correspondence theory. This is not *quite* right. One can have a correspondence theory "tacked on" to a backdrop theory. The backdrop is to give the "grounds" or "presuppositions" of language in general (and incidentally account for the *symplokē eidōn*), while the correspondence part is to give a determinate portion of the backdrop as the meaning of each ordinary sentence.

Let us start by recalling the remarks of Frede (1967: p. 43). He says that there are two types of interweaving.

1. The interweaving between predicate-forms and the form of Being.
2. The interweaving between the forms which are mentioned in the sentence.

Frede points to the first type of interweaving as meeting the requirement that discourse demands an interweaving of forms with one another. Any commentator who holds a correspondence theory can adopt this view and become a kind of mixed theorist. For example, the holders of Schemata VI and X, who do not explicitly make Being part of their correspondence theory, might adopt this in order to account for Plato's insistence on a *symplokē eidōn*.

But will it do the job? What is at issue with these kinds of mixed theories is not how well they solve Parmenides' Problem, for that is a job for their (2a$_2$) to tackle. Instead, they have to show how the interweaving of Being with every form would lead Plato to say that "the possibility of any discourse we can have *owes its existence*" to this kind of interweaving. As I said in discussing Schemata IX and XII, such a weak requirement simply does not give sufficient reason for Plato to make this bold assertion. After all, this kind of interweaving was introduced without objection as being "obvious" to everyone; if that were all there was to Plato's insistence on interweaving, he could have deleted the intervening parts of his discussion. I will not dwell further on this "weak" backdrop theory; at the very least it needs to have further kinds of blending included in its backdrop in order to account for the necessity of having such a *symplokē eidōn*. One way to add such further blend-ings is in the manner of Ackrill₂, to which I will now turn.

Ackrill₂ (1955, 1957) claims that the backdrop contains all of the various rela-tions that hold among the forms. For example, it includes the blending of Being with every form, it includes the establishment of incompatibility ranges of forms by their blending with the Different with respect to one another, and it perhaps also includes the relation among forms that has variously been called "Pauline Predication" (by Peterson [1973] and Vlastos [1972, 1973]) or "A-participation" (by Lorenz and Mittlestrass [1966b]) or "B-participation" (by Lewis [1974] and by myself in Pelletier [forthcoming]). The structure of this backdrop is more fully investigated in Pelletier (forthcoming), especially in connection with how it is to be expressed in the philosopher's language. For now I will simply note that, according to this mixed theory, the Platonic insistence upon a *symplokē eidōn* is understandable. If there were none of this kind of interweaving, then indeed language would be impossible. It is quite clear, therefore, that this mixed theory is preferable to the other mixed theory mentioned above. And, since it accords *symplokē* such a prominent role in ac-counting for discourse, it clearly is preferable to those correspondence theories that do not have a sufficient amount of interweaving (i.e., do not have at least two forms blending for every sentence), such as Schemata VI and X.

I had said before that Schema X is the best of the correspondence theories. The present considerations make the Ackrill₂ mixed theory preferable to any of the correspondence theories, so long as it retains all the advantages of Schema X. It does, of course, retain all these advantages because the correspondence portion of this mixed theory is precisely Schema X. The backdrop is to give all the relations among the forms, but for sentences about physical objects (e.g., Theaetetus) Schema X yields a translation into the philosopher's language that shows what "partakings" and so on are to be superadded to the backdrop in order to describe reality ade-quately. For this reason, the Ackrill₂ mixed theory is clearly preferable to any of the pure backdrop theories, since they do not address themselves to the issue of suf-ficient truth-conditions (or, as we might say in light of Parmenides' Problem, to the issue of sufficient meaningfulness conditions).

A few more things in favor of this view should be mentioned before I attempt to deal with the traditional criticisms: (a) It solves Parmenides' Problem. A part of the "concept-network" provided by the Forms includes the relation of incompati-bility of certain predicates. Thus, 'Theaetetus is not flying' can be treated as though it meant that Theaetetus did something incompatible with flying. (When applied to some particular sentence, the account looks very much like Schema X. But it is in-correct to say that this account is merely an account of interweaving "behind" each individual sentence; it is rather an account of what happens "behind" language in gen-eral.) (b) The account of the truth of such sentences is at least as straightforward (in contrast to, say, Moravcsik's or Lorenz and Mittelstrass₁—in Schema V or Schema XIII): Theaetetus is sitting (say) and that precludes his flying. (c) It does not make "synthetic" sentences "necessary," as some of the other semantical accounts did. (d) It does not force recourse to properties known a priori or to "unique characteristics."

(e) It does not force us to look to "all the properties a thing has," nor does it assume the well-definedness of the complement of every well-defined class—thereby neither making falsification an interminable business or "truification" an interminable business nor guaranteeing a contradictory system. (f) It does not gratuitously add new Forms to the ontology, in the way either Moravcsik (Schema V) or the believers in "negative" Forms (Lee$_1$ and Frede$_1$) want to add some unusual Forms. Remember that the existence of Forms has not really been granted yet by the Sophists—they are waiting to see whether a coherent theory can be built up out of them. If we had to make up unusual Forms, especially ones Plato's opponents would naturally be inclined not to believe in ("negative" Forms), the Sophists will have won. Ackrill$_2$'s account merely makes Plato have to point to relations that we are prepared to admit prior to philosophical wondering.

Let me now mention some of the traditional criticisms of this view and try to ease anxieties on at least a few points. The usual criticism is that Ackrill's account presupposes an "incompatibility" reading and that this is impossible. I have already dealt with this objection in Pelletier (1975), trying to show that it is possible to read the account of negation given in the *Sophist* in an "incompatibility" manner (although it is not necessary to do so). It is true that Ackrill did not try to justify it, but he could have, possibly along the lines I suggested. The same criticism, although perhaps from a slightly different perspective, is made by Lorenz and Mittelstrass (1966b). They object that, though there is incompatibility presupposed in 251–259, "interweaving" cannot be taken to include "incompatibility" since the blendings, partakings, communions, etc., mentioned in 251–259 are all "positive" and never meant as "separation" (pp. 121–22). Moravcsik makes a similar objection (1960: p. 122). He claims that the "blending and communion of Forms" in 253–258 is nonsymmetric, whereas "incompatibility" is symmetrical. Thus, interweaving cannot mean any of the relations to be found earlier.

The answer to this problem was already to be found in Ackrill (1957). The phrase 'weaving together of Forms' is obviously supposed to be a very broad concept (i.e., to contain many different subconcepts), and the concepts so contained are *all* the relations that have been mentioned as holding between the Forms (e.g., 'partakes of', 'blends with', 'blends with the Different from'). Even though the first relation might not be symmetrical, the second sometimes is and the last clearly is. This last, which is explained in 257–258C, is part of the key to the concept of 'weaving together to the Forms'. Although the first two show which (and how) Forms blend together, the last shows which (and how) Forms do not blend together. With this full sense of 'weave together', we can see how it is that this relation can be symmetrical and yet the particular subrelations into which it can be broken up (like 'partakes of') might not all be symmetrical. And, furthermore, we now know where the "separation" sense of "interweaving" is to be found: in "blending with the Different from." (Ackrill's example of this is 'is a relative of', which is symmetric, whereas particular kinds of relations, e.g., 'is a father of', are not.)

Lorenz and Mittelstrass (1966b: p. 122) also object that Ackrill's account cannot explain the later discussion of falsity. Above, I objected that Lorenz and

Mittelstrass's Schema XIII, or their backdrop theory, either cannot make sense of the meaningfulness of affirmative singular sentences or else it cannot make sense of the falsity of them. Ackrill can make sense of both. First, Ackrill's account gives direct sense to affirmative singular sentences; second, his account of Not-Being gives an indirect sense to negative singular sentences that in turn allows the falsity of an affirmative singular sentence to consist in its negation being true. As the formula at 260C puts the matter, falsity consists in Not-Being combining with *logos*.

CONCLUSION

It is clear, therefore, that a mixed theory is preferable to either a pure correspondence theory or a pure backdrop theory. Pure backdrop theories are unable to deal adequately with Parmenides' Problem because they do not give a determinate sentence of the philosopher's language (which displays the "reality" asserted by the ordinary sentence of which it is a translation) that will show how the Parmenidean argument can be avoided. Pure correspondence theories either have Plato giving philosophically implausible accounts of how to avoid Parmenides' Problem (and are thus to be ruled out by the Principles of Charity of Interpretation) or, if they give adequate accounts of this matter, find themselves unable to explain Plato's insistence on the *symplokē eidōn*. Only the mixed theories can do both; and, of the two mixed theories considered, Ackrill's is clearly superior.

We have found a way around Keyt's textual problems. Just because a number of divergent readings can be given to the text, all of which are self-consistent, it does not follow that there is no way to choose among them. We find the problem Plato thought he solved, and the Principles of Charity of Interpretation tell us that, of the textually possible solutions, we should pick the best. In my opinion, of the published works this is still Ackrill$_2$'s.

There are, however, some problems remaining. I have occasionally mentioned in passing that the structure of the backdrop needs to be more fully specified. I would lump all these sorts of deficiencies under the heading "What is the meaning of sentences with form-names in subject position?" Another problem as yet unresolved is: With what shall we replace premise (2b) of Parmendies Problem? These questions will be answered in Pelletier (forthcoming), but for now this is as far as I can go.[31]

Notes

1. See Vlastos, 1972 and 1973, and Peterson, 1973.

2. The subscripts indicate different interpretations of our commentators.

3. Some of the correspondence theories to be discussed do not, in fact, extricate Plato from Parmenides' Problem. This is presumably because they do not see Parmenides' argument to be the one given by the standard interpretation. I include them nonetheless on the grounds that we can now give a definite reason why they are incorrect in their interpretation of Plato.

4. Guthrie (1978: p. 161) echoes this objection with approval.

5. Compare Lorenz and Mittelstrass, 1966b: p. 116-17.

6. As Frede (1967: pp. 92-94) points out, the *Politicus* is later than the *Sophist* and therefore may represent yet another shift in Plato's theory of forms.

7. Lewis (1976) holds a view very similar to Lee₂'s. (See Lewis's fn. 40.) I later entertain this view, calling it Lewis₂ and Lee₂.

8. For discussion of this and how it affects the philosopher's language, see Pelletier, forthcoming.

9. Again, the various possibilities will be discussed in Pelletier, forthcoming.

10. See Lorenz and Mittelstrass, 1966b: p. 126, fn. 81.

11. Moravcsik has apparently changed his mind on some of these matters. See Moravcsik, 1976: p. 744, fn. 4.

12. This is not really Lewis's view of the matter but rather one that results from forcing him to be a correspondence theorist. His true view is what I call Lewis₂, which is discussed under "backdrop theorists."

13. Keyt's (1973) comment, that Cornford's explanation here is "incomplete" and Cornford really meant "contrariety" and "non-identity," seems to me incorrect. Cornford *explicitly* wants "blending with the Different from" to be nonidentity (1935: p. 290) — however, it is true that his later discussion of "falsity" on pp. 311–17 does not make much sense for the reasons noted in the text.

14. Frede (1967: pp. 78–79) makes a related criticism based on his analysis of two uses of 'is' in the *Sophist*. He claims that there is such a use of 'is not' but that it is so rare and artificial that one can hardly expect Plato to try to interpret all uses of 'x is not y' according to it. (Schema VII [2a₂] is Frede's 2[b] on p. 78.)

15. Note that (2a₂) of Schemata VI and VIII are not the same in spite of their superficial similarity. Schema VI says, "Here is a number of Forms, ϕ_1, ϕ_2, ϕ_3, . . . ; are they distinct from ϕ?" The answer is "yes (or no) — and necessarily so." The parenthetical remark after (2a₂) merely tells us how to take hold of the Forms ϕ_1, ϕ_2, ϕ_3, . . . but is not a part of the condition proper. This is not the case with Schema VIII. Here, thanks to the bound variable 'F', we have a nonnecessary claim in spite of the fact that the consequent is necessary for all substitution instances of 'F'. Of course, it is possible that Owen intended (2a₂) of Schema VIII instead of that of Schema VI. In such a case, this "third objection" would not hold of his view, although the first and second still would.

16. Keyt (1973), of course, claims there is no decisive way to resolve the issue on textual grounds. He feels that an ambiguity in *heteros* will allow both sides to have their day in text. Many writers (e.g., Owen, Frede) find absolutely no justification for (2a₂) of Schema IX. Frede (1967: p. 79) says that *heteron* can never be replaced by 'incompatible' and that it is neither compatible with the train of thought nor justified by the text. I think I have adequately refuted this view in Pelletier, 1975.

17. I am not sure exactly how this argument should run. In the sentences given by Plato, there is no word corresponding to 'is' (the sentences could best be translated 'Theaetetus sits', 'Theaetetus flies'), and thus the so-called "syntactic glue" is not there as a *unit* but merely in the words' interweaving. So, we have to invent our "ontological glue" anyway. But, if this is the case, it is indeed unclear why anyone would want to put the Form Being into every predication. (Moravcsik's reason was to get it "behind" the copula, but, if there is no copula, there seems no reason to get it at all.)

18. For cases I am considering, where α is taken to indicate an individual, Frede (1967) uses '... is₂ ...', which indicates that the predicate does not express what belongs necessarily to the subject (p. 33). And this I have expressed by 'partakes of Being in relation to', which seems to be what follows from his discussion on, e.g., pp. 33–44, especially pp. 37–38 and 43, and p. 82. (2a₂) is stated on p. 79 as his (1'), but see also his discussion on p. 78. The 'partakes of Being in relation to' in (2a₂) may be slightly incorrect, for Frede intends not only '... is₂ ...' but also his '... is₁ ...', where the predicate indicates *precisely* what is indicated by the subject. For the case of individuals as subjects, however, this seems to make no difference. In any case, it is probably more accurate to treat Frede as a mixed theorist.

19. In a previous publication (Pelletier, 1975), I tried to justify yet another possible reading

of this passage in terms of "incompatibility." I think that the strict textual evidence does not rule any of these out. For similar feelings, see Keyt, 1973.

20. I will here treat this term (*Prädikatsbegriff*) as though it meant the Form corresponding to the predicate, since his explanation immediately after seems to demand it ("Die erste Art von Vergindung von Formen wird von allen Sätzen vorausgestezt. Dem Prädikat muss in sinnvollen Sätzen immer eine Form zugeordnet sein, die ist"). But he does not always seem to have this in mind. Immediately before (p. 42), he seems to distinguish '*Begriff*' from 'Form': "If there is no concept or no Form corresponding to expressions like '*summexis*,' 'blending,' etc., in virtue of which they are meaningful, then to that extent all these theories are meaningless." This seems to presuppose a "building-block" role for 'blending'—something we have already discarded. Frede goes on to say (p. 43): ". . . the interweaving of motion and rest on the one hand and Being on the other in the first argument [251E7–252A11] is to be understood exactly as the interweaving between blending and Being in the second argument [252B1–252B6], namely as an interweaving between the predicate-concept and the Form of Being. As the preceding discussion on 242–250 has shown, these last two are different whenever the predicate '... is being' is not word-for-word used. Only on the grounds of this interweaving are sentences, wherein the corresponding predicate is used, meaningful."

21. I believe that Frede, (1967) actually attributes to Plato the idea that the complement of every well-defined set exists. On p. 86, he says that 'not-y' belongs to the things that have a proper essence (*eigenes Wesen*). This may also account for his belief that the *Sophist* makes use of "negative" Forms.

22. That is, we will here concentrate on the blending they think gives legitimacy to language and treat it as though it gave the precise sentence of the philosopher's language that would be required if they were correspondence theorists. Thus construed, they are Lorenz and Mittelstrass$_1$, to be distinguished from the actual position they hold, Lorenz and Mittelstrass$_2$.

23. Thus (2a$_2$) does not give the required *correspondence* for (say) 'Theaetetus sits'; rather, it gives something like "Man is compatible with Sitting" (or in their terminology, Man I-partakes of Sitting). In some sense, this gives the "grounds" for the truth of the sentence or gives a presupposition of the sentence; but it does not give necessary and sufficient truth-conditions; nor does it give the meaning of the sentence. Since Lorenz and Mittelstrass are really backdrop theorists, such objections need not tell against them, but they do tell against our straw people Lorenz and Mittelstrass$_1$, who take Schema XIII as a correspondence theory.

24. See Lorenz and Mittelstrass, 1966a; Pfeiffer, 1972; Weingartner, 1970; and Richardson, 1976 for further discussion of this matter.

25. It is possible to read many of our correspondence theorists in this manner, e.g., the holders of Schemata VII through IX, but none of them are explicit enough on the point for me to be able to decide how to take them, and so I have simply read them as correspondence theorists.

26. Reminder: (form) A I-participates in (form) B if and only if A is compatible with B (that is, if and only if some A is B).

27. It might be objected here that I have begged the question against Lee$_2$ and Lewis$_2$, since (as Lewis says in the quotation given) they hold that Plato is not concerned with trying to formulate truth-conditions for negative sentences (i.e., is not trying to give any replacement for Parmenides' premise [2]). The charge against me is accurate but is one that any of the commentators under consideration might bring up in his defense. (I suppose all the commentators would think that the failure of their schemata to solve Parmenides' Problem merely showed that Plato was not concerned with Parmenides' Problem as I gave it. To them I reissue my challenge: give a possible interpretation of Parmenides so that your schema shows how the problem is to be solved.)

28. Since the Schema VI interweaving is a logical consequence of the Schema X interweaving.

29. Lorenz and Mittelstrass (1966b) note that they have not given sufficient conditions (e.g., see pp. 142–43), but they do not see a problem here. They apparently have a different conception of what the philosopher's language is supposed to be like than what I am advocating here. (See their discussion on pp. 133–34, which, nonetheless, does not seem to me to confront the

issue adequately. Indeed, it seems only to be an argument in favor of having *some* backdrop or other and not an argument about whether correspondence theories are a necessary adjunct.) Again, I place the burden upon them to interpret explicitly Parmenides in such a way that their remarks about a backdrop (and, in particular, their specific kind of backdrop) become relevant.

30. Again, of course, a different understanding of Parmenides might make this sort of backdrop theory relevant. These writers, therefore, must give us an account of Parmenides that does this.

31. This paper has had a very long and difficult gestation period. For their help in bringing it to term, I would especially like to thank Montgomery Furth, Sandra Peterson, Frank Lewis, Alex Mourelatos, Julius Moravcsik, Richard Bosley, Alan Code, and Roger Shiner. Each, in their own way, has urged upon me one or the other of the positions rejected in this paper. Earlier versions have been read at the University of Alberta and the University of Texas. I wish to thank the University of Alberta for an EEF release time grant during which this paper was (in part) written and the Social Sciences and Humanities Research Council for a grant that allowed me to hire Joanne Freed, research assistant extraordinaire. The present paper is a version of a chapter of my forthcoming publication.

Bibliography

Ackrill, John, "*Symplokē Eidōn*," *Bulletin of the Institute of Classical Studies of the University of London* 2 (1955):31–35 (pp. 201–9 in Vlastos, 1970).

Ackrill, John, "Plato and the Copula: *Sophist* 251–259," *Journal of Hellenic Studies* 77 (1957): 1–6 (pp. 210–22 of Vlastos, 1970).

Allan, D. J., "The Problem of the *Cratylus*," *American Journal of Philology*, 75 (1954):271–87.

Bluck, R. S., "False Statement in the *Sophist*," *Journal of Hellenic Studies*, 77 (1957):181–86.

Cornford, F. M., *Plato's Theory of Knowledge* (London: Kegan Paul, 1935).

Frede, Michael, *Prädication und Existenzaussage*, *Hypomnemata* 18 (1967) (Göttingen).

Furth, Montgomery, "Elements of Eleatic Ontology," *Journal of the History of Philosophy* 6 (1968):111–32.

Guthrie, W. K. C., *A History of Greek Philosophy*, Vol. 3, *The Later Plato and the Academy* (Cambridge: Cambridge University Press, 1978).

Hackforth, R., "False Statement in the *Sophist*," *Classical Quarterly* 39 (1945):56–58.

Hamlyn, D. W., "The Communion of Forms and the Development of Plato's Logic," *Philosophical Quarterly* 5 (1955):289–302.

Keyt, David, "The Falsity of 'Theaetetus Flies' (*Sophist* 263b)," pp. 285–305 in E. N. Lee, A. P. D. Mourelatos, and R. Rorty (eds.), *Exegesis and Argument* (*Phronesis* Sup. Vol. 1 [1973]).

Kostman, James, "False Logos and Not-Being in Plato's *Sophist*," pp. 192–212 of J. M. E. Moravcsik, *Patterns in Plato's Thought* (Dordrecht: Reidel, 1973).

Lee, E. N., "Plato on Negation and Not-Being in the *Sophist*," *Philosophical Review* 81 (1972): 267–304.

Lewis, Frank, "Plato's Paradox of Being: *Sophist* 249e ff" (unpublished paper, 1974).

Lewis, Frank, "Plato on 'Not'," *California Studies in Classical Antiquity* 9 (1976):89–115.

Lorenz, K., and Mittelstrass J., "On Rational Philosophy of Language: The Programme in Plato's *Cratylus* Reconsidered," *Mind* 75 (1966a):1–29.

Lorenz, K., and Mittelstrass, J., "Theaitetos Fleigt," *Archiv für Geschichte der Philosophie* 48 (1966b):113–52.

Moravcsik, J. M. E., "*Symplokē Eidōn* and the Genesis of *Logos*," *Archiv für Geschichte der Philosophie* 42 (1960):117–29.

Moravcsik, J. M. E., "Being and Meaning in the *Sophist*," *Acta Philosophica Fennica* 14 (1962): 23–78.

Moravcsik, J. M. E., "Critical Notice of P. Seligman *Being and Not-Being*," *Canadian Journal of Philosophy* 4 (1976):737–44.

Mourelatos, A. P. D., "Some Alternatives in Interpreting Parmenides," *The Monist* 62 (1979): 3–14.

Owen, G. E. L., "Plato on Not-Being," pp. 223–67 in Vlastos, 1970.

Peck, A. L., "Plato and the *Megista Genē* of the *Sophist*," *Classical Quarterly* 2 (1952):32–56.

Peck, A. L., "Plato's *Sophist*: The *Symplokē tōn Eidōn*," *Phronesis* 7 (1962):46–66.

Pelletier, Francis Jeffry, "On Reading 'Incompatibility' in Plato's *Sophist*," *Dialogue* 14 (1975): 143–46.

Pelletier, Francis Jeffry, *Parmenides, Plato, and the Semantics of Not-Being* (forthcoming).

Peterson, Sandra, "A Reasonable Self-Predication Premise for the Third Man Argument," *Philosophical Review* 82 (1973):451–70.

Pfeiffer, W. M., "True and False Speech in Plato's *Cratylus*," *Canadian Journal of Philosophy* 2 (1972):87–104.

Philip, J. A., "False Statement in the *Sophistes*," *Transactions and Proceedings of the American Philological Society* 99 (1968):315–27.

Richardson, Mary, "True and False Names in the *Cratylus*," *Phronesis* 21 (1976):135–45.

Robinson, R., "Forms and Error in Plato's *Theaetetus*," *Philosophical Review* 59 (1950):3–30.

Ross, David, *Plato's Theory of Ideas* (Oxford: Oxford University Press, 1951).

Runciman, W. G., *Plato's Later Epistemology* (Cambridge: Cambridge University Press, 1965).

Sayre, K. M., *Plato's Analytic Method* (Chicago: University of Chicago Press, 1969).

Schipper, Edith, "The Meaning of Existence in Plato's *Sophist*," *Phronesis* 9 (1964):38–44.

Schipper, Edith, *Forms in Plato's Later Dialogues* (The Hague: Nijhoff, 1965).

Turnbull, R. G., "The Argument of the *Sophist*," *Philosophical Quarterly* 14 (1964):23–34.

Vlastos, Gregory, *Plato I: Metaphysics and Epistemology* (Garden City, N.Y.: Anchor Books, 1970).

Vlastos, Gregory, "The Unity of the Virtues in the *Protagoras*," *Revue Metaphysics* 25 (1972): 415–58.

Vlastos, Gregory, "An Ambiguity in the *Sophist*," pp. 270–322 of Vlastos (ed.), *Platonic Studies* (Princeton, N.J.: Princeton University Press, 1973).

Weingartner, R. H., "Making Sense of the *Cratylus*," *Phronesis* 15 (1970):5–25.

Wiggins, David, "Sentence Meaning, Negation, and Plato's Problem of Not-Being," pp. 268–303 in Vlastos, 1970.

Xenakis, Jason, "Plato's *Sophist*: A Defense of Negative Expressions and a Doctrine of Sense and of Truth," *Phronesis* 4 (1959):29–43.

Some Observations on Aristotle's Theory of Mathematics and of the Continuum

PAUL FEYERABEND

(1) In book ii/2 of his *Physics* and in book XIII/3 of his *Metaphysics*, Aristotle explains the nature of mathematical objects.[1] The explanation is fairly simple, but long and elaborate discussions are added to combat alternative views and to eliminate mistakes. I will not go into these discussions, nor will I mention and comment upon the modern debates about their correct interpretation. I will merely present Aristotle's statements, add clarifying remarks, examine consequences in physics, compare them with objections by later authors, and show how they are related to modern problems. In quoting Aristotle I will omit special reference to the physics and to the metaphysics — here the page numbers speak for themselves. Simple numbers in parentheses such as (14) refer to the sections of the present paper.

(2) Physical bodies, says Aristotle, have surfaces, volumes, lines, and points. Surfaces, volumes, lines, and points become the subject matter of mathematics *by being separated from bodies* (193b34).

We also read (1964a28ff.) that physics "deals with things that have principles of movement in themselves; mathematics is theoretical and is a science that deals with things that last — *but are not separate*."

"They *cannot in any way exist separately* — but they cannot exist *in* sensible objects either" (1077b13ff.; cf. 1085b35ff.).

The contradiction is resolved by realizing that "things are said to be in many different ways" (cf. *Met.* iii/2 and numerous other passages). Mathematical objects have separate existence in some of these senses but not in others.

Assume that to exist means to be an individual entity that does not depend on other objects and is as real as (or perhaps even more real than [1028b18] physical bodies. If mathematical objects exist in this sense, they cannot be *in* physical objects — for then we would have two solids in one place (1076a40ff.; cf. 998a13f.) — nor can they be physical objects ("sensible lines are not lines like those the geometer describes: there is nothing perceptible that is straight or curved in [the strict geometrical] sense, the circle touches the ruler not at a point but after the manner of Protagoras'' (998a1ff.). Neither can we assume that physical objects are *combinations* of mathematical objects: a combination of static and unperceived objects only yields further static and unperceived objects (1077a34ff.) and joining physical material (bronze, for example) and mathematical shape (an individual sphere, for example), both conceived as complete and self-sufficient individuals, yields a pair of complete and self-sufficient individuals (bronze; sphere), not a single individual having sphericity as a (dependent) property (1033b20ff.). Aristotle gives further arguments, not all of them admirable, to show that mathematical entities, interpreted as complete and independent individuals (or as 'substances', in Aristotle's terminology) are neither *in* physical objects nor *outside* of them and separate from them.

(3) Although it is not possible to have self-sufficient *objects*, either in physical bodies or apart from them, that lack important properties of physical bodies, it is possible to have incomplete *descriptions* of such bodies.

> For example, . . . there are many statements about objects considered merely insofar as they can be in motion which say nothing about their essential and their accidental properties without it necessarily following that there is motion apart from sensible things or that there is a distinct moving entity in them (1077a34ff.).

Similarly, "there are properties and domains of knowledge that treat [changing objects] not insofar as they are moving but insofar as they are bodies or only insofar as they are planes and lines and are divisible, or as indivisibles having position, or as indivisibles only" (1077b23ff.). "The same principle applies to harmonics and optics for neither of these sciences studies objects as sight or as sound but as lines and as numbers—but the latter are attributes belonging to the former. And the same is true of mechanics" (1078a14ff.). No error arises from this "any more than when one draws a line on the ground and calls it a foot long when it is not—for the error is not included in the premises" (1078a18f.; cf. Berkeley's very similar account in the introduction to his *Principles of Human Knowledge*, 1710).

Bearing this in mind, we can say not only without qualification that what is separable exists but also that what is inseparable exists and is separable by description. For example, the objects of geometry exist; *they are sensible objects* but only accidentally so, for the geometer does not treat them as sensible objects (1078a1ff.).

(4) Not all incomplete descriptions of bodies disregard motion and perceptibility. 'Straight' and 'plane' do; 'torn' and 'polished' do not—the last two descriptions contain an implicit reference to changeable physical material (Aristotle's favorite example is *simós*, meaning snub-nosed, as opposed to 'concave': "the definition of *simós* contains the matter of the object, for snubness is only found in noses, whereas the definition of 'concave' does not" [1064a23ff.]). As a result, 'straight' and 'plane' can be separated in the sense just explained, while 'torn' and 'polished' cannot. Aristotle criticized Plato for separating things such as 'flesh', 'bone', and 'man' that belong to the latter category (194a6ff.; cf. 1064a27ff.) and for trying to define "lines

[which are separable] from the long and the short [which are not], planes from the broad and narrow and solids from the deep and the shallow" (1085a9ff.).

(5) If a feature or a property or an entity is separable in the sense explained, then we can either treat it as separated, i.e., we can discuss it without paying attention to other features *that are also present*, or we can give a more complete description. However, we cannot do both at the same time, i.e., we cannot mark or subdivide a physical object by a mathematical point or by a mathematical plane. It is customary in physical calculations to 'imagine' a physical object O 'cut' by a mathematical plane P or to 'consider' a volume V in it (Figure 1). According to Aristotle, this is nonsense. Mathematical planes cannot subdivide physical objects; only physical surfaces can, and those have physical properties not present in the undivided physical body. If P is to divide O, then P must be identifiable as a surface—there must be a narrow slit at P: "whenever bodies are joined or divided, their boundaries instantaneously become one at one time namely, when they touch, and two at another, when they are divided. Thus when the bodies are combined the surface does not exist but has perished" (1002b1ff.). One should compare this account with what the quantum theory says about location and division.

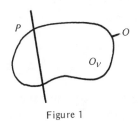

Figure 1

(6) These considerations play an important role in Aristotle's theory of place. According to Aristotle, the place of an object is the "inner limiting surface of the body that contains" the object (212a7), this inner limit being a real physical subdivision. Hence, "if a thing is not separated from its embracing environment but continues with it, then it has no place in it, but it has a place as part of the whole" (211a29ff.). For example, a bottle partly filled with water and floating in a lake has a place in the lake: the surface consists of the surface where the outside water meets the bottle—added to the surface where the outside air meets the bottle (Figure 2). The water inside the bottle also has a place, viz., the inner surface of the glass where it touches the inside water plus the surface of the inside air that touches the water. Both places are physically identifiable surfaces, however; a drop of water inside the bottle is *part* of that water; it has *no place* in that water; it has only, as part of that water, a place inside the bottle. We may say that the droplet potentially has a place inside the water of the bottle and that this potential place can be actualized when the droplet is physically separated from the rest of that water, e.g., when it freezes (212b3ff.).

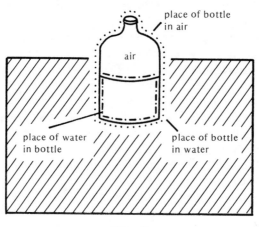

place of bottle in air

air

place of water in bottle

place of bottle in water

Figure 2

The argument of 3 also shows that place cannot be an inner extension (*diástema*) of a body that stays behind when the body has departed (as place is supposed to stay behind [208b1ff.]), for, if there were such an entity, "there would be infinitely many places in the same thing" (211b21). This argument, says H. Wagner (*Aristoteles, Physikvorlesung*, Darmstadt, 1974, 544ff.) "is one of the great cruces the Aristotelian physics has offered to its interpreters since antiquity." But the situation is rather simple, almost trivial. In the argument, the *diástema* of a particular body is viewed physically, not mathematically (place, after all, exerts a physical influence [208b11]), and it is supposed to be identical with place. Viewing the *diástema* physically implies that a real physical object is associated with it; identifying the *diástema* with place means demanding that this object behave like a place, i.e., that it stay behind when the body whose place it is supposed to be moves on (208b1ff.). Staying behind the *diástema* does not turn into a mathematical entity, nor does it change from a particular feature of a particular body into something that is shared by all bodies (every physical object has its own individual place and therefore its own individual *diástema*). Hence, every place, having been occupied and left by many different objects, contains many different *diastémata*; and, as every place is occupied by a body (there is no vacuum) and every *diástema* is a place, every body will contain an infinity of places.

(7) Similar remarks apply to the idea that the void might be an independently existing entity, similar to a *diástema* (216a23ff.). Local movement consists in one body replacing other bodies. The void was introduced not in order to be replaced by a body, but to receive it (213b5f.). It can, therefore, receive a wooden cube. In this case, there would be two things in the same place—which is impossible (216b11f.). It is interesting to see that Guericke (*Experimenta Nova* [1672] Book 2, Chapter 3) reintroduces the *diástema* as representing the vacuum without mentioning Aristotle's arguments to the contrary but with heavy sarcasm concerning Aristotle's philosophy.

(8) Aristotle's view of mathematics has especially interesting applications in the domain of motion. In 5 we saw that, in order to make physical sense, statements about parts and subdivisions must be about physically identifiable separations: a continuous body has no actual parts unless it is cut and its continuity interrupted thereby. Applied to motion, this means that part of a continuous motion can be separated from another part of the same motion only by a real modification, this time of the motion; i.e., the motion must either slow down or come to a temporary halt; it must "stop and begin to move again" (262a24f.). This is how Aristotle solves one of Zeno's paradoxes. Zeno had pointed out (263a4ff.) that a movement over a certain distance must first cover half the distance, then half of the half and so on — which means that the motion never gets completed. According to Aristotle, one subdivides the motion either by using mathematical points — then no subdivision has occurred — or by using physical ("actual" [263b6ff.]) points — then the subdivision changes the motion, turns it into an "interrupted motion" (263a30f.), which is indeed never completed.

(9) Few people are satisfied with this solution. The reason is that the idea of motion that is usually connected with the paradox differs from the idea Aristotle uses for solving the paradox. Aristotle, the critics feel, does not meet the paradox head-on, he evades it. And he evades it in a particularly simpleminded fashion, introducing acts of subdivision when the problem is the nature of a motion that proceeds without outside interference. The assumption behind the feeling is that the idea of such a motion is without fault, that the paradox arises from a mistaken use of it, and that the task is to correct this mistake and not to start talking about entirely different processes.

If this assumption is incorrect, i.e., if the view of motion involved is inadequate and perhaps even incoherent, then its replacement is not an evasive move but is a required one. Zeno's argument will then cease to be a mere paradox and will become a further contribution to its downfall. The main question is: What is the view of motion that those who speak of evasion have in mind, and how can it be defended?

Briefly, the view can be stated as follows: for every point A of the line to be transversed, the event 'passing point A' is part of the motion *whether we now interfere with it or leave it alone*. Motions consist of individual punctiform events of this type, and lines consist of individual points. This is an interesting cosmological hypothesis, but is it acceptable? Aristotle says no, and his main reason (which will be discussed in greater detail in 19 below) is very simple: a continuous entity such as a line or a continuous motion is characterized by the fact that its parts are connected, or hang together in a special way. Indivisible entities such as points or passings of points cannot be connected in any way whatsoever; hence, lines cannot consist of points and continuous motions cannot consist of passings of points.

Similar though more complex arguments are provided by the quantum theory that states that we can have pure motion (well-defined momentum) but without any passing of points or a precise passing of points, but then we have no longer any coherent motion.

The assumption is, therefore, incorrect; the view of motion implied impossible, and its removal is a necessity, not an evasion.

(10) If motion can only be subdivided by modifying it, then any clearly marked subdivision must be accompanied by a temporary change of motion; for example, the stone thrown upward must come to a halt at the highest point of its trajectory (262b25ff.; 263a4f.). Galileo (quoted from Drake-Drabkin, *On Motion and Mechanics*, Madison, 1960, p. 96) has criticized the result by criticizing what Aristotle says when introducing it. There is a temporary halt, says Aristotle, "for one point must be reckoned as two, being the finishing point of one half [of the motion] and the starting point of the other" (262b23ff.). Galileo objects that, though, the turning point may be *described* in two different ways, as the starting point of one segment and as the finishing point of another, it still *is* only one point that corresponds to one instant, the instant of reversal. But quite apart from the fact that Aristotle demands an interval (the moving object "cannot have arrived at [a certain point] and departed from [it] simultaneously for in that case it would simultaneously be there and not there at the same moment; so there are two points of time concerned with a period of time between them" [262b28ff.]), an interval is demanded also by his general account of the difference between mathematical and physical entities (cf. the quotation at the end of 5).

Galileo also uses an example to ridicule Aristotle's account: A line *ab* moves toward *b*, with the movement gradually becoming slower. A body *c* situated on the line moves toward *a*, with the movement gradually becoming faster (Figure 3).

> Now it is clear that in the beginning *c* will move in the same direction as the line. . . . And yet since the motion of *c* is faster, at some moment *c* will actually move towards the left and will thus make a change from rightward to leftward motion over the same line. And yet it will not be at rest for any interval of time at the point where the change occurs. And the reason for this is that it cannot be at rest unless the line moves to the right at the same speed as body *c* moves to the left. But it will never happen that this equality will continue over any interval of time, since the speed of one motion is continually diminished and the other continually increased.

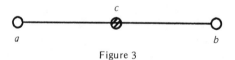

Figure 3

This remark criticizes an argument (motions can be subdivided only by introducing physical changes into them) leading to an assertion (temporary halt at points of reversal) by presenting a case that fits the argument; for it is clear that, if the argument is correct, i.e., if motions can be marked (subdivided) only by introducing physical changes such as halts, then the reversal of *c* will imply a temporary halt of *c* and, thereby, temporary halts of the two processes of acceleration that create it.

(11) Different physical entities (and different mathematical entities) may by separation yield the same mathematical entities, e.g., lines and areas, but this does not mean that they can be compared. Thus, curved angles and straight angles can be mapped (Figure 4) on to the linear continuum (or, using Aristotelian terminology, a linear continuum 'can be separated' from both of them), but there is no way of saying that a given curved angle is smaller, equal to, or larger than a straight angle (there is no way of inserting a straight angle into a curved angle [Euclid, *Elements* iii, 16]). From considerations of such cases, it is not at all obvious that the area of a circle can be said to be equal to, smaller than, or larger than the area of a polygon. Bryson's attempt to measure the area of a circle by the area of a polygon (Johannes Philoponus, *in anal. post. comment.* p. 111, 17: the circle is smaller than any circumscribed polygon and larger than any inscribed polygon; things smaller or larger than the same are equal to each other; hence, there is a polygon equal in area to the circle) was criticized by Aristotle for precisely this reason. "The equal is what is neither great nor small but could be great or small *because of its nature*" (1056a23ff.). According to Aristotle, Bryson uses "a common middle term" (*Anal. Post.* 75b42f.) — 'area' — referring to an entity that has been separated both from the circle and from the polygon but without inquiring whether before the separation this entity occurred together with furthe properties, different in both cases and preventing a comparison: "he does not deal with the subject matter concerned" (*Soph. Ref.* 171b17f.), viz., the area *of a circle*. (The geometer, says Aristotle, need not even consider Antiphon's 'exhaustion' of the circle by polygons. The procedure is not just mistaken, it misses its subject matter [185a16f.].)

Figure 4

(12) Considerations such as these may explain why Aristotle refused to measure qualitative change by length and why he thought that linear and circular motions were incomparable (227b15ff.; 248a10ff.). They also explain why the Euclidian definition of mathematical proportions (*Elements* V, Def. 3) is explicitly restricted to "homogeneous" quantities and why Greek mathematicians and later mathematicians up to and including Galileo never introduced "mixed" quantities such as velocity defined as a quotient of spatial and temporal magnitudes. But the fact that certain entities such as areas can be separated both from circles and from polygons indicates that they share some properties and that general statements can be made about them. According to Aristotle, such general statements play an important role in mathematics: "there are certain general mathematical statements which are not restricted to [special] substances" (1077a9ff.). For example:

The exchangeability of the inner terms of a proportion was in earlier times proved separately for numbers, lengths, bodies and time while this can be shown for all by a single proof. But for lack of a unified notation and because numbers, lengths, times and bodies looked so different each of them was grasped separately. Now the proof is general for what it asserts is true not only for lengths as such or numbers as such but for what is assumed to hold for the whole (*An. Pr.* 74a17ff.).

Similarly, some principles are valid for various sciences. An example is the principle that equals taken from equals give equals (*An. Post.* 76a38ff.). But the generality cannot be taken for granted and must always be ascertained by special arguments.

(13) Aristotle offers such arguments for linear extension, time, and motion. Linear extension, time, and motion differ in many respects. They are not "homogeneous" in the sense of Euclid V, Def. 3 (see 12). Yet, they have common properties. *Aristotle's theory of continuous linear manifolds* describes the properties and draws consequences from them. The remainder of the present paper will be devoted to this theory.

The existence of common properties for length, time, and movement is already hinted at by common sense. For example, "we say that the road is long when the journey is long and that the journey is long when the road is long—the time, too [is called long] if the movement and the movement if the time" (220b29ff.). We also notice that the commonsensical distinction between what is 'in front' and what is 'behind' is a distinction that applies to place and, hence, to extension and that "it must also be true of movement, for the two [extension and movement] correspond to each other. But if so, then also for time [before and after] for time and movement always correspond to each other" (219a15ff.; cf. 218b21ff.). For Aristotle such analogies are "reasonable" (220b24), for extension, time, and movement are all *continuous* and *divisible quantities* (24ff.) and are related to each other in such a way that whatever is true of one is true of all (231b19ff.). Now 'continuous', 'divisible', and 'quantity' as defined in geometry are technical terms. Moreover, Aristotle has a rather elaborate theory of continuity. It needs, therefore, special arguments to show that the analogies noticed apply to these technical entities as well and to determine their limitations.

(14) "By continuous," defines Aristotle, "I mean what is divisible into further divisibles without end" (232b25f.), the parts being "distinguishable from each other by their place" (231b6f.).

The second part of this definition (and of the arguments that surround it) restrict the discussion to linear extended continua. Other types of continua such as sounds (226b29) and further properties not related to place (31f.) are mentioned but not examined. The definition makes assumptions that may seem obvious to modern readers but that require analysis and were not regarded as trivial in Aristotle's own time. The assumptions are (1) that there are entities that can be divided at any point and in any interval, however small; (2) that the division does not change the extension of the entities and of any one of their parts; and (3) that the division does not obliterate any interval, however small.

Assumption 1 was opposed by mathematicians (Democritos perhaps included), who assumed minimal lengths or "indivisible lines." Assumptions 2 and 3 were criticized by Zeno, who denied the existence of things without thickness, mass, and extension: "For that which neither when added makes a thing greater nor, when subtracted, makes it less, he asserts to have no being—evidently assuming that whatever has being is a spatial magnitude" (1001b6ff.). During the eighteenth and nineteenth centuries, assumption 1 was often supported by reference to something called 'intuition' (*Anschauung*), and the entire idea of a continuum as a kind of "gooey substance out of which we pick a point here and a point there" (H. Weyl, "Ueber die neue Grundlagenkrise der Mathematik") was referred to this dubious source. Are there better ways of supporting the idea of a linear continuum and of the assumptions involved?

(15) One of the arguments against indivisible lines was that they provide a common measure for all lengths so that there would not be any incommensurable magnitudes. Another argument was that the laws of geometry would cease to be valid below a certain length: the line bisecting the angle of an isosceles triangle consisting of minimal sides could no longer be said to hit the middle of the opposing side (*On Indivisible Lines*, 970aff.). To see these criticisms in the proper light, let us consider an important consequence of incommensurability.

One way of finding the greatest common measure for two magnitudes was the method of *antanairesis*: subtract the smaller from the larger, the difference from the smaller, and so on until you obtain zero (Figure 5). The last number in this sequence before you reach zero is the sought after measure. The procedure was used by mathematicians, but it was also used by carpenters, architects, and geographers for finding the greatest common measure for physical lengths.

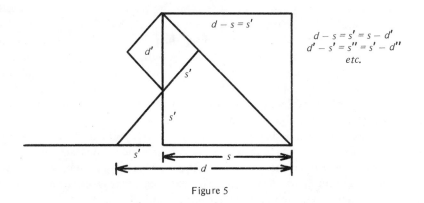

Figure 5

For incommensurable lines such as the side and the diagonal of a square, *antanairesis* has no end. According to some authors, such as Kurt von Fritz, incommensurability was discovered by discovering this property.

Incommensurability could be discovered in this manner only by people who took it for granted that geometrical relations are independent of the size of the figures described. But this was a matter that the Pythagoreans did *not* take for granted. Quite the contrary — they assumed that the void was structured by indivisible units that in turn were kept separated by the void. On such an account geometrical relations cease to be valid below a certain minimal length, and the discovery cannot be made. This is a strong argument for giving precedence to the proof reproduced in Euclid's *Elements* Book X: Assume that the relation between the diagonal D of a square and its side S can be expressed with the help of integers, d and s. Then $d^2 = 2s^2$. Reduced to the lowest form, this means that d^2 is even; therefore, d is even and s is odd. Now, since d is even, $d = 2f$ and $2f^2 = s^2$ or, reduced to lowest form, s is even. Hence, s is both even and odd.

According to Eudemus (report in Pappus, commentary of Euclid, i.44), the Pythagoreans founded not only arithmetic but also geometrical algebra. It is often assumed that they did so in order to treat incommensurables in a rigorous manner: Numbers cannot do the job, so lines are introduced in their place. But, if that was the motivation, then the conception of a line must have undergone a drastic change — from a collection of individual units separated by a void to a genuine continuum whose parts, however small, have exactly the same structure as the whole. Was this transition the result of a discovery made inside the Pythagorean school, or was it due to outside ideas?

There did exist an outside view that contained all the elements of a continuum — Parmenides' view of the One. According to Parmenides (Diels-Kranz, *Fragmente der Vorsokratiker*, Berlin, many editions, B8, 29ff.), being is "in its totality homogeneous (*homoion*), it is nowhere more or less," and it is "connected as a whole." The word Parmenides uses for 'connected', *xynechés*, is the technical term used by Aristotle in his own account. I suggest that the idea of a line as a continuous entity with the same properties everywhere, in the large as well as in the small, comes from Parmenides' account of the One. But a line can be divided and the One cannot. On the other hand, if an entity having the properties of the One can be divided (note that the division must come from the outside — it is not part of the line itself), then, if it can be divided at one place, it can be divided everywhere, and in exactly the same manner, because of homogeneity. Considerations such as these may give us some historical understanding of assumption 1 of (14). The assumption was not trivial, and it was not based on intuition.

(16) Assumptions 2 and 3 can be supported by arguments showing that the entities used for subdividing a linear continuum are unextended and indivisible. Aristotle offers such arguments for the case of the now, i.e., the instant that divides time into past and future. And, since he shows that time, extension, and locomotion are three different but structurally similar linear continua, this argument applies to all subdivisions.

To be shown: The primary now is indivisible (a moment or interval for an event or a change is 'primary' if it does not contain any interval in which the event or the change does not occur [235b34ff.]; thus, the statement that Caesar was assassinated in the year 44 B.C. does not give the primary or immediate time for the event).

Argument (233b33ff.): The now is a limit of the past, for no part of the future lies this side of it. It is also a limit for the future, for no part of the past lies beyond it. Both limits must coincide. If they are different, then either they include time or there is no time between them. If there is no time between them, then they succeed each other, but they cannot succeed each other for succession assumes separation (this point will be argued below in 21). If there is time between them, then it can be divided: part of it will be in the future, part of it will be in the past—we are not dealing with the primary now. Result: The primary now cannot be divided (and, being a limit of an extended continuum, is also without extension).

Leibniz, in a short essay on motion and continuity (*Philosophische Schriften*, ed. C. I. Gerhard, Berlin, 1885–1890, Vol. iv, 228f., esp. §4) that contains a systematic presentation of part of Aristotle's theory of motion and continuity, has improved this argument and extended it to all limits, divisions, and terminations. Take a line AB and consider its beginning, A (Figure 6). Divide the line in the middle, at C. CB does not contain A. AB is, therefore, not the 'primary' end, and CB can be omitted. Divide AC at D. CD does not contain the end; hence, AC is not the primary end and DC can be omitted—and so on as long as we are dealing with any interval, however small. Conclusion: The primary end of the line AB (or the primary division of a line that extends beyond A to the left) is indivisible (cf. also Euclid, *Elements* i, Defs. 1 and 3). This establishes assumptions 2 and 3 of 14.

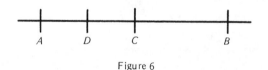

Figure 6

(17) Another argument consists in pointing out that divisions, ends, and sections do not belong to the same category as do lines: "the now is not time but an accidental property of it" (220a21f.) and "lines, or the things derived from them [such as points] are not independently existing substances but sections and divisions . . . and limits [of something else] . . . and they inhere in something else" (1060b10f.); however, they adhere "not as parts" (220a16) that could exist independently (1060b17) and could therefore obliterate a corresponding interval of a line when dividing it. Zeno's objection (1001b5f.; cf. 14) is met by noting that adding limits and/or subdivisions increases number (of subdivisions), not size. For example, a thrice-divided line is not longer than a twice-divided line, but it has different properties.

(18) In 5 division of a physical object meant separation of parts. A body divided by a plane becomes two bodies with one plane surface for each. In 10 division, this time of motion, again meant separation, on this occasion in time: the moving object comes to a stop and starts moving again. In both cases, physical division (of bodies, of motions) changes the extension (of the bodies, of the motions): the divided body becomes larger in the direction perpendicular to the plane of division; the motion takes more time.

The argument of 16 and 17 does not conflict with this result; it deals with the terminal events (points, moments) of the intervals that effect the physical separation, not with the intervals themselves. These events are indeed indivisible and unextended. However, they do not appear unless there is either an abrupt change of material, say, from water to ice, or an interruption of motion or of substance that creates an interval of which they can be ends. And, since a linear continuum is made of the same material throughout, a subdivision without change of length involves the passage of an interrupted motion alongside it. Such a motion, by creating an *interval in time*, singles out a *point on the line* without in any way affecting the extension of the line. This is not the only occasion when motion plays an important role even in the 'static' parts of geometry. (For details cf. 262a18ff.)

These remarks (and the remarks in the preceding sections) give us strong reasons for accepting assumptions 2 and 3, *provided* that there are linear Parmenidean entities that can be cut in the manner just described.

(19) I am now ready to present Aristotle's theory of continuity and motion. I will not explore all the ramifications of the theory, nor will I try to remove all the lacunae and ambiguities (there are very few of them). I will certainly not try to present the theory in a form that satisfies modern standards of mathematical rigor. To start with, there are no generally accepted versions of such standards — creative mathematicians, physicists, and systematizers have always gone different ways. Second, standards of rigor, when firmly imposed, often inhibit discoveries or make the formulation of the discoveries impossible (cf. the views of Lakatos and, to a lesser extent, of Polya). Third, dressing up Aristotle in modern garb would conceal his achievements. Aristotle was the foremost mathematical philosopher of his time, and he was well acquainted both with the technical problems and with the most precise ways of formulating them. Trying to present him in modern terms would disrupt this historical connection. Fourth, those modern thinkers who either criticize Aristotle (Galileo, for example; cf. 20) or who repeat him (H. Weyl; cf. 24) used language very similar to his own.

(20) The theory is based on a series of *definitions* (226b18f.): Things are *together* when they have the same primary place (for 'primary', see 16; for place, cf. 6); they are *apart* when this is not the case. Things *touch* when their extremes are together. *A is contiguous with B* if A touches B. *A is continuous with B* if A is contiguous with B and the ends of A and B are one "or, as the word implies, are contained in each other" (227a15f.). *Between* is defined by reference to change (as are other notions in Aristotle's physics; cf. the last but one paragraph of 18): Every change involves opposites (cf. 190b34ff.) that are contraries (227a7ff.) and as such extremes (226b26). Every stage of a continuous motion with given extremes that has passed one extreme and not yet reached the other is *between* these extremes (the extremes need not be locations; they can be sounds, colors, and other properties that admit of a linear arrangement). *A is the successor of B* if A and B are of the same kind and if there is nothing of this kind between A and B. A and B are part of a *linear continuum* if there are continua $C, C', C'', C''' \ldots C^n$ between A and B such that A is continuous with C, C is continuous with $C' \ldots$, and C^n is continuous

with *B*. From now on, the discussion will be restricted to linear continuous manifolds in this sense.

Aristotle defines 'between' after 'touching', thus assuming continuity before it has been defined. I have changed the sequence, using the definition of 'betweenness' to restrict the earlier definitions to series of events. The definitions make it clear that "continuity belongs to things which become one by touching" (227a14ff.). They thereby solve the problem as to what it is that makes a continuum such as an individual line a single individual thing (cf. 1077a21ff.). In the physical world, things become one by virtue of a functional unit or a soul—otherwise, they are aggregates. Linear continua hold together because their parts are connected in the manner just described.

(21) The definitions imply:

Proposition 1: Linear continuous manifolds do not contain (do not consist of) indivisibles.

Proof: Indivisibles have no parts, therefore they have no ends and cannot hang together in the way described.

For example, lines do not *actually* contain points though, being divisible anywhere, they contain points *potentially*. And, since points mark intervals, we must also say that the parts of a line, such as its right half or its second fifth from the left, are contained in the line only potentially, not actually. The line is one, whole, and undivided until its internal coherence is interrupted by a cut.

Galileo (*Two New Sciences*, quoted from Stillman Drake's translation, London, 1974, 42f.) ridicules this idea in the following manner.

SALVIATI: . . . I ask you to tell me boldly whether in your opinion the quantified parts of the continuum are finite or infinitely many.

SIMPLICIO: I reply to you that they are both infinitely many and finite; infinitely many before division, but actually finite [in number] after they are divided. For parts are not understood to be *actually* in their whole until after [they are] divided, or at least marked. Otherwise they are said to be *potentially* there.

SALV.: So that a line, 20 spans long, for instance, is not said to contain twenty lines of one span each, actually, until after its division into twenty equal parts. Before this, it is said to contain these only potentially. Well, have this as you please and tell me whether, the actual division of such parts having been made, that original whole has increased, diminished, or remains still of the same magnitude?

SIMP.: It neither increases or diminishes [cf. 17, especially the comments on 1001b5f.].

SALV.: So I think, too. Therefore the quantified parts in a continuum whether potentially or actually there, do not make it quantitatively greater or less. . . .

The implication of this little dialogue is that the lack of effect upon size makes the distinction between actual parts and potential parts meaningless. Stillman Drake, the translator and commentator, agrees (p. 42, fn. 27): "Here Galileo proceeds to show that the distinction is meaningless mathematically unless it affects quantity or magnitude." But a linear continuum in Aristotle's sense has not only extension, it has a structure—and this structure is changed by every division (using a similarly superficial argument, one might say that there is no distinction between a liter of wine and a liter of water because both have the same volume). The objection that Galileo is speaking as a mathematician does not remove the difficulty, for it is just Aristotle's point that mathematical entities, apart from being extended, have also a structure; otherwise, there would be no difference between the number five and a line five inches long.

Proposition 1 implies:

Proposition 2: Linear continuous manifolds (LMSs for short) are divisible into LCMs without limit and, further, that (231b5ff.):

Proposition 3: No point of an LCM can be a successor of another point of an LCM (for that would assume that the line between the two points cannot be further divided).

Propositions 1, 2, and 3 express an idea that is similar to the modern concept of an everywhere dense manifold. The difference is that the modern idea assumes the points as given while for Aristotle they are potential and have to be actualized by subdivision.

(22) If extension consists of indivisibles, then so does motion and time: A motion over an indivisible length proceeds and is completed in one single step; it is an individual unit, and this individual unit is part of the total motion just as the individual lengths are part of the total length. Moreover, the moment at which the elementary motion occurs would also be part of time. Denying any one of these consequences means denying the following assumption.

Proposition 4: Linear extension, motion, and time are all LCMs if motion is.

Note that the continuity of space, time, and motion is not shown absolutely but on the assumption that motion is continuous. There is an argument for *this* assumption, but it is cosmological (constancy of action by the prime mover), and I will not go into it.

Given the continuity of motion, length, and time, we can introduce a definition of 'quicker' that was accepted in antiquity and was still used by Galileo: Quicker is what either covers a greater distance in the same time or the same distance in a smaller time or a greater distance in a smaller time (232a23ff.). This is longer and much more clumsy than the corresponding modern definition. The 'clumsiness' is intentional: Distance and time may have some abstract properties in common (continuity, divisibility), but they are not "homogeneous" magnitudes (12). Therefore, they can only be related to themselves, distance to distance, time to time, motion to motion.

Now consider two objects, one quicker, the other slower. Assuming that any motion can take place within any period of time (232b21f.) and that for any period

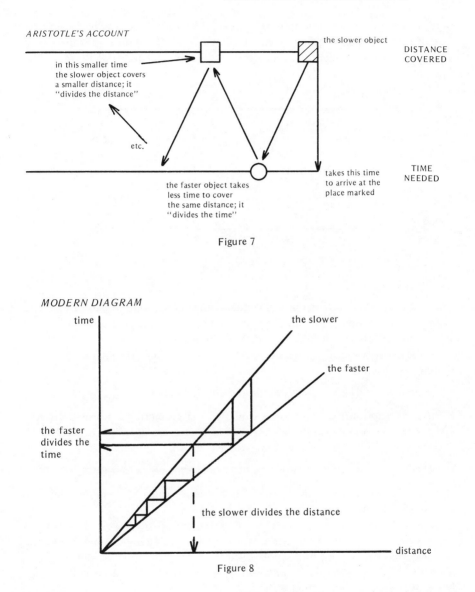

Figure 7

Figure 8

of time there can be a distinction between faster and slower (233b19f.), we see (Figures 7 and 8 and 233a8ff.) that the faster will subdivide the time and the slower, the distance, thus establishing this: if length is continuous, so is time, and vice versa.

"This conclusion follows not only from what has just been said but also from the argument that the opposite assumption implies the divisibility of the indivisible" (233b16ff.). Assume (since velocities can stand in any relation) that one body covers the distance *AB* while another body covers two-thirds of that distance in the same time (Figure 9). Let the intervals $Aa = ab = bB$ be indivisible, and let the same be true of the corresponding times; i.e., let $Rd = de = eS$. Then the slower body when arriving at the possible division a will divide the time at f, thus dividing the indivisible.

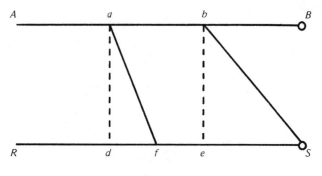

Figure 9

Remember again that the arguments of this section only try to show the coherence of the notions used and the connections established. They do not try to give an absolute proof of these notions and these connections.

(23) Next, we have a sequence of theorems concerning the relation of time to motion and distance.

Proposition 5: There is no motion in the now (234a24).

If there were motion in the now, there would be a faster motion and a slower motion and the faster motion would divide the now in the manner described in the text discussion of Figure 7. But the now is indivisible (16).

Proposition 6: Neither can anything be at rest in the now (234a33f.).

Rest can be ascribed to an object only if that object is capable of motion. But there is no motion in the now.

G. E. L. Owen, in an essay on the role of time in Aristotle's work, has criticized these two propositions as being based on a false interpretation of common sense and as having hindered scientific progress. Scientific progress, he says, occurred only when functions connecting time and velocity were introduced and used in the calculation of the movements of bodies.

The first criticism can be rejected when it is remembered that Aristotle's notion of continuity owes a debt to Parmenides (15). It is true that Aristotle occasionally uses homely examples such as glue and nails (227a17) to *illustrate* continuity. But the *content* of the notion lies in its consequences, and among those consequences we have Proposition 2 (limitless divisibility), which can be proved only via a postulate of homogenity such as the one proposed by Parmenides.

The second criticism, however, only shows that scientists can get very far by thinking very little. In 20, I quoted Galileo to the effect that what mattered was the length of a line, not its structure. This attitude served scientists well as long as the problems they encountered did not involve structure. Trouble arose in quantum mechanics, where considerations of structure became essential. In the attempt to resolve the problems connected with structure physicists introduced ideas very similar to those expressed in Propositions 5 and 6 (uncertainty relations between time and energy) and can now be said to agree with Aristotle's principle that "the motion of what is in motion and the rest of what is in rest must take time" (234b9f.).

Proposition 7: A point has no place (212b24f.).

This follows from the definition of place in 6 as the spatial correlate of Propositions 5 and 6. The three propositions (and some others that are about to follow) are anticipated in Plato's discussion of the One, *Parmenides* 137ff. This passage also contains material Aristotle seems to have used in his definition of continuity (see 20).

(24) According to 8, motion can be subdivided only by being brought to a temporary halt—the "mobile must stop and begin to move again" (262a24f.). When the motion stops, the moving object is in a well-defined place and has well-defined properties; e.g., an object is gray when it was stopped on the way from white to black (234b18f.). Being in a well-defined place and having well-defined properties is the character of an object that does not move. Moving, therefore, implies not being in a well-defined place and not having well-defined properties. It seems that Aristotle, while occasionally drawing such a conclusion (cf. Proposition 15), was not always prepared to take this step (cf. the restriction: "for as a whole [the object] cannot be in both [the initial and the subsequent state of change] or in neither" [234b17]). He concludes, rather, that "during the whole process of change [the object] must be partly under one condition and partly under another"; i.e., it must be divided into parts that are in one condition and parts that are in another condition.

Proposition 8: What changes is divisible (234b10).

Applied to locomotion, this means that we are dealing with elastic and deformable objects. Note the similarity to the relativistic account of the motion of extended objects.

Proposition 9: Whenever a change is completed, the changing thing is in the state into which it has changed (literally: what has changed is that into which it has changed [235b6ff.]).

This simply follows from the meanings of the terms.

Proposition 10: The primary time when what has changed has completed its change is indivisible.

Assume it is divisible, and change occurs in both parts. Then the change has not yet come to an end. If change occurs in one part only, then we are not dealing with the primary time (235b33ff.).

Propositions 9 and 10 are connected with the fact, emphasized in 10, that clearly marked stages of a motion are accompanied by an interruption of that motion. Now motion involves opposites (189a10); one of the opposites is the "for the sake of which" or the aim (*telos*) of the motion (194b33). When the aim is reached, the motion is completed and, therefore, interrupted; and the interruption provides an indivisible limit (236a13) for the motion. Propositions 9 and 10 express this situation.

Proposition 11: There is no indivisible primary time when what changes is completing its change (239a1ff.).

The reason is that what is completing its change is in motion and (Proposition 5) there is no motion in an indivisible moment. In a similar manner, Proposition 6 yields Proposition 12.

Proposition 12: Neither is there an indivisible primary time in which rest first occurs (239a10).

Further:

Proposition 13: Everything that changes at a certain time changed before that time.

Assume AB to be the primary time for the change. The change must occur at a point a, in between A and B, but also at b, in between A and a, and at c, in between b and A, and so on. Therefore:

Proposition 14: There is no such thing as the beginning of a process of change (236a13f.).

(25) The results of the preceding section may be summed up in the following manner. Every change is characterized by a well-defined indivisible moment, the primary moment when the change has been completed. There is no last moment when the change is still on, there is no first moment when the change starts, and there is no first moment of rest after the change has been completed.

One might be inclined to regard this situation as a trivial consequence of the fact that a series of changes terminating in an aim is closed on the right and open on the left and that it is everywhere dense (cf. Chapter iv of E. V. Huntington, *The Continuum*, Cambridge, 1917). But the comparison is misleading in various respects. To start with the structure of an Aristotelian line differs from the structure of a dense series. The elements of a dense series all exist and constitute the series. An Aristotelian line, on the other hand, is one and undivided until the parts are actualized by special means. Second, the end point of the change is actual not because all points of a change are actual and not because the change has been stopped by external means, but because of the particular way in which the change, every change, is completed: It arises because of the inner structure of the process of change. Third, it has no beginning because there is no motion in the now.

The difference between the Aristotelian continuum and the mathematical continuum has been described with great clarity by Hermann Weyl in his essay *Das Kontinuum* (Leipzig, 1919, p. 71).

There is no agreement between the intuitive continuum [which is how Weyl describes the continuum viewed as an indivisible whole] and the mathematical continuum [which consists of points] . . . ; both are separated by an un-bridgeable gulf. However we have reasonable motives which, in our attempt to comprehend nature, make us move from the one to the other. They are the same motives that directed us from the world of human experience in which we live our normal lives towards a 'truly objective', precise and quantitative physical world 'behind' experience and that made us replace the colour qualities of visible objects by aether vibrations. . . . Our attempt to build up analysis [from indivisible units] may therefore be regarded as a *theory of the continuum* which has to be tested by experiment just as any other physical theory.

The mathematical reconstruction of the continuum, Weyl says at a different place ("Ueber die neue Grundlagenkrise der Mathematik," *Math. Zs.* Vol. 10, 1919, p. 42)

selects from the flowing goo . . . a heap of individual points. The continuum is smashed into isolated elements and the interconnectedness of all its parts replaced by certain relations between the isolated elements. When doing Euclidian geometry it suffices to use the system of points whose coordinates are Euclidian numbers. The continuous 'space-sauce' that flows between them does not appear.

This is the same attitude expressed by Galileo (see the quotation in 21), except that Weyl is aware of the loss and of the possibility that its consequences may turn up in physics. The "continuous space sauce" may make itself noticed as we proceed into new domains of research. There are some physicists who think that it already appeared in microphysics.

(26) According to Propositions 5 and 6, there is neither motion nor rest in an instant; every moment fills an interval of time. The location of an object that moves in space is indeterminate in accordance with the size of this interval. If location is indeterminate, then so is length.

Proposition 15: What moves has no well-defined length [in the direction of the motion].

Conversely, a definite length can be assigned to an object only if it can be made to "cover" or "stand over against" a stationary measuring stick, i.e., if it is at rest. Being at rest takes time (Proposition 6); hence:

Proposition 16: An object can be said to have a well-defined length only if it is at rest for an interval of time, however small.

(27) I conclude with a brief account of the way in which Aristotle solves Zeno's paradoxes of motion. Aristotle describes four such paradoxes (239b10ff.). His description is the earliest detailed account we have of Zeno's arguments.

According to the first paradox, motion is impossible because before getting to a point the moving thing must first cover half the distance, then half of that half, and so on. One solution has been described in (8). Aristotle has a second solution, which he regards as less satisfactory (263a4ff.).

According to the second paradox, the "Achilles," the faster can never overtake the slower "since the pursuer must first reach the point where the pursued started, so that the slower must always hold a lead." This Aristotle regards as a different version of the first paradox, and he solves it in the same manner.

The third paradox, the "arrow," states that, as a flying arrow at any moment of its journey occupies a place equal to its own dimensions, it is at rest at any moment of its journey and therefore at rest throughout the journey. The paradox is solved by reference to Propositions 5 and 15.

The fourth paradox, which is more difficult to interpret, is supposed to show "that half the time is twice the time." There are (Figure 10) three series of masses, A, B, and C. A is at rest; and B moves to the right, C to the left, both with equal speed. While C passes all the Bs, B passes only half of the As. Assuming that passage of two masses takes the same time whether the masses are moving or at rest, we can say that B while passing half the As passes all the Cs and therefore takes half the time, while the Cs pass twice as many Bs as As and so take twice the time for the same process. Aristotle denies the assumption and so removes the paradox.

Rafael Ferber, in an interesting and provocative book (*Zenons Paradoxien der Bewegung*, Munich, 1981) has suggested a connection between this paradox and some earlier versions of the idea that what is infinitely divisible has the same number of indivisibles no matter what the size. Today, this idea is illustrated by drawings such as Figure 11. To every point of AB, there corresponds one and only one point of CD, and the two lines have an equal number of points. According to Arpad Szábo (*Anfaenge der Griechischen Mathematik*, Budapest, 1969) from whom Ferber quotes Euclid, *Elements* i, Axiom 8: the whole is bigger than the part (which in proofs is replaced by the stereotype "otherwise what is smaller would be equal to what is larger, which is impossible") was introduced because some people denied it (no other reason can be imagined for formulating such an obvious principle). One person to deny the principle was Anaxagoras (Diels-Kranz, B3).

> For any small thing there are things which are still smaller—for it is impossible that being ceases. But also for what is big there is always something bigger *and it is equal to the small in amount*. Taken for itself, however, everything is both big and small.

We may assume that this assertion underlying Anaxagoras' idea that every piece of material contains ingredients of everything else—there is flesh in metal, metal in air, air in bone, and so on—is also connected with Parmenides' assumption of the homogeneity of the One, introduced in 15 above. If the One is homogeneous throughout, then the smallest part has exactly the same structure as the whole; e.g., it has the same number of parts (subdivisions).[2] Is it possible to find an interpretation of the fourth paradox that leads to the same result? It is possible! (See Figure 12.) Take any point on C, assumed to be continuous. When this point, say O, passes the right end R of B, then R will be beneath P, half way between R and O, and so P will correspond to O. Conversely, to every point S on A there is one and only one point on C, viz., that point that is $2MS$ to the right of N. On a modern diagram

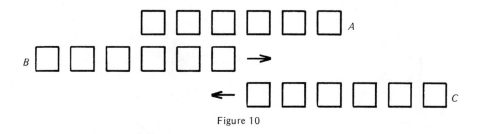

Figure 10

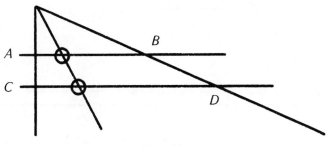

Figure 11

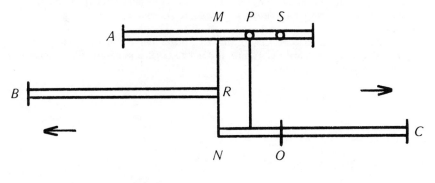

Figure 12

(Figure 13), the correlations become especially clear: The whole is mapped upon half of itself. Considering the definition in 14, we may conjecture that Aristotle might have accepted this result, *provided* that the mapping is between cuts that create points and not between preexisting points. What consequences he would have drawn from it is a different question.

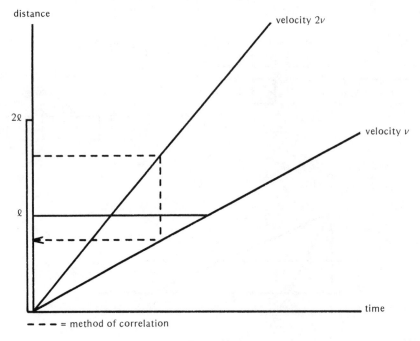

Figure 13

Notes

1. An earlier version of the paper was read by Dr. Rafael Ferber who sent an extended commentary and suggestions for improvement. I have adopted some of his suggestions and rewritten the text accordingly.

2. Of course, Parmenides' One has no parts and, therefore, no structure apart from being homogeneous. But, if we contradict Parmenides and add such a structure, then homogeneity will guarantee its presence in all parts.

Descartes's Theory of Concepts

MORRIS WEITZ

This paper, so far as I can determine, is the first attempt to show the hegemony of closed concepts (the Frege thesis) in Descartes's work.[1] Throughout, I am assuming that philosophy is conceptualization in language; that concepts are basic in philosophy; that theories of concepts—explicit or implicit—are views about the nature and role of concepts, not affirmations of their irreducibility; and that a philosopher's theory of concepts is basic to the philosopher's philosophy, determining the overall conditions of the intelligibility of thought and talk about the world.

That Descartes has a theory of concepts follows from the fact that he does philosophy at all. That this theory is made explicit by Descartes rather than intimated by some of his statements about concepts is problematic. But that Descartes has a vocabulary of conception that distinguishes conceiving, conception, and concept and that he employs this vocabulary to mark certain crucial differences between concepts and his fundamental entities of mind, matter, and God is absolutely certain, confirmed by both the Latin and French texts. It is, therefore, all the more remarkable that within the vast literature on Descartes, there is not a single essay (at least one that I have been able to find) on Descartes's theory of concepts. There are, of course, essays on his theory of ideas in which the ambiguity of "idea" as act and as object of understanding—already noted by Descartes—is resolved into a number of species, one of which is "concept," with the implication that for Descartes a concept is a variant of an idea. Whether this is Descartes's understanding of concepts is best assessed after an examination of the textual evidence, to which I now turn.

In the *Rules for the Direction of the Mind* (*Regulae ad Directionem Ingenii*, 1628), Descartes's earliest philosophical work, his main objective is to formulate and defend a method for the discovery of truth and knowledge. In presenting certain rules or principles that are to be followed if such knowledge is to be obtained, Descartes introduces a number of concepts: the concept of knowledge; the concept of method; the concepts of intuition and deduction; the concepts of understanding, sense, memory, and imagination; as well as concepts that *he* refers to as concepts, such as that of the relative, of figure, of a simple, among others. He also talks a great deal about conception (*conceptus*) and conceiving (*concipere*), distinguishing these from thought and understanding and from thinking (*cogitare*) and understanding (*itelligere*). Since he does not include conception along with sense, imagination, and memory as aids or hindrances to understanding, it is not clear what roles conception and conceiving play in Descartes's rules for directing the mind, nor is it clear what status he assigns to the concepts he calls "concepts." Are they abstractions, objects of understanding, simple natures, meanings of words, or what? If he thinks that concepts are not mental abstractions or simple natures—as he seems to in his discussion of the concept of figure as distinct from certain expressions about figure or certain conceptions of figure, as a simple nature relative to our knowledge of figure—what, then, are we to make of his concepts of method, knowledge, etc., which he does not discuss as concepts?

Basic to the *Rules* is the concept of method in achieving truth and knowledge; the concept of figure serves merely as illustrative of the method. If the concept of method is basic, then it is as important to determine what Descartes takes to be a concept as it is to ascertain what he considers the proper method.

What do the rules say about some of these problems concerning Descartes's theory of concepts? In Rule III, Descartes distinguishes between intuition and deduction, the only two mental operations that attain knowledge of things. Intuition he characterizes as "the undoubting conception (*conceptum*) of an unclouded and attentive mind, and springs from the light of reason alone."[2] Examples of these conceptions are the intuitions each of us can have that he or she exists, that he or she thinks, or that the triangle is bounded by three lines only. There is no suggestion that such conceptions involve concepts rather than things. Deduction also is conception in which we infer from our intuitions. It differs from intuition in that it includes memory, but it is like intuition in that every inference drawn by deduction is itself an intuition. One way to put together what Descartes says here is that *all* knowledge is conception.

In Rule VI, Descartes introduces a distinction between the absolute and the relative, which he restricts to deductive knowledge. By the first, Descartes means our knowledge of what is simple; by the second, our knowledge, derived from the intuition of the simple, that it is complex and is to be analyzed into the simple. The distinction itself, Descartes says, is relative to our search for truth, although the distinction upon which it rests, namely, that between the ontologically simple and complex, is not. As unclear as this distinction between absolute and relative is (since Descartes, in spite of his disavowal, does affirm the ontologically absolute, namely, pure and simple essences), it is clear (textually) that he recognizes the concepts of the absolute and relative: "But the relative is that which . . . involves in addition something else in its concept (*sed insuper alia quaedam in suo conceptu involvit*) which I call relativity" (*AT* X, 382; *HR* I, 16). Here the concept of the relative and, in its context, the concept of the absolute are whatever they may be, neither words nor things.

In Rule XII, which serves mainly as a summary of the preceding rules, Descartes discusses the roles of sense, imagination, and memory in understanding. Conception is not included, but it plays as large a role in explicating these other roles as they do in understanding. For example, Descartes asks us to conceive (*concipere*) the senses as passive, modified by their objects, as the surface of wax is altered by the applied seal. He also tells us (without asking us) that ". . . we conceive the diversity existing between white, blue. and red, etc., as being like the difference between the . . . similar figures" (which he illustrates; see *AT* X, 413; and *HR* I, 37). Not only is anything that is colored also extended but, as extended, possesses figure; but both figure and color can be abstracted, provided, Descartes adds, that we do not admit any new entity (perhaps a universal), which is abstracted. Here Descartes seems to imply that we can conceive figure and color, and can form concepts of them, by abstracting from particulars; however, abstracting is not creating or apprehending abstract entities.

He also relates conceiving to the simple and complex that he earlier calls "absolute" and "relative." We know by intuition the simples: figure, extension, motion, etc. "All others [things other than the simples] we conceive (*concipimus*) to be in some way compounded out of these" (*AT* X, 418; *HR* I, 41).

Simples are either material, spiritual, or common, such as existence, unity, or duration; or common notions, e.g., things that are the same as a third thing are the same as one another; and privative simples, such as nothing, rest, and instant. "All [the] simple natures," Descartes says, "are known *per se* and are wholly free from falsity" (*AT* X, 420; *HR* I, 42). Are simples or only compounds conceived? Descartes does not say.

Simple natures, Descartes goes on, can unite either necessarily or contingently. This union is

> necessary when one is so implied in the concept of another (*in alterius conceptu*) in a confused sort of way that we cannot conceive either distinctly, if our thought assigns to them separateness from each other. . . . Thus . . . if I say "four and three are seven," this union is necessary. For we do not conceive the number seven distinctly unless we include in it the numbers three and four in some confused way (*AT* X, 421; *HR* I, 42–43).

Descartes adds, "if Socrates says he doubts everything, it follows necessarily that he knows this at least—that he doubts." To which we may perhaps add that for Descartes, at least here, the concept of universal doubt and not only the act of proclaiming it entails, however confusedly, the existence of the proclaimer in exactly the same way that the concept of seven entails four and three. Descartes distinguishes also in this important passage "I exist, therefore, God exists" as necessary from "God exists, therefore, I exist" as contingent. Given his definition of "necessary union of simple natures," can we say that for Descartes the concept of myself entails that God exists but that the concept of God does not entail my existence? It seems to me that we can: I can no more form the concept of myself without bringing into the concept God's existence than I can exist without God or than I can understand seven without understanding four and three or than I can "conceive of a figure that has no extension nor of a motion that has no duration" (*AT* X, 421; *HR* I, 42).

Rule XII, thus, is a singularly important document for Descartes's theory of concepts. Concepts in this rule are distinct from simple natures; they are present in deduction as conception, but not in intuition as conception; they contain conceptual entailments that are based upon but not identical with necessary connections, since these connections Descartes attributes only to the relations among natures.

Rule XII also distinguishes between meaningful words and concepts, meaningless words and concepts, and words that inadequately express certain correct conceptions. Examples of meaningless, vacuous concepts are to be found in the pronouncements by some philosophers about certain truths that are nothing more than visions "which seem to present themselves through a cloud. These they have no hesitation in propounding, attaching to their concepts (*conceptus suos*) certain words by means of which they are wont to carry on long and reasoned out discussions, but which in reality neither they nor their audience understand" (*AT* X, 428; *HR* I, 47). Later, in Rule XIII, he is more generous to those who misuse words or who use wrong words, provided that they have the right concept: "Thus when people call *place* the *surface of the surrounding body*, there is no real error in their conception; they merely employ wrongly the word *place*, which by common use signifies that simple and self-evident nature in virtue of which a thing is said to be here or there" (*AT* X, 433; *HR* I, 51).

Rule XIV has a final reference to concept: the concept of body—*corporis conceptum*. Using extension as his example, Descartes is again considering the relation between our conceptions and our expressions for them. Various expressions regarding extension, e.g., "extension occupies place," "that which is extended occupies space," "body is extended," lead to no difficulties. But "extension is not body" does, for it leads us to form an image of what is pure abstraction. "Now such an idea necessarily involves the concept of body, and if they say that extension so conceived is not body, their heedlessness involves them in the contradiction of saying that *the same thing is at the same time body and not body*" (*AT* X, 444–45; *HR* I, 59).

Descartes's *Discours de la Méthode* (*Discourse on Method*, 1637), as important as it is to an understanding of Descartes's philosophy, has little to say about conception and conceiving and nothing about concepts. Of course, much is implied by Descartes's use of the concepts he discusses in the *Discourse*—about method, doubt, God, the self, and matter—concepts that are more fully developed in the *Meditations*. Here, however, I am interested only in what he says about conception and conceiving in the *Discourse*.

In Part II of the *Discourse*, having stated the four precepts of his method for arriving at the truth, Descartes writes: "And besides this, I felt in making use of it that my mind (*esprit*) gradually accustomed itself to conceive (*concevoir*) of its objects more accurately and distinctly . . ." (*AT* VI, 21; *HR* I, 94).

This use of "conceiving" as "seeing clearly" (*que je vois clairement*) Descartes formulates into a general rule "that the things which we conceive very clearly and distinctly are all true" (*ques les choses que nous concevons fort clairement et fort distinctement, sont toutes vraies*). To conceive is to see something clearly and distinctly. The certainty attributed to geometrical demonstrations, Descartes says, "is founded solely on the fact that they are conceived of with clearness" (*on les conçit évidemment*).

Is conceiving seeing clearly and distinctly, or is seeing clearly and distinctly a form of conceiving? Descartes seems to waver on this, since he also talks about conceiving the object of the geometers to be a continuous body, or a space indefinitely extended, and so on, conceptions that are neither clear nor distinct.

Descartes also says that there are ideas (*idées*) or notions (*notions*) that are clear and distinct, hence true. Since the truth of these ideas or notions as consisting in their clarity and distinctness follows from Descartes's principle of true conceptions, it is not immediately obvious that true ideas or true notions are one and the same as true conceptions.

Descartes also uses the verb *feindre*, which some translate as "conceive." If this is adequate, then Descartes sometimes means by conceiving "to feign it" or "to pretend" that it is the case. Here, conceiving slides into imagining in a conjectural, hypothetical way. This is certainly a normal use of "conceive" and one that does no justice to any of Descartes's methodological doubts. For example, "I could feign I had no body" and "I could conceive I had no body" seem to express the same state of mind.

The second edition of *Meditations* (1642), an edition that included a set of *Objections* and *Replies*, all in Latin, is, especially when the *Replies* are considered, a great source for Descartes's theory of concepts. This edition was translated into French with Descartes's revisions.

Just as the concept of method is basic in the *Rules*, the concepts of God, mind, and matter are central in the *Meditations*. Yet, Descartes nowhere in the *Meditations* refers to *these* as concepts, only as ideas. But, as surely as anything is a concept, these three are concepts; and ultimately Descartes's theory of concepts turns on them more than on what he explicitly calls "concepts."

There is much talk about conceiving in the *Meditations*, from the Synopsis through the sixth meditation. In the French the verb is *concevoir* throughout; but in the Latin—make of it what we will—there is a shift from *concipere*, used in the early *Meditations*, to *cogitare* and *intelligere*, used in the later *Meditations*. *Percipere* also serves as a synonym of *concipere*, *cogitare*, and *intelligere* more than it does elsewhere in Descartes. There is also the familiar difficulty, already in the *Rules*, about the exact nature and role of conceiving in Descartes's theory of knowledge. Conceiving does not occur in the Latin, only in the French, as a mode of a thing that thinks (*Meditation* II, *AT* VII, 28; *AT* IX, 22), and it disappears even in the French when Descartes reiterates what is included in a *res cogitans* (*Meditations* III, *AT*, IX, 27). Nevertheless, Descartes talks throughout of the importance of conceiving (perceiving) clearly and distinctly if we are to secure a criterion of truth. Is, therefore, in the *Meditations*, conceiving, thinking, intuiting, and imagining a mental operation of the forming of an idea? I do not see that Descartes gives any univocal answer.

The first provocative use of "conceive" (*concipere*, *concevoir*) occurs in Descartes's proof of his own existence: "I am, I exist, is necessarily true each time I pronounce it, or that I mentally conceive it" (*vel mente concipitur; conçoit en mon esprit*). Much has been written about this pronouncement as well as about the related *cogito*, and so perhaps a few words can be added to discuss Descartes's alternate. What does it mean to say "I am, I exist, is necessarily true each time I mentally conceive it?" First, because of Descartes's views on the relation between words and thoughts, no pronouncements or, more cautiously, not this one, can precede the conception that is prior to it and that it expresses. Second, in the sense that the utterance "I exist," though odd or unusual, is self-verifying or always self-confirming, so that its denial, "I do not exist," is self-defeating or self-contradictory, my conception of my existence does not appear to be self-verifying, nor does its opposite — my conception that I do not exist — seem to be a contradiction. Even Descartes can conceive that he does not exist without contradiction as he cannot utter "I do not exist" without contradiction. "I exist" is necessarily true every time I say it, but "I exist" is never necessarily true every time I conceive it, unless Descartes legislates a use for "conceive" that is synonymous with "intuit" so that he sees clearly and distinctly every time he forms the concept of himself that he exists. In this case, "I exist" is invariably true every time I conceive it, not necessarily true as it is every time I pronounce it. If "I exist" is necessarily true each time I mentally conceive it, it follows that the concept of myself entails the existence of myself — and we have an ontological proof of the self as well as of God. This entailment is missing from the necessary truth of the utterance: My existence does not follow from my utterance "I exist"; it is confirmed, not deduced.

Having established his existence as a thinking thing whenever he thinks, Descartes considers in turn the existence of his body, external material objects, God, the objects of mathematics, and matter. There is much talk about doubt, belief, and knowledge, but little about conception and conceiving, at least in the Latin. Descartes speaks of imagining and doubting and talks about the mind perceiving the piece of wax; he talks of the innate idea of God, of understanding and comprehending Him, but he does not ask persons to conceive (*concipere*) God as persons conceive themselves. In his discussion in the third Meditation about whether God exists, Descartes's main verb is *intelligere*, not *concipere*. In the fifth Meditation, Descartes uses *cogitare* as his verb of conceiving God. God exists because I cannot conceive God without His existence, no more than I can conceive a mountain without a valley. If we allow *cogitare*, *intelligere*, and *concipere* as equally translatable into "conceiving," as they are in the French edition's *concevoir*, then we may scratch my statement that Descartes does not ask us to conceive (*concipere*) God and substitute the statement that he does ask us to conceive (*cogitare*, *intelligere*) God and that in doing so he affirms that conceiving God is thinking of — seeing clearly and distinctly — God's attributes, including God's existence. The activity, but not the verb, of conceiving, then, remains what it is in conceiving "I exist"; intuiting, knowing something in all its simplicity or complexity with a clarity and distinctness that provide certainty and truth.

This sense of "conceiving," expressed indifferently by the Latin *concipere*, *cogitare*, and *intelligere* and by the French *concevoir*, is also employed by Descartes in his discussion of mathematical objects and of material substance. Conceiving a triangle, thus, differs from imagining it; I can conceive (*intelligo*) but not imagine a chiliagon. I can conceive myself without imagination and feeling, but I cannot conceive the latter two without me or some other spiritual substance in which they reside. Finally, Descartes allows in the sixth Meditation that we can conceive corporeal objects as distinct from our idea of them.

Conceptus, too, occurs often enough in the *Meditations*. Mostly it serves as a noun of conception, brought out in the French *conception*. Only once does it mean "concept," namely, in the sixth Meditation where Descartes borrows the scholastic tag *formali conceptu* (*concept formel*) to talk about imagination and feeling considered as formal concepts rather than as modes of intelligent substances.

Let us next look at some of the relevant textual materials in Descartes's *Replies* to the *Objections*. In Descartes's Reply to the first set of Objections, he writes ". . . We must distinguish between possible and necessary existence, and note that in the concept (*conceptu, concept*) or idea of everything that is clearly and distinctly conceived (*intelliguntur*), possible existence is contained, but necessary existence never, except in the idea of God alone" (*AT* VIII, 116; *HR* II, 20).

Here we conceive concepts or ideas of things, not things. If I have the concept of God, I see clearly and distinctly that it includes God's existence. This is not the case with any other concept. Such is Descartes's answer to Caterus, who allows only that the concept of existence is inseparably united with the concept of highest being. Caterus, Descartes implies, has the concept of God all right, but his conception or interpretation of that concept is wrong. They do not disagree about "God" or God but about the content of the concept of God. To go from words, things, and conceptions to concepts seems exactly right—as Sextus Empiricus saw long before—when replies to objections or two opposing conceptions are at stake.

In his Reply to *Objections* II (by Mersenne), there is talk of the concepts of the divine nature, an indefinitely great number, the mind, and the body and of the obscurity of some concepts (those that are not clear and distinct); and there are these stunning statements in the Appendix,[3] in which Descartes lays out his system *more geometrico*:

> When we sat that any attribute is contained in the nature or concept of anything (*Cum quid dicimus in alicujus rei natura, sive conceptu, contineri*), that is precisely the same as saying that it is true of that thing or can be affirmed of it (Definition IX).

> Existence is contained in the idea or concept of everything, because we can conceive nothing except as existent, with this difference, that possible or contingent existence is contained in the concept of a limited thing, but necessary and perfect existence in the concept of a supremely perfect being—

> In omnis rei idea sive conceptu continetur existentia, quia nihil possumus concipere nisi sub ratione existentis; nempe continetur existentia possibilis sive

contingens in conceptu rei limitatae, sed necessaria & perfecta in conceptu entis summe perfecti (Axiom X).

To say that something is contained in the nature or concept of anything is the same as to say that it is true of that being (Def. IX). But necessary existence is contained in the concept of God (Ax. X). Hence it is true to affirm of God that necessary existence exists in Him, or that God Himself exists (Proposition I).

In these quotations from the Appendix, Descartes distinguishes between the idea, the concept, and the nature of anything. In the fifth Meditation, he says that many ideas that may not exist outside his mind but at any rate are not framed by him, though they can be thought or not as he wills, "possess natures which are true and immutable" (*habent veras & immutabiles naturas*) (*AT* VII, 64; *HR* I, 180).

These four quotations raise the absolutely crucial question in Descartes's theory of concepts: Are concepts ideas or natures or both, or are they something else? If the image of a triangle contains an immutable, eternal nature, form, or essence that does not depend on its being conceived, the idea, nature, or concept of a triangle becomes as fundamental in Descartes as God, mind, or matter.

That Descartes does distinguish between conception and concept, especially when there is a dispute over contending conceptions, is manifest in one of his replies to Hobbes's objections to Descartes's distinction between mind and body. Hobbes challenges Descartes on the alleged proof of the mind as distinct from the body as presented in the second Meditation. Descartes argues that the proof is in the sixth, not the second, Meditation. Nevertheless, rather than talking about conceiving mind apart from body, Descartes talks instead of two distinct concepts—*duos distinctos conceptus*. Having formed the concept of the mind and of the body, it is easy, he says, to determine that they are distinct. Once more Descartes shifts from psychological talk of conceiving to logical talk of conceptual content when he moves from meditation to reply.

In his Reply to Arnauld (*Objections* IV), Descartes talks of the concept of the triangle—*conceptus trianguli*—not the idea, conception, or nature of the triangle. Descartes talks further of the concept of body, *corporis conceptu:* " . . . There is nothing included in the concept of body that belongs to the mind; and nothing in that of mind that belongs to the body" (*AT* VII, 225; *HR* II, 101); of the notion of substance: "No one who perceives two substances by means of two diverse concepts (*per duos diversos conceptus*) ever doubts that they are really distinct" (*AT* VII, 226; *HR* II, 101); of the concept of a superficies or of a line; and of the concept of efficient cause, *causae efficientis conceptus.*

In *Objections* V, Gassendi raises questions about what he calls "the concept of wax," "the concept of substance," and "the concept of their accidents," thereby distinguishing between Descartes's conceptions of the concepts that he challenges and the concepts that he does not. Descartes replies in kind, challenging Gassendi's (incorrect) conceptions of Descartes's (correct) conceptions regarding the *concept* of wax, not the *wax*!

For, neither have I abstracted the concept of wax from that of its accidents; rather have I tried to show how its substance was manifested by means of accidents, and how the reflective and distinct perception of it, one such as you, O flesh, seem never to have had, differs from the vulgar and confused idea (*AT* VII, 359; *HR* II, 212).

In *The Principles of Philosophy* (*Principia Philosophiae*, 1644), Descartes again talks of conceiving, conceptions, and concepts; much of this talk presupposes or implies relevant concepts. Thus, we can doubt everything, Descartes says,

but we cannot in the same way conceive (*cogitamus*) that we who doubt these things are not; for there is a contradiction in conceiving that what thinks does not at the same time as it thinks, exist. And hence this conclusion *I think, therefore I am*, is the first and most certain of all that occurs to one who philosophises in an orderly way (VIII).[4]

Here, conceiving presupposes a concept, specifically, a concept of that which thinks. This conceiving consists in seeing clearly and distinctly what is entailed by the concept, namely, that that which thinks exists.

Second, the mind has the ideas of a triangle and of God. It perceives that the three angles of a triangle are equal to two right angles. "In the same way from the fact that it perceives that necessary and eternal existence is comprised in the idea which it has of an absolutely perfect Being, it has clearly to conclude that this absolutely perfect Being exists" (XIV).[5] Here, too, conceiving (perceiving) presupposes concepts such as the concepts of a triangle or of God. Moreover, this conceiving consists in articulating the appropriate entailments.

Third, Descartes divides all objects of knowledge into things of their affections and eternal truths that exist only in our thoughts. In the *Meditations*, Descartes allows that these eternal truths might exist independently of thought; there they are in the mind, as innate, along with innate ideas. Since concepts are objects of knowledge and presumably neither things nor their attributes, the concepts involved in our apprehension of eternal truths must be construed as mental and innate.

Fourth, we have the concept of substance. "Created substances, however, whether corporeal or thinking, may be conceived under this common concept (*sub hoc communi conceptu intelligi*)" (LII).[6]

Finally, in listing the causes of error, Descartes gives as one of them: "that we attach our concepts to words which do not accurately answer to the reality" (LXXIV).[7]

Notes against a Programme (*Notae in Programma*, 1647),[8] written against Regius's manifesto on the nature of the human mind and which is quoted by Descartes, contains talk of concepts: concepts of mind, of extension, and of God. Regius calls into question Descartes's conceptions of these concepts. Descartes answers, as he does in the *Replies*, by reverting to these concepts and what is contained in them. For example, he says:

I have shown that we have a notion or idea (*notitiam, sive ideam*) of God such that, when we sufficiently attend to it and ponder the matter in the manner

I have expounded, we realize from this contemplation alone, that it cannot be but that God exists, since existence, not merely possible or contingent as in the ideas of all other things, but altogether necessary and actual, is contained in this concept (*in ejus conceptu continetur*) (*AT* VIII, 361; *HR* I, 444–45).

Descartes concludes against his opponent: "I myself . . . have founded my argument [for God's existence] entirely on this preponderance of perfections, in which our concept of God (*quo noster de Deo conceptus*) transcends other concepts" (*AT* VIII, 363; *HR* I, 445).

I hope I have covered the main textual sources of Descartes's uses of "conceiving," "conception," and "concept." As far as "concept" is concerned, his employment of this term does not seem to add up to coherent and explicit theory of concepts. Two conflicting theories emerge from the texts: first, concepts are among the innate ideas in the human mind; second, concepts are among the simple natures that exist independently of the human and divine mind and, although not substances, are entities as fundamental and irreducible as God, mind, and matter.

If we turn now, as we must, from his statements about concepts to what he implies that they are in his statements about his major concepts, what then can we say about his theory of concepts? Descartes's philosophy revolves around three fundamental entities: God, mind, and matter. Descartes believes that he demonstrates their existence and articulates their nature. Corresponding to each of these entities is an idea implanted in the human mind. And for each of these entities there is a concept of it that is not the same as the conception of it or any other thought of it, including our idea of it. God, for example, exists and has a nature that can be articulated if not fully comprehended; God exists and has a nature whether we think of God or not. Our idea of God exists when we think of such an entity or, in one version of his theory of innate ideas as potentialities (*Notes against a Programme*, *AT* VIII, 366; *HR* I, 448), when we are capable of thinking of such an entity. But the concept of God is not the nature of God; and the concept of God exists whether we think of God or not, whether our innate idea of God is activated or not. The concept of God exists but not as God exists or as our idea of such an entity exists. This concept also has a nature that is true, universal, eternal, immutable, and capable of being known clearly and distinctly. However, this concept's nature is not God's nature. The concept of God is an entity, but it is not a spiritual or corporeal entity or substance; nor is it a mode of spiritual substance, as our idea of God is. Descartes points out, especially in the *Replies*, that he cannot talk about or argue about the idea of God (which he thinks is lodged in all human minds) without the concept of God. Indeed, it seems to me that Descartes sees as clearly as he sees anything that basic in our philosophical discourse and argument about God's existence and nature (or about our idea of God) is a concept of God that, as he says of the imagined triangle in the fifth Meditation, has " . . . a certain nature, form, or essence, which is immutable and eternal, which I have not invented, and which in no wise depends on my mind . . . " (*AT* VII, 64; *HR* I, 180). There is God. There is also the idea of God. This much is clearly in Descartes. That there is also the *concept* of God as an entity that is not like God or our idea of God but that is implied by there being the idea of God and by talk about God.

Are concepts for Descartes nonspiritual, noncorporeal entities, neither substances nor modes but ontological realities nonetheless? That they are and that consequently concepts are not ideas or variants of them but are rather implied by ideas, best explains, I think, Descartes's theory of concepts as they function in his philosophy. Concepts for Descartes, on this hypothesis, are like Plato's νοητά but not like Plato's εἴδη; they are supersensible entities, not forms as universals. Neither are concepts among the ontological or epistemological simple natures or the composites for Descartes. They are not identical with common simples, common notions, simple privates, or eternal truths. An eternal truth, according to Descartes (*Principles*, XLVIII),[9] exists only in the mind (as do his common notions). But the concept of an eternal truth exists nowhere, even though that concept (as well as the concept of a contingent truth) has a nature that is as real and inviolable for Descartes as the nature of God. Concepts, thus, are not variants of ideas; rather, some ideas are variants of concepts.

One cannot have the concept of God without having the idea of God, just as one cannot have the idea of God without possessing the concept of God. But there can be the concept of God without there being the idea of God as there could not be the idea of God without there being the concept of God. This asymmetry of the existence of the concept and the idea Descartes affirms in the fifth Meditation: The nature of the triangle exists whether there are triangles or not, whether there are ideas of triangles or not. It is this nature of the triangle that serves as the concept of the triangle in Descartes, as he makes abundantly clear in his *Replies*, especially to Arnauld,[10] where he shifts from the idea of the triangle to its concept.

Concepts, for Descartes, are the natures of things, whether these things exist or not and are thought of or not. All concepts contain existence, but all concepts except the concept of God contain only possible existence. God's existence is necessary since "necessary existence is contained in the concept of God" (*Reply* II, Appendix, Axiom X).[11]

Concepts in Descartes, I submit, are fundamental, irreducible, ontological entities, distinct from simple or composite natures, spiritual or corporeal substances, or their attributes or modes, and, hence, distinct from ideas, innate or not. Does this hypothesis elucidate Descartes's major concepts: of God, mind, and matter; of truth; of method; of mathematical objects? Is there a concept of each of these in Descartes? Are these concepts distinct from their corresponding ideas? Are these concepts supersensible natures, forms, or essences?

According to Descartes, God is central in the world as the principle of order (as the principle of creation and re-creation). Therefore, God is Descartes's fundamental entity or being. This entails that the concept of God is the fundamental one in Descartes's philosophy. This concept is not the word "God," not the thing God, nor the idea of God. The word "God" expresses the concept of idea of God; the thing God is not the word or idea or concept; the idea of God exists dependently on the mind; the concept of God, expressed by the word "God" and present in the idea of God, does not depend upon the mind, no more than the properties of being a triangle do. Without the concept of God, our idea of God remains confused and obscure; it is the word "God" without a meaning and God without any adequate vehicle of talking about that entity. God is central in Descartes's world, but the concept of God is central in his philosophy.

What, then, is the concept of God? It is the independently existing object of understanding, thought, and contemplation that includes in its nature, form, or essence all the attributes of the supreme, perfect, or highest being: omnipotence, omniscience, infinity, eternality, and necessary existence. Each is contained in the concept as it is in the innate idea and in God as an entity.[12] Each is a defining property of God and a necessary feature of the concept of God. God, like mind and body, is ontologically a simple nature, although, relative to our understanding of that Being, God is a composite of simple natures, including necessary existence. Thus, the concept of God is a complex concept of a simple nature or substance. Although God is not fully comprehensible, the concept of God is fully comprehensible. Indeed, it is closed in the logical sense that it has a definitive set of necessary and sufficient properties that corresponds to the definitive attributes of God and which properties determine the criteria for the correct use of the word "God" in any language. All correct talk of God and all correct conceptions of God derive from the concept of God as it is perceived clearly and distinctly by the human mind. That God exists can be proved by certain facts: that I have the idea of God as Perfection and that I who have this idea am re-created or conserved with this idea from moment to moment. But that the concept of God has application (that it is not empty) can be proved without any facts from the nature of the concept itself. That God exists and that I have the idea of God show that the concept of God has an application, but the existence and my idea of God do not prove or demonstrate that the concept of God does have an application. For it does not follow from the existence of God or from my idea of God that God necessarily exists, that is, that the concept of God as containing necessary existence is instantiated.

The concept of God is central in Descartes's philosophy. That it is closed in the sense I have specified, that this closure is the supreme governing condition of the intelligibility of thought and talk about God, and that this closure functions as the paradigm of all Cartesian concepts, determining their logical character, illustrate further my overall thesis that basic in a philosophy is the individual philosopher's theory of concepts. In Descartes's case, that concepts as supersensible entities contain definitive sets of necessary and sufficient properties that reflect the essences of the things to which they apply and that legislate the definitive sets of criteria of the correctness of the language that expresses these concepts—all of this adds up to the theory that concepts are closed, a theory that is basic in Descartes's philosophy. Thus, his theories of God, mind, and matter (namely, his metaphysics) embody the concepts of God, mind, and matter; and these, in turn, embody his presupposition or assumption that all concepts are closed. He does not go as far as Frege in holding that "a concept that is not sharply defined is wrongly termed a concept" (*Grundgesetze der Arithmetik*, Vol. II, No. 56), but this recognition of the difference between clear and confused concepts does not deny—indeed, it rests upon—closed concepts whose definitive constituents are either clearly discerned or not. (See Reply to *Objections* II, *AT* VII, 147-48; *HR* II, 43.)

The concept of mind also is a closed concept: It is the concept of a thing that thinks and all that that includes. Here, too, as with the concept of God (I may be improvising and, no doubt, for scholars of Descartes, far worse than that) Descartes distinguishes between the concept of a thinking thing, which has a determinate nature and exists as a supersensible entity independently of our human mental apprehension of it, and our having that concept, which does depend on our minds, indeed, which is an innate idea. That there is the concept of mind as distinct from a conception of it follows from the fact that it is contingent, not necessary, that there are minds in the world whereas it is necessary, not contingent, that being a mind implies being a thinking thing. This is why Descartes can argue from the concept of mind and not from his mind and that the mind is distinct from the body. To claim otherwise (for example, to claim that the mind is not distinct from the body), would be for Descartes to violate the concept of mind, to invest it with a self-contradictory set of attributes.

That Descartes construes the concept of mind as a closed supersensible entity also can be seen in the *Cogito* of the *Discourse* and the *Principles*: "I doubt, therefore I exist." However we interpret this—as argument, intuition, or performative—presupposes the concept of mind as that which thinks (including that which doubts). The *Cogito* may prove that Descartes exists whenever he doubts (thinks), but it just as certainly shows that the concept of thinking thing is being instantiated. Descartes does not prove that the concept of mind is not empty, since that concept, unlike the concept of God, does not contain necessary existence. All he can prove regarding the concept of mind is that it contains as a constituent a "that" that thinks and can exist. His proof that he exists whenever he doubts, hence thinks, proves (provided the argument is sound) that he exists; but that he exists does not prove that the concept of mind is not empty. What it does is to provide evidence that it is not.

The concept of body or matter is for Descartes also an entity distinct from matter and our varying conceptions or ideas of it, or the word expressing the concept or used to talk about matter. It, too, is a complex concept about an ontologically simple nature but relative to our understanding of it as a composite nature. The concept is the nature, form, or essence of that which is extended and the figure, place, quantity, and motion that are implied by the extended. Here, too, one must distinguish in Descartes between this concept, the having of it, the employment of it, and the instantiation of it. In the first and second Meditations, Descartes states and formulates the concept; in the second Meditation, he employs the concept to show that he knows it more clearly than he does its application, in this case, to what he assumes to be a piece of wax; that he has the concept of that which is extended is more certain than the concept is instantiated in a piece of matter. It is only in the sixth Meditation that he proves that the concept is not empty. The proof does not derive from the concept as it does in the case of the concept of God; rather, the proof is based on his demonstration that God is not a deceiver and that his passive sense experiences, presented to his God-given faculty of sense perception, incline him to believe in the external corporeal objects that he senses. That there is matter, that the concept is not empty, that his employment of this concept is not illusory — none of these is proved from the concept; but the demonstration that there is matter and not just the concept of it requires that concept as much as it does the existence of God. In the sixth Meditation, Descartes not only proves that his employment of the concept of matter is illusory but that the concept of matter is instantiated; there really is that which is extended in the world.

Finally, the concept of matter also is closed, governed by a definitive set of predicates or properties. Descartes restricts this set to the quantitative, thereby ruling out, as neither necessary nor sufficient, all the qualitative properties in the concept having to do with color, taste, etc.

I have suggested that Descartes's meditations on God, mind, and matter best disclose his theory of concepts: that they are supersensible entities, distinct from spiritual and corporeal substances or their modes, and that they exist independently of our awareness or employment of them and of their instantiation in God, minds, and material things. I also claim that each of these concepts, in its determinate nature, essence, or form, is closed; that is, contains a definitive set of predicates, attributes, or properties. This set is the ultimate arbiter in talk, thought, and argument about God, mind, and matter. The set can be known (that is, discovered, not invented) by the human mind through clear and distinct perceptions of its members and unity. Inspired by his passion for mathematics, especially geometry and the concept of the triangle (a key concept in Descartes), his theory of closed concepts becomes the generating force of his philosophy, determining his specific doctrines about God, mind, and matter; about causality, truth, and error; about method, induction, and deduction. Some of his concepts, for example, of the relative, may not fit the pattern of a supersensible entity; however, even in their stipulative character as invented concepts (like his "formed ideas"), they are legislated as closed just as surely as his other concepts. As for the simple concepts, whether of simple natures or not, those of existence, knowledge, and certainty (*Principles*, X)[13] and of nothing, rest, and instant (*Rules*, XII)[14] these, too, are supersensible entities, intuitable by the mind but independent of it. They are also closed, not, of course, in the sense of containing definitive sets of properties, but in the sense that their unanalyzable natures preclude the definability of their corresponding terms. Their simplicity determines and legislates the necessary and sufficient criteria that govern our correct employment of these concepts and of the words we use to express them.

Notes

1. This paper was edited and prepared for publication by Theodore E. Uehling, Jr. The first paragraph was transcribed from Professor Weitz's handwritten notes, and it was necessary to make guesses concerning some words. The remainder of the paper was in typescript; some stylistic changes were introduced and the notes (2–14) added. Otherwise, the text remains essentially unchanged. All of the notes are the responsibility of the editor.

2. *Oeuvres de Descartes*, ed. C. Adam and P. Tannery, Paris, 1897–1913, X, 368 (hereinafter *AT*). For the English translation, consult *The Philosophical Works of Descartes*, ed. E. Haldane

and G. R. T. Ross, Cambridge, 1931, I, 7 (hereinafter *HR*). Further references to these two editions will remain in the text whenever possible; in a number of instances, additional notes have been given to make the references more clear.

3. Professor Weitz is here referring to that part of the *Objections and Replies* following the "Reply to Second Objections." That part Descartes entitles "Arguments Demonstrating the Existence of God and the Distinction between Soul and Body, Drawn Up in a Geometrical Fashion" and is found in *HR* II, 52-59. Definition IX is on p. 53; Axiom X and Proposition I are on p. 57.

4. The quotation is from Principle VII of the *Principles of Philosophy*, *HR* I, 221.

5. The quotation is from Principle XIV, *HR* I, 225.

6. *HR* I, 240.

7. *HR* I, 252.

8. The full title is *Notes Directed Against a Certain Programme Published in Belguim at the End of the Year 1647 under This Title:* "An Explanation of the Human Mind or Rational Soul: What It is and What it May Be" (*HR* I, 431-50).

9. *HR* I, 238.

10. "Reply to the Fourth Set of Objections," *HR* II, 96-122.

11. *HR* II, 57. The quotation should read "necessary and perfect existence [is contained] in the concept of a supremely perfect being."

12. The talk about God as an "entity" has been introduced by the editor. The typescript reads "God Himself."

13. *HR* I, 222.

14. *HR* I, 35-49, especially 40-42.

Mind, Body and the Laws of Nature in Descartes and Leibniz

DANIEL GARBER

One of the central doctrines of Descartes's metaphysics was his division of the created world into two kinds of stuff: mental substance whose essence is thought and material substance whose essence is extension. And one of the central problems that later philosophers had with Descartes's doctrine was understanding how these two domains, the mental and the material, relate to one another. Descartes's solution was to claim that these two domains can causally interact with one another, that bodily states can cause ideas, and that volitions can cause bodily states. But this claim raises a number of serious questions. The most obvious problem arises from the radical distinction that Descartes draws between the two domains and from our difficulty in conceiving how two sorts of things so different could ever interact with one another. As the Princess Elisabeth complained to Descartes, ". . . it is easier for me to concede matter and extension to the mind than [it is for me to concede] the capacity to move a body and to be affected by it to an immaterial thing."[1] Though the story is complex, it is generally held that this problem led later in the century to the doctrine of occasionalism, in which the causal link between mind and body was held to be not a real efficient cause but an *occasional* cause. Thus, it was claimed, it is God who causes ideas in minds on the occasion of appropriate events in the material world and events in the material world on the occasion of an appropriate act of will.[2] The causal link between mind and body remains but is reinterpreted as an occasional causal link, a causal link mediated by God. But Descartes's interactionism raises another problem as well. For the seventeenth-century, the material world was thought to be governed by a network of physical laws. But, it would seem, if the material world is governed by law, then there can be no room for minds to act; if minds can be *either* the efficient *or* the occasional cause of changes in the material world, then, it would seem, physical laws must fail to hold in any system that contains animate bodies, bodies under the influence of minds.[3] Particularly vulnerable to such violations are the conservation laws, laws that stipulate that certain physical quantities must remain constant over time, since it is difficult to see how a mind could influence the course of the material world, either by itself or with the intermediation of God, without altering *some* physical magnitude. Leibniz seizes upon just this feature of Descartes's position in an argument intended to persuade us to reject interactionism and accept his doctrine of pre-established harmony. Leibniz argues:

> M. Descartes wanted . . . to make a part of the action of the body depend on the mind. He thought he knew a rule of nature which, according to him, holds that the same quantity of motion is conserved in bodies. He did not judge it possible that the influence of the mind could violate this law of bodies, but he believed, however, that the mind could have the power to change the direction of the motions which are in bodies. . . . [But] two important truths on this subject have been discovered since M. Descartes. The first is that the quantity of absolute force which, indeed, is conserved, is different from the quantity of motion, as I have demonstrated elsewhere. The second discovery is that the same direction is conserved among all of those bodies taken together which one supposes to act on one another, however they may collide. If this rule had been known to M. Descartes, he would have rendered the direction of bodies as independent of the mind as their force. And I believe that this would have led him directly to the hypothesis of pre-established harmony, where these rules led me. Since beside the fact that the physical influence of one of these substances on the other is inexplicable, I considered that the mind cannot act physically on the body without completely disordering the laws of nature.[4]

Leibniz's argument is elegant and straightforward. The claim is that even though Descartes *thought* that he could reconcile the causal interaction of mind and body with the universality of physical law, he was mistaken. The true laws of nature block Descartes's solution, Leibniz argues, and lead us away from causal interactionism and directly to the hypothesis of pre-established harmony as the true account of the apparent relations that hold between the mental and the material.

In this paper, I shall explore this argument of Leibniz's in some detail. I shall begin with a careful exposition of the argument, sketching in some of the details of his position and Descartes's that Leibniz leaves out. I shall then examine the extent to which the position Leibniz attacks is the position that Descartes actually held and argue that Descartes's actual position allows him a plausible answer to Leibniz's attack on interactionism. In the end, I shall argue that the opposition between Cartesian interactionism and Leibnizian harmony is only a symptom of a much deeper difference, a difference between two opposing conceptions of the laws of nature and of the place of mind in the physical world.

1. MOTION, MOMENTUM, AND PRE-ESTABLISHED HARMONY

Cartesian physics is a physics of geometrical bodies, bodies all of whose properties are modes of extension, acting on one another through direct impact. Basic to such a physics, of course, are the laws of motion and impact, the laws that govern the only kinds of change allowed in the world of material things. And basic to the laws of motion and impact for Descartes is his conservation law, derived directly from the activity of God. As Descartes wrote in his *Principia*:

> . . . God . . . in the beginning created matter along with motion and rest, and now, through His ordinary concourse alone, conserves just as much motion and rest in the whole of it [i.e., the material world] as He put there at that time. For although that motion is only a mode of moving matter, it has a certain determinate quantity which can easily be understood to remain always the same in the totality of things, even though it is changed in the individual parts. And so, for example, we believe that when one part of matter moves twice as fast as another, and the later is twice as big as the former, there is as much motion in the smaller as in the larger; and as much motion as is lost by one part slowing down is gained by another of equal size moving more quickly.[5]

Descartes's example suggests that his conservation principle can be summarized by a simple quantitative law: the total *quantity of motion*, as measured by the mass of each body multiplied by its speed, remains constant for the whole of the material world.[6]

It is tempting, but wrong, to assimilate Descartes's conservation law to the modern principle of the conservation of momentum. The conservation of momentum, a law that entered classical physics only later in the seventeenth century, holds that the total quantity of *momentum* remains constant, where momentum is understood as mass times *velocity* and where velocity is understood as a vector quantity, speed *and its direction*. Thus, the law of the conservation of momentum governs *both* the speed *and* the directions that bodies have. So, for example, if a body moving from right to left were to reverse its direction (because of a collision with another body, say), then the conservation of momentum would require that some other body or bodies (say, the body that had been hit) would have to begin moving at an appropriate speed from left to right in order to preserve the total momentum in the world.

Descartes's conservation law is quite a different matter, though. Basic to Descartes's physics is a strict distinction between the motion or quantity of motion a body has, and its *determination* as he calls it, roughly speaking, the direction in which that body is moving.[7] Now, even though this distinction between (quantity of) motion and determination does not explicitly appear in any statement of Descartes's conservation law, it is clear both from the lack of any mention of determination in that law and from the way Descartes actually applies the conservation law that it is meant to govern the *motion alone*. Thus, for example, when discussing impact, Descartes quite carefully separates out the two factors in the physical situation, using the conservation law *only* to determine the postcollision speeds of the bodies in question.[8] So, if in a system of bodies one body changes its direction, then, as long as it maintains its original speed, there is no change in the total quantity of motion; no compensatory change in the direction of another body is required to satisfy Descartes's law, as is the case with the conservation of momentum.[9] In holding that the conservation law does not govern the directions in which bodies move, Descartes is not saying that direction is completely arbitrary. Both (quantity of) motion and direction are modes of body, and, as such, neither will change without an appropriate cause.[10] The point is just that whatever causes might result in changes in direction, such changes in direction are, by themselves, irrelevant to the law of the conservation of motion. One can alter the *directions* in which bodies in the world move as much as one likes, and as long as the *speeds* remain unchanged, the total quantity of motion will remain unaltered.

This feature of Descartes's conservation law opens an obvious possibility with respect to his account of mind-body interaction. Descartes clearly held that minds can cause events in the physical world. And it is also at least initially plausible to suppose, as Leibniz did, that Descartes wanted such interaction to take place without violating his conservation law. These two commitments can be easily reconciled, given the particular conservation law that Descartes adopted. If we suppose that mind acts on body by changing the *direction* in which some piece of matter is moving without changing its *speed*, then the problem is solved: mind can act on body without violating the conservation law. Mind can thus fit into the gap left open in Descartes's conservation law and help to determine what that law makes no pretense of governing. We will have to examine the textual evidence there is for attributing this line of reasoning to Descartes. But it is a position that he *could* have taken, and it is clearly the position that Leibniz thought that he *did* take.

However, it is just as clear that this is a position that Leibniz does not think Descartes is *entitled* to take. As the passage quoted above suggests, Leibniz's argument depends crucially on his refutation of Descartes's conservation law and its replacement by two somewhat different conservation principles. The arguments are complex, and a full examination of them would take us far beyond the scope of this paper. Put briefly, though, Leibniz was able to show that Descartes's conservation law has the absurd consequence that if it were the only law that bodies in motion were constrained to observe, then it would be possible to build a perpetual motion machine. More generally, he showed that in body-body interactions (collisions, for example) governed only by the principle of the conservation of quantity of motion, it is possible for the system to either gain or lose the ability to do work (the ability to raise a body of a given weight a given height, for example). This situation violates the principle of the equality of cause and effect, a metaphysical principle that, Leibniz held, governs this best of all possible worlds. According to that principle:

> The entire effect is equal to the full cause, and therefore, there is no mechanical perpetual motion, nor can a cause produce an active effect which can do more than the cause itself, but neither can there be an entire effect that can do less than the cause itself.[11]

Leibniz argues that if the equality of cause and effect is to be maintained, we must conserve not quantity of motion, mass time *speed*, but a different physical magnitude, living force (*vis viva*), which, he argues, is measured by mass times the *square* of the speed.[12] This new law is an improvement over Descartes's to be sure. But by

itself it does not seem to constrain directionality any more than Descartes's conservation law did. In a system of bodies, each of which is governed only by the
conservation of living force, it *seems* as if one could change the directions of the
bodies without changing the living force in the system. However, from this basic
conservation law Leibniz is able to derive a second conservation law, a new law that
constrains directionality in a way that Descartes's law does not.

Consider an aggregate of bodies in motion that constitutes a closed system,
i.e., one in which no force is being added from the outside. This system contains living
force in two different respects. First of all, each body in the aggregate has its own
force, as measured by the mass of each body times the square of its speed. The sum
of all of these individual forces is what Leibniz calls the "respective or proper force"
of the aggregate. But in addition, the aggregate has what Leibniz calls "directive or
common force . . ., that by which the aggregate can itself act externally."[13] This
force is the force that the aggregate *considered as a whole* has, and it is measured by
the *total* mass of the aggregate times the square of the speed of the *center of mass* of
the aggregate. Now, just as the force in each individual body remains unchanged if
nothing external affects it, so should the directive force of the aggregate remain unchanged if no force is added. But, Leibniz shows, this entails that *within* the aggregate any change in the direction of one body (through a collision with other bodies
in the aggregate, say) must be compensated for by a change in the direction of some
other body or bodies in the aggregate (say, the body or bodies hit), or else the speed
of the center of mass of the aggregate as a whole will change, changing the directive
force of the aggregate. Using reasoning like this, Leibniz establishes that if the total
force of an aggregate is to be conserved, then not only must the respective force be
conserved, the mass times the square of the speed of each individual body in the aggregate, but *also* the total quantity of *momentum*, mass times *velocity*, speed *and direction*! And since the universe as a whole constitutes such an aggregate, the conservation of momentum must govern the universe as a whole.[14] Thus, Leibniz argues,
the principle of equality of cause and effect governs not only the *speeds* bodies have
but their *directions as well*; a change in *either* the speed *or* the direction of a given
body not compensated for by appropriate changes in other bodies is not permitted
in the best of all possible worlds.[15]

This argument quite effectively blocks the reasoning that Leibniz attributed
to Descartes. There is no room in Leibniz's conception of the material world for
Cartesian minds to act. Cartesian interactionism is impossible without a violation of
what were for Leibniz the basic metaphysical and physical laws that govern our world.
This, Leibniz claims, led him and would have led Descartes, if he had grasped the true
laws of nature, to reject interactionism and adopt the hypothesis of pre-established
harmony. The hypothesis of pre-established harmony is, of course, one of Leibniz's
proudest inventions. In its strictest formulation, it posits a perfect correspondence
among the perceptions of all monads. As such, it is intimately connected with
Leibniz's conception of the world as a collection of monads that are, by their nature,
incapable of any genuine causal interaction.[16] But Leibniz also formulates the doctrine of pre-established harmony in a somewhat different way, a way that can be

understood, argued for, and adopted independently of Leibniz's idiosyncratic views about the ultimate nature of the world and the ultimate reduction of material bodies to well-founded phenomena grounded in a world of monads. In this version, the doctrine of pre-established harmony is less a claim about the interrelations among all created substances than it is a claim about two very special ones, the human mind and the human body. In its less rigorous formulation, the doctrine states simply that events in the mind and those in the body correspond to one another not because of any genuine causal link between the two, as Descartes held, and not because of the intervening action of God, as the occasionalists would have it, but because God, in the beginning, created mind and body independently of one another in such a way that there would always be an appropriate correspondence between what was going on in the one and what was going on in the other. As Leibniz succinctly summarized his theory:

> If we posit the distinction between mind and body, their union can be explained without the common hypothesis of influence, which cannot be understood, and without the hypothesis of occasional causes, which summons a *deus ex machina*. For GOD from the beginning so constituted both the mind and the body at the same time, with such wisdom and such skill that from the first constitution and essence of each, everything that comes about through itself in the one corresponds perfectly to everything that happens in the other, just as if [something] passed from the one into the other.[17]

This hypothesis, of course, deals neatly with the problem that had worried so many about how things as different as minds and bodies could be causally connected with one another. On Leibniz's theory they *aren't*. But, in this respect, Leibniz's theory is at best a small improvement over occasionalism, substituting one large divine labor in creating mind and body in harmony with one another for numerous lesser divine actions in coordinating the moment-by-moment states of the two. The deeper differences between pre-established harmony and occasionalist interactionism become clearer when we examine the problems raised by physical law. Although occasionalism addresses the problem of the *mechanism* of interaction, there is nothing in the occasionalist position that bears on the problem of interactionist violations of physical law. For the occasionalist, just as for the direct interactionist, every voluntary action would seem to violate some law of nature. Not so for Leibniz's pre-established harmony. If God can create a world in which events in minds and bodies can correspond with one another in an appropriate way without the necessity for either real or occasional causal links, He can also create things in such a way that this correspondence can take place without violating any of the laws that hold universally in the physical realm. Thus, Leibniz wrote:

> Minds follow their laws, which consist in a certain development of perceptions in accordance with goods and evils, and bodies also follow theirs, which consist in the laws of motion. But these two things entirely different in kind join together and correspond like two time-pieces perfectly well regulated to the same time, even though perhaps of entirely different construction.[18]

Or, even more graphically, Leibniz wrote to Arnauld:

> It is thus infinitely more reasonable and more worthy of God to suppose that He created the machine of the world from the beginning in such a way that without violating at any moment the two great laws of nature, those of force and direction, and instead in following them perfectly (excepting the case of miracles), it happens that the springs of bodies are ready to act of themselves, as is necessary, just at the moment that the soul has a volition, . . . and thus that the union of the mind with the machine of the body and the parts which it contains and the action of one on the other consists only in that concomitance which marks the admirable wisdom of the creator much better than does any other hypothesis.[19]

Given this particular statement of the doctrine, it is clear why Leibniz's reflections on mind-body interaction and physical law might have led him to pre-established harmony. Pre-established harmony seems to be an attractive way in which a dualist could account for the posited correspondence between acts of will in a nonmaterial mental substance and appropriate events in a nonmental body without violating any of the laws of nature that, Leibniz held, govern every event in the material world.

2. INTERACTION AND CONSERVATION IN DESCARTES

Leibniz's argument is an elegant one, a paradigmatic example of the interconnection between physics and metaphysics that characterizes rationalist science. And Leibniz seems to have focused on one of the central questions raised by any dualist interactionist philosophy of mind. Now, as a purely philosophical argument, Leibniz's attack on Descartes is worthy of serious consideration, to be sure.[20] But what interests me here is a somewhat more historical question: Is the position that Descartes actually held open to this kind of attack?

There is no question but that Descartes held the conservation law to which Leibniz alludes in his statement of the argument, and there is no question but that Descartes's law is wrong and the laws that Leibniz substitutes for it correct, at least within the world of classical physics. But Leibniz's attack on Cartesian interactionism makes at least one further assumption, the assumption that the laws of nature must, miracles aside, hold universally, without exception for all bodies in the material world, including animate bodies like our own. Leibniz certainly believed in the universality of natural law in this sense and attributed the same belief to Descartes, claiming that this commitment forced Descartes to hold that minds can change only the directions in which bodies move and not their speeds. But curiously enough, even though Leibniz was well versed in the Cartesian corpus, he refers to no passages from Descartes's writings to support those attributions. Nor could he have. For a close examination of Descartes's writings gives us good reason to believe that he never held the positions that Leibniz attributed to him, neither the change-of-direction account of mind-body interaction nor the universality of the laws of motion.[21]

Let us begin with the change-of-direction account of mind-body interaction.

The most striking evidence against the claim that Descartes held such a position is the simple fact that nowhere in what currently survives of Descartes's writings do we find anything like a clear statement of the account that Leibniz attributed to him; nowhere did he ever *say* that he held that minds can only change the direction in which bodies move. Typically when presenting his position he is content to assert simply that mind can cause motion in bodies. For example, Descartes wrote the following passage in a letter to the Princess Elisabeth in the context of an explanation of the primitive notion we have of the union of mind and body:

> . . . As regards mind and body together, we have only the notion of their union, on which depends our notion of the mind's power to move the body [*la force qu'a l'ame de mouuoir le corps*], and the body's power to act on the mind and cause sensations and passions.[22]

Similarly, Descartes wrote to Arnauld:

> Moreover, that the mind, which is incorporeal, can set a body in motion [*corpus possit impellere*] is shown to us every day by the most certain and most evident experience, without the need of any reasoning or comparison with anything else.[23]

And finally, consider a passage that Descartes wrote to Henry More:

> The force moving [a body] [*vis . . . mouens*] can be that of God Himself . . . or also that of a created substance, like our mind, or that of some other thing to which He gave the force of moving a body [*cui vim dederit corpus mouendi*].[24]

There is no mention of directionality in these passages. Descartes is content to say only that our minds have the ability to move our bodies. But these remarks are, admittedly, casual and were given in the context of nontechnical and almost off-the-cuff explanations of his position. However, it is significant that this casual lack of attention to the question of change of speed versus change of direction is also found in the strict and more technical accounts of mind-body interaction that Descartes gave.

Consider, for example, the discussion of interaction that Descartes gives in the *Passions de l'Ame*, a sort of auto-mechanic's manual for the mind-body union, where Descartes outlines in rather specific ways the nuts and bolts of how the mind acts on the part of the body to which it is most directly connected, the pineal gland.[25] Some of Descartes's most careful discussions of the direct action of the mind on the pineal gland there do indeed suggest that at least *sometimes* the mind acts on the human body by changing the direction in which the pineal gland is moving. Thus, Descartes writes in the *Passions* that "when the mind wants to remember something, this volition makes the gland incline successively in different directions [*vers divers costez*]."[26] Similarly, in talking about the opposition between the mind and the animal spirits, a bodily substance also capable of moving the pineal gland and, in so doing, causing both passions and involuntary movement of the body, Descartes notes that the pineal gland "can be pushed in one direction [*poussée d'un costé*] by the mind, and in another by the animal spirits."[27] But there is nothing to suggest that the *only* way that the mind acts in the pineal gland is by changing the direction of its motion. In the *Passions*, Descartes often says simply that the pineal gland "can be moved in different manners by the mind [*diversement meuë par l'ame*]" or that a volition of the mind can "make the small gland to which it is closely joined move in the manner [*façon*] that is required to produce the effect which corresponds to that volition."[28] These passages suggest that the mind can alter the state of the pineal gland in ways other than by changing its direction.

Descartes's casual talk of mind simply moving body, both in strict and technical writings and in looser, nontechnical writings, together with the lack of any clear positive statement of the change-of-direction account is evidence enough against Leibniz's attribution. But, in addition, there are some passages among Descartes's writings whose sense *seems* to run directly contrary to the account that Leibniz attributes to Descartes. Consider, for example, some passages of the *Passions* in which the mind is said to act on the pineal gland in ways that appear difficult to reconcile with the change-of-direction account of interaction. Descartes discusses in the *Passions* the circumstance in which the animal spirits are moving the gland in such a way as to cause in the mind a desire for something that the mind wants to avoid, as, for example, when the animal spirits, stirred up by the sight and smell of a glass of fine wine, cause the gland to move in such a way as to implant the passion of desire for the wine in the mind at the same time that the mind wills that the body abstain. Descartes analyzes this familiar situation as a struggle (*combat*) ". . . between the effort by which the [animal] spirits push the gland to cause the desire for something in the mind, and that by which the mind pushes it back by the volition it has to avoid that same thing."[29] Descartes gives a similar account of the conflict between the natural tendencies of the pineal gland and the volition of the mind in his account of how it is that we fix our attention: "Thus when one wants to hold one's attention to consider the same object for some time, this volition holds the gland inclined to the same side throughout that time."[30] In both of these passages, Descartes represents the mind as *resisting* the movement that the pineal gland would have, left to purely mechanical causes; our minds are *preventing* the gland from having motion that it would otherwise have. It is difficult to see how this can be reconciled with the change-in-direction account of mind-body interaction, and it seems unlikely that Descartes would have allowed such passages to creep into his most careful account of the mind's action on the pineal gland if he genuinely held the account that Leibniz attributed to him.

Or consider, for instance, the comparison that Descartes draws between the action of mind on body and the scholastic account of heaviness (gravity). According to that theory, at least as Descartes understood it, the heaviness of a body is taken to be a real quality, something real and distinct from the body itself that causes the body to move toward the center of the earth.[31] Although Descartes rejects this account of heaviness in favor of a purely mechanical account of the phenomenon in terms of the laws of motion and impact and the size, shape, and motion of the particles that make up the heavy body and its ambient medium, the scholastic theory, still familiar in his day, was of some use to Descartes in explaining his own account of mind-body interaction. For, Descartes claims, if one can understand the scholastic account of heaviness, then one ought to be able to understand how an immaterial substance can cause changes in a material substance. Thus, Descartes wrote to Arnauld:

> Many philosophers who think that the heaviness of a stone is a real quality distinct from the stone believe that they understand well enough how such a quality can move the stone toward the center of the earth, since they think that they have a manifest experience of it. I, who have persuaded myself that there is no such quality in nature, nor thus is there any true idea of it in the human intellect, believe that they use the idea which they have of incorporeal substance to represent that heaviness to themselves. Thus, it is no more difficult for us to understand how mind moves body than it is for them [to understand] how this heaviness bears a stone downwards.[32]

This example is intended to take away some of the mystery surrounding the question as to how a nonbodily thing can act on a body by giving an example of a nonbodily thing (the real quality of heaviness) that Descartes's contemporaries had no trouble accepting as a cause of motion. But this would be a curious example to use if Descartes thought that mind could change only the direction in which a body was moving. In the case of a body falling toward the center of the earth, there is no mere change in direction. Rather, the quality of heaviness is thought to produce *new motion* in the heavy body where there was none before. The implication is that mind acts on body in the same way.

This implication is clearest of all in another passage relating the action of mind on body to heaviness, this time comparing the action of mind on body not with the scholastic theory of heaviness but with Descartes's own theory. On Descartes's account of heavy bodies and free fall, the falling body is impelled downward toward the center of earth by means of collisions between that body and other smaller and more quickly moving bodies in the surrounding medium.[33] Thus he wrote in a passage, ironically enough, preserved only in a copy Leibniz made:

> If a body is pushed or is impelled to motion by means of a uniform force [*semper aequali vi*], of course imparted to it by mind (for there can be no such force otherwise), and if it is moved in a vacuum, then it would always take three times longer to travel from the beginning of the motion to the midpoint than from the mid-point to the end. However, there can be no such vacuum. . . . But suppose that the body were impelled by heaviness. Since that heaviness never acts uniformly like mind, but [acts by] some other body which already is in motion, it can never happen that a heavy body is impelled more quickly than that which moves it. . . .[34]

Descartes's main point in this passage is the contrast between the uniform acceleration due to the activity of mind, and the nonuniform acceleration due to heaviness. But it is clear from this passage that Descartes thought that the action of mind on bodies does *not* result in a mere change in direction. Rather, Descartes quite clearly thought, mind can produce a real change in the *speed* of a body, in fact, that mind is the *only* natural means by which a uniform change in speed is *possible*.

It is, of course, *possible* that all of the passages I have presented can be reconciled with the change-of-direction thesis or that Descartes *thought* they could or that he actually rendered them consistent with that thesis in some now lost fragment, perhaps even one that Leibniz saw in Paris when Clerselier showed him Descartes's literary remains. But the passages I have cited, together with the lack of any clear and positive statement of the change-of-direction account in any of the numerous writings that do survive, make it likely that Descartes just did not hold the account of mind-body interaction that Leibniz attributed to him. At the very least, the burden of proof is on anyone who wants to claim that Leibniz's account of Descartes is correct.[35] This by itself leaves us in the dark about the relations between mind-body interaction and Descartes's conservation law, however. Even if Descartes did not hold the change-of-direction account of mind-body interaction, perhaps he had some other way of rendering interactionism consistent with a universal conservation law. Perhaps he would have argued that whenever a mind puts a body into motion, something somewhere else in the material world loses the requisite quantity of motion, so that mind serves only to redistribute motion in the world, for example.[36] Although such a move is open to Descartes, there is no textual evidence that he as much as considered it. The overwhelming impression that one gets from the texts is that Descartes just was not very concerned about reconciling his interactionism with his conservation law. Now, the apparent lack of attention to this problem may be explained in a number of ways. There is always the possibility that Descartes simply neglected to see the serious problem that his position raises. But there is another, better explanation for this apparent gap in Descartes's argument. The case can be made, I think, that, from Descartes's point of view, there just *is* no problem reconciling interactionism with the laws of nature. That is, there is reason to believe that Descartes may never have been committed to the position that his conservation law holds universally and may have allowed for the possibility that animate bodies lie outside the scope of the laws that govern inanimate nature.

Many versions of the conservation law do, indeed, suggest that the law is intended to hold universally. For example, when introducing the conservation law in the *Principia*, Descartes writes: ". . . God . . . in the beginning created matter along with motion and rest, and now, through His ordinary concourse alone, conserves just as much motion and rest in the whole of it as He put there at that time."[37] It is hard to see how God could conserve "just as much motion and rest" as He initially created if minds are allowed to add and subtract motion from the world literally at will. But when Descartes is being especially careful, he seems to allow that his conservation law may admit of some exceptions. As I will discuss in some detail below, Descartes's conservation law follows from the immutability of God. Thus Descartes writes just a few lines following the passage just quoted:

> Therefore, *except for changes [in quantity of motion] which evident experience or divine revelation render certain*, and which we perceive or believe to

happen without any change in the Creator, we ought not to suppose that there are any other changes in His works, lest from that we can argue for an inconstancy in Him.[38]

Here Descartes clearly admits that there *can* be violations of the conservation law, circumstances in which motion is added or taken away. The reference to divine revelation suggests that some such violations might arise from miracles. But Descartes also makes reference to violations that "evident experience . . . renders certain." An obvious suggestion as to what Descartes has in mind here is the ability that the human mind has to set the human body in motion, which, as he told Arnauld, "is shown to us every day by the *most* certain and *most* evident experience."[39] This natural reading is confirmed a few pages later in the *Principia*, where Descartes is discussing his third law of motion, a law explicitly governed by the conservation law, in which Descartes sets out the general features of his account of impact. Descartes writes:

And all of the particular causes of the changes which happen to bodies are contained in this third law, *at least insofar as they are corporeal*; for we are not inquiring into whether or how human or angelic minds have the force [*vis*] to move bodies. . . .[40]

This is, to be sure, something less than a clear and positive statement that minds can cause violations in the laws of nature. But, together with the lack of any attempt to reconcile interactionism with his conservation law, these passages suggest that in the *Principia* Descartes, at very least, left open the possibility that the activity of minds is not constrained by the laws of nature that hold for bodies.[41]

At this point we can return to the questions raised at the beginning of this section. The passages cited earlier strongly suggest that Descartes did not hold the change-of-direction account of mind-body interaction that Leibniz attributes to him. Even more radically, although the texts are not completely decisive on the question, they do suggest that Descartes at least left open the possibility that his conservation law may be violated by animate bodies. The philosophical point should be clear. Descartes *might* have answered Leibniz's attack on interactionism by simply denying that the conservation laws must hold for animate bodies. If this were Descartes's answer, as I suspect it would have been, then even if Leibniz were to convince him of the falsity of his own conservation law, Descartes would not have been forced to reject interactionism. There is no reason to think that Descartes would have held Leibniz's conservation laws to be any more universal than he seems to have held his own to be. And if Leibniz's conservation laws are not taken to govern the behavior of animate bodies, then they pose no obstacle at all to the claim that minds can alter the course of events in the material world.

3. GOD AND THE LAWS OF NATURE

In the previous section I outlined one answer that Descartes could have given to Leibniz's argument. I have claimed that, given what he says about mind-body interaction, it is open to Descartes to deny the universality of physical law and to deny that animate bodies are constrained by the same laws that govern the purely material world. Thus, it seems, the difference between Descartes's interactionism and Leibniz's preestablished harmony comes down to a more basic difference with respect to the scope of physical law. This, however, raises still deeper questions. First of all, there is the question of the coherence of Descartes's own position. Is the position that the texts suggest consistent with Descartes's otherwise mechanistic world view? Can the exclusion of animate bodies from the laws of the material world be anything but arbitrary? And, second, there are arguments of Leibniz's to deal with. Leibniz took it for granted that the laws of nature apply to animate bodies. Are Leibniz's reasons for holding this position binding on Descartes as well? In the argument I presented at the beginning of this paper, Leibniz attempts to trace Descartes's interactionism to a relatively uncontroversial and straightforward mistake about the true laws of motion. The argument I offered in the previous section suggests that Leibniz's argument may not be applicable to the position that Descartes actually held. But Descartes's position may still rest on a mistake, a different mistake than the one that Leibniz attributes to him, to be sure, a mistake about the scope of physical law rather than its content, but a mistake nevertheless. We must, then, explore whether there is some unobjectionable way for Descartes to exclude animate bodies from the scope of physical law.

One place we might begin is with Descartes's discussion of the union of mind and body. In an interesting paper, the only discussion of this question that I know of in the literature, Peter Remnant attempts to link the exclusion of animate bodies from the laws of motion to the discussion of mind-body unity and interaction found in Descartes's celebrated correspondence with Elisabeth.[42] Remnant notes that for Descartes the world of created things is understood through three distinct primitive notions, the notions of extension, thought, and the union of mind and body. Descartes writes to Elisabeth that

> . . . there are in us certain primitive notions which are as it were models on which all our other knowledge is patterned. . . . As regards body in particular, we have only the notion of extension which entails the notions of shape and motion; and as regards soul in particular, we have only the notion of thought. . . . Finally, as regards soul and body together, we have only the notion of their union, on which depends our notion of the soul's power [force] to move the body, and the body's power to act on the soul and cause sensations and passions.[43]

These notions are primitive in the sense that they must be grasped one by one, apart from all other notions, and cannot be explicated in terms of one another. As Descartes wrote:

> If we try to solve a problem by means of a notion that does not apply, we cannot help going wrong. Similarly, we go wrong if we try to explain one of these notions by another, for since they are primitive notions, each of them can only be understood by itself.[44]

Thus, Remnant claims, "each of these primitive notions defines an autonomous sphere of knowledge."[45] We must understand mind in terms of its primitive notion and the laws that follow from it, and body in terms of *its* primitive notion and the laws that follow from it. And, most important, we must understand the animate body, the thing composed of the union of mind with body in terms of its primitive notion and the laws that follow from *it*. To impose the laws of inanimate matter on animate bodies, unions of mind and body, is for Descartes, on Remnant's reading, a basic mistake that can lead only to confusion and misunderstanding; it is an instance of attempting to apply one primitive notion (that of extension and the laws it obeys) to an object to which it does not apply. Thus Remnant concludes:

> On Descartes's view there is a system of principles which applies to all purely physical interactions among bodies (including most biological processes) and another system which describes intellectual processes. But there is also a third realm, that of animated bodies. Animated bodies can participate in purely physical interactions and when they do their behavior conforms to the laws of motion. . . . But when they are behaving *qua* animated the laws of motion do not apply to them—their behavior conforms to a different set of principles, falling under the primitive notion of the union of soul and body. . . . If all the activities of bodies consisted in animated behavior then the laws of motion would have no application; similarly, if all the activities of the soul involved its union with its body . . . the principles of intellection would have no application; it is only because bodies also behave purely *qua* bodies and minds purely *qua* minds that these two sets of principles have application. But this is consistent with the occurrence of another sort of behavior, subject to another set of principles, namely that of animated bodies.[46]

Remnant's account of the matter has the ring of truth. Descartes does, indeed, treat the union of mind and body *almost* as if it were a separate substance, and it is plausible to suppose that he thought of the animate body as satisfying different laws than the ones that inanimate bodies satisfy.[47] But this cannot be the *whole* story. Surely, *some* of the laws applicable to inanimate bodies are *also* applicable to bodies united to minds. Surely, the geometrical properties of the pineal gland are the same, whether that gland is connected to a mind or not. Surely, a living human being can no more be in two places at the same time than can a corpse. And surely, although the mind enables us to do much that cannot be done in inanimate nature, it does not allow us to create a vacuum in Descartes's world. Thus, even though animate bodies may be exempt from the laws of motion, there are many other laws that *all* bodies must obey, even those that are behaving *qua* animated, to use Remnant's phrase. And this raises a basic question: What specifically is it about the laws that govern motion that exempts the union of mind and body from their scope? Why are the laws that govern shape, for example, one mode of extension, greater in scope than the laws that govern motion, *another* mode of extension? The arbitrariness still remains on Remnant's account; there still seems no reason why Descartes can exclude animate bodies from the laws of motion. If there is any reason why animate bodies can violate the laws that hold for inanimate nature, it must concern not only the doctrine of primitive notions that Descartes expounds to Elisabeth but also his conception of the laws of motion. And if there is any way that Descartes can sustain his position against Leibniz's claims, it must be found in the different accounts of those laws that the two philosopher-scientists offer. Thus, we must for the moment turn away from minds and bodies and investigate the ways in which Descartes and Leibniz treat the laws of motion.

For Leibniz, the laws of motion, like every other contingent feature of this world, are grounded in God. In particular, they are grounded in God's *ends*, in his decision to create the best of all possible worlds. Leibniz writes:

> . . . The true physics should in fact be derived from the source of the divine perfections. It is God who is the ultimate reason of things and the knowledge of God is no less the source of sciences [*principe des sciences*] than His essence and His will are the source of beings. . . . Far from excluding final causes and the consideration of a being who acts with wisdom, it is from these that everything must be derived in physics. . . . I agree that the particular effects of nature can and ought to be explained mechanically, though without forgetting their admirable ends and uses, which providence has known how to contrive. But the general principles of physics and mechanics themselves depend on the action of a sovereign intelligence and cannot be explained without taking it into consideration.[48]

Leibniz's physics, then, begins with a consideration of God as the *final* cause of the world. Leibniz's position is, of course, that God acts in accordance with the principle of perfection, that God chose our world from among an infinity of other possible worlds because it is the most perfect, the one that has the most order consistent with the greatest variety in phenomena. Now, the order that Leibniz attributes to the world God creates is complex and involves a number of important metaphysical principles. But among these principles are the laws of nature in general, and among the laws of nature are the laws of motion and the more general metaphysical principles on which they rest. Thus Leibniz wrote in the *Principles of Nature and Grace*:

> The supreme wisdom of God has made Him choose especially those *laws of motion* which are best adjusted and most fitted to abstract or metaphysical reasons. There is conserved the same quantity of total and absolute force, or of action; also the same quantity of relative force, or of reaction; and finally, the same quantity of directive force. Furthermore, action is always equal to reaction, and the entire effect is equivalent to its full cause. It is surprising that no reason can be given for the laws of motion which have been discovered in our own time . . . by a consideration of *efficient causes* or of matter alone. For I have found that we must have recourse to *final causes* and that these laws do not depend upon the *principle of necessity*, as do the truths of logic, arithmetic, and geometry, but upon the principle of fitness [*principe de la convenance*], that is to say, upon the choice of wisdom.[49]

The laws of motion, then, are intertwined with the order that God has imposed on our world as a consequence of His decision to create the best of all possible worlds.[50]

These basic laws governing nature are not without exception, though. God, acting in accordance with some higher principles of order, principles of supernatural order that, Leibniz thought, lie beyond our comprehension, can violate the laws that He set down for finite things to observe. As Leibniz wrote in the *Discourse on Metaphysics*:

> Now, since nothing can happen which is not according to order, it can be said that miracles are as much subject to order as are natural operations and that the latter are called natural because they conform to certain subordinate maxims which we call the nature of things. For we may say that this nature is merely a custom of God's with which He can dispense for any reason stronger than that which moved Him to use these maxims.[51]

However, it is important to note, such violations of the subordinate maxims that constitute the laws of nature are miracles, happenings that, Leibniz argues, must lie beyond the capability of finite beings to bring about if miracles are to be genuinely distinct from the ordinary course of nature. Thus Leibniz explained to Clarke:

> If a miracle differs from what is natural only in appearance and with respect to us, so that we call a miracle only that which we seldom see, there will be no internal real difference between a miracle and what is natural, and at the bottom every thing will be either equally natural or equally miraculous. Will divines like the former, or philosophers the latter? . . . In good philosophy and sound theology we ought to distinguish between what is explicable by the natures and powers of creatures and what is explicable only by the powers of the infinite substance. We ought to make an infinite difference between the operation of God, which goes beyond the extent of natural powers, and the operations of things that follow the law which God has given them, and which He has enabled them to follow by their natural powers, though not without His assistance.[52]

So, even though God can violate natural law for the sake of a higher order, for the sake of *supernatural* law, nothing in nature can. These subordinate laws govern nature as a whole and without exception, save for the extraordinary (and infrequent) interference of God.

This conception of natural law and its place in the order that God imposes on nature has important consequences for Leibniz's account of mind and its relation to body. By the argument sketched in section 1, if mind could act on body, either directly or through the intermediation of God, then bodies animated by rational minds would violate the laws that govern inanimate bodies. Now, such violations are by no means impossible, even if the laws that God imposed on matter are universal in scope and make no distinction between animate and inanimate matter. But, *if* God's laws are universal in that sense, as Leibniz almost always assumes, then *any* such violations would be *miraculous*, even if such violations occurred in an entirely lawlike and regular way. Thus Leibniz writes:

. . . The common system [i.e., direct interactionism] has recourse to absolutely inexplicable influences, while in the system of occasional causes God is compelled at every moment, by a kind of general law and as if by compact, to change the natural course of the thoughts of the soul to adapt them to the impressions of the body and to interfere with the natural course of bodily movements in accordance with the volitions of the soul. This can only be explained by a perpetual miracle. . . .[53]

Though such a world of perpetual miracles is possible, Leibniz rejects such an account of the matter for both methodological and metaphysical reasons. Methodologically, the appeal to God that is required to account for the constant violation of natural law is an ad hoc appeal to a *deus ex machina* in quite a literal sense of the phrase. Leibniz writes:

Problems are not solved merely by making use of a general cause [i.e., God] and calling in what is called the *deus ex machina*. To do this without offering any other explanation drawn from the order of secondary causes is, properly speaking, to have recourse to miracle. In philosophy we must try to give a reason which will show how things are brought about by the Divine Wisdom, in conformity with the notion of the subject in question.[54]

And metaphysically, the perpetual miracle that interactionism requires is objectionable insofar as it attributes an imperfection to God's work. Thus Leibniz writes to Clarke:

But they who fancy that the soul can give a new force to the body, and that God does the same in the world in order to mend the imperfections of his machine, make God too much like the soul by ascribing too much to the soul and too little to God. For none but God can give a new force to nature, and He does it only supernaturally. If there was a need for Him to do it in the natural course of things, He would have made a very imperfect work.[55]

So, *if* the laws of motion that God decreed are universal and make no distinction between human being and stone, then order and perfection, not to mention good scientific method, require that we reject the hypothesis of interaction as miraculous. But, one might ask, how does Leibniz know that the laws of motion *are* universal? Surely, God *could* have set things up in such a way that animate bodies followed different laws than bare matter, so that it would be a *law of nature* that when a mind has an appropriate volition, the animate body to which it is attached is exempted from laws that otherwise govern its behavior. One might suggest, for example, that the laws of nature are hierarchical, as it were, that the laws of physics are dominated by the psychophysical laws of mind-body interaction in the same way that, for Leibniz, the totality of laws of nature are dominated by the supernatural laws that govern God's activity and in accordance with which He can suspend the laws of nature to satisfy higher laws.[56] What is wrong with such a conception of natural law? Although Leibniz usually takes the universality of physical law for granted, rarely arguing the point explicitly, Leibniz has an answer to this question. From Leibniz's point of view, though such a hierarchical world is *possible*, such a world is less perfect than a world governed by pre-established harmony and, thus, would not have been created. Consider two possible worlds, ω_g, a world in which there is direct or occasional interaction, a world that thus embodies a hierarchy of "gappy" laws and a world ω_h that is governed by pre-established harmony, a world governed by universal and exceptionless laws. Suppose, first, that ω_g and ω_h contain exactly the same phenomena: sensation and bodily state, volition and action correspond in *exactly* the same way in each. But, despite the agreement on the phenomena, it is obvious that ω_h, the world of universal and exceptionless laws, is considerably simpler and more orderly than ω_g, the world governed by the hierarchy of gappy laws.[57] So, from Leibniz's point of view, ω_h must be preferable to ω_g. But what if ω_g and ω_h *differ* in the variety of their phenomena? One might argue, in fact, that they *must* differ in *some* phenomena if they are to have genuinely different laws. Here the argument is more difficult. But, even in this case, Leibniz seems to hold that ω_h is the more perfect world. Leibniz's position is that simplicity is more important than variety of phenomena, so that even if the variety of phenomena in ω_g were greater than that in ω_h, the simplicity of the laws in ω_h would tilt the balance in favor of that world. The argument I have sketched is presented most explicitly in a passage from the *Theodicy*. Leibniz writes:

> Thus, it is necessary to judge that among the general rules which are not absolutely necessary, God chooses those which are the most natural, those which are the easiest to account for and which also serve to account for other things. This is doubtless most beautiful and pleasing, and were the system of *pre-established harmony* not otherwise necessary to eliminate superfluous miracles, God would have chosen it, since it is the most harmonious [system]. *The ways of God are the most simple and the most uniform: they are to choose the rules which limit one another least.* They are also the most *fruitful* with respect to the *simplicity of means*. . . . One can, indeed, reduce these two conditions, simplicity and fruitfulness, to a single advantage, which is to produce as much perfection as is possible. . . . But even if the effect were supposed greater, but the means less simple, I think that one could say that all and all, the effect itself would be less great, counting not only the final effect but also the mediate effect. Thus those who are wisest act, as much as possible, so that the means are, in a way, ends as well, that is to say, desirable not only for what they *do*, but for what they *are*. Complicated ways occupy too much ground, too much space, too much place, too much time that could have been better used.[58]

Leibniz thus concludes that the doctrine of pre-established harmony, in which the laws that govern bodies and the laws that govern minds "limit one another least," is "infinitely more reasonable and worthy of God"[59] than is any variety of interactionism. Leibniz's principle of perfection, the principle in accordance with which God creates the best of all possible worlds, demands that the laws that God decrees for inanimate nature hold for human beings as well. Human beings, complex bodies animated by rational minds, must, by the principle of perfection, be an integral part of the world of finite things governed by the simple and uniform principles that God decrees as the laws of nature, principles that only *He* can violate, principles whose violation can only be miraculous. And if the scope of natural law is to include human beings as well as tables, chairs, and potted palms, then, unless we are willing to embrace the odious hypothesis of perpetual miracle, interactionism of any sort must be out of the question.

Leibniz's position on the scope of physical law is, thus, grounded in some of his most basic metaphysical commitments, the connection between perfection and order and the principle that God creates the best of all possible worlds. Because of these principles, Leibniz must hold that the laws of nature are universal, and because of these principles, supplemented with some commonsense scientific methodology, Leibniz must reject the perpetual miracles that interactionism entails for him. But, for all that, Leibniz's position is by no means invulnerable. There are, to be sure, any number of gaps in Leibniz's arguments that a clever Cartesian might well be able to exploit in defense of a more limited scope for physical law and in support of an interactionist dualism. One might, for example, point out the ad hoc way in which Leibniz favors order over variety of phenomena in arguing for pre-established harmony over its alternatives. But Descartes himself would have found Leibniz's claims vulnerable to attack on the most basic level. The considerations of perfection, order, and God's ends in constructing the best of all possible worlds, considerations that lead Leibniz to include animate bodies within the scope of the laws of physics, and that lead him from interactionism to pre-established harmony, would have moved Descartes little, if at all. For Descartes, the immensity and incomprehensibility of God preclude *any* appeal to such reasoning to establish the laws that govern the material world. Thus Descartes wrote in response to Gassendi:

> Although in Ethics, where it is often permissible to use a conjecture, it is sometimes pious to consider what end we can conjecture for God to have set out for Himself in ruling the universe, this is certainly out of place in Physics, where everything ought to shine with the firmest reasons. Neither can we pretend that some of God's ends are better displayed to us than others; for all [of God's ends] are hidden in the same way in the abyss of His inscrutable wisdom.[60]

In fact, given Descartes's radical voluntarism with respect to the eternal truths, God *has* no aims or goals, strictly speaking. His volitions are free with a freedom of complete indifference. God did not set out to create the world that would be the most perfect; God did not create this world *because* it is the most perfect one. Rather, it is the most perfect one because God created it.[61]

The rejection of final causes in physics marks a basic difference between Cartesian and Leibnizian physics. But this does not mean that Descartes rejects Leibniz's grounding of physics in the activity of God or Leibniz's claim that true knowledge of the physical world must be derived from our knowledge of God. Neither does it mean that the laws of physics are inaccessible to rational argument or demonstration. Rather, Descartes claims, they are to be derived not from God as a *final* cause but from God as an *efficient* cause. Thus he wrote:

And finally, we shall not seek the reasons for natural things from the ends which God or nature propose for themselves in making them, since we ought not to be so arrogant as to think that we participate in their counsels. But considering Him as the efficient cause of everything, we must see what can be concluded from those attributes of which He allows us some notion, about those of His effects which the senses make apparent to us, by means of the light of nature which is innate in us.[62]

The laws of nature, then, are to be derived not from considerations of order, perfection, and God's ends in creating this world, as they are for Leibniz, but from His nature and the way in which He operates in the world. The laws of nature are not *chosen* by God and *imposed* on the world. Rather, they follow directly from the *way* in which God acts on the world. To use a distinction familiar from recent moral theory, whereas Leibniz's God is a teleologist, acting for the *end* of order and perfection, Descartes's God is a deontologist, doing the *right thing* from moment to moment, whatever might come of it. Consequently, for Descartes, one cannot appeal to order and perfection to justify one conception of the world over another.

This strategy for deriving the laws of nature is apparent in the argument that Descartes offers for his conservation law. The law is presented in the context of a discussion of the "universal and primary" cause of motion, that which is the "general cause of all motions which are in the world." This general cause is, of course, "none other than God Himself," who

... in the beginning created matter along with motion and rest, and now, through His ordinary concourse alone, conserves just as much motion and rest in the whole of it [i.e., the material world] as He put there at that time. . . . We also understand God to be perfect not only insofar as He is, in Himself, immutable, but also in that He works [*operetur*] in as constant and immutable a way as possible. Therefore, except for those changes [in quantity of motion] which evident experience or divine revelation render certain, and which we perceive or believe to happen without any change in the Creator, we ought not to suppose that there are any other changes in His works, lest from that we can argue for an inconstancy in Him.[63]

The precise intuitions behind Descartes's proof are illuminated by other passages in which Descartes discusses the operation of God in the world. Descartes notes that the nature of time is such that:

... its parts do not depend upon one another, and never exist simultaneously; and therefore from the fact that we exist now, it does not follow that we will also exist in the next following time unless some cause, indeed the same one which produced us at first, continually re-creates us, that is, conserves us.[64]

Thus, Descartes claims, God must continually re-create the world at every moment, or else it would pass into nonexistence. This provides an obvious way of seeing how God's immutability results in the conservation law for Descartes. Descartes argues: ". . . [God] conserves [motion] just as it is at the moment in which it is being conserved, without regard to what it was a bit before."[65] God's immutability requires that when He re-creates the world from one moment to the next, He must re-create it as much as possible as it was the previous moment. In part, He must re-create the world with the same quantity of motion it had the moment before.

In this argument Descartes is quite explicitly following the strategy he set out for deriving "reasons for natural things." He is considering God as an *efficient* cause, the cause of motion in the beginning, and the continuing cause of motion in the moment-by-moment conservation of the world.[66] He then considers God's attributes, the fact that God's perfection involves constancy of operation and argues from that to the conservation law. Descartes's reasoning is not without its problems here. The derivation is obscure, complex, and the conclusion ultimately wrong, as Leibniz successfully showed. But it is the strategy that I am interested in here, what Descartes thought he was doing, and that is clear enough. The conservation law for Descartes is not a law that God imposes on the world to further some end; it is intended to be a consequence of the constraints that God's nature imposes on God as an efficient cause of motion in the material world.

Descartes's conception of the conservation law and its ground in the immediate activity of God has important consequences for the way in which he conceives of mind in the context of the order of nature. The conservation law is, for Descartes, a law that follows out of the way in which God acts as an efficient cause of motion. As an efficient cause of motion, He must, by virtue of His nature, act in such a way as to preserve the same quantity of motion from moment to moment. But, Descartes says, although God is the "universal and primary" cause of motion,[67] He is not the *only* cause. As he wrote to More:

> The translation which I call motion, is a thing of no less entity than shape: it is a mode in a body. The force moving [a body] can be that of God Himself conserving the same amount of translation in matter as He put in it in the first moment of creation; or also [it can be] that of a created substance, like our mind, or that of some other thing to which He gave the force of moving a body.[68]

Now, when God causes motion, the motion He causes must observe the conservation law. But there is no reason at all to impose similar constraints on *finite* and *imperfect* causes of motion. That is, though finite, imperfect minds may act in some lawlike way, deriving from their finite and imperfect natures, the motion *they* cause need not satisfy the conservation principle. *They* may add or subtract motion from the world, even if *God* cannot. To suppose that they do argues for no change in God Himself and does not give us grounds for imputing an "inconstancy in Him."[69] Thus, it seems, there is nothing arbitrary or inconsistent with Descartes's principles to suppose that animate bodies, bodies capable of being acted upon by minds, can violate the conservation principle. Such bodies stand, as it were, outside of the world of purely mechanical nature. The conservation principle governs only *purely material* systems in nature, systems in which God is the *only* cause of motion.[70]

It should be clear by now that Descartes's interactionism rests on no simple mistake, either about the content or the scope of physical law. Because of his general rejection of final courses in physics, he has a defense against the arguments from the principle of perfection that lead Leibniz to pre-established harmony.[71] And because of his conception of the laws of motion as deriving from the action of God as an efficient cause of motion, Descartes can exempt animate bodies from the laws that govern inanimate bodies in motion in a coherent and nonarbitrary way and allow mind to affect the behavior of body. Descartes's interactionism thus rests reasonably secure against Lebniz's attack. This is an interesting conclusion in and of itself. But, I think, the defense I have sketched gives something even more interesting, an insight into the real differences that separate Descartes's and Leibniz's positions. What forces Leibniz to reject interactionism and to adopt pre-established harmony is the fact that for him mind is an *integral part* of a world governed by principles of order, overarching metaphysical principles decreed by a wise and benevolent God. In Leibniz's best of all possible worlds, simplicity and tidiness dictate that the laws of nature that God decreed must, miracles aside, govern all bodies, both animate and inanimate, thus ruling out any variety of interactionism. For Descartes, though, the wisdom of God is beyond our reach; simplicity and order are just not at issue. The laws of motion are not, for Descartes, principles of order that God imposes on the world but, rather, a direct consequence of the laws that God Himself obeys as one of a number of possible causes of motion in the world. Because mind is a cause of motion that lies *outside* the scope of the laws that govern God's activity, Descartes can maintain his interactionism in spite of Leibniz's argument. What explains Leibniz's rejection of interactionism, then, can be no simple discovery that Descartes's conservation law is wrong, as Leibniz seems to have believed. Rather, what separates Leibniz's account of the relation between mind and body from Descartes's is something much deeper and more significant, a change in the place of mind in the natural order of things, a change motivated by a fundamental shift in the very conception of what a law of nature is and how it derives from God.[72]

Abbreviations

Books and Collections

AT   Adam, C., and Tannery, P. (eds.), *Oeuvres de Descartes* (Paris: 1897–1910 and 1964–1978).

C   Couturat, L. (ed.), *Leibniz: Opuscules et Fragments Inédits* (Paris: 1903).

G   Gerhardt, C. I. (ed.), *Leibniz: Philosophischen Schriften* (Berlin: 1875–1890).

GM   Gerhardt, C. I. (ed.), *Leibniz: Mathematische Schriften* (Berlin: 1849–1855).

HR   Haldane, E. S., and Ross, G. R. T. (eds. and trans.), *Philosophical Works of Descartes* (Cambridge: 1911).

K   Kenny, A. (ed. and trans.), *Descartes: Philosophical Letters* (Oxford: 1970).

L   Loemker, L. (ed. and trans.), *Gottfried Wilhelm Leibniz: Philosophical Papers and Letters*, 2nd ed. (Dordrecht: 1969).

M   Mason, H. T. (ed. and trans.), *The Leibniz-Arnauld Correspondence* (Manchester: 1967).

NE   Langley, A. G. (ed. and trans.), *Leibniz: New Essays Concerning Human Understanding* (La Salle, Ill.: 1949).

Individual Works

DM   Leibniz, *Discours de Métaphysique*. Found in G IV 427–63 and translated in L 303–28.

Mon.   Leibniz, *Monodologie*. Found in G VI 607-23 and translated in L 643-52.
PA   Descartes, *Les Passions de l'Ame*. Found in AT XI 291-497 and translated in HR I 331-427.
Pr   Descartes, *Principia Philosophiae*. Found in AT VIII A (Latin version) and AT IX B (French translation). Partial translation into English is in HR I 203-302. Quotations are taken from the Latin version.
Theod.   Leibniz, *Essais de Theodicée*. Found in G VI 21-471.

References to books and collections are given by volume (when appropriate) and page. References to individual works are given by part (in the case of Pr) and section number. Original language citations are given first, followed by an English translation in parentheses when available.

Notes

1. AT III 685.

2. The most prominent adherent of this position is, of course, Nicholas Malebrance. See his *The Search after Truth and Elucidations of the Search after Truth*, ed. and trans. by Thomas Lennon and Paul J. Olscamp (Columbus, Ohio: Ohio State University Press, 1980), pp. 446-52 and 657-85; or *Dialogues on Metaphysics* ed. and trans. by Willis Doney (New York: Abaris Books, 1980), pp. 144-69.

3. In this paper, the term 'animate body' will be used to designate any body related in an appropriate way to a mind or soul, as, for example, the human body is for both Descartes and Leibniz. This has the unfortunate consequence that on my somewhat special use of the term Cartesian animals must be considered inanimate. But I could find no more natural way of designating the special class of bodies with which I will be concerned in this paper.

4. Theod. 60-61. See also Mon. 80; G II 94 (M 117-18); G III 607 (L 655); G IV 497-98; G VI 540 (L 587). The argument in these passages concerns only the mental causation of physical events. Consequently, I will not discuss in this paper the problems raised by the physical causation of mental events.

5. Pr II 36. The conservation law is first stated in the ill-fated *Le Monde*. See AT XI 43.

6. This is the standard reading of Descartes's law. It should be noted that my use of the term 'mass' here is anachronistic. Although it helps one to see the relations between Descartes's incorrect law and later conservation principles, such as Leibniz's, Descartes himself would have given his law in terms of 'size' rather than 'mass'. For a discussion of some of the further intricacies in interpreting Descartes's conservation law, see Pierre Costabel, "Essai critique sur quelques concepts de la mécanique cartésienne." *Archives internationales d'histoire des sciences,* Vol. 20 (1967), pp. 235-52, esp. pp. 240-51. None of these questions of interpretation are relevant to the use Leibniz makes of Descartes's conservation law in the argument under discussion, though.

7. The distinction is most clearly drawn in Pr II 41. Once again, this is the standard reading. Though it is sufficient for our purposes here, Descartes's notion of determination is much more complex than the simple equation of determination and direction would suggest. On this, see Pierre Costabel, *op. cit.*, 236-40; J. Ohana, "Note sur la théorie cartésienne de la direction du mouvement," *Les Etudes philosophiques*, Vol. 16 (1961), pp. 313-16; Ole Knudsen and Kurt Pedersen, "The Link between 'Determination' and Conservation of Motion in Descartes' Dynamics," *Centaurus*, Vol. 13 (1968-1969), pp. 183-86; A. I. Sabra, *Theories of Light from Descartes to Newton* (London: Oldbourne Press, 1967), pp. 116-27; and Alan Gabbey, "Force and Inertia in the Seventeenth Century: Descartes and Newton," in Stephen Gaukroger (ed.), *Descartes: Philosophy, Mathematics and Physics* (Sussex: Harvester Press, 1980), pp. 230-320, esp. pp. 248-61.

8. See, e.g., Pr II 41; AT IV 185-86; AT VI 94, 97.

9. This is exactly the situation envisioned in Descartes's infamous fourth rule of impact, given in Pr II 49. According to that rule, if C is larger than B and if C, at rest, is hit by B, then B will reverse its direction and rebound from the collision with exactly the speed with which it

originally approached C. Strictly speaking, though, even this very simple case would require in-numerable changes in the speeds and directions of other bodies in the system, since the Cartesian world is a plenum.

10. See Pr II 41; AT III 75; AT IV 185; AT VI 94, 97.

11. GM VI 437. See also G III 45-46.

12. This argument is implicit in the critique of Descartes's conservation law given in Leibniz's important "Brief Demonstration of a Notable Error in Descartes . . ." of 1686, the first of Leibniz's mature publications in physics. The text of this is given with a later appendix in GM VI 117-23 (L 296-302). For other presentations of the same basic argument, see, e.g., DM 17, G IV 370-72 (L 393-95); GM VI 243-46 (L 442-44); GM VI 287-92; etc. For discussions of the argument, see, e.g., Carolyn Iltis, "Leibniz and the *Visa Viva* Controversy," *Isis*, Vol. 62 (1971), pp. 21-35; George Gale, "Leibniz' Dynamical Metaphysics and the Origin of the *Vis Viva* Controversy," *Systematics*, Vol. 11 (1973), pp. 184-207; and Martial Gueroult, *Leibniz: Dynamique et Métaphysique* (Paris: Aubier-Montaigne, 1967), pp. 28-34.

13. For the distinction between these two kinds of force, see GM VI 238-39 (L 439); GM VI 462; GM VI 495.

14. The theorem is stated in numerous places. See, e.g., Theod. 61; G II 94 (M 117-18); G IV 497-98; GM VI 216-17 (NE 658); GM VI 227 (NE 667). A detailed argument is given in the *Dynamica*, GM VI 496-500. The crucial lemmas are given on GM VI 440, where Leibniz argues that "the same power [*potentia*] remains in any system of bodies not communicating with others" and concludes that, since the universe is such a system, "the same power always remains in the universe." This kind of argument is somewhat problematic for Leibniz when applied to momentum, since it is difficult to see what sense he could make of the speed of the center of mass of the universe as a whole. It should be noted that 'momentum' is not Leibniz's term for the quantity at issue. Leibniz uses a number of terms, sometimes 'quantity of *nisus*' (GM VI 462), sometimes (quantity of) 'progress' (GM VI 216-17 [NE 658]; GM VI 227 [NE 667]) but most often 'direction,' 'total direction,' or the like (Theod. 61; Mon. 80; G II 94 [M 117-18]; G III 607 [L 655]; G VI 540 [L 587]; G IV 497; etc.).

15. It *seems* as if this general kind of argument could have been used *directly* against Descartes's conservation law to show that it, too, ought to govern directionality and not just speed. Thus, Leibniz's replacement of quantity of motion by *vis viva* as the physical magnitude conserved is not, strictly speaking, relevant to the argument against interactionism.

16. This conception of the doctrine of pre-established harmony is found in G I 382-83; G II 68-70 (M 84-86); G IV 518 (L 493); G VII 412 (L 711-12).

17. C 521 (L 269). For other statements of this version of pre-established harmony, see, e.g., DM 33; G II 57-58 (M 64-65); G II 112-14 (M 144-46); G IV 483-85 (L 457-58); G IV 498-500 (L 459-60); G IV 520 (L 494); G VII 410-11 (L 710-11); etc.

18. G VI 541 (L 587).

19. G II 94-95 (M 118). See also Mon. 78; Theod. 62; G II 71 (M 87); G II 74 (M 92); G II 205-6; G IV 484 (L 458); G IV 559-60 (L 577-78); G V 455 (NE 553); G VI 599 (L 637); G VII 412 (L 712); G VII 419 (L 716-17). These passages make it evident just how deeply Leibniz was influenced by the materialism of Hobbes and the dual aspect theory of Spinoza. In these passages, Leibniz emphasizes that *every* event in the material world has an explanation in terms of the laws of physics alone.

20. For the classic examination of this objection to dualist interactionism from a purely philosophical point of view, see C. D. Broad, *Mind and Its Place in Nature* (London: K. Paul, Trench, Trubner and Co., 1925), pp. 103-9.

21. Although not generally recognized, this feature of Cartesian thought has been pointed out from time to time, only to be forgotten and then rediscovered by successive generations of scholars. On this, see Octave Hamelin, *Le Système de Descartes* (Paris: Librairie Félix Alcan, 1911), pp. 372-73; Jean Laporte, *Le Rationalisme de Descartes* (Paris: Presses Universitaires de France, 1950), pp. 245-48; Norman Kemp Smith, *Studies in the Cartesian Philosophy* (London:

Macmillan, 1902), p. 83 n.2; Geneviève Rodis-Lewis (ed.), *Descartes: Passions de l'Ame* (Paris: J. Vrin, 1970), p. 92 n.1. The most recent rediscovery is in Peter Remnant, "Descartes: Body and Soul," *Canadian Journal of Philosophy*, Vol. 9 (1979), pp. 377–86. Needless to say, there is substantial overlap between my argument in this section and the arguments presented in the other commentaries cited. However, the continued unfamiliarity of this point plus the new bits of evidence I have found make it worthwhile to review the case for this interpretation once again.

22. AT III 665 (K 138).

23. AT V 222 (K 235).

24. AT V 403–4 (K 257). This passage will be discussed in greater detail below.

25. On the direct connection between the mind and the pineal gland, see, e.g., PA 31; AT VII 86; AT XI 176–77, 183. It should also be noted that, in addition to the direct connection between mind and body, Descartes also holds that by virtue of being *directly* connected to the pineal gland the mind is *indirectly* connected to the human body as a whole. See, e.g., PA 30. Margaret Wilson sees these as two opposing conceptions of mind-body unity. See her *Descartes* (London: Routledge and Kegan Paul, 1978), pp. 204–20. I see the two conceptions as perfectly consistent and, in fact, complementary, as their juxtaposition in PA 30–31 suggests. Though I quote exclusively from the PA in discussing the action of the mind on the pineal gland, Descartes also discusses this question in the earlier *Traité de l'Homme*. But the discussions there are much less useful for our purposes. Most of the discussions that deal with the pineal gland deal with its role in sensation. See, e.g., AT XI 143–46, 176–77, 181, 183. And when volition is discussed in *l'Homme*, Descartes gives almost no detail as to how the mind actually manipulates the pineal gland. See, e.g., AT XI 131–32, 179.

26. PA 42.

27. PA 47.

28. PA 34, PA 41. See also PA 43.

29. PA 47. It is important to note here the distinction between the passion of desire and a volition, an act of the will, a distinction that is ignored in the translation of this passage given in HR I 353.

30. PA 43.

31. For a discussion of the scholastic theory of gravity and Descartes's rejection of it, in the context of his rejection of substantial forms, see Etienne Gilson, *Etudes sur le Rôle de la Pensée Médiévale dans la Formation du Système Cartésien* (Paris: J. Vrin, 1930), pp. 141–90.

32. AT V 222–23 (K 235–36). See also AT III 667–68 (K 139); AT VII 441–42 (HR II 254–55).

33. For this account of heaviness and free fall, see, e.g., Pr IV 20. Matters are complicated by a somewhat different account of heaviness that Descartes offers in *Le Monde* and mentions later in the *Principia*, in accordance with which heaviness is due to the centrifugal force that pushes the small particles of the subtle matter turning quickly around the earth away from the center of the earth. On this account, heavy bodies are pushed to the center of the earth to take the place of the subtle matter that is receding, in accordance with Descartes's claim that there can be no vacuum. For this account, see AT XI 72–80 and Pr IV 23. It is not clear how these two accounts of heaviness are related to one another.

34. AT XI 629–30. This interesting passage comes from a manuscript entitled "Problemata," preserved only in a copy Leibniz had made. Though one must use these documents with some care, the passage seems unquestionably authentic. The (mistaken) formula for the acceleration of a body in a vacuum given a uniform force is uniquely Cartesian and appears in a number of documents as the law of free fall for heavy bodies from 1618 to 1629 and is mentioned as a law that Descartes once held in a letter of 1634. See AT X 75f, 219; AT I 71–73, 304–5. For an account of Descartes's struggles with the problem of free fall, see Alexander Koyré, *Galileo Studies* (Atlantic Highlands, N.J.: Humanities Press, 1978), pp. 79–94. Dating the fragment, though, is problematic. In this fragment, Descartes is clearly distinguishing the problem of acceleration given a uniform force from that of free fall. But until at least 1629 Descartes *identified* the two

problems. See AT I 71–73. This suggests that the passage dates from later than 1629. It is also unlikely that the passage dates from later than 1640, the last date in which we have evidence of Descartes worrying about the derivation of the laws of free fall. See AT III 164–65. But it is hard to date the fragment more closely than that. It *may* be associated with a letter of 1631 in which Descartes claims that "I can now determine the proportion by which a descending stone increases its speed, not *in vacuo*, but in this air" (AT I 231). But it could just as well be associated with a letter of 1637 in which Descartes asks Mersenne to excuse him from answering a question "concerning the retardation which the movement of heavy bodies receive from the air where they move," claiming that such an account involves his whole physics and is inappropriate for a letter (AT I 392). External factors suggest a third date from the mid-1630s. One fragment in the "Problemata" is dated 5 February 1635 and corresponds to material in the *Météores* of 1637. See AT XI 626.

35. This, of course, raises the question as to why Lebniz attributed the position to Descartes. The best conjecture is that the change-of-direction account of mind-body interaction was common among later Cartesians, and Leibniz just assumed that it must have been Descartes's position as well. Norman Kemp Smith (*op. cit.*, p. 83 n. 2) cites Clauberg in this connection. Alan Gabbey has also called my attention to a letter written after Descartes's death by Claude Clerselier, Descartes's friend, translator, and editor, in which Clerselier argues that mind can change only the direction in which bodies move but cannot add motion. See Clerselier to de la Forge, 4 December 1660, in Clerselier (ed.), *Lettres de Mr. Descartes*, Vol. III (Paris: 1667), pp. 640–46. I have not been able to examine Kemp Smith's citation. But it is interesting to note that in the letter Gabbey cites Clerselier does *not* explicitly attribute the change-of-direction account to Descartes. Furthermore, the grounds on which Clerselier advances the claim involve a significant departure from Descartes's thought on motion and determination. Clerselier's argument depends on the claim that to create a motion requires as much power as to create matter itself, whereas determination "*n'adjoûte rien de réel dans la Nature*" and can thus be manipulated by finite minds (Clerselier, *loc. cit.*, pp. 641–43). But this contradicts what Descartes wrote to Clerselier in a letter 15 years earlier, a letter that Clerselier published in Volume I of his edition of Descartes's correspondence. Descartes's wrote:

> It is necessary to consider two different modes in motion: one is the motion alone, or the speed, and the other is the determination of this motion in a particular direction, which two modes change with equal difficulty (AT IV 185).

Thus, the Clerselier letter of 1660 gives us no grounds for attributing the change-of-direction account to Descartes himself.

36. This, in essence, is Broad's response to the objection. See C. D. Broad, *op. cit.*, pp. 107–9.

37. Pr II 36.

38. *Ibid*. Emphasis added.

39. AT V 222 (K 235). Emphasis added.

40. Pr II 40. Emphasis added.

41. There is one passage in *Le Monde* that seems to contradict this interpretation. In Chapter VII of that work, after having given the laws of motion and having claimed that these laws suffice for an "*a priori* demonstration of everything that can be produced" in the new world that Descartes is building in *Le Monde* (AT XI 47), Descartes says:

> And finally, so that there will be no exceptions which prevent [such a priori demonstrations], we shall add to our assumptions, if it pleases you, that God will produce no miracles, and that the intelligences or rational minds, which we might assume below [in the *Traité de l'Homme*], will not disrupt the ordinary course of nature in any way (AT XI 48).

This *might* be read as a denial that God can perform miracles or that minds can interfere in the "ordinary course of nature" in any way. But given what Descartes says about mind-body interaction elsewhere, it is more reasonable to read this as a simplifying assumption known to be false but helpful in simplifying the initial presentation of the mechanist world that Descartes intended to give in *Le Monde*.

42. See Peter Remnant, *op. cit.*

43. AT III 665 (K 138). Quoted in Remnant, *op. cit.*, p. 382.

44. AT III 665–66 (K 138). Quoted in Remnant, *op. cit.*, p. 383.

45. Remnant, *op. cit.*, p. 383.

46. *Ibid.*, pp. 384–85. Remnant, like most commentators, is too quick to trust Descartes's answer to Elisabeth here. On this point, see my essay, "Understanding Interaction: What Descartes should Have Told Elisabeth," forthcoming in a supplementary volume of the *Southern Journal of Philosophy*.

47. On the mind-body union as a substance distinct from mind and body, see, e.g., Geneviève Rodis-Lewis, *L'Oeuvre de Descartes* (Paris: J. Vrin, 1971), Vol. I, pp. 352–54, and the references cited in Vol. II, p. 543 n.29. Rodis-Lewis is quite correct to reject the claim that Descartes thought of the union of mind and body as a distinct substance, but Descartes's frequent use of the notion of "*substantial* union" in connection with the mind and body (AT VII 228 [HR II 102]; AT III 493 [K 127]; AT III 508 [K 130]; etc.) does suggest something of the sort.

48. G III 54–55 (L 353).

49. G VI 603 (L 639–40).

50. For a discussion of the contingency of the laws of nature in Leibniz, see Margaret Wilson, "Leibniz's Dynamics and Contingency in Nature," in P. K. Machamer and R. G. Turnbull, eds., *Motion and Time, Space and Matter* (Columbus, Ohio: Ohio State University Press, 1976), pp. 264–89; reprinted in R. S. Woolhouse, ed., *Leibniz: Metaphysics and Philosophy of Science* (Oxford: Oxford University Press, 1981), pp. 119–38.

51. DM 7. See also Theod. 207; G II 41 (M 44–45); G II 51 (M 57); G II 92–93 (M 115–16). Leibniz claims that the supernatural order that governs miraculous violations of the laws of nature is beyond our comprehension in DM 16 and in G III 353.

52. G VII 416–17 (L 715). See also G II 93 (M 116); G IV 520 (L 494). Leibniz sometimes also suggests a more epistemic definition of a miracle as "a divine act which transcends human comprehension." See C 508–9; G III 353.

53. G VI 541 (L 587). See also Theod. 207; G II 57–58 (M 65); G II 94 (M 117–18); G III 354. It should be noted that Leibniz recognizes a number of senses in which interactionism, particularly of the occasionalist variety, involves perpetual miracles. See M. Gueroult, *Malebranche* (Paris: Aubier-Montaigne, 1955–1959), Vol. II, pp. 241–53.

54. G IV 483–84 (L 457).

55. G VII 375–76 (L 689).

56. The position sketched here is Malebranche's. On the hierarchy of laws, see, e.g., Nicholas Malebranche, *Dialogues on Metaphysics*, ed. and trans. by Willis Doney (New York: Abaris Books, 1980), pp. 320–21. On the ability of the mind-body laws to cause suspensions of the laws of physics, see Nicholas Malebranche, *The Search after Truth and Elucidations of the Search after Truth*, ed. and trans. by Thomas Lennon and Paul J. Olscamp (Columbus, Ohio: Ohio State University Press, 1980), pp. 580–81, 594.

57. It is, of course, a commonplace observation in contemporary philosophy of science that *any* statement can be presented as a universal statement. But the distinction between universal and "gappy" laws is clear enough for our purposes here.

58. Theod. 208; emphasis added. The argument is also suggested in G II 94–95 (M 118) and G III 340–41.

59. G II 94 (M 118).

60. AT VII 375 (HR II 223). See also AT VII 55 (HR I 173).

61. See AT VII 432 (HR II 248). For Leibniz's remarks on this claim, see, e.g., DM 2.

62. Pr I 28. For Leibniz's comments on this, see, e.g., G IV 360–61 (L 387).

63. Pr II 36.

64. Pr I 21. See also AT VII 48-49 (HR I 168).

65. Pr II 39. See also the parallel passage in *Le Monde*, AT XI 44. The argument is somewhat more complex than the brief exposition I have given suggests. Since each moment is without duration, there can be no motion, strictly speaking, at any given moment, as Descartes fully realized. See, e.g., Pr II 39; AT II 215. What is preserved from one moment to the next, then, cannot be motion itself but the tendency or inclination to motion. And, Descartes would have had to have held, in order to preserve the tendency to motion from one moment to the next, God would have to create the moving body at a somewhat different place from one moment to the next if this tendency is ever to result in any *actual* motion. On the notion of momentary tendency to motion, Descartes's need for such a notion, and the problems it raises for his metaphysics, see, e.g., F. Alquié, ed., *Oeuvres Philosophiques de Descartes* (Paris: Garnier Frères, 1963-1973), Vol. I, p. 359 n. 1; Thomas L. Prendergast, "Motion, Action, and Tendency in Descartes' Physics," *Journal of the History of Philosophy*, Vol. 13 (1975), pp. 453-62; and Martial Gueroult, "The Metaphysics and Physics of Force in Descartes," trans. in Stephen Gaukroger, ed., *Descartes: Philosophy, Mathematics and Physics*, pp. 196-229. Gueroult's final judgment is that ". . . instantaneous moving force, the distinction between the instant of motion and the instant of rest, . . . pose[s] an insoluble problem for Cartesian metaphysics" (p. 222).

66. Peter Machamer argues that, whatever Descartes's intentions were, final causes inevitably creep into his derivation of the laws of nature. See his "Causality and Explanation in Descartes' Natural Philosophy," in P. K. Machamer and R. G. Turnbull, eds., *op. cit.*, pp. 168-99. Although I think that Descartes can be defended on this point, it is beyond the scope of this paper to do so. What is important in this context is simply how Descartes conceived of his enterprise.

67. Pr II 36.

68. AT V 403-4 (K 257). This position is not without its problems. This passage puts the activity of mind in causing motion on a par with that of God. But, surely, however minds cause motion, they do not do it as God does, by way of a continual re-creation. In fact, it seems difficult to see how the mental causation of motion could be reconciled with the continual re-creation picture at all. Malebranche seizes on exactly this problem, using it to push Descartes to occasionalism in the seventh of his *Dialogues on Metaphysics*. There is no reason to believe, though, that Descartes was aware of this difficulty with his position.

69. Pr II 36.

70. The precise wording in the letter to More quoted above ("the force . . . can be that of God Himself conserving the same amount of translation in matter as He put in it in the first moment of creation . . .") suggests a somewhat different conclusion than the one I have drawn. Read literally, it seems to say that what is conserved from moment to moment is *precisely* the quantity of matter that God put into the world at the beginning, implying that, even if minds could add motion in one moment, God would simply fail to preserve it in the next. If this were Descartes's position, then even though minds could, in a sense, cause motion, the motion would not persist; the conservation principle would govern all bodies, animate and inanimate, with the exception of momentary lapses. But there is no reason to attribute such a strange position to Descartes. The position that the literal reading of that sentence suggests is inconsistent with the account of God's continuous re-creation of the world given in the context of Descartes's derivation of the laws of motion, in accordance with which ". . . [God] conserves [motion] just as it is at the moment in which it is being conserved, without regard to what it was a bit before" (Pr II 39; see also AT XI 44). For God to destroy motion added by mind would require Him to "remember" how much motion there was at the beginning in deciding how much to create at the next moment. Given the central role that this conception of continuous re-creation plays in the derivation of the laws of motion, it seems most likely that Descartes's remarks to More are not meant to be read so literally.

71. There is reason to believe that Descartes may have been explicitly aware that there is some connection between the admission of final causes, the claim that God created the most perfect world, and a position much like Leibniz's pre-established harmony. In a remarkable but almost entirely unnoticed passage, Descartes wrote:

It is a strong conjecture to affirm anything which, if assumed, would make God understood as being greater or the world as being more perfect: as, for example, that the determination of our will to local motion always coincides with a corporeal cause determining motion; that miracles are always consistent with natural causes, etc. (AT XI 654).

The passage is found in a series of gleanings from Descartes's manuscripts preserved among Leibniz's papers. This portion of the manuscript is entitled "Annotations which Descartes seems [*videtur*] to have written in [or, on] his *Principia Philosophiae*" and may, I suspect, have been marginalia in Descartes's own copy. For a brief account of the manuscripts and their history, see AT X 207–10. The remark quoted is the second in a series of discrete paragraphs. The paragraph preceding the quote can plausibly be read as a comment on Pr I 26, and the paragraphs succeeding the quote link up naturally with Pr I 30, Pr I 30, Pr I 31, Pr I 33, Pr I 37, and so on in order. This suggests that the text quoted may well be a comment on Pr I 28, a passage quoted above in which Descartes explicitly rejects the appeal to God's purposes in particular and final causes in general. This, in turn, suggests that Descartes thought that *if* his structures against final causes were lifted, then pre-established harmony would be a reasonable position to adopt. Although this passage indicates that Descartes may have been aware of *some* connection between a version of pre-established harmony and the appeal to God as the creator of the best of all possible worlds, it gives us no reason to believe that Descartes was aware of the full position, as Leibniz develops it, nor does it give us any indication as to how *precisely* Descartes saw the connection between the claim that the world is perfect and the claim that "the determination of our volition to local motion always coincides with a corporeal cause determining motion." However, the fact that this passage was preserved in a copy Leibniz made during his crucial stay in Paris in 1672–1676, before Leibniz's mature system emerged, suggests that Leibniz's contact with Descartes's thought *may* have played *some* role in the formulation of the doctrine of pre-established harmony.

72. Earlier versions of this paper were given to the Seventeenth-Century Seminar, Princeton Institute for Advanced Studies, June 1981; Committee on the Conceptual Foundations of Science, University of Chicago, November 1981; Hobart and William Smith College, April 1982; the Leibniz Society, meeting with the Western Division of the APA in spring 1982; and Princeton University, October 1982. I would like to thank members of the audiences there as well as Alan Gabbey, Robert Richardson, Howard Stein, and Peter Machamer for helpful discussion, comments, and suggestions. Since Machamer is publishing his extensive comments, I have made no attempt to incorporate them into the body of the paper.

The Harmonies of Descartes and Leibniz

PETER MACHAMER

In Dan Garber's "Mind, Body, and the Laws of Nature in Descartes and Leibniz," the major claims are right and important. The problem, as I see it, lies in trying to present a better, more coherent rationale for the difference that Garber notes.

Garber is right to focus on the differences between Descartes and Leibniz as concerns the question of the interaction of the mind and body and right again to stress the consequences of this doctrine that Leibniz saw for the question of the conservation laws of motion. Leibniz does have a detailed and careful rationale that lies behind his doctrine of pre-established harmony. It does depend essentially on his conception of the manner in which God acts in the world.

To put Leibniz's theory in a way slightly different than Garber did, Leibniz's metaphysics claims there is fundamentally one stuff—monads. Minds and matter are ultimately the same, despite problematic consequences concerning conscious or self-reflecting monads. Interactionism, therefore, of mind and body is not an ultimate problem. Indeed, Leibniz's account of the passivity and activity of monads, being merely different perspectives, almost guarantees that pre-established harmony will hold at the phenomenal level of human bodies and (possibly) human minds. But Leibniz was not to see this consequence clearly until the time that he wrote the *Monadology* (1714). Up till that point, he did hold what he thought was an independent doctrine—that pre-established harmony was the best way in which God could preserve the integrity of the phenomenal laws of the physical world.

Descartes, by contrast, is often remarked as a dualist. Yet, I think that Garber is more right when he claims that Descartes holds that there are really three realms: mind, body, and the peculiar union of the two. This means ultimately that Descartes has a problem that Leibniz does not. Descartes's ontology commits him to finding an explanation that coordinates these fundamentally different sorts of entities and the relations that exist between them and that explains the nature of the union of mind and body. Here again I think that Garber's thesis is right and that he argues persuasively that Descartes restricts his concern about the laws of corporeal nature to the specific domain of corporeal nature. The laws of such nature do not apply to the other ontological realms.

This difference between Descartes's and Leibniz's ontology is also reflected in the different ways in which they view God's ordinary concourse in the world. Leibniz's God is a God of final causes. Rationalistic and moral with an eye to best outcomes, He chooses pre-established harmony as the way to relate things in this best of all possible worlds. Descartes, on the other hand, claims to eschew the attribution of final causes to God. He does not, however, fail to claim knowledge of certain of God's attributes that are relevant to His manner of working in the world. Indeed, I will argue later that Descartes's conception of God's attributes commits him to a version of harmony and principle but that it is quite different in its causal character from that later opted for by Leibniz.

According to Descartes, we cannot appeal to God's ultimate moral purposes in order to explain how God regulates and maintains the various ontological realms that He created. Descartes's God is, as Garber stresses, a supremely voluntaristic God, whose ways are best just because he chooses them. He does not choose them because they are best. Along with this voluntarism goes Descartes's insistence in the *Meditations III* that God continually creates or re-creates the world from moment to moment. His ordinary concourse in the world conservation is as much a miracle as was the first creation of it.[1] His sustaining of the world of matter and of minds is his free choice at each instant. The contrast, then, is between Descartes's God of constant miracles even in the ordinary maintenance of the world and Leibniz's clockwork God who sets the world up in the best possible way and then by non-miraculous concourse sustains it through its career.

These differing conceptions of the way in which God acts in the world lead to, or follow upon, different views concerning the nature of causal relations that obtain between God and the world and between things in the world. For both Descartes and Leibniz, understanding or explaining a phenomenon (or, better, arriving at an adequate theory about something) is tantamount to presenting a causal explanation for the phenomenon. Garber is certainly right to set Descartes's conception of causal relations against that of the occasionalists, on the one hand, and against Leibniz, on the other. Descartes's peculiar view of how God works in the world, plus certain other causal principles that he takes as basic, determine clearly what he must say about the manner in which mind interacts with body if he is to avoid both occasionalism and a monistic ontology for created entities (minds and bodies).[2]

Concerning mind/body interaction there are two cases that concern us: perception, in which the body acts on the mind, and intentional action, in which the mind acts upon the body. It is the latter, of course, that causes Leibniz to question whether the conservation of motion principle is being violated. I will argue that the two cases should be treated in parallel and in accordance with Descartes's views about causality and God. It is to the analyses of these cases that I now turn, taking perception first since it is the most discussed and the most controversial.

The basic outlines of Descartes's theory of perception are quite clear. Motions from objects affect the body in specific ways that lead to specific forms of motion in the pineal gland.[3] This he calls first-order perception, and it is what is discussed at length in the *Treatise on Man*, *Principles IV*, and many other places. Second-order perception is where the motion of the brain (pineal gland) affects the mind and causes motions in the mind. Third-order perception is where the understanding of the mind issues a judgment based on regularity of experience — corrected by reason and scientific theory — about the external object that caused the original motions.

It is the second-order connection that is our focus. How can Descartes properly say that the motions of the brain *cause* the motions of the mind? What is the causal linkage that exists between this mind-brain correlation? Leibniz's objections to interactionism take hold at just this point. Leibniz writes, as Garber quotes:

> Problems are not solved by making use of a general cause (i.e., God) and calling in what is called the *deus ex machina*. To do this without offering any other explanation drawn from the order of secondary causes is, properly speaking, to have recourse to a miracle.

Now Garber's answer to Descartes's problem is that Descartes resorts to using only efficient causes.[4] But how would the resort to only efficient causes answer the problem for perception? It could not. If efficient causes are conceived of, as Garber and others seem to do, as merely moving causes — analogous to the "bumps" and "shoves" that dictate material motion — efficient causes cannot do Descartes any good at all, for how could the body "bump" the mind? What kind of motion is involved here?

A further problem is raised by Descartes's own causal principles. For Descartes, it is a "first principle than which none clearer can be understood" that "there is nothing in the effect that has not existed in a similar or in some more eminent form in the cause."[5] Similarly, the effect is formally or eminently contained in the cause[6] and there can be no degree of perfection in the effect that has not antecedently existed in the cause.[7] On the most natural reading, this causal principle makes two claims: one about containment and one about degrees of perfection. On this reading, it is a form of the Augustinian causal principle that the perfection in cause must be equal to or greater than the degree of perfection in the effect. It is clear that God, as a cause of the material world and as a cause of our minds, is greater than either of the effects He creates. Indeed, Descartes writes that "no essence can belong in a univocal sense both to God and His creature."[8] But what about the degrees of perfection of the mind and the body? Descartes clearly holds they are separate substances (created substances), and it also seems clear that he holds that the mind is more perfect than mere matter. Thus, he is often comparing second-order perception in humans where minds are involved with first-order perceptions such as the brutes have. Similarly, his religious convictions would seem to require that he hold that minds have a higher degree of perfection than bodies (for minds have many of the properties in an equivocal way that God has, while bodies only have extension).

The upshot of the causal principle for the case of perception is that the body cannot properly be said to cause the mind to do anything since it is a lesser degree of perfection. But Descartes says in many places that the body does affect the mind.

The reconciliation of this tension lies in Descartes's more general causal principles. When Descartes speaks of the body causing the mind to have certain motions, I think he is speaking with the "vulgar," speaking a language of secondary causes. In much the same manner in his account of motion in *Principles II*, he distinguishes the true nature of motion in which nothing is passed on from body to body from the ordinary talk about motion in which such transference or action is spoken.[9] But later, when he talks about the laws of collision and throughout books III and IV, he allows himself the use of the "vulgar" idiom. Later, he rests secure in the fact that his knowing readers will realize it that this way of talking is just a *façon de parler* to make his doctrine more acceptable to ordinary readers. In the last analysis, motion cannot be characterized by such transference, but we are entitled to speak about secondary causes in this way.

The reason why motion cannot be characterized goes back to Descartes's view of the deity, God's voluntarism and continual re-creation. If there is no causal dependence between a body's existence from one moment to the next and God must re-create the body at each instant, then quite literally there cannot be anything preserved from instant to instant. To talk of such preservation of continuing motion cannot be more than just a popular way of speaking. The same can be said about the mind. Indeed, when Descartes introduces this re-creationist conception of God, he introduces it with reference to a person's existence. The person, meant here as the mind, must continually be created at each instant.

Now, if there are really no bumps or shoves that transfer motion from body to body, there certainly are none that transfer motion from body to mind. The causal connection both in the purely material mind and in the body-mind case must be explicable in other ways.

Recall two facts about Descartes's principles. First, God's continual re-creation or conservation of the world is exactly the same as was His original creation of it. If the first creation was a miracle, then each re-creation thereafter is a miracle, too. Second, all created substances, mind and matter, are created by God, and their properties are derived from Him. Descartes holds that, when a thing is derived from something else, it is derived from that as efficient cause[10] and further that perfection of form pre-exists in the efficient and not in the material cause.[11] Garber is right then in one sense: God, for Descartes, is the efficient cause of the material and mental states in the world at each instant, but at each instant He must, as efficient cause, cause them to have the form that they do.[12]

In the case of perception, God is thus causing the brain to be in a specific state of motion and is causing the mind to be in a specific state of motion. This much is required by Descartes's theological and causal principles (and consistency). If this were all there was to say, then Leibniz would be right and Descartes would have to be an occasionalist. But there is more to the story.

The form in the brain that God creates from His own essence at an instant in a case of veridical perception is identical with the form that he creates in the material object that causes that perception. Likewise, this form is identical, though of a different degree of perfection, with the form that he creates in the mind at that same perceiving instant. So there is, despite differences in degrees of perfection, an identity between the forms in God's mind, in our mind, in our body, and in the material world. The material object, when it is activating our brain in a manner specific to it, serves as an examplary or efficient cause that along with God activates the proper motions in our mind. Descartes says that for any idea we must trace its source back to the archetype from whence it came.[13] Ideas of material objects, he says, could have come from other of our ideas, but, as we find out later in the *Meditations*, God is no deceiver. So those ideas of material objects did not come from us but from without, and part of the archetype or exemplary cause of our idea of material objects, the ideas we obtain from perception, is the material object itself. It, too, of course, has a cause—viz., God—that serves as its exemplary and efficient cause. It is because God is no deceiver in most matters of perception that he activates the proper motions that preserve correspondence of form between our ideas and the material objects. Sometimes our will outstrips what is activated in perception, but this happens in the third stage of perception. This is where we make mistakes and where God, being no deceiver, has given humankind the capacity to use science to correct those mistakes.

God, being no deceiver in matters epistemological, has imposed of His own volition a harmony in the world between human ideas and the created material world. It is not done because it is good for humans to be able to know, it is good because it was imposed by God. We cannot ask questions about final causes concerning God's acts, especially final causes about their goodness.[14] It is the magicians and people who believe in animate worlds who search after final causes, who search after reasons for the goodness of this harmony.

I think this account of Descartes's view of perception makes intelligible the quotation in which Descartes is commenting on his *Principles* (which Garber cites in footnote 11, though I have changed the translation):

> God is understood to be great and the world more perfect from the following: the determination of our will to local motions always coincides with the corporeal cause that determines the motion; whereas it is miraculous that they arise at the same time as natural causes.[15]

Descartes is here talking about intentional actions, but the source of the relation between the mind and the body is the same in perception. I will turn soon to intentional action, but let me first pause to note the source of Descartes's doctrine.

Francesco Suarez, in his commentary on Aristotle's *De Anima*, claimed that a harmony exists between the soul and the body in the case of perception. Suarez claimed that the harmony was present because the forms of soul and matter involved in the act were "rooted in the same soul."[16] There is, he goes on, a natural sympathy between the soul and the body. His model to show this sympathy is not just perception but also appetite and desire.

Descartes, I believe, takes over this doctrine with a few major changes. Descartes will not talk about the forms or species involved in perception. These are replaced by motions. Also, Descartes will have no talk about natural sympathy. Such talk would smack too much of the natural magicians, alchemists, and Italian philosophers of animism. Instead, Descartes replaces natural sympathy of the soul and body, the root of the divine harmony, in the special union that God has created between the mind and the body. I said before that there was an identity of forms, in an equivocal sense, between God, the mind, the brain, and the material object. But, leaving aside God for the moment, the identity of form, despite different degrees of perfection between brain and human body, is much tighter than that between brain or body and the material object. The material object may have all sorts of other properties that are not being transmitted by the motions from that object at that instant. The coordination between the forms of mind and body at that instant are complete. This is why, at the second level of perception, there can be no right or wrong, no truth or falsity. These only enter when the mind as will begins to make judgments. It is in this strong identity that the special union exists. It is this strong identity, plus the fact that the identity has its secondary source from the material object, that keep Descartes from occasionalism.

The quotation above called this body-mind relation miraculous, and so it is. But as we saw earlier, Descartes's body-body relations are likewise miraculous for such is the nature of God. This will become clearer again when I consider intentional action.

Intentional action for Descartes is where the mind moves the body. It is this case that interested Leibniz, and Garber, for it is in this manner that the mind could add motions to the world. As in the case of perception, however, certain problems arise when one tries to understand Descartes's view of the way in which the mind, through its acts of will, can bring about bodily motion. In this case, there is no problem with the causal principle concerning the orders of perfection. The mind being more perfect than the body could cause effects in the body. But how would the causal connection work? Again, it cannot be "bumps" or "shoves" because, as we have seen, this is ultimately quite unintelligible in any case.

The model for such actions is appetitive desire. The mind forms an intention or desire concerning an object in the material world and then moves the body in order to satisfy that desire. The immediate connection between the mind and the body is the pineal gland in the brain, as it was in the case of perception. The motions in the pineal gland, in turn, activate the animal spirits that move the muscles of the body in a manner appropriate to the passions raised by the object of perception.

In ultimate terms, the causal mechanisms involved here are just the same as those in perception. The mind being re-created at each instant takes on a series of successive forms or motions and these correspond (when the mind is working right) to the series of forms or motions that God is re-creating at each instant in material substances, including our bodies. Again, however, we are entitled to speak with the "vulgar," and we do not constantly have to invoke God. Of course, God is the ultimate efficient cause of each created substance at each instant. But in dealing with the realm of created substances, where we speak just of secondary and not ultimate causes, there is no need to talk of God any more than there was in the realm of the material. Given the strict identity of form that exists between the will and the motions of the brain, we are licensed to talk about the mind's will causing the brain's motion, just as in perception we were licensed in ordinary parlance to talk about the brain's motion, and through it the material object causing the mind's motion. Again, the correspondence between the brain and the mind is closer in form than that between the mind and the material object. The mind, as moving will, must cause the brain to move the muscles in certain ways appropriate to the material object of desire. The idea of the object of desire is at the level of judgment, analogous to the third type of perception, while the idea or motion of the mind that causes the brain to move the muscles is not judgmental and is just as close in form as was the perception case. Thus, the special harmony and the special relation of union between the mind and the body are preserved.

If this is Descartes's doctrine, and I think it is, and that it must be, it helps to explain his insistence to Elisabeth and everyone else that the mind and body really have their own special sort of union.[17] It supports Garber's way out for Descartes from Leibniz's conservation problem, for the mind-body union is a really special case to which the laws of conservation (which are stated in terms of the secondary causes appropriate to the realm of inanimate matter) do not apply. The secondary causes to be invoked in explanations for each realm are distinct.

Interestingly, this reading of Descartes also helps make sense out of the analogy that Descartes always uses to explain the mind-body union. Almost universally when Descartes is queried on what he takes the mind-body connection to be, he answers by way of analogy to the scholastics' account of gravity. For them, Descartes says, heaviness is the cause of the body's downward motion. But heaviness, in the Cartesian theory, is not substance and is not independent of body, so it cannot really be a cause. But in the case of the mind moving the body, or the body the mind, there really are two separate substances, both of which have an identical form, and in the parlance of secondary causes it is the form of the one that moves the other. Ultimately, all forms derive from God; but, speaking of forms in the realm of created substance, it is the form of the material object as carried into the brain that moves the mind in perception and in action the form of the will that moves the brain and thus the body toward its object of desire.[18]

The explanation here again owes its origin to Suarez and his idea of harmony. But this harmony is part of Descartes's theory throughout. In his reliance on God's being no deceiver, in his emphasis on the role of perception and thought being for the benefit of the mind-body union, and even in his idea of conservation of material motions, Cartesian harmony, wrought by divine will for its own inscrutable purposes, is present. It is present in the conservation case because God is true to His nature as far as the relevant aspect of that nature is constancy. This is the aspect of God's form relevant to the purely material world, whereas in the epistemological realm the relevant aspect is no deception. These truths about God's nature we can know. The difference between Cartesian harmony and Leibnizian harmony lies in the "pre-established." For Descartes, whose God is constantly and continuously at work, and there is nothing pre-established. To know what was pre-established would be to know God's ends and to impute moralistic final causes to Him. For Leibniz, this is exactly what one does. But Descartes is developing a line that will later be that of Newton (who takes a good part of his conception from Descartes), a line that has a constantly active God who rules the world according to His will.

Notes

Note: Throughout I follow the same abbreviations as Garber.

1. AT VII, 50; HR 1.168.

2. Norman Kemp Smith argued strongly that Descartes was not an occasionalist. His analysis stresses the "jointly collaborative" natures of mind and body, but it does not go far enough; cf. *New Studies in the Philosophy of Descartes* (London: MacMillan, 1966), pp. 212ff.

3. Descartes calls the pineal gland the conarion. Letter to Meyssonnier (29 January 1640), p. 69. Reply to objection 6, AT 436; HR 2.251.

4. Garber is talking about the intentional action (mind-to-body) case; but, assuming the parallel between the two types of interaction, I presume he would give the same answer to the problem of perception.

5. Reply to objection 2, AT VII, 135; HR 2.

6. *Meditation III*, AT VII, 40–41; HR 1.162.

7. Reply to objection 2, AT VII, 133–34; HR 2.33.

8. Reply to objection 6, AT VII, 435; HR 2.249.

9. Principles II, XXIV, and XXV, AT VIII-I, 53–54; of also letter to More (August 1649), 1, AT V, 2 (K257).

10. Replies to objection 4, AT VIII, 238; HR 2.109.

11. AT VII 374–75; HR 2.223.

12. This view of efficient causation actually commits Descartes to a very strong thesis concerning the nature of an efficient cause. An efficient cause is not a mere moving cause obtaining its structure and direction (i.e., mode of moving) from another cause external to itself. Rather, it is an efficient cause that has its structure or principle of motion already contained in it. There is warrant for this view of an efficient cause both in Aristotle himself (see J. Lennox, "Teleology, Chance, and Aristotle's Theory of Spontaneous Generation," *Journal of Historical Philosophy*, Vol. 20 (1982), pp. 221–28, and in a more contemporary source, F. Suarez (*De Anima* [Vives edition, Paris: 1856], Book 4, Section 2, paragraph 12).

13. *Meditations III*; AT VII 40; HR 1.162–64.

14. AT VII 436; HR 2.251.

15. AT XI, 654.

16. Suarez, *op. cit.*

17. Descartes to Elisabeth, AT III 666 (K 139).

18. The story of Cartesian secondary causes actually gets more complicated, since for Descartes the ideas are already innate in the mind. Thus, God's creation of an idea is the actualizing of an innate potential. But this aspect of Cartesian thought would have to be defended at length and would take this paper far beyond its limitations.

Teleology and Spinoza's Conatus

JONATHAN BENNETT

1. SPINOZA'S CHALLENGE TO TELEOLOGY

Reports on Spinoza's views about goals or purposes or "final causes" tend to focus on his rejection of cosmic or divine purpose. But that is not all he rejected: He was opposed to all "final causes," all teleological explanation, even of human action; and that gives the *Ethics* some peculiar features that I will expound in this paper.

Spinoza has two general objections to teleology, both given in the Appendix to Part I of the *Ethics*. To get a hold on them, let us consider a small fragment of the natural world: A certain event occurs in my brain, which causes me to raise my hand, which in turn causes the deflection of a stone that has been thrown at my face. For short: Brain causes Raise, which causes Deflect. If I say that I raised my hand in order to deflect the stone, I purport to explain why Raise occurred. "Why did you raise your hand?" "So as to deflect the stone." But Spinoza thinks that to explain something is to say what causes it, and so he thinks that the above explanation purports to give Deflect a role in the causing of Raise. He objects to this on two grounds: (i) the role of "cause of Raise" is already filled, namely by Brain, and (ii) Deflect cannot enter into the causing of Raise since the causal flow runs the other way, i.e., Raise causes Deflect. I will concentrate on (ii) rather than (i). That is, I will not emphasize Spinoza's view that teleological explanations are wrong because they put items into causal roles that have been preempted by other items; rather, I will emphasize his view that they are wrong because "This doctrine concerning an end turns Nature completely upside down. For what is really a cause it considers as an effect, and conversely what is an effect it considers as a cause. What naturally comes before, it puts after." In short, Deflect cannot help to explain Raise, because Raised causes Deflect.

In an earlier treatment of this matter, I said that Spinoza's point concerned the attempt to explain an event through a *later* event, and Parkinson has criticized this on the ground that "Spinoza does not view causation in this temporal way."[1] He is right about that. Spinoza's extreme rationalism makes it hard for him to give theoretical weight to time differences, and, in particular, his conflation of causal with logical necessity forbids him to make such differences central in his account of the cause-effect relation. Still, Raise does occur before Deflect, and Spinoza would have regarded that as showing that Deflect does not cause Raise. Whatever his theoretical difficulties about time, if he were told that "something happened yesterday that caused a house to burn down two days ago," he would surely think "that can't be right!" on the ground that causes cannot postdate their effects; and so he could also give that as a sufficient reason for objecting to many teleological explanations, including the Raise-Deflect one that I have been discussing. Still, I concede that to state his entire case against teleology in that temporal way is to lose generality and to mislocate the center of gravity of his thought. In what follows, I will use the general causal statement of Spinoza's objection to teleology, though keeping the temporal version in sight as well. The choice between these makes no difference to strategy and virtually none to tactics. Spinoza says that teleological explanations order things wrongly, and we have to show that they do not: We will not be able to straighten him out unless we know what ordering of events he thought to be uniquely correct, but we do not have to know why he thought so.

Spinoza complains that a teleological explanation misrelates a pair of events, such as Raise and Deflect. Sometimes, however, there is only one event: We might say, "He raised his hand so as to deflect the stone," in a case where the hand went up too slowly and the stone got through. In this case, the charge of "misrelating a pair of events" does not get off the ground, because the only relevant event is Raise —there is no second event we could name Deflect.

Spinoza would say that there is trouble here, too, I think. He would object to our pretending to explain an item with the aid of *the concept of* something further down the causal or temporal stream, i.e., something—actual or possible—that does not lie in the causal ancestry of the item being explained. Idle mentions are harmless, of course, as in "The vase was caused to fall by a push from the man who would become President." But no tolerable explanation can *need* to mention actual or possible effects of the thing being explained—or so Spinoza thought.

Why not? It will not do merely to say that what explains Raise must cause it and Deflect cannot cause it since it is caused by it, for now we are looking at a case in which there is no such event as Deflect. Spinoza might say that that is worse than ever, for now it is being pretended that Raise is caused by a subsequent event that does not even happen! But that sounds wild and unconvincing: someone who says it, we are apt to think, *must* have gone astray somewhere in his or her thinking about teleology. Still, it is one thing to say that Spinoza no longer has a clear account of what is wrong with saying "I raised my hand so as to deflect the stone"; it is another to show what is right with it. *Can* we really explain Raise in a way that essentially involves mentioning a possible event that, if it is actual, is caused by Raise?

Yes, we can, and in section 6 I will show how. First, though, a simpler and more inviting way of dealing with Spinoza's problem ought to be discussed.

2. BRAITHWAIT'S PARTIAL RESPONSE

It seems natural to suggest that at least some teleological explanations are all right, namely, those that explain an action by reference to *thoughts about* its possible effects. Thus, according to Braithwaite:

> There is one type of teleological explanation in which the reference to the future presents no difficulty, namely explanations of intentional human action in terms of a goal to the attainment of which the action is a means. [Such] explanations are always understood as reducible to causal explanations with intentions as causes; to use the Aristotelian terms, the idea of the 'final cause' functions as the 'efficient cause'.[2]

This seems so obviously available as an answer to the question "How can an event be explained with the aid of a mention of a possible effect of it?" that one wonders why Spinoza did not avail himself of it and drop much of his opposition to teleology.

There is an easy, obvious reason why Spinoza would not accept Braithwaite's proposal just as it stands. Since Spinoza holds that there can be no causal commerce between the mental and physical realms, he could not allow that any thought or "idea" could cause Raise. But we can modify Braithwaite's proposal, consistently with Spinoza's own views, so that it clears this hurdle and yet still presents Spinoza with a teleological challenge.

The key to the modification is Spinoza's doctrine of parallelism between the mental and physical realms (2p7), which implies that physical causal chains are always matched by mental ones, and vice versa. This implies that, when Raise seems to be caused by a thought of mine, it is caused by some physical (perhaps cerebral) partner of that thought; and the thought itself does cause (not Raise itself, but) a mental partner of Raise. So there are two causal chains here, according to Spinoza. One is physical:

(1) physical correlate of thought of deflection → Raise.

The other is mental:

(2) thought of deflection → mental correlate of Raise.

Neither involves a causal crossing of the boundary between physical and mental. In thus avoiding interaction between mind and body, far from destroying Braithwaite's proposed form of teleological explanation, we have turned it into two!

If (1) and (2) above are genuine causal transactions, why can they not support teleological explanation? In each of them, an item *x is caused by* — and is thus explainable through — a previous item that somehow involves the concept of a possible *effect of x*. In (1) Raise is caused by a brain event that is, in a sense, "of" the stone's being deflected; in (2) the mental correlate of Raise is caused by a thought of the stone's being deflected. But neither of them has the faintest appearance of implying that Deflect causes Raise; so Spinoza is not entitled to say outright that they reverse the order of nature by treating effects as causes. What, then, can he say about them?

3. HOW COULD SPINOZA HAVE REPLIED?

I do not know whether Spinoza explicitly thought about this way of explaining an item with help from the concept of a possible effect of the item. If he did, he must have rejected it, and reasons for doing so can be found in his thought.

They turn on the fact that a cause of x has features that do not contribute to its causing x, including some that do not contribute to its causing anything. The fall of a vase may be caused by a push that (i) occurs across the middle of the table in a northerly direction, (ii) extends through ten inches, (iii) is accompanied by a snapping of fingers, (iv) is just like a certain movement that Olivier makes in his film version of *Hamlet*, and (v) is performed by someone who will become President ten years later. The first two of these are relevant to the push's causing the fall, the third is relevant to some of its causal powers though not to that one, and the last two are arguably irrelevant to all its causal powers.

Now, with reference to causal chain (1), Spinoza would say that the physical event that causes Raise is not helped to do so by having the feature that links it with the deflection of the stone, and in (2) he would say that the thought that causes the mental correlate of Raise is not helped to do so by being a thought of the deflection of the stone. In each case, the cause *has* a deflection-involving feature, but its other features are sufficient for it to cause Raise (1) or the mental correlate of Raise (2). Indeed, the position is even stronger than that. Spinoza, as I understand him, would say that those deflection-involving features are entirely causally impotent: They do not contribute to *any* of the causal powers of the items that have them. He would regard them as representative rather than intrinsic features of the items that have them, and he thinks that a thing's causal powers depend only upon its intrinsic nature. To get the feel of this position, consider the thesis that the causal powers of a bit of paper with ink marks on it may depend on size, shape, chemical composition, etc., but will never depend upon whether it is a map of Sussex. Though the example needs refining, even in its rough form it may help to give the general idea.

Having attributed this very strong view to Spinoza, I should defend it in more detail, taking the two cases separately.

(1) Spinoza allows that a state of one's body may be "of" something else: He calls such physical states "images." The only ones he explains are caused by what they are images of, so that my "image of" you is a state that my body is caused to be in by your body. I do not see how to extend that to cover a brain state that is "of" a nonexistent state of affairs, e.g., a possible future deflection of a stone, but I need not wrestle with that problem. What matters here is that Spinoza seems to have assumed, firmly and deeply, that the causal powers of a physical item depend wholly upon its intrinsic properties, such as the shapes, sizes, positions, and velocities of particles, and never on any representative or "of"-ish feature it might have. The physical theory expressed in the lemmas inserted between 2p13 and 14 leaves no room for doubt about this. It follows that, although the cerebral item that caused Raise is correlated with my thought of the stone's being deflected, that feature of it cannot have contributed to its causing of Raise. A fortiori, this causal transaction

does not enable us to put the concept of an effect of x *to work* in explaining x, and so it does not threaten us with teleology.

(2) I contend that Spinoza would also hold that the representative features of mental items contribute nothing to their causal powers. Thus, when I have the thought that P, this thought is a psychological particular that has various features that enable it to have various mental effects, but its representative feature—its having the content *that P*—is not causally efficacious. Spinoza is forced to accept this by pressure from his doctrine of parallelism between the mental and physical realms: "The order and connection of ideas [mental items] is the same as the order and connection of things [basically physical items]" (2p7). The very wording of this and still more Spinoza's handling of it throughout the *Ethics* imply a strict isomorphism between the mental and physical realms, with similarities in one mapping onto similarities in the other and with causal chains in one mapping onto causal chains on the other. Now, if I was right in my previous claim that Spinoza holds that a physical item's causal powers depend solely on features of it having to do with positions, velocities, shapes, and sizes of particles, then he must make the causal powers of mental items depend upon features of them that are systematically correlated with *those* physical features.

That seems to foreclose the possibility that the causal powers of mental items should depend on their content, their representative features, what they are "of" or "about" or what they "say." Spinoza's parallelism doctrine is a lot to swallow, but it would be even harder to choke down the thesis that features having to do with positions and velocities, etc., can be systematically mapped onto such mental features as *being about Vienna* or *being of the form '. . . that God is good'* or *being of the form '. . . in order to deflect the stone'*. It seems reasonable to suppose— and these days *is* widely supposed[3]—that many different kinds of cerebral event might serve in the brains of different people, or even at different times in the brain of one person, as the physical correlate of a thought about Vienna; and, if that is right, then a psychological theory that was isomorphic with some physical theory such as cerebral neurology could not have *being about Vienna* as a causally significant feature of some thoughts. The same is true for all the other representative features of thoughts.

Thus, Spinoza is pushed into denying the causal efficacy of the representative features of thoughts by his physics together with his parallelism thesis. He may also be pulled toward that denial by a certain advantage he can get out of it. I was first put onto this point by C. L. Hardin, though the details of the handling are my own. It deserves a section to itself, but readers can jump to the start of section 5 without losing the main thread.

4. WHY DO WE KNOW NO PSYCHOLOGY?

The 2p7 parallelism doctrine says that true psychology maps onto true physics, right across the board, and human psychology is just the mental special case corresponding to the physical special case of the human brain. Spinoza thought he knew some general physics but must have realized that he had no inkling of a corresponding psychology. This asymmetry makes itself felt in the *Ethics* through repeated reminders that for Spinoza the physical realm calls the tune, as is strikingly evident in the structure of Part 2 "On the Nature and Origin of the Mind." The opening propositions of this say only that the realm of thought is systematically correlated with the physical realm without interacting with it, and then 2p11 through 2p13 say that a person's mind and body are instances of this correlation. Before giving detail about the human mind, however, Spinoza breaks off at 2p13 and inserts a physics and a biology; then he returns to the topic of the human mind in 2p14, which says that the more versatile your body is, the more sensitive and capable your mind will be. As I said, the body calls the tune.

Still, Spinoza does not say outright that we have more access to the physical realm than to the mental; still less does he explain why. He ought to see this as a problem. It is understandable that the thick detail of human psychology defeats us by its complexity, matching the complexity of the still unknown fine structure of the human brain; but Spinoza should be troubled by our possessing some general physics but no corresponding general psychology.

Although this asymmetry must be an embarrassment to him, there are two things he can do to reduce it a little, making our ignorance of true basic psychology look less blankly contingent than is, say, my ignorance of economic geography or yours of New Zealand poetry.

The first is to suppose that we do not yet know how to classify mental items in a manner suitable for psychological theory: We have no glimmerings of true psychology for about the same reason that someone could have no glimmerings of true chemistry if he tried to found his chemical theory on the categories "dirt," "rock," "liquid," and "greenery."[4]

What is wrong with our present taxonomy of the mental? Does it just happen not to carve up mental reality at the joints, or has it some general feature that positively disqualifies it for scientific use? Spinoza, who hates brute facts, would prefer the latter option, and there is something he could say in support of it—this being the second of the two discomfort-reducing moves I said he could make.

It consists in the observation that we know almost nothing about our thoughts except for their representative features (i.e., what they are like *objective*), whereas what determines their causal powers, and thus what matters for science, is their intrinsic nature (i.e., what they are like *formaliter*). That is my main point in this section: If Spinoza does hold that mental items owe none of their causal powers to their representative features, i.e., to what they are "of" or "about," that can help him to explain why, although we do have physics, we do not have psychology. Of course, the explanation is incomplete, since it leaves unexplained our ignorance of the intrinsic natures of our thoughts, but it is better than nothing.

You might think that it is wrong because we really know a lot about the intrinsic natures of many mental items: the intensity of sensations, the subjective "what-is-it-like" quality of perceptual states, and so on. There is something in that, but Spinoza would attach little weight to it. His picture of our mental life is a severely intellectualist one: it is dominated by our "ideas," which tend to be *beliefs* but which, even when they fall short of that, are always *propositional thoughts* (2p49s). It is surely true that we know almost nothing about the intrinsic nature of that kind of mental item. I am now consciously entertaining the thought that I will be in New York City on Friday: that is a particular episode in the history of my mind, but, if I were asked to describe it, what could I say? I could say when and "where" it happened and what else I was thinking and experiencing at the time, but that would be all I could report, except for the episode's content, its being a thought that I will be in New York City on Friday. And so it is in general with mental items that have content: we know virtually nothing about them except their content.

There is just one feature of mental states that is intrinsic and that Spinoza does not snub. When my physical health improves, so correspondingly does my mental health, and the latter improvement is—Spinoza seems to hold—a *feeling* of pleasure. He has a general theory about pleasure and unpleasure, which he holds to be the mental sides of changes in physical health and level of vitality, and he apparently thinks there are causal laws about such kinds of feeling. That would be a start on a true basic psychology, but what a small one! It is on a par with—and indeed is really the mental counterpart of—the fragment of the science of biology that you get just from being able to tell whether a given organism is becoming more or less ill. In Spinoza's theory about feelings, all the fine detail is given in terms of the beliefs that cause the feelings, and that puts the theory out of touch with true basic psychology. But this is an aside within an aside; it is time to rejoin the main path.

5. THE REJECTION OF HUMAN TELEOLOGY

Whether or not his reasons were as I have conjectured in section 3, Spinoza does try to avoid teleological notions in his initial account of the human condition. He allows himself the term "desire," defined as "appetite with consciousness thereof"; but according to him my appetite for P's being the case amounts merely to those intrinsic features of me that cause me to act in ways that make P more likely to become the case. (That, anyway, is the best I can make of what he says in 3p9s, 3p56d, and the first of the affect definitions at the end of part 3.) Suppose that I am in a physical state S and a corresponding mental state S* and that S causes me to move in ways that increase the chance of my eating an apple; that fact can be expressed by calling S my "appetite" to eat an apple and by calling S and S* together my "desire" for an apple. But a proper (i.e., causal) explanation of my movements or their mental counterparts will refer only to S or S* itself; it will adduce only the intrinsic features of the relevant physical or mental item; the item's being an appetite or desire *for an apple* is not an intrinsic fact about it and so has no explanatory role. In short, Spinoza is resolutely refusing to let a possible effect of x have a working role in the explanation of x.

That is a pity because his account of the human condition is distorted and cramped by his refusal to allow anything teleological and his consequent inability to wield a sound concept of intention or purpose or goal. And there was no need for this, since one does not have to "reverse the order of nature" or engage in any other malpractice in order to explain an item in a manner that essentially involves mentioning items that are temporally and causally subsequent to it. In section 6 I will show how this is done. Spinoza might not have liked the procedure in question, but his own basic principles give him no reason to reject it.

There is another reason for bringing a sound theory of teleology to bear upon our study of Spinoza and comparing it with his substitute theory of "appetite." When the text of the *Ethics* is examined in the light of that comparison, we can explain a profoundly puzzling feature of that work. Spinoza says that teleological explanations are always improper; yet he attributes to organisms a drive — he calls it conatus — that in his hands becomes a principle of self-interest. But to be self-interested is to have a certain kind of goal or purpose, which is the whole essence of teleology or "final causes." What on earth is going on here? In sections 9 and 10 I will answer this question.

6. SKETCH OF A THEORY OF TELEOLOGY

A full account of teleological explanation is a lengthy affair, which I have presented elsewhere.[5] Here I will keep it brief. The crucial notion is that of an instrumental property, that is, a property attributed to x by a proposition of the form:

x is so situated and constructed that *if Fx soon then Gx thereafter.*

In shorthand, I put this by saying that F/Gx or that x has the instrumental property F/G: the animal is kills/eats, the pane of glass is dropped/shatters, and so on. Instrumental properties are not in themselves teleological. But now suppose that there is an organism x and a property G such that for *any* property f and time t,

If f/Gx at t then fx at t+d

— that is, whenever x is does-something/becomes-G, it does the "something." If Gx is "x eats," then x is an organism that does whatever leads to its eating: when it is kills/eats, it kills; when it is climbs/eats, it climbs; and so on. This would be an animal that has becoming-G as a goal, and its G-seeking conduct could be explained in those terms. Why did it do F at time T? Because then it was F/G — which is to say that at T the animal was so constructed and situated that if it did F shortly thereafter that would *lead* to its becoming G a little *later still*. That is how an event can be explained with help from a mention of a possible event that, if it became actual, would be causally and temporally subsequent to the explained event. This explanation is not causal; i.e., it is not a matter of mechanistic, efficient causation. But neither is it a rival to mechanistic causation: There is no reason why each movement that is explained in terms of a goal should not also be mechanistically explicable in terms of the animal's intrinsic states at the time.[6]

There are no interesting cases of organisms conforming to a teleological law of the kind I have given. Any non-trivial teleological law must be restricted to values of f that in some sense belong to the repertoire of the given organism; and there must be allowance for multiple goals, for the animal's being prevented from doing F, and so on. I will pretend that all of that has been silently built into the account.

7. THE COGNITIVE COMPLICATION

One complication must be treated explicitly, however. We do not expect any actual organism to do whatever *will* make it become G but only what *it thinks will* do so. We can always fix things so that an animal's doing F is the route to its becoming G (for example, walking clockwise in a circle for nine minutes is a way to get food, because we have arbitrarily chosen that reward for that performance), but we do not expect that to affect its behavior unless the relevant instrumental fact is registered upon the animal. I use "registration" to name a genus of which belief is a vaguely demarcated species. And what I am saying is that a true teleological generalization would almost certainly have to be not of the form:

If f/Gx at t then fx at t+d,

but rather of the form:

If at t x registers that f/Gx at t then fx at t+d.

That, I submit, is the fundamental source of the famous interplay between belief and desire. They are well known to be intimately tied together, at least through the formulae:

His behavior shows what he wants, if you know what he thinks;

His behavior shows what he thinks, if you know what he wants.

The ultimate source of that link is the theory of teleological explanation: The concept of *desire* comes from that of *goal*, which is defined by the teleological patterns to which the animal dependably conforms; and the basic use of the concept of *belief*—I submit—is in the antecedents of teleological generalizations, with all its other uses depending on that. Properly to explain what beliefs are, you must start with their role in the pursuit of goals.

Spinoza's rejection of teleology, therefore, deprived him of a well-grounded concept of belief. His theory of cognitive content was bound to be thin and inadequate, since he did not have the teleological context within which to launch a good theory.

Still, the cognitive element in teleological explanations is not central to my present theme: Spinoza's basic objection to teleology can be stated and rebutted without reference to anything cognitive, namely, as an objection to explaining an item with help from the concept of a possible effect of that item. This is countered by showing how teleological explanations can have that feature without thereby being guilty of misconduct, e.g., "reversing the order of nature" by treating effects as causes. The crucial idea is that of an organism's being so constructed that it can be depended upon to do whatever will make it G later.

8. DISTINGUISHING THE CONATUS FROM TELEOLOGY

From 3p4, which says that no organism can possibly destroy itself, Spinoza infers his conatus doctrine, his thesis about universal self-interest, according to which from each human's nature "there necessarily follow those things which are conducive to his preservation" (3p9s).[7] In this section, I will try to provide a clearer view of the gap between those two.

There are two elements in it. One is the difference between ". . . does not destroy x" and ". . . is conducive to x's survival." This of no great moment. If we take 3p4 as saying:

If x does f, then the doing of f does not destroy x,

we could allow Spinoza to strengthen that to:

If x does f, then the doing of f does not tend toward x's destruction,

and it would be intelligible, though wrong, to equate that with:

If x does f, then the doing of f tends toward x's preservation.

I believe that those moves are at work early in Part 3 of the *Ethics* and that we can usefully see Spinoza as having taken his no-self-destruction thesis (3p4) to imply that whatever an organism does is helpful to it in the sense of being conducive to its survival.

I will now take the conatus doctrine in that form of it. That lets us focus on the second difference, which is more interesting. We now have the strengthened conatus doctrine saying:

If he does it, it helps him,

and we have the remark in 3p9s, about each person doing "those things which are conducive to his preservation," which says in effect that:

If it would help him, he does it.

Of these, the former involves Spinoza's concept of "appetite" or "desire": the man is so constructed that what he does will tend to produce such-and-such results. The latter is genuinely teleological: the man is so constructed that, if something would tend to produce a certain result, he does it.

It is the difference between a conditional and its converse, and it is enormous. From the teleological statement we can infer positive predictions of behavior: The man *will do F* because that will help him. In contrast, the strengthened conatus doctrine supports only negative predictions: The man *won't do F* because that will not help him. Similarly, the teleological statement can explain why the man did such-and-such, while the other can only explain why he did not do so-and-so. The formal source of these differences is plain see: The teleological statement has behavior in its consequent, whereas the conatus doctrine has it in the antecedent and can move it over only through contraposition:

If it wouldn't help him, he doesn't do it.

It is because the consequent of that is negative that the conatus doctrine lets us predict and explain only negative facts about behavior.

There is no distinction between positive and negative facts in general. But I have recently established a firm grounding for a distinction between positive and negative facts about the movements of a single individual,[8] which is all I need here.

9. HOW THE TWO APPEAR IN SPINOZA'S TEXT

I have been making much of the difference between "If he does it, it helps him" and "If it would help him, he does it." It is undeniable that the former of these is the most that could with any semblance of validity be squeezed out of the thesis (3p4) that nothing can destroy itself, and I take that for granted. What about the other, teleological statement? I have equated it with what Spinoza says in 3p9s, namely, that there necessarily follow from each person's nature "those things which are conducive to his preservation." The equation would have failed if Spinoza had said: "From a man's nature there necessarily follow things that are conducive to his preservation; and so he is determined to do such things." That might mean no more than that the man is sometimes caused by his nature to do things that are helpful to him and could not mean more than that whatever he does is helpful to him. What Spinoza says, however, is not that but rather: "From a man's nature there necessarily follow *those* things which are conducive to his preservation; and so he is determined to do *those same* things"; and I cannot see how to avoid taking that to mean literally that he does *all* the helpful things,[9] which makes the statement a conditional running in the teleological direction, saying that, if something would help the man, then he does it.

Am I exaggerating tiny nuances in insisting that Spinoza's "those (same)" ("*ea*" and "*eadem*") be read as "all those"? Well, I need not rest anything on that one sentence in 3p9s, for later in part 3 Spinoza uninhibitedly employs conditionals of the teleological sort. No fewer than eleven propositions imply that the conatus doctrine predicts what people will do in certain circumstances. In fact, Spinoza always speaks of what the person will *try* to do; and, as I will explain shortly, the word "try" is essentially teleological. But never mind that just now. My present point is that in the propositions 3p12 and 13 and nine others derived from those two Spinoza accepts conditionals with the actual or attempted behavior in the consequent. These propositions say "If . . . , we try . . ." and not "Only if . . . do we try . . .", and they say "We try to do whatever . . ." and not "We try to do only what . . . ." Furthermore, in parts 4 and 5 Spinoza is clearly relying on a doctrine of self-interest that is openly teleological and predictive of behavior.

In the paper mentioned in section 1, Parkinson adopts my view about what a good teleological explanation looks like and comments: "Bennett (*Linguistic Behaviour*, p. 41) thinks that his theory is an *answer* to Spinoza's views. But is has already been argued (n. 11) that Bennett misunderstands Spinoza's views about final causation."[10] I do agree that Spinoza ends up saying things that are teleological in the way that Parkinson and I both accept, and I don't think I was clear about that until I returned to Spinoza after studying teleology. But it does not make much difference. These genuinely teleological things that Spinoza says do fall within the scope of his challenge to teleology, and he does nothing to argue that they do not, i.e., nothing to clear himself of the charge of "reversing the order of nature." In saying this, I cannot be reaping the fruit of that "misunderstanding of Spinoza's views about final causation" with which Parkinson charges me: That concerned *why* Spinoza thought that "He raised his hand so as to deflect the stone" puts Raise and Deflect in the wrong order; it did not affect my view about *what* the objectionable order is, and that is all I need to make the challenge apply to Spinoza's own teleological statements. Parkinson apparently construes the challenge as a very limited affair amounting to nothing but the point that Deflect did not cause Raise. There is very little actual teleological talk that would not be fully acceptable to Parkinson's Spinoza: He would serenely accept Braithwaite's proposal (reported in section 2) and would be under no strain in accepting a conatus doctrine that implies that, if somebody thinks that doing F would help him, then he will do F.

Well, I submit that my tougher and less consistent Spinoza is more interesting and deeper. He is also the actual Spinoza. If Parkinson were right, Spinoza would not have needed to insist upon his special notion of appetite, which is so resolutely unteleological. (Remember that to have an appetite for P's being the case is not to be disposed to do whatever will make P the case; it is merely to be in a condition in which one's behavior is apt to make P the case.) Also, I will show in my next section that Spinoza's route to his teleological conatus doctrine, in the pages of the *Ethics*, is a sequence of invalidities. I take these as evidence that Spinoza is in trouble here: he is trying to arrive at something that he has implicitly forbidden to everyone; and so it has to be developed in a twisted, tangled, illegitimate manner. I do not, of course, mean that Spinoza knew that that is what he was doing.

Having responded to Parkinson, I should say that this conflict between us affects only a tiny part of his admirable paper, whose principal aim is to set forth Spinoza's use in his moral philosophy of the doctrine of conatus, which he actually has, i.e., the teleological one to which Parkinson does and I do not think he is entitled. The question of entitlement is marginal to Parkinson's concerns, which presumably explains his not inquiring at all into the provenance of the teleological conatus doctrine in Spinoza's text and thus having nothing to say about the tissue of invalidities to which I now turn.

10. HOW DID THE MISTAKE OCCUR?

The word "conatus" is Latin for "trying." And, properly speaking, "trying" is always a matter of trying *to do x* or trying *to bring it about that P*; that involves behavior that is explained by one's thinking it may have a certain result, which is teleological and involves explaining what happens at one time by reference to what might happen later. So, Spinoza's very choice of name for the doctrine in question suggests that he has been covertly thinking of it as teleological right from the outset, and so he has. Although it is not until 3p12 and 3p13 that we see the teleological conditional openly at work, the basic malfeasance occurs in the moves from 3p4 to 3p6 in which the conatus doctrine is originally announced. I will explain how.

Spinoza's argument for his conatus doctrine starts with the no-self-destruction thesis: "No thing can be destroyed except through an external cause" (3p4). Never mind where that comes from. Our present concern is with what Spinoza infers from it, namely, "To the extent that one thing can destroy another, they are of a contrary nature, i.e. they cannot be in the same subject" (3p5). There are two ways of taking this: (1) It could be saying that, if one *thing* can destroy another, then they could not both "be in the same subject"—presumably this means that they could not be parts of a single organism. (2) It could be saying that, if one *property* can destroy another—presumably this means that a thing's acquiring one would cause it to lose the other—then nothing could instantiate both properties at once.

Of these two readings, (1) is favored by Spinoza's use of "thing" in the proposition and by the idea of one item's "destroying" the other, but (2) is favored by the phrase "be in the same subject." With regard to the credentials of the proposition, the two readings are about on a par: Neither is entailed by 3p4, though each is encouraged by it; and on each reading the proposition is in some danger of being trivially true. Nor do the five subsequent uses of 3p6 resolve the ambiguity. Two of them clearly favor reading (1), two others clearly favor reading (2), while the remaining one is perfectly neutral between them![11] Fortunately, this neutral use is 3p6d, the demonstration of the conatus doctrine, so we can examine how this makes use of 3p5 without having to resolve the latter's ambiguity. This I now do.

The most Spinoza has any claim to be saying in 3p5 is that, if x can destroy y, then they are "contrary" in the sense that they cannot coexist; i.e., they are (1) things that a single organism cannot have as parts or (2) properties that a single thing cannot instantiate. In 3p6d, however, Spinoza takes himself to have meant something very different from this, namely, that, if x can destroy y, then y is "opposed" to x in the sense that it will exert itself to reduce the threat from x. This lavish overinterpretation of 3p5 is expressed in Spinoza's concluding that each thing "tries to persevere in its being," i.e., tries to stay in existence. This has to mean that each thing acts against threats, which goes far beyond 3p5's assertion that, if one item threatens another, then they are incapable of a kind of coexistence.

Although the two are not simply a conditional and its converse, there is an element of that in the difference between them. Given that x can destroy y, all that 3p5 as originally offered says about their behavior is a conditional with behavior in its antecedent:

> (1) For any f, if y does f, then the doing of f will not result in y's coexisting with x.

But what Spinoza makes of this in 3p6d is a conditional with behavior in its consequent:

> (2) For any f, if the doing of f would tend to keep y safe from x, then y will do f.

In this analysis I am not relying just on the phrase "tries to persevere." Further support is given by Spinoza's saying at the end of the demonstration, though not in the official proposition at the head of it, that each thing, *as far as it can*, tries to persevere in its being. It is easy to fit "as far as it can" into (2), the teleological conditional: If P, then y will do f as far as it can. But there is no plausible way of fitting it into (1), the other conditional, the official 3p5 one that has behavior only in the antecedent. The only grammatically possible place for it yields the result: "If y does f as far as it can, then . . . ," which makes philosophical nonsense.

Having thus invalidly brought something teleological into his doctrinal structure, Spinoza immediately proceeds to deny that he has done any such thing. In 3p7 he says that the so-called conatus, or trying, "is nothing but the actual essence of thing," and this, properly understood, is an important disclaimer. Although it does not use the term "appetite," it amounts to the claim that the apparently teleological term "conatus" really stands only for austere Spinozist appetite: In attributing a self-preserving conatus to an organism, he wants us to believe, we are saying only that it has a nature that will cause it to behave in self-preserving ways. He is not entitled to this. Granted, the basic *causal* story concerns the organism's intrinsic nature or "essence," but that is not the whole *explanatory* story; for Spinoza has also said that the organism will "try as far as it can to preserve itself," and nothing can save this from meaning something teleological. Later on in the *Ethics*, indeed, he stops even gesturing toward Spinozistic "appetite" in preference to real goals and purposes, or toward "If he does it, it helps him" in preference to "If it would help him, he does it." Apparently, he thinks that the sequence 3p4 through 3p7, has entitled him to a conatus doctrine that will do teleological work for him without being open to his own objections to teleology.

11. COULD SPINOZA HAVE MADE SUCH A MISTAKE?

Failing to distinguish a conditional from its converse is a bad mistake. So is confusing the sense of "contrary" that operates in 3p5 with the sense of "opposed" that is needed for 3p6d. Some of Spinoza's admirers will think that these mistakes are so bad that he cannot have been guilty of making them. I see that attitude toward Spinoza as a solid obstacle to understanding his work. As I hope my new book[12] will show, to learn a lot from the *Ethics* one needs a firm general idea of what kinds of help it can give and what kinds it cannot; and that requires a just appreciation of Spinoza's own strengths and weaknesses. Above all, it has to be understood that Spinoza's mind was strong, deep, wide ranging, tough, brave, and original but not quick and not sharp. Leibniz's kind of nimble acuity was altogether foreign to Spinoza, and Leibniz himself is on record with a wry comment about the invalidity of some of Spinoza's demonstrations.[13]

Often, the trouble is merely expository: Spinoza would assert a conditional when he meant a biconditional or label as a "definition" (to be read left to right) a biconditional that turns out to be a substantive thesis that can be used in argument from right to left. Sometimes, however, it is not bad writing but error. When, for example, Spinoza moves from:

If (x resembles y, and *x thinks that* Fy) then Fx

to

If (*x thinks that* x resembles y, and Fy) then Fx,

as he demonstrably does when he purports to rely on 3p27 in 4p68s, this is incompetence. Spinoza was a genius and one of the most challenging and instructive philosophers who ever wrote, but there is a certain kind of logical competence that he lacked—falling short not only of Leibniz, who is supreme in this respect, but also of the other major figures in early modern philosophy.

With that said, I should add that the conditional conversion that is my present topic is not as blundering as my diagnosis has made it appear. One of the hazards of philosophical debate is that in philosophy, unlike some other disciplines, the best techniques for exposing error tend to make the error look elementary and its perpetrator stupid. We show something to be wrong by boiling it down to some patent absurdity, and we may tend to forget that the absurdity was perpetrated in a thick, difficult context, not in the extracted form in which we expose it. So it is with Spinoza's switch from conatus to teleology. (I certainly hope so. If the error was gross, then we who care about Spinoza's thought must be correspondingly dense. It took me more than twenty years to discover what had gone wrong in the conatus doctrine, and others seem to have been even slower.) Although it is true that the core mistake is the conversion of a conditional, generated by malpractie with "contrary" and "opposed," these mistakes are disguised—rendered easy to make and hard to discover—by the complex philosophical context in which they occur.

12. THE CONTEXT OF THE ERROR

I will sketch the context of Spinoza's mistake about conatus and teleology, trying to show that my analysis of the situation is not greatly to his discredit. This is not to persuade myself that he deserves my admiration, for I have never begun to doubt that. Nor is it to defend his reputation in the minds of others, for that is too well established to be affected by anything I might say. The point is just that one's settled admiration for a philosopher can naturally affect what interpretations of him one is repared to consider seriously, and I want to persuade Spinoza's admirers not to shut their minds against my analysis of his muddle about conatus and teleology.

The context of Spinoza's conatus-teleology muddle is created by the intersection of three big thrusts in his thought. Let us look at them one by one.

First, having had the insight to see the prima facie problem involved in our ordinary notions of goal or purpose or end, and not seeing how to solve it, Spinoza concluded that these notions—in the form in which the common person has them—must be jettisoned. Never forget that philosophers who retained these notions had that advantage because they had seen less than Spinoza did, not more, as they overlooked the problem rather than seeing the solution.

Second, Spinoza thought it to be a universal truth that humans are always self-interested. There is plenty of evidence of egoism, and Spinoza was not one to shrink from taking a widespread tendency to be a universal truth. He will have found further support in the use he could make of psychological egoism in his moral theory. Projecting from his own character and attitudes, as all sincere moral philosophers do, he wanted a moral system with a coolly unsentimental input and a morally upright and even noble output; and he thought he could achieve this remarkable result if he had egoism as his chief premise.

But the doctrine of egoism had to be freed from the taint of teleology; and Spinoza also had a need, created by his intellectual temperament, for the egoism to be shown to be somehow necessary, deeply rooted in the nature of reality. (So indeed it is, but he was in no position to give the right, *evolutionary* reason why something like self-interest runs strongly through the behavioral patterns of all organisms.) This double need was satisfied, Spinoza thought, by what comes next.

Third, he discovered the argument stretching from 3p4d through 3p6d. Wrong as this argument is, its ingenuity should not be underestimated. It starts with the argument for the thesis (3p4) that nothing can, unaided, cause its own destruction: if something destroyed itself, it would have a nature that was causally (and thus, for Spinoza, logically) sufficient for its own nonexistence; but that would be an inconsistent nature, which nothing can possibly have (3p4d). The conclusion of the argument is false, as Spinoza might have come to suspect while wrestling with the fact of suicide (4p20s), and so, of course, the argument is faulty. Where it says that, if a thing could destroy itself, its nature would be logically sufficient for its nonexistence, the argument ought to say only that, if a thing could destroy itself, its nature *at one time* would be *causally* sufficient for its nonexistence *later*. But since Spinoza conflated logical with causal necessity and, associated with that, did not generally attach weight to temporal differences, he was not well placed to see anything wrong with 3p4d. That argument is thus not a merely perverse contrivance; on the contrary, it is just what Spinoza ought to say, given his causal/logical conflation and his inattention to temporal differences. Just as his rejection of teleology arose from a real insight, so his no-self-destruction thesis arose from a brilliant exploitation of his own philosophical assumptions and attitudes.[14]

Next comes the move to 3p5. I will expound this on the basis of one resolution of the ambiguity noted in section 10; the whole story could, perhaps less plausibly, be reconstructed in terms of the other reading. The idea is that, if nothing can destroy itself, then nothing can have two parts, one of which will destroy the other. It does not quite follow, since—as Spinoza well knew—the health of a whole may require occasional destruction or atrophy of some of its parts; but in the given context, with so much at stake, the mistake is a natural one. What needs more explaining is the final mistake in the sequence, namely, moving from the premise that, if x can destroy y, then they are "contrary" in that sense, to the conclusion that, if x can destroy y, then y is "opposed" to x in the sense that it will make war on x, so to speak. Perhaps it is just a conflation of "contrary" in one sense with "opposed" in another, but there may be more to it than that. Here is a guess about what more there is.

We are to interpret 3p5 as applying to two things x and y, which are themselves "individuals" but which are also fit to be parts of larger "individuals," and Spinoza is taking the proposition to imply that, if x can destroy y, then they cannot both be parts of a single individual that is not vastly greater than either of them is. That stipulation about relative size is needed: The universe itself is an "individual" in Spinoza's sense, and 3p5 must not imply that, if x can destroy y, then they cannot coexist in the same universe. And similar considerations apply at smaller sizes. For example, if x is a person who can destroy person y, they could still belong to the same universe and even the same nation; but Spinoza might say that their belonging to the same village or to the same family would tend toward creating the impossible situation of an individual (a village or a family) that could destroy itself without outside aid. Now, approaching 3p5 in that manner, Spinoza could reasonably take it to imply that, if x could destroy y, then they must always be at a distance from one another, since, if they came too close, they would threaten to unite within a single individual that could contain both only at the risk of being self-destructible. From that he might infer that y could be depended upon, if necessary, to *keep x at a safe distance*; and from that he might drift into thinking, in 3p6, that y could be relied upon to *do whatever would reduce the threat from x* — perhaps keeping it at arm's length but perhaps instead launching a preemptive strike against it. That would be a bad mistake, but it would have more structure to it than a mere confusion would.

My overall point is just that in the sequence 3p4 through 3p6 Spinoza is arguing intricately and ingeniously and is playing for high stakes. What is at issue is the establishment of a deeply rooted egoism that is no way teleological! In such a context, even a wonderful philosopher is likely to make bad mistakes.[15]

Notes

1. G. H. R. Parkinson, "Spinoza's Concept of the Rational Act," *Studia Leibnitiana Supplementa*, Vol. 20 (1981), pp. 1-19, at pp. 6-7 (n. 11).

2. R. B. Braithwaite, *Scientific Explanation* (Cambridge: Cambridge University Press, 1953), pp. 324f, quoted with omissions.

3. See, for example, Jaegwon Kim, "Causality, Identity, and Supervenience in the Mind-Body Problem," in Peter A. French, Theodore E. Euhling, Jr., and Howard K. Wettstein, eds., *Midwest Studies in Philosophy*, Vol. IV, *Studies in Metaphysics* (Minneapolis: University of Minnesota Press, 1979), pp. 31-49, at pp. 38-39; and David Lewis, "Psychophysical and Theoretical Identifications," *Australasian Journal of Philosophy*, Vol. 50 (1972), pp. 249-58, at p. 256.

4. For a more fully worked out presentation of this general line of thought, see Thomas Nagel's intensely and helpfully Spinozist paper, "Panpsychism," in his *Mortal Questions* (New York: Cambridge University Press, 1979), pp. 181-95.

5. J. Bennett, *Linguistic Behaviour* (Cambridge: Cambridge University Press, 1976), Chapter 2. The account presented there is developed from a basic idea — which would have sufficed for my main purposes in this present paper — in Charles Taylor's *The Explanation of Behaviour* (London: Routledge and Kegan Paul, 1964).

6. See D. C. Dennett, "Intentional Systems," in his *Brainstorms* (Montgomery: Bradford Books, 1978); Bennett, *op. cit.*, section 21.

7. Although in working on the *Ethics* I rely heavily on Curley's forthcoming translation, in quoting from the work I sometimes depart from Curley, and I take responsibility for all renderings. My "are conducive to" renders the Latin "*inserviunt*," which literally means "are in the service of" or "are devoted to" or "are serviceable to." Curley's "promote" conveys the same idea.

8. J. Bennett, "Killing and Letting Die," in S. M. McMurrin, ed., *The Tanner Lectures*, Vol. II (Salt Lake City: University of Utah Press, 1981).

9. Interestingly, Boyle's translation actually uses the word "all" in rendering the passage: ". . . from the nature of which all things which help in [his] preservation necessarily follow."

10. Parkinson, *op. cit.*, p. 8 (n. 15).

11. Favoring reading (1) are 3p10d and 4p30d; favoring (2) are 3p37d and 4p7d.

12. J. Bennett, *Spinoza's Ethics* (forthcoming).

13. G. W. Leibniz, *Sämtliche Schriften und Briefe* (published by the Berlin: Akademie Verlag), Series 2, Vol. 1, pp. 379f.

14. One might think that Kant is criticizing this argument here: "The principle that realities never logically conflict with each other is entirely true as regards the relation of concepts, but has no meaning in regard to nature. For real conflict does take place; there are cases where A + B = 0, that is, where two realities combined in one subject cancel one another's effects" (*Critique of Pure Reason* A 273, quoted with omissions and one correction [minus changed to plus]). But, although this scores a direct hit on Spinoza's 3p4d and 3p5d, its intended target is Leibniz, whom it misses. See G. H. R. Parkinson's helpful paper, "Kant as a Critic of Leibniz," *Revue Internationale de Philosophie*, Vols. 136-37 (1981), pp. 302-4, at pp. 310ff.

15. I am indebted for good help with this paper to my colleagues William P. Alston and C. L. Hardin.

States of Affairs and Identity of Attributes in Spinoza

RICHARD E. AQUILA

I propose in this paper that Spinoza confuses two conceptions of identity with respect to the attributes and modes of substance. The first involves the relation between a state of affairs and the totality of its constituents. This relation is such that the former might be regarded as merely "formally," hence not "really," distinct from the latter. The second involves a stricter conception of identity. The confusion is what allows Spinoza to avoid, or to believe he can avoid, a subjectivistic view of the relation between substance and its attributes, namely, a view according to which what we know as the various attributes of substance do not correspond to a set of real distinctions internal to that substance itself.[1] The confusion may also be what allows Spinoza to believe he can avoid a certain contradiction regarding the ultimate substance or "constituent(s)" of reality. This is the contradiction between regarding the attributes as themselves the ultimate constituents of reality, with all particulars mere modifications or determinations of them, and regarding the attributes merely as the basic forms *for* all possible modification or determination of reality. In the latter case, the "material" or "content" entering into the states of affairs in question could not be provided by the attributes themselves. I suggest, finally, that the clue to comprehending Spinoza's general approach to attribute identity lies in his antecedent inclination toward a particular view of the identity of thought and its object.[2]

I

It is clear that in Spinoza's *Ethics* substance is in some way the same thing as its attributes. Thinking substance is not just a thing that thinks; it is thought itself. Extended substance is not just a thing that is extended; it is extension itself.[3] Nevertheless, it remains unclear in just what way substance is supposed to be "the same" as its attributes. The unclarity, of course, is closely connected with Spinoza's

161

view that the same substance that is the attribute thought is also the attribute extension; and it is also, apparently, other attributes as well.

Surely, one would hope, the sense in which a single substance is identifiable both with thought and with extension is not one that requires admission that thought and extension, and the other attributes, are literally identifiable with each other. If it did require that admission, then we would seem forced to deny the possibility of objective knowledge of substance through the attributes. At the very least, certainly, we would have to say that apparently distinct attributes are really just the same attribute regarded in different ways. But what then could be the *ground* for the possibility of such alternate regards? Can we, in particular, suppose that it lies in some objective properties (or facts) correlated with each form of regard? If so, then, while the attributes extension and thought would be the same thing, for example, the *difference* in question would lie in the fact that this one "thing" is considered with respect, say, to D_1 in the former case and to D_2 in the latter. If, however, D_1 and D_2 are properties or facts whose conception involves that of thought or extension in the first place, then the putative objective ground for distinguishing the latter would involve a vicious circularity. On the other hand, if D_1 and D_2 are not items whose conception involves that of thought or extension, then the distinction between thought and extension, insofar as they are in fact distinguishable, would be dependent upon an "attribute" external to either of these. This would appear to contradict Spinoza's claim that "each attribute of a substance must be conceived through itself" (Prop. X). Thus, if the distinction between attributes, insofar as they are distinguishable, is really a distinction between an attribute regarded in one way and that same attribute (and not just the same *substance*) regarded in another, we are forced to deny the very objectivity of the distinction in question. But, if each of the attributes is strictly identical with each, then it seems impossible to avoid the conclusion that each is the same attribute regarded in a uniquely distinguishable way.

It might appear that Spinoza could avoid identifying the attributes with one another, and hence subjectivism, by adopting what we may call the Totality View of the relation between substance and its attributes: a substance "is" its attributes only as a whole is identical with the totality of what constitutes it; it is not, therefore, literally identical with each of its attributes.[4] Substance "is" the attribute thought, for example, only in the sense that it is a totality comprised of attributes, among which thought is to be found. The fact that substance is identical both with thought and extension, accordingly, does not imply that these are the same thing.

Perhaps the primary difficulty with the Totality View is its failure to do justice to the unity of what Spinoza argues to be the *one* substance that there is (namely, God) and of its "essence."[5] If each of the attributes, insofar as it is distinguishable from the others, is conceivable only "through itself," then it is difficult to see why any one *set* of distinguishable attributes (or, indeed, any one of them) should have any less a claim to the title of "substance," or at least of that which constitutes the "essence" of a substance, than any other set. If, of course, each of the attributes had a merely "adverbial" or "perspectival" status, as one of the irreducibly different "ways in which" substance manifests its essence, then the unity of that substance would not conflict with the apparent lack of unity among its attributes. But it could only be in the loosest sense that a perspectival or adverbial approach is compatible with regarding substance as a "totality" of attributes. No being could really *be* a totality of the various ways in which it (*it*!) might be regarded or in which it might manifest itself or its essence.

Spinoza himself, even before attempting to show that there can be only one substance, argues for the "indivisibility" of a substance (Prop. XIII). As it stands, the proof might appear compatible with the Totality View. Spinoza simply argues that either each of the allegedly distinguishable parts of a substance would itself be a substance characterized by one or more of the original attributes (violating Prop. V, which rules out the sharing of attributes by substances) or else we are dealing with a kind of divisibility according to which, the parts in question being *separable*, the original whole would have been, absurdly, destructible (violating Prop. XI, which rules out the destructibility of substances). The argument might seem compatible with the Totality View so long as we supposed Spinoza's point to be precisely that the several attributes comprising a substance must be necessarily connected and hence *not* separable.[6] How several distinct beings, each conceived independently of the others insofar as they are distinct, could be, in turn, "necessarily connected" of course remains a mystery. In any case, Spinoza appends a note to the argument in question, according to which the indivisibility of substance is "more easily" comprehensible directly from the fact that, substance being infinite (Prop. VIII), a "part" of substance could be nothing other than something *finite*. That would plainly be question begging on the Totality View insofar as each of the infinite attributes on that view would itself be a prime candidate for a "part" of the substance in question. To insist, again, that Spinoza's point is simply that the attributes, being "necessarily connected," would not be *separable* parts would destroy the intended distinction between the more difficult and the "more easily" comprehensible consideration. However we read the former, the latter would seem most natural when read as simply ruling out a Totality approach altogether.

Now, not everyone who claims that substance is "identifiable" with the totality of its attributes subscribes to what I have called the Totality View. That view requires two things. First, a substance is identifiable with a totality of attributes; second, it is not, in the same sense, identifiable with *each* of its attributes. Some views might satisfy the first but not the second of these conditions. Consider, as suggested earlier, a view according to which the attributes are best regarded as "ways in which" a substance is regardable.[7] On this view, the attributes are not supposed to be distinguishable beings in their own right. Each of them is in a sense the same being (substance). But the multiplicity of attributes discernible with regard to this being does not involve a multiplicity of further discernible beings (attributes); it merely involves a multiciplicity of perspectives *on* the original being, or ways of apprehending it. This approach might concede that substance is in some way "identical" with the totality of its attributes. To say this, presumably, would simply be to say that the attributes just *are* substance, although substance "as grasped" from particular points of view. But the view in question implies that a substance is, in the same sense, also identical with *each* of its attributes. This distinguishes that view from the Totality View; it is obviously intimately connected with the distinction between an entitative and a merely adverbial or perspectival approach to the attributes.

It is, I think, important to formulate the perspectival or adverbial approach so as to allow it to avoid subjectivism with respect to the attributes. In that case, in order to yield objective knowledge, the multiplicity of "perspectives" on Spinoza's substance would need a grounding in a multiplicity of objective states of affairs or facts involving that substance. The attributes, accordingly, would appear to be identifiable with the totality of the most general facts *defining* the plurality of "perspectives" that are in question.[8] One might, of course, maintain that, insofar as a set of such facts can be regarded as a set of facts about a single reality, that set comprises a unity in a way that the plurality of attributes could not in the Totality View, for the plurality in question does not involve a set of distinguishable beings but merely a set of distinguishable facts (or general kinds of facts) about some being. As I will argue later, the notion of a state of affairs or a fact as not really (though no doubt "formally") distinct from the "substance" providing its content plays an important role in Spinoza's thinking. It is important to see, however, that whatever "identity" might be in question in the case of a relation between a fact and its content (constituent or constituents), it cannot be the kind of strict identity that allows us to say that a given thing and that same thing "as regarded in" a certain way are one and the same thing. Certainly, there is a sense in which a substance is the same being as that *same* substance "considered as" thinking or as extended. That is simply because, trivially, a substance is the same thing as itself. If there is a sense in which some substance and an objective *fact* about that substance are the "same thing," this could hardly be a comparably trivial matter. In any case, we cannot straightforwardly say that Spinoza regarded the attributes as the most general kinds of facts about substance. The advantage of saying this is that it allows us to regard the attributes as comprising a set of objectively distinguishable *beings*. The disadvantage is that this would require a recognition on Spinoza's part that facts are indeed some kind of being in their own right, "over and above" their content. It is, I will propose, precisely his inability to do justice to this point that accounts for an irresolvable tension in Spinoza's own theory of substance.

II

So long as one allows a distinction between a substance and the set of facts alleged to constitute its "attributes," one is unable to do justice to some of the most central arguments in Spinoza's *Ethics*. Consider, for example, the arguments for the crucial Propositions IV and V. The latter attempts to establish that there cannot be a plurality of substances sharing an attribute, a claim that is crucial in a number of Spinoza's subsequent arguments, most importantly for Proposition XIV (that there can only be one substance). The proof appeals to that of the antecedent proposition in the course of which Spinoza reads his original definition of an attribute (Def. IV) as implying that a substance is "the same" (*idem*) as its attributes. As we have seen, the "identification" of substance with its attributes might be interpreted in a number of ways. The proof, I think, requires a "strict" interpretation.

The question, as Proposition IV makes clear, concerns the ontological ground for the distinguishability of any number of beings. This ground can lie only in some diversity of attributes or in some diversity of modifications of an attribute. What is ruled out is a "purely numerical" difference. Now consider what are supposed to be two distinguishable beings. If what makes them different is a difference in attribute, then it is conceded that we have not found two substances with the same attribute. Suppose, on the other hand, that the two are distinguishable only with respect to modifications of an attribute. Then, "since substance is prior by nature to its modifications," we need to place those modifications "on one side" and consider the substance "in itself," that is, with respect to the attribute in question. Thus by supposition not differing, we have again failed to find a case in which two substances differ with respect to an attribute.

It is easy to see that this proof requires a strict identification of substance and attributes. Otherwise, one might argue as follows. Suppose two things to be distinguished only by diversity of modifications, hence, not to differ in attribute. This, it might be argued, is perfectly compatible with those two things, considered "in themselves," being different substances, for considered in themselves they do by hypothesis differ by diversity of certain modifications. Hence, so long as we do not regard substance as strictly identical with its attributes in the first place, the two may, indeed, be regarded as distinct substances. Of course, this is what Spinoza wants to rule out when he calls our attention to the fact that substance is prior to its modifications. This would seem to involve precisely the principle that mere difference in modifications could never be what makes two substances different substances. Presumably, the difference has to lie "deeper," namely in that *of* which the modifications are modifications. Having ruled out purely numerical difference, that leaves us only with attributes, which by supposition provide no ground for difference in the case at hand. However, appeal to the principle in question, which Spinoza undoubtedly accepts, seems to put the cart before the horse. *Why* must the ground for the difference between two substances lie deeper than mere modifications of an attribute?[9] Modifications, admittedly, are conceived only through some attribute and, hence, not through themselves (Def. V). It follows from this that modifications are not substances, but that does not imply that differences in modification cannot constitute *differences* in substances. What seems to rule out the latter suggestion for Spinoza is precisely the supposition that in a case in which two sets of modifications involve modifications of a single attribute there are not, *ex hypothesi*, two substances to be found, for substances are the *same thing* as attributes and no difference in attribute is at hand. As we have already noted, in any case, Spinoza's *reason* in Proposition IV for ruling out the possibility of merely numerical differences rests explicitly on the supposition that a substance is the same thing as its attributes.

It can also be seen that the proof of Proposition V requires the assumption that a substance is identical with *each* of its attributes, should it have several. To see this one must notice that Spinoza takes the proof to show that there cannot be two substances with any attributes in common, not simply that there cannot be two with *all* their attributes in common.[10] Suppose that a substance were identifiable with a complex of certain attributes but not with each singly. Then, so long as two sets of attributes differed in one member, the substances in question would seem to have an ontological ground of numerical difference. So how, by consideration of the problem of numerical difference, could Spinoza rule out the possibility of two substances sharing a common attribute (while differing in others)? Obviously, Spinoza supposes that all of the attributes of a single substance must be necessarily connected together so as to rule out this possibility. But what is the ground of that supposition? And what kind of "necessary connection" could be in question in the first place, so long as each of the attributes is, insofar as it is distinguishable from the others, conceivable only through itself? In any case, while Spinoza himself appeals to the "identity" of a substance with its attributes as the moving force of his reasoning, he makes no reference to the notion of necessary connection.

It might appear that Spinoza is reasoning in the following way. A substance is, by definition, conceivable only through itself. But if, say, there were a substance comprised of attributes A and B while another was comprised of B and C, then each of the alleged substances would have to be conceived "through the other," for in conceiving of either I perforce conceive of B, hence of a "part" of the other.[11] However, this argument rests on a pair of assumptions that Spinoza cannot consistently affirm. The assumptions are, first, that in conceiving a whole one necessarily conceives of each of its parts and, second, that in conceiving of anything that is a part of some whole one necessarily forms a conception of that whole. These assumptions, conjoined with the assumption of an objective plurality of attributes, generate a contradiction for Spinoza, for, if a whole of attributes is conceivable only by conceiving each attribute and if each attribute contained in a whole is conceivable in turn only by conceiving that whole, then it would follow that none of the attributes comprising a given substance is conceivable independently of the other, which Spinoza denies repeatedly. It would seem, therefore, that Spinoza can argue that the apparent pair of substances AB and BC really would amount to the same substance (regarded in distinct ways) only if he assumes that a substance is strictly identical with each of its attributes. In that case, he can then argue that, since the substance comprised of A and B *is* both A and B, *a fortiori* it is B. And, since B is also C (as implied by the fact that some substance that is B is by hypothesis also C), it follows that the original substance is also C. Hence, the alleged duality really pertains only to a single substance. This argument would fail, however, if the "identity" of a substance with both of two attributes were merely the sort of identity obtaining between a whole and its parts, however "necessarily" the latter are supposed to be connected (i.e., compatibly with the demand of their independent conceivability).

It is also clear that Spinoza's argument cannot rest merely on appeal to the sort of identity expressed in the claim that each of the attributes of a substance "is" that substance in the sense that each is that substance *grasped* in some particular way. On this approach, a substance whose attributes are A and B would be "identical" with each of those attributes only in the sense that it is, as we might say, a substance that can be regarded both A-ly and B-ly. From this it at most follows that we can regard the substance in question in one of the ways in which a substance whose attributes are B and C might *also* be regarded. It does not follow from this that the first substance might itself be regarded C-ly, hence, that it is a substance whose attributes also include C. The problem of partial overlapping would remain.

Consider, finally, Spinoza's inference from the identity of attributes to that of the modes of substance:

> . . . substance thinking and substance extended are one and the same substance, which is now comprehended under this attribute and now under that. Thus, also, a mode of extension and the idea of that mode are one and the same thing expressed in two different ways. . . . For example, the circle existing in Nature and the idea, that is in God of an existing circle are one and the same thing which is manifested through different attributes (Part 2, Prop. VII, Note).

The inference, or apparent inference,[12] seems to presuppose that a substance can be apprehended with respect to a plurality of attributes if and only if each *mode* of that substance can be so apprehended. This, in turn, would appear to require supposing that a substance is strictly identifiable with each of its attributes and not just with the totality of them. In that case, as noted earlier, the attributes of thought and extension would be strictly identifiable with one another. They would be the same thing (the same substance) regarded in two different ways. From this it would follow automatically that any mode of extension is the same thing as a mode of thought and vice versa, whereas apart from that assumption the possibility remains that a substance regardable both as thinking and extended substance involves thought and extension simply in the sense that some of its modes are regardable with respect to one and others with respect to the other of these attributes. Apart from an appeal to some elusive "necessary connection" among the two systems thereby in question, this would be indistinguishable from supposing that the originally given substance was comprised of two distinct substances as parts, namely, those two systems. In any case, the introduction of the needed necessary connection would, so long as we remain with distinct attributes, still leave us with no more than a necessary correspondence between a circle and an idea of a circle, not with a sense in which they are "one and the same thing." Of course, one might suggest that all Spinoza meant to hold, in claiming that modes of thought and extension are one and the same thing, is that they are all manifestations of one and the same substance. But in that case there would be no closer identity between a circle and the idea of a circle than between a circle and a square. All would equally be manifestations of a single substance.

III

It seems clear that Spinoza was guilty of some confusion. His position requires a strict identification of a substance with its attributes, but this, in turn, implies that each attribute is the same thing as all the others, except insofar as it is "regarded" in a distinguishable way. In order to avoid the subjectivism that the latter formulation suggests, Spinoza then could only suppose that each of the substantial "regards" in question rests on an objective *fact* about some single substance. Each, namely, would be in a very general and irreducible fact about what that thing is, such that all other facts (the "modes" of that substance) are merely specific cases of those generalities; they are different *ways* of that thing's being the various sorts of things it is supposed to be. Such, no doubt, is the way Spinoza very often regarded the relation between substance and its attributes. Unfortunately, this way of regarding the relation undercuts his very attempt to establish that only one substance is in question in the first place. That attempt requires a stricter conception of substance/attribute identity. In addition, the suggested approach requires that we take substance to be whatever provides the *material, content,* or *constituents* of those most general states of affairs that are to be identified with the attributes. This content presumably must contain its own internal "principle of identity," in virtue of which it *can* comprise the content of those states of affairs in the first place. In other words, if the attributes define the most general "forms" of facts regarding that content, the latter must contain in itself some ontological ground in virtue of which those forms do indeed *apply* to some particular content. This could be neither the modes nor the attributes *of* substance, insofar as it is that very substance itself. This, in turn, appears to introduce an "unintelligible" element into the heart of substance. It is precisely the exclusion of such an element that lies behind Spinoza's rejection, in Propositions IV and V, of an ontological ground of purely "numerical" difference. It seems we cannot avoid concluding that Spinoza was engaged in a futile attempt to preserve his cake and eat it, too. He attempted to regard substance as strictly the same as its attributes (hence, in principle, transparent to intellect) and yet also to construe the attributes merely as the most general ways of *regarding* substance.

This formulation seems to me to suggest precisely the *explanation* of Spinoza's confusion. Spinoza, we might speculate, had a glimpse of the necessity of introducing facts or states of affairs as an irreducible element into any adequate ontology. However, he also found it objectionable to do so. Somehow, a fact or a state of affairs does not seem to be a real entity "over and above" whatever constituents it is supposed to contain. At best it is merely "formally" distinct from them. The uneasy tension between the latter point of view and the recognition that a fact is something more (ontologically, one might say, and not merely "propositionally") than its constituents would seem to be precisely what accounts for Spinoza's vacillation between an identification of substance with its attributes and a quite different conception according to which the latter are merely the various (objectively grounded) *ways of regarding* some substance.

It might be best, at this point, to turn to the modes of substance and then ascend once more to the attributes. My suggestion rests on the fact that it is precisely Spinoza's conception of the relation between ideas and their objects that might most naturally lead us to suspect, quite independently of his general account of substance, a tendency to regard the relation between a state of affairs and its content as a relation of identity. Spinoza's inference concerning the identity of ideas and their objects appears to presuppose, as we have seen, a strict identification of substance with its attributes. It is important to observe, however, that the presupposition of this identity is not quite sufficient for his purposes. What it permits is the conclusion that every mode of extension is also a mode of thought and vice versa. What remains unexplained is Spinoza's insistence that every mode of extension is identical with a mode of thought (an idea) whose *object* is that mode of extension. Having identified modes of extension with modes of thought, in other words, and not unreasonably supposing that all modes of thought have objects, Spinoza must have had some *independent* motivation for supposing that modes of thought are, in general, "one and the same thing" as their objects. His motivation in this regard has not, I think, been sufficiently explored.

Considerations concerning the ontology of facts have been introduced in order to explain Spinoza's pronouncements concerning the identity of thought and its objects. E. M. Curley suggests, namely, that modes of extension are facts or states of affairs on Spinoza's view, and the corresponding thoughts or ideas are the *propositions* asserting these states of affairs to obtain.[13] It is well known that some philosophers tend to identify propositions (or least true ones) with facts. In any case, even for those who are not prepared literally to identify propositions and the facts that they assert to obtain, there is obviously a very close and intimate connection between the two. Curley suggests that it is the intimacy of this connection that Spinoza means to indicate by speaking of an identity between thought and its objects.

It seems to me that there are a number of problems in this approach. First of all, it does not seem plausible to say that minds are systems of propositions, though Spinoza regards all distinguishable minds as complexes of ideas (Pt. 2, Props. XI and XII). Admittedly, Spinoza is unclear concerning the relation between ideas and states of consciousness. Does he want to say, for example, that the "mind" of a stone involves conscious ideas? In any case, however we deal with this problem, it seems most reasonable to regard at least human ideas as states (or "acts") of consciousness. But it is difficult to see how any set of *propositions* could add up to a state of consciousness. Furthermore, even if the "mind" of a stone does not contain conscious ideas, Spinoza does regard the stone's *possession* of a mind, that is, the identity of its material aspect with a set of ideas, as what entitles us to regard even a stone as, at least to some degree, "animate" (Pt. 2, Prop. XIII, Note). It is difficult to see how the mere existence of a set of true propositions describing a corresponding set of facts could account for any more "animation" in the thing than would otherwise be ascribable to it. On the other hand, we might suppose that a stone is indeed conscious, at least to some degree; or, rather, Spinoza might have supposed this.

The second problem concerns the motivation for describing a proposition as identical with the fact that it asserts to obtain in the first place. Of course, one might simply *mean* by a proposition a fact that happens to obtain. That is often done, but it is difficult to suppose that Spinoza did it. Presumably, Spinoza wants to allow for more of a distinction between the "identifiable" items. Curley suggests that the distinction is merely one between "matter" and form."[14] This, as I have indicated, I also find to be a promising suggestion. However, it would appear to make more sense when applied to the relation between the (totality of) constituents of some state of affairs and that state of affairs itself than when applied to the relation between propositions (whatever they are supposed to be) and facts. Ideas, as I would suggest, are just as much states of affairs as the modes of extension that are their objects, and it is precisely Spinoza's tendency to identify a state of affairs and its constituents, or at least to regard them as merely "formally" distinct, that leads, as I will suggest, to the supposition that ideas and their objects are, in turn, merely formally distinct.

We have also seen that whatever notion of identity is operative in Spinoza's conception of ideas is intimately connected with his tendency not simply to identify ideas and their objects but also to identify any attribute of a substance with that substance. The relation between propositions and the modes of the other attributes might be supposed to shed some light on Spinoza's claim that ideas (propositions) are identical with the modes that are their objects (the corresponding facts or states of affairs). It is difficult to see what bearing the suggestion could have on Spinoza's tendency to regard an identity relation as connecting *all* of the attributes and not simply the attribute of thought with each singly. Admittedly, Spinoza's tendency in this case must be seen as counterbalanced by a tendency in the opposite direction as well, inasmuch as the strict identification of the attributes with one another appears to lead to subjectivism. But this is precisely the point. What we need is an explanation of the conflict among Spinoza's tendencies. The analysis that equates ideas with propositions does not promise to shed light on whatever more general confusion might lie behind that conflict.

There is a piece of (quasi-) historical speculation that might account for the tendency on Spinoza's part to regard the relation between an idea and its object in terms of the sort of identity in diversity relating a state of affairs to the totality of its constituents. The background involves certain elements of Spinoza's Scholastic heritage. I will limit my attention to its manifestation in Descarte's doctrine of the "objective" containment of the objects of thought in individual minds. What that doctrine amounts to, I suggest, is that thoughts (ideas) are mental "states" only in the sense of being peculiarly mental *states of affairs*. One term of that stage of affairs is a mind; the other is whatever reality, in virtue of its objective containment in a mind (i.e., in virtue of its *real* containment in the state of affairs in question), provides the mind with an object of thought on that occasion. I cannot enter into a detailed defense of the suggestion here. What is clear, however, is that Descartes takes the doctrine seriously and literally enough to insist that any idea's incorporation of such a content implies a genuine relation to some real *being* as object within that idea. The point, for example, is crucial to his Third Meditation argument for the existence of God. The argument requires, as Descartes insists, that the objective reality constituting any thought about infinite perfection is a sufficiently literal sort of reality to guarantee that its object is a real being in the idea requiring an onto-logical (causal) ground that is itself infinitely perfect.[15] In addition, Descartes is careful to assure us that the doctrine of objective containment does not imply that *particular objects* are ever contained in the mind: only "attributes" or "essences" are. Infinite perfection is objectively contained, not the infinitely perfect *being*.[16] Were the containment in question merely metaphorical, there would be no need for such assurance.

The upshot, I think, is that an act of thought for Descartes is a special sort of relational state of affairs, as suggested. This rules out two alternatives, both of them often attributed to Descartes. One is that ideas are entities that intervene as pecu-liarly mental and internal objects between the mind and its proper, that is, *transcen-dent* objects. Descartes acknowledges a sense in which ideas are themselves "ob-jects," but it is simply the sense in which genuinely (i.e., "formally") instantiable essences are objectively contained in thoughts. Otherwise, "ideas" are simply mental acts themselves.[17] The other alternative is that mental acts are not intrinsically rela-tional at all; they simply involve the informing of the peculiarly spiritual substance of the mind by various special representational *properties*. This alternative would take very seriously the suggestion that thoughts or ideas are "states" of the mind.[18] By contrast, as I have suggested, the only states in question are the peculiar sorts of relational *states of affairs* entailed by Descarte's theory of objective containment. No mental act, or mental "state," is, in turn, a constituent of such states of affairs. The only mental constituent is the mind itself.

Now, Spinoza shared the Cartesian assumption that ideas as modes of mental activity are directed toward particular objects by virtue of containing those objects — or at least their "essences" — in some way.[19] It is this assumption, combined with a crucial departure from Descartes, that leads to a kind of "identification" of thought and object in Spinoza. The ground for Descartes's formal objective distinc-tion lies in his notion of substance. Essences are "formally" real when they actually "inform" some substance. But, even when merely objectively real, their ontological status depends on their relation to a substance, namely, to some particular *mind*.

As noted earlier, however, Spinoza rejected the view that individual minds are substances in which mental activity occurs. Rather, minds are nothing, insofar as they are distinguishable from one another, over and above the ideas attributed to them. It follows that the formal/objective distinction cannot rest on the sort of ground that Descartes attempted to provide for it. An idea, qua mode of mental activity, is a certain sort of state of affairs involving the *object* of that activity. Al-though Descartes does, Spinoza cannot construe the mind itself as a *constituent* of that state of affairs. Objective containment, that is, thoughts, cannot be explicated in terms of a primitive relation between an object (or essence) and an entity that is a mind. For thoughts just *are* the "objective containments" of objects, and the existence of an individual mind is ontologically secondary to that of thoughts themselves. Spinoza, accordingly, must conclude that ideas, qua particular modes of ideational activity, are states of affairs involving "nothing" in particular beyond the objects of those ideas. To that extent, ideas can be regarded as merely "formally" distinct from their objects and hence, qua modes of ideational activity, mere "forms" in their own right: "The idea of the mind, that is to say, the idea of the idea, is nothing but the form of the idea in so far as this is considered as a mode of thought and without relation to the object" (Pt. 2, Prop. XXI, Note). We might, as suggested, then speculate that Spinoza had a tendency to regard an idea, insofar as it is only formally distinct from its object, as, therefore, really the *same* as its object (though "regarded" in a different way). That would involve a confusion of two quite different kinds of "identity."

Of course, this attempt at a diagnosis might appear to rest on the ascription to Spinoza of a thoroughly incoherent conception or, at least, the tendency toward such a conception. This is the alleged conception of a state of affairs that contains only a single constituent. Granted, if a philosopher is antecedently inclined to regard an idea as a state of affairs containing its object as single constituent, we might anticipate an at least equally strong inclination to *identify* an idea with its object/ constituent. The problem would lie not in explaining such a tendency, but in explaining the tendency to suppose there was a distinction or, at least, an ontological distinction in the first place. No amount of historical explanation, it might be urged, could let us see a "tension" in the thinking of a philosopher where one of the alleged points of tendency is so close to being inconceivable.

For my own part, I am not convinced that the notion of a state of affairs that contains only a single constituent is unintelligible.[20] Certainly, if the only reason for supposing it is unintelligible lies in some intuitive inability to *distinguish* the state of affairs from that constituent, there is no reason to suppose that this would be easier in the case of multiple constituents. No state of affairs is the same thing as the complete set of its constituents. Of course, in the case of multiple constituents we may derive some comfort from our ability to say that the state of affairs is not the constituents in question because it is these constituents in some sort of *relation*. But, insofar as the relation they are "in" is presumably just the very *state of affairs* that is in question, it is hardly clear that the comfort offered by the "because" in this case is more than apparent. It is of the essence of a state of affairs to be something (and yet also in a way "nothing") more than its content, and, once this is acknowledged, it may not, in fact, be an easy matter to exclude states of affairs with only a single constituent.

In any case, we need to remember that the object of any idea for Spinoza will *itself* most plausibly be regarded as a state of affairs. This is the portion of Curley's position that, as suggested, I do not propose to reject. Suppose then, that the object of an idea is a certain body A in a (spatial) relation to B. Spatial states of affairs, after all, presumably always involve a multiplicty of constituents, even if there are some others that do not. Now, I have suggested that Spinoza had, in general, contrary tendencies regarding the ontology of states of affairs. On the one hand, he tended to recognize their ontological "otherness" with respect to their constituents;

yet, he also tended to *identify* them with (the totality of) those constituents. Precisely what we ought to expect, accordingly, is that, insofar as spatial states of affairs can be regarded as containing a plurality of constituents, Spinoza would be inclined toward the supposition that this very same plurality also provides the content of any idea *of* that state of affairs. The tendency to identify a spatial state of affairs with its constituents, in other words, would at the same stroke *account* for a tendency to regard the idea of a mode of extension both as containing that mode as its sole constituent and yet also as containing a plurality of constituents.

Of course, the suggestion also calls our attention to a difficult question. What, if anything, could possibly be the *ultimate* constituents of state of affairs for Spinoza? However we answer this question, we should expect to encounter a critical tension precisely at this point. On the one hand, Spinoza is inclined to regard the *attributes* as the ultimate constituent(s) of reality, for Spinoza is inclined to identify substance with (each of) its attributes, and substance is obviously the ultimate "stuff" of which any genuine state of affairs must be constituted. On the other hand, Spinoza is inclined to regard the attributes not as the ultimate substance of things but as the various possible "ways of regarding," or at least as the ontological *grounds* for the various possible ways of regarding, the ultimate substance of things. Thus, we need to return to a consideration of the status (singular or plural) of the attributes on the suggested scheme.

IV

On the suggested approach, the attributes would most naturally lend themselves to an interpretation as the most general "forms" of all possible states of affairs involving substance. This, I think, would fit in well with what Spinoza says about universals. Spinoza takes pains to reject a conception of universals as "substantial" beings of a peculiar sort,[21] or, at least, he does so with regard to alleged universal beings other than the attributes. The latter are obviously in some sense both substantial beings and yet universals. With regard to them, we simply ought to expect to encounter again the ultimate tension in Spinoza's thinking. On the one hand, he has a tendency to regard the attributes as substantial particulars (or, rather, all as the same particular); on the other hand, he has a tendency to regard them as the most universal ways of *regarding* some particular or particulars. Apart from the attributes themselves, in any case, it would appear most natural to suppose that all allegedly universal beings will be able to preserve a genuine *universality* in Spinoza's system only insofar as they are construable as part of the "form" rather than the content of objective states of affairs. Some people will regard the state of affairs consisting of A at a certain distance from B as containing three constituents: A, B, and the relational universal Being-at-a-distance-from. In Spinoza's system, the latter is not a genuine term of any possible states of affairs at all. It is not enough of a real, or a really dinstinguishable, *being* for that. But to the extent that it is possible to regard the more universal attribute of extension as real enough at least to constitute the objective *form* of certain possible states of affairs, we ought to regard Being-at-a-distance-from and all other spatial universals (insofar as they are something more than the particular, but vague, mental "images" to which Spinoza would otherwise reduce universals) as mere "modifications" of that more general form. A being at a distance from B would involve A and B in a state of affairs of one recognizable form rather than another, rather than as items connected by some *additional* item internal to the state of affairs in question. Of course, we would then need to distinguish between the "forms" provided by the attributes and what we might otherwise be inclined to regard as purely "logical" forms. But it is not clear what need we would have for the presence of the latter in Spinoza's system in the first place. What we usually mean by "logical form" presumably finds its paradigm in reference to some alleged "relation" of *predication*, for example. But predicates could be real for Spinoza only insofar as they are themselves part of the form of possible states of affairs. There are no predicates *internal* to a state of affairs thus requiring some further, logical relation to connect them with the remaining constituents.

This suggestion introduces an ambiguity into the notion of a "mode" and at the same time reinforces our recognition of a fundamental difference between modes of thought and those of the other attributes. In one sense, a "mode" may be regarded as the relatively specified "form" of some states of affairs. Thus, Being-at-a-distance-from is a mode of extension, for it is not the attribute of extension itself but that attribute "modified" as the form of a particular (sort of) state of affairs. At the same time, however, states of affairs have a *content*. Thus, the state of affairs of A being at a certain distance from B would presumably have A and B as its content. In a second sense, these must also be "modes of extension," since presumably these are nothing other than the *bodies* A and B. And, finally, in a third sense, we would, of course, need to distinguish the state of affairs of A being at a certain distance from B *both* from the general "form" of that state of affairs (Being-at-a-distance-from) and from the bodies providing its content. Insofar, however, as Spinoza himself was inclined to regard a state of affairs as merely formally distinct from its content in the first place, and, hence *as* a mere "form" taken in itself, the distinction between a mode of an attribute in the first and in the third of these senses would tend to be blurred. Insofar, on the other hand, as the attributes themselves must be regarded as the universal "forms" *of* all possible states of affairs, the distinction between any actual state of affairs and its form would appear crucial. We are torn in two directions.

It would appear that in all these respects modes of thought must differ from modes of the other attributes. Consider the thought of A being at a distance from B. Its "content" is provided by a mode of extension (A being at a distance from B). This immediately seems to distinguish it from a spatial state of affairs. For the content of a spatial state of affairs would seem to involve further modes of extension or, at least, to involve modes of extension in a further *sense*, for example, the bodies A and B. In this further sense, there are *no* "modes of thought"; there are no mental particulars providing the content of ideational states of affairs in the way that spatial particulars may be regarded as providing the content of spatial states of affairs.[22] Furthermore, part of what we would ordinarily *call* the content of a particular spatial state of affairs is, as we have seen, really a matter of form. This is what allows us to say that Being-at-a-distance-from is part of the form *rather* than the content of a spatial state of affairs. There is no corresponding distinction in the case of thoughts. If there were, then being a thought about A being at a distance from B would have to involve not simply the general attribute of thought, but a specific "mode" of that attribute responsible, at least in part, for the content of the thought in question. But no special mode of thought is required in this sense: insofar as the content of the thought in question is provided by the spatial state of affairs that is its object, the only form required to distinguish the former from the latter is simply the general *attribute* of thought.

In one way, then, "modes of thought" are radically dependent upon their objects and, hence, upon modes of the other attributes. This is a respect in which thought is distinguishable from the other attributes. In the sense in question, for example, a mode of extension would depend only upon the *further* modes of extension (bodies) for its content. By this very fact, on the other hand, thought also remains radically *independent* of the other attributes. Precisely because no special form is *required*, over and above the attribute itself, in order to provide the specific content of any particular thought, *no* "mode of thought" requires specification with respect to any other attribute. Of course, the two points require distinguishing between modes of thought as specific ideational states of affairs and modes of thought as the ontological *form* of those same states of affairs. In the former sense, modes of thought are radically dependent upon modes of the other attributes; in the latter sense, qua mere forms, they are completely independent. Insofar, however, as Spinoza was inclined to regard states of affairs as mere forms, that is, as merely "formally distinct" from their content, he no doubt was unable to come to clear terms with the distinction. Precisely the same tendency inclining him to *identify* a state of affairs with its object (being merely formally distinct from and, hence, "nothing more" than it) constitutes a confirmation of the very *independence* of the corresponding attribute (containing, as a mere "form," no reference at all to modes of other attributes).

This double life of an attribute, fostered by Spinoza's tendency to identify states of affairs with, or to regard them as at most "formally" distinct from, their content, can only be reinforced by focusing on a point spotlighted by Curley. I have distinguished between, for example, a mode of extension such as A being at a distance from B and a mode of extension such as the bodies A and B themselves. The latter, it seems, are "particulars"; the former, a state of affairs for which those particulars provide the content. As Curley has suggested, however, any apparent spatial particular like A or B (say, this or that billiard ball) ought *itself* to be further reducible in terms of some state of affairs. Insofar as the particulars in question are essentially characterized with respect to the attribute of extension and to the extent that the attributes themselves function as the forms of possible states of affairs underlying the characterizations of particulars, this is precisely what we ought to expect: the attribute of extension "enters into" a spatial state of affairs only as the *form* of that state of affairs. This, of course, only brings out more clearly the difficulty alluded to earlier concerning the *ultimate* content of those state of affairs for which the attributes provide the forms. At the same time, it may allow Spinoza to overcome, or to think he can overcome, the apparent lack of symmetry between thought and the other attributes.

The "ultimate content" of reality could not be provided by a set of "basic particulars." For particulars, insofar as they are distinguishable from one another in the first place, will always be reducible in terms of further states of affairs. So where could we possibly end up? Wherever it is, obviously, we will have to end up with what can provide *equally* the ultimate content of any mode of extension and the ultimate content of any thought *about* that mode of extension. Equally obviously, if we end up anywhere at all, it has to be with "substance." But what could substance be apart from its attributes? If there is any ultimate substance of spatial states of affairs, for example, what could that substance be except indeterminate *space*? And yet what, circularly, is "indeterminate space" if not the attribute of extension? Thus, the attributes are inevitably called upon to perform a double duty. They serve both as the ultimate substance or content and also as the ultimate *forms* of substance.[23] The contradiction is clear. Yet, it is no more clear than the contradiction involved in the identification of a state of affairs and its content. This, so long as Spinoza was inclined to see the distinction in question as merely "formal" and hence not as an ontologically real one, seems not, in fact, to have been completely apparent.

Thus, the fortune of all the attributes must ultimately be the same for Spinoza. The tendency both to distinguish a state of affairs from, and yet at the same time to identify with, its content constitutes a pull in two contrary directions. The one seeks to absorb the attributes into substance, the form into the content; the other seeks to absorb the content into the form. Since, as one might say, there is form "all the way down"; that is, any discriminable content is itself resolvable into more fundamental states of affairs: content and form, substance and attribute continue to constitute, all the way down, an irresolvably ambiguous identity-in-difference. Thus, on the one hand, the many attributes will appear as so many basic forms of possible *determination* with respect to some underlying substance; on the other hand, they must appear one and all to be nothing *other* than that substance. Obviously, Spinoza must reason, whatever mysterious identity-in-difference is in question, it is not a mere illusion, but something eminently real and intimately present to all consciousness, for it is at bottom the sort of identity-in-difference whereby a distinguishable idea is both one with and yet distinguishable from its *object*. And we are all intimately aware of that sort of identity-in-difference.

Notes

1. I assume that each attribute is supposed to provide a distinct, objective knowledge of the essence of substance. An example of a subjectivist: Harry Austryn Wolfson, *The Philosophy of Spinoza* (Cambridge, Mass.: Harvard University Press, 1934), Vol. I, pp. 116, 146. Some defenses of objectivism: Francis S. Haserot, "Spinoza's Definition of Attribute," *The Philosophical Review*, Vol. 62 (1953), pp. 499-513, reproduced in S. P. Kashap, *Studies in Spinoza*

(Berkeley: University of California Press, 1972); M. S. Gram, "Spinoza, Substance and Predication," *Theoria*, Vol. 34 (1968), pp. 222-44; Alan Donagan, "Essence and the Distinction of Attributes in Spinoza's Metaphysics," in Marjorie Grene, ed., *Spinoza: A Collection of Critical Essays* (Garden City, N.Y.: Anchor Books, 1973). Some commentators consider Spinoza hopelessly committed to having it both ways at once. Cf. James Martineau, *A Study of Spinoza* (London: Macmillan & Company, 1882), p. 185: "How the essence can be one and self-identical, while its constituents are many, heterogeneous and unrelated, is a question which is hopeless of solution." Cf. H. H. Joachim, *A Study of the Ethics of Spinoza* (Oxford: Clarendon Press, 1901), pp. 103-4.

Jonathan Bennett proposes an interesting interpretation according to which an "intellectual illusion" is involved, not in supposing the attributes to be objectively *distinct*, but in supposing them to be ontologically *basic* determinations of the essence of substance. Rather, there are properties that cut across all the attributes as basic *differentiae*. These are what provide the notion of the "identity" of substance through the attributes. The properties in question could not, of course, be modes *of* any of those attributes. See "Spinoza's Mind-Body Identity Thesis," *Journal of Philosophy*, Vol. 77 (1981), pp. 573-84. For some objections, see the response by Margaret Wilson, "Notes on Modes and Attributes" (same journal, same issue, pp. 584-86; both papers were contributions to the December 1981 APA meetings). Unlike myself, Bennett takes Spinoza's belief in the unity of substance to be most fruitfully regarded as part of an explanation for psychophysical parallelism. Thus, Bennett bypasses the issues concerning the identity of the attributes by what he calls Spinoza's "most ramshackle demonstrations" (p. 575).

2. This paper extends to the general problem of attribute identity a suggestion that I previously defend with respect to the identity of ideas and their objects as modes. See "The Identity of Thought and Object in Spinoza," *Journal of the History of Philosophy*, Vol. 16 (1978), pp. 271-88.

3. "It follows, secondly, that the thing extended (*rem extensam*) and the thing thinking (*rem cogitantem*) are either attributes of God or (Ax. 1) modifications of the attributes of God" (Prop. XIV, Cor. 2); ". . . we have concluded that extended substance is one of the infinite attributes of God" (Prop. XV, Note): *Opera*, ed. Carl Gebhardt (Heidelberg: Carl Winter, 1925), II. References to *Ethica* appear parenthetically by proposition number and, unless specifically noted, are to Part One, translation by W. H. White (revised by A. H. Stirling) as included in *Ethics Preceded by On the Improvement of the Understanding*, ed. James Gutmann (New York: Hafner Publishing Company, 1949). Cf. also Letters 2 and 9, translated by A. Wolf, *The Correspondence of Spinoza* (London: George Allen and Unwin, 1928), reproduced in John Wild, ed., *Spinoza Selections* (New York: Charles Scribner's Sons, 1930), pp. 403-8.

4. Cf. Frederick Pollock, *Spinoza: His Life and Philosophy* (London: Kegan Paul, 1880), pp. 163, 179; A. Wolf, "Spinoza's Conception of the Attributes of Substance," *Proceedings of the Aristotelian Society*, Vol, 27 (1927), reproduced in Kashap; Martial Gueroult, *Spinoza* (Paris: Aubier, 1968), Vol. I, pp. 51ff.; E. M. Curley, *Spinoza's Metaphysics* (Cambridge), Mass.: Harvard University Press, 1969), p. 75.

5. Donagan (pp. 176-77) rejects the Totality View on the ground that it contradicts Spinoza's conception of each attribute as expressing "the essence" of God, hence expressing a *single* essence. This assumes that a single essence cannot be *composed* of several essences, each of which in precisely that sense "expresses" the whole in question. In any case, Donagan does not appear to do justice to Spinoza's tendency to *identify* each attribute with substance.

6. That Spinoza puts the original alternative in the terms that he does shows that he at least *assumed* that the attributes are not separable.

7. Cf. Henry E. Allison, *Benedict De Spinoza* (Boston: Twayne Publishers, 1975), pp. 59-60.

8. Cf. Curley, p. 75. Allison appears to adopt this approach as well.

9. The rejection of purely numerical grounds of difference is also highlighted by William Charlton, "Spinoza's Monism," *The Philosophical Review*, Vol. 90 (1981), pp. 511-15. In order to rule out individuation by means of discriminable *modes*, Charlton argues that a ground of

numerical difference must concern differences in "essential" properties. This is why we must "set aside" mere diversity of modifications and consider the attributes themselves. This approach seems to be question begging. Why *can't* differences defined merely modally constitute essential differences between individuals? With respect at least to finite individuals, this would seem precisely to be the case, insofar as bodies are individuated in terms of proportions of motion and rest (Part 2, arguments following Prop. XIII). We have not yet *shown*, of course, that true substances must be infinite.

10. This is clear, for example, from the use to which Proposition V is put in the proof of Proposition VI. It is also clear from the parallel formulation in Letter II, Gebhardt, Vol. IV, p. 8.

11. Cf. the proof of Propositions II and XIV.

12. Bennett argues (pp. 574-75) that no inference is intended. Perhaps the primary reason for supposing this is the absence of any clear inferential relation. I concede that the assumption of attribute identity at most implies the identifiability of a mode of thought with *some* mode of extension and vice versa. Hence, Spinoza must have had an independent motivation to identify modes of thought with their *objects* in particular. Given that, one might argue, why assign an inferential role to the doctrine of attribute identity in the first place? However, the independent motivation, as I present it shortly, is neutral with regard to the ontological status of objects of thought. Taken by itself, in particular, it is compatible with supposing that *ideas* are the proper objects of thought. The doctrine of attribute identity, combined with the independent motivation, thus allows the inference not simply that thought and its objects are identical, but that the identity in question indeed constitutes an immediate relation between thought and the other attributes.

13. Curley, pp. 122ff.

14. Curley, p. 124.

15. Descartes, *Meditations*, "Preface to the Reader," *The Philosophical Works of Descartes*, tr. Elizabeth S. Haldane and G. R. T. Ross (Cambridge: Cambridge University Press, 1970), Vol. I, p. 138; "First Replies," Haldane and Ross, Vol. II, p. 11.

16. Descartes, "Arguments" following "Second Replies," Haldane and Ross, II, p. 53. The suggested approach may appear to commit Descartes to a more Platonistic conception of universals than he was willing to countenance, since he requires the introduction of a distinct "attribute" to constitute the defining essence of any object of thought whatsoever. However, Descartes might have supposed he could make do with the general attributes of thought, extension, and infinite perfection. The apparent distinction between two *universals*, definable with regard to extension, for example, might be regarded simply in terms of two different ways in which the *single* attribute of extension is "present in thought." Cf. Descarte's reduction of all "universals" to "modes of thought" in Anthony Kenny, *Descartes: Philosophical Letters* (Oxford: Oxford University Press, 1970), pp. 187-88.

17. Descartes, "Preface to the Reader," Haldane and Ross, Vol. I, p. 138. I leave aside the sense in which ideas, *as* mental acts, may themselves be "objects" (of consciousness).

18. Descarte's claim that ideas are "forms" might suggest this reading. Cf. "Arguments" following "Second Replies" and "Fourth Replies," Haldane and Ross, II, pp. 52, 105. As I suggest, however, the notion of ideas as "forms" might also be connected with a conception of ideas as states of affairs (merely "formally distinct" from their constituents).

19. Spinoza, *On the Improvement of the Understanding*, tr. R. H. M. Elwes, in Gutmann, p. 12 (Gebhardt, Vol. II, p. 14): "The true idea of Peter is the objective essence of Peter." Cf. Letter 32: "I state that there exists in Nature an infinite power of thought, which in so far as it is infinite, contains in itself objectively the whole of Nature . . ." (Wolf translation slightly modified). Cf. also Part 2, Proposition VII, Note.

20. For a discussion of the suggestion, in connection with Sartre's theory of consciousness, see my "Two Problems of Being and Non-Being in Sartre's *Being and Nothingness*," *Philosophy and Phenomenological Research*, Vol. 39 (1977), pp. 167-86; I also discuss the

parallel between Spinoza in Sartre in "The Identity of Thought and Object in Spinoza," pp. 285-88.

21. Cf. Part 2, Proposition XL, Note 1. The present account provides a kind of middle way between a nominalistic and a realistic interpretation of Spinoza. For a discussion of the issue, see Francis S. Haserot, "Spinoza and the Status of Universals," *The Philosophical Review*, Vol. 59 (1950), pp. 469-92, reproduced in Kashap.

22. Thomas Mark, on the other hand, appears to identify Spinoza's "ideas" with object-ideas: *Spinoza's Theory of Truth* (New York: Columbia University Press, 1972), pp. 17-23. The basis for this is Spinoza's identification of an idea of Peter with the "objective essence" of Peter in the "Improvement." But, in the first place, it is by no means obvious why the "objective essence" of Peter should be regarded as an object-idea rather than an act-idea. Second, Marks's approach seems less able than mine to accommodate the possibility of ideas of ideas upon which Spinoza insists in the passage in question. An idea of an idea must be, according to Spinoza, *distinct* from the latter idea, yet also "objectively" identical with it. That is, the higher-order idea must just *be* the "objective essence" of the lower-order idea, which, in turn, is the objective essence of the original object. Unless the objective essence of the original object is itself a unique sort of *state of affairs* involving that object (and the higher-order idea in question consequently a unique sort of state of affairs involving *that* state of affairs), it is difficult to see how there could be *any* ground for distinguishing higher from lower-order ideas.

23. Evidence that Spinoza failed to distinguish clearly between attributes as special sorts of facts and as the universal forms *of* such facts may be found in Spinoza's desire in the "Improvement" to regard the ultimate "fixed and eternal things" both as *particulars* of some sort and as *universals* (Gutmann, p. 34 [Gebhardt, Vol. II, pp. 36-37]).

Infinite Understanding, *Scientia Intuitiva*, and *Ethics* I.16

MARGARET D. WILSON

I

Spinoza defines 'substance' partly in terms of the way in which substance is conceived: "By substance I understand that which is in itself, and is conceived through itself: that is, that the concept of which does not need the concept of another thing, from which it must be formed" (E I.Def. 3).[1] But the following definition of 'attribute' suggests an even more central connection between *this* concept and that of a certain way of knowing: "By attribute I understand that which understanding perceives of substance, as constituting its essence" (E I.Def. 4). And the link between attributes and understanding is emphasized by Spinoza even more strongly in an early letter to de Vries (Letter IX). He writes:

> . . . [B]y substance I understand that which is in itself and is conceived through itself: that is, the concept of which does not involve another thing. I understand the same by attribute. Except that it is called attribute with respect to understanding. Attributing to substance a certain such nature.[2]

Some scholars have held that this definition of 'attribute' in terms of the perception of understanding indicates that the attributes in Spinoza's system are merely subjective or ideal.[3] Others have argued very persuasively against this reading.[4] Perceptions of understanding—and particularly understanding's ideas of the divine attributes—are held by Spinoza to be intrinsically true and adequate (II.37, 38, 41). But a true idea by definition has an agreeing ideatum. It follows that there are (formally) attributes that correspond to understanding's perceptions of attributes. And I take it further to follow that the attributes really do constitute and "express" God's essence, for otherwise they could hardly be said to "agree" with understanding's perception of them. Indeed, *Ethics* I.15, scholium, contrasts extension or quantity as conceived *abstractly* or *superficially* ("as we imagine it"), with the same conceived by understanding ("as substance"). This contrast suggests that the stress on understanding in Spinoza's account of attributes is particularly *meant* to carry the implications of truth and adequacy.

The subjective interpretation did, of course, have a reasonable motive: it was intended to resolve the problem of reconciling the unity of substance with the plurality of attributes. This remains a very difficult problem in interpreting Spinoza —one that I will not address here. Rather, I will argue that the definition of 'attribute' in terms of understanding ties in with conspicuous but initially mysterious references to understanding and "infinite understanding" in a key proposition concerning the causality of God, *Ethics* I.16. (Though conspicuous, these references to understanding have received relatively little notice in the literature on Spinoza.[5]) My approach involves the claim that *Ethics* I.16 involves the exemplification on the level of infinity of *scientia intuitiva* or the third (and highest) "kind of knowledge." It is *scientia intuitiva* that gives rise to the intellectual love of God and our highest possible peace of mind; it is also involved in the eternity of our minds. Hence, one consequence of my argument will be the demonstration of important continuity between the latter notions, which dominate the discussion of freedom and salvation in Part V, and the more broadly "metaphysical" definitions and propositions of Parts I and II. My reading also has significant implications for the interpretation of God's causality, as asserted in *Ethics* I.16.

II

Spinoza alludes to "understanding" in several of the early propositions of Part I, as well as in the definition of attribute. I want to focus though on I.16, where the expression "infinite understanding" also appears (and for the first time). The proposition reads as follows:

> From the necessity of the divine nature, infinite [things] in infinite ways (that is, all [things] which can fall under infinite understanding) must follow.

> *Ex necessitate divinae naturae, infinita infinitis modis (hoc, est, omnia, quae sub intellectum infinitum cadere possunt) sequi debent.*

The demonstration of this proposition consists of just two sentences. In the first Spinoza asserts that the proposition "ought to be evident to anyone" who only considers that:

> from the given definition of anything understanding infers (*concludit*) a number of properties, which indeed necessarily follow from it (that is, from the essence itself of the thing), and the more, the more reality that the definition of the thing expresses, that is, the more reality that the essence of the thing involves.

But, Spinoza concludes:

> Since the divine nature has absolutely infinite attributes, each of which also expresses infinite essence in its kind [all this follows from the definition

Spinoza has given of God], from its necessity therefore infinite [things] in infinite ways (that is, all [things] which can fall under infinite understanding) must necessarily follow.

On initial reading, at any rate, *understanding* and *inference* certainly seem to be playing some important role in this proof. Comparing the first with the second sentence, we might even suppose that infinite understanding's inferential power plays some kind of *accessory* role in the derivation of things from the divine nature. But *this* cannot be right, for surely, on Spinoza's view, things just *do* follow with necessity from the divine nature: they do not need something different from that nature to bring them about. And Spinoza's remarks elsewhere clearly indicate that infinite understanding is *not* part of the divine nature: it is merely the *idea Dei* or an infinite mode under the attribute of thought.[6] So perhaps we should, taking heed of the parentheses, construe the references to infinite understanding in this proposition and proof as merely some sort of unimportant *obiter dictum*. But then why are the references there at all? Why would Spinoza muddle one of his key propositions with such distractions?

A more satisfying but (I am going to suggest) still inadequate explanation is the following. Spinoza clearly wishes to oppose the idea that God's creative activity involves a voluntary selection among the things existing in his understanding (as in the Leibnizian picture). He therefore mentions infinite understanding in the statement and demonstration of Proposition I.16 just to underline his view that God's understanding of things does not exceed in scope the things he actually brings into existence.

This explanation is inadequate because—I hope to show—the references to understanding in I.16 have a broader significance for the overall interpretation of the *Ethics*. They signal, namely, the involvement of this proposition, together with the definition of attribute, with *scientia intuitiva*.

In *Ethics* II.40 Scholium 2 Spinoza explains *scientia intuitiva* in the following terms: "This kind of knowing proceeds from an adequate idea of the formal essence of some attributes of God to an adequate knowledge of the essence of things."[7] I will argue that this definition fits exactly the role ascribed to infinite understanding in I.16—with several interesting implications for the interpretation of the content of the proposition.

As we noted in connection with the definition of 'attribute', understanding perceives the attributes adequately, and indeed can only perceive them adequately. Further, I think it is clear enough from what has been said that in perceiving the essence of substance, understanding perceives it "under" an attribute—or "attributes to substance a certain such nature." (See also E I.10S.) But the notion of inference or conclusion introduced in Proposition I.16 certainly suggests a "proceeding from . . . to."[8] So, to show that Proposition I.16 involves an exemplification, on the level of infinity, of *scientia intuitiva*, I think that we need to do only one thing. We need only show that Spinoza conceives of infinite understanding as proceeding (inferring) from its adequate ideas of the formal essences of the attributes of God *to an adequate knowledge of the essence of things*.

Now, Spinoza makes quite clear in the subsequent propositions and demonstrations that the *"infinita infinitis modis"* do at least *include* the essences of things. For example, in Proposition 25 of Part I (scholium), he observes that "God is the efficient cause not only of the existence of things but also of their essence," citing I.16. But does infinite understanding form *adequate* ideas of the essences of things that it infers from the essence of God's attributes (as the definition of *scientia intuitiva* would further require)? There are strong grounds for saying it does. According to Proposition 40 of Part II, "Those ideas are . . . adequate which follow in the mind from ideas which are adequate in it." And in I.16 *infinita infinitis modis* are precisely said to "follow" (*sequi*) from the ideas of God's attributes in infinite understanding—which, as we have noted, must be adequate. Also, Spinoza asserts in the proof of V.17 that "all ideas, as they are related to God, are true; that is to say, are adequate." I will take this as sufficient evidence at the present stage of argument. (There are some difficulties about the point, though, which I will mention later.)

It seems then that I.16 does portray infinite understanding as proceeding from the "adequate idea . . . of some attributes of God to an adequate knowledge of the essence of things"—and hence as complying with the definition of *scientia intuitiva*. But, one might object, I.16 still does not conform *exactly* to the definition. For, as we have just seen, Spinoza relates this proposition to the claim that the essences *and existences* of things follow from the divine nature. But *scientia intuitiva* seems to have to do with essences in contrast to existences.

This is a reasonable objection but one that can be answered. And the answer bears in an interesting way on the interpretation of I.16 itself.

Later in the *Ethics*, when Spinoza refers back to this proposition, he at least twice indicates the sort of existence or reality that it asserts to follow from the divine nature must *not* be confused with "existence at a certain time and place." On the contrary, it has to do with a type of existence that Spinoza gives us rather clear license to construe in terms of "essence." Consider the scholium to Proposition 45 of Part II. The proposition itself reads: "Any idea of any body, or singular thing, existing in act, necessarily involves the eternal and infinite essence of God." The scholium refers us back to I.16.

> Here by existence I do not understand duration, that is, existence as it is conceived abstractly, and as a certain kind of quantity. For I speak of the very nature of existence, which is attributed to singular things, because [*propterea quod*] infinite [things] in infinite ways follow from the eternal necessity of the nature of God (see Prop. 16., p. I). I speak, I say, of the existence itself of singular things, as they are in God. For, even though any singular thing is determined by another to a certain mode of existing, nevertheless the power, by which any thing perseveres in existence, follows from the eternal necessity of the nature of God.[9]

But the power, by which a thing perseveres in existence, is characterized by Spinoza as the "actual essence" of the thing itself (E III.7). This characterization suggests that "the existence itself of singular things, insofar as they are in God" may be identified with the essences of things (in a certain special sense). And this is just the sort of "existence of things" that I.16 asserts to follow from the attributes of God. Hence, infinite understanding's inference even of "existences" in Proposition I.16 actually is subsumable under Spinoza's account of *scientia intuitiva*.

Ethics V provides further support for the proposed interpretation of I.16. For example, Proposition 29 of Part V reads as follows:

> Whatever the mind understands under the aspect of eternity, it does not understand from the fact that it conceives the present actual existence of the body, but from the fact that it conceives the essence of the body under the aspect of eternity.

The scholium to this proposition refers specifically to II.45, which I cited just above. The scholium reads:

> Things are conceived by us as actual in two ways, either as they exist with relation to a certain time and place, or as we conceive them to be contained in God, and to follow from the necessity of the divine nature. But those which are conceived in this second way as true or real, we conceive them under the aspect of eternity, and their ideas involve the eternal and infinite essence of God, as we showed in Proposition 45 of Part II.[10]

Taken together these two passages—and others from Part V could be cited—seem clearly to indicate that Spinoza distinguishes two senses of 'existence' or 'being-actual', only one of which relates to what infinite understanding infers according to *Ethics* I.16. The "existence" of things that infinite understanding infers from the divine attributes must be distinguished from their duration through time or at a certain place. Proposition I.16 specifies the inference of the essences of things from the essence of God: it tells us that (in the words of V.22, which also makes use of I.16) "in God there necessarily exists an idea which expresses the essence of this or that body under the aspect of eternity."

If I am right, then, Proposition I.16 has considerably broader significance and implication than is usually noticed. It does not merely tell us that all things follow "from the necessity of the divine nature" (or by necessity from the divine nature)[11] and that *everything* comprehended by infinite understanding does so "follow." It also relates this fundamental statement about the origin of beings in God to the concept of the third kind of knowledge, which is only explicitly developed later. Both Proposition I.16 and *scientia intuitiva* play important roles in Spinoza's development of his ethical and (loosely speaking) eschatological views in Part V. I hope that my interpretation, by showing the connection between this key proposition of Part I and the concept of knowledge explained in Part II, will be suggestive also as to the interpretation of Part V. More particularly, I hope it will advance efforts to interpret the *Ethics* as a truly unified work, in which metaphysical, epistemological, ethical, and eschatological themes are quite rationally and purposively intermingled.

I will not attempt here to apply my interpretation of I.16 to the detailed interpretation of the proposition of Part V. However, the proposed reading of I.16 as relating to the concept of *scientia intuitiva* does have one particular implication that seems worth pointing out. I mentioned above that the references to infinite understanding in the proposition might be construed as Spinoza's way of underscoring his opposition to the voluntarist view that God *selects* the things to be brought into existence from *among* the things he understands. But, at least in its Leibnizian version,[12] the voluntarist position has to do with creation in the sense of bringing into existence at a time and place. And, according to my reading of I.16, nothing about existence at a certain time or place (or about "actual" being in the corresponding sense) is supposed to be established by I.16. If this reading is correct, then, the proposition does not establish quite as complete and direct an opposition between Spinoza's metaphysics and, say, Leibniz's as might be supposed. Spinoza need not—indeed cannot—be construed as saying that everything that falls under the divine understanding exists in the sense of being instantiated at a time and place or of "having duration." Rather, he holds that everything that falls under the infinite understanding has *some sort of being* in the divine attributes (such as extension). (This result also accords well with Spinoza's statement that the "ideas of non-existent modes" have their ideata "in the attributes of God"—a claim crucial to his proof [in Propositions V.21-40] that the human mind is eternal.) Of course, even on this reading of I.16, Spinoza still differs from Leibniz in holding that all of God's ideas have *ideata* or objects that are *in some sense* actual. However, at least as far as Proposition I.16 goes, he need not be differing from Leibniz to the extent of denying that in *one* sense of 'existent' or 'actual' not everything in God's understanding is existent or actual.[13] (What is most peculiar is that Spinoza regards the notion of existence or being-actual involved in this second, commonsensically more obvious sense as an "abstraction."[14])

Now to consider some problems.

III

The reading of I.16 that I am proposing leads us into several difficulties. I believe that only one—the first to be considered—is a problem for the interpretation itself. The other difficulties I will mention seem to arise within Spinoza's system independently of the connection I am suggesting between I.16 and *scientia intuitiva*. They are relevant to my interpretation without being generated by it.

The first problem I want to consider has both a philosophical and a textual aspect. Philosophically, one may argue that my interpretation implausibly leaves the determination of existence *in the sense of duration* (or existence at a time and place) outside the scope of Spinoza's major statement on the origin of things in God. In fact, my reading of I.16 leaves the significance of I.16 rather unclear in general, for *what is* the "very nature of existence" in contrast to "existence at a time and place" or duration? Textually, the interpretation of I.16 that I am proposing runs up against the fact that some later propositions of Part I (and Part II) seem to suggest that the "causality of God" delineated in *Ethics* I.16 does after all include the determination of things' duration. In particular, in the corollary to Proposition 24 of Part I—"The essence of things produced by God does not involve existence" —Spinoza comments: ". . . [T]he essence [of things] cannot be the cause either of their existence *or of their duration*, but God only, to whose nature alone it pertains to exist" (italics added). This statement certainly suggests that Spinoza is including the duration of things in the scope of God's causality. And subsequent propositions explicitly presuppose that I.16 has established that God is the cause of all things, *both* of their essence and of their existence.

Now, I believe that the *textual* aspect of this objection to my interpretation can be met, though admittedly not in a philosophically satisfying manner. Spinoza does indicate that God is the cause of things' duration in I.24, but he does *not* there refer us back to I.16. And the subsequent passages, which do refer back to I.16, contrast existence and essence under the divine causality but make no mention of duration. It is, therefore, possible after all to render these propositions consistent with II.45 and V.29, which I have relied on in defending the view that I.16 exclusively exemplifies the third kind of knowledge. For one can, consistent with the former texts, construe Spinoza's position in the following way: (1) Though Spinoza may assume that God is the cause of the duration of things, he does not base this claim on *Ethics* I.16. (2) When he speaks of God as cause of the essences and existence of things in the later propositions of Part I, he has in mind existence in the recherché sense he later contrasts with duration ("the very nature of existence"). Existence in this recherché sense may (according to II.45 and III.7) be identified with "the actual essence" of things.

Unfortunately, this reading does leave the reference to the causing of duration in I.24 a seemingly inexplicable loose end. But such a loose end seems unavoidable in any case, for Proposition 45 of Part II does quite explicitly imply that the divine inference of I.16 is *not* an inference to the existence of things at a certain time and place.

The second problem that needs to be considered has to do with the transition in Spinoza's system from infinite attributes to finite modes. It is a problem that is often mentioned in the literature, and it does not particularly weigh against my reading of I.16 as exemplifying the concept of *scientia intuitiva*.[15] But it does have a special connection with my reading.

How is it *possible* that infinite understanding should infer adequate ideas of the essences of things from adequate ideas of the formal essences of certain attributes of God? Spinoza tells us in I.21 that "all [things] that follow from the absolute nature of any attribute of God" must be infinite and eternal, i.e., the infinite modes. In the proof he comments: "Hence that which so follows from the necessity of the nature of any attribute cannot have determinate existence or duration." The language here is highly reminiscent of that of I.16. The statement, in fact, can happily be seen as confirming my claim that I.16 does not have to do with the origin of things' duration. Unfortunately, though, I.21 goes further than this, for it seems to indicate that only *infinite* and eternal modes—or ideas of such modes—could follow or be inferred from "the necessity of the divine nature."[16]

E I.21 thus presents grave difficulties for interpreting the *"sequi"* of I.16, difficulties that arise independently of my attempt to relate that proposition to the concept of *scientia intuitiva*. To express the point bluntly, Spinoza seems both to affirm and to deny that finite things "follow from" the divine nature. But we are now in a position to see some further complications of this problem. It is not *just* a problem for the reading of E I.16 but *also* a problem for the concept of *scientia intuitiva* — even if I am wrong in regarding the two as intimately related — for we can have *scientia intuitiva* just insofar as we *can* proceed *from* adequate knowledge of the essence of God's attributes *to* adequate knowledge of the essences of things. If this is not possible in the case of finite things, then it appears that they cannot at all legitimately be included under *scientia intuitiva* any more than under the derivation of I.16 (even if these are, contrary to my suggestion, distinct). The texts do seem to me confusing and unsettled on this point — quite a fundamental one, unfortunately, for Spinoza's "necessitarianism," his epistemology, and his theory of human happiness and salvation.

In originally relating I.16 to *scientia intuitiva* I partly relied on a proposition affirming that all ideas in God are adequate. I used this to show that infinite understanding conforms to *scientia intuitiva* in that it infers to adequate ideas of the essences of things, but I also mentioned having some reservations about the point. We have just seen that there are general difficulties in understanding the possibility of inferring, or proceeding, from the divine attributes to anything finite. It is now appropriate to note that the arguments Spinoza offers for his claim about the adequacy of God's ideas (V.17; II.36) are not very satisfactory. In these arguments Spinoza in effect holds that the *truth* of all ideas as related to God entails the *adequacy* of all ideas related to God. But God's ideas are all true just because they all have corresponding ideata. And "adequacy," as Spinoza himself defines it, seems to involve the additional condition of possessing all the *intrinsic properties* of a true idea (II. Def. 4). This awkward fallacy in Spinoza's argument may be a reflection of his deep difficulty in rationalizing the transition (in God) from infinite attribute (or its idea) to finite mode (or *its* idea).

The study of I.16 brings up another problem. This again, I think, is a difficulty that could not be avoided by any reasonable reading of I.16. As I briefly suggested in a previous remark, Spinoza clearly and firmly distinguishes the status of infinite understanding from that of the attribute of thought. He argues that infinite understanding is a *mode* of the attribute of thought. This, of course, means it is not self-caused, or "conceived through itself." Yet, by I.16 it has ideas of the attributes of God. Now, surely if it is a mode, all its ideas (including our minds) must be modes. But, famously, Spinoza holds that ideas and their ideata must be causally parallel. There seems to be an outright contradiction between the latter notion and the supposition that "other-caused" ideas take as their ideata self-caused attributes. Maybe there is an obvious answer to this dilemma, but I have not been able to see it.

Thus, my interpretation of I.16 in terms of the concept of *scientia intuitiva* by no means solves the major problems of interpretation and problems of apparent inconsistency in Spinoza's system. Indeed, it leads directly into some of them.

However, I do not think it creates any *new* problems of this sort. And it does, I hope, help to illuminate the important intimacy among the metaphysical, epistemological, and ethical aspects of Spinoza's thought.

IV

In conclusion, I wish to turn to a different sort of issue. It is, I think, a common experience of students of Spinoza to feel torn between – or to alternate between – two conflicting conceptions of his philosophical stature. Some of the time, one is mainly of the opinion that his system is just too hopelessly shot through with inconsistency, fallacy, obscurity, and idiosyncrasy to *deserve* the painstaking analysis it seems to demand of the reader. At other times, one may be more impressed with the startlingly original and even powerful character of Spinoza's underlying philosophical conceptions. The treatment of creation, or the origin of dependent being, in Part I – and perhaps particularly in I.16 – provides a good example of why this should be so. We have already surveyed a number of serious – indeed critical – problems with which it is bound up. On the other hand, the idea that things arise *necessarily*, as if by deductive inference, from God or nature is surely a bold and provocative one, however exactly it should be interpreted. It is a view that in some ways, at least, does provide a direct and intriguing alternative to the more traditional voluntarist conception defended (for instance) by Leibniz. Therefore, I would like finally to comment briefly on the following question: How successful is Spinoza in his attempt to establish that his form of necessitarianism is more in conformity with reason than is traditional voluntarism?[17]

The core of the voluntarist position is, I take it, the following: The world is, and is *as* it is, because God *chose* that this be so. He could have chosen differently and so things could have been different. It could even have been the case that he abstained from creating anything. Spinoza surely does make some cogent or plausible points against this view. Some are familiar, such as the argument that an all-perfect God would have no reason to decide to bring into being any thing outside himself. (This precise sort of difficulty does not arise for Spinoza, since his God does not do anything on purpose and hence *requires* no "reason for acting."[18]) Some of Spinoza's other objections to voluntarism are much more original. He argues, for instance, that, if God could have chosen differently, there must be more than one possible divine nature. But the ontological argument will apply to each. Therefore, there would have to be more than one God! (I. 33).[19] But one of the most interesting and fundamental points of contrast between Spinoza and his voluntarist opponents is found in their respective concepts of omnipotence. And, although Spinoza makes great fun of his opponents' views on this subject, I do not think he provides a coherent refutation.

Spinoza, as I read him, holds that God's omnipotence requires that everything in God's power actually comes into being. In other words: "G is omnipotent" entails "G brings about everything in its power to bring about." His opponents, he indicates, deny this proposition on the riduculous grounds that, unless there are unrealized possibles in God's understanding, his power to create would have come to an end! (And, hence, I suppose, be limited.)

> . . . [A]lthough they conceive God as actually understanding to the highest degree, they nevertheless do not believe he can bring it about that all [things] which he actually understands, exist; for they think they would in that way destroy God's power. They say that if he had created all [things] that are in his understanding, then he would be able to create nothing more, which they believe is inconsistent with God's omnipotence . . . (E I.17s).

Now, I do not know whether any of Spinoza's contemporaries actually argued like this, but certainly the voluntarist position can be stated in more plausible terms. The voluntarist may contend that omnipotence requires the power *to bring about or prevent* any possible state of affairs and therefore requires choice—the choice of which to do. In other words: "G is omnipotent" entails "it is in G's power to determine, for any possible contingent state of affairs, whether or not it obtains."[20] Presumably, Spinoza would insist that such a conception of omnipotence rests on an illegitimate anthropomorphization of God, an extrapolation from a common conception of human power to God. But he does not systematically defend or explain his own intuition. Perhaps he supposed that the demonstration of I.16 was sufficient to settle the issue in his favor. If so, I think he was wrong.[21]

Notes

1. E is used as abbreviation of *Ethica*. Translations are my own. Geb. (below) refers to *Spinoza opera*, ed. C. Gebhardt (Heidelberg: Carl Winters, 1926) (4 vols.).

2. Geb. IV, p. 46. (The peculiar punctuation follows Gebhardt's text.) Throughout the paper I translate '*intellectus*' as 'understanding'. In an earlier version of the paper, I frequently used 'the understanding'. At a Spinoza symposium, E. M. Curley objected to this phrasing on the grounds that it introduces a specious definiteness where (on Curley's view) Spinoza is only talking about *an* understanding or *some* understanding or other. (The Latin, of course, has no article at all.) Curley made this point in connection with more substantive criticisms. Although I was not persuaded by his other substantive criticisms, I have dropped the definite article throughout for the sake of consistency and to avoid the appearance of question-begging on the issue.

3. See especially H. A. Wolfson, *The Philosophy of Spinoza* (Cambridge, Mass.: Harvard University Press, 1934), pp. 142-57.

4. See especially Francis S. Haserot, "Spinoza's Definition of Attribute," in S. Paul Kashap, ed., *Studies in Spinoza* (Berkeley: University of California Press, 1972, originally published 1953); Martial Gueroult, *Spinoza: Dieu (Ethique, 1)* (Paris: Aubier-Montaigne, 1968), p. 50.

5. One exception is an unpublished manuscript by Genevieve Lloyd, *The Eternity of the Mind: A Study of Spinoza's Ethics*. Lloyd's approach is in some ways congruent to mine, though there are also substantial differences between our interpretations.

6. Cf. E II.4; 1.34.

7. Geb. II, p. 122.

8. My linking of the third kind of knowledge with E I.16 seems to entail a different understanding of 'proceeds' in the definition of the former than that sketched by Guttorm Fløistad, "Spinoza's Theory of Knowledge Applied to the *Ethics*," in Kashap, pp. 271-72. Fløistad, incidentally, provides a useful gloss on the term 'formal essence'.

9. Cf. E V.22. See also E. M. Curley, *Spinoza's Metaphysics* (Cambridge, Mass.: Harvard University Press, 1969), pp. 141-42.

10. This passage is also cited, in a similar connection, by Joel I. Friedman in "Spinoza's Denial of Free Will in Man and God," in Jon Wetlesen, ed., *Spinoza's Philosophy of Man: Papers Presented at the Scandinavian Spinoza Symposium, 1977* (Oslo: 1978), pp. 51-84.

11. It is not unreasonable to wonder whether "follow *from the necessity* of the divine nature" implies "follow *with necessity from* the divine nature"; however, both the demonstration of E I.16 and Spinoza's subsequent use of the proposition idicate that he does intend this implication.

12. I mention Leibniz in this connection because his philosophy seems to provide in some ways an excellent *example* of the *type* of view Spinoza wants to oppose (and one with which I happen to be familiar). I do not mean to suggest that Spinoza was reacting against his successor!

13. I have learned in discussion that quite a few people want to attribute to Spinoza the view that everything in God's understanding has temporal or durational existence at some time or other. This issue seems to me an obscure one textually. There is also the problem of compossibility: Is it reasonable to hold that everything in God's understanding is compossible with everything else in the sense that, given enough time, it is possible that all these things exist? Alan Donagan attributes to Spinoza a view about incompatible essences in "Spinoza's Proof of Immortality" (*Spinoza: A Collection of Critical Essays*, Marjorie Grene, ed. [Notre Dame, Ind.: University of Notre Dame Press, 1979; originally published 1973], pp. 253-55). (Like Fløistad [see n. 8], Donagan gives some help with the concept of "formal essence," which he contrasts with "actual essence." However, Donagan does not appear to take note of the fact [argued above] that Spinoza recognizes *two* senses of 'actual',)

14. '*Abstracte*' and '*abstractus*' are not words that Spinoza uses often. See, however, E I.15S (Geb. II, p. 59), and Letter XII (to L. Meyer) (Geb. IV, pp. 56-57).

15. See, for instance, Alasdair MacIntyre, "Spinoza, Benedict (Baruch)," *The Encyclopedia of Philosophy*, ed. Paul Edwards, (New York: Macmillan, 1967), Vol. 7, p. 535.

16. In "The Causality of God in Spinoza's Philosophy," *Canadian Journal of Philosophy*, Vol. II, No. 2 (December, 1972), A. J. Watt argues that the direct causality of God, as asserted in E I.16, should be understood as the causing of *essences*. On this point, of course, my own interpretation largely follows his. But Watt also seems to hold—what I would deny—that this construal of 1.16 helps avoid problems about the emergence of the finite from the infinite.

17. Of course, if my foregoing argument is right, there is not a *complete and direct* opposition between Spinoza and traditional voluntarism, at least as far as E I.16 goes (since Spinoza is not there concerned with the bringing about of temporal existence). I think there is still enough opposition to consider intelligibly the issue taken up in this section.

18. However, the problem about "how" the finite modes arise from the infinite attributes in his system may perhaps be regarded as somewhat parallel.

19. I sketch a similar line of reasoning in relation to a problem of interpreting Leibniz's views about modality in "Possible Gods," *The Review of Metaphysics*, Vol. XXXII, No. 4 (June, 1979), pp. 717-33.

20. Curiously, Spinoza himself touches on this conception at the beginning of the scholium to E 1.17.

21. I am grateful to more people than I could reasonably name here for helpful comments on earlier versions of this paper, many of which have led to changes in argument and structure. But I must particularly thank Eyjolfur Emilsson, E. M. Curley, George L. Kline, and Joel Friedman for detailed comments and criticisms.

Leibniz on the Two Great Principles of All Our Reasonings

R. C. SLEIGH, JR.

In the *Monadology*, Leibniz said:

> 31. Our reasonings are based on two great principles; the *principle of contradiction*, by virtue of which we judge to be false that which involves a contradiction, and true that which is opposed or contradictory to the false;

> 32. and the *principle of sufficient reason*, by virtue of which we consider that no fact can be real or existing and no proposition can be true unless there is a sufficient reason, why it should be thus and not otherwise . . . (G/7/612 *Monadology* § 31, § 32).

Similar remarks are to be found in a number of works completed in the 1680s, for example, G/7/199 (Schrecker 13), where Leibniz said: "I use two principles in demonstration . . . ," and *A Specimen of Discoveries* (G/7/309 [MP75]), where Leibniz said: "There are two first principles of all our reasonings . . . ." These passages might suggest that Leibniz viewed the principle of contradiction and the principle of sufficient reason as principles of inference governing reasoning much in the manner in which we might view *modus ponens*, for example. I think, however, that so construing Leibniz would be incorrect. No doubt Leibniz made original contributions to logic, but most of his contributions presuppose that the basic concept of validity is captured by standard syllogistic inference. Leibniz was not of the opinion that the classic rules governing syllogistic inference could be reduced to the principle of contradiction and the principle of sufficient reason.

So, when Leibniz said, "Our reasonings are based on two great principles . . ." (*Monadology* § 31), he was not construing the principles of contradiction and sufficient reason as rules of inference that govern our reasonings. What then? As premises that occur in our reasonings? Recollect our passage from *Specimen* (G/7/309 [MP 75]: "There are two first principles of *all* our reasonings" (emphasis mine). This quantifier is implicit in the other passages noted. Surely Leibniz was not expressing the absurd view that there is no case of correct human reasoning lacking both the principle of contradiction and the principle of sufficient reason as premises. Hence, there is a problem of interpretation concerning the sense of the expression "based on" in the claim that "our reasonings are *based on* two great principles" (emphasis mine).

It is reasonably clear in the passage cited that Leibniz intended to claim that there are *exactly* two great principles upon which all our reasonings are based. He was not there claiming that there are these first principles, contradiction and sufficient reason, and, perhaps, thirty-two others as well. But, when we explore the relevant texts in detail, we find other candidates. The law of contradiction remains ensconced in its position, secure from rivals. By contrast, sufficient reason appears to have supplementers, perhaps even competitors. The principal ones are the principle of perfection (fitness, best) and what I call experimenta. (In the Latin texts propositions that would normally be expressed by first-person, present-tense sentences about immediate experience are called "experimenta.")

Consider this representative text:

There are two primary propositions: one, the principle of necessary truths, *what implies a contradiction is false*, the other, the principle of contingent truths, *what is more perfect, i.e. has a greater reason, is true* (Grua 287).

This passage contains an intriguing blend of the principles of perfection and sufficient reason. Do we have two principles here? One and a half?

Then there is the following passage from a study of Locke:

My opinion is therefore that one must take nothing for a first principle except experiences and the axiom of identity or (what comes to the same thing) of contradiction (A/6/6/4 [Langley 13-14]).

What happened to the principle of sufficient reason?

We seem, then, to have problems concerning just what are the fundamental principles as well as what it might mean to say that our reasonings are based on them. There are more problems.

Many of Leibniz's pronouncements about first principles are accompanied by an assignment of a realm to each principle—a realm the elements of which are said to be based on or to depend upon the principle in question. These assignments are of three types.

In the first type, the realms are characterized in terms of the modality of the propositions falling under them. In all instances of this type, necessary propositions are assigned to the realm of the principle of contradiction and all contingent propositions to another principle (or principles). Compare G/7/301 (L 349/227), where contingent propositions are assigned to the principle of sufficient reason, with Grua 301, where contingents are assigned to the principle of perfection.

In the second type, the realms are characterized in terms of standard areas of human inquiry. Thus, in his second paper to Clarke (G/7/355-6 [LC 15-16]), Leibniz stated that the principle of contradiction is the foundation for all of mathematics, whereas the principle of sufficient reason is the foundation for metaphysics, natural theology, and ". . . the physical principles independent of mathematics, i.e., the principles of dynamics or force." A similar distribution of areas of inquiry occurs in *The Principles of Nature and Grace* with the exception that some of the principles of force (specifically, conservation principles) are ascribed to the principle of perfection (G/6/603 [MP 200-1]).

In the third type, the realms are characterized in terms of the kind of knowledge that correct application of the relevant principles yields. Thus, at C 515 (MP 9) contradiction and sufficient reason are said to be first principles of a prior knowledge, whereas experimenta are said to be first principles of a posteriori knowledge.

The slightest acquaintance with Leibniz's views about the modality of propositions within the various sciences and the relation of the a priori/a posteriori knowledge distinction to the necessary/contingent proposition distinction will suggest problems of interpretation.

We must also be sensitive to a distinction Leibniz utilized between the domain in which a principle *holds* and the realm of propositions that *depend* on that principle. Thus, in a book review appended to *The Theodicy*, Leibniz claimed that both contradiction and sufficient reason hold for all true propositions but that necessary truths depend upon contradiction, whereas contingent truths depend upon sufficient reason (G/6/413 [Huggard 419-20]). A slight variation on this theme may be found in *De Contingentia* (Grua 303), where Leibniz claimed that necessary truths depend upon the principle of contradiction, that contingent truths depend upon the principle of sufficient reason, but that there must be something in common between necessary and contingent truths (presumably since both are truths). What is common, according to this text, is given by the principle of sufficient reason.

Many of Leibniz's pronouncements about first principles mention, or at least allude to, hierarchical relations holding among them. The most familiar pattern is that found in *The Monadology*, where contradiction and sufficient reason appear to be presented as independent principles, with the principle of perfection supplementing or falling under sufficient reason in some way. But in Section II we will consider a text that suggests that the principle of contradiction is king and that sufficient reason may be derived from it.

Various familiar interpretative strategies may be applied to this farrago. Recent scholarship has made it abundantly clear that Leibniz's views altered and developed over time. Indeed, careful scrutiny of the dates of the relevant texts does, I believe, mitigate the problem posed by the role of experimenta as first principles (see Section IV). But the most assiduous care with respect to chronology and possible development will leave us with much of our tangled web. Recent scholarship has also made it clear that Leibniz was quite capable and, indeed, prone to carry on simultaneous discussions (with himself as well as others) of the same topic at a number of different levels of sophistication. Knowing the various levels of analysis on which he tended to operate, we can formulate plausible hypotheses that will serve to unravel some of the knots involved without the need for excision. In addition, close textual scrutiny will show that some of the principal phrases in this matter, e.g., 'principle of sufficient reason,' 'based on,' are systematically ambiguous as employed by Leibniz, independent of the level of analysis involved.

My supposition is that careful study of the relevant texts, employing the ideas sketched above, would permit us to escape the interpretive labyrinth outlined. This essay focuses primarily on a sophsticated level of analysis to be found in Leibniz's writings after 1678 — the connection of the "great principles of reasoning" with the concept-containment account of truth. Various "deep forms" from this level of analysis will be compared with more common forms.

Distinct principles were cited by Leibniz as *the* principle of contradiction; the same holds for the principle of sufficient reason. Let us note some and winnow the field a bit.

THE PRINCIPLE OF CONTRADICTION

(a) For any proposition p, p is either true or false.
(b) For any proposition p, p is not both true and false (G/7/299 [L 347/225], C 401 [MP 93]).
(c) For any proposition p, if p implies a contradiction, then p is false.
(d) For any proposition p, if p is false, then not-p is true (*Monadology* § 31, G/7/199 [Schrecker 13], Grua 287).
(e) For any proposition p, if p is an identical proposition, then p is true (G/7/309 [MP 75], C 183, G/7/355 [LC 15], C 1).

Each of these may be a distinct proposition; (a) through (d) seem to involve a combination of what we might call the law of noncontradiction and the law of excluded middle; (e) appears to be a separate matter. Leibniz saw a connection. (See *Monadology* § 51.) Consider any identical proposition; its opposite is an express contradiction; hence, via (c), it is false; so, via (d), the original identity must be true.[1] Indeed, in terms of Leibniz's various claims about the connection of the principle of contradiction with the concept containment account of truth, it is (e) that is fundamental.

THE PRINCIPLE OF SUFFICIENT REASON

Paragraph 32 from the *Monadology* (previously quoted) provides in one breath two versions of the principle of sufficient reason: one a quasi-causal principle, the other a principle concerning the truth conditions for propositions. Consider:

(f) For any fact (or event or entity) e that obtains (or exists), there is some reason why it obtains (or exists) and is not otherwise.
(g) For any proposition p, if p is true, then there is a sufficient reason why p is true.

Obviously, these principles are closely related. It is from (f) that Leibniz derived a causal principle; it is clearly close in form and content to (g). More will be said on the relation of (f) to (g) at the close of Section II. For the present, given our focus on Leibniz's conception of truth, we will concentrate on (g).

Leibniz regarded (g) as a "common axiom." (See G/2/56 [M 64].) There is a deeper version of the principle of sufficient reason to be found in Leibniz, namely:

(h) For any proposition p, if p is true, then there is an a priori proof that p is true (G/7/300-301 [L 348-49/266], G/7/44, C 513 [MP 7]. Grua 287, G/7/295 [MP 14], C 402 [MP 94], Le Roy 47 [DM 18-19], G/4/438 [DM 22], G/2/62 [M 71], C 518 [MP 87], G/7/309 [MP 75]).

(h) is based on an equivalence, which Leibniz expressed in this passage from the correspondence with Arnauld: ". . . nothing exists without a reason, i.e., every truth has its a priori proof . . ." (G/2/62 [M 71]). The equivalence is:

(i) For any proposition p, there is a sufficient reason why p is true if and only if there is an a priori proof of p (G/7/301 [L 349/226], C 513-14 [MP 7-8], Grua 287, G/7/295-96 [MP 15], C 519 [MP 88], C 402 [MP 93], G/4/438 [DM 22], G/2/62 [M 71], G/7/309 [MP 75]).

(i) involves contentious doctrines from the very depths of Leibniz's system. My view is that Leibniz ultimately rejected (h) and (i), replacing them by more subtle principles. This view is outlined at the close of Section I.

(e), our preferred form of the principle of contradiction, and (g), the "common form" of the principle of sufficient reason, both bear centrally on the notion of truth. In a book review appended to *The Theodicy*, Leibniz stated, ". . . one may say in a sense that these two principles are contained in the definition of the true and the false" (G/6/414 [Huggard 419]). In Section I, I say something about my understanding of the development of Leibniz's conception of truth. In Section II, I return to the questions previously noted concerning Leibniz's two great principles.

I

In this section, an account of the development of Leibniz's views on truth (better, one strand thereof) is developed. The account is controversial, and yet little supporting evidence is presented. Some of the evidence and considerable textual support is to be found in "Truth and Sufficient Reason in the Philosophy of Leibniz" (my contribution to *Leibniz: Critical and Interpretive Essays*, edited by Michael Hooker, published by the University of Minnesota Press in 1982).

To make matters manageable, attention is restricted to propositions in subject-predicate form that are categorical, affirmative, and either singular or universal. Sentential letters employed below are to be replaced by sentences expressing such. A basic, noncontroversial account of truth that Leibniz accepted throughout his career is this:

(1) P is true if and only if the predicate of p is in the subject of p.

Here, by the subject of a proposition Leibniz meant that of which the proposition predicates something, and by the predicate he meant that which is predicated of the subject. (See, for example, G/4/438 [DM 21] and G/2/52 [M 58].)

A more daring account of truth to be found in Leibniz's writings after 1678 is this:

(2) p is true if and only if the concept of the predicate of p is contained in the concept of the subject of p.

Propositions (1) and (2) are equivalences with the same left-hand component. One would hope to find textual evidence for the following equivalence:

(3) The predicate of p is in the subject of p if and only if the concept of the subject of p is contained in the concept of the predicate.

One does. I would draw particular attention to C 401-2 [MP 93-94], G/2/43 [M 47], and G/2/56 [M 63-64]. These passages suggest that Leibniz took the right-hand side of (3) as providing an analysis of the left-hand side. At G/2/56 [M 63-64] Leibniz stated: ". . . there must always be some foundation of the connection of the terms of a proposition which must be in their notions. *This is my main principle*" (emphasis mine). I take it that in this quotation the "terms" of a proposition are the entity (or entities) of which something is predicated and the entity predicated; the "notions" are the concepts that are constituents of the proposition. What Leibniz's "main principle" requires, then, is that the connection between substance and attribute, as well as the notion of truth, be explained in terms of relations internal to concepts. Why Leibniz held this "main principle" is one of the deepest questions that can be asked about his philosophy. The subject runs deeper than I intend to go in this paper.

Proposition (2) expresses an account of truth to which Leibniz was firmly committed from 1679 on. Clearly, (2) (particularly the implication from left to right) is the ground on which commentators have based the claim that Leibniz accepted the view that all true propositions (of the relevant variety) are analytic. (Whether that is a justifiable attribution will not be discussed here.) At approximately the same time, Leibniz formulated a doctrine about concept containment that, when applied to constituent concepts of a proposition (of the relevant variety), may be expressed thus:

(4) The concept of the predicate of p is contained in the concept of the subject of o if and only if there is an a priori proof of p.

Propositions (4) and (2) combine to yield what many regard as Leibniz's deepest account of truth, namely:

(5) p is true if and only if there is an a priori proof of p.

What is an a priori proof? That is a question worth a paper unto itself. Here is a rough account that will do for present purposes: Think of a proposition p (of the relevant variety) as an ordered pair whose first term is the subject concept of p and whose second term is the predicate concept of p. Think of the concepts involved as sets of properties. On this construal, an identical proposition is an ordered pair whose terms are sets of properties where the second term is a subset of the first. Think of complex concepts as arising from simple concepts by conjunction, and think of an analysis of a concept as a step-by-step decomposition of that concept into simpler components. An analysis of a proposition p is a sequence of ordered pairs the first term of which is p, with each subsequent pair just like its predecessor except that one concept is replaced by a set that constitutes a one-step analysis of it. Finally, we may say that such a sequence is an *a priori proof* of p provided that it commences with p and terminates with an identical proposition.

The process of proof just outlined is what Leibniz called reducing a proposition to an identity. (See, for example, C 518 [MP 87].) Not surprisingly, then, we find textual support for the following:

(6) p is true if and only if p is, or is reducible to, an identical proposition.

Consider the following *slight* extension of (e):

(e′) For any proposition p, if p is or is reducible to an identical proposition, then p is true.

Suppose we take (e′) as the principle of contradiction. We note that (e′) may be put equivalently as:

(e″) For any proposition p, if there is an a priori proof of p, then p is true.

Recollect:

(h) For any proposition p, if p is true, then there is an a priori proof of p;

and

(5) p is true if and only if there is an a priori proof of p.

Taking (e″), (h), and (5) as Leibniz's deep forms of, respectively, the principle of contradiction, the principle of sufficient reason, and the concept-containment account of truth, we arrive at Couturat's classic account: The two great principles are indeed "contained in the definition of the true . . ." because each is half (so to speak) of the deep account of truth and conjoined they yield the whole. (See Louis Couturat, *La Logique de Leibniz* [Paris: Presses Universitaires de France, 1901; reprinted in Hildesheim: Georg Olms, 1969, pp. 214-15].)

Unfortunately, it is not quite that simple. Leibniz thought of (1) as noncontroversial, as a datum requiring philosophical elucidation. He formulated (2) as a partial elucidation of (1); he never rejected (2) or (3). At about the same time, he formulated (4) and ancillary doctrines setting out the notions of concept analysis and a priori proof as elucidations of (2) (and, hence, as further elucidations of (1)). Almost immediately he came to see that (5) (and, hence (4)) lead to serious difficulties. The fundamental problem is to maintain a distinction between necessary and contingent truths. The problem is clearly displayed in *General Inquiries about the Analysis of Concepts and Truths*. Paragraph 40 (C 369 [P 59]) gives us essentially (6); i.e., a proposition is *true* just in case it is reducible to an identity; paragraphs 133 and 134 (C 388 [P 77]) give us essentially this: a proposition is *necessarily true* just in case it is reducible to an identity. One hopes something drastic has happened between paragraphs 40 and 133. It has. The doctrine of infinite analysis has been set forth.

A word about infinite analysis: Recollect the notion of an analysis of a proposition previously sketched. Recall that an *a priori proof* was characterized as a sequence of ordered pairs (of the appropriate sort) commencing with the proposition to be proved, with each subsequent pair just like its predecessor except that one concept is replaced by another constituting a one-step analysis of it, terminating in a pair that is an identical proposition. Think of a *proof sequence* for a proposition p as a sequence generated in the same way where there is some identical proposition q such that either the sequence terminates with q or, although it fails to terminate, it converges on q.[2] Notice that every a priori proof is a proof sequence, but not conversely.

Using the concepts described above, we may formulate the doctrine of infinite analysis as consisting in the following theses:

(7) p is true if and only if there is a proof sequence for p.

(8) p is necessarily true if and only if there is an a priori proof of p.

(9) p is contingently true if and only if there is a proof sequence for p but there is no a priori proof of p.

There are numerous passages in the texts that sustain the attribution of part of the doctrine of infinite analysis to Leibniz.[3] Here is a good example from the important essay "On Freedom."

A necessary proposition is one whose contradictory implies a contradiction, such as all identical propositions and all derivative propositions which are analyzable into identical propositions. . . .

But in the case of contingent truths, even though the predicate is in the subject, this can never be demonstrated of it, nor can the proposition ever be reduced to an . . . identity. Instead, the analysis proceeds to infinity . . . (FC 181, 182 [MP 108, 109]).

Note that these passages refer to the infinite analysis idea but that they make no *direct* reference to the notion of convergence that is central to our notion of a proof sequence. Direct reference and detailed discussion of convergence (with respect to the analysis of propositions) is to be found in *General Inquiries* (C 356-99 [P 47-87]) and *The Origin of Contingent Truths from an Infinite Process* (C 1-3). These texts support attributing (7) through (9) to Leibniz.

The doctrine of infinite analysis was Leibniz's official view by the end of the eighties. He never abandoned it. My claim is, then, that Leibniz retained (a) through (g), rejecting (h) and (i); that he retained (1) through (3), rejecting (4) through (6). In place of (some of) the rejected doctrines, he accepted (7) through (9). I suggest that in place of (h) and (i) we have, respectively:

(j) For any proposition p, if p is true, then there is a proof sequence for p;

and

(k) For any proposition p, there is a sufficient reason why p is true if and only if there is a proof sequence for p.[4]

Note, in passing, that (e″) may be sharpened to the following equivalence:

(e‴) For any proposition p, there is an a priori proof of p if and only if p is *necessarily* true.

Taking (e‴), (j), and (7) as Leibniz's revised deep forms of, respectively, the principle of contradiction, the principle of sufficient reason, and the concept-containment account of truth, we arrive at something like Rescher's account of the matter. (See Nicholas Rescher, *Leibniz: An Introduction to His Philosophy* [Totowa, N.J.: Rowman and Littlefield, 1979, pp. 23-25]). Rescher puts particular emphasis on one-half of (9), i.e., the implication from right to left:

(ℓ) For any proposition p, if there is a proof sequence for p but no a priori proof of p, then p is contingently true.

Rescher calls (ℓ) Leibniz's "principle of perfection." Perhaps, in fairness to Rescher, it should be said that he sees (ℓ) as a *deep form* of the principle of perfection. An important thesis of Rescher's account is the claim (p. 35) that the principle of perfection cannot be derived from the principles of contradiction and sufficient reason and that the three principles are logically independent. In Section II, I say something about the relations between the principles of contradiction and sufficient reason; in Section III, the focus is broadened to include the principle of perfection.

II

In an interesting paper, "An Unpublished Leibniz Manuscript on Metaphysics" (*Studia Leibnitiana*, Band II, Heft 2, 1975, pp. 161-89), Prof. Nicholas Jolley translates from a marginal comment in the manuscript, *Ad Christophori Stegmanni*:

> On several occasions I have observed that there is a pair of supreme principles of all our knowledge of things that is deduced a priori: the principle of contradiction, to avoid arguing against ourselves, and the principle of reason, to avoid judging that anything ever happens without a sufficient reason. It arises from the principle of contradiction.

Professor Jolley notes that Leibniz bracketed this marginal comment and added this note for a copyist: "Omit what is enclosed." Jolley comments on the passage that:

> Despite the impression he [Leibniz] conveys of repeating familiar ideas, the last statement here is puzzling, and is to my knowledge unparalleled in all Leibniz's writings which have so far appeared in print: indeed it gives an account of the relationship of the two great principles which is in conflict with Leibniz's standard pronouncements on the subject. Even in the texts published by Couturat, Leibniz constantly treats the principle of sufficient reason as logically independent of the principle of contradiction. Leibniz tells us again and again that the principle of sufficient reason is one of the two primary

principles of all our reasoning. Even when he declares it subordinate in importance to the principle of contradiction, Leibniz still insists on its logical independence (*ibid.*, p. 165).

The view that Professor Jolley is expressing in this passage is the standard one, i.e., that the two great principles are logically independent. Is there good textual evidence for this claim?

Suppose we take the following as our versions, respectively, of the principle of contradiction and the principle of sufficient reason.

(e) For any proposition p, if p is or is reducible to an identity, then p is true.

(g) For any proposition p, if p is true, then there is a sufficient reason why p is true.

Obviously, these are distinct propositions; we have *two* great principles. Many of the texts cited to establish that Leibniz regarded the two great principles as logically independent only show that he regarded them as *two*. If they are both necessarily true then, although two, they are not logically independent. Indeed, if Leibniz thought of the principle of sufficient reason as necessarily true, then he thought of it as reducible to an identity and, hence, dependent in a nontrivial way on the principle of contradiction. But did he?

In *De Contingentia*, Leibniz explicitly raised the question that concerns us: ". . . it can be asked whether this proposition is necessary—*nothing exists without a greater reason for existing than not existing*" (Grua 304). Unfortunately, Leibniz failed to provide a straight answer to his own question in this context. We do find a straight answer to a somewhat different question Leibniz posed.

It is to be seen whether, this proposition having been assumed to be necessary: *a proposition holds whose reason for holding is greater*, it follows that a proposition whose reason for holding is greater is necessary. But the inference is rightly denied. For if the definition of a necessary proposition is that its truth can be demonstrated with geometrical rigor than it can indeed happen that this proposition can be demonstrated—*all and only truths have a greater reason*. . . . But it will not therefore be possible to demonstrate this proposition: *contingent proposition A has the greater reason*. . . . And hence it does not follow that contingent proposition A is necessary (Grua 305).

I take it Leibniz was drawing our attention to the following form of inference.

(i) Necessarily, p is true if and only if there is a sufficient reason why p is true.

(ii) There is a sufficient reason why p is true.

(iii) Necessarily, p is true.

And he was claiming that it is an invalid form, that an instance of it would have premises entailing its conclusion only if what replaces p is necessary.

Parenthetically, there is an important point worth noting here. I intend (i) to capture the idea that "all and only truths have a greater reason" is necessary; this, in turn, is Leibniz's way of formulating the claim that the principle of sufficient reason is necessary. Consider the argument minus its modal operators; so construed it is valid. Only half of (i) is required—the implication from right to left. But the implication from right to left is the *converse* of what we have been calling the principle of sufficient reason. I think that this observation is significant. My view is that frequently, when Leibniz said that the principle of sufficient reason is the first principle of contingent truths, he had in mind the equivalence from which both what we have been calling sufficient reason and its converse may be derived, i.e., (9).

Although Leibniz did not provide a direct answer to his own question of whether the principle of sufficient reason is necessary in *De Contingentia*, a careful reading of the entire text suggests that he thought an affirmative answer was the right one. Fortunately, we can do better than this. There are a number of texts in which Leibniz provided just the sort of argument, based on definitions, that his own theory requires in order to show that the principle of sufficient reason can be reduced to an identity. Consider the following passage from Leibniz's fifth paper in the Leibniz-Clarke correspondence:

> . . . 'Tis very strange to charge me with advancing my principle of the want of sufficient reason, without any proof drawn either from the nature of things, or from the divine perfections. For the nature of things requires, that every event should have beforehand its proper conditions, requisites, and dispositions, the existence whereof makes the sufficient reason of such an event (G/7/393 [LC 60]).

This same argument is mentioned in *Confessio Philosophi* (CP 34-35), *Catena Mirabilium Demonstrationum de Summa Rerum* (Grua 263), *De Existentia* (Grua 267), and *On Freedom* (FC 178 [MP 106]); it is stated in considerable detail in an early work, *Demonstratio Propositionum Primarum* (A/6/2/479-86). The entire proof is short and worth quoting.

Proposition:
Nothing exists without a reason
or whatever exists has a sufficient reason.
Definition 1. A sufficient reason is something which having
been posited, the thing exists.
Definition 2. A requisite is something which if not posited
the thing does not exist.
Demonstration:
whatever exists has all its requisites.
For, if one is not posited, the thing does not
exist per Definition 2.
All requisites having been posited, the thing exists.
For, if the thing does not exist, something will
be lacking in virtue of which it does not exist,
i.e., a requisite.
Therefore, all the requisites constitute a sufficient
reason per Definition 1.

Therefore, whatever exists has a sufficient reason.

Q.E.D.

Leibniz's intent here was to derive the principle of sufficient reason from acceptable definitions of "sufficient reason" and "requisite." Success would have permitted him to reduce the principle of sufficient reason to an identity. A difficulty with the argument stares one in the face. Note that the reason given for the second step — i.e., the collection of all the requisites of a thing constitutes a sufficient condition of it — is not a consequence of either definition. Indeed, when applied in the present case, the aroma of question begging fills the air.

It may be objected that the argument above applies directly to sufficient reason in the form of a causal principle, something like (f), rather than (g). My response is this. First, just on their faces (f) and (g) are exceedingly similar. When (g) is recast in the light of the concept containment account of truth as (j) they become nearly indistinguishable. In particular, the notion of a requisite, as well as the suppositions about requisites utilized in the argument, have their analogues with respect to concept containment, as understood by Leibniz (see, for example, G/7/293 [MP 11-21]).

III

Leibniz took the principle of contradiction to be secure in its realm, not requiring supplementers, not brooking competitors. His treatment of it remained fixed throughout his mature period, with the exception of some vacillation concerning its vindication. Hence, noting the senses in which Leibniz took necessary truths to depend on it will provide a model for exploring similar matters with respect to sufficient reason and perfection.

Consider, again, a deep form of the principle of contradiction, i.e.,

(e''') For any proposition p, there is an a priori proof of p if and only if p is necessarily true.

So stated there is an obvious sense in which necessary truths depend on the principle of contradiction; it provides necessary and sufficient conditions for necessary truth. It provides what Leibniz viewed as a deep semantic analysis of necessary truth. It is important to note that in this form the principle of contradiction also functions as an epistemological principle in Leibniz's system. Not only can we humans come to know (any) necessary truth by coming to know that the left side of (e''') is true of it, according to Leibniz, but in numerous passages he exhorted us to employ this method to the full. See, for example, C 539, where Leibniz set out to demonstrate Euclid's axiom that the whole is greater than a part by the method of reduction to an identity. The idea here is that we know the axioms and, hence, theorems of geometry only to the extent to which we have reason to believe that the project of reduction to identicals is feasible. Therefore, the principle of contradiction plays a significant epistemological role in Leibniz's full system as well as a semantic role. Can the same be said for the principle of sufficient reason?

Initially it will be useful to consider the principle of sufficient reason in its common form and then to consider our deep form, which is more intimately related to Leibniz's mature account of truth.

How did Leibniz employ the principle—if p is true, then there is a sufficient reason why p is true and not otherwise—in actual cases of reasoning? The strategy appears to be this: Suppose we want to prove that p is true. Assume that p is false; then show that if p were false some state of affairs would obtain for which there would be no sufficient reason. But the principle of sufficient reason precludes this outcome. Therefore, p is not false, that is, p is true. Here is an instance of this pattern of reasoning from *The Nature of Truth* (C 402 [MP 94]) that employs one of Leibniz's favorite examples.

> . . . It is assumed by Archimedes, as one of the foundations of the whole of statics, that two equal weights A and B, which are equally distant from the center of motion C, are in equilibrium. This is a corollary of our axiom; for if there should be any diversity, then some reason can be given for it (by our axiom). But this cannot be given (by hypothesis), for everything on both sides is assumed to be in the same state, and so nothing diverse can follow from this.

Note that Leibniz claimed that the proposition purportedly established by this procedure is "one of the foundations of the whole of statics." It is plausible to suppose that this common form of the principle is what Leibniz had in mind when he claimed that the transition from mathematics to natural philosophy requires the principle of sufficient reason.

A similar pattern of reasoning is exhibited when Leibniz set out ot prove that a necessary being exists by employing the principle of sufficient reason. He reasoned in this manner: Suppose there is none such. Then there is a state of affairs, consisting in the entire series of contingent things, for which there is no sufficient reason. So, via the principle of sufficient reason, we conclude that there is a necessary being. Leibniz said of the principle of sufficient reason in its common form," . . . without this great principle one cannot prove the existence of God, nor account for many other important truths" (G/7/419 [LC 95]; similar remarks are to be found in Grua 268, A/2/1/117 [L 226/146], G/7/301 [L 349/227], and G/6/127 [Huggard 148].[5] Leibniz also purported to derive metaphysical conclusions from sufficient reason in its common form. The Leibniz-Clarke correspondence contains a number of instances, e.g., an argument against the thesis that space is an absolute being (G/7/364 [LC 26]), an argument against atomism (G/7/408 [LC 79]), and an argument against the thesis that there are distinct, but indiscernible, individuals (G/7/393 [LC 60-1]).

We have found that Leibniz purported to derive from sufficient reason in its common form some propositions from physics (in particular, statics), some from natural theology, and some from metaphysics. It is plausible to assume that the propositions purportedly derived are knowable a priori, if known at all. That fits nicely with Leibniz's claim that both the principle of contradiction and the principle of sufficient reason are principles of a priori knowledge. Indeed, Leibniz may have regarded all the conclusions reached in our examples as necessary truths. He certainly so regarded the proposition that God exists. This feature is not surprising given the form of argument involved and the difficulty of proving the *lack* of a sufficient reason. The principle of sufficient reason in its common form does not seem to be related to contingent truths in anything like the way the principle of contradiction in its deep form is related to necessary truths.

Consider, again, the principle of sufficient reason in our deep form, formulated specifically in order to provide necessary and sufficient conditions for contingent truth.

(9) p is contingently true if and only if there is a proof sequence for p but there is no a priori proof of p.

Leibniz regarded it as providing a deep semantic analysis of contingent truth, just as he regarded the principle of contradiction as providing a deep semantic analysis of necessary truth. Did he assume that (9) has epistemological significance with respect to knowledge of contingent truths? He assumed so for God, not for us. Leibniz took seriously the idea that we (humans) might be able to establish a priori that a given sequence is a nonterminating proof sequence for a given contingent proposition (e.g., at C 374 [P 63]). Of course he was perfectly clear that neither we nor God can complete a nonterminating proof sequence. What he took seriously was the notion that we might be able to prove that a given proof sequence, although nonterminating, nonetheless converged on some identical proposition. His considered opinion was that this is not in our power.

> . . . Just as a larger number contains another which is incommensurable with it, although even if one continues to infinity with a resolution one will never arrive at a common measure, so in the case of a contingent truth you will never arrive at a demonstration. . . . The sole difference is that in the case of surd relations we can, none the less, establish demonstrations, by showing that the error involved is less than any assignable error, but in the case of contingent truths not even this is conceded to a created mind (C 18 [MP 97]; cf. C 272-73, C 388-89 [P 77-78]).

In the paragraph after that just quoted, Leibniz said of contingent propositions that ". . . their truth is understood a priori by the infinite mind alone" (C 18 [MP 98]). Here and elsewhere Leibniz appears committed to the doctrine that no created mind knows a contingent proposition a priori. (See, also G/7/44, G/7/220 [Schrecker 13], FC 181 [MP 108].) Whether this thesis is consistent with Leibniz's views about the uses of the principle of perfection is a difficult question deserving attention.

We have already noted that Leibniz employed a principle of perfection as a supplement to sufficient reason. It is important to weigh its relevance to the matters at hand.

Consider:

. . . All contingent propositions have reasons for being so rather than other-wise . . . ; but they do not have demonstrations of necessity, since these reasons are founded only on the principle of contingency or of the existence of things, i.e., on what is or appears best among several equally possible things (G/4/438 [DM 22]).

Similar passages can be found in Grua 301, 305; FC 182 (MP 109); G/6/413 (Huggard 418); *Monadology* § 46, § 53, § 54 (G/6/614-16), *Principles of Nature and Grace* (G/6/603), and G/7/390 (LC 57). In many (most) cases, Leibniz referred to this principle without stating what the principle asserts. The quotation above from the *Discourse on Metaphysics* is particularly helpful in this regard. The most general form of the principle of perfection seems to be this:

(m) Every mind wishes to choose what appears best to that mind.

Applied to God (taking into account his wisdom and his power), (m) yields:

(n) God always chooses the best.

We may think of (n) as Leibniz's "common form" of the principle of perfec-tion. The sense in which it serves as a supplement to (g), i.e., to sufficient reason in its common form, is well known. The principle of sufficient reason requires that God have some reason for choosing *this* world; the principle of perfection supplies that reason. In the *Discourse on Metaphsyics*, Leibniz attempted to explain the rela-tion of the principle of perfection in its common form to the principle of sufficient reason in a deep form. In Article 13 of the *Discourse*, Leibniz argued that truth is always a matter of containment of the concept of the predicate in the concept of the subject but that in the case of contingent truths proof of containment requires appeal to the principle of perfection. But in the *Discourse* Leibniz did not provide any details explaining how the principle of perfection (in any form) could be rele-vant to an analysis of concepts. That topic is reserved for the *General Inquiries*. I consider it after a discussion of deep forms of (n).

Given that some world is actual and God chose it, (n) has the following con-sequence.

(o) For any proposition p, if p holds in the best possible world, then p is true.

In order to have a version comparable to (9), consider:

(p) p is contingently true if and only if p holds in the best possible world and there is no a priori proof of p.

Questions naturally arise about (p) analogous to those we asked about (9). We want to know whether Leibniz thought of (p) as having an epistemological func-tion relative to contingent truths analogous to the role of the principle of contradic-tion with respect to necessary truths.

Did Leibniz think that an explanation of all our knowledge of contingent truths can be based on (p)? He certainly did not. Did he think that some interesting portion of our knowledge of contingent truths can be based on (p)? This is an exceedingly difficult and yet important question. It concerns the role of reasoning by final causes in Leibniz's philosophy of science. My intention is to outline one aspect of the problem.

Consider:

(10) p holds in the best possible world.

Put aside theological and ethical propositions, and consider only propositions that Leibniz viewed as contingent and a part of physics. Did Leibniz believe that there are propositions fulfilling those conditions such that we can know (10) to be necessarily true of them? There are plausible candidates of two types: conservation principles and principles of order. Something needs to be said about these principles and about how Leibniz understood the expression "the best possible world."

Leibniz distinguished between metaphysical and moral perfection. However, he claimed that there is exactly one world that is both metaphysically and morally the most perfect. Fortunately, God created it. Leibniz understood the metaphysically most perfect world to be ". . . the one which is at the same time the simplest in hypotheses and the richest in phenomena" (G/4/431 [DM 10]). Hence, the expression "the best possible world" had considerable content for Leibniz, including the ideas just noted plus various items entailed by the creator's perfection.

Conservation principles and principles of order are to be distinguished from lower-level generalizations applying directly to the phenomena of physics. Leibniz stated, ". . . All natural phenomena could be explained mechanically if we understood them well enough, but the principles of mechanics themselves cannot be explained geometrically, since they depend on more sublime principles which show the wisdom of the Author in the order and perfection of his work" (G/7/272 [L 779/478]). By a mechanical explanation Leibniz meant an explanation in terms of efficient causation referring to the contribution of various parts of the agent to the phenomenon to be explained (L 447/289).

Conservation principles (for example, the entire effect is always equal to its full cause) and principles of order (for example, the law of continuity) are instances of "the more sublime principles" he thought essential to explain the lower-level mechanical laws. (See, for example, G/6/603 [L 1039/639] and G/3/52 [L 539/351].) Leibniz employed the conservation principle, the entire effect is always equal to its full cause, and the principle of order, the law of continuity, as tests for the acceptability of proposed laws of impact and motion. In fact, Leibniz found Descartes's rules of impact unacceptable, in part, because they violate these principles (G/3/52 [L 540/352]). Our examples of a conservation principle and a principle of order have been selected, in part, because Leibniz said explicitly of each that it is contingent (see, G/6/319-20 [Huggard 332-3] and G/2/168 [L 837/515-16]).

Is there textual support for the thesis that Leibniz thought it necessary that the conservation principle cited and the law of continuity would hold in the best possible world, i.e., the world created by a perfect being? There is. In a letter to Malebranche, Leibniz argued against the laws of impact formulated by Descartes and subsequent revisions formulated by Malebranche on the ground that both sets of laws conflict with the principle of continuity. He concluded his discussion of the principle of continuity with this remark: ". . . We see . . . how the true physics should in fact be derived from the source of the divine perfections" (G/3/52 [L 541/353]; see also G/4/360 [L 637/387]).

However, none of the passages cited settles absolutely the question with which we began. Many other passages, directed to a consideration of the same matter, suggest that Leibniz held that careful study of God's perfection has a heuristic value in the formulation of scientific hypotheses—that a consideration of final causes will often suggest a hypothesis more readily than a consideration of mechanical, efficient causation. But, of course, that is quite distinct from the claim that these hypotheses can be deduced from the perfections bestowed by a perfect creator on his creation.

The tension in Leibniz's thinking on this matter is vividly displayed in *Elements of Natural Science* (L 426-47/277-89). After distinguishing between two methods of discovering causes in physics, one a posteriori, the other a priori, Leibniz contrasted two a priori methods, one "certain," the other "conjectural," in the following manner: "The apriori method is certain if we can demonstrate from the known nature of God the structure of the world which is in agreement with the divine reasons and from this structure, can finally arrive at the principles of sensible things" (L 436/283). By contrast, Leibniz said, "The conjectural method a priori proceeds by hypotheses, assuming certain causes, perhaps, without proof, and showing that the things which now happen would follow from these assumptions" (L 437/283).

Leibniz's elaboration of the conjectural method a priori sounds like a textbook description of the hypothetico-deductive method. It fits perfectly with a heuristic use of knowledge of God's perfection. However, our concern is with his attitude toward the certain method a priori. His attitude here, as in many other texts, is equivocal in the extreme. He began by saying that it is difficult but that it does not seem entirely impossible. He then said that it is perhaps too long to be completed by humans and concluded, ". . . We believe that the absolute use of this method is conserved for a better life" (*ibid.*). This last sounds definitive, but it would be hasty to conclude that Leibniz intended to reject the method outright in this passage. The phrase "absolute use" is difficult to interpret. He may have intended to reject the idea that use of this method may be expected to get us beyond a knowledge of structure, i.e., beyond a knowledge of conservation principles and principles of order, in order to "finally arrive at the principles of sensible things," i.e., lower-level generalizations applying directly to the phenomena of physics.[6]

It may be that Leibniz held different attitudes toward this matter at different times. Only detailed investigation of his philosophy of science will settle this question. My present inclination is to suppose that his mature view was that we (humans) are restricted to the conjectural method a priori, hence, that (p), like (9), lacks epistemological significance for us.

(9) and (p) are equivalences that play important roles in Leibniz's scheme. They have a common left-hand member but distinct right-hand members. One

would expect Leibniz to offer a detailed explanation of the relation between the right-hand members, but there is surprisingly little on this topic in the texts of which I am aware. Our problem is what the principle of perfection has to do with non-terminating, but convergent, proof sequences, i.e., sufficient reason in its most austere form.

Rescher supplies an answer. He says:

> The principle of sufficient reason demands definiteness: it states that a contingent truth is susceptible of an analysis which, though infinite, converges on something. . . . The principle of perfection shows how this is the case. [It says] . . . all infinitely analytic propositions—and thus all propositions whose infinite analysis converges on some characteristic of the best of all possible worlds—are true. . . . [An] infinite comparison process is involved, one on whose basis it is exhibited that the truth at issue is one of the characteristics of a "best possible" arrangement of a world (Rescher, 34-45, 38).

There is considerable textual support for the idea that is involved here. At C 19 (MP 99) we find this remark:

> . . . Even if someone could know the whole series of the universe, even then he could not give a reason for it, unless he compared it with all other possibles. From this it is evident why no demonstration of a contingent proposition can be found, however far the resolution of notions is continued.

Similar ideas are expressed at C 405, Grua 288, C 9 (MP 134), and G/7/309 (MP 75-76). But Rescher's account needs supplementation. His notion of an analysis of a proposition is similar to that outlined in Section I. In particular, he is quite clear that the analysis of a contingent truth converges on an identical proposition (see, for example, Rescher, p. 23). An identical proposition is a "characteristic" of every possible world, not just the best possible world.

In order to see how the idea of infinite comparisons, based on the principle of perfection, may be related to nonterminating proof sequences, we need to pull together some seemingly disparate aspects of Leibniz's thought to be found in the *General Inquiries*, the main source of Leibniz's views concerning infinite analysis, convergence, and the like. Our problem is to find a textual basis for maintaining that 'there is a proof-sequence for p' is equivalent to 'p holds in the best possible world'. In what follows attention is restricted to the case where p is a categorical, affirmative, singular proposition. I believe Leibniz was of the opinion that, if this case is handled satisfactorily, the rest will fall into place.

Consider:

(11) The a is f.

In the *General Inquiries*, Leibniz explained that "from every proposition tertii adjecti a proposition secundi adjecti can be made, if the predicate is compounded with the subject into one term and this is said to exist" (C 392 [P 81]). Applied to (11), this procedure yields:

(12) The thing that is both a and f exists.

Here the grammatical subject is the entire sentence less the last word, which is the grammatical predicate. So, the subject concept is the concept of the thing that is a and f and the predicate concept is the concept of existence. In order to apply the machinery of Leibnizian analysis with the aim of generating proof sequences, we need a Leibnizian characterization of existence that makes reference to perfection in such a way as to involve infinite comparisons. Such a characterization would provide the required link between the principle of perfection and nonterminating proof sequences. But that is what we find in the *General Inquiries* at C 360 (P 51) and, particularly, C 376 (P 65-66). Various accounts of existence are considered at C 376; the basic idea is that a thing exists just in case it would not be absolutely displeasing to the most powerful mind, were there such. A complementary idea is found at C 9 (MP 134): ". . . All that can be explained in existence is being an ingredient in the most perfect series of things." Similar remarks are found at C 405, Grua 325, and G/7/195.

My suggestion is that the characterization of existence to be found at C 376 of the *General Inquiries* may be a crucial element in Leibniz's scheme. It provides a possible basis for understanding why Leibniz might have taken 'there is a proof sequence for p' to be equivalent to 'p holds in the best possible world,' at least in the case of singular propositions. Note that it does so only if the complementary idea connecting the notion of existence with the idea of being an ingredient of the most perfect series of things is itself connected with what God finds pleasing and, hence, chooses. Otherwise, the account of existence outlined at C 376 will not yield comparisons among infinitely many possible entities and, hence, will not yield the connection with nonterminating proof sequences that is essential to my account of Leibniz's strategy. The connection between what pleases God and the most perfect series of things is discussed briefly at the close of this section.

There are numerous objections to my account that have been brought to my attention. Some here suggested that the account of existence offered at C 376 is not to be given the importance I attribute to it because the full discussion contained there is tentative in the extreme. What we find are three or four seemingly distinct explications of existence, one after another. It has the appearance of someone trying out ideas without reaching closure. My reply is this: We certainly find a series of characterizations of existence, but it is not simply a series hit or miss. Leibniz discarded earlier characterizations in the series because of alleged counterexamples. He seemed satisfied with the final results.

Others have argued that not much importance should be attributed to the account of existence offered at C 376 because the ideas involved are rarely found elsewhere in Leibniz's writings. My reply is this: It is true that the ideas involved here are rarely found elsewhere in his writings; it is also true that most of his major ideas are frequently repeated in various texts. But that is not true of other important elements of Leibniz's scheme to be found in the *General Inquiries*. For example, the idea of convergence in propositional analysis, an idea central to Leibniz's account of contingent truth, rarely occurs in his writings other than the *General Inquiries*. Of course the idea of an infinite analysis occurs frequently in his writings, but the fact that a proposition has an infinite analysis does not distinguish contingent truth from contingent falsehood. To mark this distinction, convergence is the key.

Some have objected that the passage at C 376 ought not to be taken too seriously since it conflicts with various texts in which Leibniz claimed that existence cannot be defined. For example, at Grua 325 we find "Existence cannot be defined . . . so that some clearer concept can be exhibited." In *De Libertate*, an interesting essay previously cited for its blending of perfection with sufficient reason, we find this: "The reason why some contingent thing exists rather than another is not to be sought from its definition alone . . ." (Grua 288). Furthermore, 'existent' is one of the terms listed by Leibniz as a *primitive simple term* in the *General Inquiries* at C 360 (p 51). My reply is this: Note that C 360 (P 51) and Grua 325 are texts previously cited as favoring my interpretation! What is going on here? At C 360, Leibniz listed certain words as ". . . *primitive simple terms*, or those to be assumed for them in the meantime." When he listed 'existent', he then added the parenthetical remark "'existent' can be defined as 'that which is compatible with more things than anything else which is incompatible with it.'" The passage from Grua 325 occurs five lines after the following: "'Existent' compossible with the most perfect," which occurs in an array of definitions. It may have been Leibniz's intention simply to point out that the ideas involved in the purported definition of existence are no clearer than what is being defined. The passage from *De Libertate* only establishes that Leibnizian analysis must be applied not only to the subject of a singular proposition such as (12) but to the predicate 'exists' as well. Indeed, the full sentence in final form (taking into account Leibniz's additions and deletions) is this: "The reason why some contingent thing exists rather than another is not to be sought from its definition alone *but by comparison with other things*" (emphasis mine).

There are many more passages bearing on this issue that require exegesis. My belief is that the interpretation here recommended will survive that exegesis as a possible, if somewhat strained, reading of the texts.

Others have argued that the suggested interpretation ought to be rejected because the doctrine thereby ascribed to Leibniz on admittedly thin textual evidence is incompatible with another Leibnizian doctrine well entrenched in the texts, namely, that only in God's case does essence involve existence; for contingent beings, existence does not follow from essence. (See, for example, *De Contingentia*, Grua 302-3.) Two replies, leading to the same conclusion, may be offered to this argument. One involves bringing the apparatus of infinite analysis to bear by maintaining that, when Leibniz claimed that existence does not follow from essence in existent contingent beings, he was referring to what may be derived from the concept of an individual via a finite analysis. Some textual support for this approach may be found in *De Libertate Fato Gratia Dei*; see particularly Grua 309. The other reply leans on a distinction Leibniz sometimes drew between the complete concept of an individual and its essence (see, for example, *De Libertate Creaturae et Electione Divina*, particularly, Grua 383). At Grua 383, Leibniz maintained that only necessary properties belong to a thing's essence whereas contingent properties as well belong to its concept. Unfortunately, there are texts in which Leibniz identified essence with complete concept (see, for example, G/4/441-42 [DM 27-28]). Truth to tell, both of these replies have problems. It is not clear that, when Leibniz said that existence does not follow from essence in contingent beings, he was using either 'follow from' or 'essence' in the sense the suggested replies require.

Independent of the details of my exposition there is a general objection to efforts to show that Leibniz regarded 'there is a proof sequence for p' as equivalent to 'p holds in the best possible world'. It is this: Leibniz took (9) to be necessarily true. So, if he took the right-hand components of (9) and (p) to be equivalent, he would have been forced to regard (p) as necessarily true. But it may be argued that Leibniz did not regard (p) as necessarily true because he thought the inference from right to left required (n) (i.e., God always chooses the best [possible world]), and he thought of (n) as contingent. Deep water. For an excellent discussion of the relevant issues, see Robert Adams, "Leibniz's Theories of Contingency," in *Leibniz: Critical and Interpretive Essays* (Minneapolis: University of Minnesota Press, 1982), edited by Michael Hooker. I am happy to settle for this: Leibniz saw 'p holds in the best possible world' and 'there is a proof sequence for p' as equivalent in the presence of (n).

IV

We have found that Leibniz's "two great principles" turn out to be at least three, the principles of contradiction, sufficient reason, and perfection. Each has a number of distinct forms. Apparently there is more to come. In an essay entitled "On Principles," Leibniz said:

> These two first principles: one of reason; identicals are true . . . , the other of experience; various things are perceived by me, are such that it can be demonstrated concerning them that a demonstration of them is impossible; secondly, all other propositions depend on them (C 183).

We have noted that both the principle of sufficient reason and the principle of perfection receive various formulations in the texts but that 'various things are perceived by me' is not one of them. Essentially, the same division is to be found in the passage from an essay on Locke previously quoted.

In a marginal note appended to *Introduction to a Secret Encyclopedia*, Leibniz listed the principles of contradiction and sufficient reason under the heading "first principles a priori"; under the heading "first principles of a posteriori knowledge" he listed "Every perception of my present thinking is true" (C 515 [MP 9]). As previously noted, in the Latin texts propositions that would normally be expressed by first person, present-tense sentences about immediate experience are called "experimenta." Our current problem concerns where experimenta fit into Leibniz's scheme of first principles. It is not only Leibniz's account of first principles that appears to be infected by experimenta; his account of truth appears involved as well. In a letter of March 1678 to Herman Conring, Leibniz offered what he clearly intended as a definition or characterization of truth: "All truths are resolved into definitions, identical propositions and experimenta (although purely intelligible truths do not require experimenta" (A/2/1/348 [L 286/187]). One idea involved here—that truth is a matter of reducibility to specific types of propositions—was pervasive in his thinking. In the letter to Conring, identicals served as the base for reductions of necessary truths; experimenta served as the base for reductions of contingent truths. By 1679, Leibniz was fully committed to the concept-containment account of truth. Thereafter, only identicals served as the reduction base in accounts of truth. As we have noted, his account of reduction (and, hence, containment) changed from that embodied in the notion of an a priori proof to that embodied in the notion of a proof sequence. Leibniz recognized that the latter notion could not be used to account for our *knowledge* of contingent truths. For this purpose he reintroduced experimenta as "first truths according to us."[7] After 1679, there are frequent references to experimenta in connection with the foundations of knowledge but not in connection with the analysis of truth.

We have noted that some of Leibniz's statements about sufficient reason and perfection apply to these principles in their "common form." Others apply only to those principles in "deep forms" drafted with explicit attention to their relevance to the notion of contingent truth. In the years after full commitment to the concept-containment account of truth, but prior to full commitment to the doctrine of infinite analysis as the mark of contingency, Leibniz utilized a notion of a priori proof with respect to truth, necessary or contingent, that had both semantic and epistemological significance. The need to preserve contingency, to ward off the dreaded disease of necessitarianism, led to a bifurcation in the account of contingent truth, yielding an epistemological account based on experimenta (supplemented by the conjectural method a priori), and a semantic account based on infinite analysis and convergence. The latter provides help in epistemology only to God, who, after all, needs no help.

Abbreviations

A/K/ℓ/m = *Gottfried Wilhelm Leibniz: Samtliche Schriften und Briefe* (Academy Edition: Darmstadt and Berlin 1923 –), series K, volume ℓ, page m.

C = *Opuscles et fragments inédits de Leibniz*, ed. Louis Couturat (Paris: Alcan, 1903; repr. Hildesheim: Georg Olms, 1961).

CP = *Confessio Philosophi*, trans. Yvon Belaval (Paris: Vrin, 1970).

DM = *Leibniz—Discourse on Metaphysics*, trans. Peter Lucas and Leslie Grint (Manchester: Manchester University Press, 1953).

FC = *Nouvelles Lettres et Opuscles inédits de Leibniz*, ed. Foucher de Careil (Paris: Librairie Philosophique de Ladrange, 1854, repr. Hildesheim: Georg Olms, 1975).

G/m/n = *Die Philosophischen Schriften von G. W. Leibniz*, ed. C. I. Gerhardt (Berlin: Weidmannsche Buchhandlung, 1975-1890; repr., Hildesheim: Georg Olms, 1965), volume m, page n.

GM/m/n = *Die Mathematische Schriften von G. W. Leibniz*, ed. C. I. Gerhardt (Berlin-Halle: Ascher, Schmidt, 1849-1863, repr., Hildesheim: Georg Olms, 1971), volume m, page n.

Grua = *Leibniz, Textes inédits*, ed. Gaston Grua (Paris: Presses Universitaires de France, 1948).

Huggard = *Leibniz-Theodicy*, transl. E. M. Huggard (New Haven, Conn.: Yale University Press, 1952).

Langley = *New Essays Concerning Human Understanding by Gottfried Wilhelm Leibniz*, trans. Alfred Langley (LaSalle, Ill.: Open Court Publishing Company, 1949).

L/m/n = *Leibniz—Philosophical Papers and Letters*, ed. and trans. Leroy E. Loemker (1st edition, Chicago: University of Chicago Press, 1956; 2nd edition, Dordrecht, Holland: D. Reidel Publishing Company, 1969), page m of the 1st edition and page n of the 2nd edition.

LC = *The Leibniz-Clarke Correspondence*, ed. H. G. Alexander (Manchester: Manchester University Press, 1956).

Le Roy = *Leibniz—Discours de Métaphysique et Correspondance avec Arnauld*, ed. Georges Le Roy (Paris: Vrin, 1970).

M = *The Leibniz-Arnauld Correspondence*, trans. H. T. Mason (Manchester: Manchester University Press, 1967).

MP = *Leibniz—Philosophical Writings*, trans. Mary Morris and G. H. R. Parkinson (London: J. M. Dent and Sons Ltd, 1973).

NE = *G. W. Leibniz—New Essays on Human Understanding*, trans. and ed. Peter Remnant and Jonathan Bennett (Cambridge: Cambridge University Press, 1981).

P = *Leibniz—Logical Papers*, trans. and ed. G. H. R. Parkinson (Oxford: Oxford University Press, 1966).

Schmidt = *Gottfried Wilhelm Leibniz—Fragmente zur Logik*, trans. and ed. Franz Schmidt (Berlin: Akademie Verlag, 1960).

Schrecker = *Leibniz—Monadology and other Philosophical Essays*, trans. Paul Schrecker and Ann Martin Schrecker (Indianapolis: Bobbs-Merrill, 1965).

W = *Leibniz—Selections*, ed. Philip P. Wiener (New York: Charles Scribner's Sons, 1951).

Notes

Acknowledgments: Some of the research for this paper was done at the Institute for Advanced Study, Princeton, N.J. I thank the institute and the members of the Seventeenth Century Study Group who met there and discussed these topics with me. I am especially grateful to Martha Bolton, Vere Chappell, Willis Doney, Michael Hooker, Ruth Mattern, Fabrizio Mondadori, and Margaret Wilson. Earlier versions of the paper were read at Arizona State University, Brandeis University, and Dartmouth College. Comments received on these occasions were helpful. Willis Doney's comments, offered when I read the paper at Dartmouth College, were particularly useful. Passages taken from Leibniz are given in English and are followed by a reference to a source containing the quoted passage in the original language and by a reference (in brackets) to a source containing a translation of the passage into English in those cases in which I know of a published translation into English. In some cases, the words in a passage quoted in the paper will not be exactly the same as those in the English translation cited. Citations to unquoted material follow the same format.

1. For Leibniz the general form of an affirmative identical proposition was AB is B (see, for example, C 369 [P 58]).

2. For an attempt to indicate what Leibniz may have had in mind here, see my paper, "Truth and Sufficient Reason in the Philosophy of Leibniz," mentioned above.

3. Here are some of the more significant ones: G/7/309 (MP 75), C 371 (P 61), C 387 (P 77), C 17 (MP 96), G/7/200 (Schrecker 13), C 270, C 1, and Grua 305.

4. (k) is speculation about what Leibniz would have said in place of (i) once the infinite analysis doctrine had been firmly grasped.

5. It seems surprising that Leibniz would say (in so many places) that without the principle of sufficient reason we cannot prove the existence of God. What about the ontological argument? In one text, Leibniz modified the claim. He said of the principle of sufficient reason,

". . . Without it, indeed, the existence of God cannot be proved *from his creatures* . . ." (G/7/301 [L 349/227]; emphasis mine). That sounds more like it.

6. There are a number of passages that suggest that even matters of *detail* can be reached via final causes. Leibniz's favorite example was his theory of optics. See, for example, "Unicum Opticae Catoptricae et Dioptricae Principium" in *G. G. Leibnitii Opera Omnia*, ed. L. Dutens (Geneva, 1768), Vol. 3, pp. 145-51. Note also the following passages in which Leibniz commented favorably on its use of reasoning from final causes: G/4/446-47 (DM 37), GM/6/243 (L 723/442), G/7/273-74 (L 781/479), A/6/6/423 (NE 423), and C 13 (MP 174).

7. See C 515 (MP 9), G/7/296 (MP 15), C 220, C 17 (MP 97), G/7/44, G/3/258-59, and, especially, A/6/6/367 (NE 367), A/6/6/411 (NE 411), and A/6/6/434 (NE 434). The last three references are to the new Remnant and Bennett translation of the *New Essays*. Gloriously, the pagination of their translation matches that of the Academy edition. The translation is admirable. Notes appended to the text provide information about persons, events, and ideas alluded to therein. The notes are extraordinarily helpful and interesting in their own right.

Phenomenalism and
Corporeal Substance in Leibniz

ROBERT MERRIHEW ADAMS

The most fundamental principle of Leibniz's metaphysics is that "there is nothing in things except simple substances, and in them perception and appetite" (G II,270/L 537).[1] This implies that bodies, which are not simple substances, can only be constructed out of simple substances and their properties of perception and appetite. ('Constructed' is our word for it. Leibniz commonly says that bodies or phenomena "result" from simple substances and their modifications; but resulting is not what we would call a causal relation in this context.)[2]

How, according to Leibniz, are bodies constructed out of simple substances and their properties? Two theses frequently asserted by Leibniz—that bodies are phenomena and that bodies are aggregates of substances—have been thought to represent incompatible theories of the construction of bodies. Interpreters have spoken of a vacillation in Leibniz or have tried to document a change of mind, assigning the different theories a predominant role in different periods of the philosopher's career.[3] I was once inclined to do that myself, but I have now become convinced that Leibniz did not vacillate or change his mind on this point. To be sure, he is often careless or imprecise, saying things in ways that ignore aspects of his views that he does not want to present at the moment. But if there are two theories here, Leibniz believed (rightly or wrongly) that they are consistent, and he held both of them throughout the mature period of his thought (say, from 1686 on).

In this paper I will try to show how he wove the theses that bodies are phenomena and that they are aggregates of substances, into a single, phenomenalistic theory, which seems to me to be reasonably coherent. In section 3 I will try to explain why Leibniz thought that, precisely *as* aggregates of substances, bodies are only phenomena; and in section 4 I will examine the distinction between real and imaginary bodies in his system, which is the principal point at which he might be suspected of using two or more mutually inconsistent constructions. First, however, I must try to explain what Leibniz does and does not mean by calling bodies "phenomena." Section 1 will be devoted to this topic, which contains (in my opinion) some of Leibniz's most valuable contributions to metaphysics.

In order to understand Leibniz's views about corporeal aggregates, it will be important to know something about the relation between a simple substance, or "monad," and "its" body. This relation, which is the topic of section 2, is fundamental to the structure of what Leibniz calls a "corporeal substance." And this brings us to another theme, which I think Leibniz was not so successful in harmonizing with the rest of his philosophy. He held that a corporeal substance, composed of a monad (something like a soul) and its organic body (an aggregate or phenomenon), is one per se as no aggregate can be. As I will argue in my fifth and final section, the nature of this unity is puzzling and Leibniz himself seems to have been troubled about it during the last years of his life; he has left us, indeed, more evidence of vacillation on this point than on any other part of his philosophy of matter. In this connection I will examine the notorious conception of a substantial bond (*vinculum substantiale*) that appears in his letters to Des Bosses.

Thus, this paper will be concerned with three Leibnizian theses about the physical world that seem at first glance to be flatly inconsistent with each other: (1) that bodies are phenomena, (2) that bodies are aggregates of substances, and (3) that there are corporeal substances that, though composite, are one per se. And I will be arguing that Leibniz held all three of them at once and was reasonably successful in integrating the first two of them with each other, but not with the third.

1. PHENOMENA

Leibniz's phenomenalism is quite different from the sorts of phenomenalism with which English-speaking philosophers are likely to be most familiar. It is, therefore, important to clear our minds of preconceptions when we consider what Leibniz meant by calling bodies phenomena. 'Phenomenon' is a Greek word that means 'appearance,' or more literally 'thing that appears'. Things that appear are objects of awareness. The first thing that I want to say about phenomena, as Leibniz conceives of them, is that they are *intentional objects*.[4] Bodies, as phenomena, may be thought of as the objects of a story — a story told or approximated by perception, common sense, and science. In calling them phenomena Leibniz means that they have their being in the awareness that perceivers have of this story.

Leibniz spoke of phenomena as "*objects* of limited minds" (G VII, 563, my emphasis). This should not be taken to imply that he thought of phenomena as fully distinct from the acts or properties of our minds by virtue of which we are aware of them, for he also said that "phenomena are nothing but thoughts" (G II,70/L-A 86) and that the "phenomena" that are always produced in us when we see bodies "are simply new transitory modifications of our souls" (G VI,591/L 626). On the other hand, it is difficult to accept that Leibniz simply identified bodies, as phenomena, with perceptions; for the properties he ascribes to these two sorts of entities are quite different. For example, he ascribes size, shape, and motion to bodies but not to modifications of the mind as such. And, conversely, bodies are not said to be distinct or confused, although those are salient properties of perceptions of bodies for Leibniz.

I believe the solution to this problem is that, when Leibniz speaks of material things as phenomena, he usually thinks of those phenomena as qualities or modifications of a perceiving substance *considered only in a certain respect*. Specifically, corporeal phenomena are perceptions considered with regard to their objective reality or representational content or insofar as they express some nature, form, or essence.

Here I am extrapolating from things Leibniz says about "ideas." His notion of idea is by no means the same as his notion of phenomenon. The latter notion is more closely connected with perception than the former, and some phenomena are transitory, whereas ideas in general are not. But ideas, like phenomena, are both properties and objects of the mind; and Leibniz gives much fuller discussion to the relation between ideas and the mind than I have found him to give to the relation between phenomena and the perceiving substance.

A famous controversy between Malebranche and Arnauld provides the starting point for much of Leibniz's thought about ideas. Malebranche held that ideas of bodies are objects of awareness distinct from the modifications of our minds by which we are aware of them. He had to regard them as distinct, since he held that the ideas are in God's mind and not in ours. Arnauld maintained not only that we have ideas of bodies in our own minds but also that they are modifications of our minds. Leibniz declared himself for Arnauld in this debate: "It suffices to consider ideas as Notions, that is to say as modifications of our soul. That is how the school, M. Descartes, and M. Arnauld take them" (G III,659; cf. G IV,426/L 294).[5]

This declaration does not fully reflect the complexity of Leibniz's position, however. In the first place, he agreed with Malebranche that, *if* ideas are taken "as the immediate external object of our thoughts, it is true that they could only be placed in God, since there is nothing but God that can act immediately upon us" (RML 317, cf. 490). And in conciliatory moods he was prepared to say that "it can very well be maintained in this sense that we see everything in God" (RML 490). But Leibniz insists that we also have an immediate *internal* object of our thought (RML 317). "I hold, however, that there also is always something in us that corresponds to the ideas that are in God as well as to the phenomena that take place in bodies" (RML 321f.) In this sense we have our own ideas in our own minds (DM 28-29), and our ideas are modifications of our minds, or relations of correspondence to God's ideas, which are included in those modifications (RML 490).

In the second place, Leibniz's calling ideas modifications of the soul should not lead us to suppose that he identified them with conscious episodes. In section 26 of the *Discourse on Metaphysics*, he distinguishes two sense of 'idea':

Some take the idea for the form or difference of our thoughts, and in this way we have the idea in our mind only insofar as we think of it, and every time we think of it anew, we have other ideas of the same thing, although similar to those that went before. But it seems that others take the idea for an immediate object of thought or for some permanent form which remains when we do not contemplate it.

Leibniz prefers the second of these conceptions. An idea, properly speaking, is a "quality of our soul," but a permanent quality and not a transitory modification (DM 26). It manifests itself in distinct successive modifications when we think of it consciously; and even when we are not thinking of it, there remains in us a property (*habitudo*) that expresses the content of the idea (G VII,263/L 207). The concrete reality of the idea in our minds is thus quite different at different times.

In the third place, it is only considered in a certain respect that modifications or qualities of the soul are ideas. If we ask what it is that is permanent in an idea that takes such different forms as the conscious and the unconscious at different times, the answer is first that the representational content, or in Cartesian terms the objective reality, of the idea is constant and second that the mind always has in it a certain potentiality for making that content conscious, "the quality," as Leibniz puts it, "of representing to itself whatever nature or form it is, when the occasion arises for thinking of it" (DM 26). Leibniz himself, in the passage quoted, connects the permanence of the idea with its character as object of thought. We may say that the idea is a permanent quality of the mind considered with regard to its objective reality or representational content; Leibniz says, "This quality of our soul *insofar as it expresses some nature, form, or essence*, is properly the idea of the thing, which is in us, and which is always in us, whether we think of it or not" (DM 26, my emphasis). "An idea is that in which one perception or thought differs from another by reason of the object" (RML 73).

Similarly, I believe that when Leibniz speaks of material things as phenomena he usually thinks of those phenomena as qualities or modifications of the perceiving substance considered with regard to their objective reality or representational content or insofar as they express some nature, form, or essence. Adapting Cartesian terms, one can say that, in their objective reality or as phenomena, perceptions have properties that they do not have in their formal reality or as modifications of the mind, and vice versa. Among the most important of these properties, for Leibniz, are causal properties, for they are the basis of the preestablished harmony between body and soul. Many philosophers have wondered what the things are that need to be harmonized, if bodies are phenomena and phenomena are modifications of the soul. Leibniz holds that corporeal phenomena as such are caused mechanically by preceding corporeal phenomena, whereas modifications of the soul as such are to be explained teleologically by preceding appetites (Mon. 79, 87; GV IV,391/L 409f.; C 12). God preestablishes a harmony between soul and body by so programming perceptions that, while their formal reality follows from the formal reality of previous perceptions and appetites of the same substance by laws of teleological explanation, their objective reality follows from the objective reality of previous perceptions by laws of mechanical explanation.

In spite of these fundamental differences between perceptions as phenomena and perceptions as modifications of the perceiving substance, Leibniz will resist any attempt to treat them as fully distinct entities. The point of his saying that phenomena are modifications of our souuls is that as a conceptualist about all sorts of abstract entities and merely intentional objects, he does not believe that phenomena have any being except *in* the existence or occurrence of qualities or modifications of perceiving substances. The existence of a phenomenon must consist in the occurrence of certain perceptions.

Nonetheless, Leibniz distinguishes, among phenomena, between *real* and merely imaginary material objects and holds that some stories in which the real ones figure are *true*. The task of Leibnizian phenomenalistic analysis is to explain what this reality and truth consist in. It is not to analyze the content of the true stories. I can discover no phenomenalistic analysis in Leibniz that does not *presuppose* the concept of spatially-extended-objects-appearing-to a perceiver. There is no attempt to break that down into supposedly more primitive concepts of sensory impressions. This is a principal difference between Leibniz and many other phenomenalists.

This point may be pursued by asking whether the objective reality of perceptions must *result*, in Leibniz's sense, from their formal reality. Must phenomena be constructible, by sufficient conditions, from the nonintentional properties of the relevant perceptions? One might expect Leibniz to answer this question in the affirmative, and perhaps he would if pressed; but I have not found that he did. He is committed, I think, to the view that the objective reality of a perception must be *expressed* by the formal reality of the perception (cf. RML 321f.); but that is not clearly more than a *necessary* condition on a perception's having a certain objective reality. For one thing to express another, according to Leibniz, is for there to be a one-to-one mapping from elements of the latter to elements of the former according to appropriate rules. (See, for example, G VII,263f./L 207f.) This appears to be a transitive and symmetrical relationship, which does not provide a *sufficient* condition for perception. Since any two actual substances (Ronald Reagan and Leonid Brezhnev, for example) are expressions of the same universe, according to Leibniz, it would seem they must also express each other, and my perception of Reagan must express Brezhnev as well as Reagan—by virtue of the transitivity and symmetry of the expression relation. Yet, I doubt that Leibniz would be willing to say that my perception of Reagan is a perception of Brezhnev, too.

So far as I know, Leibniz neither demands nor promises nor begins to give an account of sufficient conditions for a perception's having a certain objective reality, in terms of its formal reality. I think his philosophy is best interpreted as one that treats the objective reality or representational content of a perception as a primitive feature of that perception, at least for all purposes that actually arise in the philosophy. Leibniz provides at least one analysis of the notion of the *reality* of a corporeal universe that appears to us (as we will see in section 4, below). But he provides no *analysis* of the notion of a corporeal universe's appearing to us (as opposed to something else appearing to us). He thus treats the notion of a corporeal universe's appearing to us as conceptually prior to the notion of such a universe's being real.

For further exploration of the distinctive features of Leibniz's conception of phenomena, let us turn to his explicit disagreements with Berkeley. His best-known comment on Berkeley, in a letter of 15 March 1715 to Des Bosses (G II,492/L 609), suggests that Leibniz failed to realize the strength of Berkeley's desire to be found in agreement with common sense and overlooked Berkeley's efforts to define a sense in which bodies can be called "real." Other evidence does not contradict these suggestions but does make clear that Leibniz actually read Berkeley and saw more than he is commonly thought to have seen of the similarities as well as the differences between Berkeley's views and his own. This evidence is provided by the following comments that Leibniz wrote on the last page of his copy of Berkeley's *Treatise Concerning the Principles of Human Knowledge*:

> Much here that's right and agrees with my views. [*Multa hic recte et ad sensum meum.*] But too paradoxically expressed. For we have no need to say that matter is nothing, but it suffices to say that it is a phenomenon like the rainbow; and that it is not a substance, but a result of substances; and that space is no more real than time, i.e. that it is nothing but an order of coexistences as time is an order of subexistences. The true substances are Monads, or Perceivers. But the author ought to have gone on further, namely to infinite Monads, constituting all things, and to their preestablished harmony. He wrongly or at least pointlessly rejects abstract ideas, restricts ideas to imaginations, despises the subtleties of arithmetic and geometry. He most wrongly rejects the infinite division of the extended; even if he is right to reject infinitesimal quantities.[6]

Leibniz did not fail to see that he and Berkeley were fundamentally on the same side. He thought much of their disagreement was in presentation, style, and tactics. Berkeley "expressed" their common beliefs "too paradoxically." Several substantial disagreements are reflected in Leibniz's critique, however. I will discuss three of these.

(1) The perceptual atomism of Berkeley's construction of physical objects evokes Leibniz's strongest protest. Berkeley "most wrongly [*pessime*] rejects the infinite division of the extended." For Berkeley, extended things are ideas or collections of ideas, and these ideas in turn are composed of parts that are only finitely small because they cannot be smaller than the mind in which they exist can discriminate (*Principles*, § 124). In dividing any extended thing, therefore, we come eventully to parts that are still extended but so small that they cannot be divided any further; and Berkeley maintains that there are no distinct parts within these smallest discernible parts, on the ground that as an idea exists only in the mind, "consequently each part thereof must be perceived" (ibid.).

For Leibniz, on the other hand, it is of the very essence of the extended as such to be continuous and therefore infinitely divisible. Because there are indefinitely many ways in which it can be divided in parts (G VII,562) and no parts in it that cannot themselves be divided in parts, it has no parts of which it is ultimately composed as Berkeleyan extended things are ultimately composed of the smallest perceptible parts of ideas. There may indeed be indivisible, unextended substances that are in some sense "in" an extended thing, but the extended thing cannot be composed of them precisely because a continuous quantity cannot be composed of elements that have no parts. "Just as a part of a line is not a point, but a line in which the point is, so also a part of matter is not a soul but the body in which it is" (FC 322; cf. G VII,268/L 536). This is one of the reasons why the extended as such can only be a phenomenon. "From the very fact that a mathematical body cannot be analyzed into first constituents, it follows that it is not real at all, but something mental and designating nothing but the possibility of parts, not something actual" (G II,286/L 535f.). Another inference that Leibniz draws from his thesis that an extended whole has, as such, no first constituent parts is that it is not constructed out of its parts at all but is prior to them. "In the ideal or continuous the whole is prior to the parts, as the Arithmetical unit is prior to the fractions that divide it, which can be assigned arbitrarily, the parts being only potential; but in the real the simple is prior to the groups, the parts are actual, are before the whole" (G III,622; cf. G VII,562; G II,379). Here, therefore, is another way in which bodies as phenomena are not constructed according to Leibniz.

(2) Leibniz can take this position only because he also thinks Berkeley is wrong to "restrict ideas to imaginations"—or, in other words, because he rejects the sensationalism of Berkeley's theory. If bodies are phenomena for Leibniz, these phenomena are objects of the intellect as well as of sensation. Both faculties play a part in our perception of corporeal phenomena.

The intellect's part is particularly important and includes both mathematics and physics. Berkeley was right in insisting that no sensory image is infinitely divisible into parts that are still sensory images. Leibniz would certainly grant that the lines without breadth by which a continuous surface can be divided into parts indefinitely small can neither be imagined nor perceived by sense. We conceive of them, rather, by mathematical reason. Hence, body as an infintely divisible phenomenon is "mathematical body" for Leibniz.

Among the features of phenomena that are not directly perceived by sense at all are *forces*. Force is characteristic of monads, but there are forces that are properties of phenomena. "As matter itself is nothing but a phenomenon, but well founded, resulting from the monads, it is the same with inertia, which is a property of this phenomenon" (G III,636/L 659; Cf. G II,275f.). Certainly, Leibniz did not think we have a sensory image of inertia. (Cf. G VII,314f.) We perceive it or conceive of it only by rudimentary or sophisticated scientific thinking. Indeed, I believe that for Leibniz the universe of corporeal phenomena is primarily the object not of sense but of science. The *reality* of corporeal phenomena depends, as we will see in section 4, on their finding a place in the story that would be told by a perfected physical science.

Leibniz may well be committed to regarding corporeal phenomena as objects of a third faculty, unconscious perception, as well as of sensation and intellect. But the notion of an unconscious perception having a representational content is difficult to understand, and Leibniz does little to explain it. I will not take the time to speculate about it here but instead will pass now to a third disagreement.

(3) Part of Leibniz's point in saying that extended things as such are phenomena is to claim that they have their existence only in substances that perceive

them, and in this he agrees with Berkeley. But there is also something else going on in Leibniz's talk of phenomena, something that is reflected in his comment that Berkeley "ought to have gone on further, namely to infinite Monads, constituting all things." 'Phenomenon' contrasts not only as intramental with 'extramental'; it also contrasts as apparent with 'real'. Part of what is going on in Leibniz is that he does assume that in our perception of bodies we are at least indirectly perceiving something that is primitively real independent of our minds, and he is asking what sort of thing that may be. His answer is that it is "infinite Monads," whose harmonious perceptions are the "foundation" of corporeal phenomena.

This answer, however, does not adequately represent the interplay of appearance and reality in Leibniz's thought. Like almost all modern philosophers, Leibniz thought that good science requires us to suppose that there are very considerable qualitative differences between bodies as they appear in naive sense perception and bodies as they exist independent of our minds — if they do exist independent of our minds. In the corporeal world as described by modern science, there is, in a certain sense, no part for colors and the other so-called "secondary qualities" to play. And, on the other hand, modern science postulates vast numbers of motions of minute particles in portions of matter that appear to our senses to be perfectly quiescent internally. This was true of what Leibniz viewed as modern science, and it is true of what we think of as modern science.

Many among us respond to this situation by supposing that, whereas what we perceive naively by our senses is only an appearance, what is described by science — or what would be described by a perfected science — is reality. Leibniz has a fundamental reason for rejecting this thesis of scientific realism — a reason for not expecting science to give us knowledge of reality as it is in itself. Scientific knowledge, as Leibniz sees it, is relatively distinct but buys its distinctness at the price of studying a mathematical idealization. Reality, he thinks, is infintely complex, intensively as well as extensively. It is not just that there are infinitely many objects in infinite space; even when we perceive a body of limited extent, such as the body of a human being, Leibniz believes that the reality represented by our perception is infinitely complex and that all of that infinite complexity is relevant to the explanation of some of the salient features of the body's behavior. Human minds are finite, however; and the definitive mark of finite minds is that they cannot distinctly know an infinite complexity. So, if science is distinct knowledge, the only sort of science that is possible, even in principle, for human beings will have as its immediate object a finitely complex representation of the infinitely complex reality. At least to this extent, the objects of scientific knowledge will be phenomena. Leibniz's opinion, that the object of scientific knowledge is not reality as it is in itself but a mathematical abstraction from its infinite complexity, is plausible enough in its own right, I think; but it is also rooted in other aspects of his metaphysics, which need not be rehearsed in detail here — in his theory of free action and infinite analysis conception of contingency, for example, and in his doctrine that each thing expresses the whole universe.

Leibniz's treatment of the relation of the primary and secondary qualities to reality can be understood in this light. In section 12 of the *Discourse on Metaphysics*, he wrote:

> It can even be demonstrated that the notion of size, shape, and motion is not so distinct as is imagined, and that it includes something imaginary and relative to our perceptions, as are also (though much more so) color, heat, and other similar qualities of which it can be doubted whether they are really found in the nature of things outside us.

Many similar statements are found in other places in his work. It seems to be implied here that the secondary qualities are even less real than the primary, although both are apparent rather than ultimately real. The primary are more real only in the sense that they represent reality more distinctly than the secondary qualities. The primary qualities "contain more of distinct knowledge" than the secondary, although they both "hold something of the phenomenal" (G II,119/L-A 152).

According to Leibniz, the perception of secondary qualities, as they appear to us, is a confused perception of minute motions or textures—a confused perception of primary qualities that are too small for us to perceive them distinctly by sense (NE II,viii,13, 21). We might put this by saying that the secondary qualities are appearances *of* primary qualities—and as such are appearances of appearances. I do not know that Leibniz ever said exactly that, but in the last letter that he wrote to Des Bosses (29 May 1716) he did suggest relating secondary qualities to the corresponding primary qualities as "resultant phenomena" to "constitutive phenomena." Thus, the "observed perception" of white and black results from tiny, unobservable bumps and depressions that reflect and trap rays of light, respectively; but these geometrical textures themselves are still only phenomena (G II,521; cf. C 489).

Even within the realm of primary qualities there are veils behind veils of appearance between us and reality in the Leibnizian universe. Inspect a leg of a fly with the naked eye and under a microscope; you will see rather different shapes. Yet Leibniz would surely say that what you see with the naked eye is a confused representation of the more complex shape that appears under the microscope and that the latter is still not complex enough to be more than an appearance. This is indeed one of Leibniz's reasons for holding that shape is only a phenomenon.

> For even shape, which is of the essence of a bounded extended mass, is never exact and strictly determined in nature, because of the actual division to infinity of the parts of matter. There is never a sphere without inequalities, nor a straight line without curvatures mingled in, nor a curve of a certain finite nature without mixture of any other—and that in the small parts as in the large—which brings it about that shape, far from being constitutive of bodies, is not even an entirely real and determined quality outside of thought (G II,119/L-A 152; cf. G VII,563).

One of the reasons, I take it, why Leibniz thought that finitely complex shapes cannot be "entirely real outside of thought" is that they cannot express a relation to every event in an infinitely complex universe as the qualities of a real thing ought to. "There is no actual determinate shape in things," he wrote, "for none is able to satisfy infinite impressions" (C 522/L 270). The conclusion Leibniz draws is not that real shapes are infinitely complex (though some things he says might leave us with that impression) but rather that shape as such is only a phenomenon. I suppose that an infinitely complex shape would involve a (finite) line segment that changes not merely its curvature but also the direction of its change of curvature infinitely many times and that Leibniz would have thought that an absurd and impossible monstrosity. What I assume he would say, instead of postulating infinitely complex shapes, is that for every finitely complex shape that might be ascribed to a body there is another still more complex that more adequately expresses reality. Every shape in the series of more and more adequate expressions, however, will still be only finitely complex and for that reason among others will still be an appearance, qualitatively different from the reality expressed, which is infinitely complex and does not literally have a shape at all.

Bodies—organic or living bodies in particular—are appearances of monads.[7] A monad is represented by its body; we perceive it by perceiving its body. This is possible because the monad and its body express each other; the body is the expression of the soul. We have just seen, however, that a body as a phenomenon having a certain definite extension, shape, and motion is not complex enough to be an adequate expression of any real thing, according to Leibniz. It is not complex enough to express something that expresses the whole universe as a monad does. It is a mathematical abstraction. Perhaps the body that adequately expresses a monad is an infinite series of such abstractions, each more complex than its predecessors.

This discussion of bodies as appearances *of* monads has already led to questions about the relation of monads to "their" bodies. These are questions about the structure of Leibnizian corporeal substances. It is time to examine that subject more closely.

2. CORPOREAL SUBSTANCE (I): MONADIC DOMINATION

"I call that a *corporeal substance*," says Leibniz, "which consists in a simple substance or monad (that is, a soul or something analogous to a Soul) and an organic body united to it" (G VII,501). The corporeal substances are "bodies that are animated, or at least endowed with a primitive Entelechy or . . . vital principle"; they can, therefore, be called "living" (G II,118/L-A 152). When Leibniz says that corporeal substances are living things and that "all nature is full of life" (PNG 1), he emphatically does not mean that every material object is alive. He rejects the view of "those who imagine that there is a substantial form of a piece of stone, or of another non-organic body; for principles of Life belong only to organic bodies" (G VI,539/L 586). Here, as in many other places, Leibniz uses the Aristotelian term 'substantial form' to signify the soul, or that which is analogous to a soul, in any corporeal substance.) He adds that

it is true (according to my System) that there is no portion of matter in which there is not an infinity of organic and animated bodies; among which

I include not only animals and plants, but perhaps other sorts as well, which are entirely unknown to us. But it is not right to say, on account of that, that every portion of matter is animated—just as we do not say that a lake full of fishes is an animated body, although the fish is (G VI,539f./L 586).

Stones and lakes, then, are not corporeal substances. "Each animal and each plant too is a corporeal substance" (G III,260); I believe that they are the only corporeal substances of which Leibniz claims empirical knowledge, if we include among animals and plants the tiny living things whose discovery under seventeenth-century microscopes so excited Leibniz (G II,122/L-A 156). In a lake full of fishes the water between the fishes is not a corporeal substance, but it is composed of corporeal substances, which may be very different from the things that we know as animals and plants (Mon. 68). In particular, they may be even smaller than microscopic organisms; there is indeed no minimum size for corporeal substances.

Still, all corporeal substances are alive, in a broad sense. And Leibniz seems to have assumed that we can detect the presence or absence of life in bodies large enough to be distinctly perceived by our senses. He speaks of a study of nature that would enable us to "judge of the forms [of corporeal substances] by comparing their organs and operations" (G II,122/L-A 155f.).

The principal characteristic of living bodies that Leibniz mentions as distinguishing them from other portions of matter is that they are "organized" or "organic." There is . . . no animated body without organs" (G II,124/L-A 159); "I restrict corporeal or composite substance to living things alone, or exclusively to organic machines of nature" (G II,520). I have found little explanation in Leibniz of what distinguishes organic from inorganic bodies. It is not a radical difference in the kind of causality that operates in them. Leibniz always insists that everything can be explained mechanically in organic as well as in inorganic bodies. There is no need to refer to the substantial forms or souls of corporeal substances in explaining their physical behavior (e.g. G II,58, 77f./L-A 65f., 96). "And this *body* is *organic* when it forms a kind of Automaton or Machine of Nature, which is a machine not only as a whole but also in the smallest parts that can be noticed" (PNG 3; cf. G III,356). Presumably, an organic body is one so organized mechanically that it continues over time to cohere and retain a sort of unity in physical interactions. But stones have that property, too; so it is not enough to distinguish organic bodies from others.

Perhaps the best account that can be given of the notion of organism here is that an organic body is a body so structured mechanically that it can be interpreted as always totally expressing and being expressed by the perceptions and appetites of a soul or something analogous to a soul. We recognize living things by observing that their behavior can be interpreted as a coordinated response to their environment on the basis of something like perception of the environment together with a tendency toward something like a goal—though Leibniz would insist, of course, that their behavior can *also* be explained mechanically. This account fits animals better than plants, but it is clear in any case that Leibniz's principal model of corporeal substance is the animal; he mentions plants only occasionally and seems favorably disposed toward the suggestion that they "can be included in the same genus with animals, and are imperfect animals" (G II,122/L-A 156).[8]

Leibniz's fullest statement about the structure of a corporeal substance is in a letter of 20 June 1703 to De Volder:

> I distinguish therefore (1) the primitive Entelechy or Soul, (2) Matter, i.e. prime matter, or primitive passive power, (3) the Monad completed by these two, (4) the Mass or secondary matter, or organic Machine, for which countless subordinate Monads come together [ad quam . . . concurrunt], (5) the Animal or corporeal substance, which is made One by the Monad dominating the Machine (G II,252/L 530f.).

The first three of these items can be discussed quite briefly here. The monad (3) is "a simple substance . . . ; *simple*, that is to say without parts" (Mon. 1). The primitive entelechy and prime matter must not, therefore, be conceived as *parts* that compose the monad, but rather as aspects or properties of the monad. In particular, prime matter (2) is not to be understood here as a substance or an extended stuff. It is the primitive passive power that is a fundamental property of the monad. 'Entelechy' (1) is sometimes used by Leibniz (as in Mon. 62-64) as a synonym for 'monad' or 'simply substance'; but here the entelechy clearly is not the complete monad, but a property of it. Since it goes together with primitive passive power to form the monad, the entelechy here is presumably the monad's primitive active force. Leibniz held that "the very substance of things consists in the force of acting and being acted on" (G IV,508/L 502; cf. G II,248f./L 528). The properties possessed by monads as such are perceptions and appetites, or analogous to perceptions and appetites, as Leibniz often says. As properties of monads, therefore, "primitive forces manifestly cannot be anything but internal tendencies of simple substances, by which according to a certain law of their nature they pass from perception to perception" (G II,275). As we saw in section 1, Leibniz also spoke of certain forces as properties of bodies, but this is not the place to try to understand the connection he saw between forces as properties of bodies and forces as properties of monads.

My present purpose demands a fuller discussion of the mass, or secondary matter (4), which combines with the monad to form the complete corporeal substance. This mass is, as Leibniz says here, an organic machine or, as he more often says, the organic body of the monad. Not every mass of secondary matter is an organic body; inorganic bodies are also masses of secondary matter. But only an organic body combines with a single monad to form a corporeal substance. No mass of secondary matter, organic or inorganic, is in itself a substance. The organic body, "taken separately, that is, apart from the soul, is not one substance but an aggregate of several" (G IV,396). "And *secondary matter* (as for example the organic body) is not a substance, but for another reason; it is that it is a heap of several substances, like a lake full of fishes, or like a herd of sheep, and consequently it is what is called *One per accidens* —in a word, a phenomenon" (G III,657). The mass of secondary matter that, as an organic body, combines with a monad to form a corporeal substance is thus merely a phenomenon *because* it is an aggregate of substances. The connection between being an aggregate and being a phenomenon will be the topic of section 3; for the present, I must simply note that the organic body, apart from its "soul" or dominant monad, is characterized both as an aggregate and as a phenomenon.

According to Leibniz, *every* created monad has an organic body of this sort with which it combines to form a corporeal substance (G IV,395f.; G VII,502, 530; cf. Mon. 62-63). The monad *always* has its body, and hence the organic body is an enduring object permanently attached to its dominant monad (G II,251/L 530). Even in death, it does not cease to exist, it does not cease to be organic; it just undergoes a sudden, drastic reduction in size and a change in its operations (e.g., PNG 6). The parts of an organic body do not belong to it permanently, however. "It is true that the whole which has a true unity can remain strictly the same individual even though it loses or gains parts, as we experience in ourselves; thus the parts are immediate requisites only for a time" (G II,120/L-A 153). The substances that are included in an organic body can be replaced with other substances so long as the body retains the necessary organs and the same dominant monad (Mon. 71-72).

In the outline I have been following, Leibniz clearly distinguishes the corporeal substance (5) both from its organic machine and from its dominant monad. It is something formed by the combination of those two. This appears to rule out one tempting interpretation. Cassirer identified corporeal substance with the monad itself "insofar as it is endowed with a particular organic body, according to which it represents and desires."[9] Cassirer added that this corporeal endowment is "only a determination of the *content of the consciousness*" of the monad. On this reading, the corporeal substance is a substance because it is a monad and corporeal because it is endowed with an organic body.

This conception of corporeal substance agrees admirably with other aspects of the philosophy of Leibniz and is suggested (though I think not unambiguously asserted) by some passages of his writings (G VII,314; G IV,499, 395f.). It would provide the simplest explanation of the per se unity of a corporeal substance. Unfortunately, the weight of the evidence is against Cassirer's interpretation. Leibniz seems, at least usually, to have thought of a corporeal substance as including a mass or organic body as well as a dominant monad. We have seen that he defined a corporeal substance as consisting "in a simple substance or monad . . . and an organic body united to it" (G VII,501). In other passages, he speaks of "the complete corporeal substance, which includes the form and the matter, or the soul with the organs" (G VI,506/L 551), or of "corporeal substance" as "composed of the soul and the mass" (G VI,588/L 624), and says that "a true substance (such as an animal) is composed of an immaterial soul and an organic body, and it is the Composite of these two that is called *One per se*" (G III,657). The corporeal substance is formed by the coming together of the subordinate monads with the primary monad (G II,252/L 530).

The corporeal (or composite) substance thus formed is not an aggregate, but one per se, according to Leibniz. Hence, it is not a mere phenomenon; corporeal substance is regularly contrasted with the phenomenal (G II,77/L-A 95; G VII, 314,

322/L 365; G III,657; C II,435/L 600). But corporeal substance certainly is not simple, as monads are. How then can it be one per se? Leibniz stated to De Volder that the corporeal substance "is made One by the Monad dominating the Machine" (G II,252/L 531). This statement gives rise to at least two questions: (a) how does a monad "dominate" its organic body or "Machine"? (b) How does this domination make the corporeal substance one per se? The second of these questions, as the center of the gravest difficulties and instabilities in Leibniz's theory of the physical world, will be reserved for the final section of this paper. But the first question will be discussed now. I think it can be answered in terms of the perceptions of monads in a way that is consistent with Leibniz's phenomenalism. This answer will be important in section 3 for understanding why Leibniz thought that corporeal aggregates, as such, are phenomena.

In what sense, then, does a monad "dominate" or rule its organic body? In what sense does it dominate or rule the subordinate monads, as Leibniz more often says?

In a letter of 16 June 1712 to Des Bosses, Leibniz says, "The domination, however, and subordination of monads, considered in the monads themselves, consists in nothing but degrees of perfection" (G II,452/L 605). Clearly, the dominant monad must be more perfect than the monads subordinate to it. And perfection of monads, for Leibniz, is measured by distinctness of perceptions; so the dominant monad must perceive some things more distinctly than the subordinate monads.

What must the dominant monad perceive more distinctly than the subordinate monads? Everything that happens within its body, suggested Bertrand Russell. But that does not adequately explain the sense in which Leibniz thought the dominant monad rules the body. In particular, the sufficient condition for domination that Russell seems to propose is not plausible. He says:

> If, then, in a certain volume, there is one monad with much clearer perceptions than the rest, this monad may perceive all that happens within that volume more clearly than do any of the others within that volume. And in this sense it may be dominant over all the monads in its immediate neighborhood.[10]

But suppose that a certain volume of air immediately adjacent to my right eye contains no monad that perceives anything in that volume or in my body as distinctly as I do. By Russell's criterion, if I dominate as a monad over my body, I will dominate also over all the monads in that adjacent volume of air, and it will presumably form part of my body. The incorporation of such volumes of air in my body would surely be an unacceptable consequence for Leibniz. He might try to avoid it by insisting that in any such space there would always be a monad that perceived something in the space as distinctly as I. But I would expect him to base his strategy more directly on the offensive feature of the example, which is that the volume of air does not seem to be part of the organic structure of my body.

In a letter to De Volder, Leibniz says, "Nay rather the soul itself of the whole would be nothing but the soul of a separately animated part, were it not the dominant soul in the whole *by virtue of the structure of the whole*" (G II,194/L 522, emphasis mine). I believe that a correct understanding of Leibniz's conception of monadic domination depends on the relation of the dominant monad to the structure of its organic body no less than on the superior distinctness of the dominant monad's perceptions. There are two main points to be discussed here.

(1) In a preliminary draft of his *New System*, Leibniz says that the perceptions of a monad correspond "to the rest of the universe, but particularly to the organs of the body that constitutes its point of view in the world, and this is that in which their union consists" (G IV,477). Every monad expresses everything in the whole universe, according to Leibniz; but each monad expresses, and is expressed by, its own organic body in a special way. A monad and its organic body both *contain* expressions of an infinity of things; but each *is*, as a whole, an expression of the other, and this relationship of mutual expression is peculiarly direct. An organic body stands in this relation to its dominant monad alone, not to the subordinate monads in it—though they do, of course, contain expressions of it. This is an important part of the structural relationship between a monad and its organic body by which monadic domination is constituted.

An organic body is an expression of its soul or dominant monad. Leibniz has less to say about this than about the soul's expressing its body, but expression as he understands it is a relation of one-to-one mapping, which will normally be symmetrical. So, if each monad is an especially good expression of its body, the organic body will be, reciprocally, an especially good expression of its dominant monad. I believe that in the most natural development of Leibniz's system this explains how one perceives another monad. There is only indirect textual support for this interpretation, but how else would Leibniz think that we perceive other monads?

Suppose I see a kitten jumping off a chair to pounce on a piece of string. Leibniz will surely say that I perceive certain internal properties of the kitten's soul: its seeing the string and intending to seize it. And how do I perceive those psychological properties? By far the most plausible answer is that I read them off certain properties of the kitten's body: its structure, posture, spatial position, and movements.

According to Leibniz, the subordinate monads in the kitten's body also have internal properties analogous to the seeing and intending in the kitten's soul. And since I perceive everything, at least unconsciously, I must perceive these perceptions and appetitions of the subordinate monads. But it would not be plausible to say that I perceive them by perceiving physical properties of the whole body of the kitten. Rather, I perceive the subordinate monads by perceiving *their* organic bodies, which most directly express their perceptions and appetitions. Perhaps I do not usually perceive them consciously; but with a suitable microscope, for example, I might observe one of the kitten's white blood cells reacting to a bacterium in its vicinity. In this case, I may be taken as perceiving a perception of the bacterium and an appetition for its obliteration that are present (confusedly, no doubt) in the dominant monad of the white corpuscle. And I would be reading these internal properties of the monad off movements and other physical properties of the cell. If

I understand Leibniz correctly on this point, each monad is perceived by perceiving *its* organic body, and perception of an organic body directly yields perception of its dominant monad but not of its subordinate monads.

My claim that for Leibniz one perceives a monad by perceiving its body is somewhat speculative, but he explicitly holds that each created monad expresses and perceives everything else *by* expressing and perceiving its own organic body.

> Thus although each created Monad represents the whole universe, it represents more distinctly the body which is particularly assigned to it and of which it constitutes the Entelechy; and as this body expresses the whole universe by the connection of all matter in the *plenum*, the Soul also represents the whole universe in representing this body, which belongs to it in a particular way (Mon. 62; cf. G II,90f., 112f./L-A 113f., 144f.; G II,253/L 531; G IV,530ff., 545; NE II,vii,21; C 14; G VII, 567).

The Leibnizian harmony is a system of infinitely many models—or even a system of systems of models. Each model perfectly, if perhaps obscurely, expresses all the others; but some express each other with a special closeness or directness. Perhaps Leibniz would explain this special closeness in terms of distinctness of perceptions; I find it a point of obscurity in his philosophy. One system of models occupies a peculiarly central role, although it does not have a high status ontologically. This is the universe of organic bodies, considered as phenomena and continuously extended in space and time. They are involved in all of the modeling in the whole harmony; for each of the ultimately real models, the monads, stands in a direct modeling relationship only to its own organic body. The organic body, however, is also a model of the whole universe of organic bodies. Leibniz thought that in a physical universe with no empty space every physical event would have some effect on each infinitely divisible organic body and that each such body would, therefore, always bear in itself traces from which, in accordance with the mechanical laws of nature, an infinite mind could read off all past, present, and future events in the spatiotemporal universe. Since my organic body expresses in this way the whole corporeal universe and also expresses me as its dominant monad, I perceive the whole corporeal universe in perceiving my own body. And, since the other organic bodies in the universe express their own dominant monads and since each finite monad is expressed by its own body, I perceive each monad by perceiving its organic body and I perceive the whole system of finite monads by perceiving the whole system of organic bodies. And I perceive all of this by perceiving my own organic body. (So far as I can see, the thesis that I perceive other monads by perceiving their bodies is needed here if the idea that I perceive *everything* by perceiving my body and the effects of other bodies on it is to be carried through.)

Obviously, I do not consciously perceive all these things. Because I am finite, I perceive most of them much too confusedly to be conscious of them, Leibniz would say. His scheme is at least initially less plausible if we attend mainly to conscious perceptions. When I am reading a page, do I really perceive the letters on the page by perceiving what is going on in my eye? It seems that I can see perfectly well what is on the page without consciously knowing anything at all about what is going on in my eye (and without even being able to become conscious of the inner workings of my eye by paying attention to them). If my perception models what is going on in my eye more *directly* than it models the surface of the page and if conscious perceptions are always more *distinct* than perceptions that cannot even be brought to consciousness by attending to them,[11] then this case shows that Leibniz cannot consistently explain directness of the expression and perception relations wholly in terms of distinctness of perceptions. Perhaps directness and indirectness of perception in such a case are founded on explanatory relations rather than on degrees of distinctness. I perceive what is going on in my eye more directly than what is on the page because the psychophysical laws that correlate corporeal phenomena with what happens in monads relate visual perceptions more directly to events in the eye than to events at a distance.[12] The distant events are related to visual perceptions by virtue of their connection, under mechanical laws, with events in the eye.

The task of providing a satisfactory account of the relation of directness of expression will not be pursued further here, but clearly it is an important problem. The idea that each monad and its organic body express each other with a unique directness plays a pivotal role in Leibniz's philosophy. As we have seen, it is used to explain how every monad perceives everything else. I think it plays an essential part in determining which monad has, or dominates, which organic body. That is my present concern; in addition, I will argue in section 3 that the spatial position, or "point of view," of a monad depends in turn on which organic body it has, while any aggregation of monads to form bodies depends on their spatial position. Thus, a great deal depends directly or indirectly on the relation of directness of expression.

(2) Leibniz does imply that a dominant monad perceives some things more distinctly than the monads subordinated to it do. What remains to be explained here about monadic domination is how the greater distinctness of the dominant monad's perceptions is related to the structure of the organic body and why these relationships should be expressed by an idea of domination, that is, of rule or control. The hypothesis I propose to answer these questions is that what the dominant monad as such perceives more distinctly than any other monad in its body is an appetite or tendency for perceptions of the normal organic functioning of the body. I call this a hypothesis because I have not found any place in which Leibniz explicitly asserts it, but it seems to me to provide the best explanation of much that he does say.

In developing the hypothesis, I begin with a passage of an early draft of section 14 of the *Discourse on Metaphysics*:

> It is sure above all that when we desire some phenomenon which occurs at a designated time, and when this happens ordinarily, we say that we have acted and are the cause of it, as when I will that which is called moving my hand. Also when it appears to me that at my will something happens to that which I call another substance, and that that would have happened to it in that way even if it had not willed, as I judge by frequent experience, I say that that substance is acted on, as I confess the same thing about myself when that happens to me following the will of another substance.

I believe that these statements reveal the intuitive origins of the idea that activity and passivity can be explained in terms of distinctness of perceptions. Voluntary agency provides the paradigm of activity. It is characterized by consciousness of a tendency or appetite that has a certain event as its goal. The goal is described by Leibniz here as a "phenomenon," a certain event as perceived by the voluntary agent. The whole passage is stated very much in terms of what appears to the agent; that Leibniz was thinking in those terms is confirmed by the fact that he initially wrote "perception" where "phenomenon" stands in the text as I quoted it and that he initially wrote "when I will that it appear to me" in describing the willing of a motion of his hand. A substance that is conscious of an appetite for a perception of a certain event is active in producing the event, if the appetite does indeed produce the perception; whereas other substances involved in the event are acted on if they are not conscious of such an appetite for their perceptions of the event. According to Leibniz's philosophy, they must have had appetites for those perceptions, but they were not conscious of them; that is, they were much less distinctly aware of them than the active substance was of its corresponding appetite. I believe that for Leibniz activity and passivity in the production of an event consist in more and less distinct perception of a monad's own appetite for perceptions of the event, although this distinctness does not reach consciousness in most cases as it does in the case of voluntary action.

My hypothesis is that Leibniz saw the dominant monad as active, in this way, in the normal functioning of its organic body, the functioning that fits the body constantly to be the direct expression of the dominant monad. This is connected with Leibniz's speaking of the monad as the "soul" or "substantial form" of the body or of the corporeal substance. He was consciously and professedly adopting or adapting Aristotelian and scholastic terminology here, and he explicitly took a position, in the famous scholastic dispute about the unit or plurality of substantial forms, for those who held that there is only one substantial form or soul in each substance. He considered himself to be in agreement with theological authority on this point (Gr. 552), and to Queen Sophia Charlotte he wrote:

> I have read the sheet that Your Majesty was kind enough to send me on the subject of my letter. It is very much to my taste, when it says that the immaterial is active, and that the material is passive. That is exactly my idea. I also recognize degrees in activites, such as life, perception, reason, and thus believe that there can be more kinds of souls, which are called vegetative, sensitive, rational, as there are kinds of bodies which have life without sensation, and others which have life and sensation without reason. I believe, however, that the sensitive soul is vegetative at the same time, and that the rational soul is sensitive and vegetative, and that thus one single soul in us includes these three degrees, [13] without its being necessary to conceive of three souls in us, of which the lower would be material in relation to the higher; and it seems that that would be to multiply beings without necessity (G VI,521).

Two points in this text are important for my present purpose: that I am the vegetative and sensitive soul of my body, as well as a rational soul, and that the functions of a vegetative and sensitive soul are the activites of life and sensation. If I am the vegetative soul of my body, that is presumably because I am active in the nutritive functioning of my body — for example, in particular events of sugar metabolism in the cells of my body. And, if I am active in those events, that is because I perceive my preceding appetite for my perception of them and that perception, though unconscious, is more distinct than the perception any other monad in my body has of its corresponding appetite.

This hypothesis allows, but does not require, that the dominant monad perceives *all* events in its body more distinctly than any other monad in the body does. All that is required is that it have more distinct perceptions of its appetites for all events of *normal* functioning of the body. I see no reason why the soul must be similarly active with respect to traumas of disease or injury in the body. In fact, I suspect Leibniz would deny that it is. His fullest discussion of the soul's role in the production of such traumas is in response to a criticism by Bayle. Bayle had asked how the theory of preestablished harmony could explain the sudden transition from pleasure to pain in a dog that is struck unexpectedly by a stick while eating (G IV,531). What is the previous state of the dog's soul from which the sudden pain results, according to Leibniz? Leibniz replies:

> Thus the causes that make the stick act (that is to say the man positioned behind the dog, who is getting ready to hit it while it eats, and everything in the course of bodies that contributes to dispose that man to this) are also represented from the first in the soul of the dog exactly in accordance with the truth, but weakly by little, confused perceptions, without apperception, that is to say without the dog noticing it, because the dog's body is also only imperceptibly affected. And when in the course of bodies these dispositions finally produce the blow pressed hard on the body of the dog, in the same way the representations of these dispositions in the dog's soul finally produce the representation of the blow of the stick. Since that representation is distinguished and strong, . . . the dog apperceives it very distinctly, and that is what makes its pain (G IV,532).

This explanation, according to which perceptions produce one another in the soul by virtue of their representing corporeal events that follow from one another by the laws of the corporeal universe, is reminiscent of Spinoza's version of psychophysical parallelism. But what I want to emphasize in this text is that the soul's prior tendency to have the pain that is its perception of the trauma in its body is based on its unconscious perception of events outside its body.[14] It perceives these events indirectly by perceiving its own body; I cannot see that Leibniz is committed to saying that the soul perceives those external events more distinctly than the subordinate monads do. At any rate, a more distinct perception of external events, or of the causes of traumas, is not obviously connected with the functions of a vegetative soul.

This hypothesis about the nature of the rule that the dominant monad bears in its body confirms and illuminates my interpretation of the nature of organism in Leibniz. An organic body is one of many of whose operations, in its parts of all sizes, can be explained not only mechanically but also *teleologically*, as directed in accordance with the active appetites of a soul that is at least vegetative and may also be sensitive and rational. And the active appetites of a vegetative soul are for states that contribute to the maintenance of the body as a direct expression of a monad and a perfect expression of the whole corporeal universe, according to certain laws of nature.

3. AGGREGATES

Leibniz says that "the body is an aggregate of substances" (G II,135/L-A 170). We may be tempted to think this contradicts the thesis that bodies are phenomena, but Leibniz did not think these views inconsistent. He speaks of masses as "only Beings by aggregation, and *therefore* phenomena."[15] (G II,252/L 531, my emphasis; cf. G VII,344). In order to understand this doctrine—frequently asserted by Leibniz—that precisely as aggregates of substances, bodies are phenomena, we must first consider how these aggregates are constituted. There are two questions here: of what sort of substances are bodies aggregates, and what is the principle of aggregation that determines which substances are grouped together to form a particular aggregate?

Leibniz is commonly read as holding that bodies are aggregates of *monads*. A question naturally arises: how could an aggregate of those ultimately real substances be only an appearance? But it is not entirely clear that he did think of bodies as aggregates of monads or simple substances. There are indeed places in his works where he speaks of a corporeal mass as aggregated from "unities" (G II,379) or, more clearly, as "a result or assemblage of simple substances or indeed of a multitude of real unities" (G IV,491; cf. G VII,561; G III,367; G II,282/L 539; G III,622). I think there are more texts, however, that support the view that "a mass is an aggregate of *corporeal* substances" (G VII,501, my emphasis; cf. G III,260; G IV,572; G II,205f.; G VI,550; C 13f.; L-W 139). We have seen that, according to Leibniz, a corporeal substance is composed of a monad and the organic body of that monad and that in his opinion the organic body is a phenomenon (G III,657). This might suggest to us that Leibniz thought corporeal masses are phenomena *because* they are aggregates of corporeal substances that are partly composed of phenomena.

This explanation of Leibniz's belief in the phenomenality of corporeal aggregates is unacceptable, however, for at least four reasons. (1) If masses are phenomena because they are composed of corporeal substances that are partly composed of phenomena, the corporeal substances themselves should also be phenomena because they are partly composed of phenomena; but Leibniz did not hold that corporeal substances are phenomena. (2) So far as I know, Leibniz never says that corporeal aggregates are phenomena because they are partly composed of phenomena; but he often says they are phenomena because they are aggregates. (3) Indeed, a vicious-looking circle would arise if Leibniz tried to explain the phenomenality of corporeal aggregates on the ground that they are partly composed of organic bodies that are phenomena, for he explains the phenomenality of organic bodies on the ground that they are aggregates. (4) Leibniz did write to De Volder that "accurately speaking, matter is not composed of" monads "but results from them" (G II,268/L 536). Elsewhere, however, it seems that the treatment of bodies as aggregates of *corporeal* substances is not meant to exclude the claim that at bottom they are entirely reducible to *simple* substances or monads, related in certain ways. Thus, Leibniz can say that every body is "an aggregate of animals or other living and therefore organic things or else of concretions or masses, but which also themselves are finally analyzed into living things"—where I take the living things to be corporeal substances; but he adds immediately that "the last thing in the analysis of substances is simple substances, namely souls or, if you prefer a more general word, *Monads*, which lack parts" (C 13f.). For all of these reasons, I think we must try to understand why Leibniz would have thought that aggregates as such cannot be more than phenomena even if they are aggregates of *simple* substances.

First, however, we have to consider what is the principle that determines how substances—simple or corporeal, as the case may be—are grouped together to form a body. Although Leibniz does not give much explanation on this point, I think it is fairly clear that a body will be an aggregate of all or most of the substances whose positions are within some continuous three-dimensional portion of space. What portion of space that is, and which substances are members of the aggregate, may change over time, of course. This spatial togetherness is a necessary condition for any corporeal aggregation, but it is presumably not a sufficient contin for even the accidental unity that Leibniz ascribes to a stone. For such unity, additional, quasi-causal conditions on the way in which the members of the aggregate change their positions relative to each other will also be necessary.[16]

If the aggregation of substances into bodies depends on the positions of the substances, the next thing we will want to know is what determines the positions of the substance in space. It is not hard to answer this question if it is about *corporeal* substances. A corporeal substance is composed of an organic body and the dominant monad of that body. The position of the corporeal substance will surely be the position of its organic body. The organic body is a phenomenon, spatial position is a phenomenal property, and the spatial position of the organic body is *given* in appearance. The spatial position of a corporeal substance is thus the one it appears to have, or perhaps the one it *would* appear to have in a perfected science.

If we think of bodies as aggregates of *simple* substance, we will need to have spatial positions for the simple substances as well as for corporeal substances. But this can be accomplished by assigning to each simple substance the spatial position of its organic body (cf. G II,253/L 531), for, according to Leibniz, each simple substance is the dominant monad of an organic body.

This construction of bodies as aggregates of either corporeal or simple substances has the metaphysical peculiarity that the grouping of the substances into aggregates depends on the spatial appearance of the bodies. Those who seek a less phenomenalistic reading of Leibniz might wish to find a construction of corporeal aggregates that is independent of such phenomenal properties of bodies. I once thought I had discovered such a construction. It starts with Bertrand Russell's statement that for Leibniz "places result from points of view, and points of view involve confused perception or *materia prima*."[17] In this construction, all spatial relations are to be defined in terms of the points of view of monads. These points of view will be the positions of the monads and will be conceptually prior to the positions of bodies. The points of view of monads will be positions determined by comparison of the degree of confusion of their perceptions of each other, in accordance with the principle that, if monad A's perception of monad C is more obscure than monad A's perception of monad B, then monad A is closer to monad B than to monad C.

William Irvine[18] has persuaded me that this construction is mathematically possible. That is, if we are given a monad corresponding to every point of space, plus, for every triple of monads, A, B, and C, the information whether the distance AB is greater or less than, or equal to, the distance AC, that will suffice for the construction of all spatial relations. Furthermore, Leibniz often indicates that distance is correlated with obscurity of perception. Nevertheless, I have not found this construction in Leibniz, and I have come to believe that it does not correspond to his intentions, for several reasons.

(1) It is not plausible to suppose that we always perceive nearer things more distinctly than anything that is farther away, and Leibniz does not seem to have believed it. In response to a related objection by Arnauld, he wrote that in distinctness of perception "the distance of some is compensated for by the smallness or other hindrance of others, and Thales sees the stars without seeing the ditch in front of his feet" (G II,90/L-A 113). In other places, he says that the things a monad perceives distinctly are "some that are nearer *or more prominent, accommodated to its organs*" or "the nearest, *or the largest* with respect to each of the Monads" (C 15, Mon. 60, my emphasis). Thus, distance and obscurity of perception are not always directly proportional to each other, and it is not clear that degrees of obscurity of perception will provide enough data for a mathematically satisfactory construction of spatial relations.

(2) In order to make the points of view of monads completely prior to bodies, I was trying to define them in terms of monads' perceptions *of each other*, rather than in terms of their perceptions of bodies. But I have not found any indication that Leibniz thought that any monad, except God, ever perceives any other monad directly. In section 2, I have argued for an interpretation of his system according to which I perceive every other created monad by perceiving, more or less distinctly, its organic body.

(3) The construction of all spatial relations, and therefore of bodies, from the points of view of monads depends on assigning to each monad a point in space as its precise position. Leibniz noted in 1709, however, that, although he had once "located Souls in points," that was "many years before, when his philosophy was not yet mature enough" (G II,372/L 599). In the last decades of his life, he seems

to have thought that the only spatial position that could correctly be assigned to monads is that of "the whole organic body that they animate" (G II,371/L 598; cf. G IV,477; NE II,xxiii,21; G III,357).

I conclude that the first construction I gave of the spatial positions of simple and corporeal substances is the one intended by Leibniz. These positions and, therefore, the aggregation of substances into bodies are dependent on the apparent position of bodies as phenomena. Having come to this conclusion, I am ready to try to explain why Leibniz would have thought that corporeal aggregates cannot be more than phenomena even if they are aggregates of simple substances. There are two sorts of reason to be considered here: Leibniz has (1) a reason for thinking that *all* aggregates as such must be merely phenomena and (2) a special reason for ascribing phenomenal status to *corporeal* aggregates.

(1) The reason that he usually gives for thinking that aggregates as such are only phenomena is that they are not one per se. "Finally, bodies are nothing but aggregates, constituting something that is one *per accidens* or by an external denomination, and therefore they are well founded Phenomena" (G VII,344). The unity of an aggregate comes to it by an "external denomination" — namely, by relation to a mind that perceives relationships among the things that are aggregated. And, since Leibniz adhered to the Scholastic maxim that 'being' and 'one' are equivalent [*"Ens et unum convertuntur"* (G II,304)], he inferred that aggregates that have their unity only in the mind also have their being only in the mind.

This reasoning is clearly expressed in Leibniz's long letter of 30 April 1687 to Arnauld.

> To be brief, I hold as an axiom this identical proposition which is diversified only by accent, namely that what is not truly *one* being [*un* estre] is not truly a *being* [un *estre*] either. It has always been believed that these are mutually convertible things. . . . I have believed therefore that I would be permitted to distinguish Beings of aggregation from substances, since those Beings have their unity only in our mind, which relies on the relations or modes of genuine substances (G II,97/L-A 121).

Leibniz's claim is that aggregates have their unity and, therefore, their being only in the mind and that this is true even of aggregates of real things.

Why did Leibniz think that aggregates have their unity only in the mind? Another passage in the same letter to Arnauld reminds us that Leibniz is a conceptualist about abstract objects in general and also about relations (G II,438), believing that they have their being only in the mind (especially in the divine mind). (Cf. NE II,xii,3-7.) The same treatment is to be accorded to the unity of an aggregate and, hence, to the aggregate itself.

> Our mind notices or conceives some genuine substances which have certain modes; these modes include relations to other substances, from which the mind takes the occasion to join them together in thought and to put one name in the accounting for all these things together, which serves for convenience in reasoning; but one must not let oneself be deceived into making of

them so many substances or truly real Beings. That is only for those who stop at appearances, or else for those who make realities out of all the abstractions of the mind, and who conceive number, time, place, motion, shape, sensible qualities as so many separate beings (G II,101/L-A 126f.).

In Leibniz's ontology, the only things that have being in their own right are particular "substances, or complete Beings, endowed with a true unity, with their different successive states" (ibid.). Everything else, including universals and also including aggregates, "being nothing but phenomena, abstractions, or relations" (ibid.), is at best a being of reason (*ens rationis*), existing in the mind and dependent on being thought of.

(2) There is another reason for assigning the status of appearances to *corporeal* aggregates in particular. "Mass is nothing but a phenomenon, like the Rainbow," wrote Leibniz to Des Bosses (G II,390). The rainbow provides Leibniz with a favorite example of a phenomenon to which he frequently likens bodies. His treatment of the example is not perfectly consistent. At least once (G II,58/L-A 66), he contrasts the rainbow with aggregates, but more often it is presented as something that is a phenomenon because it is an aggregate (e.g., G II,306). "The rainbow," Leibniz says, "is an aggregate of drops which jointly produce certain colors that are apparent to us" (Gr. 322). "The rainbow is of diminished reality under two headings," Leibniz says, "for it is a Being by aggregation of drops, and the qualities by which it is known are apparent or at least of that kind of real ones which are relative to our senses" (Gr. 322). The first of these reasons for the diminished reality of the rainbow is simply Leibniz's general thesis of the phenomenality of aggregates; it is the second reason that we must now develop.

This reason has to do with the perceptual relativity of colors. Colors, Leibniz indicates in the same text, are "apparent qualities" in the sense that they are "not in things absolutely, but insofar as they act on us; thus the same water will seem cold or tepid or hot according to the disposition of my hands. Yet this is real in it, that it is naturally apt to produce this sensation in me when I am thus disposed" (Gr. 322). Colors in general are apparent qualities in this sense, according to Leibniz; but he neglects to emphasize that the colors of the rainbow are even more than ordinarily relative to perception. Any particular aggregate of drops of water will be colored as a rainbow only relative to perceptions from a particular place. And, on the other hand, Leibniz thinks that spatial properties, too—such as size, shape, and position—are not in monads absolutely but can be ascribed to monads or aggregates of monads in a derivative sense defined in terms of the way the organic bodies of the monads are perceived. Because the aggregation of drops in a rainbow, and of monads in a body, is based on properties that are relative to perception in this way, he infers that the rainbow and the body are phenomena and have diminished reality.

It is misleading, I think, that Leibniz says in presenting this argument that the qualities by which the rainbow is *known* or recognized (*noscitur*) are apparent or relative to our senses. What is crucial here is not that we know or recognize the rainbow by merely apparent qualities. We know or recognize other monads generally by properties of their bodies that are merely apparent, according to Leibniz, and the monads are not less real for that. The crux of the argument is that the *existence* of the aggregate depends on properties that are relative to our perceptions. The relation to perception provides the principle of grouping that defines the aggregate. If we think of a rainbow as an aggregate of drops, what is it that picks them out from all the other drops of water in the sky and groups them as an object that we call a rainbow? It is their relation to the color perceptions that an observer (in one place but not in others) would have. It is only in appearance that there is more reason to aggregate these drops together than to form any other group from the drops in the sky. Likewise, the aggregation of monads as belonging to a single corporeal mass depends entirely on their bodies' *appearing* to occupy contiguous or overlapping spaces.

Suppose through a cleverly contrived network of glass fibers the images of a thousand different people walking, talking, and gesturing on a thousand different streets of a hundred different cities were combined to give you an image of an angry mob. This "mob," we might say, is an aggregate of real human beings, but the reality of the individual persons does not keep the mob as such from being a mere phenomenon. This is because the existence of an aggregate (in the Leibnizian sense) depends on relations among its members in a way that the existence of a set does not. If sets exist at all, the existence of all the members of a set suffices for the existence of the set. But that Leibnizian paradigm of an aggregate, a pile of wood, ceases to exist when the logs in it are scattered, even though the logs are not destroyed. A pile or mob exists only while its members are grouped by a certain proximity. In the case that I described, the mob is a mere phenomenon because its grouping is merely apparent and exists only in the image presented to you by the optical apparatus. This would be an apt example for Leibniz, because in his opinion the aggregation of monads by spatial relations, to form bodies, is no less dependent on perception since monads do not have spatial properties in their own right but are spatially represented in our perceptions. (Cf. G III,623.) "And the aggregates themselves are nothing but phenomena," Leibniz says, "since besides the monads that enter into them, the rest is added by perception alone, by the very fact that they are perceived together" (G II,517).

Doubts may remain, nevertheless, as to whether this conception of bodies as aggregates and therefore phenomena is completely consistent with the account I gave in section 1, according to which bodies, as phenomena, are perceptions considered with regard to their objective reality or representational content. Several questions arise here. (1) Does Leibniz think that aggregates of monads, or of corporeal substances, as the case may be, are perceptions or modifications of the mind (considered with regard to their objective reality or representational content)? Yes, he seems to be saying that in his conceptualism about aggregates. (2) If bodies as phemonena are the objects of stories told by perception, by common sense, and especially by science, as I suggested earlier, can they also be aggregates of substances? Certainly they can also be aggregates, for, according to Leibniz, it is part of the story told by science, and less clearly also by common sense and perception, that every extended thing is composed of parts into which it could be divided; and that is enough to make extended things aggregates in Leibniz's book. On the other hand, it does not seem to be part of the story told by perception, common sense, or science that extended things are composed of *monads*, nor perhaps even that they are composed of *substances* at all. To this I think Leibniz might say that those stories do not *exclude* the thesis that bodies are aggregates of substances. It is at least vaguely part of the stories told by common sense and science that the appearances of bodies have or may have some further foundation in reality. But no hypothesis of the nature of that foundation is part of the stories of Leibnizian science and common sense; it is left to metaphysics to consider what the foundation might be.

(3) Can aggregates of substances possess the physical properties that bodies have in the story told by science? It might seem, in particular, that an aggregate of *simple* substances would not be *continuous* because it is composed of parts that cannot be divided again into parts and that do not adjoin or overlap each other. Leibniz seems to say as much himself in his last letter to De Volder (G II,282/L 539); but that passage is a difficult one in which he also appears to have forgotten his doctrine that aggregates, even aggregates of real things, are phenomena.[19] We could say, however, that, though monads may be *elements* of corporeal aggregates, the relevant *parts* of the aggregate are not monads but subaggregates containing infinitely many monads. The aggregate will be divisible in indefinitely many and various ways into subaggregates of this sort, which will themselves be similarly divisible into subaggregates and which may overlap each other in their membership or may share a common "boundary" of monads. In this way, the aggregate as such can have the mathematical structure of continuity. This distinction between the role of monads and the role of subaggregates in the composition of corporeal aggregates seems to me to be approximately what Leibniz was after when he wrote to Fardella, in March 1690:

> Meanwhile it should not therefore be said that an indivisible substance enters into the composition of a body as a part, but rather as an essential internal requirement. Just as a point, although it is not a component part of a line, but something heterogeneous, is still necessarily required, in order for the line to be and to be understood (FC 320; cf. G II,436/L 600).

Just as the parts of a line are not points but lines, so the parts of a corporeal aggregate are not monads but (I suggest) subaggregates.

Continuity is not the only physical property, of course, but there are natural enough ways of assigning other physical properties to any aggregates of monads that might constitute bodies. Although monads do not have any primitive spatial properties, Leibniz assigns them, in a derivative sense, the spatial positions occupied by their organic bodies. I have argued, further, that the principle of aggregation by which Leibniz thinks monads are grouped to form a corporeal mass provides that the monadic membership of a particular corporeal mass at any given time includes all or most of the monads whose spatial position at that time, in this derived sense, is within a certain region of space. And it seems natural to say that the size and shape of such an aggregate are the size and shape of the space in which the member monads have their positions. The positions are resultant or constructed properties of the monads, but the size and shape are constitutive properties of the aggregate. That is indeed one reason why the aggregate is only a phenomenon, since size and shape are phenomenal properties. Motions can be ascribed to corporeal aggregates on an analogous basis.

I am guilty of some oversimplification here, however. It was pointed out at the end of section 1 that for Leibniz the spatial representation of a monad is defined, not by any single shape, but by an infinite series of increasingly complex shapes. Presumably, the same will be true of aggregates of monads; instead of a single determinate shape, they will have an infinite series of shapes that increase in complexity as they increase in accuracy.

4. THE REALITY OF PHENOMENA

Phenomenalists and idealists do not generally leave us without a systematic difference between the physical objects that appear to us in normal experience and those that appear to us in dreams and hallucinations. In Leibniz's thought, there is a distinction between "real" phenomena and "imaginary" (G VII,319/L 363) or "apparent" or "false" phenomena (Gr. 322). As I stated in section 1, it seems to be part of Leibniz's projects to analyze this distinction in a way that he does not attempt to analyze the *content* of physical phenomena.

His principal account of what it is for phenomena to be "real" or "true" is classically phenomenalistic in the sense that it is in terms of the contents of perceptions and their agreements with other perceptions. "Matter and motion are . . . phenomena of perceivers, whose reality is located in the harmony of perceivers with themselves (at different times) and with other perceivers" (G II,270/L 537). This account can be found in works of all periods of Leibniz's thought—in the Paris years,[20] in 1686 in section 14 of the *Discourse on Metaphysics*, in criticisms of Descartes about 1692 (G IV,356/L 384), in a letter to De Volder in 1704 (G II,270/L 537), and in a sketch of his metaphysics prepared for Remond in 1714 (G III,623), to mention only a few texts.

The criteria for reality of phenomena are most fully spelled out in an essay "On the Method of Distinguishing Real from Imaginary Phenomena" (dated to 1684 by Hochstetter).[21] They are similar to criteria proposed by other early modern philosophers. The internal marks of a real phenomenon are that it is *vivid, complex*, and *harmonious (congruum)*.

> It will be vivid if qualities such as light, color, heat appear intense enough. It will be complex if they are varied, and suited for setting up many experiments and new observations, for example if we experience in the phenomenon not only colors but also sounds, odors, tastes, tactile qualities, and that both in the whole and in various parts, which we can investigate again according to various causes (G VII,319f./L 363).

These first two marks do not usually figure in Leibniz's formulations about the reality of phenomena, but *harmony* is stressed repeatedly. Internally, "a phenomenon will be harmonious when it is composed of several phenomena for which a reason can be given from each other or from some sufficiently simple common hypothesis" (G VII,320/L 364).

The main external mark, and the most important mark, of the reality of a phenomenon is also a sort of harmony:

> if it keeps the custom of other phenomena that have occurred to us frequently, so that the parts of the phenomenon have the same position, order, and outcome that similar phenomena have had. . . . Likewise, if a reason for this [phenomenon] can be given from those that precede, or if they all fit the same hypothesis as a common reason. The strongest proof, however, is surely agreement with the whole series of life, especially if most other [people] affirm that the same thing agrees with their phenomena. . . . But the most powerful proof of the reality of phenomena, which even suffices by itself, is the success of predicting future phenomena from past and present ones (G VII,320/L 364).

The notions of complexity and harmony are clearly connected here with notions of causal order. Real phenomena are those that form part of a *causally* coherent, *scientifically* adequate story that appears all or most of the time, at least in an obscure or fragmentary way, to all or most perceivers. That is the story that would be told by a perfected physical science. Imaginary phenomena are those that do not fit in this story.[22]

There is a problem about how Leibniz can admit imaginary phenomena in this sense at all, for he holds that every monad always perceives the whole universe. It follows that the true physical story appears at *all* times to *all* perceivers, not just to most of them at most times. How then can there be any false phenomena? I have not found Leibniz dealing explicitly with this problem, but we can conjecture what his answer might have been. In the first place, I think he believed that all perceptions of every monad do express something that is in the monad's organic body. Suppose I seem to see a pink rat. Leibniz would say that this perception expresses, and is a perception of, some event in my body. As a perception of that event it is a true, not a false, perception, and the event is a real, not an imaginary, phenomenon. What appears to me consciously, however, is not the event in my body, but a pink rat. In this case, I think Leibniz has to say that my perception has two different objective realities or representational contents. The first, an event in my body, is a phenomenon that certainly coheres with the story told by a perfected physical science. The second, a pink rat, may or may not cohere with that story; it is real if it does and an hallucination if it does not.

There are many passages in which Leibniz seems to say that internal and external harmony, supplemented perhaps by vividness and complexity, is a sufficient condition for the reality of a phenomenon. In the essay "On the Method of Distinguishing Real from Imaginary Phenomena," however, he speaks more cautiously.

The marks of reality are presented as epistemic criteria by which we may tell when a phenomenon is real; it is not asserted that they define what the reality of a phenomenon consists in. Indeed, it is virtually implied that a phenomenon could possess the marks of reality and yet not be fully real. "It must be admitted that the proofs of real phenomena that have been adduced thus far, even taken in any combination whatever, are not demonstrative." They have "the greatest probability," or "moral certainty," but not "Metaphysical" certainty; there would be no contradiction in supposing them false. "Therefore it cannot be absolutely demonstrated by any argument that there are bodies; and nothing keeps certain well ordered dreams from being the object of our mind, which we judge to be true and which are equivalent for practical purposes to true things because of their mutual agreement." Leibniz rejects Descartes's claim that in such case God would be a deceiver. "For what if our nature happened not to be capable of real phenomena? Surely God should be thanked rather than blamed in that case; for by causing those phenomena at least to agree, since they could not be real, he has furnished us with something equally as useful, for all of life, as real phenomena" (G VII,320f./L 364; cf. G I,372f.; NE IV,ii,14).

It has been thought that Leibniz vacillated or changed his mind about the sufficiency of the harmony and agreement of phenomena for their reality, but it seems to me more probable that he used 'real' in stronger and weaker senses in expressing different aspects of a fairly constant system of opinions. A statement in the previous paragraph of the same essay is particularly revealing: "Indeed even if it were said that this whole life is nothing but a dream, and the visible world nothing but a phantasm, I would call this dream of phantasm real enough if we were never deceived by it when we used our reason well," that is, if predictions reasonably based on past experience generally succeeded so far as future experience is concerned (G VII,320/L 364). To say that this whole life is a dream is presumably to say that its phenomena lack a kind of reality that phenomena could have, but Leibniz indicates another sense in which our phenomena would still be "real enough," provided only that our experience had all the internal marks of reality.

This helps to explain the fact that Leibniz seems to offer two other accounts of what the reality of bodies consists in. These accounts, I suggest, should be seen as stating additional conditions that harmonious phenomena must satisfy in order to be real in the fullest sense, although their harmony is sufficient for their reality in a weaker sense that is enough for all practical purposes. It must be admitted, however, that all three accounts—the one in terms of the harmony of perceptions as well as the other two—are usually presented as if they were completely independent.

One of the other accounts is theological. In a study for a letter to Des Bosses, Leibniz wrote:

If bodies are phenomena and are evaluated on the basis of our appearances, they will not be real, since they appear differently to different people. Therefore the reality of bodies, space, motions, and time seems to consist in their being God's phenomena, or the object of intuitive knowledge [*scientia visionis*] (G II,438).

This is an exceptional text in two respects. In the first place, it seems to deny that there is enough agreement among human perceivers for their phenomena to satisfy the intersubjective harmony condition for reality. Elsewhere Leibniz seems to assume that the required agreement does exist (DM 14), especially if unconscious perceptions are taken into account. Even in writing to Des Bosses just a few months later, Leibniz says that on the hypothesis that there is nothing outside of all souls or monads, "when we say that Socrates is sitting, nothing else is meant than that those things by which we understand Socrates and sitting are appearing to us and to others who are concerned" (G II,451f./L605), which surely implies enough agreement in the perceptions of those "who are concerned" to distinguish a real from a merely apparent sitting of Socrates.

In the second place, the explanation of the reality of phenomena in terms of God's phenomena is rare in Leibniz's work. It occurs in other letters to Des Bosses (G II,474, 482/L 607f.), but I have not found it elsewhere. There are many unanswered questions, also, about what God's corporeal phenomena would be.[23] For these reasons, I will largely ignore this second, theological account of the reality of phenomena.

The third account applies chiefly to aggregates as such and says that their reality consists in the reality of the substances that enter into them. Aggregates "have no other reality than that which belongs to the Unities that are in them" (G II,261; cf. G VII,314). Given that Leibniz says that bodies *are* aggregates of substances, indeed, it is hard to see how he could fail to think that their reality consists at least partly in the reality of the substances that are aggregated in them. And this thesis plays a part in the argument for monads. It is partly because an aggregate "has no reality unless it is borrowed from the things contained" in it that Leibniz "inferred, therefore there are indivisible unities in things, since otherwise there will be in things no true unity, and no reality not borrowed" (G II,267).

There are several reasons for thinking that this is not a completely independent account of the reality of bodies, that it does not conflict with the account in terms of harmonious perceptions but supplements it and even depends on it. (1) Leibniz seems to have regarded the two accounts as consistent. He sometimes gives both of them in the same document. I have quoted expressions of both of them from his letter of 30 June 1704 to De Volder (G II,267, 270/L 537). And in a single two-page piece written in 1714 Leibniz says both that bodies *are* assemblages of monads and that material things "have their reality from the agreement of the perceptions of apperceiving substances" (G III,622f.).

(2) I think Leibniz believed that the two accounts are at least materially equivalent—that there is a true scientific story that is always at least unconsciously perceived by all monads, that most of what appears consciously to conscious perceivers fits at least approximately into that story, that there are infinitely many monads whose properties are expressed by organic bodies that would figure in a sufficiently detailed extension of the true scientific story, that aggregates of these monads (or of the corporeal substances that they form with their organic bodies) can, therefore, be regarded as the bodies that figure in the true scientific story,

and thus that the bodies of the true scientific theory are real according to both accounts, both as coherent phenomena and as aggregates of real things.

(3) The claim that the reality of bodies consists in the reality of the substances that are aggregated in them presupposes that substances *are* aggregated in them, and this aggregation presupposes the harmony of perceptions. As I argued above, the grouping of substances into corporeal aggregates depends on the spatial positions their organic bodies appear to have. If a single system of aggregates of substances is to be real, as opposed to any others, which may be imaginary, it is surely not enough that the substances that belong to the real aggregates be real; it is also required that the aggregates themselves represent the *true* grouping of the substances. In particular, the true grouping of the substances can hardly depend on the positions the substances' organic bodies appear to have just a little of the time to just any perceiver. Rather, it depends on the positions the organic bodies have in a coherent system of phenomena that are represented by most of the perceptions of all perceivers—or else perhaps by all the perceptions of a single authoritative perceiver (God). In order for there to be corporeal aggregates that are real by virtue of the reality of the substances aggregated in them, they must appear as material masses in this coherent system of phenomena and, therefore, they must satisfy the harmonious perceptions condition for reality—or else the theological condition, but the latter usually seems to play no role in Leibniz's thought.

Considering all these reasons (and ignoring the theological account), I think we find in Leibniz, not two competing analyses of the reality of corporeal phenomena, but one analysis in two layers. Phenomena are real, in a weak sense, if and only if they fit into a single scientifically adequate system of harmonious phenomena of all perceivers.[24] Those phenomena—and only those—that are real in this weaker sense are also real in a fuller sense to the extent that there exist real monads that are appropriately expressed by organic bodies belonging to the system of phenomena that is at least weakly real.

5. CORPOREAL SUBSTANCE (II): PRINCIPLES OF UNITY

There are many texts in which Leibniz says that corporeal substances are distinguished from mere aggregates by a profounder sort of unity. Writing to Arnauld late in 1686, he said, "if there are no corporeal substances, such as I wish, it follows that bodies are nothing but true phenomena, like the rainbow," for on account of the infinite divisibility of the continuum, "one will never come to anything of which one can say, 'Here is truly a being,' except when one finds animated machines of which the soul or substantial form constitutes the substantial unity independent of the external union of contact" (G II,77/L-A 95). This statement implies, first, that there cannot be a corporeal substance without a "substantial unity" stronger than the unity that many aggregates have by the bodily contact of their members with each other and, second, that such a substantial unity is somehow provided by the dominant monad. And this is only one of a number of texts in which the dominant monad, or perhaps sometimes the active entelechy in the dominant monad, is characterized as the principle of unity of the corporeal substance. A corporeal substance is "actuated by one Entelechy, without which there would be in it no principle of true Unity" (G II,250/L 529); "the Monad dominating the Machine makes [the corporeal substance] One" (G II,252/L531; cf. G II,120/L-A 154; L 454; G III,260f.; G II,314; PNG 3).

It may be doubted, however, whether on Leibniz's showing the dominant monad gives to the composite that it forms with the organic body a unity fundamentally different in kind from the unity of an aggregate. As Leibniz himself said, monadic domination and the unity that springs from it consist at bottom only in certain relations among the perceptions of monads. "The agglomeration of these organized corporeal substances which constitutes our body is not united with our Soul except by that relation which follows from the order of the phenomena that are natural to each substance separately" (G IV,573). Aggregates, too, are united (accidentally, Leibniz says) by relations among the perceptions of monads. So at bottom it would seem that the unity of an aggregate and the unity of a corporeal substance are of the same kind.

To be sure, the perceptual relations involved in monadic domination are more direct, in a puzzling sense that I have discussed in section 2, and they play a more basic part in explanation in the Leibnizian system than those that constitute aggregates. They also give rise to interesting properties of a corporeal substance; Leibniz mentions indivisibility, natural indestructibility, and the property of completely expressing its whole past and future, as distinguishing a corporeal substance from a mere aggregate (G II,76/L-A 94). But these properties belong to the organic body, which is not a substance, as well as to the corporeal substance; and they merely result, for Leibniz, from the fact that the organic body, as a phenomenon, is a perpetual perfect expression of the dominant monad, which possesses analogous properties. Given Leibniz's doctrine that "there is nothing in things except simple substances, and in them perception and appetite" (G II,270/L 537), there is no way for the unity of a corporeal substance to be anything over and above the system of relations among the perceptions of monads. By stipulation, of course, Leibniz would be free to define a difference between unity and accidental unity in terms of different patterns of relations among perceptions. But does this add up to such a fundamental metaphysical difference as Leibniz seems to wish to assert between corporeal substances and aggregates?

There is evidence that Leibniz himself worried about this issue, at least in the last ten or twelve years of his life. This evidence is connected with his correspondence with the Jesuit Fathers Tournemine and Des Bosses. Leibniz wrote a note for Tournemine, probably in 1706, in which he acknowledges that his preestablished harmony cannot account any better than the Cartesian philosophy for "a true Union" between the soul and the body. He excuses himself from giving such an account:

> I have tried to give an account only of Phenomena, that is to say, of the relation that is perceived between the Soul and the Body. But as the Metaphysical Union that one adds to it is not a Phenomenon, and as an intelligible

Notion has not even been given of it, I have not taken it upon myself to seek the explanation of it. I do not deny, however, that there is something of that nature (G VI,595).

It is hard to interpret this statement. It certainly does not constitute an affirmation that there is, over and above the relations of perceptions of monads provided by the preestablished harmony, a metaphysical union of soul and body. In fact, Leibniz plainly denies that such a union is part of his philosophy. But is he tactfully muffling his belief that it is an unintelligible absurdity? Or is he more straightforwardly acknowledging that there may be something in the universe that cannot be understood in his philosophy?

The more cynical reading of the text is supported, in my opinion, by the last letter he wrote to De Volder, dated 19 January 1706, in which he reports an interchange with Tournemine. What he wrote to De Volder agrees closely in substance with what he wrote for Tournemine but is noticeably less respectful and more ironic in tone. It is introduced with the remark, "The scholastics commonly seek things that are not so much beyond this world [*ultramundana*] as Utopian. An elegant example was recently supplied to me by the Jesuit Tournemine, an ingenious Frenchman" (G II,281/L 538). The "example," stigmatized as "Utopian," is Tournemine's demand for an account of a union, different from agreement, between body and soul. By itself, therefore, the interchange with Tournemine is not much evidence that Leibniz had serious misgivings about his own philosophy.

The evidence of Leibniz's correspondence with Des Bosses, however, cannot be disposed of so easily. That correspondence is voluminous and in large part devoted to the nature of the union between soul and body. It is in writing to Des Bosses, probably in 1712, that Leibniz introduced the notorious concept of a *substantial bond (vinculum substantiale)*. The substantial bond is "a certain union, or rather a real unifier superadded to the monads by God"; it is "something absolute (and therefore substantial)" (G II,435/L 600). It "will not be a simple result, or will not consist solely of true or real relations, but will add besides some new substantiality or substantial bond; and it will be an effect not only of the divine intellect but also of the divine will" (G II,438) — or, as we might say, it will not be a mere logical construct out of monads and the relations of their perceptions. A subsantial bond never unites spatially scattered monads; it unites only "monads which are under the domination of one, or which make one organic body or one Machine of nature" (G II,438f.; cf. G II,486/L 609). And each substantial bond is permanently attached to a single dominant monad (G II,496/L 611). It is only by the order of nature, however, and not by absolute necessity, that the substantial bond thus requires the dominant monad and its organic body. Supernaturally and miraculously, God can separate the bond from the monads (G II,495f./L 610f.) and perhaps does so in transubstantiation, in the Eucharist.

The conception of the substantial bond includes some of the properties that Leibniz previously ascribed to the dominant monad. It is "the very substantial form of the composite" (G II,516; cf. G II,504/L 614) and apparently "consists in the primitive active and passive power of the composite" (G II,485f./L 609). "This bond will be the source [*principium*] of the actions of the composite substance" (G II,503/L 613). It is to the substantial bond that the properties of the composite substance are to be ascribed; "it will be necessary that the accidents of the composite be its modifications" (G II,486/L 609).

Unlike any monad, however, the substantial bond is metaphysically acted on by other finite things. It does not change anything in the monads (G II,517; cf. G II,451/L 604), for that would be contrary to their nature. But it unites them by being influenced by them (G II,496/L 611).

"If that substantial bond of monads were absent, all bodies with all their qualities would be nothing but well founded phenomena, like the rainbow or the image in a mirror" (G II,435/L 600). But, if there were substantial bonds, then corporeal substance would be "something making phenomena real outside of Souls" (G II,451/L 604; cf. G II,515f., 519). Among phenomena made real are not only bodies but their qualities of continuity and extension. "Real continuity cannot arise except from a substantial bond" (G II,517).

The question of the extent to which Leibniz personally accepted this theory of substantial bonds is extremely controversial. Some interpreters have taken the theory straightforwardly as a part of his philosophy in its final form. I believe the majority view, however, is typified by Russell's statement, "Thus the *vinculum substantiale* is rather the concession of a diplomatist than the creed of a philosopher."[25]

Several reasons can be given for not taking the substantial bond very seriously as a part of Leibniz's thought. (1) The most important reason is that it is blatantly inconsistent with other parts of his philosophy. The theory of substantial bonds postulates something ultimately real in things besides "simple substances, and in them perception and appetite" (cf. G II,270/L 537). It also postulates a continuous extension that is not a phenomenon but is real. Both of these positions are emphatically rejected in many other places in Leibniz's writings, late as well as early (e.g., in G III,622f. and E 745f., written in 1714 and 1716, respectively).

(2) Russell says that "nowhere does Leibniz himself assert that he believes" the doctrine of substantial bonds.[26] This could be disputed. In a letter of 16 January 1716, he refers to "the primitive passive and active powers of the composite" and says to Des Bosses, "the complete thing resulting from them I really judge to be that substantial bond which I am urging" (G II,511). This certainly looks like an endorsement of this doctrine. It could be read, however, as a statement only of what Leibniz thinks should be said about primitive passive and active powers *if* they are ascribed to a composite substance as such. And it is true that Leibniz more commonly speaks of substantial bonds in a more tentative way that seems to leave open the alternative hypothesis that bodies are in fact only phenomena. He even explicitly expresses to Des Bosses some preference for the phenomenalistic view (G II,461).

(3) A particularly important indication of Leibniz's intentions is found in a passage, cited by Russell, from Leibniz's letter of 30 June 1715 to Des Bosses:

Whether my latest answer about Monads will have pleased you, I hardly know. I fear that the things I have written to you at different times about this subject may not cohere well enough among themselves, since, you know, I have not treated this theme, of Phenomena to be elevated to reality, or of composite substances, except on the occasion of your letters (G II,499).

The theme (*argumentum*) mentioned in this text is certainly the doctrine of substantial bonds. Leibniz is telling Des Bosses, in effect, that he has not thought enough about it and does not have the ideas clearly enough in mind to be confident that he has been consistent in what he has said about it from one letter to another. Whatever may have seemed plausible to Leibniz in those hours that he spent writing to Des Bosses, a theory that he did not "treat" except in this correspondence, that he did not keep clearly in mind, and that is blatantly inconsistent with important doctrines that he asserted in many other places and continued to assert during this period of his life, cannot be counted as a part of his philosophy.

There is quite a range of attitudes, however, that a philosopher may have toward ideas that are not a part of his philosophy. He may be sure they are false. He may be afraid they may be true or wish they were true. He may think they present an intriguing or perhaps even a promising alternative to some of his own views. He may be playing more or less seriously with the thought of trying to incorporate them into his philosophy. He may be completely confident of the correctness of his own theories; but, if he is worried about their adequacy in some respect, that will affect his interest in alternative theories.

In trying to discover Leibniz's attitude toward the theory of substantial bonds, we must form some assessment of his motives in discussing it with Des Bosses. Russell's claim that the *vinculum substantiale* is "the concession of a diplomatist" reflects a cynical assessment. It is based on the idea that the theory "springs from Leibniz's endeavour to reconcile his philosophy with the dogma of transubstantiation." Not that he meant at this stage in his life to accept the dogma. As a Lutheran, he was quite frank with Des Bosses that he did not accept it (G II,390). But "he was extremely anxious to persuade Catholics that they might, without heresy, believe in his doctrine of monads," suggests Russell.[27]

There are at least four reasons for regarding Russell's explanation of Leibniz's motives as implausible. (1) Leibniz was certainly capable of concealing part of his position in order to make the rest of it more palatable to others. He has even left behind some indication that he believed in doing so.[28] But one at least must wonder why he would be interested in selling to Catholics what is left of the theory of monads after abandoning the claim that the world is constituted by monads alone.

(2) I must record my own impression that Leibniz strikes me as comparatively candid, rather than cautious, in his correspondence with Des Bosses. His very inability to remember exactly what he had said to Des Bosses supports the suggestion that he was not carefully shaping diplomatic missives but rather was freely and casually playing with ideas in letters to a good friend. It is worth noting that the more phenomenalistic aspects of Leibniz's thought find much fuller expression in his letters to Des Bosses than they do in his publications and his letters to most correspondents, though Leibniz withheld from Des Bosses a full endorsement of phenomenalistic views that he did endorse in writing to some others.

(3) The doctrine of the substantial bond was proposed by Leibniz, not forced

on him by Des Bosses, although the term 'bond' (*vinculum*) in this context does have resonance with Jesuit metaphysics of the seventeenth century.[29] Indeed, Des Bosses showed a rather persistent preference for accidental or modal bonds, against which Leibniz had to defend his substantial bonds. And Des Bosses did not react with horror to the phenomenalistic alternatives offered by Leibniz. If the *vinculum substantiale* was a concession, it was not in any simple way a concession to Des Bosses.

(4) Except in one of Leibniz's letters, neither he nor Des Bosses seems to have believed that the doctrine of transubstantiation could not be accommodated without the substantial bonds. Leibniz did once say that he could hardly see how the dogma could be "sufficiently explained by mere monads and phenomena" (G II,460). But he subsequently proposed two different theories of transubstantiation based on the assumption that only monads and their phenomena exist (G II,474/L 607f.; G II,520f.), and the availability of these theories did not seem to diminish his interest in substantial bonds.

Des Bosses also proposed to Leibniz a theory of transubstantiation based on "the Hypothesis of bodies reduced to Phenomena" (G II,453-55). He did not endorse this theory, but he liked it better, in one way at least, than Leibniz's substantial bond theory of transubstantiation. In Leibniz's theory, the substantial bonds of the sacramental bread and wine, or of the corporeal substances contained in them, are miraculously destroyed, but the monads of the bread and wine endure and are miraculously united to the substantial bonds of the body and blood of Christ. Des Bosses objected to the survival of the monads of the bread and wine as inconsistent with "the dogma of the Church . . . that the whole substance of the bread and wine perish" (G II,463; cf. 474, 480). In Des Bosses's theory based on monads and phenomena alone, the monads of the bread and wine are destroyed and the monads of the body and blood of Christ take their place. Leibniz was averse, of course, to the destruction of monads; but Des Bosses forced him to admit, in the end, that the destruction of substantial bonds would be just as unnatural (G II,481f.).

There is more than one alternative, of course, to a cynical reading of Leibniz's discussion of substantial bonds. He could largely have been playing, in a friendly discussion, with ideas that he did not believe for a minute. But there is something to be said for the view that Leibniz was influenced to some extent by worries about the adequacy of his philosophy to account for certain types of union.

I have already argued that he had reason to be uneasy about the adequacy of his account of the special unity that he wished to ascribe to corporeal substances. A few hints of such uneasiness may be found elsewhere (e.g., the mention of "metaphysical union of the soul and its body" in G III,658), but the major evidence for it is in the letters to Des Bosses.

This evidence is independent of the question whether Leibniz accepted the theory of substantial bonds. Even if he did not, he seems at least to have asserted to Des Bosses that without the bonds there would be no corporeal substances that would be one per se because the monads and their subordination would not be enough to constitute such composite substances (G II,435,444,511,517f./L 600,602). This is clearly inconsistent with Leibniz's oft-repeated claim that the dominant monad is the principle of unity that makes a corporeal substance one per se.

It would be neat and tidy if it could be shown that these statements to Des Bosses represent a change of mind on Leibniz's part. But, in fact, there seems not to have been a settled change in his views on this point. Even after he began to make these statements to Des Bosses, he wrote in *The Principles of Nature and of Grace* that the dominant monad of a composite substance "makes . . . the principle of its unicity" (PNG 3).[30] We have to do here with a vacillation, at most, rather than a change of mind.

I believe that Leibniz's deepest grounds for misgivings about the adequacy of his treatment of concepts of union were theological. The theory of substantial bonds is introduced under the condition, "if faith leads us to corporeal substance" (G II,435/L 600), though the allusion there may be more to Des Bosses's theology than to Leibniz's own. In any event, Leibniz alludes to problems about the relation of his philosophy to dogmas to which he was committed as he was not committed to transubstantiation, problems about the need for a strong concept of union or something similar. The Lutheran doctrine of the Eucharist, as he explained it to Des Bosses, does not involve transubstantiation but does involve a real "presence of the body of Christ," and he acknowledged that this presence "is something Metaphysical, as union is: which is not explained by phenomena" (G II,390/L615n8; cf. G VI,595f. and Gr. 449).

Still more important is a problem about the doctrine of the Incarnation. He wrote to Des Bosses:

> If an account could be thought out for explaining the possibility of your transubstantiation even with bodies reduced to phenomena alone, I would much prefer that. For that Hypothesis pleases in many ways. Nor do we need anything else besides Monads and their internal modifications, for Philosophy as opposed to the supernatural. But I fear that we cannot explain the mystery of the Incarnation, and other things, unless real bonds or unions are added (G II,461).

This is not the only text in which Leibniz suggests something like this about the Incarnation. There is an obscure but fascinating theological fragment, not addressed to any correspondent, in which he brings the Incarnation together with the union of soul and body: "Everything can be explained by adding one thing to those things which can be explained from phenomena—namely, by adding the *union* of God with the creature in the incarnation; of the soul with the body to make the human suppositum; of the monads among themselves to make the secondary substance or organic body" (RML 414, Leibniz's emphasis). I take it that the human suppositum and organic body mentioned here are the human nature and human body of Christ, but it is striking that the idea of a union of body and soul, and of monads, that cannot be explained in terms of phenomena is once more linked with the union of divine and human in Christ.

Perhaps there was a reason for this linkage. A long tradition has seen the relation of divine and human in the Incarnation as analogous to the union of body and soul in a human being. The so-called "Athanasian Creed" states, "For as the reasonable soul and flesh is one man, so God and man is one Christ."[31] The analogy was familiar to Leibniz. In a study for a letter to the Electress Sophia in 1702 he wrote, "For as an active thing joined to the animal makes the man of it, so the Divinity joined to the man makes of it the man that is God's [*l'homme à Dieu*; or the man-god (*l'homme-Dieu*) as Leibniz actually wrote to the Electress]" (G VI, 521).

There are two reasons why Leibniz might have thought that the doctrine of the union of divine and human natures in the Incarnation requires another conception of union than that which monadic domination provides in his philosophy for the union of body and soul. The first reason is simply that, as we have seen, the union provided by monadic domination is not very strong. The second reason is that applying the Leibnizian conception of domination directly to the Incarnation leads to heresy. According to Leibniz, the dominant monad is the *sole* substantial form of a corporeal substance. If it is a rational soul, it is the sensitive and vegetative soul of its body as well. By analogy, if the second person of the holy Trinity were united with a human nature as a dominant monad in a corporeal substance, the divine nature would be the only substantial form or soul of that substance. It would take the place of the rational as well as the sensitive and vegetative souls. But that is an extension of the Apollinarian heresy. Orthodoxy requires, as Leibniz surely knew, that the single person of Christ include a complete human soul distinct from the divine nature.

If Leibniz believed, at the end of his life, that the doctrines that are most satisfactory in philosophy as such are not adequate for theology, that would not have been an unprecedented belief. It was held, before Leibniz, by many philosophers whose loyalty to Christianity was sincere. That would have been an uncomfortable position, however, for a philosopher who held in his *Theodicy*, in the "Preliminary Discourse on the Conformity of Faith with Reason" (§ 63), that "the Mysteries surpass our reason, . . . but they are not at all contrary to our reason." Leibniz would surely have preferred to think that the central dogmas of Christianity can be reconciled with the views to which a rational examination of the nature of substance would lead us. But it is not clear that he saw how that could be done to his own satisfaction.[32]

Notes

1. The works of Leibniz are cited by the following abbreviations: C = *Opuscules et fragments inédits de Leibniz*, ed. by Louis Couturat (Paris: Alcan, 1903). DM = *Discourse on Metaphysics*, as ed. by Henri Lestienne (Paris: Vrin, 1975) and trans. by P. G. Lucas and L. Grint (Manchester: Manchester University Press, 1953), cited by section number. E = *Opera philosophica*, ed. by J. E. Erdmann (Berlin: G. Eichler, 1840). FC = *Nouvelles lettres et opuscules inédits de Leibniz*, ed. by Foucher de Careil (Paris: Aug. Durand, 1857). G = *Die philosophischen Schriften von Gottfried Wilhelm Leibniz*, ed. by C. I. Gerhardt (Berlin: Weidmannsche Buchhandlung, 1875-1890), cited by volume and page. GM = *Leibnizens mathematische Schriften*, ed. by C. I. Gerhardt (Berlin: A. Asher, and Halle: H. W. Schmidt, 1849-1863), cited by

volume and page. Gr. = *Textes inédits*, ed. by Gaston Grua (Paris: Presses Universitaires de France, 1948). L = Leibniz, *Philosophical Papers and Letters*, trans. and ed. by Leroy E. Loemker, 2nd ed. (Dordrecht and Boston: Reidel, 1969). L-A = *The Leibniz-Arnauld Correspondence*, ed. and trans. by H. T. Mason (Manchester: Manchester University Press, 1967). L-W = *Briefwechsel zwischen Leibniz und Christian Wolf*, ed. by C. I. Gerhardt (Halle: H. W. Schmidt, 1860). Mon. = *Monadology*, cited by section number from Leibniz, *Principes de la nature et de la grace fondés en raison* and *Principes de la philosophie ou Monadologie*, ed. in one volume by André Robinet (Paris: Presses Universitaires de France, 1954). NE = *New Essays Concerning Human Understanding*, cited by book, chapter, and section from G, V. PNG = *The Principles of Nature and of Grace*, cited by section number from the same edition as Mon. RML = André Robinet, *Malebranche et Leibniz: Relations personnelles* (Paris: Vrin, 1955). All works are cited by page number unless otherwise noted above. Entries separated by a slash refer to the original and an English translation of the same passage. I take responsibility for the English translation of all quotations, although I have made some use of existing English versions.

2. "In actual realities the whole," for example, "is a result of the parts" (G VII,562), but that does not mean that the parts are (efficient) causes of the whole. I think that if *b* results from *a* in Leibniz's sense, then *a* entails *b* and *b* adds nothing to reality over and above *a*. The data from which something "results" are jointly *sufficient* for the result. (L 699 seems to say that the "result" is *uniquely* determined by the data, which must, therefore, be sufficient for it. In the original Latin of this mathematical context [GM VII,21f.], however, the word whose meaning is explained is the unusual *'prostultare.';* and it is not clear to me whether what is said here implies anything about the meaning of *'resultare'*, *'resultatum'*, and *'resultat'*, which are more usual in metaphysical contexts. Even if this text is not directly relevant, I think it is most plausible to take Leibniz as supposing that the data must be sufficient for a "result" in metaphysics.) Perhaps the data will also be individually *necessary* for the result, but I doubt that that is implied in the notion of "result." Certainly, the result need not be capable of definition in terms of the data, in a finite language, for the data will commonly be infinite. Leibniz is not committed to the possibility of translating talk about bodies into talk about simple substances and their perceptions.

3. For example, Erich Hochstetter, "Von der wahren Wirklichkeit bei Leibniz," *Zeitschrift für philosophische Forschung*, Vol. 20 (1966), pp. 421-46 (see especially the references to Leibniz's "Schwanken," pp. 422 and 440); and Louis Loeb, *From Descartes to Hume* (Ithaca, N.Y.: Cornell University Press, 1981), pp. 299-309 — to mention two works that I hold in high regard.

4. Cf. Montgomery Furth, "Monadology," *The Philosophical Review*, Vol. 76 (1967), p. 172.

5. On Leibniz's relation to this controversy, see RML 133ff. Even before seeing the documents, Leibniz wrote in a letter that "Mons. Arnauld writes with more judgment" than Father Malebranche (RML 150).

6. Published, with a full report of the discovery, by Willy Kabitz, "Leibniz und Berkeley," *Sitzungsberichte der preussischen Akademie der Wissenschaften*, Philosophisch-historische Klasse N. xxiv, (Jahrgang 1932), p. 636.

7. Here I disagree with Hochstetter, "Von der wahren Wirklichkeit bei Leibniz," p. 436. It must be granted to Hochstetter that Leibniz did not explicitly speak of phenomena as "appearances of monads."

8. In writing to Arnauld, Leibniz expressed some agnosticism, or at least some hesitation, about whether there are any "true corporeal substances" besides those that have "souls" or whether it is enough for them to have something analogous to a soul. (See G II,76f./L-A 95.) If sincere, this uncertainty seems not to have endured.

9. Ernst Cassirer, *Leibniz's System in seinem wissenschaftlichen Grundlagen* (Marburg: N. G. Elwert'sche Verlagsbuchhandlung, 1902), p. 408. Cassirer represents this phrase as a quotation from E 678, but he seems to me to be mistranslating and misapplying the text.

10. Bertrand Russell, *A Critical Exposition of the Philosophy of Leibniz*, 2nd ed. (London: George Allen and Unwin, 1937), p. 148.

11. I believe consciousness and distinctness were linked in this way in Leibniz's mind (see Mon. 19-24), but the question could be raised whether his theory of perception would not go better if distinctness and consciousness were allowed to be two dimensions in which perceptions can vary independently—distinctness being a feature of the structure of the perception and consciousness being, as it were, the light that is turned on it. (I am indebted to Jeremy Hyman for this image.) Separating these dimensions would give the theory more flexibility.

12. As Wallace Anderson has pointed out to me, it is also true that visual perceptions are *more fully* correlated with the eye than with the page. There are features of my visual perception that express features of my eye without expressing features of the page (e.g., the dots that are swimming across my image of the page).

13. The mention of "degrees" in the soul here might serve to place Leibniz more precisely in the complex Scholastic debate about the unity or plurality of substantial forms, but I will not pursue that historical relationship here.

14. Despite what Leibniz says here, it will be difficult for him to refuse to distinguish my perceiving my appetite for a certain event from my perceiving the corporeal causes of that event, for I may perceive the latter much more distinctly than the former, as when I perceive that I am falling and about to strike the ground with considerable force. (I owe this observation to Timothy Sheppard.)

15. I take these phrases to apply only to masses. Literally, Leibniz says this about "the rest" (*reliqua*) by contrast with "simple things." "The rest" might be taken to include corporeal substances (which are composite), but I find it hard to believe that Leibniz meant to say that corporeal substances are "only Beings by aggregation, and therefore phenomena," given other things that he says about corporeal substances.

16. For this last point I am indebted to Wallace Anderson. Cf. G II,100/L-A 126.

17. Russell, *A Critical Exposition of the Philosophy of Leibniz*, p. 147.

18. In unpublished papers written at UCLA.

19. A much earlier text in which there is at least a suggestion that aggregates of true substances might not be phenomena is G VII,322/L 365 (dated to 1684 by Hochstetter; see note 21).

20. See Hochstetter, "Von der wahren Wirklichkeit bei Leibniz," and Hector-Neri Castaneda, "Leibniz's Meditation on April 15, 1676 about Existence, Dreams, and Space," *Studia Leibnitiana, Supplementa*, Vol. XVIII (1978) (*Leibniz à Paris*, Tome II), pp. 91-129.

21. Hochstetter, "Von der wahren Wirklichkeit bei Leibniz," p. 431f. This dating presumably reflects the thinking of the staff of the Academy edition as of 1966.

22. This is a convenient way of talking. Leibniz's conceptualism might give rise to some problems about the ontological status of such a story, if we rely heavily on 'would be told'.

23. In G VII,563, Leibniz seems to equate "phenomena" with "objects of limited spirits" —which could be taken as implying that God has no phenomena.

24. Perhaps Leibniz recognizes a still weaker sense in which phenomena are "real enough" if they belong to a scientifically adequate system of the harmonious phenomena of a single perceiver.

25. Russell, *A Critical Exposition of the Philosophy of Leibniz*, p. 152.

26. *Ibid.*

27. *Ibid.*

28. See Lestienne's edition of DM, p. 14*n*, in the 1952 or earlier edition (missing from the 1975 edition, in which a new introduction by Andre Robinet replaces some of Lestienne's introductory material).

29. A. Boehm, *Le "vinculum substantiale", chez Leibniz: Ses origines historiques* (Paris: Vrin, 1938)—a very useful book, though Boehm takes remarkably little note of the reasons for denying that the doctrine of the *vinculum* was part of Leibniz's philosophy.

30. Leibniz first wrote 'unity' ('*unité*') and then changed it to 'unicity' ('*unicité*'). '*Unicité*'

was an unusual word, but the best evidence I have found suggests that the change did not weaken the claim of unity but was meant to emphasize that the unity here is original rather than produced. (Cf. the *Oxford English Dictionary* on seventeenth-century use of 'unicity'.) I am indebted to Nicholas Rescher for a comment that helped straighten me out on this point.

31. H. Denzinger, *Enchiridion symbolorum, definitionum et declarationum de rebus fidei et morum*, 11th ed. (Freiburg-im-Breisgau: Herder, 1911), p. 19; trans. in the (proposed) *Book of Common Prayer of the Episcopal Church* (1977), p. 865.

32. Drafts of parts of this paper have been read to several scholarly gatherings, and the material has been discussed with my Leibniz class at UCLA. Many people have helped me with their comments. I am particularly indebted to Nicholas Jolley, Louis Loeb, J. E. McGuire, and the late Wallace Anderson for giving me written comments, which have been of great use for my revisions.

Locke on Clear Ideas, Demonstrative Knowledge, and the Existence of Substance

RUTH MATTERN

Locke sometimes asserts that clear knowledge requires clear and distinct ideas:

> . . . Each of those Simple Ideas, which are the ingredients of our Complex one, should be clear and distinct in our Minds. For it being evident, that our Knowledge cannot exceed our Ideas; as far as they are either imperfect, confused, or obscure, we cannot expect to have certain, perfect, or clear Knowledge.[1]

> . . . Ideas, which by reason of their Obscurity or otherwise, are confused, cannot produce any clear or distinct Knowledge; because as far as any Ideas are confused, so far the Mind cannot perceive clearly, whether they agree or disagree. . . .[2]

Sometimes, however, he allows the possibility of clear knowledge with obscure and confused ideas. For example:

> But since our Knowledge is founded on, and employ'd about our Ideas only, will it not follow from thence, that it is conformable to our Ideas; and that where our Ideas are clear and distinct, or obscure and confused, our Knowledge will be so too? To which I answer, No: For our Knowledge consisting in the perception of the Agreement, or Disagreement of any two Ideas, its clearness and obscurity, consists in the clearness or obscurity of that Perception, and not in the clearness or obscurity of the ideas themselves. . . .[3]

And, in his very lengthy correspondence with Stillingfleet, Locke reiterates again and again his contention that knowledge "lies in the perception of the agreement or disagreement of ideas, such as they are, and not always in having perfectly clear and distinct ideas."[4] "In some cases," Locke writes, "we may have certainty about obscure ideas."[5]

Stillingfleet, troubled by the obvious appearance of conflict between these two assertions, presses Locke to clarify his belief in the possibility of knowledge with obscure and confused ideas. "How can I clearly perceive the agreement or disagreement of ideas," Stillingfleet asks, "if I have not clear and distinct ideas?"[6] Locke employs two strategies in defending the possibility of knowledge with obscure ideas, and specifically knowledge of the existence of substance. He contends that such knowledge is *exempt* from the requirement for clear and distinct ideas pertaining to knowledge of "general propositions"; he also writes that knowledge with obscure ideas is possible because such ideas are *partially* clear and distinct.

Locke appeals to the distinction between propositions that are concerned with *existence* and those that are not in his reply to Stillingfleet's comments on an *Essay* passage beginning, "For the attaining of knowledge and certainty, it is requisite that we have determined ideas. . . ."[7] Locke writes that

> the certainty here spoken of, is the certainty of general propositions in morality, and not of the particular existence of any thing; and therefore tends not at all to any such position as this, [that] we cannot be certain of the existence of any particular sort of being, though we have but an obscure and confused idea of it: though it doth affirm, that we cannot have any certain perception of the relations of general moral ideas (wherein consists the certainty of general moral propositions) any further than those ideas are clear in our minds.[8]

He also gives knowledge of existence special attention at many points in his defense of the possibility of knowledge with obscure and confused ideas. Certainty about the truth of the proposition "that there was substance in the world," he states, is consistent with the fact that "we have but an obscure and confused idea of any substance at all."[9] Similarly, he writes: "I am certain, that I have evident knowledge, that the substance of my body and soul exists, though I am as certain that I have but a very obscure and confused idea of any substance at all."[10]

What is the significance of Locke's special treatment of knowledge of existence; why does he exempt it from his rule that clear knowledge requires clear and distinct ideas? One natural hypothesis is that Locke gives it special status because such knowledge falls outside the scope of his comparison-of-ideas model of knowledge. *Some*, but not all, knowledge is *based on* the perception of agreement or disagreement of ideas in the sense that comparison of ideas leads one to the state of cognition.[11] As paradigmatic cases of knowledge based on the comparison of ideas, Locke cites (a) knowledge of propositions such as "white is white" and "blue is not yellow," interpreting these as cases of knowledge of the "identity and diversity of ideas,"[12] and (b) knowledge of mathematical propositions, which are known either by immediate comparison of ideas or by chains of intuitions.[13] Locke's interpretation of such claims as known by comparison of ideas contrasts sharply with the formalistic approaches advanced by the Scholastics and by Leibniz.[14] That this "comparison-of-ideas" or "intuitivist" model of knowledge requires clear ideas, according to Locke, is apparent from his claim that bringing moral propositions within the scope of demonstrative science requires clear moral ideas.[15] Locke may, then, exempt knowledge of the existence of substance from the requirement of clear ideas because he does not think that existence claims can be assimilated to the comparison-of-ideas model of knowledge.

However, Locke also defends the possibility of knowledge of the existence of substance by appeal to the *partial clearness* of obscure ideas, and this approach seems quite different from the other one. He contends that an obscure idea may enter into known propositions only when it is partially clear and distinct:

> An idea that is not in all its parts perfectly clear and distinct, and is therefore an obscure and confused idea, may yet with those ideas, with which, by any obscurity it has, it is not confounded, be capable to produce knowledge by the perception of its agreement or disagreement with them. And yet it will hold true, that in that part wherein it is imperfect, obscure, and confused, we cannot expect to have certain, perfect, or clear knowledge.[16]

This appeal to the partial clearness of obscure ideas is puzzling, because it is natural to interpret it as showing that the comparison-of-ideas model of knowledge can apply even to obscure ideas. The model applies to obscure ideas, he seems to be saying, because we can compare the clear parts of obscure ideas with other clear ideas. Note, for example, how a typical statement of his appeal to partial clearness refers to the comparison of ideas; Locke denies that it is a contradiction to say

> that an idea, which cannot be well compared with some ideas, from which it is not clearly and sufficiently distinguishable, is yet capable of having its agreement and disagreement perceived with some idea, with which it is not so confounded, but that it may be compared.[17]

Locke has two different answers to Stillingfleet's question "How can I clearly perceive the agreement or disagreement of ideas, if I have not clear and distinct ideas?" These two answers seem to stem from conflicting views about the status of knowledge of the existence of substance in relation to the comparison-of-ideas model of the basis of knowledge. This essay will attempt to resolve this conflict, using it to clarify Locke's conception of knowledge through the comparison of ideas. In Section 1, I will attempt to elucidate Locke's interpretations of the contrast between ideas that are clear and distinct and those that are obscure and confused. In Section 2, I will try to provide a better understanding of the way in which the comparison-of-ideas model of knowledge relates to knowledge of the existence of substance in Locke's philosophy. The conclusion will comment briefly on the relation between Locke's conception of demonstrative knowledge and existence claims and Hume's treatment of these matters.

1. DIFFERENT USAGES OF "CLEAR AND DISTINCT"

Locke writes that "all the ideas we have in our minds, are, as far as we have them there, clear and distinct."[18] This reference to the clearness and distinctness of all our ideas expresses the same point that he makes in the first draft of the *Essay*, where he writes of the

cleare and destinct knowledg that every man hath of his owne Ideas where by
he most evidently and perfectly knows every one by its self and destinguishes
it from others, and soe haveing universally neither ignorance of any one of
them nor confusion about them but when any one of them is present in his
understanding he knows evidently and clearly what it is, and when more then
one is there he knows them as destinctly and unconfusedly one from an
other. . . .[19]

That is, in speaking of all our ideas as clear, Locke is affirming his belief that all the
ideas of the mind are present to it and recognized by it; in applying the term "distinct" to all our ideas, he is expressing his view that all of them are infallibly distinguished from one another by virtue of the mind's recognition of them. As he writes
in the published versions of the *Essay*, "there can be no Idea in the Mind, which it
does not presently, by an intuitive Knowledge, perceive to be what it is, and to be
different from any other."[20] Presumably, Locke thinks that ideas are *clear* in this
sense insofar as they are perceived to be "what they are" and *distinct* insofar as
they are perceived to be different from one another.

Though all ideas are clear and distinct in this sense, Locke does want to say
that some ideas are confused in *some* sense. He allows for this possibility by suggesting a usage of "confused" and "distinct" that is relative to words.[21] Confusion,
he writes, "carries with it a secret reference to names."[22] In the letters to Stillingfleet,
he interprets obscurity in this way, too, and indicates two ways in which an idea
may fall short of being verbally "clear and distinct"; those ideas

> which we would suppose the terms in the proposition to stand for, may not
> be clear and distinct: either
>
> 1.   By making the term stand for an uncertain idea, which we have not
> yet precisely determined in our minds, whereby it comes to stand sometimes
> for one idea, sometimes for another which by this use of a name undeter-
> mined in its signification, come to be confounded.
>
> 2.   By supposing the name to stand for something more than really is in
> the idea in our minds, which we make it a sign of, v.g. let us suppose, that a
> many many years since, when he was young, eat a fruit, whose shape, size,
> consistency, and colour, he has a perfect remembrance of; but the particular
> taste he has forgot, and only remembers, that it very much delighted him.
> This complex idea, as far as it is in his mind, it is evident, is there; and as far
> as he perceives it, is in all parts clear and distinct: but when he calls it a pine-
> apple, and will suppose, that name stands for the same precise complex idea,
> for which another man (who newly eat of that fruit, and has the idea of the
> taste of it also fresh in his mind) uses it, or for which he himself used it, when
> he had the taste fresh in his memory: it is plain his complex idea in that part,
> which consists in the taste, is very obscure.[23]

As I understand Locke here, in both of these cases the language user has violated
the rule that one should use a word to stand for a single definite idea. In the first
case, it sounds as though no definite stipulation about the meaning of the term was

made; in the second case, there was a definite assignment of a meaning to the term but the speaker fails at times to use the term with the assigned meaning. The verbal interpretation of "clear and distinct" is also stated explicitly in the *Essay*'s fourth-edition Epistle to the Reader. There, Locke advises that the meaning of the phrase "clear and distinct" is conveyed better by the term "determined" or "determinate" and that

> This, I think, may fitly be called a determinate or determined idea, when, such as it is at any time objectively in the mind and so determined there, it is annexed and without variation determined to a name or articular sound, which is to be steadily the sign of that very same object of the mind, or determinate idea.[24]

Locke's verbal account of "clear and distinct" provides a clever way for him to hold both that (a) we know all our ideas "distinctly and unconfusedly one from another"[25] and that (b) there are some confused ideas, ideas that are "not sufficiently distinguishable from another"[26] because they are not as distinguishable as they *should be*. This move is made possible by suggesting, in effect, that, in addition to the natural distinctions that ideas have from one another without words, a second standard for individuating ideas is imposed by language. Since ideas are not always as finely distinguished as the different names applied to them, ideas can be confused relative to these names. Consider one example of confusion that Locke gives in the *Essay*.

> He, that has an Idea made up of barely the simple ones of a Beast with Spots, has but a confused Idea of a Leopard, it not being thereby sufficiently distinguished from a Lynx, and several other sorts of Beasts that are spotted. So that such an Idea, though it hath the peculiar name Leopard, is not distinguishable from those designed by the Names Lynx, or Panther. . . . When the Ideas, for which we use different terms, have not a difference answerable to their distinct Names and so cannot be distinguished by them, there it is that they are truly confused.[27]

The idea of a spotted beast is distinguishable from all other ideas that one has in mind, but, if one uses this same idea as the meaning of both the terms "leopard" and "lynx," then one's *idea of a leopard* is not sufficiently distinguishable from one's *idea of a lynx*.

So far, I have indicated two interpretations that Locke gives to the contrast between "clear and distinct" ideas and "obscure and confused" ones. But he has a third usage as well. For example:

> suppose you should in the twilight, or in a thick mist, see two things standing upright, near the size and shape of an ordinary man; but in so dim a light, or — at such a distance, that they appeared very much alike, and you could not perceive them to be *what they really were*, the one a statue, the other a man; would not these two be obscure and confused ideas?[28]

Locke does not call these ideas "obscure and confused" because the mind fails to recognize and distinguish its own contents; he is not denying that the two blurred images are perceived, recognized, and distinguished from each other. Nor is there mention of words here, as we would expect there to be if it were the second usage of "clear and distinct" that he had in mind. Rather, the ideas fall short of being clear and distinct because they do not tell us what the objects "really were"; what the ideas represent is not apprehended well or well enough to distinguish one thing from another. This usage of "obscurity" is more like the *Essay*'s notion of inadequacy of ideas than anything else I find in Locke. "Inadequate ideas are such which are but a partial or incomplete representation of those archetypes to which they are referred," where the term "archetypes" designates those things that the ideas are supposed to represent.[29]

Locke does not explicitly define the term "clear" as it appears in this context. Two possible ways of doing so come to mind. One is to say that an idea is clear *to the extent* that it represents what it is supposed to represent.[30] Clearness in this sense would be a matter of degree. But another approach would be to reserve the term "clear" for ideas that are fully *adequate*, so that no partial or incomplete representations would count as clear.[31] Probably Locke has such a usage in mind when he writes that, because of our incapacity to discover the minute parts of physical things, we do not have "cleare adequate ideas of the essences of natural bodies."[32] It is natural to interpret this reference to clearness as tantamount to "clear, i.e., adequate."[33]

I have distinguished three main usages of the "clear" and "obscure" contrast in Locke, but in some cases the last two are closely related. Inadequacy for mode ideas, Locke writes, can only be a matter of failure to conform to language conventions,[34] and so obscurity and confusion for these ideas are merely a matter of failure to use words as they are supposed to be used.[35] In cases in which an idea has an external archetype, however, adequacy and inadequacy will not be mere verbal clearness and obscurity. For example, Locke writes of the idea *pineapple* as obscure when a man leaves out one of the components of the idea that he initially associated with the word or that his society associates with the word.[36] But even if the man's ideas of a pineapple contained all the components required by the linguistic conventions about "pineapple," his idea would not be adequate; i.e., it would still fail to represent pineapples completely because it would lack many of the indefinite set of properties common to pineapples. The distinction between the second and third usages of "clear and distinct" is as deep as the difference between conformity to nominal conventions and conformity to independent archetypes.

2. THE RELEVANCE OF CLEAR IDEAS TO CLEAR KNOWLEDGE

Now that we have some understanding of the usages of "clear and distinct" and "obscure and confused" in Locke, let us determine which of these are relevant to his claims that clear knowledge requires clear ideas but that some knowledge is possible with obscure and confused ideas. Sometimes he seems to be talking about the verbal notion of "clear and distinct," the second usage, when he writes that knowledge presupposes clear ideas.

> Ideas, which by reason of their Obscurity or otherwise, are confused cannot
> produce any clear or distinct Knowledge: because, as far as any Ideas are con-
> fused, so far the Mind cannot perceive clearly whether they agree or disagree.
> Or to express the same thing in a way less apt to be misunderstood. He that
> hath not determined Ideas to the Words he uses, cannot make Propositions of
> them, of whose Truth he can be certain.[37]

This injunction pertains equally to all sorts of knowledge, including knowledge of
existence.[38] However, some of Locke's other comments about the need for clear
and distinct ideas do not use the verbal sense of "clear and distinct" and do not pertain in the same way to all types of knowledge.

Locke's first sort of knowledge, knowledge of the identity and diversity of
ideas, requires clear and distinct ideas in the first sense; it requires that the ideas are
recognized and distinguished in the mind. But since such recognizability is auto-
matic for all our ideas on Locke's account, this sense of "clear and distinct" can
play no role in his recommendations that we clarify our ideas. Locke also thinks
that knowledge of the second sort, demonstrative knowledge of relations of ideas,
presupposes clear ideas. For example, he requires that we have clear ideas in order
to arrive at mathematical knowledge by the comparison of mathematical ideas. It
is the sense of clarity relating to adequacy, the third usage of the term "clear," that
Locke has in mind when he writes that

> he that has not a perfect and clear idea of those angles or figures of which he
> desires to know anything is utterly thereby incapable of any knowledge about
> them. . . . Suppose a man not to have a perfect exact idea of a right angle, a
> scalene, or trapezium; and there is nothing more certain than that he will in
> vain seek any demonstration about them. . . .[39]

Also, Locke says concerning moral knowledge (which he construes on the model
of mathematical knowledge) that it requires clear ideas: "We cannot have any certain perception of the relations of general moral ideas (wherein consists the certainty
of general moral propositions) any farther than those ideas are clear in our minds."[40]
The notion of clearness that Locke refers to here cannot be either the first or the
second sense of "clear and distinct," for he says that this sort of clearness is a prerequisite for knowledge of moral propositions, but not for knowledge of existence;
there would be no reason for him to say this if he had in mind either of the first
two senses of "clear and distinct." Locke writes that there would be no knowledge
at all without the ability to recognize and distinguish our ideas,[41] and, as I have indicated, the need for verbal clearness is not restricted to some types of knowledge
rather than others. It must be clearness in the third sense, then, that Locke thinks
relevant to intuitive and demonstrative knowledge in ethics.

Why does Locke contrast the need for this sort of clear idea in moral and
mathematical knowledge with the lack of need for such clearness in existence
claims? To see this, let us look more closely at the sort of adequacy of ideas that
Locke requires for intuitive and demonstrative knowledge and the reason why he
thinks it relevant. He believes that mathematical and moral knowledge presuppose

ideas that are adequate in the sense of representing mathematical and moral real essences. The significance of such adequacy is that these ideas give us access to the properties that have interesting necessary connections with a very large set of other properties; Locke thinks that these real essences are identical with the "foundation" from which other properties "flow," i.e., follow demonstratively. For example, he writes of our idea of a triangle in the following way:

> A Figure including a Space between three Lines, is the real, as well as nominal Essence of a Triangle; it being not only the abstract Idea to which the general Name is annexed, but the very Essentia, or Being, of the thing it self, that Foundation from which its Properties flow, and to which they are all inseparably annexed.[42]

Locke also cites the fact that we have clear ethical ideas (at another point he describes these as "adequate and complete ideas"[43]) as the grounds for his optimism about the possibility of a deductive science of ethics similar to mathematics: those ideas

> would, I suppose, if duly considered, and pursued, afford such Foundations of our Duty and Rules of Action, as might place Morality amongst the Sciences capable of Demonstration: wherein I doubt not, but from self-evident Propositions, by necessary Consequences, as incontestable as those in Mathematicks, the measures of right and wrong might be made out, to anyone that will apply himself with the same Indifferency and Attention to the one, as he does to the other of these Sciences.[44]

Locke does not require this sort of adequacy for the ideas correlating with subject terms in existence claims, however. There would be no point in his requiring that these ideas express the "whole essence" of the thing in question, as the ideas in mathematics and ethics supposedly do. Locke does not believe that *existence* is a property that "flows demonstratively" from any real essence at all; he never admits the possibility of any necessary-existence claims. He rejects the ontological argument explicitly in the First Letter to Stillingfleet[45] and in a later essay.[46] The fact that he does not think existence follows necessarily from any real essence makes intelligible his contrast between the relevance of clear moral ideas to moral knowledge and the irrelevance of this sort of clearness to knowledge-of-existence claims, a contrast expressed in a quotation given earlier; he says of his *Essay* passage beginning "For the attaining of knowledge and certainty, it is requisite that we have determined ideas . . ." that

> the certainty here spoken of, is the certainty of general propositions in morality, and not of the particular existence of any thing; and therefore tends not at all to any such position as this, [that] we cannot be certain of the existence of any particular sort of being, though we have but an obscure and confused idea of it: though it doth affirm, that we cannot have any certain perception of the relations of general moral ideas (wherein consists the certainty of general moral propositions) any farther than those ideas are clear in our minds.[47]

This contrast makes sense if we interpret the clearness of ideas relevant to moral claims as adequacy, the sort of adequacy that Locke thinks essential to the demonstrative sciences of mathematics and ethics. Clearness in this context is not partial; nothing less than full adequacy will do. Either we have a grasp of the mathematical and moral real essences – the "whole essence"[48] – or we do not.

We saw, though, that in his correspondence with Stillingfleet Locke retains his comparison of ideas model of knowledge, even in propositions with obscure ideas, by appealing to the partial clearness of such ideas. Why does he do this, if not to protect the applicability of this model of knowledge to claims such as "substance exists"? The answer, I think lies in a distinction between stronger and weaker versions of the comparison-of-ideas model of knowledge. Locke does refer explicitly in the *Essay* to some *demonstrative* knowledge of existence, specifically, knowledge of the claim that God exists.[49] "Demonstration" in this context does not mean the derivation of necessary consequences from real essences, but demonstrative inference in a broader sense. The inference resulting in knowledge that God exists proceeds, in Locke's view, by the intuition of necessary connections between steps. It uses the comparison of ideas rather than a formalistic proof procedure; Locke thinks that all demonstration involves chains of intuitions.

The demonstration of the existence of substance parallels in general strategy Locke's proof of the existence of God. In both cases, Locke thinks that we should begin from an existential premise known by experience and that we can derive from this claim a belief in something that stands in a special relation to what is experienced. In the proof of the existence of substance, Locke thinks that knowledge of the existence of thinking or of any qualities will lead us to posit something standing in the relation of support; we conclude that substance exists even though we do not have a clear idea of it beyond an idea of its function.[50]

I am suggesting, then, that Locke has both a broader conception of demonstrative inference that can apply to arguments with existential premises and a narrower conception of demonstration that applies only to arguments drawing out the implications of real essences. Both sorts of demonstration require clear and distinct ideas in the second sense; the equivocal or indeterminate use of words can preclude certainty in either case. But there is a distinction in the degree of the third sort of clearness required for each type of demonstration. The broader sort of demonstration requires some degree of clearness, but this might be merely a clear apprehension of some aspects of the things concerned in our demonstration. The sort of demonstration that draws out implications of real essences, though, requires the highest degree of clearness of the third sort; it requires adequacy, so that our ideas give us access to the *fundamental nature* of the thing under investigation. In claiming that knowledge of the existence of substance is exempt from the need for a clear idea of substance, I think that Locke is using "clear" in this sense, i.e., "adequate." Denying that this idea is adequate is consistent with affirming that it has some clearness and that this clearness is necessary for demonstrating the existence of substance.

When Locke writes of the idea of substance as "obscure and confused," it sometimes sounds as though he thinks that the term "substance" has not been assigned a meaning at all. He writes that the idea of substance would be useful if we had it and that we "signify nothing by the word *substance* but only and uncertain supposition of we know not what."[51] However, even in this passage Locke acknowledges that the idea of substance is not completely uninformative. The problem is only that our characterization of substance is a relational one, since we do not know what performs the function of supporting properties; our idea of substance is an uncertain supposition of "something whereof we have no particular distinct positive idea, which we take to be the substratum, or support, of those ideas we do know."[52] In the correspondence with Stillingfleet, Locke claims that we do have a clear *relational* idea of substance; he thinks that we can be sure of the existence of substance because we know that there is something that performs the function of supporting accidents.

> In some cases we may have certainty about obscure ideas; v.g. by the clear idea of thinking in me, I find the agreement of the clear idea of existence, and the obscure idea of a substance in me, because I perceive the necessary idea of thinking, and the relative idea of a support; which support, without having any clear and distinct idea of what it is, beyond this relative one of a support, I call substance.[53]

Our idea of substance, Locke thinks, has *some* degree of clearness because it represents one property of substance—the relational property of the power to support accidents. It is not *adequate*, however, because it does not represent the fundamental nature of substance; the idea of substance does not give us access to a real essence from which derivative properties may be seen to flow.

CONCLUSION

Locke's discussion of substance has been a focus of considerable controversy ever since the *Essay* was published. I have made no attempt in this essay to travel well-worn paths of controversy but have concentrated instead on one aspect of Locke's commitment to the existence of substance that has been neglected in the literature. I have tried to use a puzzle about his defense of knowledge of the existence of substance as an avenue to clarification of Locke's general views about knowledge.

I indicated initially that in his correspondence with Stillingfleet Locke claimed both that knowledge of the existence of substance was exempt from the requirement for clear and distinct ideas and that it fulfilled the requirement for clearness by virtue of the partial clearness of the idea of substance. What is particularly troubling and interesting about these two different lines of defense is that they seem to imply two conflicting views about the relation of this knowledge to the comparison-of-ideas model of knowledge. I have tried to show, though, that the two sets of comments in response to Stillingfleet's query are complementary rather than incompatible. The reconciliation was achieved by interpreting Locke as talking about two different requirements for clearness of ideas. The idea of substance is exempt from the need for clearness that applies to ideas involved in demonstrations from real essences; the idea of substance does not need to be adequate. It does need to be clear in the weaker sense relevant to Locke's broader concept of demonstration; it needs to be a determinate idea and to represent accurately some property (a relational property) of substance.[54]

If my interpretation is correct, then we need a distinction between two sorts of Lockean demonstration; this distinction has not received sufficient attention so far from historians of philosophy. One commentator claims, for example, that Locke's concept of demonstration "inevitably restricts the range of demonstrative knowledge to a very narrow field" since Locke ignores demonstrations with contingent premises.[55] But Locke does attempt to provide a model of knowledge that accommodates demonstration with contingent premises, and this attempt needs recognition and discussion.

Roger Woolhouse has concentrated on Locke's narrower conception of demonstration in his study of Locke's theory of knowledge and has suggested that it illuminates important parts of his philosophy.[56] However, Woolhouse's interpretation does not provide an account of Locke's other concept of demonstration, the sort of demonstration that does not require knowledge of real essences. Much remains to be done in interpreting and evaluating both of Locke's versions of his idea-oriented view of demonstration. Realizing that a distinction should be drawn between the two conceptions of demonstration is at least a first step toward understanding them.

The problems discussed here involve issues whose significance goes beyond matters of interpreting Locke to broader concerns in early modern philosophy. His position represents an interesting stage in the development of awareness of the special status of existential propositions. We find in Locke a distinction between existential claims and relations-of-ideas claims that foreshadows Hume's and Kant's assertions of the impossibility of demonstrating existence propositions. Years before Hume's distinction between relations of ideas and matters of fact, Locke presented his own distinction between two sorts of knowledge "founded upon two different principles, i.e. true ideas and matter of fact or history."[57] However, Locke does differ from Hume significantly in his commitment to a broader sense of "demonstration" that differs from the narrower one confined to a priori knowledge. Hume includes in the category *relations of ideas* "every affirmation which is either intuitively or demonstratively certain."[58] Locke, however, counts as demonstratively certain some propositions that are not Humean relations-of-ideas claims. Locke thinks that, once one has certain existential claims, one can use those certain propositions as the starting point for chains of demonstrations. Hume, asserting that all inferences concerning matters of fact are merely causal, rules out the Lockean category of existential propositions derived by demonstration.[59]

Notes

1. John Locke, *An Essay Concerning Human Understanding*, ed. P. H. Nidditch (Oxford: Clarendon Press, 1975), 4.12.14. References to the *Essay* will be cited by book, chapter, and section number from this edition.

2. *Ibid.*, 4.2.15.

3. *Ibid.*, 4.2.15.

4. Locke, "Correspondence with the Bishop of Worcester" (Letters to Stillingfleet), *The Works of John Locke* (London: W. Otridge et al., 1812), Vol. 4, p. 42. Also, for example, pp. 29, 56, 103, 104, 118, 123, 222, 236, 269, 345.

5. *Ibid.*, p. 42

6. *Ibid.*, p. 220.

7. *Essay*, 4.4.8

8. "Correspondence with the Bishop of Worcester," p. 239.

9. *Ibid.*, p. 236.

10. *Ibid.*, p. 345.

11. Although Locke does say that in some sense *all* knowledge is the "perception of the agreement or disagreement of ideas," this broader claim is best interpreted as the assertion that the state of cognition is the perception of the truth of propositions. See R. M. Mattern, "Locke: 'Our Knowledge, Which All Consists in Propositions,'" *Canadian Journal of Philosophy*, Vol. 8 (1978), pp. 677-95.

12. *Essay*, 4.1.4., 4.1.7., 4.2.1.

13. *Ibid.*, 4.2.2.-4.2.7.

14. For a discussion of the contrast between the intuitivist and formalist approaches in Locke and Leibniz, see Margaret D. Wilson, "Leibniz and Locke on 'First Truths,'" *Journal of the History of Ideas*, Vol. XXVIII, No. 3 (July-September, 1967), p. 351.

15. "Correspondence with the Bishop of Worcester," p. 239.

16. *Ibid.*, p. 241.

17. *Ibid.*, p. 241.

18. *Ibid.*, p. 380.

19. Locke, "Draft A of the *Essay*," in Richard Aaron and Jocelyn Gibb, eds., *An Early Draft of Locke's Essay together with Excerpts from His Journal* (Oxford: Clarendon Press, 1936), p. 42.

20. *Essay*, 4.3.8.

21. *Ibid.*, 2.29.6ff.

22. *Ibid.*, 2.29.12.

23. "Correspondence with the Bishop of Worcester," p. 380.

24. *Essay*, Epistle to the Reader.

25. *Ibid.*, 4.7.4.

26. *Ibid.*, 2.29.4.

27. *Ibid.*, 2.29.7.

28. "Correspondence with the Bishop of Worcester," pp. 221-22; emphasis added.

29. *Essay*, 2.31.1.

30. Also, an idea is *distinct* if it is clear enough to permit a distinction to be drawn between what this idea represents and what other ideas represent.

31. "Distinct" could still be defined as above (footnote 30).

32. Draft C of the *Essay*, 2.33.18.

33. *Ibid.*, 2.33.18.

34. *Essay*, 2.31.

35. *Ibid.*, 3.11.15.

36. "Correspondence with the Bishop of Worcester," p. 380.

37. *Essay*, 4.2.15.

38. Sometimes, however, Locke asserts that knowledge would be achieved more readily if words were not attached to ideas: "Though the examining and judging of Ideas by themselves, their Names being quite laid aside, be the best and surest way to clear and distinct Knowledge: yet through the prevailing custom of using Sounds for Ideas, I think it is very seldom practised" (*Essay*, 4.6.1).

39. *Essay*, 4.12.15.

40. "Correspondence with the Bishop of Worcester," p. 239.

41. *Essay*, 4.2.1.

42. *Ibid.*, 3.3.18.

43. *Ibid.*, 4.4.7.

44. *Ibid.*, 4.3.18.

45. "Correspondence with the Bishop of Worcester," pp. 53-56.

46. "Deus: Des Cartes' proof of a god from the Idea of necessary existence examined 1696," in Peter King, *Life of Locke* (London, 1858), pp. 313-16.

47. "Correspondence with the Bishop of Worcester," p. 239.

48. *Essay*, 2.31.11.

49. *Ibid.*, 4.9.2.

50. "Correspondence with the Bishop of Worcester," p. 42.

51. *Essay*, 1.4.19.

52. *Ibid.*, 1.4.19.

53. "Correspondence with the Bishop of Worcester," p. 42.

54. Locke's statement of the need for clear and distinct ideas at *Essay* 4.2.15 refers to the need for determining ideas to words; the second usage of "clear and distinct" is the relevant one here.

Ideas, which by reason of their Obscurity or otherwise, are confused, cannot produce any clear or distinct Knowledge; because as far as any Ideas are confused, so far the Mind cannot perceive clearly, whether they agree or disagree. Or to express the same thing in a way less apt to be misunderstood. He that hath not determined the Ideas to the Words he uses, cannot make Propositions of them, of whose Truth he can be certain.

55. Frederick Copleston, *A History of Philosophy* (Garden City, N.Y.: Doubleday, 1959), Vol. V., p. 120.

56. Woolhouse discusses the relevance of Locke's real essence model of demonstration to his philosophy in "Locke on Modes, Substances, and Knowledge," *Journal of the History of Philosophy*, Vol. 10 (1972), p. 422, and in *Locke's Philosophy of Science and Knowledge: A Consideration of Some Aspects of an Essay Concerning Human Understanding* (New York: Barnes and Noble, 1971).

57. Locke's Journal entry for June 26, 1681, in Aaron and Gibb, *op. cit.*, p. 116. See also *Essay* 4.11.13.

58. David Hume, *An Inquiry Concerning Human Understanding* (New York: Bobbs-Merrill, 1955), p. 40. (First published in 1748.)

59. *Ibid.*, p. 41.

Acknowledgment: A much earlier version of this paper was discussed by the Seventeenth Century Study Group. I am grateful to Willis Doney, Michael Hooker, Robert Sleigh, and Margaret Wilson for comments. I am also grateful to the Pierpont Morgan Library for permission to consult and quote from the unpublished manuscript of the 1685 draft of Locke's *Essay*.

Locke's Theory of Personal Identity

MARGARET ATHERTON

Locke's theory of personal identity has been a very fruitful one. It has provided the seed for a great deal of discussion, and there have been many theories of personal identity that can appropriately be regarded as descendants of Locke's theory.[1] But I think many of these descendants may be illegitimate ones, for I suspect the theory discussed as Locke's is more legendary than real. And, although this heavily discussed theory has undoubtedly proved interesting, I think at the very least there is another reading of what Locke is saying that is equally interesting and provocative.

The salient characteristic of the view generally attributed to Locke is its use of memory or remembering in order to construct a theory of personal identity. Locke's theory is thought to be something like this: ". . . X at time two is the same person as Y at time one if and only if X and Y are both persons and X can remember at time two (his doing) what Y did or felt or what have you at time one."[2] The basic idea, then, on this reading, is that a person's identity with its former selves is guaranteed just when that person remembers what the former self thought, felt, or did.

According to the standard view, Locke's use of memory is in the service of a basically phenomenalist conception of the problem of personal identity. Locke, it is said, noticed that the problem of personal identity requires a way to unify a self that does not, in fact, remain the same, but, as a federation of experiences, is always changing. His solution to this problem is held to be the characteristically phenomenalist one. The purpose of memory, therefore, is that it provides a pattern or a way of relating or tying together otherwise distinct experiences. A final feature of the standard view is that it assumes that Locke intended the notion of personal identity to serve essentially practical ends. He wanted to help us discover who is responsible and thus who should be rewarded or punished.[3] Locke's solution and his way of conceiving the problem have been found to be problematic. But it seems to me that, if we try to get at what is said to be problematic and to think about why Locke would have held such a view, it turns out that he never did, in fact, hold a memory theory in this phenomenalist sense. What I want to show is that Locke was not trying to provide a criterion to use in reidentifying other people bur rather that he was trying to say something about what the identity of a person consists in, that his general claims about identity are incompatible with the sort of phenomenalist account that is generally given of the memroy theory, and that an account of personal identity that is more nearly coherent with the rest of what Locke has to say about identity requires taking seriously Locke's claim that a person is a single center of consciousness.

I

Locke's theory has generally been assumed to be offering a way of telling how one ought to go about reidentifying other people. Conceived as a practical suggestion about how to reidentify people, it has been thought to be problematic because it relies exclusively on a psychological rather than a physical criterion. That is, Locke is frequently thought of as giving us a criterion by means of which we can decide whether some person, Perkin Warbeck, say, is the same as little Prince Richard in the Tower. (Another way of expressing this is to say Locke is giving us a way of knowing what evidence is needed in order that we might know some person is the same as some earlier or later person.) And the thrust of his remarks is thought to be that, since psychological clues, that is, memories, take precedence over physical ones, then people are essentially minds and dualism rather than materialism is the correct account of people and their behavior. Because of the kind of evidence that is appropriate, the correct concept of personal identity must be a mental concept.

Locke's evidence for his claim is thought to come primarily from his famous puzzle case, the story of the exchange of souls between the prince and the cobbler: "For should the Soul of a Prince, carrying with it the consciousness of the Prince's past Life, enter and inform the Body of a Cobler as soon as deserted by his own Soul, every one sees, he would be the same Person with the Prince, accountable only for the Prince's Actions . . . ."[4] The point of this story is thought to be that our intuitions will show us that memories are a better criterion for us to use in reidentifying persons than physical clues, like the continuity of physical characteristics. And against this it has seemed reasonable to object that our intuitions also tell us that, even if, to use my example, Perkin Warbeck's memories were flawlessly like those we would assume Prince Richard to have, we would still prefer to use things like fingerprints and dental records to establish his identity and that, if these proved to be other than those of the prince, we would not accept Perkin Warbeck as Prince Richard, despite his memories. Furthermore, we would only have reason to suppose that Perkin Warbeck's memories were trustworthy if we had independent evidence that Prince Richard's body had been present and doing the things Perkin Warbeck remembered. So physical clues must ultimately prevail over psychological ones.

These arguments, however, are irrelevant to Locke's actual purpose here. He is using the prince-cobbler story to show that the criteria for 'same person' are not the same as those for 'same man', that is, the same living organism of the human species.[5] Just after he tells the story of the exchange, Locke goes on to say: ". . . But who would say it was the same Man? The Body too goes to the making the Man, and would, I guess, to every body determine the Man in this case, wherein the Soul, with all its Princely Thoughts about it, would not make another Man: But he would be the same Cobler to every one besides himself" (2.27.15). The criterion of *personal* identity that Locke is establishing is not meant to solve third-person problems about whether our friends or Perkin Warbeck or the Princess Anastasia are the same when encountered today as someone encountered earlier. These are all problems that come up for us, in Locke's terminology, about the "man" and are to be solved in terms of bodily clues, so the Prince's soul in the cobbler's body is correctly identified as the man, the cobbler.[6] Only the prince is in a position to say that he, the prince's soul, although the same person as before, is not the man he once was. So, although the criterion of personal identity does have ultimate application for questions of responsibility, for the cobbler should not be held responsible for what the prince's soul does while in his body, the criterion will be of no particular practical help to the detective or judge trying to discover who is responsible for the crime. It is not supposed to be used in reidentifying other people. Locke's criterion of personal identity is intended only to explain how it is that I am the same person that I was before, not how other people make this judgment, for he says that the prince's soul in the cobbler's body alone is able to recognize that he remains the same person as the prince. Only I can encounter the bearer of *my* personhood; everyone else proceeds on the generally justified assumption that the same man is also the same person. Thus, everyone else will make use of the physical evidence they directly encounter to establish the identity of the same man, something defined quite differently than the same person.

There is nothing in any of this, moreover, that amounts to or points to a defense of dualism. Locke is in general pretty cagey about whether his conceptual distinctions indicate a difference in kind. Although he thinks we can distinguish immaterial from material substance, still he thinks we have no evidence to show whether matter can or cannot think. There is no reason to believe, therefore, that, for Locke, the most interesting question would be 'Is a person something physical or something mental?'[7]

II

But by far the most serious complaints about Locke's theory have centered around the role of memory. Locke is thought to be claiming that my present identity with my past selves is a matter of my currently remembering (or my present experiences containing among them memories of) my past experiences. Proponents as well as opponents of a theory of this sort agree there are several problems that must be solved before the theory can be allowed to stand, problems Locke does not seem to have considered, for either we must assume that my present self is gifted with total and absolutely accurate recall or else the criterion seems to leave out of the concept of personal identity bits of what we generally take to be a part of ourselves, namely, the things we thought or did we do not remember. Even though I do not now remember where I was and what I did on December 14, 1949, nevertheless, I think my present self is identical with some self who was somewhere and did some things on that date. The criterion seems too broad as well, for it includes all the things we claim to remember doing and thinking that in fact did not happen. That is, in common with phenomenalist attempts to define objects in terms of relationships among our experiences of them, Locke's account of personal identity as it stands seems to suffer the two-fold disability of being gappy and yet including illusions. Nor does it seem that Locke has tried to avoid the charge that any attempt to specify the experiences that are included (as when the definition of personal identity is amended to include not just the experiences the present self does remember but those it is capable of remembering) results in circularity.[8]

What makes this account initially odd as an account of Locke's theory of personal identity is that there is no reason to believe that Locke was unaware of the points that cause difficulty for this theory or that he would have considered a theory acceptable that ignored these difficulties.[9] Locke certainly did not think we have total recall. He remarks more than once how liable we are to forget things.[10] Thus, there is no reason to believe Locke would think that an idea of personal identity based on memory would not be gappy and, moreover, subject to alteration, since what we could or could not remember can change from one time to the next. Locke himself does not state unequivocally that forgetting means a loss of personal identity. There are even passages in which he says that the kinds of gaps caused by forgetting do not raise problems for personal identity.[11] But surely these gaps do cause difficulties for the memory criterion.

If we take a look at what Locke himself says about personal identity, it seems his account does not by any means unequivocally depend upon memory. There are two longish passages in this chapter on personal identity containing summary statements that I want to quote in their entirety. The first is at 2.27.9, where Locke tells us first what he takes a person to be and then how we can derive from it the idea of personal identity. A person, Locke says:

> is a thinking intelligent Being, that has reason and reflection, and can consider it self as it self, the same thinking thing in different times and places; which it does only by that consciousness, which is inseparable from thinking, and as it seems to me essential to it: It being impossible for anyone to perceive, without perceiving, that he does perceive. When we see, hear, smell, taste, feel, meditate, or will any thing, we know that we do so. Thus it is always as to our present Sensations and Perceptions: And by this every one is to himself that which he calls *self*: It not being considered in this case, whether the same *self* be continued in the same, or divers Substances. For since consciousness always accompanies thinking, and 'tis that, that makes everyone to be, what he calls *self*; and thereby distinguishes himself from all other thinking things,

in this alone consists *personal identity*, i.e. the sameness of a rational Being: And as far as this consciousness can be extended backwards to any past Action or Thought, so far reaches the Identity of that *Person*; it is the same *self* now as it was then; and 'tis by the same *self* with this present one that now reflects on it, that the Action was done.

Slightly later on, in the same chapter, at 2.27.17, Locke gives another summary statement. He is more interested in this passage in the relationship between self and substance, and he also gives a gloss on what he means by saying the self "extends itself":

Self is that conscious thinking thing, (whatever Substance, made up of whether Spiritual, or Material, Simple or Compounded, it matters not) which is sensible, or conscious of Pleasure and Pain, capable of Happiness or Misery, and so is concern'd for it *self*, as far as that consciousness extends. Thus every one finds, that whilst comprehended under that consciousness, the little Finger is as much a part of it *self*, as what is most so. Upon separation of this little Finger, should this consciousness go along with the little Finger, and leave the rest of the Body, 'tis evident the little Finger would be the *Person*, the *same Person*; and *self* then would have nothing to do with the rest of the Body. As in this case it is the consciousness that goes along with the Substance, when one part is separated from another, which makes the same *Person*, and constitutes this inseparable *self*: so it is in reference to Substances remote in time. That with which the *consciousness* of this present thinking thing can join it self, makes the same *Person*, and is one *self* with it, and with nothing else; and so attributes to it *self*, and owns all the Actions of that thing, as its own, as far as that consciousness reaches, and no farther; as everyone who reflects will perceive.

The first thing to notice about these passages is that Locke nowhere uses the words 'memory' or 'remember'. In fact, this is generally the case throughout his discussion of personal identity. He speaks, as he does here, only of consciousness. In some places in these passages, moreover, it is quite clear that he cannot be talking about memory but only about consciousness, as in the definition of a person that begins at 2.27.9, where he says that present consciousness is what makes everyone to be a self. Here, of course, he is talking about what characterizes a person and not what preserves identity (although later he indicates they are one and the same); Locke says it is thanks to consciousness that a person is a person, and there is no obvious reason to understand him here as saying that memory creates a present self. Thus, it seems to me the text provides reasons for trying to develop an account of Locke's theory of personal identity that uses the concept of consciousness and not that of memory.

Right off, there will be difficulties in such an attempt, for the notion of consciousness is not a clear one. In this context, it is even ambiguous, for Locke could be talking about plain consciousness, that is, the registering or becoming aware of, in his terminology, ideas, or he could be talking about self-consciousness. He could be saying we come by or build up an idea of ourselves by observing our first-order mental activities. Although I think it is clear from the passage quoted above that self-consciousness is, according to Locke, one of the distinctive activities of a person, I think it is also clear that it is not the only distinctive activity and that he does not mean to restrict the term 'consciousness' to this kind of reflective activity.[12] Rather, according to Locke, we do not have mental contents except by being conscious; thus, to hear a sound or to see a color or to feel a pain is to be conscious of that sound, color, or pain. Locke is saying a person is something capable of a distinctive range of activities, reflecting, perceiving, etc., all of which, in one way or another, consist in being conscious of, that is, having, ideas. So Locke's consciousness that constitutes the person is not some one mental activity over and above the rest of the person's mental activities. Instead, no mental act can occur without consciousness; as Locke says in 2.1.19, "thinking consists in being conscious that one thinks."

But, even if we are to interpret Locke's term, 'consciousness' in this manner to mean awareness, then, of course, this is still not incompatible with the claim that memory has a large role to play in the concept of personal identity. Many of those who interpret Locke as a memory theorist permit an interpretation of consciousness as awareness insofar as he is talking about the present self. Memory comes in when we ask how this present self can be said to be identical with past selves. It is his term 'extended' in the passage on identity (2.27.9), "as far as this consciousness can be extended backwards to any past action of thought, so far reaches the identity of that person," that is generally taken to be about memory. On this interpretation, the self at the present time consists in whatever experiences are going on, and this self is extended to its past selves by including experiences it remembers.

Although this is a plausible reading of this passage, I do not think it is the only reading. Locke still could be talking about consciousness throughout, considered as whatever it is about us that enables us to register or to be aware of ideas. That is, he could be saying not that the present self consists in a set or federation of experiences each of which possesses the property of being conscious but rather that to be a self is to have a particular kind of capacity, the capacity to have or to register experiences. The consciousness that is peculiar to each self is whatever it is about a person that enables it to have ideas. It is because people are conscious that things look red, taste sweet, or feel warm to them. It is thanks to their being conscious that physical stimulation striking them turns into ideas for them, as it does not for a rock. The notion of consciousness I am attributing to Locke is primarily a notion of that which is responsible for awareness; it is not intended to be just another term for all the ideas we are aware of. So, on this interpretation, to say the self is extended would be to say the same self is found wherever thoughts, perceptions, or whatever are due to that same consciousness.

There are various passages that would tend to support this attempt to read Locke as talking about consciousness and not about memory. For example, the passage already quoted from 2.27.17 supports this reading rather than an interpretation in terms of memory, for there Locke says consciousness extends itself to different parts of my body. He says I count my little finger as a part of myself if events happening to it are registered in my consciousness, in the same consciousness that receives ideas from the rest of my body. Locke says, moreover, if my consciousness ceased registering events from anywhere except my little finger, my self would extend only into my little finger. Some additional evidence against the memory interpretation comes in 2.27.26, where Locke says the self owns its past actions "just upon the same ground, and for the same reason, as it does the present." This would again suggest (although in this case not unequivocally since memory is a species of consciousness) that Locke does not think we own our present actions through having them, being conscious of them, and our past actions by remembering them since these would seem to be different grounds. Thus, it seems to be not incompatible with the text to try to develop for Locke a theory of personal identity that hinges on the notion of consciousness, interpreted as that which is responsible for registering ideas, in which memory enters only in ways that are compatible with taking this notion of consciousness as the primary identification of personal identity. For, in fact, to treat Locke instead as a memory theorist does not always result in the most natural reading of what he is saying.[13]

III

Nevertheless, it is easy to see why it has seemed so natural to read Locke as a memory theorist, for it has been thought that Locke's construal of personal identity was a notion compatible with diversity. It is assumed that, according to Locke, what we have is a series of changing experiences and that these must somehow be tied together to make the person. But then it seems reasonable to ask what else could unite in consciousness my present experiences with my past ones except memory, for what on earth could 'tie present experiences with past ones' mean except 'to remember today what happened yesterday'? So long as it is assumed that what Locke is looking for is a pattern or way of relating together our different past and present experiences, then memory is a very plausible candidate for the criterion to pick out the pattern. In addition, of course, Locke does seem to think that some losses of memory, in particular those we call amnesia, do raise serious problems of continued identity. So it does seem natural to read 'memory' where Locke puts 'consciousness'.

It is worth noticing, however, that it is a little odd of Locke to have been willing to have settled for a purely phenomenalistic account of personal identity. For, in general, he adheres to a more realist position, as reflected in his claim that complex ideas of substances each have attached to them the idea of substance, that is, of some permanent core responsible for the different ideas we get of things. So it is difficult to see why, in the case of personhood, Locke would be inclined to phenomenalism or why he would want to say that it is each person's experiences of themselves as reflected in memory that constructs the self. Penelhum, for example, in his *Encyclopedia of Philosophy* article (p. 92), remarks on the fact that Locke is carrying two different criteria of unity, one in terms of substance and the other in terms of patterns among changing experiences. It is true Locke says the same self is not necessarily the same substance, but this does not itself explain why Locke thought a phenomenalist account would do for selves, although it would not for anything else. It is widely assumed[14] that Locke's point is that, since we can never have any information about substances, our notion of personal identity would always have to be independent of substance and would never be evidence for the same substance. But such an approach is quite antithetical to Locke's usual practice. This would be a reason for never making reference to the notion of substance at all, since we are ignorant, according to Locke, of the nature of substance in any circumstance. But Locke typically takes our ignorance of substance to be evidence for limitations we must recognize to exist for the kinds of knowledge we can have, and he shows no inclination in general to argue that our ignorance of substance can be circumvented through phenomenalist means. So it is difficult to see what would have motivated Locke to abandon his realism for phenomenalism in this one case only.[15]

There is in fact a further problem that suggests that this phenomenalist line of approach to Locke is misguided, for, according to this reading of Locke, the notion of identity must be ambiguous. It must mean one thing when we are talking about things like rocks, which on Locke's terms are substances that persist from one moment to the next, and something else when we are talking about people, which, if they are federations of experiences, must be literally new entities from moment to moment, since Locke says thoughts come in and out of existence as one has them and that they do not repeat themselves. That is, it must make sense to talk of strict identity when we are talking about some kinds of things and to have some looser notion when we are talking of the identity of other kinds of things. But Locke explicitly subscribes to a contrary view. He says in a summary paragraph at the end of his chapter on identity, in 2.27.28, that the notion of identity is not ambiguous but refers to the same sort of thing in each case and that we follow the same sorts of processes whenever we try to uncover the relevant concept of identity. So it seems unlikely that Locke would have one sort of notion of identity for rocks and quite another for entities that do not strictly persist but are actually changing collections of one sort or another.

This is not to say, of course, that Locke thought it did not make any difference at all whether the identity in question was that of a rock of a person, for rocks and people are very different kinds of things. But what he seems instead to be saying is that the preservation of identity happens in the same sort of way with rocks, people, or whatever, even though what it is that preserves identity will vary widely. He makes clear when he introduces the notion of identity in 2.27.1. that the primary notion involved is that a thing must at all times be different from anything else except itself. Then, when we call a thing at one time identical with something at a later time, we need a guarantee that the thing has preserved its identity in a way that continues to distinguish it from anything else. Locke says we derive our notion of identity first by considering the existence of something at a particular place and time, which must, therefore, be other than anything else existing at that time, and *next* time by asking whether it is the same thing now as it was then. This, Locke says, will be true whenever the thing we are considering now had the same beginning as that thing whose identity with it we are trying to establish, for at its beginning that thing was clearly other than anything else. So A and B can be identical only if they share a common beginning, but, if they have different beginnings, they are not one thing but two, however closely related or resembling they might be.

This approach to the problem would seem to rule out, as Locke himself points out, trying to establish identity by means of some unique set of properties, or properties related in some unique order, since it is always possible for two otherwise indistinguishable things to exist at the same time. This fact raises grave doubts about a pattern of memories as a suitable criterion for Locke, since it is perfectly possible for there to be two distinct persons with qualitatively exactly identical memories. Locke would find unacceptable any theory that would have this result.[16] He would also find unacceptable any theory that permitted the fusion of two people into one person identical with both or the fission of one person into two, both identical with the original. His appeal to a single origin as a criterion of identity would certainly rule out cases of fusion, and I think also cases of fission as well, since the event of fission would constitute an origin of one if not both of the resulting entities. On the whole, then, Locke's stated criterion of identity in general, that of a common origin, is uncongenial with the theory attributed to him for persons, that of a continuity of memories.

But, even if having a common origin is the root notion of identity, no matter what we are talking about, Locke thinks that what preserves the identity of a thing from its origin will differ widely. It seems that what we must do in each case is to consider what makes a thing distinctive, for a thing's existence will be preserved so long as it continues to exist after its own particular manner. Thus, for each thing, there will be some individuating way of being, the preservation of which constitutes the continued existence of the thing in question from its origin. Locke is not saying, then, that things are called identical on different kinds of grounds. Things are always identical when they have a common origin, even though what keeps them in existence from their origin will differ from kind to kind. Because a thing's way of existing will differ, it is important in every case to know what we are talking about, but this is not because conditions of identity change or because we call some things the same that are "really," or on another criterion, different.

Confusions on this issue have arisen because of some of the things Locke says when he is trying to explain about what preserves existence, for he is anxious that it be clear that what it is that, for some kinds of things, may be that which preserves its existence from its beginning, may be quite irrelevant for other kinds of things. Thus, he says in 2.27.2 that, if we are considering the possible identity of a mass of matter at one time with a mass of matter at another time, what is relevant is whether all the same particles of matter have continued in existence. From a common origin some alterations then will not destroy the identity of the mass of matter; for example, if the particles are rearranged but if so much as one particle is added or taken away, then we are no longer confronted with the same mass of matter. However, as Locke says, when we think about living creatures, the situation is very different, for we know quite well that the material parts are constantly being removed and yet the organism remains the same. There is no need, however, to in-terpret Locke as saying that the organism is not really the same over time or that we have looser standards of identity for organisms than we do for masses of matter. Locke is simply saying it is something else besides the continued existence of par-ticles of matter that preserves the identity of the organism. Instead, he argues that what individuates an organism is that all the changing parts give rise to and support the same life.[17] It is the life that differentiates one organism from another, no mat-ter how similar. My life is different from anyone else's life. So the principle of in-dividuation that begins with the beginning of the organism and continues to its end is its life.

Thus, the idea is not that identity of living organisms is different from that of masses in that organisms unlike matter are collections of changing things. In both cases, some kinds of things can differ or alter so long as some other kinds of things remain the same. The organism's life is not the same as the organization of its parts, even though created and maintained by those parts. For example, a replica of an organism could reproduce its organization of parts, and its parts could do all the things the parts of the organism do, at the proper times, but the replica would not reproduce the life of the organism. So the identity of both the mass of matter and the organism is discovered by locating some particular individuating feature that preserves existence, but, in the one case, this is the particles of matter and in the other case, its life.[18]

It is true that the notions of "a life" and in particular that of the "same life" are not entirely clear, and there are a number of questions I do not know how to answer. What, for example, is the relationship between the organization of an or-ganism's parts and the life they give rise to? Is it impossible for a donkey to have the life of a flea or an apple tree to have the life of a string bean? That is, are the lives of things whose parts and organization differ also qualitatively different from each other, or are they merely numerically distinct?[19] One might also wonder whether, if I take a living organism, kill it, and then somehow succeed in reanimat-ing its organized parts, it is the same organism or a different one. Must we say the life and hence the organism has a new beginning, or does it make sense to think of the parts of the organism as picking up the life where they left off? It seems likely that as far as Locke is concerned in this situation there are two organisms, since he does not suggest any other way of counting lives except for looking for the origin. Nevertheless, the life is more than just a way of talking about the organization of parts or the events in their history; it is something else, over and above the organiza-tion of parts of the organism, whose continued existence counts as the continued existence of one single organism.

It seems reasonable to assume that, in his criterion for the identity of persons, Locke is looking for something analogous to his criterion of 'one life' for organisms. If so, there is no reason to assume he is trying to find a pattern among changing ex-periences. Instead, what he will be looking for is some individuating way of being, whose presence from the beginning of the person will differentiate that person from all others and the continued existence of which will preserve the continued existence of the distinctive person. It is not necessary to assume that Locke is introducing a phenomenalist account of the self or to assume that his idea of personal identity is as a relationship serving to tie all the different experiences of a person into a bundle. It is sufficiently clear, I think, that such an approach would be antithetical to Locke. What is needed instead is an interpretation of what he is saying about personal identity that will be about something that continues throughout the different experiences of the person and constitutes his or her way of existing in the way the organism's life continues throughout its existence.

The concept of memory has been found to be incompatible with Locke's general account of identity, but the concept of consciousness is not. Locke's idea of what preserves personal identity can be understood simply in terms of consciousness by interpreting this as playing a role analogous to life for an organism. If we look at Locke in this fashion, then what he is saying is that what makes me different at this moment from any other person is that *my* thoughts are identical with *my* consciousness of them. No one else can have my consciousness, any more than any other organism can have my life. Even if two of us both have the same idea of red, we each have it via a different consciousness. Thus, consciousness, like life for an organism, is an individuating feature of a person, present from the beginning of the person.

If this is the correct approach to take to what Locke is doing, then his account of personal identity could be seen to be something like this. What I call my self refers to my consciousness and derives from the fact that all my experiences are had by a consciousness that is different from any one else's way of having experiences. One thing this will mean is that how things look and feel and smell for me will be the result of my consciousness of them, the way they are registered for my consciousness. So it would seem that one feature of this would be that, while any act of thinking or feeling is such that I cannot avoid knowing what it is like for me to have it for this is what my thinking or feeling amounts to, I cannot know what this is like for anyone else.[20] Of course, if I take our two mechanisms of consciousness to be similar, then I will assume that what it is like for me to have a pain is similar to what a pain is like for you. Nevertheless, we will want to talk about how the pain seems for each of us, and you will be able to compare how the pain in your knee feels to how your headache feels but not to how my headache feels. Thus, because each person has his or her own consciousness, each has his or her own distinctive internality. We might even imagine that each consciousness registered things differently, that my headache felt differently from yours. If consciousness worked this way, if how things were registered reflected the individuality of each consciousness, then each center of consciousness would also be qualitatively distinctive. But under these circumstances, if I started to have your sort of headache, this still would not make me you so long as it was my consciousness having the headache.

One way of thinking about this (suggested to me by Robert Schwartz) is to imagine what it would be like to exchange properties or experiences with some other person. Even though we have no difficulty in supposing we might acquire one person's beauty or another's experience on waking up to find oneself famous, we nevertheless expect to retain our own internality, our own consciousness of these changes or events. It is much harder to imagine a lack of continuity in our registration of things. This situation is quite different, of course, from that of our memories. We can imagine all too readily having memories other than our actual ones, or even having some other person's memories, but we would expect them to be incorporated into and had by our own individuating consciousness.

Since, on this account, what is distinctive about each person is that each is a consciousness constituting an individuating center of consciousness and not that a person has been collected together from a distinctive history of experiences, it is easy to see why the existence of gaps in the series of experiences recorded by our consciousness would not be a problem. It ought not to be necessary that I remain conscious of my consciousness for the actions of my past self to remain actions of my present self. This is presumably Locke's point when he says (2.1.11) that the sleeping Socrates will be identical with the waking Socrates so long as the sleeping Socrates is not assumed to be having experiences of which the waking Socrates is unaware. If it were, then this would constitute the presence of two distinct consciousnesses and so would amount to two different people, but mere absence of consciousness, the fact that our consciousness is not always in operation, has no effect on the functioning of our consciousness.

One would think also simple forgetting would be no problem, so long as the events we cannot recall were registered by our present consciousness and not by anyone else's. Locke's discussion of memory is not easy to understand, however, since his attention is very much taken up with extreme cases in which, he thinks, we ought to want to say we are dealing with two people and not with only one. So he says that one would remain the same man but would not be the same person if "I wholly lose the memory of some parts of my life, beyond a possibility of retrieving them, so that perhaps I shall never be conscious of them again" (2.27.20). If he means here that anything forgotten was not done by a present you, that remembering is a necessary condition for being the same person, then he has fallen into the difficulty Berkeley and Reid pointed out[21] of having an identity that alters depending upon what one happens to remember. But I am not entirely sure of what Locke means here. Locke's intuition seems to be that, since the present you has a consciousness that cannot communicate with the consciousness of a past you, there must be two distinct consciousnesses. He thinks that, wherever consciousnesses are incommunicable, they are distinct. The clearest example of incommunicability among consciousnesses occurs presumably when we consider two persons at a single time. One person might be conscious of a headache among many other things, while the other might be conscious of an itch between the shoulder blades. The person with the headache is not conscious of the itch. This is a clear case, presumably, of incommunicability. Locke also thinks, as I said, that, if I were assumed to be having in sleep thoughts I did not perceive, this would be another case of incommunicability. (Because to think is to be conscious one thinks, this assumption requires the existence of a second consciousness incommunicable with my own.) This case is just like the first, except that the thoughts I do not perceive do not happen to be occurring simultaneously with the same ones I do perceive. Locke talks about not being able to recall such thoughts. This brings memory into the picture, but possibly in a misleading fashion. There is a difference between not being able to remember what color the book was I saw on the table and not being able to say what color it was because I never saw it in the first place. The role of memory will be much more important if Locke is assumed to be saying that the things you thought or did but cannot remember are no longer a part of you than if he is saying that the things you never thought or did and hence cannot remember are not a part of you. It seems to me that, when Locke is talking about amnesia or when he is talking about a sleeper who develops a consciousness its waking self is unaware of, he can be understood as having this latter type of case in mind. He could be saying that, if, for example, the body associated with your consciousness develops a second consciousness, in-communicable with the first, then the acts of this second consciousness are not yours, since your consciousness does not extend to them, even though we might want to say that a part of you did them, namely, your body. Locke, for example, compares the case in which the sleeper has a distinct consciousness to the case in which your arm becomes divorced from your consciousness. We would not attribute the actions of your arm to you under these circumstances. The comparison with the arm suggests that what is important in attributing actions to persons cannot be memory. But, since action occurring to consciousness distinct from yours are actions of which you are not aware, they will be actions you cannot remember.

Perhaps the most troublesome passage for reading Locke's views on memory in the way I have suggested comes at 2.27.23. Locke says:

> For granting that the thinking Substance in Man must be necessarily suppos'd immaterial, 'tis evident, that immaterial thinking thing may sometimes part with its past consciousness, and be restored to it again, as appears in the forgetfulness Men often have of their past Actions, and the Mind many times recovers the memory of a past consciousness, which it had lost for twenty Years together. Make these intervals of Memory and Forgetfulness to take their turns regularly by Day and Night, and you have two Persons with the same immaterial Spirit, as much as in the former instance two Persons with the same Body. So that *self* is not determined by Identity or Diversity of Substance, which it cannot be sure of, but only by Identity of consciousness.

So long as by "the former instance" Locke means to pick out amnesia, then my interpretation can stand. If he is not distinguishing amnesia from ordinary forgetting, then Berkeley's and Reid's objection will hold. Notice, however, that the issue here is whether Locke intended remembering to be a test for a continuing consciousness, which is a sufficient condition for personal identity. There is no suggestion that he might have been a memory theorist as traditionally conceived.

If an account of Locke's theory of personal identity based on consciousness is correct, then it will become important to work out how consciousness can be thought to constitute something individuating for each person. Certainly there are problems involved in the notion of a distinctive consciousness, as there were for the concept of a distinctive life. There are clear difficulties in expressing what it is for a consciousness to be continuing and what is involved when a consciousness is not communicating. These sorts of issues would have to be resolved before one could get clear on what might be meant by saying a person is distinctive in that all its experiences are registered by and thus unified in its own consciousness.

IV

There is, however, a general problem for this interpretation of Locke's theory in terms of a distinctive consciousness. This arises because of Locke's claim that being the same person does not necessarily entail having the same immaterial substance. This means the consciousness criterion must be interpreted in such a way as to individuate persons but not immaterial substances, for, in making this claim, Locke is not saying we should not make use of the notion of immaterial substance for any purpose. Locke in several different passages defends the idea of immaterial substance as being quite as justified as our idea of material substance and derived in the same way; he says this in 2.23.5, for example, and in 2.23.15, where he says, "And thus by putting together the *Ideas* of Thinking, Perceiving, Liberty, and Power of moving themselves and other things, we have as clear a perception, and notion of immaterial Substances, we we have of material." That is, 'immaterial substance' is just Locke's term for mind, and we derive our idea of it apparently by observing the existence of mental events or processes. Nor does he think there is any particular problem with the notion of 'same immaterial substance', for he says he thinks the criterion of having a common origin is quite sufficient (2.27.2). But, so long as we take it that what Locke thinks individuates a person is having a distinctive consciousness, it becomes a problem why he thought being the same person did not necessarily result in having the same mind, for he says the concept of mental substance is derived by putting together mental acts. But what could this mean except that these acts are observed to occur to the same consciousness?

Shoemaker[22] finds Locke's view to be entirely incoherent. He says that, since Locke has identified persons as thinking things and since thinking things are substances, persons are substances. I do not think Locke would disagree with this; that is, he need not claim that each consciousness does not belong to some substance, just that the same consciousness need not necessarily belong to the same substance. To illustrate this contention, Locke introduces a story of a day-person and a night-person, as well as a version of the prince-cobbler story (2.27.23).

> Could we suppose two distinct incommunicable consciousnesses acting the same Body, the one constantly by Day, the other by Night; and, on the other side the same consciousness acting by intervals two distinct Bodies: I ask in the first case, whether the *Day* and the *Night-Man* would not be two as distinct Persons as *Socrates* and *Plato*; and whether in the second case, there would not be one Person in two distinct Bodies, as much as one Man is the same in two distinct clothings. Nor is it at all material to say, that this same, and this distinct *consciousness* in the cases above mentioned, is owing to the

same and distinct immaterial Substances, bringing it with them to those
Bodies, which whether true or no, alters not the case: Since 'tis evident the
personal Identity would equally be determined by the consciousness, whether
that consciousness were annexed to some individual immaterial Substance or
no.

Thus, it is not necessary to imagine in these examples that consciousness occurs
without an immaterial substance any more than it occurs without a body. But what
is plausible, according to Locke, is that we imagine the day-man and the night-man,
for example, to have the same immaterial substance but different consciousnesses.[23]

Shoemaker also questions the plausibility of this idea, that it be possible for
the same person not always to be annexed to the same substance. Since we must
say, for example, both persons and substances think and feel, we must either say
persons and substances both think but in different senses, in which case we must
specify those different senses, or else we must say they both think in the same
sense, which seems an unnecessary duplication of effort. It seems to me, moreover,
if persons and minds both think in the same sense or if our evidence for the presence of a thinking person and a thinking mind is the same, namely, a unified consciousness for thinking activities, then Locke could have no possible reason for
saying the day-man and the night-man could have the same mind but different consciousnesses. Our reason for saying there are two people, namely, that the thinking
events are occurring in two distinct consciousnesses, would also be a reason for saying the thinking events are not occurring concomitantly, and so that there are two
different minds.

For Locke to have made this claim it would seem what he must have had in
mind is that there is another interpretation of the concomitance of mental acts besides their occurring in the same consciousness. The 'putting together' he says
comes about when the ideas of the various mental operations are combined to form
the notion of immaterial substance is not grounded in the observation of the unity
of consciousness. What Locke might be thinking of can be made relatively clear if
we keep in mind the circumstances under which he liked to talk about substances.
In making use of the notion of substance, Locke is saying he thinks there is a real
basis or cause of our mental activity, just as there is for the activities of material
objects. He calls something a substance to indicate that the various properties and
powers found to go together are taken to be part of a real, natural unity, for Locke
speaks of substance as "the peculiar internal constitution, or unknown essence,"
from which flow the powers from which we derive our ideas of things (2.23.3). We
require the notion of substance because powers must be grounded in some constitution, unknown to us, that is their cause. Thus, it is not every concomitance that
gives rise to the idea of substance but only those that seem to require some natural
causal basis.[24]

It is not unreasonable to suppose our mental powers are all powers of some
single cause, for our various powers all work together to produce a thoroughly integrated set of mental operations or behavior. We have every reason to believe that
our perceptions causally affect our beliefs and memories and that these, in turn, can

be used in explaining the outcomes of our power to move in action. That is, people seem to be able to reach for what they see, to reach for what they see when they want it; their wants are connected with what has given them pleasure or pain, and yet they also refrain from wanting as a result of certain kinds of beliefs or trains of reasoning. We cannot help but be aware of the mutually interlocking nature of our various mental events. This sort of integrative unity is clearly not the same as the unity of consciousness. Suppose it so happened that, whenever I thought 'salt', you thought 'pepper', or when you felt pain, I cried. We might well imagine it ought to be possible to discover some underlying cause of these phenomena, but we could still distinguish two seats of consciousness. Thus, it seems reasonable for Locke to have supposed the interdependence of our thought, desires, and powers to move in action provides sufficient reason for assigning all of them to a single causal basis. But he is very anxious to argue against Descartes that we can have no reason for claiming that we know the essential property of this causal basis of immaterial substance to be thinking or conscious thought.

This means that we can talk about the items of our mental life in two different ways. We can consider each mental event as an instance of a family of interlocking powers whose unifying cause is unknown, or we can consider the qualitative nature of each mental event as it occurs in each individual's consciousness, such as a seeing of red or a hearing of B-flat. Thus, we might talk about a wine lover's breathing in the bouquet of the wine and then rolling it on her tongue as the result of the causative powers expressed in certain beliefs and desires, but we will also talk about how the wine smelled and tasted to her in terms of her instrument for registration, her consciousness. An account, if we had one, of the causes of our mental powers and how they are integrated would not tell the whole story of our mental operations for Locke. We must still include reference to that aspect of thinking and feeling that can be considered the peculiar province of the individual person, for, of course, Locke has said there is no thinking without consciousness, that thinking and being conscious of a thought are one and the same (2.1.19). Or, again, with reference to sensations, he says all the right physiological things can be happening to us in the presence of some object but, unless we are paying attention, there will be no sensation, for nothing will have entered our consciousness. Thus, for Locke, there is a second indispensible aspect to thinking and feeling besides the causative, for we must also talk about the way the various contents of thought end up seeming to us, the manner in which they get registered together in consciousness.

This kind of account, then, requires us to be able to say something about the unique contribution of consciousness to our mental life. There are a number of different activities that Locke might have had in mind. The first is obvious: that, unless we have become conscious of something or some kind of thing, we cannot think about it. This is, of course, Locke's famous point with regard to simple ideas (2.2.2). Unless we have had the experience of being conscious of, for example, colors, we can do no thinking about colors; they will not be available as a category to us. And one might also imagine that what has been experienced in the past will affect what will be paid attention to and, hence, what will enter into consciousness. In addition, unless we have reflected on our ideas in certain ways, we will not have become conscious of particular relationships among them, and these categories will not be available to us.[25] And, since we can reflect on any number of different relations, we can each of us enlarge our experience in any number of different ways. Finally, Locke says almost every experience we have is accompanied by a consciousness of pleasure or pain and this pleasurable or painful coloring could shape what we pay attention to and what we do and, in so doing, be of great importance for the nature of the person. It should be clear that these various ways of establishing a conscious framework of experiences, on which our mental powers then operate, will be dependent on individual features of our experience—what each person has paid attention to, thought about, and enjoyed or disliked. Thus, the effect of having experiences or registering experiences via consciousness will be to build up a distinctive outlook. It is natural to think of the establishment of this conscious outlook as being the contribution each person makes to his or her own mental life. Thus, we can solve the dilemma that Shoemaker raised by saying that, for Locke, there are indeed two different aspects to thinking and feeling. The first is the integrated set of powers we attribute to immaterial substances, and the second is the conscious outlook we attribute to persons. It might be tempting to try to develop an account of the continuity and individuation of each consciousness in terms of the causal relations among experiences that lead to a distinctive outlook. But, as an account of what individuates a person, this will ultimately conflict with Locke's claim that identity requires a common origin. Consider a case of fission, by which it seems that at least one of the resulting entities does not share a beginning with the original. Nevertheless, the causal relations and distinctive outlook will, at least at the time of the fission, be the same in both.

It is easy to see why Locke thought that anything other than one mental substance giving rise to one consciousness was highly unlikely. But is it possible, using this account of the difference between mind and person, to think of cases in which we would be willing to say there was only one mind but more than one person? What this would require is that we think of cases in which we could find integration of mental operations but more than one center of consciousness. Interestingly, these features seem to characterize the situation of some recent surgery cases who have had their corpus collosum severed as a cure for epilepsy. Such people with split brains are in general indistinguishable from the rest of the population because of the successful integration of their mental operations, but careful experimentation reveals the two halves of the brain are no longer mutually coconscious. Only one half of the brain still has the power to produce speech, and this verbal half is unable to report on and denies the existence of experiences occurring to the other half of the brain, although the verbal half does exhibit behavior caused by experiences to the half of which it is not conscious. Thus, such people seem to represent an actual realization of Locke's day-man and night-man case. It is also interesting that it is just these features, namely, mental integration together with absence of coconsciousness, that lead Nagel[26] to conclude that it is impossible to count the number of minds a person has in any meaningful way. But Nagel is apparently assuming we will count minds and persons in the same way, that the same concept will do for both. Locke's distinction would enable him to describe the situation of the split brain by saying they have only one mind but are nevertheless two persons, even though these two persons are, under most circumstances, very much alike.

C. O. Evans has pointed out[27] that most theories of the self, in particular Pure Ego and Bundle theories, are merely adaptations of theories about material objects. ". . . The Pure Ego Theory," he says, "is simply the application to the self of the general doctrine of substance and attribute." Thus, if Locke were prepared to treat the self like any other object, one would expect him to have proposed some sort of pure ego theory. But instead Locke has chosen to treat mind and self quite differently. He is prepared to agree with a pure ego theorist like Descartes that it is the fact of consciousness that is to be identified with myself but is not prepared to agree with Descartes that consciousness can be seen as the essential property of mental substance. Thus, Locke's notion of consciousness is to be distinguished from a basically unknown mental substance, but, for Locke as for Descartes, being conscious is the same as having ideas. For Locke to have distinguished immaterial substance and person in this way, moreover, seems to me to lend further plausibility to I. C. Tipton's suggestion[28] that Berkeley's notion of spiritual substance is actually much closer to that of Locke's person than to Locke's immaterial substance. Pretty clearly, Berkeley could not have adopted Locke's concept of immaterial substance as distinguished from the person without laying himself open to inconsistency. But the identification of the person with that which is responsible for consciousness seems to pave the way for Berkeley's agent-self.

These final remarks are speculative merely and intended only to show the kinds of areas to which this way of construing Locke's theory of personal identity might direct attention. All I hope to have shown is this. Theories of personal identity in terms of mental continuity as located in memory (and sometimes character) have loomed very large over discussions of personal identity, and Locke is generally taken to be a speaker for this memory view. I think it is not only possible to conceive of quite different theories of personal identity than the dominant views, I think it is likely that Locke himself held that the identity of each person consists, not in their memories, but in their possessing from the moment of their birth their own consciousness.

Notes

Note: A version of this paper was an invited paper at the Eastern Division American Association meetings in December, 1978. Martha B. Bolton was the commentator, and I am very grateful to her for her helpful response. Earlier versions were read at Columbia University, CUNY Graduate Center, University of Maryland, University of Rochester, and University of North Carolina, Chapel Hill. I owe special thanks for their help to Dennis Ahern, E. M. Curley, Richard Feldman, Daniel Hausman, Arnold Koslow, Jerrold Levinson, David Rosenthal, and Robert Schwartz.

1. For example, H. P. Grice, "Personal Identity," reprinted in John Perry, ed., *Personal Identity* (Berkeley: University of California Press, 1975), pp. 73-95; Anthony Quinton, "The Soul," *Journal of Philosophy*, Vol. 59 (July, 1962), pp. 393-409.

2. This formulation is from Anthony Flew, "Locke on Personal Identity," reprinted in C. B. Martin and D. M. Armstrong, *Locke and Berkeley* (Garden City, N.Y.: Anchor Books, 1968), p. 157. It is representative of a number of accounts of Locke, although there is disagreement about how Locke's memory criterion should be formulated. See Bernard Williams, "Personal Identity and Individuation," *Problems of the Self* (Cambridge: Cambridge University Press, 1973), pp. 1-18; or Baruch Brody, "Locke on the Identity of Persons," *American Philosophical Quarterly*, Vol. 9, No. 4 (October, 1972), pp. 327-34.

3. I do not want to suggest that all these views have been held by every commentator on Locke, but they are characteristic of most discussions of Locke and form a kind of "general knowledge" picture of Locke's theory of personal identity. All these points were mentioned, for example, by Terence Penelhum in his article on "Personal Identity" for the *Encyclopedia of Philosophy* (New York: Collier-Macmillan, 1967), pp. 95-107.

4. *An Essay Concerning Human Understanding* (2.27.15). All references are to the edition edited by Peter H. Nidditch (Oxford: Oxford University Press, 1975). It is not, of course, strictly accurate, although usual, to describe this event as an exchange, since Locke never mentions what happens to the soul of the cobbler.

5. The exact nature of this distinction will, I hope, become more clear later. It may well be that the 'person' and 'man' are not the best words, in terms of our ordinary feelings about their use, to capture Locke's distinction. This is particularly so since feminist consciousness has encouraged us to substitute 'person' whenever 'man' is not being used to refer to the male sex only. Probably the best way to capture Locke's meaning comfortably would be to use 'person' for what he calls 'man' and to use 'self' for 'person', for we typically speak of the self as what is encountered in self-awareness, while persons are what we meet on the street. But to adopt this terminology would unduly complicate any exegesis of Locke. (Locke himself uses 'self' and 'person' interchangeably.)

6. In his controversy with Stillingfleet, Locke points out that it is a convenience when resurrected saints appear to their still-living friends in the body they had when alive so that they might be recognized as the same man who was dead and is now resurrected. Presumably, he does not suppose that a different body with the same memories as a former friend would be accepted as convincing proof of resurrection. The relevant passage from the Second Reply to the Bishop of Worcester appears on p. 186 of *The Locke Reader*, ed. John W. Yolton (Cambridge: Cambridge University Press, 1977).

7. Some contemporary discussions of these issues have tended to adopt Locke's disinterest in the question of dualism and have talked about brain transplants rather than soul transplants.

8. These are just some of the many criticisms that have been brought against the view that memory can be used as a criterion of personal identity, for this claim has been a popular target. A sampling of these criticisms can be found in: Joseph Butler, "Of Personal Identity," Appendix to the Analogy of Religion, reprinted in John Perry, ed., *Personal Identity* (Berkeley: University of California Press, 1975), pp. 99-105; Thomas Reid, "Of Mr. Locke's Account of Our Personal Identity," from *Essays on the Intellectual Powers of Man*, reprinted in John Perry, ed., *Personal Identity* (Berkeley: University of California Press, 1975), pp. 113-18; Sidney Shoemaker, *Self-Knowledge and Self-Identity* (Ithaca, N.Y.: Cornell University Press, 1963); Anthony Flew, "Locke and the Problem of Personal Identity," in C. B. Martin and D. M. Armstrong, *Locke and Berkeley* (Garden City, N.Y.: Anchor Books, 1968), A. B. Palma, "Memory and Personal Identity," *Australasian Journal of Philosophy*, Vol. 42, No. 1 (May, 1964), pp. 53-68, Williams, "Personal Identity and Individuation."

9. John Perry, in fact, suggests that Locke may be defending this theory "in the spirit of conceptual innovation," since Locke was certainly aware of the counterexamples to it. "The Problem of Personal Identity," p. 15.

10. For example, in 2.10.5 he says, "But yet there seems to be a constant decay of all our Ideas, even of those which are struck deepest, and in Minds the most retentive; so that if there be not sometimes renewed by repeated Exercise of the Senses, or Reflection on those kinds of

Objects, which at first occasioned them, the Print wears out and at last there remains nothing to be seen."

11. ". . . This consciousness, being interrupted always by forgetfulness, there being no moment of our Lives wherein we have the whole train of all our past Actions before our Eyes in one view: But even the best Memories losing the sight of one part whilst they are viewing another: and we sometimes, and that the greatest part of our lives, not reflecting on our past selves, being intent on our present thoughts, and in sound sleep, having no thoughts at all, or at least none with that consciousness, which remarks our waking thoughts. I say, in all these cases, our consciousness being interrupted, and we losing sight of our past *selves*, doubts are raised whether we are the same thinking thing; i.e., the same substance or no. Which, however, reasonable or unreasonable concerns not *personal identity* at all. The question being what makes the same *Person*, and not whether it be the same Identical Substance, which always thinks in the same Person" (2.27.10). A full interpretation of this passage must await a discussion of Locke's distinction between person and substance, for which see below.

12. Thus, I am disagreeing with Harold Noonan ("Locke on Personal Identity," *Philosophy*, Vol. 53, No. 205 [July, 1978]), pp. 343-51, who states, without argument, that Locke is concerned with the self-conscious subject.

13. Sometimes it results in somewhat cavalier treatment. Flew, for example ("Locke and the Problem of Personal Identity," p. 159), notes that Locke sometimes seems to be using consciousness to mean awareness, sometimes self-consciousness; announces that we can nevertheless substitute 'remember' for 'consciousness' throughout; and then berates Locke for not saying what he meant. A. B. Palma ("Memory and Personal Identity") also notices that several of Locke's references to consciousness, such as the little finger example, cannot be interpreted as memory and suggests that they mean something like awareness.

14. Shoemaker, *Self-Knowledge and Self-Identity*, p. 71; Perry, "The Problem of Personal Identity," p. 25; and Penelhum, "Personal Identity," p. 96, for example, all make this assumption.

15. It might be thought that Locke had special reservations about the idea of substance underlying psychological qualities, but, in fact, this is not so. I will say more about this later.

16. This, I think, also rules out that his point is, as M. W. Hughes suggests in "Personal Identity: A Defense of Locke" (*Philosophy*, Vol. 50 [1975], pp. 169-87), that a contemporary man with Homer's memories and Homer's talents is so indistinguishable from the old Homer as to make the question of their identity uninteresting or unnecessary.

17. "That being then one Plant, which has such an Organization of Parts in one coherent Body, partaking of one Common Life, it continues to be the same Plant, as long as it partakes of the same Life, though that Life be communicated to new Particles of Matter vitally united to the living Plant, in a like continued organization, conformable to that sort of Plants" (2.27.4).

18. Therefore, considered as a 'man', a living organism, the cobbler retained his identity, even when his soul was replaced by that of the prince, for his organization of parts, which, after all, always includes the replacement of some parts by others, continued unabated to give rise to life.

19. Although the notion of lives as being of different qualitative sorts or as continuing to exist in qualitatively distinct manners might be attractive, it is important to realize that we cannot use these qualitative differences to individuate organisms and remain true to Locke's picture of identity, for it would be possible for two lives to be qualitatively identical and yet have different origins.

20. See Thomas Nagel, "What Is It Like to Be a Bat?" *Philosophical Review*, Vol. LXXXIII, No. 4 (October, 1974), pp. 435-50.

21. Berkeley's objection is found in *Alciphron* 7.8, Reid's in his *Essays on the Intellectual Powers of Man*, reprinted in John Perry, ed., *Personal Identity* (Berkeley: University of California Press, 1975).

22. *Self-Knowledge and Self-Identity*, pp. 45-55.

23. This is not the only passage in which Locke asserts that the same person does not

necessarily go along with the same immaterial substance. He said it before in 2.27.21 and says it again in 2.27.24, adding immediately afterward in 2.27.25 that he thinks it extremely unlikely that consciousness ever occurs except as "annexed to and the affectation of one individual immaterial substance."

24. For Locke's theory of substance, see in particular, M. R. Ayers, "The Ideas of Power and Substance in Locke's Philosophy," *The Philosophical Quarterly*, Vol. 25, No. 98 (January, 1975), pp. 1-27; Martha Brandt Bolton, "Substances, Substrata and the Names of Substances in Locke's Essay," *The Philosophical Review*, Vol. LXXXV, No. 4 (October, 1976), pp. 448-513.

25. Yolton has made the point in "Locke's Concept of Experience," in Martin and Armstrong, that Locke's concept of experience must be enlarged to include explanatory concepts as well as directly experiential concepts.

26. In "Brain-Bisection and the Unity of Consciousness," reprinted in John Perry, ed., *Personal Identity* (Berkeley: University of California Press, 1975), pp. 229-45.

27. *The Subject of Consciousness* (London: Geo. Allen and Unwin, 1970), p. 29.

28. "Berkeley's View of Spirit" in *New Studies in Berkeley's Philosophy*, Warren E. Steinkraus, ed. (New York: Holt, Rinehart and Winston, 1966), pp. 59-71.

Berkeley's Argument against Abstract Ideas

WILLIS DONEY

I n the Introduction to the *Principles*, Berkeley argues in several ways against the "patrons" of abstract ideas.[1] I will be concerned with his line of reasoning in Section 10. The view that I attribute to Berkeley is that an argument in Section 10 can be used to prove the impossibility of abstract ideas. In the first part of my paper, I give what I believe is a prima facie plausible reading of Section 10. Many commentators would disagree with this interpretation, and, in the remaining sections, I distinguish and try to answer three objections based on contrary opinions in the literature. I conclude that, since my reading can be defended against these objections, it stands a chance of being the correct interpretation of this important passage.

1

In Sections 6 through 9, Berkeley is at pains to expound the view or views of his unnamed adversaries. Naturally enough, what he regards as weak points are exposed; and, when in Section 10 he begins his actual attack, he travels very rapidly. I distinguish four moves that he makes in this passage and mark them with the letters A, B, C, and D.

> 10 [A] Whether others have this wonderful faculty of *abstracting their ideas*, they best can tell: for my self I find indeed I have a faculty of imagining, or representing to my self the ideas of those particular things I have perceived and of variously compounding and dividing them. I can imagine a man with two heads or the upper parts of a man joined to the body of a horse. I can consider the hand, the eye, the nose, each by it self abstracted or separated from the rest of the body. [B] But then whatever hand or eye I imagine, it must have some particular shape and colour. Likewise the idea of man that I frame to my self, must be either of a white, or a black, or a tawny, a straight,

or a crooked, a tall, or a low, or a middle-sized man. I cannot by any effort of thought conceive the abstract idea above described [i.e., "the abstract idea of *man*" described in the preceding Section 9]. And it is equally impossible for me to form the abstract idea of motion distinct from the body moving, and which is neither swift nor slow, curvilinear nor rectilinear; and the like may be said of all other abstract general ideas whatsoever. [C] To be plain, I own my self able to abstract in one sense, as when I consider some particular parts or qualities separated from others, with which though they are united in some object, yet, it is possible they may really exist without them. But I deny that I can abstract one from another, or conceive separately, those qualities which it is impossible should exist so separated; or that I can frame a general notion by abstracting from particulars in the manner afore-said. Which two last are the proper acceptations of *abstraction*. [D] And there are grounds to think most men will acknowledge themselves to be in my case. The generality of men which are simple and illiterate never pretend to *abstract notions*. It's said they are difficult and not to be attained without pains and study. We may therefore reasonably conclude that, if such there be, they are confined only to the learned.

The three sentences following C in this passage are from the errata in the first edition. A question can be raised whether they were inadvertently omitted by the printer or were added by Berkeley, and the answer to this question will be of some importance when an alternative interpretation is considered. Since my interpretation is compatible with either possibility, I will say no more about the question until I consider that interpretation.

When in Section 6 Berkeley introduces the view that he is going to attack, it is "the opinion that the mind hath a *power* of framing *abstract ideas* or notions of things" (my emphasis of "*power*"). It is important to note that the question to which he addresses himself at the outset in Section 10 is not whether there are abstract ideas or whether we are aware of abstract ideas but rather as in Section 6 whether we possess that "wonderful faculty" of abstracting posited by his adversaries. In A, he describes various feats of framing or conceiving ideas that he is able to perform. He can, he says, "imagine a man with two heads or the upper parts of a man joined to the body of a horse"; and he "can consider the hand, the eye, the nose, each by it self abstracted or separated from the rest of the body." His claims of success in performing these feats seem to be intended to illustrate and to confirm his general observation at the beginning: "I find indeed," he writes, "I have a faculty of imagining, or representing to my self the ideas of those particular things I have perceived and of variously compounding and dividing them."

Having found in A that he possesses this faculty, he goes on to argue in B that he lacks another imputed faculty or faculties, namely, the faculty or faculties of abstraction posited by his opponents.[2] Here he reports failures in attempts to form ideas of each of the three types that he distinguishes in Sections 7, 8, and 9. With regard to the abstract idea of man described in Section 9, he finds that he "cannot by any effort of thought conceive the abstract idea above described." In the sentence that follows, he alludes to procedures for forming ideas described in Sections 7 and 8: "And it is equally impossible for me to form the abstract idea [as suggested in Section 7] of motion distinct from the body moving, and [as suggested in Section 8] which is neither swift nor slow, curvilinear nor rectilinear. . . ." He seems to be of the opinion that his classification of ideas in Sections 7, 8, and 9 is exhaustive and that, after reporting failures in the three cases, he is in a position to conclude that he lacks the ability to form any abstract idea; for he says at the end of B, "and the like may be said of all other abstract general ideas whatsoever."

Although the discussion in A and B is explicitly about faculties that he does and does not possess, it is, I believe, clearly implied in B that, when the lack of a faculty of abstracting is established, the nonexistence of the ideas that are supposed to issue from the faculty is also proved. Berkeley does not explicitly draw that conclusion, however; and, considered as an argument against the existence of abstract ideas, the argument stated in B is incomplete. The conclusion that Berkeley thinks he proves in the Introduction is that abstract ideas are impossible. Thus, in Section 21, he claims to have "shewn the impossibility of *abstract ideas*." And, to get to that conclusion, it seems that the premise we need to supply is a principle that Berkeley relies on in other places and that he seems to have regarded as self-evident, namely, that what is inconceivable is impossible.[3] Supplying that principle, we get the following argument. The first two steps are simply his more-or-less explicit way of arguing in B that he lacks the ability to form ideas described by his adversaries. (1) "When I attempt to follow the procedure described for forming e.g. an abstract idea of man, I find that I fail." From 1 he concludes: (2) "I lack the ability or power to form such an idea." These steps are compressed in Berkeley's assertion, "I cannot by any effort of thought conceive the abstract idea above described." From his assertion here that the *idea* in question cannot be conceived, it seems that 3 is intended to follow from 2: (3) "The supposed idea of man cannot be conceived" or −shortly−"The supposed idea of man is inconceivable."[4] Supplying the principle, (4) "What is inconceivable is impossible," we get the implied conclusion, (5) "The supposed abstract idea of man is impossible."

This is the argument against abstract ideas that I believe is implied in Section 10. I will call this way of reasoning the Argument from Inconceivability. It differs in an important respect from another argument that it is tempting to ascribe to Berkeley and with which the Argument from Inconceivability can easily be conflated. Both are ostensibly based on a kind of self-observation or introspection, but the other argument, which I will call the Argument from Unobservability, does not lead to the conclusion that Berkeley claims to have established in the Introduction, namely, that the existence of abstract ideas is an impossibility. The Argument from Unobservability has three steps. (1) "When I survey the contents of my mind, I fail to observe ideas of the kinds described by the proponents of abstract ideas." (2) "What is supposed to exist in the mind but cannot be observed there does not exist." Therefore, (3) "Ideas of the kinds described by the proponents of abstract ideas do not exist." It can be argued that Berkeley uses the Argument from Unobservability as well as the Argument from Inconceivability in Section 13, where he says, "What more easy than for any one to look a little into his own thoughts, and there try whether he has, or can attain to have, an idea that shall correspond with the description that is here given of the general idea of a triangle. . . ." The phrase "can attain to have" echoes the Argument from Inconceivability in Section 10, whereas "try whether he has" suggests the Argument from Unobservability.

Whether Berkeley does in fact employ the Argument from Unobservability is a question that I will leave open.[5] What seems quite clear to me, however, is that the Argument from Inconceivability is the argument to be found in Section 10 and that it is on this argument that Berkeley relies in trying to show that the existence of abstract ideas is an impossibility. To put my contention in a few words: it is not from the unobservability of abstract ideas but from their inconceivability that he infers their necessary nonexistence. The arguments are sufficiently alike that they might seem to be fundamentally or really of the same sort. Both might be called empirical or perhaps "quasi-empirical" since they purport to be based on a kind of self-examination. But it is a different sort of self-examination proposed in the two arguments. In the Argument from Unobservability, it is a kind of looking and observing or rather failing to observe; in the Argument from Inconceivability, an attempt is made to perform a thought experiment and that "effort of thought" fails. Moreover, the conclusion reached in the Argument from Unobservability is weak by comparison with the strong conclusion of the Argument from Inconceivability. I believe some commentators have failed to distinguish the two arguments, and it is for this reason that they have supposed that the "psychological" or "quasi-empirical" argument in Section 10 could not yield the conclusion that Berkeley claims to reach and they have then cast about—rather desperately and wildly—for another argument to fit that bill.[6]

2

If my reading of Section 10 is correct, the Argument from Inconceivability is presented succinctly (if elliptically) within B. But Section 10 does not end when Berkeley says, "and the like may be said of all other abstract general ideas whatsoever," and there are problems to be considered about the relationship of what he goes on to say in C and D to what, on my interpretation, he has already said in A and B.

It might at first seem that in C Berkeley is simply making explicit some general conclusions that are implied but not stated in B. When he asserts in B that the alleged abstract idea of man is inconceivable and implies that it is impossible, he also implies that any idea that is supposed to have been formed in similar fashion by the procedure or procedures described in Section 9 is impossible; and it seems that, when he denies in C that he "can frame a general notion by abstracting from particulars in the manner aforesaid," he is just making explicit the general conclusion implied but not stated in B. But, in what comes before this in C, it is not clear that that is all that he is doing. No doubt, he does intend to make explicit that it is not just "the abstract idea of motion distinct from the body moving" that he wishes to repudiate but any idea formed in similar fashion in the way or ways described in Section 7. In Section 7, the view ascribed to his antagonists is that "qualities or modes of things" that cannot exist apart can nonetheless be abstracted and conceived apart, and he is clearly rejecting that view in the first sentences in C:

> To be plain, I own my self able to abstract in one sense, as when I consider some particular parts or qualities separated from others, with which though they are united in some object, yet, it is possible that they may really exist without them. But I deny that I can abstract one from another, or conceive separately, those qualities which it is impossible should exist so separated. . . .

But, in the second sentence, it seems that Berkeley is not just saying that any idea formed in the way or ways described in Section 7 is impossible: he also seems, roughly speaking, to be specifying the bounds of conceivability in terms of possibility. Somewhat less roughly, he seems to be asserting that, if it is possible for a quality $Q1$ to exist apart from a quality $Q2$, then it is possible for $Q1$ to be conceived apart from $Q2$, and, if it is impossible for a quality $Q1$ to exist apart from $Q2$, then $Q1$ cannot be conceived apart from $Q2$. This conclusion does not seem to be clearly implied in B, and it is difficult to see how, if indeed it is intended to be a conclusion, Berkeley can have thought that it could be established by reasons stated in A and B.

It is difficult to see how he could have thought this since it seems to have been his view that the only way in which we can come to know that it is impossible for $Q1$ to exist apart from $Q2$ is by finding that $Q1$ cannot be conceived apart from $Q2$.[7] From this view, it follows that we cannot know that $Q1$ and $Q2$ cannot exist apart without knowing that $Q1$ and $Q2$ cannot be conceived apart. But then no sense can be made of the supposition that a person can come to know that what is impossible is inconceivable. Yet it is precisely that which someone would have to come to know if we suppose that this conclusion is supported by the reasons given in A and B. And it is perhaps the problem that arises when we take Berkeley to be stating a conclusion here that has encouraged some commentators to believe that that is not what he is doing.[8]

When I consider objections, I will argue against the proposed alternative interpretation of this passage. But I want to offer an explanation of why Berkeley might not have been troubled by the problem that I have just raised. As Berkeley describes his opponents' view in Section 7, it is part of that view that it is impossible for certain qualities to exist apart. The view that is ascribed to them is that, though a certain quality $Q1$ cannot possibly exist apart from $Q2$, $Q1$ can nonetheless be conceived apart from $Q2$. Moreover, in the description of this view, it is implied that there is complete agreement as to which qualities can and which cannot exist apart.

> *It is agreed on all hands* [my emphasis], that the qualities or modes of things do never really exist each of them apart by it self, and separated from all others, but are mixed, as it were, and blended together, several in the same object. But we are told, the mind being able to consider each quality singly,

or abstracted from those other qualities with which it is united, does by that means frame to it self abstract ideas. For example, there is perceived by sight an object extended, coloured, and moved: this mixed or compound idea the mind resolving into its simple, constituent parts, and viewing each by it self, exclusive of the rest, does frame the abstract ideas of extension, colour, and motion. *Not that it is possible for colour or motion to exist without extension* [my emphasis]: but only that the mind can frame to it self by *abstraction* the idea of colour exclusive of extension, and of motion exclusive of both colour and extension.

Berkeley professes to be in agreement with his adversaries as to which qualities can and cannot exist apart, and the question is not raised here, or indeed anywhere else in the Introduction, as to how this is to be determined. What Berkeley thinks he shows in Section 10 is that the qualities that admittedly or on all accounts cannot exist apart cannot, as his adversaries maintain, be conceived apart. If the question had been raised as to how we ascertain that a quality Q1 cannot exist apart from another quality Q2, I think Berkeley would have had trouble answering that question and justifying his procedure in Section 10.[9] But that question was not raised, and Berkeley seems to have experienced no qualms about the possibility of a discovery that what is impossible is inconceivable.

There is a second problem to be raised about the last sentences of Section 10. Berkeley tells us in D that others should be able to find in their own cases what he has found in his, and he tells us he has "grounds to think most men will acknowledge themselves to be" in the same situation as he. That situation is presumably one of not being able to conceive the abstract ideas described by the learned. But what exactly are the "grounds" that he has in mind? If indeed he thinks he has shown in Section 10 that abstract ideas are impossible, it seems that he would not need any other *grounds* for supposing that others cannot conceive these ideas. Berkeley's statement here poses a problem for my interpretation, for it can be argued that, since he thinks he has grounds for thinking that others lack the power he finds lacking in his own case, he does not, or at any rate does not clearly, think that the argument in Section 10 proves the *impossibility* of abstract ideas. I will tackle this problem when I try to answer objections, pointing out there what I take Berkeley to have in mind by "grounds" and why I think his saying that he has these grounds is not incompatible with my interpretation of Section 10.

One last point about Section 10 is worth noting. Commentators have called attention to irony in this passage,[10] but it is not altogether clear what they take the irony to consist in. Section 10 begins and ends with ironical statements; and, to complete my interpretation, I will say what, on my view, the irony is and also what it is not. In the last sentence, "We may therefore reasonably conclude that, if such there be, they are confined only to the learned," the irony involves the false supposition that it is *possible* for the learned to possess abstract notions. In the opening clause, "Whether others have this wonderful faculty of *abstracting their ideas*, they best can tell . . . ," the irony here rests on the false supposition that others really *are* best able to tell whether they have this faculty, for it is Berkeley's view that "the learned" are not best able to tell. Though it should have been evident to them that they do not possess this faculty, they nonetheless persist in thinking that they do possess it. It is important to distinguish the irony here from a quite different implication in Section 13, where he says, "All I desire is, that the reader would fully and certainly inform himself whether he has such an idea [the abstract idea of a triangle] or no. . . ." The falsehood here is that there is some *need* for the reader to "fully and certainly inform himself" since, as that supposed idea is described, it is manifest from the description that it is an "inconsistent idea,"[11] and this apparent inconsistency obviates the need to attempt a thought experiment to show that the supposed idea is impossible. If I am right, that suggestion is not made in Section 10. On the contrary, an attempt to conceive the ideas described by his adversaries is at the very heart of Berkeley's reasoning in Section 10.

3

Turning to objections, I shall begin with an objection that is related to this last point about the irony in Section 13. It has not gone unnoticed that, when Berkeley quotes Locke's description of the abstract idea of a triangle in Section 13, the idea described by Locke and the process by which it is supposed to be attained differ markedly from the abstract ideas and the procedure or procedures by which they are reached described in Sections 7, 8, and 9.[12] In Sections 7, 8, and 9, the process of abstraction is represented to be one of separation and elimination, and the products are supposed to be truncated or mutilated ideas from which something has been removed. When Berkeley makes the transition from ideas described in Sections 7 and 8 to the ideas described in Section 9, he implies that it is one and the same process that is supposed to yield ideas of all three types: "And as the mind frames to it self abstract ideas of qualities or modes, so does it, *by the same precision or mental separation*, attain abstract ideas of the more compounded beings [e.g., the idea of man], which include several coexistent qualities" (my emphasis). The procedure described by Locke in the passage quoted from the *Essay*, IV, vii, 9, seems to differ importantly in that it involves "putting together" as well as leaving out. In Locke's words, the abstract idea of a triangle is "an *Idea* wherein some parts of several different and inconsistent *Ideas* are *put together*" (my emphasis of "put together"),[13] and, when Berkeley ridicules the view in Section 14, he observes that "numberless inconsistences" are supposed to be "*tacked together*" (my emphasis).

In an important paper, E. J. Craig claims that the "Full Representation View" of abstract ideas discussed in Sections 13 and 14 differs from the views described earlier in Sections 7, 8, and 9 and that Berkeley's argument against the Full Representation View is not the same as his arguments against the views described earlier. He implies in this paper that the listing of ideas in Sections 7, 8, and 9 is not intended to be exhaustive and also that there is no one argument that Berkeley wields to show the impossibility of abstract ideas in general, i.e., the impossibility of abstract ideas of all the various types distinguished.[14] Although I agree with the claims that Craig makes about the Full Representation View," my interpretation of Section 10 is incompatible with what he implies. For, on my interpretation, the classification of various types of ideas in Sections 7, 8, and 9 is intended to be exhaustive, and one argument — the Argument from Inconceivability — is supposed to tell against all the various kinds or types of abstract ideas that Berkeley distinguishes.

Is the view described in Section 13 intended to be a new and different view? The section begins: "To give the reader a yet clearer view of the nature of abstract ideas . . . ." When Berkeley begins in this way, it seems to me that he clearly implies that he is going to elaborate on and clarify the view or views described earlier. But Craig claims that Berkeley is mistaken here.[15] I want to suggest that he is not. Although the idea of a triangle described in Section 13 has one feature distinguishing it from the ideas described in Sections 7, 8, and 9, it also has one feature in common. It is an idea that is "*neither oblique, nor rectangle, equilateral, equicrural, nor scalenon* . . ."; that is, it is an idea like the ideas in Sections 7, 8, and 9 from which particularities or specificities are supposed to have been removed. Though it is also said to be "all . . . of these at once," it shares one feature with the ideas described earlier of being "none of these at once," and it is by virtue of this feature that the idea can be fitted into the classification in Sections 7, 8, and 9. Presumably, it could be put with the ideas listed in Section 8 (or possibly Section 9). Though Craig is certainly right in pointing out that it differs with respect to "putting together," it is misleading to suggest that it cannot be included within the compass of the view or views stated earlier. It would perhaps be more exact to say that the view in Section 13 is indeed a view described earlier but with an additional feature.

It is apparent in Craig's article why he is insistent that the view in Section 13 is new and different. He thinks that Berkeley employs an argument here that could not be used against the views described earlier. It could not be used because the additional feature of "putting together" is required to show that the idea of a triangle is an idea of something that is supposed to be both Q and not-Q and can arguably be said to "infringe the Law of Non-Contradiction." Craig is certainly right in saying that an argument along these lines could not be used against ideas that are supposed to be formed exclusively by "taking away." But it does not follow that an argument used against these ideas could not also be used against the supposed idea of a triangle in Section 13. It seems clear that Berkeley thinks the Argument from Inconceivability can be so used. Indeed, the last sentence of Section 13, as I noted earlier, echoes that argument in Section 10.

> What more easy than for any one to look a little into his own thoughts, and there try whether he has, *or can attain to have*, an idea that shall correspond with the description that is here given of the general idea of a triangle, which is, *neither oblique, nor rectangle, equilateral, equicrural, nor scalenon, but all and none of these at once*? [my emphasis of "or can attain to have"].

As I also noted earlier, however, there is irony in this passage. Berkeley suggests that, though the supposed idea could be shown to be impossible by virtue of its inconceivability, it is not necessary to proceed in this way. Here, from a manifest inconsistency or contradiction in the description of the idea, we can conclude that it is impossible. But the Argument from Inconceivability, though it is not needed, is nonetheless available. That Berkeley thinks it can be applied to the idea described in Section 13 is, in my opinion, evident from the last clause in B, which completes the statement of the argument: "and the like may be said of all other abstract general ideas whatsoever."

4

In his *Berkeley*, George Pitcher contends that the main line of argument against the possibility of abstract ideas is an argument that proceeds from the impossibility of an object or state of affairs to the impossibility of an idea of such an object or state of affairs.[16] The sort of argument that he attributes to Berkeley—a way of arguing that I will call the Argument from Impossibility—is worded as follows:

(a) There can be no idea of x if it is conceptually (or logically) impossible that x should exist.

(b) It is logically impossible that (bare) motion should exist—i.e., that there should be a motion that is "neither swift nor slow, curvilinear nor rectilinear," . . . that is not the motion of any moving thing at all, and so on.

(c) The abstract idea of motion is the idea of (bare) motion.

(d) So, the abstract idea of motion is the idea of something that cannot—conceptually (or logically)—exist.

Conclusion: Therefore, there can be no abstract idea of motion.[17]

Pitcher says that this argument is "implicit" in the Introduction,[18] but he also cites two sentences in Section 10. "But I deny that I can abstract one from another, or conceive separately, those qualities which it is impossible should exist so separated . . ." is taken to be a statement of premise a; and, in the second premise (b), he cites, "And it is equally impossible for me to form the abstract idea of motion distinct from the body moving, and which is neither swift nor slow, curvilinear nor rectilinear. . . ."[19] In addition, he calls our attention to a passage in the draft of the Introduction in which an argument that is indeed very like his Argument from Impossibility is stated.

It is, I think, a receiv'd axiom that an impossibility cannot be conceiv'd. For what created intelligence will pretend to conceive, that which God cannot cause to be? Now it is on all hands agreed, that nothing abstract or general can be made really to exist, whence it should seem to follow, that it cannot have so much as an ideal existence in the understanding.[20]

That this passage was scratched out in the draft of the Introduction is, I believe, a significant fact of which Pitcher does not inform us.[21]

If Pitcher is right, my interpretation of Section 10 and of the Introduction as a whole is clearly wrong. I will, therefore, try to impugn his evidence. From the draft of the Introduction, we know that at one time Berkeley did indeed formulate an argument like Pitcher's Argument from Impossibility, but it is also evident that Berkeley had a very good reason for jettisoning that argument. If he argued in the Introduction that a primary quality like motion cannot be conceived apart because it cannot exist apart, he could not consistently argue in Section 10 of the body of the *Principles* that a primary quality like motion cannot exist apart, i.e., apart from sensible qualities, because it cannot be conceived apart. The circularity of that procedure would have jumped to the reader's eye, and I conjecture that it was for this reason that there is no counterpart of that early argument in the Introduction.[22]

When we examine the two sentences cited from Section 10, we find that neither supports Pitcher's attribution of the Argument from Impossibility. In the sentence from B, "And it is equally impossible for me to form the abstract idea of motion distinct from the body moving, and which is neither swift nor slow, curvilinear nor rectilinear . . . ," the claim that Berkeley makes is that an *idea* of motion distinct from the body moved is inconceivable and by implication impossible and not, as on Pitcher's reading, that *motion* distinct from the body moved is inconceivable and by implication impossible. When Berkeley writes in C, "But I deny that I can abstract one from another, or conceive separately, those qualities which it is impossible should exist so separated . . . ," there is a good reason for denying that he is giving a reason, or stating an argument, directed against the patrons of abstract ideas. If that were what he was attempting to do, he would be flagrantly guilty of *ignoratio elenchi*. The view of the opposition as described in Section 7 is that, although motion by itself is impossible, it can nonetheless be conceived. On the assumption that an argument against a view cannot contain a premise in which that view is simply rejected, it will clearly not do to begin an argument against the view set forth in Section 7 by saying that, since motion by itself is impossible, it cannot be conceived. Furthermore, it is possible, as I mentioned at the outset, and there is some reason to believe that the sentences in C were added by Berkeley and were not left out by the printer.[23] If Berkeley did add these sentences, Pitcher's interpretation seems most implausible, for we would have to suppose that Berkeley had at first omitted what Pitcher takes to be a crucial step in his main argument against the possibility of abstract ideas.

5

A final objection to my interpretation of Section 10 is that Berkeley would have realized that the Argument from Inconceivability would be ineffectual against the defenders of abstract ideas and hence would not have relied on it to prove that abstract ideas are impossible. It seems that the Argument from Inconceivability would clearly be ineffectual because the defenders of abstract ideas could and would simply reject the first step in the argument. They would deny that, when they attempt to follow the procedure that is supposed to lead to an abstract idea, they fail. Perhaps they would argue that, though they cannot *imagine* something satisfying the description of an abstract idea, they can nonetheless conceive the ideas described; and they might question Berkeley's non-Cartesian assumption that all ideas are images. Pitcher does not distinguish the Argument from Inconceivability from the Argument from Unobservability, but it seems that he would be prepared to raise an objection of this sort against any supposed "quasi-empirical" line of reasoning as the mainstay of Berkeley's attack.

> The great trouble with this kind of quasi-empirical support, however, is that it is extremely weak. One can take a first-hand survey of one's own mind, and then ask a few friends what sorts of ideas they find in theirs—but even if we obtained in this way a completely Berkeleyan result, this would provide no answer at all to the abstract idea theorist when he confronts us with the remark "Ah, but you see I *do* find abstract ideas in my mind." So more substantial backing is needed.[24]

Not only could Berkeley's adversaries react in this way, it seems that Berkeley himself was well aware of this line of defense.[25] But, if the Argument from Inconceivability is vulnerable in this way and Berkeley was aware of the danger, it seems unlikely that he would have made it the mainstay of his attack.

The objection has some weight if we suppose that Berkeley's only ploy against the patrons of abstract ideas is the Argument from Inconceivability. If I am right, he does think it proves that abstract ideas are impossible, but he also realizes that it would be ineffectual by itself against opponents who think there *must* be abstract ideas and who deceive themselves into thinking that they can form and have formed them. Berkeley's strategy in the Introduction is, in fact, in three stages. The Argument from Inconceivability is the first. He then asks why, when it can be so easily shown that abstract ideas are impossible, the patrons of these ideas persist in this view; and his answer is in part that they think there *must* be these ideas if there is to be "enlargement of knowledge" and "communication." Thus, in a second stage, he argues in Sections 14 through 17 that abstract ideas are not necessary for either of these purposes. In the third stage, he exposes (Sections 18 ff.) "the source of this prevailing notion." In the second and third stages, he in effect attempts to show how the learned have come to deceive themselves about having abstract ideas when it should have been plain as a pikestaff that abstract ideas are impossible. When Berkeley speaks of "grounds" in Section 10 for supposing that others will find in their case what he finds in his own, the grounds that I believe he has in mind are the considerations that he gives in the second and third stages against the supposition that there *must* be abstract ideas. What he does is to attempt to remove misunderstandings that have blinded his adversaries and that would keep them from accepting the Argument from Inconceivability.

Notes

1. *A Treatise Concerning the Principles of Human Knowledge* is in Volume II of the standard edition: *The Works of George Berkeley Bishop of Cloyne*, ed. by A. A. Luce and T. E. Jessop (Edinburgh: Thomas Nelson, 1948-1957). References to the Introduction and to the body (Part I) of the *Principles* will be by Berkeley's section numbers. Berkeley speaks of the "patrons" of abstract ideas in Section 21 of the Introduction. I have used similar expressions—"adversaries," "opponents," etc.—though a comparison with *An Essay Concerning Human*

Understanding, especially Book III (ed. by Peter H. Nidditch [Oxford: Clarendon Press, 1975]), makes it apparent that Berkeley has John Locke in mind when he describes his adversaries' position. Earlier versions of this paper were read at Edinburgh, York, University College, London, and Hull and at a metting at the Institute for Advanced Study in Princeton in June 1982. I am grateful to many people for comments and criticism but particularly to Ruth Mattern, Robert Sleigh, and Margaret Wilson. I wish I had been able to show the paper to Morris Weitz, whose generosity and encouragement in the past have been greatly appreciated.

2. C ends, "Which two last are the proper acceptations of *abstraction*," and this might lead us to suppose that, as Berkeley describes his opponents' position, there are two sorts of abstraction. But, when in Section 9 he turns from ideas of "qualities or modes" to "ideas of the more compounded beings," he writes, "And as the mind frames to it self abstract ideas of qualities or modes, so does it, by the same precision or mental separation, attain abstract ideas of the more compounded beings, which include several coexistent qualities." Because of this unclarity, I use "faculty or faculties."

3. This is clearly implied in Part One of the *Principles*, Sections 5, 6, 10, 22, and 23.

4. It can be argued that 3 should read: (3') 'The supposed idea of man is inconceivable by me.' The principle to be supplied would then have to be: (4') 'What is inconceivable by me is impossible.' That is a principle to which, I believe, Berkeley is also committed.

5. George Pitcher thinks that he does. In his *Berkeley*, p. 73 (London: Routledge and Kegan Paul, 1977), Pitcher writes, "It comes as no surprise to find Berkeley sometimes saying, in effect, 'If you look into your mind, you will find images there, but no abstract ideas.'" To illustrate this point, however, he quotes a passage from the first of the *Three Dialogues between Hylas and Philonous*, in which it seems to me that Berkeley presents the Argument from Inconceivability and not the Argument from Unobservability:

> Philonous. But for your farther satisfaction, try if you can frame the idea of any figure, abstracted from all particularities of size, or even from other sensible qualities.

> Hylas. Let me think a little—I do not find that I can (Vol. II, p. 194, of the Luce-Jessop edition).

6. See Pitcher, *Berkeley*; and also E. J. Craig, "Berkeley's Attack on Abstract Ideas," *The Philosophical Review*, Vol. LXXVII, No. 4 (October, 1968). pp. 425-37. Craig observes (p. 431):

> It should also be noted that his objections are put in empirical psychological terms, sometimes tinged with irony, as in: "Whether others have this wonderful faculty of *abstracting their ideas*, they best can tell: for my self I find indeed I have a faculty of imagining, or representing to my self . . ." [Section 10; original italics]. But they are always capable of translation into the logical mode as points about the a priori impossibility of there being images of certain kinds, and it will be more profitable for us to take them in this way.

One wonders whether accuracy may not have been sacrificed for "profitability."

7. See Berkeley's argument against the possibility of separating primary qualities from all sensible qualities in Section 10 of the body of the *Principles*. Although he thinks his arguments from relativity (Sections 11-15) tell against such a separation, the impossibility of the separation is established on the ground of inconceivability.

8. Both Pitcher (*op.cit.*, p. 68) and Craig (*op. cit.*, p. 431) take Berkeley to be arguing against his adversaries in this passage and not, as I have suggested, stating a conclusion.

9. I have discussed the problem in "Is Berkeley's a Cartesian Mind?" *Berkeley: Critical and Interpretive Essays*, ed. by Colin M. Turbayne (Minneapolis: University of Minnesota Press, 1982), pp. 273-82.

10. Cf. Pitcher, *op. cit.*, p. 77, and Craig, *op. cit.*, p. 431.

11. Berkeley emphasizes *"inconsistent"* in *"inconsistent ideas"* in the quotation from Locke in Section 13; in Section 14, he speaks of tacking together "numberless inconsistences"; and, in Section 16, we find "an abstract general inconsistent idea of a triangle." In the *Philosophical Commentaries*, No. 687 (Volume 1 of the Luce-Jessop edition, p. 84), Berkeley reminds

himself: "Mem: to bring the killing blow at the last v.g. in the Matter of Abstraction to bring Lockes general triangle at the last." This, on my interpretation, would be a killing blow since it could be used against an opponent who insists that he *can* follow the procedure or procedures for forming abstract ideas described in Sections 7, 8, and 9. Even he would have to admit that this idea qua inconsistent is inconceivable and impossible.

12. Notably by Craig, *op. cit.*, pp. 425-37.

13. In the Nidditch edition, p. 596. Berkeley emphasizes the word 'inconsistent' when he quotes this sentence in Section 13.

14. Craig, *op. cit.*, locates the "Single Property View" in Section 7 and the "Common Property View" in Section 9. It is not clear to me what he would do with the "determinable" ideas in Section 8, e.g., "a most abstract idea of extension," "an idea of colour in abstract," and "the abstract idea of motion."

15. Craig, *op. cit.*, p. 429.

16. Pitcher, *op. cit.*, pp. 62-90.

17. Pitcher, *op. cit.*, pp. 67-68.

18. Pitcher, *op. cit.*, p. 67.

19. Pitcher, *op cit.*, pp. 68 and 67. Pitcher also cites Section 5 of Part I of the *Principles*. But, in Section 5, Berkeley is not arguing against the doctrine of abstraction but explaining how it has worked to obscure the truth of the view that the *esse* of sensible things is their *percipi*.

20. "First Draft of the Introduction to the Principles," in Volume II of the standard edition, p. 125.

21. Prof. T. E. Jessop does not indicate this change in the manuscript in the standard edition. It is pointed out in the older edition of A. C. Fraser, *The Works of George Berkeley, D.D.*, Vol. I, pp. 413-14 (Oxford: Clarendon Press, 1871). Professor Jessop's statement in the Editor's Introduction, p. 117, that "compared with the printed Introduction, the draft neither adds nor omits anything of substance" can hardly be justified. About the argument that was scratched in the draft of the Introduction, two additional points are noteworthy. First, it was stated tentatively, ". . . it should seem to follow. . . ." Second, the statement of the argument is preceded by a sentence in which he implies that he has already given his primary reason for rejecting abstract ideas: "For besides the incomprehensibleness of abstract ideas to my understanding (which may pass for an argument, since those gentlemen do not pretend to any new facultys distinct from those of ordinary men), there are not wanting other proofs against them" (*loc. cit.*).

22. Apparently, Berkeley could not resist using his early Argument from Impossibility in *Alciphron* VII (though the passage was deleted in the third edition):

Euphranor. Pray, Alciphron, which are those things you would call absolutely impossible?

Alciphron. Such as include a contradiction.

Euphranor. Can you frame an idea of what includes a contradiction?

Alciphron. I cannot.

Euphranor. Consequently, whatever is absolutely impossible you cannot form an idea of.

Alciphron. This I grant.

Euphranor. But can a colour or triangle, such as you describe their abstract general ideas, really exist?

Alciphron. It is absolutely impossible such things should exist in Nature.

Euphranor. Should it not follow, then, that they cannot exist in your mind, or, in other words, that you cannot conceive or frame an idea of them? (Volume III, pp. 333-34, of the Luce-Jessop edition).

23. There is no counterpart of these sentences in the fuller draft of the Introduction, and Section 10 reads easily and smoothly without them.

24. Pitcher, *op. cit.*, p. 73.

25. The passage from *Alciphron*, VII, continues: "Alciphron. You seem, Euphranor, not to *Three Dialogues between Hylas and Philonous* (pp. 193-94 of the standard edition). Hylas asks, ject of pure intellect, which may conceive them although they cannot perhaps be imagined." It is against this position that Euphranor wields the Argument from Impossibility: "I do not perceive that I can by any faculty, whether of intellect or imagination, conceive or frame an idea of that which is impossible and includes a contradiction." Alciphron's suggestion is also made in *Three Dialogues between Hylas and Philonous* (pp. 193-94 of the standard edition). Hylas asks, "But what say you to *pure intellect*? May not abstracted ideas be framed by that faculty?" It is, I believe, significant that in the *Dialogues* Berkeley does not allow Philonous to use the Argument from Impossibility.

Hume and Contemporary
Ethical Naturalism

S. D. GUTTENPLAN

I

A good way to understand what many ethical naturalists are up to is to consider what goes on in cases of reductive explanation in science. As an example —and without paying too close attention to historical details—take the case of the explanation of genetic facts by their reduction to facts of molecular biology. Mendel and others made claims and discoveries about heredity and could even be said to have offered theoretical explanations of these using the notion of the *gene*. Statements about genes, in a rudimentary way, explained many features of the transmission of characteristics between generations of organisms. Nonetheless, these facts and their genetic explanations remained somewhat mysterious inasmuch as they were not yet anchored in facts about the physical makeup of organisms. The eventual identification of genes with stretches of DNA molecules provided us with a largely satisfactory answer to the mystery. All of this is, of course, quite familiar, and, even though it is no more than a philosopher's textbook example, it will serve my purposes in this paper.

Two features of this sort of reductive explanation that I want to stress are as follows: (i) the reduction is, in general, conservative of the original body of theory and fact, and (ii) such reduction does not commit us to any semantical connection between elements of the two bodies of knowledge. The molecular account of genetic claims makes it possible for us to understand why these claims are true by showing their dependence on what are for us the less mysterious facts of cellular chemistry. In doing so, the earlier genetic theory is, in a way, conserved. Additionally, as this example makes obvious, reductive explanation neither requires nor even has to allow that proponents of the one set of beliefs are in any sense 'really' speaking of items in the other set. Genes are stretches of DNA molecules, but 'gene' does not mean 'stretch of a DNA molecule'. (That it could come to mean this is not to the point here.)

309

It hardly needs saying that facts about morals or, more generally, values are considerably more complex and mysterious than facts about heredity. That human beings value certain actions, characters, and lives; that their so valuing is intricately connected with their behavior; and that, in their discourse about such valuation, they adopt the apparently theoretical stances they do,[1] these phenomena which together make up what might be called the institution of value, are as mysterious as any feature of the natural or social world. Yet, for all its complexity, it has seemed to many that we can make at least a start toward understanding this institution by seeing it as rooted in features of human life, no less complex but somewhat less mysterious. Such writers are ethical naturalists, and I think that the program of providing a naturalist account of morality shares, with reductive explanation, among others, the two features mentioned above. It requires that we explain why the institution is as it is (allowing, of course, for the fact that there can be controversy about the description of the institution), and it does so in a way that need not commit us to seeing the language of value as a disguised way of talking about other matters. Ethical naturalism, in short, should aim to be conservative of as much of the institution of value from which it starts, and it should be semantically neutral.

The program of naturalism is hardly new, but in recent years, and after a period in which it was held in disrepute for what I regard as bad reasons, it has acquired new champions. No contemporary naturalist writer has provided anything like a detailed reduction of all the features of morality, but the general outline of the program is clear enough. Warnock, for example, writes:

> It seems reasonable, and in the present context highly relevant, to say, without going quite so far as Hobbes did, that the human predicament is inherently such that things are liable to go badly. This seems to be inherently so, but not completely hopelessly so; that is, there are circumstances, not in the least likely to be changed significantly or to be changed by our own efforts, which cannot but tend to make things go badly, but also something at least can be done, many different things in fact, to make them go at least somewhat better than they would do, if no such things were done at all. . . .
>
> . . . The general suggestion that (guardedly) I wish to put up for consideration is this: that the 'general object' of morality, appreciation of which may enable us to understand the basis of moral evaluation, is to contribute to the betterment — or non-deterioration — of the human predicament.[2]

Other writers, without Warnock's excessive caution, have made a similar claim, and contemporary moral writing is dotted with expressions such as 'human welfare', 'human good and harm', and 'human flourishing' — these playing the role of Warnock's 'non-deterioration' of the human condition. In all these cases, the program is the same, namely, to explain moral institutions by appeal to some notion of human flourishing that these institutions can be understood to serve; and, in the words of one writer, the goal of the program is to 'de-fictionalise' morality.[3]

My aim in this paper is to show that Hume saw, even if not in a clear way, a profound difficulty in this whole project — a difficulty that shows up most prominently in his distinction between the natural and artifical virtues. What I hope is both that an appreciation of this difficulty can be used for interpretative purposes in regard to Hume *and* that a close discussion of Hume can improve our understanding of ethical naturalism. Quite clearly, these dual aims will force me to be somewhat freer in my view of Hume than his text would everywhere support; as is usual in these cases, I appeal to the desire to have a view of Hume closer in spirit to what he thought than to the letter of what he wrote.

II

I will begin by describing briefly, and without reference to Hume, the difficulty that I see as inherent in the sort of ethical naturalism adumbrated above. That given the human condition things are liable to go badly seems true enough. Additionally, it does not seem at all implausible that the institution of morality, and value generally, go some way to improving life. In terms Warnock's views invite, it does not seem unreasonable to say that things go better with morals or, perhaps with more gravity, that morality is essentially connected to, and given point by, human good and harm.

What makes such views reasonable, and have always done so, are the pictures that philosophers paint of life without the guidance of morality. Perhaps not all of nasty, poor, brutish, and short, but it would certainly be uncomfortable. Against this background, the more obvious moral guidance that encourages cooperation and puts some check on unbridled pursuit of self-interest seems unquestionably a contribution to human flourishing. Can there be any doubt that rules, appropriately inculcated, that encourage the cultivation of virtuous dispositions in my fellow human beings make my life and theirs better than they would otherwise have been? Still, without doubting this, one can still have the following doubt about this account of morality; a doubt that centers on the naturalist's central idea of the betterment of human life.

Integral to the institution of values of which the moral rules that enjoin unlicensed self-assertion are part is the idea that some lives are better than others. That is, part of what we are expected to recognize when we have a developed moral view of the world is that pursuing certain goals, and pursing them in some ways rather than others, is better than not having them or than pursuing them in other ways. I do not mean here, it should be said, that these goals and the means of achieving them are bound up with the moral outlook that, as agreed above, is needed to make human life more tolerable than it would otherwise be. One can perfectly well imagine that, within the framework provided by the morality of social interaction, there still remain questions—moral and evaluative—about how to live one's life and how to deal with others. The worry is that the ethical naturalist is not in a position to explain the origin of this sort of evaluation. The ethical naturalist seeks to provide us, in one way or another, with an *explanation* of value in terms of human flourishing. I cannot see how one could reasonably spell out a notion of human flourishing that did not presuppose value in the first place. I can certainly see, in the cruder sort of case that is given prominence in most discussions, that life is better for the organisms we are if we do not go in for too much killing and injustice. However, I could not begin to fill out the notion of human flourishing without using in its description the very values this notion is appealed to in order to explain.

Mrs. Foot, in defense of her more recent account, writes of the man who, in a particular case, has no direct egocentric reason to act honestly: "He wants to live openly and in good faith with his neighbours; it is not all the same to him to lie and conceal."[4] One cannot but agree to this, but, on reflection, this sentiment is the beginning of my puzzle. It just is the case that living and acting morally in any sufficiently rich sense is itself part of any state that deserves to be called "human flourishing." But it is far from clear that this is because the moral life contributes to a state we could, independently of moral values, distinguish as one of human flourishing. Yet, in the absence of such independent specification, it is hard to see how the notion of human flourishing could help us to explain morality, could help us to "de-fictionalise" it.

No doubt there are things a naturalist could say in reply to this. I do not pretend what I have said by itself constitutes an *argument* against naturalism; it is a *worry*, though one I think insufficiently recognized by writers in the contemporary naturalist tradition. In what follows I should like to show that the recognition of some such worry is implicit in Hume's quite complex attempt to explain moral phenomena in the *Treatise*.

III

My primary interest in Hume's ethical views will center around his distinction between the natural and artificial virtues. Hume obviously thought this distinction was important; indeed, the prominence he gives to it prompts one to think that he saw it as a distinctive part of his theory of morals. After all, he gave the distinction this prominence even though he seems to have been concerned that his making of it would lead some readers to think he was undermining morality; the subversion of morality, however, was the last thing Hume intended. Worried by this thought, he ends Book III of the *Treatise* with the following analogical defense of his views—a defense that follows by two paragraphs his forceful reassertion of the natural/artificial distinction.

> The anatomist ought never to emulate the painter: nor in his accurate dissections and portraitures of the human body, pretend to give his figures any graceful and engaging attitude or expression. There is even something hideous, or at least minute in the views of things, which he presents; and 'tis necessary the objects shou'd be set more at a distance, and be more covered up from sight, to make them to the eye and imagination. An anatomist, however, is admirably fitted to give advice to a painter.[5]

Additionally, Hume not only used the artificial/natural distinction throughout Book III of the *Treatise*, he provided an argument—albeit a sketchy one—that purports to show that such a distinction is necessary to his naturalist project. I will discuss this argument in due course, but let us begin with a quite specific example of what Hume would most certainly regard as an exercise of a natural virtue. (It is also, and not coincidentally, the sort of example Hutcheson uses at the center of his moral theory.)[6]

Suppose that, in appropriate circumstances, you witness a parent helping his or her child though this help costs him or her some sacrifice. Let us further suppose that you, not implausibly, regard the parent's act as virtuous. Two typically Humean questions about this are: (i) Why does the parent act this way, what is his or her 'motive' (Hume's word)? (ii) Why do you, as a witness, think of this act as virtuous? Constraining answers to the first of these questions, Hume offers the following argument.

It appears, therefore, that all virtuous actions derive their merit only from virtuous motives, and are consider'd merely as signs of these motives. From this principle I conclude, that the first virtuous motive, which bestows merit on any action, can never be a regard to the virtue of that action, but must be some other natural motive or principle. To suppose, that the mere regard to the virtue of the action, may be the first motive, which produc'd the action, and rendered it virtuous, is to reason in a circle. Before we can have such a regard, the action must be really virtuous; and this virtue must be deriv'd from some virtuous motive: And consequently the virtuous motive must be differet from the regard to the virtue of the action.[7]

Antecedent to consideration of (i) above against the background of this argument, two interpretative comments are in order. First, I do not think that Hume should be understood here as appealing to the unacceptable (or, at least, highly contentious) claim that our actions depend for their merit only on their motives. In view of what Hume actually wrote, this might seem highly paradoxical, but the paradox is no more than word deep. Contemporary philosophical wisdom tends to think of an action as a piece of behavior characterized in intention-loaded terms. This is not very precise, but it will do for what follows. Hume, being a complete stranger to our more sophisticated usage, thinks of an action as something characterizable in intention-free language. In a paragraph before the above, and in support of it, he refers to an action as an 'external performance' that is, as such, neither virtuous nor vicious. What he is aiming at in using the word 'external' can be illustrated most simply in a nonmoral context.

Suppose that it is judged foolish of me to have signaled a left turn while riding my bicycle in heavy traffic. That is, my *action* is judged foolish. Still, it would be very odd indeed to say that my left hand's horizontal extension, what I think Hume would call the "external performance," was foolish. In this context where Hume uses the word 'motive', we would be more comfortable with 'intention'. In other contexts, Hume's use of motive is closer to ours, though in these other instances he does not distinguish, as he should have, between the actual motivation of an act and the reason an agent has to perform it. Here, however, I do not think

that Hume would say that the foolishness of my action (in our sense) does not reside in it but in the motive from which it was performed. If I had what we might
call the 'motive' of signaling in order to frighten a car driver whose behavior I had
noted to be inconsiderately aggressive, then Hume would not say that this motive
was foolish and that the action of signaling was only the sign of the motive. What is
foolish is the intention that I carried out, i.e., signaling a left turn, and the external
performance here, the extension of my left arm, is in some sense a sign of that intention. This leaves us with problems about intentions that are not translated into
actions, but these need not detain us since for purposes of discussion what is at issue are actions, i.e., behavior, that occurs and is intentionally undertaken. In sum,
as I have explained it, the premise of Hume's argument could be read as: Virtue is
in the intentionally characterized actions we perform and not in their intention-free
descriptions.

The second point of clarification arises out of Hume's use of the phrase "the
first virtuous motive." This phrase makes it sound as though Hume's argument is
restricted to some hypothetical past in which the first virtuous item appeared. In
spite of this appearance, though, his object in using the phrase is more subtle. He
is, I think, making a conceptual point about the content of our 'motives' (intentions in acting). Precisely what that point is will emerge shortly, but that it is a conceptual and not an imaginary historical point seems to me obvious enough, especially in the light of the obsession of eighteenth-century theorists with asking conceptual
questions as if they were about the 'origins' of various things.

Given my remarks above, the question to which Hume's argument is applicable
is: With what intention does the parent act in his or her behavior toward the child?
The argument is intended to show that the content of this intention cannot, without
vicious circularity, be something like "to bring into existence some virtuous item."

To make this more plausible, let us consider an interesting paragraph in which
Hume qualifies but does not substantially alter the thrust of his argument. On p.
479, he asks, "But may not the sense of morality or duty produce an action without any other motive?" And his somewhat paradoxical answer is "It may: But this
is no objection to the present argument." His defense of this point is not altogether
clear, but I think that a reasonable view of what he is getting at is as follows. A
parent may undertake some behavior (read "external performance") with the intention of acting virtuously; in contemporary usage, it would be appropriate to say of
this behavior that "x did his or her parental duty." Equally, however, this behavior
can be given other intentional characterizations; that a stretch of behavior can be
given various intentional descriptions has become (rightly) almost a datum of contemporary philosophy of action. So, we can say of the parent that he or she gave
food to his or her son, that he or she helped his or her son, and, of course, that he
or she did his or her duty. Hume's point is that even in cases in which what we may
call the primary intention is "to do one's duty," this can only make sense if there is
some appropriate intentional designation of the behavior in respect of which the
behavior comes to be thought of as dutiful in the first place.

More concretely, his claim would be that even in cases of cold-hearted but adequate parental support, it only makes sense to see the specific behavior as dutiful because, for example, it is helpful to a child in need. There is no virtue, for Hume, in the mere transfer of food from the hand of the parent to the child. Any virtue must be based on the possible characterization of this phenomenon as "helping the child" and, in most cases, this is all there is to the parent's primary intention; we are so built that we undertake to help and care for our children. In the much rarer case in which natural parental affection is lacking, the primary intention may shift "outward" to the more general motive "doing one's duty," but this intention is parasitic on the availability of the intentional description "helping one's child." Hume puts it this way: "But tho', on some occasions, a person may perform an action merely out of regard to its moral obligation, yet still this supposes in human nature some distinct principles, which are capable of producing the action, and whose moral beauty renders the action meritorious."[8]

So interpreted, I think that Hume's argument here is perfectly reasonable and that we can use it in our background to answering the first of the two questions we began with: What, in the exercise of a natural virtue such as parental care, is the motive for acting? The answer Hume gives, in my terms, is that human beings are so constituted that their primary intentions in the performance of what we call (for reasons to be discussed) natural virtues such as caring for one's children are such things as "wanting to help," "easing the misery of," etc. These are other regarding 'motives' that Hume rightly thinks are simply a feature of human life, part of human psychological equipment. Also, and importantly, these motives are characterizable without reference to the natural duty that, in pursuing them, we undertake. And this last point is in no way undermined by the undoubted fact that some parents simply lack any such motivation even though they take care of their children out of a sense of duty or a "regard to the virtue of their action."

I turn now to consider the second question raised above: Why do you—the witness of an act of parental care—regard the act as virtuous? Given the previous discussion, Hume thinks that insofar as you would regard it as virtuous it would be because of the motive of the act; in my view, this means that you would regard as virtuous the act of "helping the child" when the intention in acting is included in the act's description. Moreover, as the well-known discussion in III,I,ii of the *Treatise* makes clear, Hume's full answer to the question of why we regard such intentions in acting as virtuous would be, roughly: We are so constituted that witnessing a parent helping a child gives us a particular sort of pleasure and the concept of virtue becomes annexed to the items that give us this sort of pleasure.

Much has been written about this view, and I do not wish to add to it nor to discuss the account of sympathy that Hume brings into it. However, it is important to see how this answer to our question relates to another one that Hume sometimes appears to accept. Someone might explain the virtue of parental care as follows: Acts of parental care contribute to human flourishing, and we are so constituted that we take pleasure of a particular sort in such contributions. This answer to the question is not far from things Hume does say, but it is a way of putting his position that must be treated with caution.

On one "reading," this answer commits us to a view Hume definitively rejected, viz., the matter of fact objectivity of virtue. This is so because someone might understand the above as involving the claim that human flourishing, or what contributes to it, is an empirically discoverable matter of fact. If this were so, then, insofar as parental care contributes to human flourishing, we would have made virtue a feature of the world contrary to Hume's well-known strictures about this. I think that Hume would have thought that there is nothing empirically accessible to an independent observer that, even in the parental case, would show this as contributing to human flourishing. Such an observer could witness the parent's act and even be aware that the intention was that of helping but still see nothing that would make it a matter of fact that the act, and others like it, contributed to human flourishing. The proverbial Martian observer could very well think such acts — on any but the smallest scale — were, in fact, detrimental to human beings. After all, and canvassing only one possibility, goods on this earth are relatively scarce; creating and supplying more mouths to feed might strike the Martian as highly dysfunctional behavior.

Thus, there seems to be a tension between Hume's allegiance to the role of human flourishing in the exploration of virtue and his undoubtedly subjectivist view of such matters. The way out, as should by now be obvious, is to see Hume as committed to a subjective view of what constitutes (and contributes to) human flourishing. Not only do we call individual actions virtuous because of their effect on us, constituted as we are, we also project onto certain states of affairs the idea that they are or are not part of the flourishing of our species. In themselves these states do not have such features; a creature not endowed with our conative nature would not be able to discover, from the states of affairs themselves, which did and which did not contribute to human flourishing. So understood there is on this point no tension in Hume's views, and, faithful to Hume's subjectivism, we can accept either of these explanations of why the parent's act is virtuous: (i) we are so constituted that the act gives us a particular sort of pleasure; (ii) such acts contribute to a state we project onto the world — human flourishing — and we are so constituted that we take a particular pleasure in such contributions.

Before proceeding to discuss the artificial virtues, I must make one observation about Hume's subjectivism, which will have an important bearing on what follows. Hume's subjectivism is not itself central to anything I want to say in this paper, though, as I will show, it does connect with his distinction between natural and artificial virtues. There can be no doubt that Hume is an ethical naturalist, though, unlike the naturalist discussed in section II, his is a more complicated form of naturalism. Hume's subjectivism does not allow him to think of virtuous intentions as possessed of some property that constitutes their virtue. Nor does his subjectivism allow him to think of the factors in human flourishing as a matter of discovery in principle available to any observer. The complete account of human flourishing must for him take account both of the way things are and of the particular conative equipment of human beings. Given our passions, we do just see certain states of affairs as in our interest as human beings and others as not. In the next section, I will discuss how this subjectivism forced Hume to give an account of the relationship between human flourishing and virtue that, if not wholly successful, can nonetheless be seen as an attempt to deal with the difficulty discussed earlier. Even so, the acceptability of the subjectivist element in Hume's naturalism is not what will be at issue.

IV

Hume's discussion of artificial virtues begins, as mine of the natural virtues did, with a specific example: "I suppose a person to have lent me a sum of money, on condition that it be restor'd in a few days; and also suppose that after the expiration of the term agreed on, he demands the sum: I ask, *What reason or motive have I to restore the money?*"[9] To this question Hume first replies, as he supposes we all would, that our regard to justice would provide the needed reason, but he immediately sees something wrong with this reply: ". . . this answer, no doubt, is just and satisfactory to a man in his civilised state, and when train'd up according to a certain discipline and education. But in his rude and more *natural* condition, if you are pleased to call such a condition natural, the answer would be rejected as perfectly unintelligible and sophistical."[10] Hume then goes on to apply the previously discussed argument about the need for independent motivation to this case. The motive for restoring the money must be something other than the regard to justice, since it is only the motive that makes an act a just one and it would be circular to at the same time insist that the motive was regard to justice and the justice was in the motive. He then canvasses various possible sources of such independent motivation and comes up empty-handed; self-interest in various forms would hardly lead us to restore the money, and our concern for others is implausibly weak for this purpose.

In the end, Hume claims that justice is an artificial virtue—one that human beings have invented—and he apparently argues that, in spite of his previous remarks, the motive to justice is part of, or grafted on to, the powerful impulse of self-interest.

Seen this way, Hume's position is not all that different from writers like Hobbes, and Hume's distinction between the natural and artifical virtues comes to something like this: We do not need to be trained to act virtuously in the former cases, though we do in the latter. Mackie sees the distinction this way and unsurprisingly complains that "[w]hereas Hume offers a sociological explanation of the artificial virtues but a psychological explanation of the natural virtues, it is now clear that an at least partly sociological explanation is needed for the natural virtues."[11] That is, we need to be trained to some extent (socialized), for example, to be dutiful parents and friends and that, in this respect, such virtues do not differ except perhaps in degree from virtues such as honesty and the like. On this view, Hume is, in making his distinction between the virtues, not saying anything particularly important. I will take issue with this, but in doing so I must admit that there are many passages in Hume that support this view. My hope is that by offering a way to understand the distinction as more substantive—a way itself supported at places in the text—we can connect Hume's discussion with my worry about naturalism and justify the importance that Hume gave to the distinction between the virtues. The issue of whether Hume "really" should be read my way, as if he clearly saw and followed one line, will then lapse.

Hume asks, in his specific example: What reason or motive has one to restore the money? Given my earlier remarks, I take this to be the question: How can it be made plausible that the agent who originally received the money will form the intention to restore it? Hume rightly insists that we are so socialized that, in the circumstances he describes, we will form this intention, but he is clearly unsatisfied by this appeal to training, though precisely why this is so can be brought out only after some further discussion.

Any explanation of our forming intentions in cases such as the one exampled above is governed by Hume's earlier argument about the potential circularity of the motive "regard to justice." Whether by appeal to training or by some other route we want to explain why the agent comes to intend the restoration of the money, we must not simply credit the agent with the general intention of doing what is just or virtuous.[12] Justice for Hume is a "general scheme" made up of infinitely many acts of which restoring the money in this case is one. In order that there is such a scheme in operation, it must be shown plausible to credit agents with the capacity to form the many specific intentions that produce these acts; that any one of these is virtuous depends on the intention with which it is performed and, hence, we cannot intelligibly credit ourselves with the "motive" regard to the virtue of the acts in the absence of the more specific intentions that make the acts virtuous.

This being so, why could not we say that human beings are so constituted that, in the various circumstances they find themselves, they tend to form the specific intentions requisite to the virtue of justice? Hume rejects this as implausible, but I think it worth being careful about his grounds. Mackie writes: ". . . Hume thinks there is no such special natural disposition . . . and indeed that honesty is so strange and *prima facie* pointless a behavior pattern that there could not be an instinct . . . . (This is a weak argument, but it is excusable, since Hume could not have known what strange and elaborate instincts many animals have been given by natural selection and evolution)."[13] However, I think Hume need not be excused on this point, since, even if he had known about evolution, he would have found it beside the point. Hume's real worry about the "natural instinct" account of our forming the myriad intentions that together make up justice is contained in this (rather "modern") argument; ". . . 'tis absurd to imagine, that in every particular instance, these sentiments are produced by an original quality and primary constitution. For as the number of our duties is, in a manner, infinite, 'tis impossible that our original instincts should extend to each of them."[14] What Hume thinks necessary is that some smaller number of principles be described that will make plausible the potential infinity of intentions with which we undertake virtuous actions. Thus, whether by natural instinct or training we possess the requisite capacity to form the panoply of necessary intentions, we are owed some plausible account of what that capacity consists in. Let us consider each of these in turn.

Hume, with some detailed discussion, rejects the possibility that our usual and presumably instinctual source of motivation can *directly* provide us with the needed explanation as they did in the parental care case. We do not pay back our debts because we, in doing so, are showing our love for our creditor or ourselves. Still, might it not be said that we do such things out of "regard to the public interest"? Might we not, in the more contemporary idiom, be credited with a concern for human flourishing or welfare? One thing Hume certainly urges here is that there is just "no such passion in human minds."[15] Any explanation of our coming to have the intentions requisite to justice cannot merely credit us with this concern.

Nonetheless, and without abandoning the appeal to human welfare or public interest, why could not we tell the following story? Human beings, though lacking a direct instinctual concern for human welfare, are trained up in a society that has evolved in such a way that the training provides them with motivation toward acts —acts of justice—that themselves serve human welfare. From this vantage point, we can answer with respect to justice the two Humean questions we put earlier with respect to the natural virtues? (i) Why do we perform just acts (ii) Why are just acts virtuous? The answer to i is: because of our education and training; and to ii: because these acts serve human flourishing. Also, on this view, the only real difference, if difference it is, between the natural and artificial virtues is the role of training in the one.

I indicated earlier that I think Hume rejects this view but, having arrived at it as we have, his reasons will be easier to appreciate.

Hume says that "public interest is not naturally attach'd to the observation of the rules of justice; but is only connected with it, after an artificial convention for the establishment of these rules . . . ."[16] Connecting this with the previous discussion of Hume's subjectivism encourages the following gloss. Human flourishing is not an objective state of affairs; rather, it is a matter of how human beings 'see' the world through their own conative (and cognitive) equipment. Any explanation of why we perform acts of justice that appeals to the notion of human flourishing must, therefore, explain how creatures such as we can see these acts as part of the requisites for human flourishing. That is, given that we are largely self-interested and that our concern for others tends to extend only rarely beyond family and friends, how is it that we come to see the public interest as what it no doubt is, i.e., as bound up with a whole range of things that we call acting morally? Put another way, how can any appeal to human flourishing explain the nature of the training we receive in society when the very idea of human flourishing depends, in part, for its *content* on our training?

Hume's answers to these questions contained in *Treatise* III,II,ii, are, I think, highly unsatisfactory; but my interest has been in showing that he raised them rather than in looking at his answers. Hume's subjectivism together with his detailed arguments about the motivation and explanation of virtue led him to recognize that a large class of what we call virtues is deeply mysterious. The artificial virtues for Hume are not merely, I would suggest, those virtues for which we have to be socialized. Rather, they are the virtues for which the training is problematic. We may well need education to be virtuous parents or friends (or, indeed, to be prudent)—though, admittedly, Hume does not emphasize this point. Still, in these cases, it is quite clear both which features of the human personality the training is grafted on to and how such a personality could come to view the behavior as part of the flourishing of our species. In the case of the artificial virtues, matters are quite different. There is no doubt that we do care about justice and that our training supports this. What is not clear, however, is how to explain this. Acting justly is not merely contributory to human flourishing, it is part of it. Yet, because of this, we cannot easily explain by reference to human flourishing how society should have evolved so as to lead us to act justly. Hume thinks that the answer lies in a complex account of how self-interest and convention "artificially" work to connect our notions of justice and human flourishing. Without accepting this, I still think one can profit from Hume's thought that there is a real problem here, a problem shown up by his distinction between the artificial and natural virtues. Moreover, it is a problem that does not genuinely rely, though I think it did for Hume, on subjectivism. Any naturalist attempt to explain morality by appeal to a notion of human flourishing is going to have to give us a plausible account of what human flourishing consists in that does not itself appeal to moral values.

Notes

1. In saying this, I mean to point out that some element of so-called "metaethics" seems to me a part of the institution of value.

2. G. J. Warnock, *The Object of Morality* (London: Methuen, 1971), pp. 17 and 26.

3. P. Foot, *Virtues and Vices* (Oxford: Basil Blackwell, 1978), p. 174.

4. *Ibid.*, pp. 165-66.

5. Hume, *A Treatise of Human Nature*, pp. 620-21. (All page references are to the Selby-Bigge edition of 1888.)

6. F. Hutcheson, *An Inquiry Concerning Moral Good and Evil* (1738), p. 327.

7. *Treatise*, p. 478.

8. *Ibid.*, p. 479.

9. *Ibid.*

10. *Ibid.*, pp. 479-80.

11. J. L. Mackie, *Hume's Theory of Morals* (London: Routledge and Kegan Paul, 1980), p. 123.

12. I use these in this way even though it needs an argument, which Hume tries to give, to show that justice is a virtue. Nothing important for the purposes of this paper hangs on this looseness.

13. Mackie, *op. cit.*, pp. 80-81.

14. *Treatise*, p. 473.

15. *Ibid.*, p. 481.

16. *Ibid.*, p. 480.

Hume's Distinction between Genuine and Fictitious Identity

ELI HIRSCH

I

Hume held that virtually all of our ordinary judgments about identity through time are mistaken.

> We have a distinct idea of an object, that remains invariable and uninterrupted thro' a suppos'd variation of time; and this idea we call that of *identity* or *sameness*. We have also a distinct idea of several different objects existing in succession, and connected together by a close relation. . . . But tho' these two ideas of identity, and a succession of related objects be in themselves perfectly distinct, and even contrary, yet 'tis certain, that in our common way of thinking they are generally confounded together.[1]

The one case of identity that Hume regards as genuine or "perfect" is that of a "mass of matter, of which the parts are contiguous and connected" and which persists without gaining or losing any parts (pp. 255-56). On the other hand, "the identity, which we ascribe to the mind of man, is only a fictitious one, and of a like kind with that which we ascribe to vegetables and animal bodies" (p. 259). Hume also implies that the identities of artifacts such as ships and inanimate natural things such as mountains and planets are merely fictitious (pp. 256-57).

Whereas Hume's aspersions on the "fictitious" cases of identity may strike us as the most problematic aspect of his position, a prior question needs to be raised whether, given some of his own philosophical assumptions, he was entitled even to the one case of genuine identity that he credited. According to Hume's theory of ideas, any intelligible idea must derive from our immediate experience, our "impressions." It is not clear, however, how the idea of identity through time derives from our experience. Barry Stroud, in his recent study of Hume, concludes that Hume fails to explain how we get the idea of identity through time, for "[a]ccording to Hume, we do not get it directly from the senses. Our experience is in fact

321

nothing but a sequence of momentary, internal impressions, so even when we have an uninterrupted series of exactly similar impressions we are not actually surveying an identical object."[2]

Stroud evidently assumes that, according to Hume, we have no impression of identity through time.[3] Later I will question that assumption. Even granted the assumption, however, it may seem that Hume could meet Stroud's challenge by maintaining that our idea of the identity through time of an intact bit of matter is logically complex and can be analyzed in terms of other ideas that do derive from experience.

It may seem indeed that Hume attempts to offer us such an analysis when he repeatedly connects identity to the two conditions of *invariableness* and *uninterruptedness*. The connection is stated in the passage quoted earlier (*Treatise*, p. 253) and even more clearly in the following.

> Thus the principle of individuation is nothing but the *invariableness* and *uninterruptedness* of any object, thro' a supposed variation of time, by which the mind can trace it in the different periods of its existence, without any break of the view, and without being oblig'd to form the idea of multiplicity or number (p. 201).

By "uninterruptedness" Hume seems to mean something very much like spatiotemporal continuity, for it is only when an object traverses a continuous space-time path that we can trace it "without any break of the view." The previous passage does not make clear what Hume means by "invariableness," but it seems plain that in many contexts what he means by this is qualitative constancy.[4] So it may seem that he is in effect analyzing or defining the "perfect" identity of matter in terms of the two conditions of spatiotemporal continuity and qualitative constancy.

This cannot be quite right since Hume acknowledges the obvious fact that a mass of matter can maintain its identity while its parts are rearranged in such a manner as to alter its shape or size. "[W]e must attribute a perfect identity to this mass, provided all the parts continue uninterruptedly and invariably the same, whatever motion or change of place we may observe either in the whole or in any of its parts" (p. 255). This seems to suggest that we have the same mass of matter if and only if either the mass satisfies the two conditions of spatiotemporal continuity and qualitative constancy or it consists of parts that satisfy the two conditions.

If that is what Hume thought (as I suspect), then he was wrong, for the fact is that spatiotemporal continuity together with qualitative constancy do not suffice for the identity of matter. As Russell pointed out, "[W]e can travel by sensibly continuous gradations from any one drop of the sea at any one time to any other drop at any other time."[5] Russell speaks of continuity, but we can easily secure the condition of constancy by imagining a stretch of water that is qualitatively homogeneous. The general point is that a space-time path that is perfectly continuous and qualitatively constant may begin at one bit of matter and end at another.

Now Hume in fact held that the ultimate constituents of matter are minimally sized objects and that any finite quantity of matter is composed of a finite number of these minimal atoms (pp. 26-30). He may then have supposed that the identity of a minimal atom is defined by the conditions of spatiotemporal continuity and qualitative constancy, and the identity of a composite object is defined by its containing the same atoms. But Russell's problem applies even at the level of the atoms. If the atoms that comprise a qualitatively homogeneous stretch of water are in contact, then we can pass from one atom to the next without sacrificing spatiotemporal continuity or qualitative constancy. It would seem farfetched to suggest that on a priori (conceptual) grounds we must exclude the possibility of qualitatively similar atoms touching each other; anyway, Hume does not exclude this possibility.[6]

Even if it is agreed that there must be more to our idea of the identity of matter than continuity and constancy, it might still be suggested that Hume missed this complication and that he did intend to provide an analysis of the identity of matter in terms of those conditions. I suspect that Hume did, in fact, miss this complication, but I think that it is wrong for another reason to interpret him as intending to provide an analysis of the identity of matter. What is the basic contrast that Hume draws between a genuine case of identity and a merely fictitious case? It is that in the latter case identity amounts to nothing more than "several different objects existing in succession, and connected together by a close relation" (p. 253). But if we attempt to analyze the identity of matter in terms of continuity and constancy, then we are in effect saying that the identity of matter amounts to nothing more than a succession of momentary stages that are interrelated by continuity and constancy. This point was somewhat obscured in the previous discussion because I deliberately avoided talk of "successions of stages." I did, however, talk of "space-time paths," which comes to much the same thing. It seems that any analysis or definition of the identity of matter must in one way or another be couched in terms of some characteristic interrelationship between the successive stages (or states or parts or events) in the history of a persisting bit of matter. But that would make the identity of matter fictitious in Hume's terms.

Butler and Reid were two other philosophers who maintained a distinction between genuine or perfect identity (identity in the "strict and philosophical sense") and fictitious identity (identity in the "loose and popular sense").[7] They apparently disagreed with Hume only about the case of personal identity, which they regarded as genuine. Now in these two philosophers the point emerges rather clearly that a genuine case of identity must be ultimate and unanalyzable. As Reid says, "If you ask a definition of identity, I confess I can give none; it is too simple a notion to admit of logical definition."[8] I think we should assume that for Hume, too, a case of identity is genuine only if it is indefinable.[9]

II

If this is so, then one question we are left with is how to understand his oft-repeated connection between identity and the two conditions of uninterruptedness and invariableness. But a more urgent question is Stroud's challenge, which is now left unanswered. If the idea of identity is indefinable, then how can we ever get the idea?

I suggest that Hume would answer that we get this idea directly from our experience; in other words, that we have an impression of identity through time. Stroud's reason for thinking that this is impossible is that Hume believed that "our experience is in fact nothing but a sequence of momentary, internal impressions"[10]; and a momentary impression, Stroud assumes, cannot give us the idea of identity through time.

If "momentary" means literally without duration (or temporally indivisible), then it is doubtful that Hume believed that all of our impressions are momentary. It is true that he says in a famous passage that our perceptions "succeed each other with an inconceivable rapidity" (p. 252), and this may (though need not) suggest that all impressions are without duration. But there are other passages in the *Treatise* that imply the opposite. Hume says that we get our idea of time from "some *perceivable* succession of changeable objects" (p. 35, Hume's emphasis). To say that the succession is perceivable ought to imply that it is possible for us to have an impression of the succession, an impression, that is, that is temporally extended. Hume seems to make this point explicit when he says that a person can get the idea of time by having "a certain sensation or impression, the parts of which are successive to each other" (p. 56).

Let us note that Hume's theory of ideas states only a necessary condition for acquiring an idea; it does not state a sufficient condition. It seems clear that if someone has two impressions that are separated by a sufficiently long time, then even if these impressions are related in some distinctive way, the person will not acquire the idea of the relation—and the theory of ideas does not say that he will. In order for the person to acquire the idea of the relation, he must be aware of the two impressions "together," in some sense. (Some philosophers would say that the impressions must both belong to a single "specious present.") Now in the passages just cited Hume seems to imply that in order for the two impressions to be present together in someone's awareness, in the sense required to generate the idea of their relationship, they must both be parts of a longer impression.

I do not suggest that Hume had worked out the details of a theory of the duration of impressions. It seems clear, in fact, that his remarks on this issue are extremely haphazard.[11] But what he does say does not support Stroud's interpretation.

Details aside, Stroud's assumption that our impressions cannot directly generate the idea of identity through time can be decisively rebutted simply by comparing the idea of temporal succession to the idea of identity through time. Clearly, Hume must hold that our impressions can generate the idea of successive events being temporally ordered. But then our impressions can also generate the idea of successive events belonging to the same persisting object. There does not seem to be any relevant difference between the two cases.

There are several passages in the *Treatise* in which Hume virtually says outright that identity through time is given in our experience. He explains the difference between *perceiving* a relation and *reasoning* about a relation as follows: "When both the objects are present to the senses along with the relation, we call this perception rather than reasoning; nor is there in this case any exercise of the thought, . . . but a mere passive admission of the impressions thro' the organ of sensation" (p. 73). If Hume held that identity is given in experience, then one might have expected him to go on to mention identity as an example of a perceivable relation. And that is precisely what he does: "[W]e ought not to receive as reasoning any of the observations we may make concerning *identity*, and the *relations* of *time* and *place*; since in none of them the mind can go beyond what is immediately present to the senses . . ." (*ibid.*). That seems almost completely clear.[12]

But there is an even clearer passage, and this one is well known: "[T]here are three different kinds of impressions convey'd by the senses. The first are those of the figure, bulk, motion and solidity of bodies" (p. 192).[13] It seems obvious that to have an impression of the motion of a body is to have the impression of identity through time; it is to have the impression of a body at one time and place being identical with a body at another time and place.

III

I am attributing the following two views to Hume: first, that the identity of matter is ultimate and unanalyzable and in particular that it is not analyzable in terms of continuity and constancy; second, that the identity of matter is immediately given in sensory experience. The conjunction of these views, however, may seem to imply a consequence that one would not want to attribute to Hume. The consequence seems to be that we find in our sensory experience facts over and above the spatio-temporal and qualitative relations of momentary stages. This position seems both inherently implausible and distinctly non-Humean. Imagine that we have been given a description of everything that could be known about the qualities and spatiotemporal relations of all the momentary stages within a certain region of space-time. Hume might allow that there are additional facts about that space-time region (e.g., facts about causal relations) that are still unknown to us. But he would not be likely to suggest that we could find out these additional facts by direct observation. For it does not seem that there could be anything given in immediate experience beyond the facts about the qualities and spatiotemporal relations of the stages. Therefore, if Hume held that identity goes beyond the facts about continuity and constancy, it seems that he ought not to have held that identity is given in experience.

That is one serious difficulty. Another difficulty that I mentioned earlier is how to explain the connection that Hume draws between identity and the conditions of uninterruptedness (continuity) and invariableness (constancy), if he is not analyzing identity in terms of these conditions.

I will now suggest a philosophical position that could resolve both of these difficulties. Since this position has some inherent interest and reconciles at least many things that Hume said, we might take it as his implicit position. (I do not suggest that Hume explicitly addressed these difficulties.)

Hume may have implicitly held both that (a) identity cannot be analyzed in terms of continuity and constancy and (b) identity consists in nothing more than continuity and constancy. These propositions are by no means incompatible. To say that identity consists in nothing more than continuity and constancy only implies that propositions about identity are logically equivalent to propositions about continuity and constancy. But that need not imply that identity can be *analyzed* or *defined* in terms of continuity and constancy. To analyze a proposition, at least in one traditional sense, is to present another proposition that is not only equivalent to the first but is in some sense more *basic* than the first. Hume may have held that propositions about continuity and constancy are *not* more basic than propositions about identity. When he equates identity to the two conditions, that may only imply an equivalence, not an analysis to something more basic. And the equivalence is enough to explain how he could think that identity is given in experience.

An example that may be partially analogous to the situation I am here envisioning is the following. It seems trivially correct to say that something's being green consists in nothing more than (is logically equivalent to) its being either grue and examined before the year 2000 or bleen and not so examined. But that does not make us want to say that being green can be analyzed in such terms.

If a philosopher holds that the identity of matter is equivalent to the occurrence of a succession of stages that is spatiotemporally continuous and qualitatively constant, then there are several reasons why he might not regard this equivalence as constituting an analysis. First of all, he might question the basicness of "stages"; if these are construed as abstract items—say, ordered pairs of bits of matter and moments of time—then the equivalence obviously cannot qualify as an analysis in any sense that might imperil the genuineness of identity. An even more obvious question can be raised about the basicness of spatiotemporal continuity. This condition is typically defined in terms of a framework of persisting places, and this framework is typically relativized to some persisting objects, perhaps indeed to some persisting bits of matter. Given these assumptions, it would be blatantly circular to attempt to analyze the identity of matter in terms of spatiotemporal continuity.

Hume related the condition of spatiotemporal continuity ("uninterruptedness") to the fact that an object can be traced "without any break of the view" (p. 201). But it is not logically possible that the successive perceptions of a single self might jump discontinuously from place to place (so that there is no "break of the view" even in the absence of spatiotemporal continuity)? Hume, I think, might readily have conceded this possibility. His point might only have been that if we presuppose our ordinary spatial framework and also presuppose that human bodies move continuously through space, then it seems correct and illuminating to relate the condition of continuity to the fact that there is no "break of the view." And it might also have seemed to Hume correct and illuminating to relate this condition to the identity of matter. But none of this need imply that the condition is independently intelligible in such a manner that it might figure as part of a definition of identity.

IV

The view I am attributing to Hume—that propositions about the identity of matter are equivalent to, though not analyzable in terms of, propositions about the two conditions of spatiotemporal continuity and qualitative constancy — is refuted by Russell's argument, which shows that the equivalence claim is mistaken. Assuming that the identity of matter goes beyond continuity and constancy, let us now consider what alternatives there are to Hume's position. I am particularly interested to see what alternatives there may be compatible with Hume's theory of ideas.

Some philosophers have suggested that the identity of matter is analyzable in terms of the distinctive causal relations that obtain between the successive stages of a bit of matter.[14] This account would conform to the theory of ideas, assuming that the theory can accommodate causality. But it seems to me that the account is vulnerable to much the same kind of objection as that raised by Russell. Russell shows that there seems to be no a priori constraints on the qualitative and spatiotemporal relations that might obtain between different particles of matter. By the same token, there seems to be no a priori constraints on the causal relations that might obtain between different particles of matter. It seems possible that two particles of matter may interact in such a manner that the early stages of one affect the later stages of the other as much as, or even more than, the later stages of itself.[15]

I suspect that some proponents of the causal account may be confusing two positions. One position is that the identity of matter consists in the occurrence of a succession of stages that are causally related in some distinctive way. That position seems to me wrong. A second position, which I think may be correct, is that our judgments about the identity of matter ultimately depend on our attempt to provide the best (causal) explanation of what we experience. The second position evidently does not imply that identity consists in a causal relation; it does not suggest any account of what identity consists in.

Let us suppose that the identity of matter goes beyond any facts about spatiotemporal continuity or qualitative constancy (or continuity) or causal connectedness. Can our possession of such an idea of identity be reconciled with the theory of ideas? Let me explore several ways in which this might be attempted.

One interesting possibility is that our idea of the *diachronic unity* of a bit of matter — i.e., its identity through time — derives from our idea of the *synchronic unity* of its contemporaneous parts and qualities, the latter idea deriving directly from our experience. This suggestion may initially seem wildly wrong, since it may seem obvious that our idea of identity through time introduces something essentially new, something that is not present at the synchronic level. But it is on further reflection not clear why this has to be so.

At the synchronic level, we acquire the idea of a thing with several properties. If we already have the idea of "different times," what can now prevent us from forming the idea of a thing with several properties *at different times*, which is of course the idea of identity through time? Note that this would not involve analyzing identity through time in terms of a succession of suitably interrelated momentary stages. Rather, one takes the unanalyzed idea of unity that has operated in the synchronic context and applies that idea within the new diachronic context. It is not clear that the theory of ideas ought to prevent this.

Let me pose this issue in slightly different terms. To have the idea of the unity of a thing is to have the idea of a certain kind of *conjunction*. We can distinguish between *external* and *internal* conjunctions, depending on whether the conjunction occurs within the context of a bound variable. In "Something is A and something is B" the conjunction is external, whereas "Something is A and (that same thing is) B" involves an internal conjunction. Now the synchronic level provides us with the general idea of internal conjunction, as exemplified in propositions of the form "Something is A at t and B at t." Once we have this general idea (and also the idea of different times), it seems that we might automatically be in the position to frame propositions of the form "Something is A at t and B at t'," where t is distinct from t'. These propositions would express identity through time.

My contention is that there is nothing in Hume's theory of ideas as such that could decisively block the extraction of the idea of diachronic unity from the experience of synchronic unity. But I am not suggesting that the theory of ideas *forces* us to countenance this extraction. Consider that Hume would certainly not have allowed that we can acquire the idea of grue by experiencing some green (and hence grue) things. This is because the class of grue things seems to divide into two cases (those examined before the year 2000 and those not) that have nothing essentially in common; in this sense, "grue" does not seem to be a "proper" idea. The crucial question then would seem to be whether "unity" (or "internal conjunction") is a proper idea, whether, in particular, the synchronic and diachronic cases of unity are essentially alike. If one holds that "unity" is in this sense a proper idea, then the theory of ideas ought to allow us to acquire the idea of unity from the synchronic case and then apply it to the diachronic case.

The prospect for such an approach seems most favorable if it is held that unity is unanalyzable in both the diachronic and synchronic cases. The approach would seem to be blocked, however, if it is held that one case is analyzable and the other not or that both cases are analyzable but in different ways.

Hume apparently held that the synchronic unity of a thing's parts and qualities is in every instance analyzable (and hence "fictitious"). He says rather little about the unity of parts but seems to hold that a genuine case of unity "must be perfectly indivisible, and incapable of being resolved into any lesser unity" (p. 31). The unity of an ordinary composite thing he seems to regard as "merely a fictitious denomination, which the mind may apply to any quantity of objects it collects together" (p. 30). He is more emphatic about the unity of a thing's qualities, insisting repeatedly that "our ideas of bodies are nothing but collections form'd by the mind of the ideas of the several distinct sensible qualities, of which objects are compos'd, and which we find to have a constant union with each other" (p. 219). The nature of this "constant union" seems to be analyzed essentially in terms of contiguity and causation (p. 16). Note how in the following passage, which challenges almost any ordinary idea of unity, he still retains his commitment to identity through time in the one "perfect" case.

> But however these qualities of an object may in themselves be entirely distinct, 'tis certain we commonly regard the compound which they form, as *one* thing, and as continuing the *same* under very considerable alterations.

The acknowledg'd composition is evidently contrary to this suppos'd *simplicity*, and the variation to the *identity* (p. 219).

Even here Hume implies that where there is a lack of qualitative variation, identity may be genuine. However, the synchronic unity of the qualities is apparently always fictitious. (Hume's overall position then may imply that when an intact bit of matter persists, what really persists are certain unchanging qualities.)

Hume's account of synchronic unity is not plausible. It may possibly be correct to define the unity of a thing's parts in terms of causality and contiguity, but these conditions have no straightforward application to the unity of a thing's qualities. An object's shape and color or color and texture may stand in no special causal relationship; it is not even clearly meaningful to say that these qualities are contiguous (that they *touch*). Perhaps we can say that the color and texture pervade the same place, but even this could not be said of shape and color or shape and size.

But even if Hume's account is mistaken, there may be enough truth in it to discourage the suggested derivation of the idea of diachronic unity from the idea of synchronic unity. Even if we regard the synchronic unity of qualities as ultimate and unanalyzable, which does not seem implausible, we may yet want to acknowledge that this mode of unity essentially involves a distinctive kind of "spatial togetherness"—something that does not seem to figure in diachronic unity. It may strike us that there is an essential contrast between the way in which a thing's simultaneous states hang together and the way in which its successive states hang together, even if no analysis seems possible in either case.

The derivation of diachronic unity from synchronic unity has to my knowledge never been entertained by anyone. But there is a comparable maneuver that may have been attempted. Philosophers such as Butler and Reid, who regarded self-identity as unanalyzable, may have held that we derive the idea of the identity of matter from the idea of the identity of the self, the latter idea deriving directly from experience.[16] This maneuver can be challenged, however, in the same general sort of way that has just emerged. Even if we accept the premise that both the identity of the self and the identity of matter are unanalyzable, the cases may yet strike us as essentially different, in such a way as to block the derivation of one idea from the other. A point to note, however, is that Hume's theory of ideas does not itself block the derivation.

V

Suppose we assume that the idea of the identity of matter cannot be derived from any other case of unity. And we continue to assume that the identity of matter goes beyond qualitative or spatiotemporal or causal factors, this assumption presumably implying that the identity of matter is neither given in experience nor definable in experiential terms. Might we then be forced to conclude that our possession of this idea refutes the theory of ideas? This depends, I think, on what sort of idea we have of the identity of matter.

There are a number of passages in the *Treatise* where Hume seems to allow that we can refer in a general way to kinds of phenomena that are not given in experience or definable in experiential terms. "[T]here may be several qualities both in material and immaterial objects, with which we are utterly unacquainted" (p. 168). It apparently is all right for us to talk about such "unknown qualities" so long as we do not pretend that we have a "clear idea" of what they are (*ibid.*).[17]

Hume's position can be related to certain contemporary treatments of theoretical terms (especially the Ramsey treatment). Let us say that the general term 'F' (or the abstract noun 'F-ness') is theoretical if we use 'F' to refer to that phenomenon, whatever it might be, that stands in certain specified relations (e.g., causal relations) to various other things that we refer to. In using 'F' we do not claim to know what the phenomenon of F-ness is; we do not claim to grasp the essential nature of F-ness but only its contingent relations to other things. The theory of ideas implies that we cannot acquire the idea of any phenomenon—an idea, that is, of what the phenomenon consists in (what its essential nature is)—unless we derive this idea from our experience; but this need not exclude the possibility of our referring to a phenomenon whose nature we do not grasp. (Consider the sense in which someone blind from birth can refer to the color red as, for example, a quality that makes people react in a certain way.) The theory of ideas therefore might not prevent us from treating identity through time as theoretical in this sense.

Suppose that we are initially confronted with momentary things and their qualitative, spatiotemporal, and causal interrelations. Perhaps we find that the coherence of our explanations could be enhanced by positing some new phenomenon, some "unknown quality." This new phenomenon, whose nature we do not grasp, is what we call the identity through time of matter.

The suggestion that the identity of matter is a theoretical posit can apparently be developed in two ways. One approach would be to imagine an intermediary stage between the initial level of momentary things and the final level of persisting matter. At the intermediary stage, we posit a new theoretical relationship between the momentary things. Let us call this relationship 'genidentity'.[18] We then go on to *define* the identity of matter in terms of a genidentically interrelated succession. Essentially this definition would involve adopting a transformation rule that substitutes statements of the form "Something is A at t and (that same persisting thing is) B at t'" for statements of the form "Something is A at t and something is B at t' and these (momentary) things are genidentically interrelated."

The second approach would be to skip the intermediary stage and posit the identity of matter directly. We can do this by introducing theoretical terms of the form "A at t and B at t' (and C at t'', etc.)." The introduction of these terms alters our ontology because these terms cannot apply to our erstwhile momentary things. We might still retain the momentary things, at least as stages (or states or events) of the persisting things; we can even define a relationship of genidentity as holding between those momentary things that constitute persisting things; so perhaps we wind up saying precisely (the same sentences as) what we say in the first approach. But there may still seem to be a significant difference between the two approaches, if one can take seriously the question whether identity is analyzable. The first approach seems to imply that it is, and the second approach that it is not. In Hume's terms, the first approach seems to imply that the identity of matter is "fictitious," whereas the second approach seems to sustain his view that this case of identity is genuine. (I will return to this point in the next section.)

Let me note a certain puzzle with respect to the second approach. Obviously we want to be able to say that "Something is A at t and B at t'" entails "Something is A at t." But how can this be justified if it is held that the predicate "A at t and B at t'" signifies something-we-know-not-what?[19] If the predicate signifies an "unknown quality," what sense can we make of its logical structure? To put the question differently: what sense can it make to apply the logical structure of internal conjunction to the diachronic case if we have no idea what the diachronic case consists in?

Perhaps one might answer that we use the synchronic case as a model, though without implying (as in the suggestion considered in Section IV) that our experiential grasp of synchronic unity provides us with an idea of what diachronic unity is. We are initially confronted with diachronic facts of the form "Something is A at t and something is B at t'"; we have a theoretical need for a new kind of diachronic fact that would go beyond these external conjunctions. At the synchronic level, we are familiar with a kind of fact, expressed by an internal conjunction, that entails, but is not entailed by, the corresponding external conjunction. So we now posit a new kind of internal conjunction, "Something is A at t and B at t'," as entailing, but not being entailed by, its corresponding external conjunction.

It seems then that we might be able to accommodate the identity of matter to the theory of ideas, if we regard the identity of matter as theoretical in the sense of referring to something whose essential nature we cannot grasp. And perhaps we can even sustain the view that the identity of matter is ultimate and unanalyzable, if we can make out the second approach outlined above. But if a philosopher thinks that we do grasp the essential nature of the identity of matter—that the identity of matter is not for us merely "something-we-know-not-what"—then he or she might have to reject the theory of ideas and the kind of empiricism that goes with it. (This is perhaps the basic thrust of Descartes's argument about the identity of the bit of wax at the end of Meditation II.[20])

Hume himself could not have been sympathetic to a theoretical account of the identity of matter, even if he had recognized the error of his own observational account. For though he did apparently allow that we can frame ideas of "unknown qualities," he treated such ideas with disdain, as "unclear" and "imperfect" and as being unable to figure in any reasonable beliefs (see especially p. 172). His disdain for ideas of "unknown qualities" shows itself in his onslaught against the Lockean notion of substance as something-we-know-not-what that unites the qualities of a thing; Hume seems to dismiss this as so much mystification (p. 16). But if we respect the theoretical level, it is not immediately clear that we need to reject this notion. Even Hume's attack on self-identity may partially depend on his antitheoretical attitude. The attack consists primarily in his insistence that we are not aware of an ultimate kind of self-identity, that we are aware of nothing beyond the qualitative interrelations of our perceptions. But what about the possibility that self-identity is theoretically posited as something-we-know-not-what? This, too, Hume would apparently dismiss as mere mystification, though the theory of ideas as such does not seem to require this dismissal.

VI

A basic premise of Hume's discussion of identity through time is that a genuine case of identity must not be analyzable in terms of a succession of interrelated things. The premise can be questioned in two ways. First, we can question whether it makes good sense to distinguish between cases of identity that are and cases that are not analyzable in terms of a succession. And, second, even if we grant this distinction, we may question the assumption that a genuine case of identity must be unanalyzable. In the present section I will make a few brief comments about the first question and then turn to the second question in the next section.

It may initially seem that an identity statement is unanalyzable in the relevant sense if it is not logically equivalent to a statement reporting the occurrence of a succession. The inadequacy of this explanation, however, emerged earlier when I suggested that Hume may have held that the identity of matter is equivalent to, but not analyzable in terms of, the continuity and constancy of a succession. Of course this equivalence might be denied, as, in fact, I think it should be. But a more general difficulty that emerged in the preceding section is that the notion of "genidentity" can be introduced in such a manner that any identity statement is trivially equivalent to a statement about a genidentically interrelated succession. If it is nevertheless held that an identity statement is not analyzable in terms of a succession, the explanation must be that the identity statement is more "basic" than any equivalent statement about a succession, that in particular the identity statement is more "basic" than the equivalent genidentity statement. (So the contrast between the two approaches of the last section boils down to the question of whether identity or genidentity is more basic.)

But do we really understand what this notion of "basicness" means? It would surely not suffice to explicate this notion in terms of some contingent facts about the order in which human beings acquire their concepts—in terms, for example, of the fact that human beings acquire the ordinary concept of identity before they acquire the technical concept of genidentity—for Hume is evidently trying to establish a metaphysical (ontological) distinction between genuine and nongenuine cases of identity. This metaphysical distinction cannot rely on some merely contingent facts about how human beings happen to acquire their concepts.

There are cases in which we do seem to have very strong intuitions about "basicness" in the relevant metaphysical sense. Probably everyone is strongly inclined to hold that "grue" is less basic than "green" in some metaphysical sense. But do we have the same kind of intuition about "genidentity" and "identity"? I doubt it.

In the case of "grue," our intuition seems to say that it is logically impossible for any thinking creature, human or otherwise, to acquire the concept of grue without already having the concept of green. And this intuition seems to be closely related to the following idea: Any creature capable of thought must classify things on the basis of their similarities and make rational predictions on this basis, but a creature who treats "grue" as primitive would not be classifying things on the basis of their similarities and would not make rational predictions. Now I am not here trying to defend our intuitions about grue. My point is that we have no comparable intuitions about genidentity. If there were a creature who treated "genidentity" as primitive and who described the world in terms of genidentically interrelated successions, he might note all of the similarities that we do, and his inductive predictions might be in every detail equivalent to ours. Why should it be logically impossible for there to be such a creature? And if there could be such a creature, what sense does it make to say that his judgments of genidentity are less "basic" than our equivalent judgments of identity?

These questions, I think, should generate some serious skepticism about Hume's (and Butler's and Reid's) assumption that certain cases of identity through time enjoy the special status of not reducing to a mere succession of interrelated things. It may be that no case of identity can be ultimate in this sense.[21]

VII

But suppose that, for the sake of argument, we grant the assumption that certain cases of identity—the identity of matter for Hume and self-identity for Butler and Reid—are ultimate. Hume did not simply want to distinguish neutrally between ultimate and nonultimate cases of identity. His main point rather was that all of our ordinary identity judgments, except for the few ultimate cases, are *mistaken*, that we are *wrong* to make identity judgments in the ordinary way about ships and stones and trees.

> [T]he objects, which are variable or interrupted [i.e., the objects that do not perfectly retain their material composition], and yet are suppos'd to continue the same, are such only as consist of a succession of parts, connected together by resemblance, contiguity, or causation. For as such a succession answers evidently to our notion of diversity, it can only be by mistake we ascribe to it an identity (p. 255).

Hume might simply have distinguished between two kinds (or senses) of identity, the ultimate and the nonultimate. Why does he instead draw the startling conclusion that our identity judgments in the latter cases are mistaken?

In the writings of Butler, one finds it said that our typical identity judgments are not about identity in the "strict" sense. Butler says that "when a man swears to the same tree, as having stood fifty years in the same place, he means only the same as to all purposes of property and uses of common life, and not that the tree has been all that time the same in the strict philosophical sense of the word."[22]

Butler's position seems to be less extreme than Hume's, for Butler does not say that the identity statement about the tree betrays a mistaken belief; he says only that it involves a loose use of language. Hume might almost be addressing himself to Butler when he insists that "when we attribute identity, in an improper sense, to variable or interrupted objects, our mistake is not confin'd to the expression, but is commonly attended with a fiction" (p. 255).

Butler's position, though less immediately paradoxical than Hume's, may be ultimately more puzzling. Part of what Butler seems to be driving at is that our identity statements about ordinary bodies like trees are rather vague and may admit of borderline cases. Reid brings this point out clearly when he observes that "the changes which in common language are made consistent with identity differ from those that are thought to destroy it, not in kind but in number and degree . . . and questions about the identity of a body are very often questions about words."[23] This point may be readily acceptable. But Butler and Reid seem also to imply that there is, besides the loose sense, a strict sense of our identity statements about ordinary bodies. Consider the statement "This tree is the one that stood here 50 years ago." Butler and Reid seem to imply that strictly speaking such a statement is never true because in the strict sense the statement is equivalent to "The matter that makes up this tree is the matter that made up the tree that stood here 50 years ago." But this seems plainly wrong. It seems plain that there is no ordinary sense, let alone a strict sense, in which these statements are equivalent.[24]

Now Hume might be interpreted as believing in this dubious equivalence, with the added twist of not even allowing that there is any (loose) sense in which the equivalence fails to hold. It is clear that according to Hume what we treat as the identity of an ordinary body like a tree is nothing more than a succession of interrelated things and that consequently an ordinary identity statement expresses a mistaken belief. But what is this mistaken belief? Hume says that "tho' these two ideas of identity, and a succession of related objects be in themselves perfectly distinct, and even contrary, yet 'tis certain that in our common way of thinking they are generally confounded with each other" (p. 253). Perhaps the most obvious interpretation of Hume's meaning is that, when we are confronted with a succession of different bits of matter in close relation, we somehow confuse ourselves into thinking that the matter remains the same. And this confusion underlies our ordinary identity statements because these statements are equivalent to statements about the identity of matter. For example, the statement "This tree is the one that stood here 50 years ago" is equivalent to "The matter that makes up this tree is the matter that made up the tree that stood here 50 years ago"; we mistakenly accept the former statement because we somehow delude ourselves into accepting the latter.

If this was what Hume meant, then I think that his doctrine of "fictitious identity" would have little interest. Not only is the posited equivalence extremely doubtful, as I have already stated, but it seems quite absurd to suggest that we are normally deluded in the manner just described. It seems that people typically make statements like "This tree is the one that stood here 50 years ago" without being in the least confused about the fact that a tree's material composition alters. As an even clearer example, consider a statement like "This tree is the one that lost a branch." Is it conceivable that in the very course of making this statement someone is deluded into thinking that the tree's material compositon never changes? This seems even beyond the reach of human folly.

But I think that we can interpret Hume as suggesting a more interesting position. His remark that we normally confuse the case of a succession with the case of genuine identity need not imply that, when we are confronted with a succession, we confusedly think that this is a case of an intact bit of matter. His point might rather be that, when we are confronted with a succession, we confusedly think that, though this is not a case of an intact bit of matter, it is something more than a mere succession. Our confusion consists in according to the identity of a tree, for example, the metaphysical status of ultimacy that properly belongs only to an intact bit of matter. What we treat as the identity of a tree is in truth merely a succession of interrelated things, but we suffer from the illusion, the fiction, that the tree's identity is an ultimate fact. On the present account there is no equivalence between a statement about the identity of a tree and a statement about the identity of matter. But both statements commit us to a claim of ultimacy, which can, in fact, be sustained only for the latter statement.

It is the illusion of ultimacy that I think Hume is primarily trying to expose. And it seems to me that we may indeed have a tendency to suffer from such an illusion. One way to bring this out is by considering our natural response to the following question: Is it possible for there to be an intelligent creature, with our sensory apparatus, who when confronted with a tree conceives of this not as a unitary persisting object but rather as lots of different bits of matter interrelated in various complicated ways? Our immediate response is that this is not possible, that any intelligent creature with our sensory intake would necessarily have to conceive of the tree as we do. But this response may be mistaken and may merely betray the illusion that the tree's identity is an ultimate fact. For if the truth is that what we call the identity of a tree is merely an interrelated succession, it surely seems to follow that there easily could be an intelligent creature who does not synthesize this succession in the special way that we do.

The illusion of ultimacy is probably strongest with respect to self-identity, if, that is, Hume is right in holding that self-identity consists in nothing more than a succession of interrelated perceptions. We seem to have the strongest inclination to suppose that any intelligent creature must operate with our concept of self-identity. But that, too, is an illusion, if self-identity is not an ultimate fact.

What could make us suffer from these illusions of ultimacy? Let me suggest the sketch of an explanation, which I think is roughly akin to Hume's own explanation. It seems to be a basic fact about the perceptual and cognitive structures of the human mind (a basic fact about the workings of our "imagination," as Hume might say) that we see the world in terms of ordinary bodies. Hume remarks that we feel a "smooth" "passage" of the mind from one stage to the next of those interrelated successions that we treat as persisting bodies; this action of the mind requires virtually no "effort of thought" (p. 245). I think we can understand this obscure but suggestive remark by considering how natural it is for us to trace the contours of ordinary bodies with our eyes and to track the bodies as they move; even new-born infants are said to do this. It seems indeed that the human eye — and one might say the "mind's eye" — is geared toward moving along the paths of ordinary bodies smoothly and without effort. Our natural propensity to focus on ordinary bodies might be regarded as the most primitive expression of our ordinary identity concept.[25]

It may be, I suggest, the felt naturalness of our ordinary identity concept that deceives us into regarding the concept as ultimate. In the nonultimate cases (which, as I have suggested, may actually turn out to be *all* of the cases), the application of our identity concept is metaphysically arbitrary; where identity through time is not an ultimate fact but consists in merely an interrelated succession, there are no metaphysical constraints that require the succession to be synthesized in an identity concept. But we confuse psychological constraints with metaphysical constraints. Since we feel that it is absolutely inevitable *for us* to see the world in a certain way, we are deluded into thinking that the world needs to be seen that way. We wind up feeling that there is more to identity than there really is.[26]

Interpreted along these lines, it seems to me that there may be a great deal of merit in Hume's ideas about the "fictitious" character of our ordinary identity judgments. Let me conclude, however, by indicating one major reservation that I have about Hume's position. There is on the face of it a distinction between holding that our identity judgments are "attended by a fiction" — which is the way that Hume puts it at one point — and holding that these judgments are mistaken and ought to be discarded. Many of Hume's remarks indicate that he held the latter, more extreme view. I think, however, that we should consider the less extreme possibility. The illusion of ultimacy that attends an ordinary identity judgment need not be seen as infecting the content and truth-value of that judgment. The illusion might rather be located at the meta- level. We may be right in what we judge about the identity of a tree but wrong in what we implicitly hold about the nature (the analysis) of that identity judgment. If this is so, then we might be able to ward off the confusions that surround our identity judgments without being required to give up these judgments. This modification of Hume's position would, of course, need to be elaborated. In the topic of identity, as elsewhere, Hume's discussions challenge us to clarify perhaps better than he did the variety of ways in which our ordinary judgments might be off the mark.[27]

Notes

1. David Hume, *A Treatise of Human Nature*, ed. L. A. Selby-Bigge, as revised by P. H. Nidditch (Oxford: Oxford University Press, 1978), p. 253. All parenthetical page references to Hume will be to this text.

2. Barry Stroud, *Hume* (London: Routledge and Kegan Paul, 1977), p. 102. Stroud does not mention the case of an intact bit of matter, and he seems often to imply that, according to Hume, *every* judgment of identity through time is mistaken. But the passage I cited (*Treatise*, pp. 255-56), and others like it, indicate that Hume was committed to the identity of matter. (He at least was committed to this as the best philosophical position, though at some points he

does seem to treat even the best philosophical position about external reality as ultimately un-founded.) Stroud is apparently influenced by the passage in the *Treatise*, p. 201, where Hume distinguishes obscurely between "identity" and "unity" (see *Hume*, p. 103); but I do not think that this passage indicates that Hume would deny the strict truth of statements about the iden-tity (or persistence or unity) through time of matter.

3. Cf. *Hume*, p. 119: "The identity of an object through time is not something we ever find in our experience. . . . [I] t is not something we directly observe."

4. This is surely what he means when he says that "the constancy of our perception makes us ascribe to them a perfect numerical identity, tho' there be very long intervals betwixt their appearance, and they have only one of the essential qualities of identity, *viz. invariableness*" (p. 202).

5. Bertrand Russell, "The Relation of Sense-Data to Physics" in *Mysticism and Logic* (London: George Allen and Unwin, 1917), p. 171. For further discussion of the relationship between identity and continuity, see my *The Concept of Identity* (New York and Oxford: Oxford University Press, 1982), especially Chapters 1, 4, and 7.

6. Hume does suggest that someone who is trying to conceive of the atoms in contact "can aid his fancy by conceiving these points to be of different colours, the better to prevent their coalition and confusion" (p. 41). But it seems clear that we are ultimately to conceive of atoms of any sort as capable of contact. Note that the possibility of continuously passing from one (whole) atom to another arises only for Hume's minimal atoms, not for the physicist's ex-tended atoms and subatomic particles. But it seems doubtful that we can analyze the identity of matter in terms of the physicist's particles, for we would then have to regard it as a priori that matter is (at every level) particulate rather than (at some level) continuous.

7. *The Whole Works of Joseph Butler* (London, 1836); Thomas Reid, *Works* (Edinburgh, 1863). Relevant excerpts from Butler and Reid are found in John Perry, ed., *Personal Identity* (Berkeley: University of California Press, 1975).

8. Reid, *Works*, p. 344 (in Perry, ed., *Personal Identity*, p. 108). Cf. *The Whole Works of Joseph Butler*, p. 263 (in Perry, ed., *Personal Identity*, p. 99): "Now, when it is asked wherein personal identity consists the answer should be the same as if it were asked, wherein consists similitude or equality; that all attempts to define, would but perplex it." That Butler held that the identity of matter is genuine comes out clearly in *The Whole Works of Joseph Butler*, p. 265 (in Perry, ed., *Personal Identity*, p. 101).

9. However, we cannot say that the idea of identity is "simple" in Hume's terminology, for he apparently makes the blanket assumption that all relations are "complex" (p. 13), pre-sumably on the grounds that the idea of a relation must involve at least the idea of the things related. But it seems clear that he regards the most basic spatial and temporal relations as inde-finable; on my suggestion, he regards identity in the same way. (He includes identity "in its strictest sense" together with the spatial and temporal relations in his list of "the sources" of all relations [p. 14]. I can draw no clear support from this fact, however, since he also includes causality on that list, though he presumably goes on to treat causality as definable.)

10. Stroud, *Hume*, p. 102.

11. One might perhaps have expected him to hold that an impression can have duration only if it is the impression of persisting matter. That cannot be correct, however, since in the passage last cited from the *Treatise*, p. 56, he is describing someone who has only kinesthetic experience and hence no experience of space or matter.

12. See also his statement on the following page that we make a judgment of identity about an object that is not continuously present to our senses "whenever we conclude, that if we had kept our eye or hand constantly upon it, it wou'd have convey'd an invariable and uninter-rupted perception" (p. 74).

13. Stroud, *Hume*, p. 98, cites this passage but apparently without seeing its implications.

14. See Sydney Shoemaker, "Identity, Properties, and Causality" in Peter A. French, Theodore E. Uehling, Jr., and Howard K. Wettstein, eds., *Midwest Studies in Philosophy*, Vol. IV, *Studies in Metaphysics* (Minneapolis: University of Minnesota Press, 1979), pp. 321-42.

Note that, though Hume relates causality to the "fictitious" cases of identity (e.g., on p. 255), causality does not seem to figure in his account of the identity of matter.

15. Another major difficulty with the causal account of identity is that the causal laws required by the account seem already to presuppose identity. See Shoemaker, "Identity, Properties, and Causality," p. 337.

16. See Reid, *Works*, p. 345 (in Perry, ed., *Personal Identity*, p. 111): "We probably at first derive our notion of identity from that natural conviction which every man has from the dawn of reason of his own identity and continued existence." It is, however, unclear whether Reid intends the maneuver I am concerned with.

17. Elsewhere he says that "we may suppose, but never can conceive a specific difference betwixt an object and an impression" (p. 241), and "[t] he farthest we can go towards a conception of external objects when suppos'd *specifically* different from our perceptions, is to form a relative idea of them, without pretending to comprehend the related objects" (p. 68).

18. For this common use of 'genidentity', see, e.g., Rudolph Carnap, *Introduction to Symbolic Logic* (New York: Dover Publications, 1958), p. 198.

19. The difficulty does not arise for the first approach because the rule that transforms genidentity statements into identity statements ensures the entailment.

20. If our idea of the identity of matter is not definable in experiential terms, must we then say the same even of our idea of the ("fictitious") identity of an ordinary body? Only if the latter idea depends upon the former. If the latter idea is definable on the basis of spatiotemporal and qualitative continuity (under a sortal), then there may be no such dependence, unless, of course, spatiotemporal or qualitative continuity depends upon the identity of matter.

21. There are some complicated possibilities that I here ignore. It might be suggested that a statement of identity is "ultimate" if it is not equivalent to any statement about a succession that is *more* basic than it, even if it is equivalent to a statement about a succession that is *equally* basic. Hence, if identity statements and genidentity statements are equally basic, perhaps *both* kinds of statements could be regarded as "ultimate" in this sense. But neither kind of statement would be ultimate in the stronger sense of being ineliminable in terms of an equally basic statement.

22. *The Whole Works of Joseph Butler*, pp. 264-65 (in Perry, ed., *Personal Identity*, p. 100).

23. Reid, *Works*, p. 346 (in Perry, ed., *Personal Identity*, p. 112).

24. Is it possible that Butler and Reid were swayed by either of the following fallacious arguments? *A*: (1) Identity statements about matter are strict, whereas identity statements about ordinary bodies are loose. (2) Therefore, there is a strict sense of identity statements about ordinary bodies in which they are equivalent to identity statements about matter. (Even if [1] is true, [2] does not follow.) *B*: (1) Identity statements about ordinary bodies are loose. (2) Since they are loose (and hence not strict), they are not strictly correct. (3) Since they are not strictly correct, they are strictly incorrect, i.e., their denials are strictly correct. (Compare this with arguing that since "Reagan is rich" is loose, "Reagan is not rich" is strictly correct.)

25. For further elaboration of this idea, see my *The Concept of Identity*, Chapter 8.

26. Hume explains the illusion by saying that the felt "smoothness" of our thought in the ultimate (genuine) case is very similar to what we feel in the case of an interrelated succession, so that we confuse the two cases (pp. 253-54). But why should this confusion generate the illusion that both are ultimate cases of identity rather than the *opposite* illusion that neither is? On my suggestion, the felt "smoothness" of our thought is just the felt naturalness of applying our identity concept, and this is what deceives us.

27. My thanks to Lloyd Carr, William James Earle, and Elinor West for their helpful suggestions on this paper.

Kant on Intuition

ARTHUR MELNICK

K ant characterizes sensible intuition as an immediate representation, where one is affected by what is represented and where what is represented must be present.[1] This looks very much like a characterization of the use of a demonstrative term such as 'this'. For Kant, space and time are the forms of intuition and sensation its matter. If we identify this as what goes on around me (here) now, we do connect the demonstrative with space and time. On a relational theory, what is here could be roughly interpreted as what is near to me (to my body), and what is here now as what is near to me and simultaneous with my being affected. In this way, the demonstratives of space and time (here and now) are "reduced" to the demonstrative of things (this) and to spatio-temporal relations. On one version of an absolute theory, what is here is what is at this place and what is here now is what is at this place at this time. Demonstrations of space and time (here and now) are on a par with those of things (this). It should be clear that Kant can accept neither of these views, since he rejects any objectivist accounts of space and time, whether relational or absolute.

A third alternative is to insist that the use of demonstratives involves besides affection by or sensation of things, accompanying gesturing behavior. Thus, one is to point or sweep out or to circumscribe, and it is this latter behavior that "converts" mere sensation into singular representation. On this view, here is replaced by spatial *behavior* introduced by the subject. If we consider this behavior to be carried out in imagination, we can talk of pointing or sweeping out or drawing out our attention in order to be affected. For the rest of this paper, however, I will stick to publicly observable behavior. On this view, the spatial component of immediate representation is what prefixes being affected. What of the temporal component? Suppose I am writing and marking time by tapping and at a certain stage (tap) I circumscribe, thus drawing out my attention and being affected by something. Here, temporizing behavior governs or prefixes the spatializing-cum-being-affected. At least on this analysis of immediate representation, space and time are neither things nor relations of things but rather behavior contributed by the subject.

Demonstrative representation is singular representation par excellence. We ought, however, to be able to singularly represent what is absent (either spatially or temporally remote). Suppose, then, we try to generalize the relational and absolute views to cover what is, say, spatially remote. When the object is present I can say, 'This which is near to me (to this body)', with sensation covering the use of 'this'. Suppose, however, the object is spatially remote so that sensation cannot be had. Then we are left with the mere conceptual indication of the object as 'The x such that x is so-and-so spatially related to me'. In the attempt to generalize upon demonstratives, we are brought to conceptual representation or representation by thought (definite descriptions). The same situation occurs in the absolute case. Absent places cannot be sensed (even if present places can) and so 'This which is at this place' can only be extended as 'The x such that x is at the place y such that y is so-and-so related to this place'. On the behavioral view, however, we can extend, so to speak, the behavior. A generalization of circumscribing, for example, is to move about or to take steps and then to circumscribe. Pointing or circumscribing or finger gesturing, that is, can be extended by foot behavior. *Mere* finger gesturing, then, becomes just a special case of spatial behavior that is not prefixed by other (moving-about) spatial behavior. Moving about, circumscribing, and being affected is a Kantian intuition (outer intuition). Our capacity to be affected is just such moving about.

The reason neither the relational nor the absolute versions of immediate representation can be generalized to encompass the absent is that both invoke only passive sensation in the singular terms that indicate what is present. On the relational view, what is before me and its spatial relation to me is sensed; on the absolute view, what is before me and where it is, or its place, is sensed. It is the sensation alone that has a role in the use of demonstrative terms. Since *ex hypothesi* what is absent (whether thing or place or spatial relation) cannot be sensed, there is nothing to underlie the use of a demonstrative term with respect to what is absent, and so we are left with only a conceptual means of reference. On the behavioral view, the absent is "covered" by, in effect, the behavior that makes it present.

Moving about and then circumscribing in order to be affected is a generalization with regard to the absent of simply circumscribing and being affected with regard to what is present. One may object that this is not much of a generalization, for what we really wanted was a mode of singularly representing the absent that did not require making it present. Besides one may object, what we really wanted to generalize to the absent was not demonstratives but singular representation, and definite description either as on the relational or absolute view provided for such singular representation of the absent. Let us consider the first objection. What is demanded, we may say, is that our representations be 'spontaneous'; i.e., that independently of my accidental situation in the world I be able here and now to represent what is absent. Animals, after all, can move about and be affected. What is required (and what constitutes thought) is the ability to represent the absent without actually changing our position vis-à-vis things. This means that we must superimpose thought upon

Kantian intuition. How then is thought to be related to or imposed upon behavior? The answer seems obvious. Thought must provide the rule for or guide behavior. Thus, we can prescribe 'Move about Circumscribe and Be affected'. This prescription is spontaneous in the sense we want, namely, giving the prescription does not require actually changing our position, rather it is what produces or guides or provides the rule for such behavior. Since we move in steps (by taking steps), we can write instead as a schema for a singular thought 'Take n steps Circumscribe Be affected'. The special case, then, of representing what is present will just be 'Take 0 steps Circumscribe Be affected'. Here, the role of thought is to direct or to govern or, indeed, to produce behavior. The first objection, then, is unfair in demanding spontaneity of representation of the generalizations ('Moving about Circumscribing Being Affected') without thought being added or imposed. The behavioral generalization comes in two steps. First, intuition apart from thought (viz., behavior-cum-affection) is generalized and *then* thought is brought in as the rule or guide that allows spontaneity. In the behavioral case, there is a pure manifold (spatial behavior) for prescriptions (thought) regarding the absent to govern or bear upon (by producing the behavior), which is an extension of what thought regarding the present governs or bears upon. It is this that is missing in the relational or absolute cases, for in these cases thought regarding the absent is radically distinct from thought regarding the present. Reference to the present is mediated by sensation, whereas reference to the absent is purely conceptual (unmediated by sensation or anything else with respect to the absent except predicative [conceptual] conditions). What we have in the behavioral case is parity of reference. The thought in all cases is simply a referral to things via the performance of behavior. The difference is simply how much behavior is prescribed.

The second objection, recall, was that definite descriptions provide the generalization to singular representation of the absent, and that this, not some generalization of demonstrative representation, is all that is important. I think for Kant it is false that thought can go beyond intuition as required in definite descriptions. There is nothing extraconceptual that backs up or interprets the specification of the subject in a definite description. It has to be a case, then, of thought itself being adequate to give itself (us) an absent object. But for Kant thought without intuition is empty. The definite description selects an object from a range of objects. Unless the range (the candidates for selection) is somehow provided, the description merely provides the idea of being an (only) object of a certain (*infima*) sort. If the candidates for selection are all before me in sensation, then a description can pick out one of them by conceptual discrimination. In the case of what is absent, one may say the range for all our descriptions are just the actual objects or the objects there are, etc. This latter specification, however, is itself a plural selection (or selection of a collection) that merely provides the idea of being a plurality or set of actual objects without there being anything to which to apply the idea. Definite descriptions are supposed to extend the scope of reference beyond the present by specification of predicative conditions. Whether these conditions invoke spatial terms or not, they are predicative (include relations) conditions. Predicative conditions require, they do not provide, a range of potential satisfiers. Descriptions (whether singular or plural) are by themselves *implicit* definitions of objects, specifying standards or requirements for how things must be for the description to refer. Unless, however, the range of things that are to be assessed (selected) by such standards or requirements can be represented, there is no relation of the description to any object.

In short, definite descriptions do not provide singular reference to the absent at all. On the relational and absolute views, the role of space in relation to the representation of absent objects is as being part of a relational condition conceptually specifying objects. On both views, then, singular representation of the absent is impossible. On Kant's behavioral view, the role of space is to be that behavior that enable us to obtain affection. In what sense can the behavioral prescriptions be regarded as singular representations? Note, first, that we have something like a causal theory of reference, only the direction of causation is from the representer to the represented rather than vice versa as on a causal theory of names. The prescription to take steps and be affected produces the behavior that leads to the represented. Second, the causal relationship is encompassing, systematic, and in the grasp of the individual subject. We do not have names for everything, and what we have names for is accidental or circumstantial. There will be spatially remote objects for which there are no names but that are in the compass of one's directed behavior. We do not have a way of creating new names systematically (independent of the accidents of our circumstances), but we do (if we can recite numerals) have a way of systematically creating new prescriptions ('Take n steps', 'Take n + 1 steps', etc.). Even if I am causally attached to an object in my use of a name, via the community, I may not grasp that I am nor is there anything in my state (the use of the name) that I am thereby conscious of as putting me in a relation to the object. Either of these would require representing the causal attachment itself, which would have to be done apparently by definite description. Reference is a peculiarly unself-conscious affair on the causal theory of names. On the behavioral theory, the prescription-cum-thereby-subsequent-behavior is all in my ken. Further, the prescription is syntactically structured to mirror or to picture (viz., to produce) corresponding elements in the subsequent behavior. The prescription is not only productive of the behavior but systematically isomorphic to components of that behavior. For example, the order of behavior corresponds to the order of utterance in the prescription. In these ways the prescriptive theory combines the systematicity and the structuredness of descriptions, with the "going beyond mere (internal) thought" of names.

All this, of course, does not show that the behavioral theory suffices as a general theory of singular representation. There is, for example, singular representation of the (remote) *past* to consider. Note, however, that it is an extension of demonstratives that, then, are not just the singular terms par excellence but the singular terms tout court. These episodes of prescription-guiding behavior are extensions, for example, of Russell's logically proper names in that what affects (the upshot of the entire episode) is literally a component of the representation (the episode). Further, these representations (like good demonstratives) are preontological; they do not invoke any settling of issues of identity. Not only are they demonstratives, they are pure demonstratives in that it is circumscriptive behavior alone that delineates the referent without sortal accompaniment. Finally, and most importantly, these terms are not eliminable in favor of names and or definite descriptions (of the speaker, the time, etc.). A representative or exhibitive use of 'this' (involving sensation) cannot be analyzed as 'The x such that x is present to the y such that y is a "this" utterer'. Description of (thought of) exhibiting or sensing will not make do for actually doing it, for it is only the latter that gives an object (as a satisfier of the description). Similarly, in our generalization, the prescription-cum-behavior is not eliminable in favor of the *thought* of carrying out the behavior ('the x such that x would be met with if I were to take n steps'). This latter definite description, no more than any other, can provide singular reference.

One may now reraise the issue of whether we have provided for the spontaneity of representation. In our discussion so far, the actual compliant behavior has been considered as a literal part of the singular representation. In one sense, the representation episode is spontaneously initiable, without first making the object present, but is not completable except by the behavior that makes the object present. Connected with this is the point that thought (even referential thought) is not always productive of behavior but is information that can be held in reserve. The way to separate the thought from the behavior is to defuse the prescriptive force in favor of the *legitimacy* of so behaving. We would have then as a canonical singular representation 'It is legitimate to take n steps Circumscribe Be affected'. In effect, then, singular thought is inhibited action or behavior.[2] Note that, unlike the relational or absolute views, there is in the case of the absent as well as the present something, some behavior, to inhibit. It is not true that what underlies definite descriptions is inhibited sensation, for example. The behavioral theory, that is, retains parity as between the present and the remote even in achieving full spontaneity.

The issue, as we have presented it, is not how thought can relate to reality but how thought can be separated from reality. On the behavioral view, it is not a matter of thought itself being adequate to represent or reflect reality, but a matter of thought producing contact with reality. This productive capacity is then overridden or inhibited by other purposes, for it may be important to know what to do even if it is also important that one does not do it. The push to defuse prescription in favor of legitimacy comes also from another source. Not all spatial prescriptions are compatible. Suppose we prefix rotation to step taking so as to encompass (for Kant, produce) different spatial directions. Then the following two prescriptions are incompatible.

(1) Rotate r_1 units Take n steps Circumscribe Be affected.

(2) Rotate r_2 units Take n steps Circumscribe Be affected.

Indeed (1) and (2) are *alternative* prescriptions that cannot both be performed. What is true, however, is that both (1) and (2) are legitimate. It is legitimate to do (1) and also it is legitimate to do (2).

Singular terms enter into atomic propositions by being combined with predicates. How is a prescription to behave and be affected to be completed into a bipolar atomic representation? The answer surely has to be further behavior predicated upon the spatial-behavior-cum-affection. For example, one is to 'Take n steps Circumscribe Be affected React ϕ', where to react ϕ is a way of reacting that is an empirical (as opposed to a Kantian pure) concept. An atomic *relational* representation could be expressed as:

(3) Take n steps Circumscribe Be affected (while you)

Take m steps Circumscribe Be affected (and then) React ϕ^2.

Here we have a two-place reaction, or a reaction to be made only upon a dual circumscription-cum-affection. Predication itself then is put into prescriptive form (reaction predicated upon other action).

Prescriptions or legitimations can be completed in ordinary language descriptively. One can say, 'Go to the store. You'll see they have new shoes', in which what is in effect a prediction expresses the consequence of behaving. Suppose we attempt in a similar manner to graft predication onto prescriptions to spatially behave. We would have then:

(4) Take n steps: Be affected: The x such that x affects there (then) is ϕ.

Since a predicate in descriptive form requires a subject, we have grafted on a subject as well as predicate. Example (4) is approximately of the form 'Go to the store. The clerk you will meet is nervous'. In this latter, the prefixed prescription might even be regarded as a way of fixing the referent of the otherwise ambiguous description 'the clerk' (or 'the clerk will meet you'). Generalizing, we might say that in (4) itself the prefixed prescription provides the range of potential satisfiers for the consequent descriptive term, thus avoiding our objections against definite descriptions. Note, however, that what comes with this grafting is a grafting back on of objectivist views of space, for in the description itself is a spatial cross-reference back to the prescription, and the means of this cross-reference will either be relational or absolute. We will either have 'The x such that x is at that place and affects is ϕ' or 'The x such that x is then in front of you is ϕ' or some such term. For Kant it is not only true that space is the form of our capacity to be affected but also that space is *merely* or *nothing but* this form. It is not (even *also*) a determination of things. This latter, of course, is the aspect of Kant's position that gave rise to Trendlenburg's famous objection. It is further part of Kant's position that thought pertains only to appearance. Now, appearance is what corresponds to the matter (the passive component) of intuition, whose form is productive spatial behavior. Appearances exist only in (in our case, outer) intuition, only in what Kant calls the 'regress' of representations. Further, Kant warns us not to anticipate "what is present in the object as it is in itself, prior to all regress"[3] Being affected upon circumscribing is something that obtains or occurs only in (actually carrying out) the regress, whereas the descriptive consequent in (4) is an attempt to anticipate (by thought) the object that is there to be met with upon carrying out the regress. Not only does (4) then also make space an objective determination, but it makes appearance (what is given only in passive affection subsequent to spatial behavior) *also* a thing in itself (a thing represented as *also* existing independent of or prior to the behavior-cum-affection as waiting to be met with). It should be clear then that Kant is absolutely commited to denying the feasibility of (4) and thus denying (in our terms) that prescription and behavior simply provide the range of potential satisfiers for descriptive reference.

Kant's argument against (4) is just the argument of the First Antinomy. The mathematical antinomies concern not singular representation but general representation. We have to understand first what a general prescription is. What we are asking for is the prescriptive version of the universal and existential quantifiers. A universalization of the prescription to 'take n steps' is not to take all steps, for we suppose the latter, which directs us to complete an infinite task, is absurd. If we just drop the limitation n, we have the unlimited prescription to take steps. In a straightforward sense, there is no limitation in the prescription. We can write this lack of limitation explicitly by prescribing to *take steps freely*. An alternative way of expressing the sense we want is to direct (oneself or others) to *keep taking steps*. The former is analogous to 'any', whereas the latter is the analogue of 'all', but for present purposes we will treat them as equivalent. We can then transcribe '$\forall x \phi x$' as:

(5) Take$_x$ steps freely (as you do keep) Be$_x$ (ing) Affected (keep) React (ing) ϕ.

In (5) the parenthetical additions are used to fill in the prescriptive sense of the cross-reference between step taking and the consequent affection-cum-reaction. They are only parenthetical in order to keep things syntactically 'close to' formal quantification. The 'x' appears, as in quantification theory, simply to keep track of the cross-reference (of consequent affection-cum-reaction) to different quantifiers (step takings). Note that what plays the role of the *free* variable 'x' is 'Be$_x$ affected'. 'React ϕ', of course, is the prescriptive transcription of predication. The transcription of the atomic 'ϕa_m' is:

(6) Take m steps Be affected React ϕ.

The individual constant 'a_m' in (6) is 'Take m steps Be affected.' Suppose now one wants to transcribe prescriptively '$\forall x \forall y \ \psi^2 xy$'. Let us first write an instance.

(7) Take m steps Be affected (while you) Take n steps Be affected React ψ^2.

To generalize, replace the individual constants in (6) by free variables; i.e., replace the step-taking prefix in the constant to the left with 'Be affected', which is approximately a blank space that can then be labeled 'x', 'y', etc. We get then the analogue of the open sentence '$\psi^2 xy$', viz.:

(8) Be$_x$ affected Be$_y$ affected React ψ^2.

We then prefix the prescriptive quantifiers to get the generalization:

(9) Take$_x$ steps freely Take y steps freely Be$_x$ affected Be$_y$ affected React ψ^2.

The sense of (9) is "Keep taking steps being affected. As you do keep taking the steps being (secondly) affected and Reacting ψ (on the basis of a double affection)."

Note that the universal prescription is not a prescription to complete an infinite task; rather it is an incomplete prescription. I realize there are deep issues over the sense of such a prescription, but for our purposes the only matter we insist on is, whatever else, it is not a prescription to *complete* a task.

The transcription of '∃xφx' can be written:

(10) Take$_x$ steps until Be$_x$ affected React φ.

In (10) the consequent affection-cum-reaction limits which (number of) steps to take. There is no definite prescription to take K, K + 1, or K + 2 steps. Instead of "naming," so to speak, how many steps to take, one "indefinitely" specifies it as "however many steps are needed to . . . ." This, I think, is thoroughly analogous to the relation between specifying an individual descriptively by predicative condition (∃xφx or perhaps ∃!xφx) versus naming an individual (φa).

I will simply report that one can devise a complete prescriptive quantification theory incorporating analogues of truth-functional connectives operating between open sentences and also between closed sentences. One can assign semantic values to prescriptions ("it is legitimate to," "it is not legitimate to") and devise a classic two-valued logic and a Tarskian semantics that uses a prescriptive metalanguage. In general, what plays the role of a domain is a staged ordered activity (step taking, reciting numerals, bisecting, and making free choices of zeros and ones to form a sequence would all be examples). If so, note one surprising consequence. On the behavioral view, we can achieve full quantificational generality without any ontological commitment or any settlement of identity issues. The general representations are as neutral as the singular representations. The cross-referential role of variables then is severed from any ontological burden.

Let us return now to the issue. Recall that the singular representation alternative to treating predication as a consequent prescription to react was: (4) Take n steps: (1x) (x is there then) is φ. Suppose now we try to generalize (4). We get:

(11) Take steps freely: The x's that are along the way are φ (or some equivalent form that has a descriptive consequent).

Recall that the prescription to take steps was meant to provide a range for selection (a range of potential satisfiers) for the descriptive consequent. In (11), however, there is no definite (completed) range provided, so that the *totality* expressed in the consequent would have to be an incomplete totality or plurality of objects. But the notion of an incomplete or unfinished plurality of entities is absurd. Indefiniteness or incompletability (the potential infinite) can pertain to rules or directions or prescriptions, but it cannot pertain to things. "The x's that are along the way" in (11) comes out referring to an increasing totality. Now to say it is an increasing reference is all right, but that is just to say the right hand side of (11) is not a definite reference but an open scheme for reference. But then (11) ought to be written:

(12) Take steps freely: It keeps being legitimate to say 'These x's so far are φ'.

However, (12) has an essentially metalinguistic component that demands some sort of disquotation. What we have just seen is that it cannot be disquoted as (11) without commitment to the absurd notion of an indefinite totality of things. One could avoid this objection by converting (11) into:

(13) Take *all* steps: The x's that are along the way are ϕ.

In (13) we have a definite ("completed" infinite) totality, which by itself is not absurd but does require the prefixed infinite prescription to finish, which is absurd. Thus, if we try to represent descriptively things waiting there to be met with then in the general case, we either have an indefinite totality of things (as in [11]) or an infinite prescription to behave (as in [13]), both of which are absurd. Thus, on pain of failure in generalizing, even the singular representation must have a prescriptive, rather than a descriptive, consequent. We have then an "indirect" proof (through the detour of universalization) that terms such as (4), which (a) treat what exists in appearance as also a thing in itself (there to be met with) and which (b) make space a determination of things in addition to the mere form of behavior that makes us liable to be affected, are impossible. This argument can be extended to the Second Antinomy by considering bisection (dividing) as the activity rather than step taking.

Prescriptive generality then does not invoke any notion of totality. The reason, of course, is that it does not invoke or presuppose any notion of individual entities at all. The individuation in purely prescriptive generality is all in the *staging* of the activity (moving about, for example, is marked out into steps or units). Where then does ontology (issues of what counts as one thing) come in, in a prescriptive language? It cannot be by the grafting of descriptive reference onto prescriptions. How can there be issues of identity, then, if there are no individuals? Before answering this question, let us ask it in other (equivalent) ways. How is it possible to represent the past if the only function of thought is to guide behavior? No prescribing or legitimizing (permitting) of behavior seems to be able to cover the past. We cannot be directed to what was. So far, moving about and being affected (a Kantian intuition) has been unified by Kant's concepts of quantity and quality. The moving about has been demarcated into units (steps), and sensation has been incorporated into singular representation by the prescription to be affected. What, however, is the role of dynamical categories such as substance? These three issues of identity, the past, and substance are obviously interconnected. We will see now that they really are the same issue.

Let us begin with representation of the past. The closest thing we have to a demonstrative in ordinary language is a term such as 'that, which just went by'. Once again, there can be both relational and absolute versions of this term, but, once again, such versions when extended to the remote past give us only definite descriptions. The latter not only fail to be an extension of demonstratives, they fail to be an extension of singular representation, period. With respect to the immediate past, 'the x that just went by' together with sensation or being affected could be interpreted along the lines of Kaplan's D that operator[4] as a definite description involving the referent itself in its semantics. This formal semantics has application in this case via the sensation of the referent that is a crucial (even semantic) feature of the use of the term. With regard to the remote past (too remote for any baptism), there is nothing to give application to the formal idea of the D that operator. The D that operator converts definite descriptions into what we can say, are extensions of ordinary demonstrative terms (or at least into extensions of singular representation not open to our charges against definite descriptions). The only trouble is it gives no sense to how there could be such terms when the crucial role of sensation, which gives application to the formal semantics, is dropped.

Let us attempt then a behavioral interpretation of the demonstrative with respect to the immediate past. Roughly, thought governs past behavior by summarizing rather than by prescribing, which summarizing is marked by gerundive phrases. Suppose we try then as an interpretation of the demonstrative something like:

(14) Taking 4 steps Up to 4 Being (first) affected Reacting ϕ.

Example (14) is meant to correspond to the atomic sentence 'That which just went by is ϕ'. We are to assume that for (14) one recites numerals as one takes steps and summarizes what one has just been doing, how and at what stage of proceeding one has passively reacted. A special case of (14) would be where one has not been taking steps at all but has just been marking one's time. We can write this as:

(15) Taking 0 steps Up to 4 Being (first) affected Reacting ϕ.

The situation envisaged for (15) is as follows. Instead of reacting ϕ (actually verbalizing 'ϕ' upon being affected), one delays or temporizes in one's reaction while one marks time and then verbalizes (15). In this way, *temporizing behavior* underlies the training in and use of summarizing forms such as (14) and (15). We have then in these cases a Kantian outer intuition governed by time (spatial behavior governed by temporal behavior) and then unified by thought (by the summary). There is being affected, moving about (or not) and delaying all brought under the unity of (summarizing) thought.

How, however, can (14) be extended to the remote past? One can no more summarize behavior-cum-affection that one has not performed than one can sense the remote past. Recall that in the future-oriented (prescriptive) case, we defuse the necessity of *actually* behaving by defusing the prescription in favor of mere legitimacy to so-and-so. Suppose, then, we try this with (15). We get:

(16) It is legitimate to be Taking 0 steps (to be) Up to 4 and (to be first) reacting ϕ.

In (16), we have defused the summarizing force, but in favor of what? In the future-oriented case, legitimacy was, in effect, still a permission whose realization still lay in behavior open to us to perform. What makes it legitimate to so-and-so can still be shown by proceeding to actually behave.

Consider now the following situation. There is a disordered array of blocks in a room and a person arranging them in a certain pattern, say, as follows:

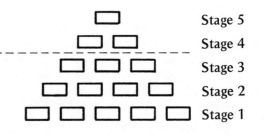

A child (who is being trained in the use of gerundives) enters the room, say, at stage 4. He or she watches the person pile on the two blocks and then finally the top block. The child can be trained to represent what he or she is coming in upon as a procedure that extends back beyond anything he or she has done or seen done, i.e., back to what relative to him or her is the remote past. He or she sees these stages but also sees the whole product (the arrangement). With respect to the product he or she sees, he or she understands that a procedure extending back beyond the stages he or she sees is a (the) legitimate procedure (for producing the product). Alternatively, he or she understands (via the apprehension of the product) that a way of proceeding is legitimate that goes beyond (and indeed is required in order for) the stages he or she sees. He or she understands, that is, that he or she is coming in upon (*in medias res*) a legitimate procedure. We can express this as: 'Upon Seeing the Product, it is legitimate to be Piling, to be Up to 5, and to be first grouping five blocks together'. Let us regard now taking steps and reciting numerals and reacting as a procedure (of reacting, rather than piling blocks). To regard then what we are presently affected by as (also) what we come in upon (*in medias res*) is to regard it as what legitimates a procedure of reacting that goes back (has stages) beyond any actual reactions of ours. Instead of being prompted to legitimate summarizing by our present sensitivity to what we have (just) done, we are prompted to legitimate a way of proceeding based on how we are now affected by what is around us. Then, for example, instead of (or in addition to) (14) and (15), we may write:

> (17) Upon Being affected, it is legitimate to be Up to 4 (first) Circumscribing Reacting σ.

In (17) the reality that presently affects us (that is given in sensation) is the basis for a procedure which extends back before our coming in upon it (at stage 4); (17) is the behavioral analogue of this (before me) was σ (at an earlier time). Our original problem, however, was to transcribe that (which just went by) was ϕ. This can be done if we allow an extension of (17) whereby alternate spatial behavior (alternate circumscription) is also legitimated. We can write then, for example:

> (18) Upon Being affected, it is legitimate to be Up to 4 (and first) Circumscribing Reacting σ and (also) it is legitimate to be Up to 4 and First Rotating Circumscribing Reacting ϕ.

In (18) an alternate piece of behavior-cum-reaction (a "separate" circumscription that for simplicity, we have indicated merely by the instructions to perform it in a different direction) is also legitimated at the first stage. We can diagram (18) as follows:

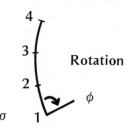

Thus, (18) can be extended in three ways. First, instead of merely alternate circumscriptive behavior, one may legitimate alternate step-taking-cum-circumscriptive behavior. Second, one can prefix (18) with step-taking behavior. Third, one can extend the temporizing backward by increasing and ultimately even generalizing the temporizing behavior legitimated. These extensions are pictured respectively as follows:

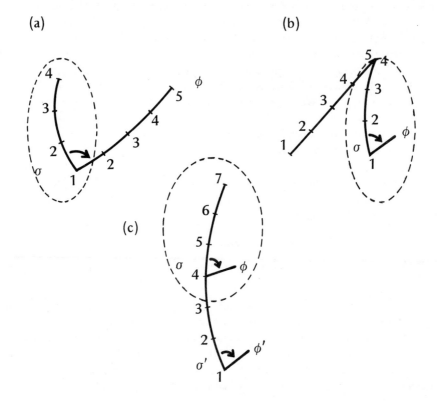

The original representation (18) is circled in each of these three extensions. These extensions of (18) have the following analogues:

(a) 'That (which was 5 units away) is ϕ'.

(b) 'That (over there 5 units away) was ϕ'.

(c) 'That (which was near 7 units ago) is ϕ'.

The latter two in particular are the direct extensions of 'That which was *just near* is ϕ', our original temporal demonstrative as interpreted behaviorally in (18). For example, (b) unloosens the 'near' restriction and (c) unloosens the 'just' restriction.

Past representation then is (i) coming in upon or (ii) taking steps to come in upon what legitimates (i)′ a procedure of reacting or (ii)′ of coming in upon or (iii)′ of taking steps to come in upon that which legitimates . . . . To express this nesting rigorously and in full generality is beyond the scope of this paper.[5]

It is with respect to what is before me that it is legitimate to be up to such and such a stage of reacting in a procedure that has previous stages. This is just what it means (prescriptively) to say that this very reality before me (what affects me) extends backward in time. We have then for the first time in (16) or (18) made an ontological move in that each of these is an expression of coming in upon what lasts or endures. That is the only way to represent the past on our view, and so to this extent there is no inscrutability or lax or relativity with respect to ontology. Only if we come in upon substances (enduring reality) can we "extend" temporizing behavior backward and so "extend" time backward.

That we have really invoked a substance ontology can be brought out as follows. Recall that for us the analogue of predication is, say, Reacting ϕ or Reacting ψ. The procedure legitimated in (16) is such reacting governed temporally (by temporizing behavior). This then would be a prescriptive analogue of *tensed* predication. Tensed predication is precisely the mark of a substance ontology as opposed to, say, a point event or a stage ontology. A nonprescriptive tensed predication theory would not have been sufficient, however. We can say 'This was ϕ' and so represent the past in terms of what is present to us. That is an improvement over a stage ontology where the best one could say is 'The stage x such that x is so-and-so related to this stage before me is ϕ', and so one would have to employ definite description to represent the past. But the tensed theory will also have to employ such description in representing the past or the history of an entity that is *not* before me. For consider the following diagram:

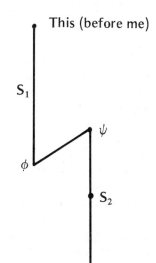

This (before me)

S_1

ψ

ϕ

S_2

where S_2 is a substance distinct from S_1 (= this) and is ψ at some step. On a non-prescriptive tensed view, we should have to represent this by 'The substance x such that x was so far from this when this was ϕ is ψ, and we still have the old problem that definite description presupposes a range of satisfiers be somehow provided. On our view, what enables us to "jump" world lines is nesting of behavioral procedures.

The prescriptive analogue of a stage or point-event ontology would be:

(19) It is legitimate to be up to 4, First Reacting ϕ,

where there is nothing with respect to which the procedure is legitimated. One is not coming in upon anything in (19), and so the legitimacy (which is in effect a modal notion) is not based in any reality or actuality. Of course, it will not do to try to legitimate the procedure in terms of the (past and gone) stage, for then one should have to say 'Upon ____, it is legitimate to be – – ing', but there is no way to fill in the first blank, except (circularly) by the very legitimacy extending backward, which one is trying to base.

Consider now the following special case of (12):

(20) Take 0 steps Circumscribe: (then) it is legitimate to say 'The x there was ϕ'.

We have argued that (20) cannot be homophonically disquoted without commitment ultimately to an indefinite totality of things upon universalization (or generality). We have now also seen that it must be disquoted not only behaviorally, but, if representation of the past is to be possible for me here now (and for who else when and where does it matter), it must be disquoted in terms that legitimate my coming in upon a procedure. The disquotation of (20), that is, is:

(21) Take 0 steps Circumscribe Upon Be affected it is legitimate to be temporizing Up to K, first Reacting ϕ.

If we consider (20) to involve the "subject-predicate" syntactic function of judgment, then its disquotation in (21) is its schematization in terms of behavior. The schema in this particular case is the permanence of the real (of what affects) that is equivalent to the legitimation of a temporizing procedure with respect to what affects. Legitimation (rules) is the province of thought as opposed to (pure or empirical) sensibility. One mode (category) of this legitimation must be of a procedure of reacting with stages precedent to what I can now perform or be up to. Note that what gets legitimated is a staged procedure of temporizing behavior-cum-reacting. What thought governs (is the rule for), then, is pure temporizing behavior (which corresponds to the form of reacting) and so thereby the reactions themselves. In (21), that is, reacting ϕ (a merely empirical reaction) is governed by temporizing behavior that in turn is *legitimated*, all of which in turn is the schema of subject-predicate. Put simply, thought pertains to or governs reactions by pertaining to or governing the behavior (spatio-temporal) in the course of which reactions can be made.

What makes the permanence of the real a *dynamical* as opposed to a *mathematical* mode of unity is that it cannot be constructed.[6] Mathematical unity (as in quantity governing one's steps) pertains to what can actually be generated by *going ahead* and behaving. This is *not* the case in (21), where one cannot *go ahead and do* anything. The dynamical modes of unity, that is, pertain to the past and "carry over" (or project) spatio-temporal behavior "into" the appearances. The behavior that is not open to us to perform is, nevertheless, legitimated with respect to what appears or what affects. We have, thus, answered our questions over how ontology, representation of the past, and nonconstructive dynamical notions arise on a behavioral theory and have validated that they are one and the same issue.

Even though dynamical unity as in (21) is not constructive (does not direct me to do or generate anything) it is, nevertheless, behavioral. The view I have been attributing to Kant looks in some respects like a version of either pragmatism, operationalism, or verificationism. It differs, however, in at least three crucial ways. First, it is not exclusively future oriented. If it is pragmatism, it is not that sort that analyzes past-tense statements in terms of present and future verifying behavior. Summarizing and coming in upon procedures are a second independent way that thought pertains to (guides, unifies, or is the rule for) behavior that is not to be "reduced to" prescription. Second, if it is operationalism, it is not that sort that is meant to provide the meaning of general terms. It is the very referential-ontological form of language (subject-predicate, quantification, etc.) that is operationalized or schematized in terms of behavior. It is as guiding behavior that thought (rules) becomes representative or referential or bears on reality at all. Third, it is not that there is a world of objects "stretched out in space and time" that we behave in in order to come to know, for space, time, and objecthood itself first get their sense from that behavior and its unity.

That it is the referential apparatus itself that is schematized (as in disquoting from [20] to [21]) in terms of *behavior* leads to the idea that not only is one ontology (substance) to be preferred to another (stages) as permitting representation of the past but also that ontology (reference) is determinate (across translation).[7] Though reference is underdetermined by the totality of stimulation, it is not underdetermined by the behavior and the unity of behavior that enables us to represent remote stimulation in the first place. Let us imagine we are allowed to observe the (idealized) language *training* as well as language use of the foreign native. The entire development of the behavioral language we have outlined can, I claim, be recognized in observable stages of idealized training. For example, we can watch the native child being trained to take steps and to associate sounds (his or her numerals) with such step takings. As he or she takes steps, he or she says "ba, be, bi, Gavagai" (for our 1, 2, 3 Rabbit*ish*). Instead of Quinean stimulations, we are beginning with Kantian intuitions. We can further observe his or her producing the right behavior in response to commands whose verbalizations share structural features with those verbalizations that, at the first stage of training, accompanied that behavior. Once we have the child prescribing and summarizing his or her own behavior as well as producing it in response to verbalization, we can begin to *observe* his or her getting the idea of the past by observing him or her completing (with verbalization) behavior that he or she did not begin. Thus, consider the case of the blocks in the room on p. 349 above. We know (hypothesize) from the first stages of observing the child's training that 'bo' is 4 and 'bu' is 5. He or she comes in the room and is trained to complete the array of blocks while verbalizing 'bo' and 'bu', and he or she appends or prefixes to it the same verbal indication as is appropriate when he or she is summarizing his or her own behavior (rather than prescribing). He or she can be so trained, and we can observe the upshot of that training and "read off" the translation of our gerundive form ("ing"). His or her novel and continued use of this form in regard to what affects him or her is then to be translated along the lines of (16) above, so that finally his or her Gavagai now indicates a permanent reality (substance).

The foregoing is to be taken as the merest sketch or outline of the observation required to "scrute" the native's reference. It is both a highly idealized and a longitudinal picture (observing the native from babyhood to adult usage). Neither of these aspects, however, is the issue. Quine's indeterminacy thesis (as pertaining to reference) is supposed to hold even for idealization (no *possible* behavior can be evidence for the native's reference) and even if observation of training is added. Quine's thesis holds because he focuses only on verbal behavior plus stimulation. He leaves out that nonverbal productive behavior (temporizing and spatializing) that verbalization in its referential aspect primarily pertains to. In Kant's terms, Quine tries to bring the logical functions of judgment to bear on sensation (Kant's "matter of intuition").

We began by equating Kant's intuition with demonstratives, but demonstratives understood as involving spatializing and temporizing behavior as well as affection or sensation in the course of such behavior. We were then able to develop a full account of singular representation as simply thought being the rule for intuition. Along the way, we have defended Kant's metaphysics of space and time. If space and time were either relational or absolute, all singular reference would have to be by definite description, which by itself (without a range of potential satisfiers) is the mere idea of *an* x that, alone among *a* set of x's, should be such and such. This is, for Kant, empty thought without content or even intellectual intuition (the idea that discursive thought itself can provide an object). Metaphysically, then, we need space and time to provide or to be the pure manifold (behavior) that supplies the content for thought (which thought serves as the rule for the behavior *and so* for the affection obtained in the course of such behavior). If singular representation is to be possible, then (if thought is to relate to reality) space and time must be the forms of (the capacities to be) affected. That space and time then are constructions rather than objective features is established on metaphysical grounds. There is a second tier, however, to any theory of space and time, namely, their status vis-à-vis mathematics and physics. We conclude by briefly considering these issues.

Of the three "classical" metaphysical theories of time (the relational, the absolute, and the tense theories), we have presented a behavioral (nondescriptive) analogue of the tense theory. The tense theory in its descriptive form treats time as being almost syncategorematic and also (thereby) as radically different than space. In our analogue version, however, neither of those two (unsatisfactory) features hold. What our analogue version shares with the classical tense theory, however, is what we can call the idea that time is, at the basis, local to or relative to substance. The basic notion, that is, is not the one time (one system of moments or the one system of relations) that stretches out (spatially) to cover everything; rather, the basic notion is the *time-of-S* (the history, or the temporal extension of a bit of reality). It is not, that is, at its base a system approach but a piece approach out of which "one single time covering everything" is to be constructed. This feature of the tense theory seems to me to make it the prime candidate for incorporation into general relativity.

We have already seen that nesting of prescriptions and gerundives can represent a topology of branching world lines up to closure under the ancestral of the relation 'can (could have) influence or can be (could have been) influenced by'.[8] What would correspond to the geometry of such a space-time is when different spatio-temporal instructions *coincided* (ended up at the very same space-time point). Let us go back to two-dimensional space. I assume that the complete geometry of the space is determined by the totality of triangles that are possible. A triangle for us is simply when two prescriptions of certain sorts coincide. Thus, to say space is Euclidean is to say (in part) that the two prescriptions:

(a) Take K steps,

(b) Rotate 90°. Take ℓ steps. Rotate 30° (in the opposite sense). Take n steps. Rotate 60°.

produce coincidence if and only if $\ell = K\sqrt{3}$ and n = 2K. Each of (a) and (b) are interpretable (with the consequent prescription to be affected) as singular representations. In this way, geometry has as its subject matter the coincidence of singular representations. The very topic of geometry is not how entities are related in themselves (to each other or to points or instants) but how singular representations are related. In the four-dimensional space time, singular representation involves three spatial parameters and an accompanying time parameter for each prescription or gerundive. The same principle holds, however, that the geometry of space-time is the coincidence of alternate singular representations. Nothing in this implies that the geometry must be Euclidean.

Kant was certainly not a relativist. He believed that the coincidence results would be the same independent of the time parameter (of how quickly one took a path), which therefore could be filtered out altogether. He believed the remaining spatial-coincidence results to be at all times Euclidean and independent of material density. Kant believed the former because local behavior (with paper and pencil, say) validates Euclidean geometry, and he simply *presumed* space to be homogeneous with respect to magnitude (what holds locally must hold in the large). Therefore, he believed, we could anticipate a priori (by carrying out local constructions) what the coincidence results of *extending* these constructions would be (or would have been). He had no good grounds, we now know, for any of these beliefs. Nevertheless, the heart of his theory of space and time survives what we now know and can provide an interpretation of what space-time is compatible with the canons of general relativity.[9] One can express the geometrical claims regarding coincidence, and that coincidence depends on the local distribution along the paths in a purely prescriptive-gerundive language. Note that, if such a language were not adequate to the expression of general relativity, that would force us to a relational or an absolute theory of space-time. Our metaphysical argument, however, would then leave us with the unsatisfactory conclusion that general relativity is incompatible with being able to extend singular representation beyond what is here now or what just went by.

APPENDIX

We would first need the gerundive existential and universal quantifiers that, without here defending, we write as follows:

Universal $\forall x \phi x \rightarrow$ Taking steps Up to x Being$_x$ affected Reacting ϕ.

Existential $\exists x \phi x \rightarrow$ Taking steps From x Being$_x$ affected Reacting ϕ.

We then need to nest prescriptions and gerundives arbitrarily via the legitimacy connection. For example, a prescription is legitimate (consequent) upon a gerundive, etc. We can motivate our rendering of the legitimacy operator as follows. Suppose I say:

(1) "If it were the play *Hamlet*, Ophelia would be going to a nunnery."

Here the fictional "reference" is in the scope of a subjunctive conditional, and we would not want to allow such reference other than in that scope. We would, however, want to allow generalization both without and within the scope to get:

(2) "For any play, if it were that play, the protagonist would not be alone." Or

(3) "If it were the play *Hamlet*, every character would be murdered."

We do not want the latter *quantification* to appear outside the scope of the subjective prefix either. If we write for (1), (2), (3), respectively:

(4) T(h,ϕo) (It is true in *Hamlet* that . . .).

(5) ($\forall$x T(x, ψ(wϕw)) (For any play, it is true in that play that . . .).

(6) T(h, $\forall$wϕw) (It is true in *Hamlet* that . . .),

then we interpret the subjunctive as a two-place operator whose first place is for an individual (constant or variable quantifiable from without) and whose second place is sentential or propositional with "exclusively in-scope" variables w. It turns out that one can provide a syntax, rules of inference, and a (homophonic in T) semantics that provide a complete theory of how quantification (both in and out) comports with the T operator. The prescriptive analogue then is as follows. Consider:

(7) Take$_x$ steps freely Upon Be$_x$ affected, it is legitimate to (be) Taking steps From$_w$ Being$_w$ affected Reacting ϕ.

We already know the steps takings are analogues of quantifiers. We take legitimacy to be the analogue of the T operator to get that (7) is the intended translation of the formal sentence:

(8) $\forall$x L(x, $\forall$wϕw),

when the quantifiers are given a prescriptive semantics and L is taken as a homophonic two-place operator. Arbitrary (*finitely* arbitrary) nestings of legitimacy are then allowable with all degrees of relative constraining of variables to scope. We get, for example:

(9) $\forall x\, L(x,\, \exists w\, L(w,\, \forall z \psi z))$

as the formal representative of extending (7) by another legitimacy, viz., of:

(10) Take$_x$ steps Freely Upon Be$_x$ affected, it is legitimate to (be) Taking$_w$ steps From Being$_w$ affected, *it is legitimate to Take$_z$ steps freely Be$_z$ affected React ψ.*

It turns out that if we try to give a multiple quantification rather than a homophonic semantics, we wind up prescribing (or permitting) *incompatible* behavior. We want rather the consequent legitimations to be in force *only* upon the prefixed behavior that legitimates it. To take them out of context is analogous to taking reference to Ophelia out of the *Hamlet* context.

Even a single language that allows arbitrary finite nesting of L's is not sufficient for full spatio-temporal generality, for no one such sentence, no matter how many L's there are in it, covers paths beyond the last nest. This is remedied by going to another interpretation (model) of the same formalism (snytax + formal semantics) in which one is told to produce nests of *instructions*, and, consequent upon each instruction, it is legitimated to carry them out. If then one allows freely producing in order finite instructions (composed of prescriptions and gerundives), one can represent complete spatio-temporal generality in single sentences. For example, "Everything (in space-time) is ϕ" gets written prescriptively as:

(11) Take$_x$ steps freely (in producing instructions for doing and summarizing) Upon Produce$_x$ it is legitimate to Take$_w$ steps freely (in carrying out instructions) Be$_w$ affected React ϕ.

where (11) can be expressed completely within *first*-order quantification theory with the L operator. Intuitively, (11) says that, no matter how often one zigzags or cuts from one world line to another (*beginning*, of course, with where/when one is) and no matter how far one follows (forward or back) such branching world lines, one is affected so as to react ϕ. Pictorially, we have, for example:

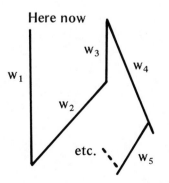

where each branching corresponds to a switch from prescription to gerundive in the instructions. Any branching from any point of any world line is also covered. Physically, this corresponds to the scope of reality being closed under the *ancestral* of the relation 'could have or could yet signal (influence) or be signaled (influenced) by'. Only topologies that allow reality that is infinitely disjoint (beyond the reach of the ancestral of the relation) are not covered. Still, we have allowed for world lines that are forever disjoint from a world line such as w_1 going back or forward from me now. Of course, it is to be understood throughout this appendix that one is to add other local parameters of rotation, marking time, etc., to get the full dimensionality of space-time.

Notes

1. Immanuel Kant, *Critique of Pure Reason*, trans. Norman Kemp Smith, (MacMillan & Co., London, 1963), p. 65, A19, B33.

2. I owe this point, as well as many others in this paper, to David Shwayder.

3. *Critique of Pure Reason*, p. 450, A509, B537.

4. David Kaplan, "Dthat" in *Contemporary Perspectives in the Philosophy of Language*, Peter A. French, Theodore E. Uehling, Jr., and Howard K. Wettstein, eds., (Morris: University of Minnesota, Morris, 1979), pp. 383-400.

5. See the Appendix (pp. 356-58) for a rough outline.

6. *Critique of Pure Reason*, p. 210, A179, B222.

7. I have in mind, of course, Quine. See Willard Von Orman Quine, *Word and Object* (Cambridge, Mass.: MIT Press, 1960), Chapter 2.

8. See the Appendix (pp. 356-58).

9. By this I mean that the *statement* that two prescriptions coincide, as well as the dependency of coincidence upon where and when prescriptions are made and upon the local distribution of matter, can be expressed purely in the language outlined in the Appendix. Whether this is sufficient to interpret the full formalism of Riemannian geometry in relativity theory is a more difficult matter.

The Skeptical Attack
on Substance: Kantian Answers

MOLTKE S. GRAM

Kant has commonly been said to have attempted a refutation of skeptical doubts about both the existence and the perceptual availability of substances. The complexity and force of that answer has, however, gone largely ignored. Giorgio Tonelli has given us the first thorough review of pre-Kantian attacks on substance and its place in Kant's thought in 1769. He summarizes the standard, received view as follows: For the Kant of 1769, "we are not able to know a subject independently of its predicates"; "[t]he idea of substance arises in the internal sense when we want to represent to ourselves something as distinct from us"; and, finally, "[t]he notions of a subject and a predicate are metaphysical notions, dictated by the nature of our reason (and they are therefore subjective)."[1] Tonelli concludes that "Kant took over the essence of traditional objections to the theory of substance, and enriched them by several original considerations which depend on the rest of his methodological and metaphysical theories at that time."[2]

This is the standard account of Kant's theory of substance and the skeptical doubts about the existence of substances. It contains conspicuous lacunae, however, which prevent our understanding of what he ultimately held about the existence of substances, how he undertook to answer the skeptic, and why he changed his mind about the defense of the existence of substances from 1769 to 1781. What he says around 1769 is an accurate account of what had become of the notion of substance by the time it had reached Kant's lectures. But that account, so far from discrediting that notion, can be transformed into an implicit defense of the existence of substance against the skeptic. This is what Kant in fact did. Understanding this is a first step toward an appreciation of the force of his 1781 defense of substance. And this has both historical and philosophical significance: historical, because it enables us to see how Kant goes, not from the adoption of a skeptical account of substance in 1769 to a properly critical account of that notion in 1781, but rather how both the 1769 and the 1781 accounts of substance are two historical stages of the development of what is fundamentally a unified view of substance and the possibility of answering skeptical doubts about its existence; philosophical, because a proper understanding of the development from 1769 to 1781 shows that Kant's argument in the First Analogy is an adequate answer to skepticism with regard to the existence of substances.

I. THE HISTORICAL BACKGROUND

Consider the skeptical situation that faced Kant in 1769. The basic theme is this: Either substances cannot be known, or they cannot exist, or, if they do exist, they are merely properties of the mind. The answer to each of these alternatives was the same. We must reconstruct what we ordinarily take to be substances so as to show that we do not have to assume the existence of entities that are not available to experience or the description of which entails contradictions. The following are the historical variations of this theme.

1. We cannot know substances immediately but only their appearances or attributes. We cannot separate a substance from all of its properties; hence, we cannot be perceptually acquainted with substances.[3]
2. We cannot distinguish one substance from another except by means of their accidents and modifications; therefore, substance without accidents is a meaningless notion.[4]
3. Substance is a case of prime matter. But prime matter is not an entity. Substances lack any entitative status; hence, they do not exist.[5]
4. Substances are essences. But essences are merely modifications of the thinking subject. Substances are, therefore, not qualities of things, but rather of our minds. Things we ordinarily but erroneously *call* substances are merely modifications of the thinking subject.[6]
5. The very notion of substance entails a contradiction. To claim that substances exist is just to say that there are continuants, entities that are numerically the same through time. But we have no right to claim that there are continuants. This would require us to verify their existence. But since everything we perceive lasts only so long as we perceive it, we cannot perceive any object that endures through time because we would then have to be able to perform the impossible epistemic task of observing an object while we are not observing it. In claming to perceive continuants, we are claiming the impossible; namely, that we can perceive a thing that cannot be perceived.[7]
6. Every statement of identity implies the existence of two relata. And this generates a paradox. If identity is a relation, it entails the numerical diversity of its relata. If there is no such diversity, then there is no identity. The notion of a continuant and the notion of identity underlying it entail a contradiction. For they require us to believe that an object is not identical with itself.[8]

Enter Kant. In 1769 he holds that we cannot be aware of a subject independently of its properties, that the properties are *all* we can know of the subject in which they inhere, and the the subject-predicate distinction is subjective and not a characteristic of things in the extramental world.[9] The *Reflexionen zur Metaphysik* is the principal source of this version of Kant's account of substance. Admittedly, the group of passages assembled there echoes the complaints about the notion of substance that Kant inherited from the tradition. Substances do not exist because either they are essence or prime matter or they require self-contradictory descriptions. They cannot be objects of possible perceptual awareness because they necessarily have properties or accidents. And these are the only objects of perceptual awareness available to us. Both of these objections force the skeptical account of substance as a mere mental figment enshrouded by philosophical pretension, which, when once exposed for what they are, leave us no alternative but to relegate them to the status of a concept and nothing more.

There is, however, a striking difference between what happened to those complaints in the hands of Kant's predecessors and what even the Kant of 1769 made of them. None of the passages that occur in the *Reflexionen zur Metaphysik* denies us an epistemic access to substance. Yes, we cannot be acquainted with a substance without its properties. And, yes, its properties are all that we can know of a substance. And, finally, the distinction between a subject and a predicate is subjective and does not obtain between things *in rerum natura*. But Kant does not conclude from any of these claims that substances do not exist, that they are unknowable if they do exist, or that they are at most characteristics of our cognitive apparatus. Let me explain.

It may be true that we cannot be presented with a substance totally devoid of any of the properties that it instantiates. But this does not prevent us from being presented with a substance when we are acquainted with whatever properties it has. We may also truly say that we require an acquaintance with the relational and non-relational properties of a substance to distinguish one substance from another. This, however, is only a fact about our epistemic habits. It does not tell us what it is for one substance to be numerically distinct from another. And the relation between the subject and the predicate of a judgment may be subjective in that it is different from the relation between a substance and any one or more of its accidents. So far from inviting the inference that the substance-accident distinction is merely subjective, it forbids us to assimilate that distinction to the subject-predicate distinction, which is for Kant subjective. All of this enables Kant, ironically, to accept the premises of what I have labeled versions (1) through (4) of the traditional skeptical attack on the notion of substance and to show that they merely spell out the conditions under which we are presented with substances. They do not prove that there are no substances.

Kant's reflections of 1769 on the concept of substance are, then, well within the tradition. Yet he does not draw skeptical conclusions from them. Those very premises can be used in order to state the epistemic limitations of our acquaintance with substances and not as a means of discrediting that concept. But this is only part of the story. The evidence of Kant's 1769 reflections does show how some of the premises governing skeptical attacks on the notion of substance can be turned against those attacks. What seems to be an acceptance of the skeptical tradition is, as we will see, really a statement of the conditions under which substances exist or are perceptually available to us. Kant thus turns the tables on the skeptic by admitting the major parts of the skeptical critique of the notion of substance and demonstrating, not that substance cannot exist or be perceived, but rather the conditions under which substances do exist and can be perceived.

The evidence for this claim lies partly in the instructive ambiguity in Kant's own early formulation of the notion of substance and partly in what he later says a substance is in the first *Kritik*. The pre-Critical Kant shows that an awareness of some properties or others is a necessary condition of an awareness of any substance. This claim is the 1769 precursor of his 1781 description of the category, not of substance, but rather of substance and inherence that he gives in 1781.[10] This explains how Kant can turn the skeptical claim that all we can know of a substance is its properties against him. This is the precursor of the Critical distinction between our awareness of particulars (*Anschauung*) and our knowledge of objects (*Erkenntniss*).[11] Substances are given to us by a mode of apprehension different from the mode in which we cognize them.[12] And Kant's early distinction between a subject and a substance is the predecessor of his Critical distinction between the pure concept of substance and the schematized form of that concept.[13] These connections between the 1796 descriptions of the substance notion and the 1781 elaboration of those descriptions have a common feature. Each exposition makes a distinction that emerges again in 1781. And each distinction is an illustration, not of the impossibility of our own awareness of substance or its existence, but rather a condition of the possibility of that awareness.

There is, as I have said, a significant lacuna in this story. What I have labeled as versions (1) through (4) of the skeptical assault may be dispatched in this way. But nothing that Kant says in his reflections on substance in 1769 undermines versions (5) and (6) of the skeptical argument. He is still faced by two cases of an alleged contradiction in the notion of substance. Substances endure through time. We perceive the history of a substance only one stage at a time. But stages of substance are momentary entities: They last only as long as they are perceived. If we are to be acquainted with a substance, we must perceive it between the times that we are aware of any two of its stages. And this requires that we perceive it when we are not in a position to perceive it. That, as we already know, is the alleged contradiction.

The second such contradiction is this. If substances endure through their various temporal stages, we must say that a substance at one stage is numerically identical with itself at another stage. But the stages are numerically diverse; hence, no substance can be identical with itself through numerically distinct stages just because those stages are themselves numerically distinct one from another. These versions of skepticism are structurally responsible for the strategic change in Kant's view of what substance is from 1769 to 1781. His previous answers to skepticism had been based on conditions that can be fulfilled by a world in which there is no time. They require only the minimal notion of an object bearing properties. Nothing about this characterization nor the relevant answers to it need turn on whether it is numerically identical through time. Whether a substance can be presented to us directly, together with whatever properties it has, or only by inference from the properties that we do directly perceive is an issue that can be raised with respect to a substance at each stage of its history. The issue does not concern, say, the relation between the temporal stages of the substance that has properties. How we determine the numerical diversity of one substance from another is no exception to this. The individuation of substances by reference to relational or nonrelational properties is an issue that can be raised and settled without any reference to time. Nor, finally, is time relevant to deciding whether what we ordinarily call a substance is vacuous because it can be shown to be indistinguishable from prime matter or that it is really an essence. These issues are independent of any account of what it is for a substance to exist continuously from one stage to another. All of these issues can be raised and settled within the context of a timeless world. The introduction of what I will call the continuant notion of substance radically changes the conditions of argument about the existence of substances.

II. KANT'S "KEHRE"

The Kant of 1781 implements his strategy. He had already disposed of versions (1) through (4) of the pre-Kantian skeptical doubts about the existence of substances. But this was only a propaedeutic to what he had to do in order to demonstrate that substances exist. What he had done before 1781 was to explicate the conditions under which we can be acquainted with substances. This, however, is a far cry from showing against the skeptic that *knowledge* of substances is possible. This requires an answer to versions (5) and (6) of the skeptical complaint.

The Kant of 1781 formulates his claim in the First Analogy. He does this in two ways and offers two arguments for it. In the *A* edition of the *Kritik*, he says this: "All appearances contain the permanent (substance) as the object itself, and the transitory [*das Wandelbare*] as its mere determination that is, as a way [*eine Art*] in which the object exists."[14] He changes this in the *B* edition to read: "In all change of appearances substance is permanent; its quantum in nature is neither increased nor diminished."[15] Admittedly, the formulations are different. The former tells us that there are individual beings that come into and go out of existence; the latter, that the total amount of matter in the universe is constant. For my purpose, however, this difference makes no difference. The issue affecting versions (5) and (6) of the skeptical complaint is whether there is something permanent, whether it is a plurality of individual substances or merely one substance.

Kant supplies two different proofs for the First Analogy. In *A* it runs like this:

1. All appearances are in time.

2. Time is permanent because it is that in which change is measured.

3. The permanent or substratum in terms of which we distinguish between change and succession is substance.

4. Our apprehension of the manifold is always successive.

5. Therefore, our apprehension of the manifold alone does not enable us to determine whether its elements are merely sequential or whether they are instances of change.

6. Our ability to make this distinction assumes the existence of something that exists at all times.

7. This something is time in general.

    Scholium: If we say that time itself changes, we must represent to ourselves yet another time in which we measure such a change. And this ultimately assumes a time which is itself changeless.

8. We cannot perceive time itself; but we are given continuants *in* time which are necessary conditions of our ability to measure time.

    Scholium: Alteration [*Veränderung*] can be perceived. But it cannot be perceived unless there are continuants.

9. Therefore, the existence of substances is a necessary condition of the possibility of our ability to distinguish between genuine change and mere succession.[16]

But Kant does not let it go at that. He gives another argument that contains a crucially different premise. This is the argument:

1. All appearances are in time.

2. They are either successive or co-existent.

3. As successive, the parts of time constitute a series.

4. As co-existent, the parts of time constitute a time volume [*Zeitumfang*].

5. We can distinguish between succession and co-existence.

6. But the co-existence in time of the parts of a manifold assumes the existence of something that is permanent through time.

7. Therefore, there are substances.[17]

The arguments differ because Kant infers the existence of substances from two different epistemic abilities. The first argument turns on the assumption that we can distinguish between change and succession of the elements in our manifold (premise 4); the second, on our ability to distinguish between parts of a manifold that are merely successive and those that exist simultaneously even though they are apprehended successively (premise 5).

These, then, are Kant's answers to versions (5) and (6) of skepticism about the existence of substances. Both of them, however, are in danger of imminent collapse. There is, first of all, a difficulty that threatens to erode both alike. Local differences aside, each of them is supposed to demonstrate the existence of things that are permanent *through* time. But Kant appears to be trying to show that there is a substance —namely, time itself—that is what I will call sempiternal. These conclusions involve two very different concepts of what a substance is. A skeptic could concede the latter and quite consistently hold that the former conclusion does not follow from it.

The objection is plausible; it is not wrong. But it is wrongheaded. It feeds on a serious misconception of what Kant must do if he is to undermine the skeptical argument against the existence of substances. *He is not required to show that any particular substance or other must exist if we are to be able to distinguish, for one thing, between alteration and succession and, for another, between coexistence and succession.* He can meet this requirement if he can show that there is at least one thing that is changeless in the world.

Whether relative permanence can be inferred from what I have called sempiternal permanence is, however, the least of the problems surrounding Kant's defense of substance in the First Analogy. Someone might argue that Kant tries to infer the existence of continuants from two different premises neither of which seems to support his conclusion. He appeals, as we have seen, first to our ability to distinguish between a mere succession of events in the manifold and a genuine case of change. The former gives no evidence for the existence of continuants. The latter requires it. If we are able to detect a change in something from one state to another, then we must assume that there is something that exists from one time to another. True enough. But the argument begs the question. We must show rather than assume that there are cases of alteration in the manifold of perception. The appeal to such a fact suffers from what appears to be a critical defect. If we allow the assumption that there are cases in which we experience alteration rather than mere succession in the manifold, then we smuggle the conclusion of the First Analogy into the premise set from which you are supposed to be deducing it. If we remove that premise from the argument, the conclusion does not follow.

But this is not all. Consider again the distinction Kant makes between succession and coexistence. This, too, is supposed to show that there must be continuants in our experience as a necessary condition of our ability to distinguish a mere succession of occurrences in the manifold and a simultaneity of existence of the parts of the manifold that lasts even after you have experienced its parts serially ordered in time. The reasoning here is plain enough. Suppose that two or more elements in a perceptual manifold can exist simultaneously although we are aware of them only successively. What happens to the element that we have perceived at one time but that we no longer perceive at a later time because we have moved on to another stage of synthesis? If it does not cease to exist, it must then be a continuant. It must continue to exist despite the fact that somebody has moved on to other parts of the manifold.

This distinction is initially as troublesome as its predecessor. It cannot be inferred without circularity from the fact with which Kant prefaces the argument of the First Analogy; the fact, namely, that every manifold is successive.[18] He must, on his own showing, establish existence of coexistent elements in the manifold from the very premise that would seem to rule out the possibility of experiencing them. It may be true that the parts of a house continue to exist simultaneously even though you are not perceiving all of them at the same time. But this truth cannot be inferred solely from the fact that we always perceive those parts successively[19]—thus, the opposition.

These have traditionally been the strongest objections to the conclusion of the First Analogy. Their strength is deceptive. The objections against the use of the succession-alteration and the succession-coexistence distinction feed on a false assumption about the way in which those distinctions enter Kant's argument. Kant need not and does not use either as a premise from which he tries to conclude that there are continuants. He cites our ability to apply those distinctions as a consequence of the fact that time itself is changeless. What I have called the sempiternity of time is the condition without which both distinctions would collapse. This is just how Kant constructs both of the arguments I have canvassed. He begins by showing the sempiternity of time and only then moves to the applicability of the two distinctions to the time series. He does not—what is significant here—move the other way around. He does not attempt to show either that there are individual continuant substances or that they are perceptually available. He shows that both are possible and that the transcendental ground of that possibility is sempiternity. The objections, then, do not undermine the thrust of Kant's argument. They merely obscure its logical structure.

Kant bequeaths us, however, not only what I have called the sempiternity strand in his defense of the First Analogy, but also a quite different line of argument, which I call the transtemporality strand. Both strands are to be found in the A and B statements of the argument alike. But the transtemporality strand differs in each of the statements. In A it is the premise that we can be aware of the difference between change and succession. In B it is the claim that the coexistence of the manifold is distinguishable from the succession of the parts of the manifold. Both premises assume the sempiternality strand, without which neither would be possible as a fact of experience, for both of them assume that the manifold, whether we apprehend as merely successive or as an instance of change or coexistence, is a part of one enduring temporal framework. Thus, the very possibility of transtemporality assumes sempiternity.

The transtemporality of substance continuants cannot upset either version (5) or version (6) of the skeptical attack. The facts of coexistence and change rather than mere succession can simply be denied by the skeptic and explained away by the appeal to gentle laws of association, facts about our habits of awareness, or some other structure of our perceptual apparatus that is a fact about our awareness of objects without having any foundation in the structure of the objects themselves. But the objective fact of sempiternity cannot be denied because it is assumed by the very fact of the perception of what may only be a case of mere succession. And this shows that the existence of transtemporal substances must be possible if we are to describe the skeptical alternative without inconsistency. That is all that Kant requires in order to answer versions (5) and (6) of the skeptic's dubiety.

The point can be made differently but equivalently. The argument of the First Analogy shows that we can perceive substance continuants. But, in order to show that the objects we perceive are continuant substances, Kant is under no obligation to show that we perceive such objects under the description of being continuant substances. This fact circumvents an assumption crucial to version (5) of the skeptical attack. The skeptic lays down the condition that the perceptual availability of continuant substances assumes that we can perceive the substance during the interval that takes place between any two stages on the history of our perception of it. But the sempiternity of time guarantees the possibility of continued existence from one occasion of perception to another. And the fact that we can perceive a continuant substance even though we do not, *per impossibile*, perceive it between stages in its history is guaranteed by the fact that we need not perceive it under that description in order to perceive it at all.

III. VERSIONS (5) AND (6) REVISITED

We have seen that the distinction between transtemporal and sempiternal identity does not undermine the argument of the First Analogy. Once you have established the latter, you can infer to the *possibility* of the former. We have also seen that the introduction of the notions of alteration and coexistence in time into the argument does not make it circular. These are facts that do not function as premises from which Kant immediately infers the existence of substances. They are conclusions the possibility of which follows from an independent demonstration of the sempiternity of time itself.

This prepares the way for the refutation of versions (5) and (6) of the skeptical argument. These conclusions must now be applied to the most serious skeptical doubts facing Kant's defense of continuant substances. To understand how Kant's argument need not directly answer either of these versions is the first and major step to understanding the importance of the sempiternity strand as over against the transtemporality strand in that argument. Kant's argument in the *Kritik* meets the skeptical challenge by attacking, not its claims about the existence of transtemporal substances, but one of the presuppositions on which the whole attack is predicated, namely, the implicit denial of the sempiternity of the time order.

Consider version (5) first. We are told that any claim to an ability to perceive continuants requires us to perceive what cannot be a possible object of perception. Version (5) rests on the assumption that whatever exists must be what Hume calls a perception and what Kant was later to call an object of possible experience.[20] If there are continuants, they should be objects of possible experience. Yet, the very notion of a continuant caught in this state allegedly assumes that we are in a position to perceive something going from one stage to another in its history when we must alledgedly be forced to admit that the transition from one state to another is not itself an object of perceptual acquaintance.[21]

That is the condition that version (5) of the skeptical argument imposes on anybody wanting to defend the conclusion of the First Analogy. But does Kant have to meet it? The transtemporality strand in Kant's argument does not. But the sempiternity strand of that argument does meet the condition set by verison (5). He must show only that nothing the skeptic clinging to version (5) of the argument against substances precludes the perceptual availability of a substance through time. All Kant needs to show is that the discontinuity of perception through time does not imply a discontinuity of what is perceived. The sempiternity of time shows the possibility of continuity through time for continuants. Whether Kant can show that there are any such continuants is irrelevant. In order to break the skeptical grip of version (5), all he needs to do is to demonstrate the possibility of continuants. To claim that continuants exist is not to claim that there are unperceived percepts.

But the skeptic still has version (6) of his dubiety. The charge is that nothing can be numerically one through time without contradiction because such a claim implies that two things are one. To say that an object at time t is the same as an object at time t' is to imply that the object at t and the object at t' are both the same and yet numerically diverse. The relation of identity assumes two relata. This assumption is carried into the argument that there are continuants. The very notion of a continuant thus allegedly implies a contradiction.

Version (6) must go the way of its predecessors. The relation of identity may require two terms. It does not, however, require that the first must be identified with the second term in this relation. What occurs in this argument against the possibility of continuants is a shift in the application of the word "term" to the perceptual situation as the skeptic describes it. Assume that identity is a relation and requires, as any relation does, at least two terms. Are we to apply the notion of a term to the content we perceive or, rather, to the occasion on which the content is perceived? The skeptic's argument holds if we apply the notion of a term to the occasion or act of perceiving. If that notion is applied to what is given to us by each of these numerically discrete acts, there is no implication of diversity.

To say that the terms of the identity relation are the two occasions or events of perceiving a perceptual content rescues the notion of identity from internal contradiction once we say that one and the same perceptual content can be perceived on two different occasions. To say that the perceptual content we are given on these two occasions supplies us with two numerically different terms succeeds only in generating the contradiction that version (6) requires. No, the contents of two perceptual acts cannot be both two and one without contradiction. But the *acts* can be numerically diverse—which accounts for the diversity of terms—even though the *contents* of those acts can remain numerically the same while constituting the content of two separate acts—which accounts for the numerical indivisibility of the perceptual content. Version (6) shows only that we cannot perceive continuants when we are not looking. It does not show that we fail to perceive continuants when we do look. This is just a further consequence of Kant's argument for the sempiternity of substance in the First Analogy.

But this is not all that the sempiternity of time allows Kant in his defense of continuant substances against version (6) of the skeptical attack. Kant's argument allows him to concede that there is a paradox involved in the very notion of identity. But that paradox is irrelevant to the possibility either of the existence or of the perceptual availability of continuant substances. The paradox of identity applies to each stage of the history of a continuant substance as much as it applies to the relation between any two stages in that history. This fact does not, to be sure, remove the paradox that the skeptic foists on the notion of a continuant substance. But it shows the irrelevance of such a paradox to the issue that the skeptic raises, for it shows that the skeptical application of the paradox of identity to the issue of continuant substances applies to momentary and transtemporally continuous items alike. Version (6) thus undermines the possibility of continuant substances at the prohibitive cost of undermining the existence or perceptual availability of any perceptual object at all, including the momentary items that the skeptic has historically been willing to concede as the only viable alternative to the notion of a continuant substance.

Notes

1. An earlier version of this paper was delivered at the memorial symposium for Giorgio Tonelli at the 1980 meetings of the American Philosophical Association in Boston. The references to Tonelli are to his paper, "Critiques of the Notion of Substance Prior to Kant," in *Tijdschrift voor Philosophie*, Vol. XXIII (1961).

2. *Ibid.*, p. 300.

3. The source of this version of skepticism about substance closest to Kant is Rene Descartes, *Oeuvres*, Adam and Tannery, eds. (Paris, 1904), Vol. III, p. 222 (*Meditationes metaphysicae, Responsiones Quartae*). Cf. also Nicolaus of Autrecourt, *Nicolaus von Autrecourt: Beiträge zur Geschichte der Philosophie des Mittelalters*, J. Lappe, ed. (Münster, 1908), Vol. VI, Pt. 2, p. 12, for one of the older sources of the same criticism.

4. Henry More, *Opera omnia* (London, 1679), Vol. II, p. 294. Cf. George Berkeley, *Works*, Campbell Frazer, ed. (Oxford: 1901), Vol. I, p. 266.

5. For a standard statement of this view, see Christian Scheibler, *Opera philosophica* (Hagae Com., 1892), Vol. II, L. I. Cap. xxii, Tit. xv, Art. I pp. 167ff. (*Metaphysica ad mentem peripateticam*). The argument goes back to Augustine, *Confessiones*, L. XII, Cap. 7, as well as to Porphry, *Liber de Occasionibus*, c. XXI.

6. Cf. A. Geulinex, *Opera philosophica* (Hagae Com., 1892), Vol. II, (*Metaphysica ad mentem peripateticam*, Vol. I, ¶ I, pp. 212-13). See also the otherwise obscure John Clericus, *Logica, sive ars ratiocinande* (Leipzig, 1710), Vol. I., Ch. III, ¶ 5, for the same line of argument.

7. David Hume, *Treatise of Human Nature*, Bk. I, Pt. iv, Sec. 1.

8. *Ibid.*, Bk. I, Pt. iv, Sec. 2.

9. The main passages that document these three claims are in I. Kant, *Gesammelte Schriften*, the Prussian Academy Edition (Berlin and Leipzig, 1926), Vol. XVII. For the claim that we cannot be aware of a subject independent of its properties, see N. 3921:

> Die Empfindung selbst ist kein object des Verstandes, sondern die Merkmale derselben; daher ist z.E. der Begrif vom Menschen nichts anders als die Vorstellung von etwas, welches die Prädicate hat, darin wir den Begrif eines Menschen auflösen können. Daher in idem Urteile des subject Uberhaupt Etwas ist = X, welches, unter dem Merkmale *a* erkannt, mit einem andern Merkmale verglichen wird. Daher auch kein Wunder ist, dass wir kein subject vor allen Pradicaten erkennen, als bloss das Ich, welches gleichwohl kein Begrif, sondern eine Anchauung ist.

> [Sensation itself is not an object of the understanding but rather its marks. Therefore, the concept of man, for example, is nothing but the representation of something that has the predicates into which we can analyze the concept of a man. Therefore, in the judgment of a subject in general there lies something = x that is known by the mark *a* and compared with another mark. No wonder, then, that we cannot know any subject prior to all predicates except the pure ego that, although not a concept, is nonetheless an intuition.]

For the claim that properties are *all* that we can know of a subject, see N. 3921:

> Daher erkennen wir durch den Verstand an den Körpern nicht die eigentlichen subiecten, sondern die Pradicate der Ausdehnung, soliditat, Ruhe, Bewegung *etc*.

> [Therefore we do not know by the understanding the real subjects in bodies but the predicates of extension, solidity, rest, motion, etc.]

For the claim that the subject-predicate distinction is subjective, see N. 4052:

> Weil logische subjecte wiederum können praedicate sein, so sind wir nach Gestzen der Vernunft genöthigt, uns ein letztes subiect zu denken; dieses ist substanz.

> [Since logical subjects can be predicates, we are constrained according to the laws of reason to conceive of an ultimate subject. This is substance.]

And again, N. 4054:

> Der Begrif der substanz hat ausser der idee des subjects noch den Begriff der Beharrlichkeit bei dem, was auf einander folgt, und der Einerleiheit bei dieser Folge, welche man darum Veränderungen eben desselben Dinges nennt, bei sich.

> [Besides the idea of subject, the concept of substance still contains the concept of endurance in the transitory and identity in this succession that is therefore called changes of one and the same thing.]

10. A80-B106.
11. B350.
12. Cf. my "The Sense of a Kantian Intuition," in *Interpreting Kant*, Moltke S. Gram, ed. (Iowa City: University of Iowa Press, 1982).
13. A70-B93ff.
14. A182.
15. B224. I mention this only in order to dismiss the dispute in the literature about whether the two arguments for the First Analogy mark a distinction between the *A* and *B* edition of the *Kritik* or whether they are two parallel arguments that appear in both editions of the *Kritik*. H. J. Paton, *Kant's Metaphysic of Experience* (London: George Allen & Unwin, 1951), Vol. II, pp. 186ff., wants us to distinguish the two arguments Kant gives for the First Analogy in terms of their place in the two editions of the *Kritik*. In edition *A*, Paton tells us, Kant moves from the possibility of objective time relations to the conclusion that only in the permanent are these time relations possible. In edition *B*, however, Paton reports that Kant moves from the premise that succession and simultaneity can be known to the conclusion that there must be a substratum —namely, time itself—as a necessary condition of our ability to perceive the difference between simultaneity and succession. Paton's separation of the two arguments breaks down. For one thing Kant does not argue in either the *A* or the *B* edition of the *Kritik* merely from the stipulation that there are objective time relations or merely from the assumption that we can distinguish between simultaniety and succession in our perceptual manifold. Both of these facts that Kant introduces into his argument as conclusions from the prior demonstration of the sempiternity of time. They do not themselves constitute a demonstration of that claim. For another, the distinction that Paton claims to have found in Kant's text cannot distinguish the argument by reference to the two additions of the *Kritik*. The objectivity theme is contained in other editions of the defense of the First Analogy.

Norman Kemp Smith, *A Commentary to Kant's "Critique of Pure Reason"* (New York: Humanities Press, 1962), pp. 358ff., argues differently. He claims that there are proofs that run parallel to each other in both editions of the *Kritik*. He tells us that the first proof moves from our ability to distinguish succession and permanence in the elements of the manifold to the necessity of assuming the existence of substance; the second, from the distinction between coexistence and succession of those elements to the existence of substances. Kemp Smith is right about the presence of both arguments in each of the editions of the *Kritik*. He is, however, wrong in claiming that the arguments move solely from the alleged perceptibility of the distinctions between coexistence and alteration on the one hand and succession on the other. Cf. C. D. Broad, *Kant: An Introduction*, C. Lewy, ed. (Cambridge: Cambridge University Press, 1978), pp. 158ff., for a further argument supporting Kemp Smith's view. See also Jonathan Bennett, *Kant's Analytic* (Cambridge: Cambridge University Press, 1966), pp. 182ff.; T. H. Weldon, *Kant's "Critique of Pure Reason"* (Oxford: Clarendon Press, 1958), pp. 186ff.; Edward Caird, *The Critical Philosophy of Immanuel Kant* (Glasgow: James Maclehose and Sons, 1909), Vol. II, pp. 508ff.; and A. C. Ewing, *A Short Commentary on Kant's "Critique of Pure Reason"* (Chicago: University of Chicago Press, 1974), pp. 150ff., who unfortunately claim that Kant's argument purports to establish the objectivity of time relations. Nothing in the argument shows that he claims to do this. You can, for all Kant shows in this part of the *Kritik*, accept the conclusion that substance is sempiternal and even that there are transtemporal substances without having to conclude that either exists apart from your own experience. A solipsist could endorse both of Kant's arguments without contradiction.

16. A182ff.

17. A182-B235ff.

18. *Ibid*.

19. Cf. H. A. Prichard, *Kant's Theory of Knowledge* (Oxford: Clarendon Press, 1909), pp. 269, argues this and then proceeds predictably and irrelevantly to overturn that argument. He, along with others, overlooks the rather plain fact that sempiternity is logically prior to transtemporal identity and not the other way around. Kant repeatedly reminds us of this fact. He begins at A49-B67 of the Transcendental Aesthetic. He repeats this reminder at A187-B231 and again at A188-B232. Cf. *Reflexionen zur Metaphysik*, in *Gesammelte Schriften*, the Prussian Academy of Sciences (Berlin: Walter de Gruyer, 1928), N. 631 and N. 6503 for confirmation of this view. Cf. Laird Addis's insightful article, "Kant's First Analogy," *Kant-Studien*, Vol. 54 (1963), pp. 337ff., for an anticipation of this point. Cf. also my *Kant, Ontology, and the A Priori* (Evanston, Ill.: Northwestern University Press, 1968), Chap. 6, *passim*, for a discussion of the same topic.

20. Cf. A106, A108, A109, B137, B138, B139, A202-B248, and *Prolegomena*, ¶ 22.

21. See my contribution, "Substance," to *Substances and Things*, M. L. O'Hara, ed. (Washington, D.C.: University Press of America, 1982), pp. 120ff., for an expanded defense of this line of argument.

Kant on Objectivity

T. E. WILKERSON

1. TWO KINDS OF OBJECTIVITY

Since the first *Critique* is devoted to an examination of the ways in which we must, and the ways in which we must not, make objective judgments, it is hardly surprising that "object," "objective," and cognate expressions occur with considerable frequency. Equally, since Kant has a lot of important and difficult things to say, it is hardly surprising that his notion of an object proves to be a complicated one. A comprehensive account of his views would uncover different senses of "object" and "objective"; it would include an account of that curious animal, the transcendental object = x; it would trace the role of the concept of an object in transcendental idealism and explore the alleged ambiguity in the claim that there are objects "outside us" (A373). Unfortunately, neither I nor my editor can afford the space for a comprehensive account, and I will concentrate on one central problem. Some readers may regret the absence of any discussion of transcendental idealism, but the problem I will consider is of general philosophical interest and can be discussed quite independently of any Kantian idealism.

The problem concerns Kant's central claim that we must make objective judgments. As Ralph Walker points out, there is a crucial ambiguity in the expression "objective," an ambiguity that Kant "seems never fully to have appreciated."[1] Thus, Kant's claim — and the contrast between "subjective" and "objective" judgments — can be understood in two quite different ways. In the first sense of "objective," the distinction between subjective and objective judgments is merely a distinction between how the world appears to be and how it really is. Subjective judgments merely express how the world appears to be, or, to use another idiom, they merely express someone's beliefs, whereas objective judgments (purport to) express how the world actually is. Kant's point is not very happily expressed as a distinction between two kinds of judgment, for objective judgments are judgments and therefore express someone's beliefs, express how the world appears to be. But there is no doubt that the point is important, however Kant chooses to make it. If we are to have any beliefs at all, we must use a distinction between what we believe and what is actually the case. An "objective" judgment does not merely express a belief; it purports to be true irrespective of what I or anyone else believes. That is surely one central thread in the puzzling passage in the *Prolegomena* (Ak.298) about judgments of perception and judgments of experience and in the marginally clearer corresponding passage in the first *Critique*, at B142.

> [T]o say "the body is heavy" is not merely to state that the two representations have always been conjoined in my perception, however often that perception be repeated; what we are asserting is that they are combined *in the object*, no matter what the state of the subject may be.

Thus, in the first sense of "objective," Kant's claim that we must make objective judgments is to be interpreted as a claim that we must use a distinction between what we believe and what is actually true. Ralph Walker points out[2] that such a distinction is not a distinction between sense data and external objects. Indeed, without further argument it does not even imply any sort of distinction between sense data and external objects. One needs an argument to move from the claim that we must use a notion of objective truth to the claim that we must use the notion of an external object. A phenomenalist might reasonably argue that he distinguishes belief from truth (e.g., he sometimes fails to identify his sense data correctly) but has no use for the notion of an external object.

The notion of an external object yields the second and more prominent sense of "objective": in this sense, an objective judgment is a judgment about external objects. In other words, when Kant argues that we must make objective judgments, he is claiming that we must believe that there are objects external to us and logically independent of us. More specifically, it appears, we must believe that they are in space and time, that they are substances, that they obey causal laws, and so on. In this second sense of "objective," the distinction between subjective and objective judgments is indeed parallel to the distinction between sense data and external objects, for subjective judgments merely record the intentional content of our experience and objective judgments (purport to) record the features of external objects such as tables and chairs. And self-conscious experience would be impossible without such objective judgments. As Kant expresses it crisply in the Refutation of Idealism, "the consciousness of my existence is at the same time an immediate consciousness of the existence of other things outside me" (B276).

Those, then, are the two senses of "objective" that I will examine in the rest of this paper. Before closing this section, I want to draw attention to a passage in which Kant appears to be using both notions simultaneously and clouding the discussion completely by talking about "necessary universal agreement." The passage is to be found in the *Prolegomena* immediately after Kant's attempt to distinguish judgments of perception from judgments of experience: "All our judgments are at first merely judgments of perception; they hold good only for us (that is, for our subject), and we do not till afterward give them a new reference (to an object) and desire that they shall always hold good for us and in the same way for everybody else; . . . there would be no reason for the judgments of other men necessarily agreeing with mine if it were not the unity of the object to which they all refer and with which they accord; hence they must all agree with one another." (Ak.298). The argument seems to be as follows: All our beliefs are initially mere beliefs, which we may not share with anyone else. Yet, we presumably strive to hold beliefs that are true, beliefs that "always hold good for us and in the same way for everybody else." But such general agreements could not be secured unless at least some beliefs were about objects external to us, objects that have properties independent of any of our beliefs about them. In short, the notion of belief requires the notion of objective truth, objective truth implies necessary universal agreement, and necessary universal agreement can only be secured by our regarding certain beliefs as beliefs about an external world.

As soon as one ventures into that argument, chasms open in all directions. In particular I do not understand what it is to desire that certain judgments will always hold good for us and in the same way for everybody else. It cannot mean simply that I desire that my beliefs should be true, for that desire could be satisfied without any reference to other people at all. Kant might be claiming that I can use the notion of objective truth only if I suppose a measure of universal agreement, a set of shared beliefs. But that claim seems obviously false. That is, without further argument it seems clear that we might fail to reach substantive agreement on anything whatever. Perhaps the passage only makes sense in conjunction with the general Kantian claim that certain judgments—namely, judgments about the essential Euclidean and Newtonian structure of the world—are judgments that all of us must make if experience is to be possible at all. They are judgments to which all human beings necessarily subscribe, because they provide the essential framework of human experience. As Kant remarks in the Aesthetic, there is something in appearances that "holds for sense in all human beings" (A45/B62).

We might, therefore, construct a slightly different argument. It would yield necessary universal agreement as a corollary and would go as follows. If we are to believe anything at all, we must have certain Euclidean and Newtonian beliefs about an external world; so all self-conscious human beings will share certain beliefs. Unfortunately, although that argument is very interesting and related to arguments that I will consider later in the paper, it does not correspond at all closely to the passage from the *Prolegomena*. Moreover, it is still not clear how we might guarantee that such necessary shared beliefs are objective in our first sense of "objective." That is, we cannot guarantee that they are true. After all, many modern physicists would claim that the Euclidean and Newtonian beliefs in question are actually false. Hence, even if we could show that there must be certain universal beliefs and even if those beliefs are beliefs about an external world, it would not follow that they are true. Presumably, Kant's radical idealism would allow him to move from necessary agreement to truth, but I would argue that this is one of many occasions when the tensions between empirical realism and transcendental idealism reach breaking point. I will, therefore, be content merely to note that Kant does occasionally attempt to connect objectivity in our first sense and objectivity in our second with necessary universal agreement, and I will return to the central area of discussion.

2. THE TRANSCENDENTAL DEDUCTION

So far I have argued that Kant's central claim—that we must make objective judgments—can be interpreted in two quite different ways: first, as the claim that we must use a distinction between what we believe and what is actually the case and, second, as the claim that we must believe that there are external objects that are independent of our perceptions and that have certain general features. As I have indicated, Kant appears to make both claims, appears to believe that we must make judgments that are objective in both senses of "objective," though he may, of course, have failed to detect any ambiguity at all. I have also pointed out that it is far from clear that objectivity in the first sense even implies objectivity in the second. That is, it is far from clear that, in using a distinction between belief and objective truth, we are committed to a belief in an external world. For example, one can apparently construct a story in which the whole world consists of a person and his experiences. He might occasionally wonder whether he has misidentified his experiences, whether his memory is deceiving him, and thereby use a distinction between belief and truth, without ever believing that there are external objects. And one can imagine several quite different versions of the story. In one version, he simply does not possess the concept of an external object and cannot even speculate about the possibility of there being tables and chairs. In other versions, he possesses the concept of an external object but never finds anything answering to it. Perhaps his experience is not sufficiently orderly to lend itself to explanation in terms of a realist science. Alternatively, perhaps his experience is just as orderly as ours, but he has been so impressed by the philosophical arguments against representative theories of perception that he has taken refuge in an obstinate egocentric idealism. In all the versions of the story, he uses a distinction between belief and truth, because he has beliefs about his experiences, some of which he suspects to be false, but in no version does he believe that there are external objects.

In the rest of this paper, I will consider various attempts to show that such a story, in whatever version, is incoherent, that we must make objective judgments in both senses of "objective." At the risk of offending some readers, I will not try to argue for objectivity in the first sense, to show that we must distinguish what we believe from what is actually the case, for I think it is an essential feature of the notion of belief that beliefs may be true or false and that, therefore, there is a clear distinction between what is believed and what is actually the case. So the main burden of the paper falls on objectivity in the second sense, on the claim that we must believe that there are external objects.

Kant offers us two main arguments. One is the main argument of the Transcendental Deduction and the three Analogies of Experience. In the barest outline it goes as follows: Experience does not consist merely of a series of discrete and varied representations. If a series of representations is to count as a single coherent experience, they must be united or combined as the experiences of a single self-conscious person.

But there are no observable features of the representations themselves sufficient to yield such unity of self-consciousness. "Consciousness of self according to the determinations of our state in inner perception is merely empirical, and always changing. No fixed and abiding self can present itself in this flux of inner appearances" (A107). Indeed, without some other principle of unity, "I should have as many-coloured and diverse a self as I have representations of which I am conscious to myself" (B134). The notion of a fixed and abiding self can be secured only if the representations are brought under rules, only if they are necessarily interrelated. The rules of such necessary connection are the categories, a priori concepts of objects. It is by uniting representations in the concept of an object that we guarantee the unity of self-consciousness: "The transcendental unity of apperception is that unity through which all the manifold given in an intuition is united in a concept of the object" (B139).

Undoubtedly, that argument is an important landmark in the history of philosophy. In direct opposition to empiricists, Kant insists that experience does not consist in the purely passive reception of information about the world around us but rather consists in an active attempt to bring raw data under intellectual control. The central Kantian picture is that of a self-conscious person struggling to construct a coherent view of the world. The argument turns on the thought that there are certain rule-governed, necessary connections between my experiences, connections that are quite independent of any purely contingent connections (e.g., purely personal associations of ideas). Thus, whatever the incidental contingent features of my experiences may be, I find that I can bring them under certain laws. For example, I can discover instances of causal laws or can connect different perceptions as perceptions of a single, persisting object.

However, the argument is notoriously full of obscurities and difficulties. For example, disciples of Hume would be quick to deny that unity and connectedness are necessary features of experience and also to deny that there are any necessary connections between distinct existences (e.g., between distinct representations). Moreover, I have argued elsewhere that self-consciousness strictly is not a necessary feature of our experience.[3] But I will concentrate on the difficulty that is most important for our purposes, namely, that the argument fails to explain why the categories are concepts of external objects. Indeed, this is perhaps one of the places in which there is a definite slide from objectivity in the first sense to objectivity in the second. Suppose for the purposes of argument that self-consciousness is necessary for experience, that our experience must be rule governed, and that we must connect and unite our experiences under rules that are independent of any purely contingent principles of association: "[T]he object is viewed as that which prevents our modes of knowledge from being haphazard or arbitrary, and which determines them a priori in some definite fashion" (A104). Already, then, we have a distinction between the purely contingent and haphazard features of our representations and their necessary and rule-governed features, those features that lend themselves to intellectual control by means of the categories.

Kant wants to insist that the necessary connections in question incorporate the thought that the objects of perception are *external* objects. And it is extremely difficult to see why. That is, it is extremely difficult to see why the categories, the rules that articulate necessary connections between representations, are concepts of *external* objects. The solipsist in our story might make generalizations about his experiences, might connect them together, without in any way committing himself to the existence of external objects. Perhaps, like Berkeley, he attaches a special significance to certain experiences only because they are more vivid, belong to orderly and coherent bundles, and typically cannot be controlled in the way in which, say, thoughts or eidetic images can be controlled: "[W]hatever power I may have over my own thoughts, I find the ideas actually perceived by sense have not a like dependence on my will. . . . The ideas of sense are more strong, lively, and distinct than those of the imagination; they have likewise a steadiness, order and coherence, are not excited at random, as those which are the effects of human wills often are, but in a regular train or series" (*Principles of Human Knowledge*, §§ 29, 30). Unlike Berkeley, however, our solipsist will not be tempted to explain those facts by appealing to certain external spirits, and in particular to an external infinite spirit. Even if he talks with the vulgar and applies nouns such as "apple," "table," and "chair" to such interesting bundles of experiences, he will regard the nouns only as shorthand for much longer sense-datum expressions and, in effect, will not be using the concept of an external object at all.

At this point we might follow Strawson and reconstruct Kant's argument in an effort to remedy its deficiencies.[4] The reconstructed argument goes as follows: Experience is necessarily the experience of a single, persisting, self-conscious subject. But, if he is to be aware of himself and his experience, he must distinguish himself from other things. That is, self-awareness and awareness of other things are interdependent. Since the only materials available for making such a distinction must be in the series of his experiences, his conscious mental states, he must regard some of his experiences as perceptions of external things. He must use certain rules—to wit, the categories—rules that connect and unite various experiences. To sustain his awareness of himself, he must, in the Kantian phrase, unite his representations in the concept of an object.

There is an important difference between Kant's own argument and the reconstruction. Kant certainly argues that self-consciousness and consciousness of external objects are connected, but the reconstructed argument explains the connection. Self-consciousness and consciousness of objects together form a single distinction, and we cannot use one-half of the distinction without using the other:

> [E]xperience must be such as to provide room for the thought of experience itself. The point of the objectivity-condition is that it provides room for this thought. It provides room, on the one hand, for "Thus and so is how things objectively are" and, on the other, for "This is how things are experienced as being"; and it provides room for the second thought *because* it provides room for the first.[5]

But it is just at that point that the argument is open to two serious objections. First, Strawson, like Kant, seems to be trading on the ambiguity in the expression "objective." It is one thing to insist on a distinction between experiencing the world as so-and-so and its objectively being so-and-so. It is quite another thing to insist that there are external objects. Second, Strawson seems to be trading on another ambiguity, namely, an ambiguity in the expressions "having a concept" or "having a thought" or "using a distinction." There are many ways of using a distinction or having a concept. Consider, for example, the concept of a unicorn. I use it whenever I entertain the possibility that unicorns exist, wonder whether they exist, imagine what it would be like for them to exist, deny that they exist, or assert that they exist. Yet, in only one case do I use the concept of a unicorn in a way that commits me to their existence. Similarly, a Kantian self-conscious subject may use the distinction between himself and external things. He might wonder whether external objects exist, imagine what it would be like for them to exist, deny that they exist, or assert that they exist. But in only one of those cases is he committed to their existence. Thus, the reconstructed Kantian argument does not after all demolish our story about the solipsist. At the very most, it shows that the solipsist must have the concept of an external world. And that is very far from showing that he must believe that it exists. As in one version of our story, he may indeed believe very firmly that it does not. The whole world, he believes, consists of him and his experiences. Although in a spirit of frustrated sociability and intellectual curiosity he would like to encounter something else, he can never persuade himself that he has succeeded.

Before closing this section, we should briefly consider one argument that was fashionable some years ago, particularly in Wittgensteinian circles. To have a concept, it was said, is to have a grasp of certain contrasts, and without the contrasts one would simply lose the concept altogether. Fake coins make sense only against a background of solid currency. For example, hallucination makes sense only against a background of veridical perception; indirect perception is possible only if there are clear cases of direct perception; there can be false memories only if most of our memories are correct; and so on. Similarly, it might be said, self-consciousness requires just such a contrast, albeit a contrast of a very high level of generality. I must be able to contrast what is myself with what is not, must be able to tell where I stop and the rest of the world begins. A world that consists entirely of me and my experiences is incoherent simply because there is no alien background against which I can pick out myself.

Although that argument has been defended by many distinguished philosophers, it is not itself very distinguished. There are many concepts that we use with no apparent difficulty and yet that rest on no such contrast between cases that fall under the concept and cases that do not. One example I have already used: we can certainly use the concept of a unicorn without contrasting unicorns with nonunicorns. *Mutatis mutandis* the same is true of the concept of phlogiston, the ether, a frictionless body and (some would say) God. In a fit of desperation, one might argue that the argument does apply to concepts at a very high level of generality, such as the concept of self or the concept of an external object, but the desperation would be misplaced. One highly general concept is that of the universe, which astronomers and cosmologists use with little apparent difficulty. Yet, they clearly do not need or want to employ any contrast between what is part of the universe and what is not. Sadly,

Kant's reference to empty space and empty time in the discussion of the antithesis of the first Antinomy (A431/B459f.) shows that such self-denial has been far from universal!

3. THE REFUTATION OF IDEALISM

Let us review the state of play. First, I argued that there is a crucial ambiguity in Kant's notion of objectivity. When he claims that we must make objective judgments, he sometimes means that we must use a distinction between what we believe and what is actually the case, and sometimes means that we must hold certain beliefs about an external world distinct from ourselves and our experiences. He does not distinguish the two claims and appears to slide cheerfully from one to the other. But, since it is far from clear that our using a notion of objective truth commits us to beliefs about external objects, I then examined possible ways of moving from one to the other. I suggested that no comfort will emerge from the main argument of the Transcendental Deduction, whether in its original form or in Strawson's reconstruction.

However, Kant offers us another argument in the Refutation of Idealism (B274-279). In many respects, it anticipates Wittgenstein's private language argument, and much of what I have to say takes us into the territory mapped out in the relevant sections of the *Philosophical Investigations*. Although the Refutation of Idealism presumably is meant to be quite general, Kant focuses on a particular problem, that of measuring time. In outline the argument is as follows: I am aware of my own existence in time. But we can measure time only in terms of the successive changes of a persisting thing, "something *permanent*." The permanent cannot be in me, for I have to measure my own existence in time *against* the permanent. Thus, the permanent, the persisting thing that represents time in general, must exist outside me. "In other words, the consciousness of my existence is at the same time an immediate consciousness of the existence of other things outside me" (B276).

I have tried to keep fairly close to Kant's own words, or rather to those of his translator, but the general thought is fairly clear. The argument hinges on the claim that there is something intrinsically absurd about my treating myself and my experiences as a clock, for there is something intrinsically absurd about measuring the temporal duration of myself and my experiences against myself and my experiences. The crucial sentence is this: "This permanent cannot, however, be something in me, since it is only through this permanent that my existence in time can itself be determined" (B275). In the Preface to the second edition, Kant suggests that the sentence might be changed to the following:

> But this permanent cannot be an intuition in me. For all grounds of determination of my existence which are to be met with in me are representations; and as representations themselves require a permanent distinct from them, in relation to which their change, and so my existence in the time wherein they change, may be determined (Bxxxixa).

But how are we to interpret the argument? What precisely is wrong with using one's own representations or experiences as a clock? One obvious suggestion is that it involves circularity, for one would in effect be measuring a clock against itself, and that is as absurd as measuring a ruler against itself. We do not obtain a proper *measurement*. The length of the ruler turns out to be . . . the length of the ruler, and the duration of my experiences turns out to be . . . the duration of my experiences. We can presumably only break out of the circle and thereby obtain a proper measurement if we measure experiences against something other than themselves. In other words, we measure their duration against an external clock.

However, the charge of circularity is too quick. There is just the same sort of circularity in our "objective" methods of measurement. In the days when a bar in Paris was the standard meter, or the distance from the king's nose to the king's thumb was a yard, the bar was inevitably a meter long when measured against itself and the king stretched exactly two yards when measured against himself. Similarly, when we used a solar clock the Earth inevitably completed one orbit in a year when measured against itself. *Mutatis mutandis* the same apparent circularity afflicts more modern rulers and clocks. But the crucial point is that we should not be disturbed by such apparent circularity. The only philosophers who should be disturbed are radical verificationists who insist that the expressions "year" or "meter" or "yard" *have the same meaning* as the expressions "time taken for the Earth to complete one orbit" or "length of Parisian bar" or "distance between regal nose and regal thumb."

It is important to resist such radical verificationism for a very simple reason. We can easily imagine circumstances in which we would be entitled to say that the Earth had taken rather longer than usual to complete its orbit (e.g., because of the gravitational influence of a large asteroid passing through the solar system) or that the bar was no longer a meter long (e.g., because of a heat wave in Paris) or that the king could stretch farther than two yards (e.g., because of surgery). We may use the objects in question as standards of measurement, but it does not follow that expressions referring to what is measured and expressions referring to certain relevant features of the standards have the same meaning. We can stand back from time to time and decide that the standard clock or standard ruler is no longer up to standard. One possibility (the one that I have just illustrated) is that measurements yielded by the standard no longer sit comfortably with our scientific theory. Another possibility is that we have been using a number of standards of measurement simultaneously and that they are no longer in step—the most notorious example being the simultaneous dating of events by the Julian and Gregorian calendars.

Let us now apply those remarks to the clock in which we are interested, the clock that consists of a series of representations or experiences. There is no doubt an apparent circularity involved in measuring the duration of my experiences against themselves. But the circularity will only be disturbing to those who insist that expressions such as "hour," "minute," and "second" have the same *meaning* as expressions referring to certain relevant features of experiences. The rest of us will regard the succession of my experiences merely as the *standard* of measurement. Hence, I can stand back from time to time and ask whether the standard is up to standard. And

I might decide that its measurements sit awkwardly with my scientific theory. For example, for scientific reasons I decide that a certain pain could not possibly be as prolonged, or as brief, as my internal clock would suggest. Or I might have been using a number of internal clocks and eventually discover that they are not quite in step. The recurrent-pain clock, the recurrent-drowsiness clock, and the recurrent-image clock do not quite correspond, and I may decide to adjust the measurements yielded by one or more of them.

I conclude, therefore, that any circularity that afflicts internal or private clocks is at least as virtuous as the circularity afflicting external or "objective" clocks. Perhaps we should consider a second interpretation of the Refutation of Idealism, an interpretation that compels us to discuss Wittgenstein's private-language argument. Perhaps Kant's thought is this. If I am to hold genuine beliefs at all, and particularly beliefs about the temporal features of myself and my experiences, then I must use the notion of objectivity in the first sense of "objective." That is, I must use a distinction between my beliefs and their truth or falsehood. Thus, I must in principle be able to discover that some of my beliefs are false; for example, that a belief about the duration of an experience is false. But, if the only standards of truth and falsehood are purely private or internal, then I cannot even in principle discover that a belief is false. Such a "discovery" would amount merely to confronting one belief with another, not to falsifying a belief. That is, I would be no nearer giving content to the notion of something's being the case irrespective of my beliefs about the matter. "One would like to say: whatever is going to seem right to me is right. And that only means that here we can't talk about 'right.' "[6] Nor can I appeal to memory to check the truth of my beliefs, for there is similarly no independent check of the correctness of any memory. But by normal contraposition it follows that the "beliefs" are not genuine beliefs at all. If I cannot give content to the notion of a belief's being true or false, I cannot sustain the notion of a belief. The moral of that is that I must ground my standards of truth and falsehood in something objective in the second sense of "objective," in certain features of an external world.

One incidental advantage of that interpretation of the Refutation of Idealism is that to some extent it protects Kant from the charge of failing to distinguish the two senses of "objective." If successful, the argument shows that objectivity in the first sense requires objectivity in the second, that we can use a notion of truth and falsehood only if we have certain beliefs about an extenal world. Unfortunately, the argument fails. Its failure becomes manifest as soon as we attempt to remedy the alleged deficiencies of a private language. It might seem that we need merely to introduce external objects. That is, our solitary language user makes "objective" judgments in the second sense, judgments that express or imply beliefs about the existence and nature of objects independent of any perceiver. Similarly, the meaning of words and sentences and the standards of truth and falsehood are grounded in features of such objects rather than in introspectively discernible features of the observer. In particular, the notion of time is given content in terms of the regular changes of external objects rather than in recurrent features of the observer's experiences.

Sadly, we are no further forward. The main weakness of the private language, it was argued, was that it left no room for a mistake. But, even when we have populated the world with external objects and insisted that the meaning rules of the language must be grounded in features of such objects, our observer is no better off. Suppose, for example, he notices a recurrent physical object, such as the sun, and records the fact in sentences that others could learn, if only there were others. It is still difficult to see how, entirely unaided, he could give content to the notion of his misidentifying the sun or to the corresponding distinction between his beliefs and their truth or falsehood. Whether he is speaking a private language or a public language, he has to count as right whatever seems to him to be right.

Of course, the standard reply is that the public language grounded in features of external objects could be learned by others and that, even though a solitary language user might not *in practice* have grounds for thinking he had made a mistake, he has grounds *in principle*, for the objects in which he is interested are in principle accessible to others and others could presumably tell him that he has made a mistake. But I cannot see that help in principle is any help at all. In our example, the solitary language user is the only person in a world of public objects and is, therefore, no better equipped to spot his own mistakes than the speaker of a private language. If we say that a private language is impossible, we must also say that a public language spoken by a solitary is impossible.

That leaves us with two alternatives. One is to press the argument even further, to populate the world not merely with external objects but with other people. By introducing other people we can give some content to the notion of a mistake, for other people can disagree with me. I may not be prepared to admit that I am mistaken, but nonetheless I can understand the notion of a mistake because I can appreciate that there are two incompatible beliefs, one held by me and one held by someone else. As we have seen, a solitary language user, whether he speaks a private or a public language, cannot sincerely disagree with himself and, therefore, apparently lacks the obvious support for the notion of mistake. In contrast, a language spoken by more than one person allows disagreement and, therefore, mistake. If the crucial weakness of a private language is that it leaves no room for mistake, then Kant's Refutation of Idealism will force us not merely to believe in external objects but also to believe in external (and articulate) people.

I am reluctant to take such an extravagant step, and not merely because it is extravagant. Much more important, it has very paradoxical consequences. For example, it would seem to imply that if the rest of the human race disappeared, I would be unable to hold any coherent beliefs about anything. Indeed, one way of ridding myself of disagreeable experiences such as toothache would be to murder everyone else. There may be philosophers who are prepared to accept such views, but I confess that I am not so sanguine. I would prefer to explore a second alternative by looking more critically at the early stages of the private-language argument. First, we must examine an important assumption that is commonly held by both parties to the dispute, namely, the assumption that we have incorrigible access to our experiences. It seems obvious that there is no distinction between the apparent and actual features of experience. If I believe that I am in pain, then I am; if I believe that I have a green afterimage, then I have; if I believe that I am thinking about Kant, then I am; and so on.

On historical grounds alone, it is likely that Kant accepted the incorrigibility thesis, and there are passages in the first *Critique* where he comes close to asserting it explicitly—for example, at A371, where he talks of "the immediate witness of my self-consciousness" and claims that "the immediate perception" of representations is "a sufficient proof of their reality." But, as we have seen, incorrigibility provides security that is entirely empty, for, if there is no distinction between the apparent and the actual features of my experiences, I lose the essential tension between my beliefs and their truth and falsehood. Thus, incorrigibility rules out mistake and thereby rules out a private language. Furthermore, even if we do not press the assumption of incorrigibility, it is very difficult to see how the notion of a mistake might be introduced at all, for the Cartesian private language turns very much on our spotting certain features of our experiences and on our associating words with certain such recurrent features. But a mistake is simply not a *feature* of our experiences. For example, there is no observable difference between a sensation that is correctly identified and one that is incorrectly identified. Similarly, my memories are not labeled "true" or "false" and, even if they were, I could not suppose that those labeled "true" were indeed true, those labeled "false" were indeed false. Mistakes are simply not objects of introspective observation.

The private language has two main, and connected deficiencies: the assumption of incorrigibility rules out mistakes, and the Cartesian framework of the language makes it difficult to provide any alternative notion of a mistake. I now want to remedy those deficiencies by arguing that we should abandon incorrigibility and that we should adopt a more sophisticated account of mistakes. First, I will discuss the incorrigibility thesis, the claim that necessarily my beliefs about my experiences are true. If I believe that I am in pain, then I am in pain; if I believe I want a drink, then I want a drink; if I believe I am thinking about the private-language argument, then I am thinking about the private-language argument, and so on. The thesis looks attractive no doubt if we concentrate on experiences that are very familiar and obtrusive, such as pains and thoughts about Kant. Many philosophers would concede that we can misidentify certain of our mental states, notably those that do not involve the occurrence of any characteristic experiences. For example, notoriously we are often poor judges of our own motives, desires, and character traits and are easily misled by excessive modesty, vanity, stupidity, or self-deception. But I want to suggest that we can misidentify any mental state, including all those that are or involve characteristic experiences. For example, we can make mistakes even about our pains. Some may be mild or may not wholly occupy our attention and may be wrongly classified. Some may be so confidently expected that their absence is not noticed: if the interrogator tells me that I will feel pain, I may well believe that I feel pain when he merely touches my hand. And even if we were to consider less recondite examples, I can see no reason to suppose that I must identify my pains correctly. In short, there is a considerable looseness of fit between the apparent and the actual features of my mental states, and there is no logical guarantee that my beliefs about them are true.

Now let us consider what is involved in making mistakes, in misidentifying experiences. No doubt it is true that there is no discernible difference between a correctly identified experience and a misidentified experience; a mistake *as such* is not an object of introspective awareness. But equally mistakes as such are not objects of any sort of awareness. Whether I am speaking a private language or a public language, I do not spot my mistakes in the way in which I spot the redness or the roughness or the stickiness of a thing. The moral to be drawn is not that a private language is impossible but rather that we must provide a more sophisticated account of mistakes. In a public language, we spot our mistakes in various ways. We might abandon a belief because it is inconsistent with most of our other beliefs or because it is inconsistent with certain central or very important beliefs or because it is simply an unusual or eccentric belief and so on. Nothing counts as spotting a false belief *as such*. A belief is taken to be true or false insofar as it sits comfortably or uncomfortably with other beliefs.

Once we abandon incorrigibility and once we accept a more sophisticated account of mistakes, there is nothing to prevent our private language user from revising his beliefs in the light of other beliefs, just as public linguists do. He does not need to spot mistakes as such. Nor does he have to fall back on "acts of recognition."[7] Since it is always possible for him to misidentify his experiences, it is possible for him coherently to wonder whether a certain experience is as he supposes, and it is in turn possible for him to revise any existing theories he may have about his experiences. As long as he has no Cartesian attachment to incorrigibility, he can appreciate the crucial distinction between his beliefs and their truth or falsehood. So, the solipsist in our story can make judgments that are objective in the first sense, judgments that reflect a distinction between what is believed and what is actually the case. But he does not make judgments that are objective in the second sense, judgments that are or imply claims about the existence of external things. If we interpret Kant's Refutation of Idealism as anticipating Wittgenstein's attack on the notion of a private language, it fails to earn its title.

4. AN AFTERTHOUGHT: EPISTEMOLOGY AND THE CARTESIAN BASIS

In this paper I have argued that Kant's notion of objectivity is crucially ambiguous and that he fails to show that we must make objective judgments in the more important second sense. Neither the Transcendental Deduction nor the Refutation of Idealism gives us conclusive grounds for supposing that we must believe in an external world independent of our perceptions. In the course of examining the Refutation of Idealism, I also argued that we must abandon the incorrigibility thesis, the claim that necessarily my beliefs about my experiences are true. I want now to point out very briefly an important consequence. I want to suggest that, if we do indeed abandon incorrigibility, we need to approach Kantian problems about the existence of external objects in an entirely different way. Whatever their various disagreements, many philosophers since Descartes have shared the "Cartesian basis," as Jonathan Bennett puts it. That is, they have agreed that our experiences form a sure and certain foundation for our knowledge of the world. Beliefs about external objects may need justification, but beliefs about experiences do not. Thereafter, of course, their paths diverge. Some, like Berkeley, argue that an object is a collection of experiences; some, like Russell in some moods, argue that an object is a "logical construction" out of experiences; some, like Putnam, argue that our belief in the external world is the best theory available to explain our experiences; Kant insists that such a belief is a necessary condition of our having experiences at all. All agree on the starting point, whatever happens thereafter. But, once we abandon incorrigibility, there is no longer an agreed, secure starting point. If all our beliefs are corrigible, including our beliefs about our experiences, then beliefs about the external world are no more in need of a general justification than beliefs about experiences. Furthermore, there is no general reason to suppose that one set of beliefs must form the *basis* of another set. We must, once and for all, abandon the picture of knowledge as having foundations in the form of utterly secure beliefs about our experiences.

Notes

1. R. C. S. Walker, *Kant* (London: Routledge and Kegan Paul, 1978), p. 76.
2. *Ibid.*, p. 117.
3. T. E. Wilkerson, "Kant on Self-Consciousness," *Philosophical Quarterly* (1980), pp. 54-60.
4. Cf. P. F. Strawson, *The Bounds of Sense* (London: Methuen, 1966), pp. 89-112, and T. E. Wilkerson, *Kant's Critique of Pure Reason* (Oxford: Clarendon Press, 1976), pp. 54-61.
5. Strawson, *op. cit.*, p. 107.
6. L. Wittgenstein, *Philosophical Investigations* (Oxford: Basil Blackwell, second edition, 1958), Pt. I, § 258.
7. A. J. Ayer, "Could There Be a Private Language?" in *The Concept of a Person and Other Essays* (London: Macmillan, 1964), p. 42n.

Kant's Philosophy of Science

PHILIP KITCHER

Contemporary philosophers are not usually enthusiastic about Kant's philosophy of science, and it is not hard to understand why Kant's discussions of science meet with a lukewarm reception. In the first place, Kant seems to be committed to the idea that some substantive scientific principles can be known a priori. Second, his apparent attempt to do a priori science, the *Metaphysical Foundations of Natural Science*, contains some very unpromising arguments, and its relation to the first *Critique* is highly obscure. In this paper, I will explore some of Kant's ideas about science, with the aims of understanding whether he is really an advocate of a priori science and of exposing the intended relation between the *Critique* and the *Metaphysical Foundations*. I also want to see whether there is anything we can learn from Kant's doctrines about science.

I

Kant's apparent commitment to the existence of a priori science is expressed in the early pages of the *Critique* (and in parallel sections in the *Prolegomena*). Despite the fact that his assertion that synthetic a priori judgments exist in natural science is more outré than the companion claim about mathematics, Kant offers little by way of defense or explanation. He states bluntly that two propositions are necessary and a priori and that this status is evident. Kant's propositions sound like general truths of physics: "In all changes of the material world the quantity of matter remains unchanged" and "in all communication of motion, action and reaction must always be equal" (B17-18).[1]

Later in the *Critique* there are passages that seem to retract this bold doctrine. At the height of the *Deductions*, Kant declares that only laws "which are involved in a *nature in general*" are knowable a priori (B165; also A127-28). The *Antinomies* section is more forthright. Drawing an invidious contrast with pure mathematics and pure ethics, Kant declares: "In natural science . . . there is endless conjecture, and certainty is not to be counted upon" (A480, B508). Since he firmly believes that all a priori knowledge is certain, this passage implies that natural science is not a priori.

We can easily reconcile the contrary indications by drawing a distinction that Kant sometimes makes explicitly. Perhaps *most* of natural science is empirical, and Kant's remarks in the *Deductions* and the *Antinomies* are prompted by consideration of empirical natural sciences. What is distinctive about Kant's philosophy of science is the idea that natural science contains a pure part, and the Introduction to the *Critique* is intended to advertise the existence of pure natural science.

Since it is evident that Kant does not believe all natural science to be a priori, this distinction has to be drawn. Yet, it does not resolve all our problems. Does Kant's a priori science include anything more than the very general propositions about nature that he tries to prove in the Transcendental *Analytic*? If not, then Kant's doctrine loses its provocative character, and the claim that there is a priori science is exposed as based on a dull pun. The Introduction to the *Critique* suggests a way to restore the excitement. Kant's examples sound like central laws of Newtonian physics, so we might attribute the view that central parts of Newtonian physics belong to a priori science.

This attribution has been popular. It rests on three pieces of evidence. Besides the Introduction to the *Critique*, there is a section in the *Prolegomena* that appears to sketch an a priori route to the law of universal gravitation[2] and an entire work, the *Metaphysical Foundations of Natural Science*, seemingly devoted to the task of proving many basic Newtonian principles. However, taken individually, these three pieces of evidence are inconclusive and, taken collectively, there are internal tensions among them.

Kant's use of terms like 'matter', 'action', and 'reaction' is not clearly explained in the *Critique*, and, although the propositions enunciated in the Introduction sound like principles of Newtonian science, we might easily reinterpret them as the more general claims for which Kant argues in the *Analogies*. In #36 of the *Prolegomena*, Kant does indeed outline what looks like an attempt at a priori argument for the law of universal gravitation. But he characterizes it by saying that it explains why the law "is usually propounded as capable of being known as a priori." This characterization stops short of endorsing the argument as an a priori proof. Finally, despite the fact that the *Metaphysical Foundations* does claim that there is a pure part of natural science to which basic Newtonian principles belong, Kant clearly distinguishes between the status of those principles and the propositions established in the *Critique*. Indeed, the more detailed articulation of his views about science that is given in the later work suggests that we *must* reinterpret those parts of the *Critique* and the *Prolegomena* that seem to claim the apriority of Newtonian science. Kant maintains that *some* general Newtonian principles are knowable a priori, *given the empirical concept of matter*, but his discussion of the law of gravitation does not even attribute this status to it.

These jumbled doctrines about Newtonian science are best understood if we adopt an interpretative hypothesis. Kant does not believe that principles like that of the conservation of matter and that of the equality of action and reaction are fully a priori. Nor does he think that these principles are best described simply by declaring them to be empirical. Instead, he takes them to admit of *something like* a priori proof. Introducing a label, let us say that, for Kant, parts of Newtonian science are *quasi a priori* and that the *Metaphysical Foundations* is his attempt to display their quasi apriority. I want to see whether we can give sense to the idea of quasi apriority in a way that will illuminate what Kant says about Newtonian science.

II

Our chief clue comes from the announcement of his project that Kant provides at the beginning of the *Metaphysical Foundations*. After attempting to explain why there can be no "natural science proper" without a pure part, Kant continues by elaborating on the nature of this "pure part."

> . . . [It] must indeed always contain nothing but principles which are not empirical (for that reason it bears the name of a metaphysics). But either it can treat of the laws which make possible the concept of a nature in general even without reference to any determinate object of experience, and therefore undetermined regarding the nature of this or that thing of the sense-world—and in this case it is the transcendental part of the metaphysics of nature—or it occupies itself with the specific nature of this or that kind of things, of which an empirical concept is given in such a way that besides what lies in this concept, no other empirical principle is needed for cognizing the things (MFNS 6).

This passage represents a division of labor between the *Critique* and the *Metaphysical Foundations*. The task of the *Critique* is to set forth those principles that apply to nature in general. The later work is to expound those quasi-a priori principles obtained by introducing an empirically grounded concept.

What exactly does this mean? There is an obvious, and trivial, way to relativize the notion of apriority. We can say that a proposition is a priori relative to a theory if, given knowledge of the theory, we can obtain knowledge of the proposition without further reliance on experience. This is trivial because most empiricists will concede that any theorem of any knowable theory is a priori relative to that theory. However, Kant seems to be after something different. He does not say that the law of conservation of matter is a priori relative to Newtonian theory but that this, and other Newtonian principles, are a priori relative to an empirical concept.

The trivial relativization of apriority just considered presupposes a particular way of thinking about science that is deeply embedded in contemporary empiricist philosophy of science but that is at odds with Kant's approach. We find it natural to view science as a collection of theories and to identify a theory as a deductively organized set of propositions. Kant does not explicitly consider the question "What is a scientific theory?" but I believe that he would reject the standard empiricist idea that the epistemologically interesting questions about science should be addressed by taking theories to be organized sets of propositions.[3] By understanding how an alternative approach to theories might be developed, I think we can obtain a clearer view of that relativization of the notion of apriority that Kant intends to employ.

Let me begin obliquely. It is standard practice to use two different notions of scientific theory. In our more restrictive usage, we talk about theories as short-lived entities; thus, we might speak of Newtonian theory, intending to refer to the particular set of propositions put forward by Newton in a particular work (*Principia*). I will call such entities *theory versions*. We also talk of theories as enduring entities, and we identify different, incompatible theory versions as belonging to the same theory. In this usage, we envisage something that stands behind the sets of propositions accepted by successive generations of scientists and that unites those sets of propositions as versions of a single theory.[4]

At any stage in the history of a scientific field, we can identify the set of statements that practitioners of the field accept. For *some* epistemological purposes, it may be useful to axiomatize (a subset of) these statements. However, I believe that there are some epistemological inquiries and some fields of science for which the focus on statements (rather than on questions or on procedures for answering questions) is inappropriate. But, even if we concede the traditional idea that epistemological questions about the science of a time can take the set of accepted statements as an index of the state of science, there still remains the question of what unites the sets of accepted statements (theory versions). What is the larger entity, the one theory that embraces the different versions? One suggestion is to identify a set of core propositions that persists through the sequence of theory versions. Another answer — the answer I attribute to Kant — is that a temporally enduring theory is constituted by a *projected order of nature*.[5]

A projected order of nature is a scheme for classifying and explaining natural phenomena. Kant's presentation develops the idea in a particular way. Think of a concept as a rule for marking out a set of things (the extension of the concept) by specifying certain properties that the members of the extension are to have. A theory, or projected order of nature, presents a hierarchy of concepts. At the top of the hierarchy is a concept, whose extension is the set of *fundamental entities* with which the theory is concerned and which marks out those entities according to their *fundamental properties*. As we move down the hierarchy, we encounter concepts that apply to *derivative entities* (or perhaps to subsets of the fundamental entities) and that identify those entities by *derivative properties*. What this means is that, if a concept C_{n+1} occurs immediately below a concept C_n, then the fact that the entities actually belonging to the extension of C_{n+1} have the properties C_{n+1} attributed to them is to be explained by appealing to the fact that the entities in the extension of C_n have the properties C_n attributes to them. On this account, a theory is something that tells us how to group things together and that presents the skeletal structure of explanations.

It is easy to see that a theory, or a projected order of nature, can give rise to different theory versions. The theory may tell us that a particular property (or set of properties) is dependent on another property (or set of properties). But the exact form of the dependence need not be specified. So, for example, Dalton's atomic theory proposed to explain chemical reactions in terms of molecular rearrangements.

This theory generated a number of different versions, each of which was characterized by precise claims about how the molecules combine in particular cases.

I claim that, if Kant had addressed the question "What is a scientific theory?" his answer would have been "a projected order of nature." In introducing this answer, I have begun from a problem that has recently interested many philosophers of science, the problem of how to understand scientific change. This is not a problem that would have motivated Kant. He would have been concerned to emphasize two respects in which the account of theory just sketched is superior to the standard empiricist analysis: (1) It provides a more accurate picture of the methodology of empirical science; (2) it allows us to understand how pure natural science—quasi-a priori science—is possible. I will elaborate both points, concentrating primarily on the second.

III

Kant's discussion of the confirmation of theories hardly amount to a systematic treatment. Nevertheless, his remarks indicate that he views theories as subject to judgment according to a number of different criteria. Most obvious is an emphasis on the predictive success of theory versions. Indeed, Kant sometimes sounds like a proponent of twentieth-century hypothetico-deductivist orthodoxy: we support our theory versions by verifying their observational consequences (Bxii-xiii; A646-47, B674–75). Yet, there are more distinctive suggestions about confirmation. Kant appears to believe that there are principles that we can use to assess the merits of theories directly, prior to our enunciation of theory versions. One principle enjoins us to prefer theories that give rise to theory versions that are more subject to test. Others, presented in an appendix to the *Ideal of Pure Reason*, direct us to choose theories with special properties: for example, we are to search for unified theories. I believe that these principles can be understood if we attribute to Kant the perspective on theories that I indicated above.

Toward the end of the second chapter of the *Metaphysical Foundations*, Kant considers the merits of two rival explanatory schemes.[6] One of these, the "mechanical way," proposes that the phenomena of nature are to be understood by tracing them to the interactions among atoms, each of which is viewed as having certain fundamental properties, including impenetrability. The alternative, which Kant favors, is the "dynamical way." On this conception, we are to understand natural phenomena by regarding them as the results of the distribution of centers of fundamental forces. As Kant puts it, the goal of science lies in "explicating all varieties of matter through the mere variety in the combination of the original forces of repulsion and attraction" (MFNS 90). Although the details of this proposal are far from clear, it is not hard to identify the merits that Kant takes it to enjoy. He is worried that it is too easy to construct theory versions that conform to the "mechanical philosophy." The use of the concepts of "absolute density" and "absolute emptiness" allows too much freedom to the scientific imagination (MFNS 90). As he puts it positively:

A dynamical mode of explication . . . [is] more favorable to experimental philosophy inasmuch as it leads directly to the discovery of the moving forces proper to matters and the laws of such forces, but restricts the freedom of assuming empty intermediate spaces and fundamental particles of determinate shapes, neither of which can be discovered or determined by an experiment . . . (MFNS 91-92).[7]

Because the "dynamical mode of explanation" is a cloudy notion, it is not easy to evaluate Kant's application of the criterion invoked here. However, what concerns me is the criterion rather than its employment. The rival hypotheses are both projected orders of nature. We are invited to compare them independently of the specific versions of them that may be available. Kant envisages a situation in which, given one account of the hierarchy of concepts, we see how to proceed experimentally to identify precise versions of the relations of dependence, while, on the other account, we have no similar experimental procedure for isolating the correct version. The methodological directive is to prefer those explanatory schemes that focus our explanation-seeking questions, making them accessible to empirical investigations. To use Kant's famous terminology from the Preface to the second edition of the *Critique*, some projected orders of nature teach us how to interrogate nature, and such theories are intrinsically more worthy of acceptance than those that do not.

The idea of comparing theories, rather than theory versions, is also fundamental to the Appendix to the *Ideal*. Kant identifies three "regulative principles," the principles of "*homogeneity, specification*, and *continuity* of forms" (A658, B686). Neither the content of these principles nor their intended status is made particularly clear by Kant's remarks. However, both kinds of obscurity can be lessened if we understand this section to be concerned with criteria for judging theories. Consider first the maxim on which Kant places most emphasis, the directive to "bring . . . systematic unity into our knowledge"[8] (A650, B678). I interpret this as enjoining us to prefer theories that put forward a smaller number of fundamental entities and properties. (How precisely the accounting is to be done is a tricky business; I will not explore this issue here.[9]) The second maxim directs us to "attend to the diversity no less than to the identity" (A654, B683). Here, Kant seems to be insisting that the bottom level of the hierarchy must be sufficiently fine to accommodate the variety of natural phenomena. Finally, he adds a law of "the *affinity* of all concepts," directing us to group together concepts into families at each level of our conceptual hierarchy, so that "all the manifold differences are then related to one another, inasmuch as they one and all spring from one highest genus, through all degrees of a more and more widely extended determination" (A658, B686). When we combine the three principles, we can easily obtain a picture of the type of theory (projected order of nature) that is intrinsically worthy of acceptance (see p. 393). Kant's own summation itself suggests this picture (A660, B688).

I believe that the account of theories attributed to Kant makes sense of his attempts to explain how theories are confirmed. Kant thinks of a theory as something like a taxonomy. A theory is a hierarchy of concepts that exposes the direction of explanation. The passages that I have cited articulate this conception in terms of the Aristotelian logic that Kant knew. As I will suggest in the final section, contemporary

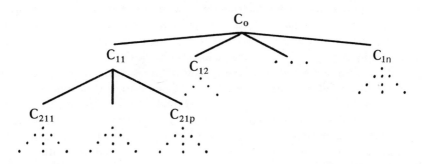

(The numbers n, p are large, so that the tree branches considerably at each node)

logical views may enable us to provide a more sophisticated development of the basic Kantian idea. First, however, I want to see how Kant's views about the methods of empirical science provide a framework within which his conception of quasi-a priori science can be set.

IV

Two related definitions of quasi-a priori science present themselves. The first begins from the apparent possibility that, having adopted a theory, we might be able to proceed, without any further assistance from experience, to arrive at a particular theory version. The second involves something even more ambitious. Suppose that we had empirical reason to believe that it is appropriate to conceptualize the entities we are interested in investigating as having certain properties (not necessarily fundamental properties). Then, on the basis of this, but using no further empirical information, we might be able to construct parts of a projected order of nature and even to arrive at parts of a particular theory version. I think that Kant conceives of this possibility as genuine and that he takes it to be realized in Newtonian science. The *Metaphysical Foundations* is his attempt to display how quasi-a priori science, in the more ambitious sense, is possible.

It will be useful to have a more precise characterization of the bolder notion. I begin from the ideas of an *a priori procedure* and of an *empirically legitimzed concept*. Quasi-a priori science consists of two types of activity: (1) using a priori procedures to construct a hierarchy of concepts that will include the empirically legitimized concept; acceptance of this hierarchy is justified by the empirical evidence that supports the concept and the a priori procedures employed; (2) using a priori procedures to reason from the hierarchy of concepts constructed in (1) to a determinate theory version. We will see that, in the *Metaphysical Foundations*, Kant tries to engage in both kinds of activity.

Two central Kantian themes need to be tackled before this project will be fully comprehensible. Consider first the notion of a priori procedure.[10] Early in the *Critique*, Kant identifies a priori knowledge as knowledge that is independent of experience. His definition is best understood by supposing that a priori knowledge is knowledge obtained by following an a priori procedure and focusing on the concept of a priori procedure. An a priori procedure for a proposition is a type of process such that, given any experience that would be sufficiently rich to enable someone to entertain the proposition, a process of the type would be available to the agent and, if it were followed, would generate knowledge of the proposition. (The function of the restriction to "sufficiently rich experiences" is to allow for the possibility that we know a priori propositions involving concepts that are not innate. Kant plainly wants to allow that there are a priori propositions containing concepts that we can only acquire with the aid of experience. See, for example, his characterization of the proposition that every alteration has its cause as impure but a priori [B3].)

The basic idea of this notion of a priori procedure is easily explained. Picture a person as a device endowed with a set of cognitive capacities. Consider all the possible streams of experience that the person could have. Some of these will be long and complicated; others will be very short. With respect to any proposition, we restrict our attention to those streams of experience that would enable the person, constituted as she is, to entertain the proposition. A type of process is an a priori procedure for the proposition, if, given any experience in the restricted class, the person could undergo some process of the type, and, if she were to undergo such a process, she would achieve knowledge of the proposition.

What kinds of procedures might count as a priori? In the *Critique*, Kant divides a priori procedures into three main types. Conceptual analysis is a procedure, about which Kant says very little, that is supposed to yield knowledge of analytic truths. Two procedures give us a priori knowledge of synthetic truths. Construction in pure intuition is the route to a priori mathematical knowledge. So, for example, Kant believes that by constructing geometrical figures and inspecting them with the mind's eye we expose to ourselves the features of space and thus gain a priori knowledge of geometrical truths. A different kind of a priori procedure consists in analysis of the conditions of possible experience. The arguments advanced in the *Principles* chapter of the *Analytic* are intended to exemplify this kind of procedure. They are attempts to show that certain conclusions must be true if experience is to be possible for us, and Kant seems also to believe that they supply routes to those conclusions that would yield knowledge of them whatever (sufficiently rich) experience we might have.[11] There is an obvious difference between the theses about a priori procedures advanced in the *Aesthetic* and the *Analytic*. Whereas the process of pure intuition is *described* and its epistemological credentials are analyzed, the procedure of analysis of the conditions of possible experience is *displayed*, and Kant does not examine carefully whether it will really satisfy his constraints on a priori procedures.

Let us now turn to the issue of conceptual legitimacy. Throughout the *Critique*, Kant insists on the importance of establishing that the concepts we use are rightfully employed. How does this inquiry arise? Kant's basic idea is that concepts of certain kinds are so deficient that, if a person believes a proposition involving such concepts, then that person's belief is ipso facto unjustified. Consider a simple example. If I maintain that all round squares are round, you might be willing to credit me with a piece of knowledge, even a piece of a priori knowledge, on the grounds that I have followed an a priori procedure, analysis of concepts, to obtain a true belief. Kant would deny that this attribution is correct. Concepts, like that of a round square, that cannot be exemplified, are not constituents of propositions that one can justifiably believe. Analysis of a *legitimate* concept counts as an a priori procedure, but not every concept is legitimate.

It is important to note that there are two separate questions that Kant would be prepared to ask about a given concept. We could inquire whether some experience of a particular kind is needed to *acquire* a particular concept. Or we could inquire whether some experience of a particular kind is needed to *justify our use* of a particular concept. Kant *allows* for a priori knowledge of propositions containing concepts that can only be acquired on the basis of particular kinds of experience. But I take him to *deny* that we know a priori propositions containing concepts whose use could be undermined by experience. Part of this doctrine about mathematics, that part that gives point to the *Axioms of Intuition*, is that we cannot have empirical justification for abandoning the concepts involved in mathematical judgments. (These concepts are *a priori concepts*.)

Kant's interest in the issue of conceptual legitimacy (so prominent in the *Analytic*) makes his views about the a priori much more complicated than they are often taken to be. Allowing that a priori knowledge is knowledge obtainable given any *sufficiently rich* experience opens the possibility of a priori knowledge of propositions including concepts that can only be acquired empirically. Demanding that the concepts that figure in items of knowledge be legitimized entails that we cannot know a priori those propositions that contain concepts that experience could justify us in discarding. Implicit in the *Critique* is the denial that all analytic propositions are a priori. Kant is working his way toward a Quinean insight. Experience can undermine our beliefs by showing that we should abandon a particular way of thinking about the phenomena.[12]

In the *Critique*, Kant's touchstone for conceptual legitimacy is possible exemplification in experience. Although this test is adequate to his principal epistemological purposes, I do not think it really captures his central insight. Kant sees that it is possible to employ crazy concepts and that someone who does so makes no contribution to human inquiry. But instantiation in actual experience (or in possible experience) is neither necessary nor sufficient for conceptual sanity. Idealizations are properly employed in our investigations. Concepts that intersect natural kinds in bizarre ways are not.

There is a brief discussion of the use of idealization in science in the Appendix to the *Ideal*, a discussion that indicates an improved criterion for conceptual legitimacy. Kant suggests that the drive for a unified system of knowledge warrants us in abstracting from some of the conditions we encounter in experience (A645-6, B673-4). Generalizing this suggestion, we may propose that a concept is legitimate if and only if it belongs to (or further extends) a well-confirmed theory, that is, to a well-confirmed projected order of nature.

This proposal will help us to explicate the notion of an empirically legitimized concept and also to see why Kant stresses the importance of the "pure part" of natural science. Consider a responsible scientist. She will want to use the evidence available to her to assess the adequacy of the concepts she employs. Can she succeed without having at her disposal a well-confirmed theory? I believe that Kant's answer would be that it depends on the concepts in question. *Some* concepts, the more special ones, may not be subject to legitimization except by noting that they belong to a successful theory. However, I think Kant would claim that the credentials of some concepts can be established even prior to our articulation of a full theory. The idea would be that, even before we have developed a projected order of nature, we may be able to recognize, empirically, that certain concepts must figure in any successful theory. So, for example, experience might teach us that *all* the entities with which our science will be concerned will have particular properties. Thus, the concept that marks them out as having these properties must find some place in our theory — though not necessarily as a fundamental concept.[13] Let us call concepts whose use can be justified by experience prior to the articulation of a theory *empirically legitimized concepts*.

The doctrine that natural science must have a pure part can now be explained. Kant would suggest that proper scientific investigation should exemplify the following pattern. One begins by using experience to legitimize certain concepts. On the basis of these concepts, one uses a priori procedures to construct a theory and, possibly, even parts of a theory version. Once this stage has been reached, one has achieved a framework within which the experimental interrogation of nature can profitably begin. *Pure natural science is important because it takes us from a position in which naive observation teaches us that some concepts are legitimate to a situation in which we can propose and test precise technical hypotheses.*

In developing my interpretation of Kant's thesis that natural science must have a pure part, I have adopted a particular construal of the Kantian notions of a priori knowledge and a priori concepts. There is an alternative approach to these notions that can justifiably be traced to the first *Critique*, and, in the remainder of this section, I will outline this approach, contrast it with my own, and suggest why my construal offers a more promising reading of Kant's philosophy of science.

Like Kant's own introduction of the concept of apriority, I have begun with the idea of a priori *knowledge*.[14] However, it is quite apparent that the *Transcendental Analytic* is primarily concerned with a priori *concepts* and with a priori principles involving those concepts. If one begins with Kant's remarks in the *Analytic*, taking these usages as primary, a different picture of apriority emerges. This picture has been sketched in papers by Hilary Putnam and Manley Thompson.[15] On the Putnam-Thompson picture, *a priori propositions* are those propositions that cannot be defeated by experience because, given any possible experience, we must believe those propositions if we are to be capable of rational thought at all. *A priori concepts* are concepts that must figure in our beliefs if rational thought is to be possible for us. I think that it is relatively easy to discern these conceptions of a priori propositions and a priori concepts in some of the discussions of the *Transcendental Deductions* and the *Principles* chapter of the *Analytic*.

Let me note first that the Putnam-Thompson characterization of a priori propositions does not seem to be equivalent to mine. My approach allows in principle for the apriority of propositions that are, as it were, luxuries of our belief system. Thus, on my account, it would be possible to hold that a recondite logical or mathematical truth is a priori in that there is a procedure that we can follow that will warrant belief in it, given any sufficiently rich experience, even though it is acknowledged that it is not a prerequisite of rational thought that one believes the logical or mathematical truth in question. We can simultaneously hold, for example, that Gödel's theorems for elementary arithmetic can be known a priori and that people (like Hilbert) who believed propositions incompatible with those theorems were capable of rational thought. (This is not to maintain that, on my account, Gödel's theorems will turn out to be a priori truths. My point is just that, on the approach to apriority I have developed, the conclusion that Gödel's theorems are not a priori does not follow from the premises that Hilbert believed a proposition inconsistent with the theorems and that Hilbert engaged in rational thought.)

The Putnam-Thompson criterion for a priori propositions diverges from mine in a different respect. It is possible that a person may not be justified in believing a proposition that is a prerequisite of rational thought. Consider the following scenario. Humans come into contact with a race of aliens who quickly seem to learn how to communicate with us. The aliens teach us many remarkable things, clear up longstanding problems in mathematics and science, and introduce us to concepts that make it possible for us to develop entirely new fields of inquiry. One day they tell us that the time has arrived to correct a fundamental misapprehension. Our standard logical system, including a principle that we (rightly) take to be a fundamental prerequisite of rational thought, should be abandoned. The aliens explain that our old system has foundations that are conceptually flawed, and they offer to teach us something better. Unfortunately, when we are shown their "logic," we find it incomprehensible. The aliens profess disappointment and provide apparently conclusive demonstrations that their "logical" perspective has led them to solve important problems. Yet we are still unable to learn.

Will we be justified in believing the propositions of our logic — including those that are indeed prerequisites for rational thought — given the type of experience I have described? The first point that I want to make is that the mere fact that the propositions we are asked to abandon are prerequisites of rational thought does not make us justified in continuing to believe them. A lazy dogmatist among us, someone who simply ignored the alien challenge, would not be justified in his belief. As in more mundane cases, whether we are justified depends on how our belief is generated.[16] But now a second point arises. It is conceivable that there is no procedure that we can use to turn back all the challenges that the aliens can muster. They may offer excellent reasons for believing that our inability to learn their "logic" reflects the same psychological difficulties encountered by our ancestors in coping with non-Euclidean geometry or quantum physics. Perhaps they may dupe us into thinking that members of our own species have been able to gain entry to their logical system with remarkably liberating results. Under these circumstances, though we might have no option but to continue using our old system, we would not be justified in believing its principles. Our position would be an extreme version of predicaments in which human inquirers have sometimes found themselves: we would feel compelled to carry out our investigations within a system that, quite reasonably, we believe to suffer from serious defects.

If these arguments are correct, then the Putnam-Thompson conception of apriority will identify as a priori a rather different class of propositions than those countenanced by my analysis. Now I have already recognized the existence of both notions in Kant's *Critique*. I think it is likely that Kant took the two conceptions to be equivalent and that, when he claims that the principles of the *Analytic* are a priori, he thinks that they are both items of a priori knowledge (in my sense) and that they are prerequisites of rational thought. (Of course, given his early linking of the notions of necessity and apriority, he also contends that the principles are necessary truths. As Kripke and others have argued, this equivalence is also faulty.[17]) The question that now confronts us is whether, in Kant's discussions of pure natural science, we should read him as maintaining that the propositions hailed as a priori are being celebrated as items of a priori knowledge or as prerequisites of rational thought.[18]

An interpretation of Kant's claim along Putnam-Thompson lines could proceed as follows. What Kant asserts is that any rational investigator who forms judgments involving particular concepts must have certain beliefs. In particular, to form judgments involving the concept of matter (more exactly, the concept(s) of matter articulated in the *Metaphysical Foundations*) one must believe that there are attractive forces that act at a distance, that matter obeys Newton's laws of motion, and so forth. Now this interpretation appears extremely implausible. The Putnam-Thompson conception of apriority is geared to the explanation of the status of beliefs that are so fundamental to our thinking that they appear undeniable. It is not well adapted to understanding the status of scientifically controversial propositions. Kant would be hard pressed to defend the idea that Leibniz and other opponents of Newtonian principles, opponents who advanced judgments about matter, had abandoned prerequisites for rational thought. My rival interpretation appears far more likely. Given their acceptance of the concept of matter, Newton's detractors ought to have withdrawn their criticisms. For, on Kant's view (as I construe him), there are procedures that can be followed independently of experience that will lead from acceptance of the concept of matter to endorsement of Newtonian judgments. Rather than being scientific analogues of those who try to flout the principle of noncontradiction (or Putnam's "minimal principle of non-contradiction"),[19] anti-Newtonians are like those who fail to appreciate the subtle consequences of their beliefs. (They do not recognize the presuppositions of their own criticisms.)

I think that the characterization of quasi-a priori science that I have given can best be defended by showing how it illuminates the enterprise of the *Metaphysical Foundations*. Kant claims that certain concepts of matter are legitimized by experience. Spatial objects that are to affect us must have certain properties; we learn this by discovering very general facts about how our senses are affected (MFNS 13–14; see also MFNS 20). The properties in question are known on the basis of experience to apply to all objects of outer experience. If one supposes that a concept that applies to all objects that fall within the domain of physical science must find a place within our physical theory, then it is possible to conclude that the concepts that ascribe the relevant properties are empirically legitimized.

What are the properties that Kant selects? The concept of matter is developed in sequence through the chapters of the *Metaphysical Foundations*. Kant begins with the concept of matter as "the movable in space," arguing forthrightly that what is not movable cannot affect the "external senses" (MFNS 14). Subsequent chapters add the properties of "filling a space" (glossed as the property of resisting intrusion) and of "having a moving force" (construed as a power to impart motion). (In the final chapter, he adds the definition of matter as that which "can as such be an object of experience," but it seems to me that this characterization is redundant. The earlier chapters appear to be an attempt to specify the conditions that have to be met if something is to be an object of experience. I will henceforth ignore the final chapter, which, like the *Postulates* section of the *Principles* chapter of the *Critique* to which it corresponds, seems to have been introduced solely to fill a vacant gap in Kant's all-too-tidy system.)

Whatever the merits of his reasons for thinking that the concepts of matter he chooses are empirically legitimized, the central doctrine of the *Metaphysical Foundations* is an interesting one. Given that it is appropriate to characterize the objects of physical science as movable, as able to fill space and to transmit motion in impact, we are to construct a priori a projected order of nature and to justify a priori certain Newtonian principles. Specifically, we are to show a priori that diverse natural phenomena are to be understood by advancing hypotheses about the distribution of centers of fundamental forces, that the impenetrability of matter is explained by the fact that matter is endowed with a fundamental repulsive force, that gravitational phenomena result from the fact that matter has a fundamental attractive force; and we are to reason a priori to the truth of a principle of mass conservation and of Newton's first and third laws. This is quite an agenda.

Kant has a clear conception of how the conclusions are to be reached. The *Critique* identifies two types of a priori procedures for synthetic truths. Believing that one of these, the analysis of the conditions of possible experience, takes precedence over the other, the construction of concepts in pure intuition, Kant asserts that the initial stage of pure natural science must consist in "metaphysical constructions." Hence, even though the *Metaphysical Foundations* attempts something very ambitious, Kant restricts himself to using only part of his arsenal of a priori procedures, namely, the procedures of the *Transcendental Analytic*. Throughout the work, Kant is faithful to the self-imposed prohibition against the use of mathematics,[20] and I will argue below that his policy leads him into serious errors. However, he does not succeed in restricting himself to applying the conclusions of the *Analytic*, since the regulative principles of the Appendix to the *Ideal* play an important part in developing his explanatory scheme. (See MFNS 48, 90-4.)

When we look at seventeenth- and eighteenth-century speculative natural philosophy, examining the writings of Descartes, Leibniz, Euler, Boscovich, or Kant, there is a strong temptation to dismiss the enterprise as thoroughly confused. However, I think that Kant offers an interesting theory of a type of scientific activity in vogue among his predecessors and that the *Metaphysical Foundations* represents his own attempt to practice it. (Given his belief that the critical machinery provides a detailed account of the activity, he was also confident that he could do it properly.) I want also to suggest that the activity is as much a part of our own science as it was of the science of Kant's day. Anyone who has taken a standard college course in special relativity or electromagnetic theory or fundamental particle physics will have heard arguments that, beginning from a particular conceptualization of the phenomena, proceed, by steps that make no obvious reference to empirical findings, to striking conclusions. Similarly, derivations of the central equations of population biology seem to adopt a particular description of the situation to be studied and then to advance to the enunciation of precise laws without further recourse to experience. In the "thought experiments" of contemporary physicists and the "modeling" of contemporary biologists and social scientists, we find the present versions of that part of scientific activity that Kant's account of pure natural science tries to characterize.

Empiricists are likely to respond either by denying that the activity has any epistemological significance or by proposing an alternative account of it. In the final section of this paper, I will take a brief look at this empiricist response. Before I do so, however, I want to show that Kant's execution of the project of quasi-a priori science in the *Metaphysical Foundations* is a disaster. In trying simultaneously to exemplify his philosophical theory and to resolve substantive scientific questions, Kant fails to achieve either goal.

V

The scope of the intended conclusions of the *Metaphysical Foundations* makes it impossible for me to examine in detail all the arguments that Kant offers. I will focus on one example that represents both the merits of the work and its shortcomings. The example is Kant's treatment of attractive force.

The main direction of argument in Chapter 2 of the *Metaphysical Foundations* is as follows. Kant begins with the definition of matter as the movable that fills a space. On the basis of this conception, he argues that we should attribute as a fundamental property of matter the property of being a seat of repulsive force. (This argument endeavors to move from a concept to a projected order of nature. It is presented briefly early in the chapter [MFNS 42, 48] and in a more extended form in the concluding "General Observation" [MFNS 77-94], part of which I have mentioned above.) After a sequence of propositions characterizing this fundamental force, Kant claims that "the possibility of matter requires a force of attraction, as the second fundamental force of matter" (Proposition 5, MFNS 56). He believes that he cannot only prove quasi a priori the existence of this attractive force but that he can establish some of its general properties, in particular that it acts at a distance. However, Kant denies that he can demonstrate quasi a priori the specific mathematical form of the law of gravitation. On his account, to show that the attractive force is inversely as the square of the distance requires further assumptions.

Let us consider one step in this sequence of arguments, the attempt to show that matter must be a seat of attractive force. The proof of Proposition 5 begins as follows:

> Impenetrability, as the fundamental property of matter whereby it first reveals itself as something real in the space of our external senses, is nothing but matter's capacity of extension (Proposition 2). Now, an essential moving force by which parts of matter recede from each other cannot, firstly, be limited by itself, because matter is impelled by such a force to continuously expand the space that it occupies, and cannot, secondly, be fixed by space alone at a certain limit of extension. This second is so because even though space can indeed contain the ground of the fact that with the increase in the volume of a matter extending itself, the extensive force becomes weaker in inverse proportion; yet inasmuch as smaller degrees of every moving force are possible to infinity, space cannot anywhere contain the ground of the ceasing of such a force. Therefore, matter by its repulsive force alone (which contains the ground of its impenetrability), and if no other moving force counteracted this repuslive one, would be held within no limits of extension, i.e., would disperse itself to infinity, and no assignable quantity of matter would be found in any assignable space. Consequently, with merely repulsive forces of matter, all spaces would be empty; and hence, strictly speaking, there would be no matter at all (MFNS 56-7).

Kant then goes on to argue that the dispersal of matter could only be prevented if matter were endowed with a fundamental attractive force.

Like most of the attempts at proof in the *Metaphysical Foundations*, this argument is a failure. Instead of reveling in its inadequacies, I will try to understand why Kant produced so misguided a piece of reasoning. Let us begin by noting that, notwithstanding the reference to the theory of space in the opening sentence, Kant does not use his favored a priori procedures to reach his conclusion. The argument belies the advertisement for "pure natural science" that we find in the Preface to the *Metaphysical Foundations*. What Kant appears to be doing is engaging in a clumsy thought experiment. We are asked to imagine a situation in which matter, endowed only with repulsive force, is present; Kant tries to show us that the situation must develop into a state in which space is empty.

The trouble is that the original situation is hopelessly underdescribed. Kant has forbidden himself the use of mathematics, and his qualitative formulations permit him to neglect a myriad of alternative possibilities. The claim that matter is the seat of repulsive force seems to amount to supposing that, when a particular volume of space is occupied by matter, a field of repulsive force takes on nonzero values through the volume. Kant seems to make the following assumptions: (1) the field is uniform through the volume; (2) because the force is repulsive, at later times the matter will be dispersed and the associated force field will take on nonzero values on a larger volume; (3) the intensity of the repulsive force varies inversely as the volume occupied; (4) the sequence of volumes occupied at successive times is not bounded above. Lacking a precise specification of his premises, Kant produces a sketch of an argument instead of a proof.[21]

It is interesting to compare the proof of Proposition 5 with the far more explicit discussion of the law of universal gravitation. Kant emphasizes that we cannot attempt to establish precise quantitative force laws in the same way that we can prove the existence of a fundamental attractive force (MFNS 69, 76). So, his argument for the inverse square law of gravitation (the same argument canvassed in #36 of the *Prolegomena*) is supposed to have a second-rate status. Ironically, because this argument is liberated from the theoretical constraints on quasi-a priori proofs, he is able to expose more clearly the assumptions on which his reasoning depends.

I suggest that Kant's efforts at thought experimentation go awry because of his beliefs that he must operate in purely qualitative terms. Operating in vague and general terms, he smuggles in assumptions galore. However, this does not explain the fact that, in the proof of Proposition 5, and in many other parts of the *Metaphysical Foundations*, the principles and procedures of the *Analytic* are conspicuously absent.[22] To see why Kant compromises his official theory of quasi-a priori science, we must recognize that he intends not merely to reconstruct but to *advance* Newtonian science. The long "General Observation on Dynamics" that ends Chapter 2 of the *Metaphysical Foundations* sets forth a program for extending physical science. There Kant outlines proposals for explaining phenomena in several fields (for example, hydrodynamics, the theory of elasticity, and chemistry). Besides these suggestions about how Newtonian science should develop, Kant believes that he has advanced beyond Newton in laying to rest certain misguided criticisms. Specifically, the popular objection that action at a distance is inconceivable is to be met by a typical Kantian strategy. The objector believes that the concept of matter as that which fills a space is legitimate. However, when we apply correct methodological principles, we find that the concept commits us to a theory that attributes to matter a fundamental repulsive force. This commitment brings others in its train. Matter must be endowed not only with a fundamental repulsive force but also with an equally fundamental attractive force that acts at a distance. Hence, like so many of the skeptics whom Kant wants to refute, the envisaged objector finds himself attacking a doctrine that is presupposed by his own formulation of the objection. To worry whether *matter* can act at a distance is confused because matter, to fill a space, *must* act at a distance.

VI

I want to conclude by suggesting how, despite the failure of the *Metaphysical Foundations*, Kant's philosophy of science contains insights that are relevant to contemporary thinking about science. Kant offers an interesting approach to scientific justification that recognizes features of scientific practice often neglected by his empiricist successors. His basic insights are developed by adding two more dubious theses: (1) The justification of specific versions of scientific theories involves the use of a priori procedures, and (2) the *Critique* provides an exhaustive account of our a priori procedures and of their interdependence.

Fundamental to Kant's philosophy of science is his view of a scientific theory as a *projected order of nature*. Many twentieth-century philosophers of science have debated the possibility of axiomatizing various pieces of science. However, when we turn away from the standard examples from physics to consider theories in biology or geology, the issue of axiomatizability frequently appears irrelevant. A more fundamental problem is to decide what corpus of statements we are trying to axiomatize. Biological and geological theories do not come neatly presented as collections of displayed formulae—like Newton's laws of motion or Maxwell's equations. Attempts to force contemporary evolutionary theory or plate tectonics into the standard empiricist mould inevitably strike practitioners of the theories as producing caricatures. They do so not because of sophisticated worries about the observation-theoretic distinction but because the theory is not adequately represented as a set of statements.

Kant's approach to theories does better. If we think of scientific theories as schemes for classifying and ordering phenomena, then we can make sense of theories that appear problematic when viewed from the empiricist perspective. We can think of contemporary plate tectonics, for example, as a collection of strategies for answering questions about a variety of geological phenomena—such as mountain building, sea floor spreading, and earthquakes—by tracing those phenomena to the motions of plates. What is fundamental to the theory of plate tectonics is its classificatory and explanatory scheme, the way in which it formulates geological questions and the way in which it directs us to answer such questions.

Kant's own presentation of the idea of a theory as a scheme for classification and explanation is not readily adapted to reconstructing contemporary science. In the Appendix to the *Ideal*, the fundamental idea of theories as directives for describing and explaining is transmuted into the view of theories as conceptual hierarchies. Perhaps this metamorphosis is to be understood in terms of the influence of Aristotelian logic on Kant's thought. In any case, we can achieve a more flexible presentation of the fundamental insight. Theories can be identified by the questions they address and the patterns of reasoning they use to answer those questions. The classification of natural phenomena is reflected in the questions posed, while the patterns of reasoning used in giving answers reflects the projected dependencies of phenomena on one another.

The Kantian approach to scientific theories just sketched serves as the basis for a Kantian account of scientific justification. Kant's minimal claim is that, given empirical justification for using a particular concept within a field of science, there are procedures for justifiably adopting a particular theory and for accepting specific principles, procedures that can be carried out in advance of testing those principles. On Kant's account, there is a rationale for embryonic science.

I believe that this minimal claim is correct. Scientists working in fields as diverse as fundamental particle physics and population ecology frequently advance arguments that justify the acceptance of particular methods of problem solving, and even of particular conclusions, on the basis of an initial acceptance of some conceptualization of the phenomena under study. Kant's philosophy of science is motivated by his awareness of the eighteenth-century versions of this practice (primarily in the development of Newtonianism). His thesis is that the gathering of experimental evidence presupposes a framework that is rationally adopted before the work of experimentation is begun.

Some empiricists might deny that the *Gedankenexperimente* of the physicist or the "model building" of the population ecologist serve anything more than a heuristic function. The heuristics merely induce us to fancy certain theories that receive their support only from the subsequent experiments. I believe that this version of empiricism is incorrect. Embryonic theories are rationally adopted, and it would be foolish to condemn as unreasonable those who were persuaded by Darwin's "long argument" for his programmatic theory or those who were convinced by Einstein's thought experiments in advance of the experimental determinations.

Kant adds to his minimal claim two further suggestions about the rationale of immature science. The first is the idea that there are methodological directives, such as the directive to obtain "systematic unity in our knowledge," that enable us to evaluate scientific proposals even before those proposals can be put to the test. Darwin's argument for the theory of evolution by natural selection illustrates two of the methodological canons to which Kant draws attention: Darwin is justly proud of the unifying power that the explanatory scheme of the *Origin of Species* supplies, and he defends his view by pointing out how it gives direction to biological research by identifying the ways in which we should interrogate nature.

More problematic is the contention that there are a priori procedures that play a critical role in the rational genesis of theories. Kant supposes that a proper reconstruction of the scientific arguments for proposals that are justified in advance of experimentation will reveal the operation of those a priori procedures whose workings are described in the *Critique*. As we have seen, his efforts to resolve some scientific controversies of his day by applying this general thesis about scientific justification succeed neither in confirming his own philosophical theory nor in settling the scientific issues. I suggest that the fundamental flaw is the imposition of the apriorist machinery of the *Critique* on the sensible idea that the rational acceptance of theories —that is, schemes for classification and explanation—is a crucial step in the justification of scientific claims through *subsequent* experimental investigation.

Some philosophers and historians of science are drawn to the idea that experimental confirmation of hypotheses presupposes acceptance of a framework and that decisions to accept such frameworks cannot be understood as completely rational. Kant's philosophy of science is built upon endorsing the first part of this idea and providing a particular way of denying the second, skeptical, claim. The choice of a framework (or of a projected order of nature) can be completely rational because scientists can use a priori procedures to arrive at their choices. I think that a thoughtful empiricist should accept neither of these accounts. When the arguments that figure in embryonic science are analyzed, they are seen to turn on very general considerations about the world that have been inherited from previous pieces of successful science. The physicists who appeal to symmetries in nature or the population biologists who propose that the differential equation for the growth of a population will take a particular form are neither making assumptions that involve "leaps of faith" nor appealing to a priori principles about the universe. Their arguments extend the findings of previous scientists—including scientists working in apparently unrelated areas—to justify a new scheme for problems and problem solving within their field. It may be that such principles are *relatively* immune to disconfirmation. But they do not meet the conditions that Kant requires of the a priori.

This evaluation is admittedly short and speculative. I have tried to outline a view of scientific justification that has some affinity with Kant's and to motivate some of its elements. Quite evidently, my remarks do not amount to a defense. But, if I am right, then traditional appraisals of Kant's philosophy of science get things almost exactly backward. Orthodox Kantians are wrong to dismiss Kant's views about science as an embarrassing addendum to the central achievements of the *Critique*.[23] Taking the project of isolating items of a priori knowledge to be worthwhile, they suppose that assigning substantive scientific principles to the category of the a priori is misguided. I doubt that there is much that answers to Kant's conception of the a priori. However, the approach to scientific justification on which Kant imposes his apriorist views—the approach that I have tried to indicate in this section— is both interesting and important. Furthermore, the general assumptions about nature that scientists so frequently use in justifying embryonic theories may come as close to the ideal of the a priori as anything in which we are likely to be interested.

Notes

Acknowledgment: I am grateful to Patricia Kitcher for many valuable criticisms of drafts of this paper. Earlier versions were read at Temple University and at Cornell University, and a number of people made helpful suggestions. In particular, I would like to thank Charles Parsons (who commented on the version read at Cornell), Richard Burian, Michael Friedman, and Ralf Meerbote for comments that have caused me to abandon or to amplify previous formulations. This is not, of course, to imply that *anyone* accepts my interpretation of Kant's philosophy of science or my assessment of its importance.

1. All references to the *Critique of Pure Reason* will be to the Norman Kemp-Smith translation, and I will follow standard practice in giving parenthetical references in the text, using the pagination of both first and second editions. I will refer to the *Metaphysical Foundations* by giving page references to the James Ellington translation, cited as MFNS in the text.

2. *Prolegomena* #36.

3. This is a *minimal* empiricist view shorn of all the standard claims about the theory-observation distinction(s), axiomatizability, and so forth. Even though many philosophers have abandoned those extra claims, I think that the minimal view remains very popular.

4. I take it that Kuhn's concept of a paradigm, Lakatos's notion of a research program, and Laudan's idea of a research tradition attempt to do justice to this usage. (See T. S. Kuhn, *The Structure of Scientific Revolutions* [Chicago: University of Chicago Press, 1970]; I. Lakatos, *Philosophical Papers*, Vol. I [Cambridge: Cambridge University Press, 1978]; L. Laudan, *Progress and Its Problems* [Berkeley: University of California Press, 1977].) Whatever the difficulties of these particular notions, I think that there are genuine philosophical problems that require us to introduce something similar.

5. The principal passages in which Kant advances this answer occur in the Appendix to the *Ideal* (which I will discuss below) and in the Introduction to the *Critique of Judgment*. For a striking discussion, see p. 21 of the Bernard translation of the latter work.

6. These two schemes have an obvious connection to the two major Newtonian traditions of the eighteenth century: the corpuscularian program and the movement to develop field theories. For discussion, see Mary Hesse, *Forces and Fields* (London: Sheed and Ward, 1961) and,

especially, R. Schofield, *Mechanism and Materialism* (Princeton, N.J.: Princeton University Press, 1969).

7. Given the history of the corpuscularian program in the eighteenth century, Kant's judgment is hardly unfounded!

8. Kant's terminology in the Appendix is somewhat ambiguous. 'Systematic unity' is usually employed to cover the maxim that requires us to reduce fundamental entities, but sometimes it is used to identify what we achieve by following all three maxims in conjunction.

9. For one way to analyze the notion of systematic unification, see my paper "Explanatory Unification," *Philosophy of Science*, Vol. 48 (1981), pp. 507-31.

10. The account that follows recapitulates the analysis given in my paper "A Priori Knowledge," *Philosophical Review* (1980), pp. 3-23.

11. Thus, in two places, Kant hails the conditions of possible experience as the "third thing" that enables us to link subject and predicate to arrive at a priori knowledge of a synthetic truth. See A156-7, B195-6, and A216-8, B263-5.

12. I would thus argue that Kant recognizes that analyticity is not the key to solving the problem of a priori knowledge. For passages that support this attribution, see footnote a to A242, A252-4, B308-10, and especially Kant's reply to Eberhard. (Henry Allison, ed., *The Kant-Eberhard Controversy* [Baltimore: Johns Hopkins University Press, 1973], p. 175; see also L. W. Beck, "Can Kant's Synthetic Judgments Be Made Analytic?" in R. P. Wolff, ed., *Kant* [New York: Doubleday, 1967], pp. 3-22.) I have defended the attribution at some length in "How Kant Almost Wrote 'Two Dogmas of Empiricism' (And Why He Didn't)," *Philosophical Topics* (December 1981).

13. Thus, a concept that is universally instantiated would be assured a place in our projected order of nature because it would be immune from the two most obvious ways in which concepts fail to be legitimate — namely, by not being instantiated and by cutting across natural kinds.

14. In this I follow the approach taken by Saul Kripke. See *Naming and Necessity* (Cambridge, Mass.: Harvard University Press, 1980), p. 34.

15. Putnam, "There Is at Least One A Priori Truth," *Erkenntnis*, Vol. 13 (1978), pp. 153-70; "Analyticity and Apriority: Beyond Wittgenstein and Quine," in Peter A. French, Theodore E. Uehling, Sr., and Howard K. Wettstein, eds., *Midwest Studies in Philosophy*, Vol. IV, *Studies in Metaphysics* (Minneapolis: University of Minnesota Press, 1979), pp. 423-41; Thompson, "On A Priori Truth," *Journal of Philosophy*, Vol. LXXVIII (1981), pp. 458-82.

16. For a defense of this general point about justification, see Gilbert Harman, *Thought* (Princeton, N.J.: Princeton University Press, 1973), Chapter 2. I draw the moral for a priori knowledge in "A Priori Knowledge" pp. 21-23.

17. *Naming and Necessity*, pp. 55-57, 97-105. I have tried to extend Kripke's argument in "Apriority and Necessity," *Australasian Journal of Philosophy*, Vol. 58 (1980), pp. 89-101.

18. I should note explicitly that many traditional interpretations of Kant's epistemology and philosophy of science seem to me to err in failing to give any adequate analysis of what Kant might have meant in hailing a particular proposition as a priori. Kant's conception of apriority may be muddled or ambiguous, but I do not believe that one can understand his doctrines about pure natural science (for example) by refusing to analyze it. Hence, I believe that a crucial step in interpreting Kant's philosophy of science is to identify the relevant notion of apriority, and, to the best of my knowledge, the Putnam-Thompson approach and my own treatment in "A Priori Knowledge" provide the only clear analyses currently available.

19. "Analyticity and Apriority: Beyond Wittgenstein and Quine," pp. 440-41.

20. As Michael Friedman pointed out to me, there is one place in the *Metaphysical Foundations* where the prohibition seems to be relaxed. In the first part of the work, Kant appears to try to prove a mathematical result, the parallelogram law for the composition of velocities (MFNS 34-35). However, as I interpret this discussion, the main point is to establish a proposition that will make the application of mathematics to experience possible. Kant's goal appears to be that of showing how we have to represent composite velocities to ourselves (MFNS 31-32),

and he introduces geometrical notions only insofar as they are needed to classify the possible to forms that the representations can take. Thus, I construe his argument not as a mathematical proof of a mathematical result but as drawing on mathematical concepts to formulate what he views as a metaphysical argument. The status of this argument would be parallel to the treatment in the *Axioms of Intuition*, where mathematical notions are discussed but mathematics is not done.

21. If we were to continue with the proof we should discover that Kant's qualitative formulations disguise even more assumptions. For example, when he investigates the possibility that the dispersal of matter might be checked by a balance of repulsive forces, he writes as though pieces of matter would have to be introduced one by one and would be subject to instantaneous dissipation. It would be interesting to try to mathematize Kant's "dynamical conception of matter" and to see what further premises are needed to make the sequence of arguments of Chapter 2 go through. However, some of Kant's claims about "filling" and "occupying" space are hard to construe on any simple field theory of matter.

22. The link between the *Metaphysical Foundations* and the *Analytic* is most evident in Chapter 3. There Kant does try to apply the principles of the *Analogies* to derive substantive laws. So, for example, the principle of the First Analogy serves as a premise for a law of mass conservation. This argument fails to fit the format of quasi-a priori science for a slightly different reason: Kant seems to make no use of the specific property of matter attributed in the definition that begins Chapter 3. The argument deserves analysis, but I do not have space to investigate it here.

23. Of course, some commentators have tried to reconstruct Kant's ideas about science. There are scholarly discussions of the *Metaphysical Foundations* and its relation to the *Critique* by Jules Vuillemin, Hansgeorg Hoppe, and Peter Plaass (J. Vuillemin, *Physique et Métaphysique Kantienne* [Paris: Presses Universitaires, 1955]; H. Hoppe, *Kant's Theorie der Physik* [Frankfurt: Vittorio Klosterman, 1969]; P. Plaass, *Kant's Theorie der Naturwissenschaft* [Göttingen: Vandenhoeck and Rupprecht, 1965]). Unfortunately, I think none of these works succeeds either in making clear what the project of pure natural science is supposed to be or in identifying any Kantian insight about science. More successful, to my mind, are two recent works in English. In the long final chapter of his *Metaphysics and the Philosophy of Science* (Oxford: Blackwell, 1969), Gerd Buchdahl gives a sympathetic exposition of many of Kant's discussions of science. Buchdahl is very clear in his contention that Kant does not believe he can deduce Newtonian science a priori. Buchdahl proposes that there is a "looser relation" between the *Critique* and Newtonian science, but I do not see that he has given any clear account of this relation. In *Kant's Theory of Science* (Princeton, N.J.: Princeton University Press, 1978), Gordon Brittan is more forthright. He maintains that the goal of the *Metaphysical Foundations* is to show that certain concepts must be instantiated in any world in which science is to be possible. Although I believe that Brittan's discussions, like Buchdahl's, are sometimes illuminating, I think that he does not achieve a satisfactory view either of Kant's project or of Kant's practice of it and that the trouble stems from Britton's explicit dismissal of some of Kant's central epistemological notions (for example, p. 24, footnote 43).

Constitution and Structure of Self-Identity: Kant's Theory of Apperception and Hegel's Criticism

KLAUS DÜSING

The philosophy of modern times since Descartes starts from the principle of self-identity or from the principle of self-consciousness and develops different models of a theory of subjectivity. But, since the end of the nineteenth century, the concept and theory of self-consciousness and of the ego have been criticized from almost every side, though by quite different arguments. It is not always clear whether the critique specifically points to a concept of empirical self-consciousness, understood as self-referential subject of its experiences, or points to a concept of pure self-consciousness, conceived as subject of pure thinking of the logical rules and categories, or points to both of them. An objection to one of the concepts is not in general simply transferable to the other. Furthermore, a criticism of one of the historical theories in which one of these concepts has its place, even if convincing, is not necessarily valid for the other.

So Ernst Mach[1] — to indicate some of these objections — declares generally and without reference to a specific theory of subjectivity that the ego is irrecoverable. This is meant of the empirical as well as of the pure ego, because neither of them is to be found as simple fact in psychological descriptions. For the early Husserl, before he founded the transcendental phenomenology, an ego that glides over the psychical occurrences and ostensibly connects them cannot be proved; he thereby rejects a pure ego a priori as well as an empirical self-consciousness insofar as it goes beyond the totality of psychical events. In the same manner, William James criticizes the assumption of a pure ego, both in the transcendental sense Kant taught and in the substantial sense as Descartes advocated. James claims that the empirical ego is only a stream of consciousness in which different phases of psychical events have only a relative identity. He integrates this view into the theory of neutral monism, according to which consciousness is not an independent entity.

Later on, Bertrand Russell takes up James's neutral monism[2] and from this standpoint criticizes especially Descartes's conception of the "Ego cogito," which is a substance with an independent existence, and also the idea that thinking generally is performed only by an ego. Why should it be impossible to say "it thinks" just as "it rains here"? Russell here follows a reflection of James, as well as unknowingly an ingenious vote by Lichtenberg in which the statement "it thinks" is thought of in an analogy to "it lightens." Thinking here is understood as a temporal psychical occurrence that is to be stated empirically, and in this way the concept of an empirical ego is challenged by this impersonal formulation. A fortiori then, Russell rejects the notion of a pure ego a priori. More radically, Gilbert Ryle in his behavioristic theory puts aside the ego as an independent entity, since, unlike James and Russell, he rejects the validity of introspection. Ryle, of course, attacks the Cartesian theory as well, which in his opinion introduced the myth of the mental world as a kind of second theater with an existence opposed to and independent of the physical world. Mental performances are, as he stresses, of a higher order than physical ones because of their different logical type. But at the same time mental performances are dependent on preceding physical facts. So the ego, which is empirical, is self-consciousness only in the sense that reflection is of a higher order than simple representations and their contents. Therefore, it avoids itself again and again when it endeavors to comprehend itself as an object; it is said to be systematically elusive and finally inconceivable. This criticism rejects any kind of original self-representation of the ego.

A different sort of objections to the ego is to be found in what is called the ontological critique. Here the ego is rejected as the fundamental principle in modern philosophy because, as for Nicolai Hartmann,[3] the general ontological sense of the categories of being is prior to the ego or because, as for the later Heidegger, the being and its history are prior to any attempt to give a foundation of knowledge and prior even to any attempt at a theory of subjectivity, which is itself a historical position. Still another critique is the Marxian objection according to which the doctrine of self-consciousness, especially of the pure ego a priori, is a hypostasis of the civil subject abstracted from the civil society and their contradictions.

The premises of these objections are rather divergent and in part incompatible with one another. One objection, however, is independent of these premises because it calls into question the logical possibility of the self-comprehension of the ego. It is developed as such by Henrich, but it is also contained in Ryle's thesis of the elusiveness of the ego and, in fact, is stated in a similar way much earlier already by Plotinus in connection with the possibility of thinking on thinking.[4] According to this objection, self-representation of self-thinking already is to be presupposed for the performance of distinguishing and identifying in the self-representation of the ego; and, if this presupposed self-referential representation or thinking is to be thought as such, again it presupposes the same, and so forth in an infinite regression. This objection may be called an argument from infinite iteration, because it is always the same ego that wants to conceive itself, and for that each time must presuppose itself. The objection can also be formulated as an argument of circularity. Every theory of subjectivity has to take account of this argument. Contrary to the view of those who advocate it, in idealistic theories of subjectivity it is invalid.

In the other objections, the spectrum of differentiations in the concept of subjectivity represented by different theories is often not suffficiently taken into consideration. So, in the objections to Descartes's philosophy, understood as objections to the theory of subjectivity in general, the subsequent critiques and systematic developments of the Cartesian doctrine up to Kant are often neglected. The philosophical foundation and explanation of the internal structure of the pure, transcendental ego, which is the work of Kant, as well as the disclosure of gaps in this theory and the consequent amendment in Hegel's logic, are often unrecognized in modern critiques of the theory of subjectivity. Therefore, Kant's doctrine of pure apperception will be discussed here with regard both to the possibilities and to the deficiencies of the critical theory of subjectivity. Hegel's objections to Kant's theory will be considered in the light of further developments in the theory of subjectivity, which Kant did not complete. Also Hegel's deflecting speculative premises and his own speculative theory of subjectivity will be contrasted with the critical philosophy. If Kant's and Hegel's arguments are valid, then subsequent accounts on which the ego is denied will probably seem less striking.

I

Considering the overwhelming number of inquiries into this subject, research in Kant's theory of pure apperception might appear to be either superfluous or, for skeptics, without prospects. The Kantian theory, however, will be discussed here from a specific and somewhat novel perspective, that is, from the point of dispositions, problems, and gaps of a critical transcendental exposition of the internal structure of pure subjectivity and its constitution. The idealists, especially Fichte and Hegel, deal with these questions in their critique of Kant. Recent interpretations of this idealistic critique of Kant, some of which are to be mentioned later on, mostly proceed from a Fichtean or Hegelian position. Here, however, the arrangement of, and the problems for, Kant's theory will be outlined by scrutinizing his own explanations and by considering the evolution of his thought, independent of idealistic interpretations.

In Neokantianism, for instance, in Cohen's commentary, pure apperception is understood as the highest principle of the theory of knowledge and science; it is a principle that makes the use of general rules and thus objective knowledge possible.[5] On the other hand, Heimsoeth stresses the close connection of pure apperception with personal existence. Similarly for Heidegger, pure apperception as a part of traditional ontology is a concept of human existence, which constitutes modes of time as ontological determinations. Paton is not involved in these discussions between different Neokantian and ontological interpretations of Kant; he gives an internal commentary on Kant's theory of apperception. De Vleeschauwer proceeds in a similar way, while emphasizing the evolution of Kantian thought. Ebbinghaus and Reich save the sense of the metaphysical deduction of the categories and interpret the concept of pure apperception as a principle of logic and epistemology; they avoid the Neokantian circle of proceeding from experience as real knowledge to the conditions of its possibility but in which the same knowledge is considered. The critical analytic interpretations, especially those of Strawson and Bennett, hold that Kant's concept of an a priori synthetic unity of apperception with its pure synthesis a priori is meaningless. In an analogous manner, Hossenfelder systematically criticizes the Kantian theory of constitution in general and especially the doctrine of pure apperception and its synthesis. Dryer, however, in the historical framework of Kant's question whether scientific metaphysics is possible, outlines and determines the sense of the Kantian doctrine of judgment and pure self-consciousness. In a detailed, historically reconstructing analysis, Henrich designs a theoretical structure on the basis of Kant's explanations about apperception and synthesis. In the matter of which questions to pursue, this reconstruction is similar to our exposition. Kant in his formation of the doctrine of pure apperception, a doctrine that is significant for his whole philosophy, is seen here predominantly neither as an analytical theorist of experience nor as a rather cautious reserved metaphysician, but as an idealist within critical limits.

The proof of the ideality of space and time necessarily precedes Kant's transcendental deduction of the categories, how and in which contexts objects are to be known by categories. Spatial and temporal intuitions as subjective representations must be combined in such a way that an object can be known. Object as such then is not given in intuition, nor indeed found at all, but is the product of a constitution by intellectual synthesis, which is according to Kant the origin of the idea of necessity in the connectedness of sensible intuitions. This connectedness only comes about by pure intellectual and spontaneous synthesis and synthetic unity. The performance of such a synthesis is thinking; and thinking and its action, which in itself is uniform and based on a guiding synthetic unity, are to be founded in pure apperception. So Kant gives a basis for pure thinking that itself is fundamental, the basis of pure self-consciousness. A decisive step in the deduction of the categories, therefore, depends on Kant's theory of pure self-consciousness, at least on that part of this theory in which the constitution of objectivity is explained.

In Kant's view, intellectual synthesis of representations as well as its synthetic unity are attributed to pure apperception. These determinations, however, are not identical. The intellectual synthesis is an act of the spontaneity of thinking;[6] the manifold of representations that are to be connected, of course, must be given; it is not produced in the act of synthesis. The synthesis further combines representations guided by a prospect of a unity of their various contents. So the unity of a topic is brought about by the synthesis of a given manifold. But the synthesis itself is possible only by the unity of consciousness,[7] which guarantees the performance and the unity of the synthesis of representations. Kant has indicated a subordination of synthesis under synthetic unity within the pure consciousness as such. The basic unity of consciousness in Kant's thought is simplicity; for, if this unity were produced by collected disparate moments, the consciousness that is the constituting basis would not be united in itself and could not produce the primitive unity of a thought and of its intellectual content.

The connection between these concepts is only partly described or signified by Kant but is not expressly developed into a theory of subjectivity. Some ideas that are employed there are self-evident for him but not explained. So, for instance, not the awareness of the idea "I think" or of the unity of the self in actual presence, but only the *possibility* of such a synthetic unity is necessary in Kant's view for the performance of the synthesis. Therefore, self-consciousness as such does not need to be present at certain psychical acts of representation; it is only necessary that it could be present. But, if it proves in a synthesis of representations that this is impossible, these representations either are self-contradictory or at least are nothing for the self. Further, Kant in the second edition of the *Critique of Pure Reason*, which my research follows, more clearly than in the first one distinguishes between intellectual synthesis, which belongs to the understanding, and figurative synthesis, which belongs to the imagination. In the first edition, Kant occasionally claimed the imagination is the faculty of synthesis in general; but consistent metaphysical judgments, even if they do not establish knowledge, and pure practical knowledge both presuppose a pure intellectual synthesis without imagination.

Kant's identification, however, of pure synthesis with synthesis of understanding is in need of further reasons, for the synthesis of understanding, which brings about the logical unity in *theoretical* judgments, in the first place is only one kind of pure synthesis; there is also, for instance, a synthesis that produces the unity in aesthetic judgments. So in this theory of Kant, which results from the goal of showing the objective reality of the categories, the meaning of the subject that performs that theoretical pure synthesis is limited from the outset. Second, the assumption of such a pure synthesis of understanding is not as unquestionable as Kant thought. But there are good reasons for it, if this consideration, which can only be outlined here, is taken into account, namely, that logical determinations and rules, presupposing their apodictic validity and hence their apriority, were valid in themselves but unthinkable and unthought, provided that a pure synthesis of understanding is not accepted. The apodictic validity and apriority of logical rules are a premise that cannot be defended here. But, if it is right, these rules only can be valid if they are thinkable and also thought. Something thinkable and thought without thinking would be only an arbitrary product of abstraction; but the thinking, the pure intellectual synthesis, employed here is not an empirical psychical occurrence; it is a pure mental act, a performance of pure spontaneity, which becomes a thought by correspondence with a priori logical rules. In Kant's view, a separated real existence is not to be ascribed to these a priori acts; they are only the ideal principles of the constitution of those psychical events that, unlike sense perceptions or dreams, can be determined with some legitimacy as actually occurring acts of thinking.

Kant, moreover, assumes a *subject* of these pure a priori acts of thinking, the pure ego or self-consciousness, for first a pure act of thinking is performed spontaneously, so it cannot be conceived as effected by something else. Therefore, the Neoplatonic argument, that thinking is brought about by emanation from the one, as well as the theological argument, that it is an effect of God in the ego, are void. What is acting spontaneously, only by itself and so to speak autonomously, is nothing else than a subject of its own activity. So only such a subject is able to perform these spontaneous acts of thinking. Connections with the pure will of a moral person here are obvious, as Kant hints, but they are not developed on the basis of the unity of subjectivity.[8] Second, an anonymous occurrence of pure thinking without an ego is

likewise not possible because the logical unity of judgments that is constituted by intellectual synthesis must be comprehended as such as a necessary and valid one.[9] So
the thinking, which is the reflective consideration of the logical unity and of the unifying synthesis, refers to the thinking that establishes this intellectual synthesis, and
it knows itself in both sorts of thinking, even though at different levels, as the same
thinking. Hence, it is pure self-consciousness that knows its own synthesis as regular,
that is aware of it as its own performance, and that, thus, as Kant hints, does think
of itself.

This problem of the relation between synthetic unity and thinking self-reference
of pure self-consciousness also is the basis of Kant's account of the relation between
synthetic and analytic unity of apperception.[10] Representations do not already belong to the unity of self-consciousness in that each single representation, as clear and
distinguished from others, itself is perceived with consciousness; but one has to be
added to other representations, and so a connection among them must be brought
about. Such a synthesis gets to be a uniform action in itself only by the synthetic
unity of apperception. Contents of representations, for instance, that successively
come into consciousness and that might be clear in themselves by regular synthesis
are brought in a necessary connection of chronological order according to the unity
that establishes the category of causality, and this unity itself is based on the synthetic unity of self-consciousness. The analytic unity of apperception, however, in
Kant's view, is a certainty that the ego possesses in thinking of its own identity in
various representations and in different phases of the synthesis of them. Thus, it is
in virtue of this certainty that the ego is thinking of itself. But Kant is less interested
in this meaning of the analytic unity that here proves to belong to a theory of subjectivity; he more considers the analytic unity in a fundamental epistemological sense.
According to this sense, it is the basis of a tenor that remains one and the same in
various representations; that means it is the basis of an analytic identity of a general
concept.

These determinations of the analytic and synthetic unity belong to the structure of pure self-consciousness. Neither the act of pure synthesis that becomes uniform in itself by the guiding synthetic unity nor this unity itself is to be understood
as an anonymous matter without any subject; they are to be ascribed to pure self-
consciousness. So the self-consciousness must know the act as its own performance,
the unity as its own unity, and its own unity in both of them. But Kant places the
analytic unity of apperception behind the synthetic one, for, in his view, only by the
synthesis of various representations and their synthetic unity can a consciousness of
the identity of the ego within these synthesized representations and thus a thinking
self-reference of the ego be achieved, or better—constituted. In this argument, however, there is no discussion of how it is possible that, without the analytic unity of
self-identity knowing self-consciousness, the synthesis and the synthetic unity, which
according to Kant precede the analytic unity, might be internal determinations of the
pure self-consciousness that is to be defined by thinking self-reference. So Kant has
broached the problem of structure and self-constitution of apperception in its synthesis and its thinking of itself. He has indicated a solution that, however, leaves

undiscussed certain questions and that is not systematically developed in a general theory of subjectivity.

In the transcendental deduction of the categories, the structure of pure subjectivity is involved only insofar as the *objective reference* of the categories results from it. This objective reference is implied in the determinations of the unity of pure self-consciousness. By an intellectual synthesis under the guiding synthetic unity of apperception, the manifold of given intuitions is brought into a regular or necessary connection. This connection, according to Kant's theory, already is the object in general that is constituted by the regular synthesis.[11] The idea of necessity in this connection, as well as of the regularity of the synthesis, is well founded as a logical unity in the conception of the synthetic unity of self-consciousness. Corresponding to the basic kinds of logical unity as thought in the forms of judgment, the necessary connection, which is produced within the given manifold by the synthesis of understanding, is differentiated in diverse kinds of logical unity as various determinations of intuition, that is, in diverse categories, for the forms of logical unity in the functions of judgment and in the categories are identical. So, if a given manifold of intuitions belongs to the unity of self-consciousness, it is to be united and to be ordered in a way that is provided for by one of the logical functions of judgment conceived as a rule for the synthesis. Consequently, the first and decisive answer to the question how the categories might have objective validity reads as follows: categories refer to an object generally, because as unifying concepts they themselves together with the intellectual syntheses constitute the object as such. In this argument, the limitation of the objective reality of the categories is clearly implied, for the syntheses presuppose something to be synthesized, namely, the given manifold of sensible intuitions. So the categories are valid only for those sensible intuitions, but not beyond that region.

This argumentation is sufficient for the proof of the objective validity of the categories; but it leaves unresolved the basic question that belongs to a theory of subjectivity and that is raised by that argument, the question of how a necessary relation between thinking self-reference and constitution of an object might follow from the structure of pure self-consciousness. Whereas for Kant the constituted connection is the object in general, Hegel in discussing the subjectivity problem claims, as will be shown, that the constituted object is nothing else than the subject that is thought and that is thinking of itself.

The constituted necessary connection, the object according to Kant's theory, is to be conceived as a topic of science. So the object is not a thing simply given in sense-perception and to be found in daily environment, but a regular unity of given intuitions, that means a space-time-content determined by rules or a law of nature.[12] This lawfulness in Kant's theory is marked in a special manner; it is principally a logical unity in judgments that determines the manifold of intuitions. As has been mentioned, the logical unity in judgments according to Kant is the same one as in ontological determinations, i.e., in the categories. This idea forms the conception of Kant's "metaphysical" deduction of the categories and is principally Aristotelian. Plato or Hegel generally do not establish fundamental ontological determinations with regard to the functions of judgment. But for Kant, as well as for Aristotle, the sense of being is to be drawn primarily from the sense of judgment and its different functions. Therefore, in the light of the forms of judgment and their system, Kant is able to outline a system of categories or an ontology that is consistent but by itself falls short of knowledge. Indeed, the questions now arise whether the correspondence between particular forms of judgment and categories is to be carried out in detail and whether the forms of judgment are to be developed out of their principle, that is, the synthetic unity of apperception. The idealists, and especially Hegel, argue that Kant has not explained such a systematic deduction of the plurality of the categories or of the forms of judgment from the unity of pure self-consciousness.[13]

Just as the object that is not simply a sensible thing to be met in our everyday world, but a lawfully constituted and determined unity, so the basic pure self-consciousness is not a psychical ego that represents itself in the inner sense but is the principle of logical unity in general. Therefore, it is conceived as a principle of formal logic, and along with the forms of pure sensible intuitions as a principle of the transcendental logic. The often discussed questions of the problem of immediate self-certainty of the ego feeling its own states or of the problem of an empirical ego that is separated from its psychical occurrences do not arise here. But the question does arise as to how the pure self-consciousness, which is the principle of logical unity as well as pure spontaneity of thinking and intellectual self-reference, is related to the empirical self-consciousness that exists in an individual person. The pure self-consciousness must be a basis for, and an ideal principle of, the constitution of thinking and intellectual self-reference as psychical acts, and so also of the intellectual performance that is an essential part of empirical self-knowledge.

This determination of the principal meaning of pure self-consciousness belongs to Kant's critical philosophy in which theoretical knowledge, including self-knowledge, is limited. A pure intellectual knowledge of the existence of the pure self-consciousness a priori therefore is impossible. In reflections about the 1770s, on the other hand, Kant designs a theory of the ego, which can only be sketched here, in which such an *intellectual self-knowledge* is assumed. This theory is important not only as a precursor of the *Critique* but also as a document of an idealistic conception that later was developed by Fichte, although he was not aware of the earlier Kantian outline. In the lectures about metaphysics, edited by Poelitz, Kant affirms that the ego, the "absolute subject" of all predications, is substantial, "the only case in which we are able to have an immediate intuition of the substance."[14] This statement pertains to the systematic context of rational psychology in which the substantiality of the soul and thereby its immateriality was to be proved. The demonstration against the material composition and for the simplicity of the soul, according to a reflection of Kant, amounts to the point that the soul "is an immediate intuition of itself by the absolute unity, the Ego, which is the singular of the actions of thinking."[15] As a kind of knowledge, this self-representation of the ego is such an intuition, which cannot be material or sensible. So he speaks in the *Träume eines Geistersehers* about the intellectual self-knowledge as an "immaterial intuition" ("immaterielles Anschauen"). Here the Platonic background is clear: we have a pure spiritual intuition of the intellectual world in a pre-existence. And he adds with moderate skepticism that human beings are without reminiscence of this spiritual intuition. According to him, in the field of morality the supposition of a spiritual world and the idea that the subject is a member of it are allowed; concerning theoretical knowledge, however, Kant there abstains from judging, perhaps out of a consideration of Swedenborg. This holding back is not to be found in the mentioned reflections and lectures about metaphysics.

In these reflections, but in the different systematic context of the problem of freedom, Kant unambiguously assumes an intellectual intuition that the ego possesses of itself: "The Ego is an inexplicable idea. It is an intuition which is immutable." We have "a concept" of freedom and its reality "by our intellectual inner intuition (not the inner sense) of our activity which can be moved by intellectual motives."[16] The theory of the early Fichte is closely connected with this Kantian conception. The ego immediately and intuitively is certain of its own spontaneous activity, but, since this certainty is not conditioned by senses or by receptivity, it is intellectual. In this way, the ego knows its own intellectual being that is determined by real freedom. The self-knowledge of the ego is immediate and intuitive because the ego, conceived as an absolute subject of all predicates that in itself is simple, cannot be a predicate and consequently cannot be a concept because furthermore, according to Kant, it is immediately accessible to itself in its real spontaneity and freedom. Therefore, in these reflections Kant adopts, as did Fichte later on, an intellectual self-intuition of the ego. In the *Critique*, however, Kant argues against such an intellectual self-intuition, for the self-consideration of the ego requires the presupposition that representations in accordance with the form of time are *given* in the inner sense as sensible receptivity. Hence, the possibility of intellectual self-intuition cannot be shown for this limited faculty of knowledge that is dependent on a given manifold. Therefore, the claimed insight into the intellectual existence of the ego and beyond it into the intellectual world is not to be justified. In his critical philosophy, Kant does not reject intellectual self-reference; it is, however, no longer an intellectual self-intuition, a kind of knowledge, but only a self-thinking without knowledge.[17]

In the *Opus postumum*, Kant, motivated probably by a vague information about the beginning idealistic discussion of the ego, stresses the self-reference of the thinking of pure apperception: "The first act of the representative faculty is the consciousness of myself which is a mere logical act basic for all other representations and by which the subject itself makes an object."[18] The self-representation of the pure ego according to the critical philosophy continues to be a mere thinking. But now, in the ideal arrangement of conditions of knowledge, self-reference belongs expressly to the first act, which is a pure logical act of thinking. In these latest reflections, Kant distinguishes clearly between the objectification in which pure apperception makes itself an object by thinking of itself and the constitution of knowable objects. But even here Kant does not reach a developed theory of the internal structure of pure self-consciousness and of its relation to the constitution of objects of knowledge in general. Essential for his conception, however, is the view that the original act of apperception is not, as it is for Fichte, a deed-action ("*Tathandlung*") that precedes the logic and is basic for logical determinations but that it is a pure act of thinking, an act determined by a logical unity. So pure apperception remains a principle of logic in Kant's later writings.

It remains, though, a problem in Kant of how in detail thinking self-reference of pure apperception as a principle of logic is to be determined. He finds this self-reference to be possible even in the *Critique of Pure Reason*. (We will return after this overview of previous history and the later development of the Kantian discussion of that question to the first *Critique*.) But here Kant declares that pure self-consciousness, being the subject of the categories, cannot determine itself by the categories as an object, that is as a knowable existence, because it just is the principle of the kinds of logical unity that are thought in the categories. As the context confirms, Kant's opinion is here that self-consciousness cannot know itself in this way. But it can try merely to *think* of itself by categories, understood as kinds of logical unity. The thinking, however, which is the subject of the categorical thought founded on the pure ego and forming its moments, leads to a circle, according to Kant.[19] From his earlier outline, mentioned above, Kant maintains in the *Critique* the view that the pure ego, being the absolute simple subject of all predicates, cannot be comprehended by predicates and consequently not by categories. But, because, in contrast to his earlier conception, an intellectual self-intuition is not available for it, its self-reference can only be a thinking of itself. The circle that Kant points out does not eliminate self-thinking; it is not a circle in the definition of thinking self-reference but only makes impossible any advancement of knowledge of it, so that Kant regards it as "inconvenience."

Here likewise the argument from an infinite iteration mentioned at the beginning is obvious: each time the ego intends to comprehend itself in categories, it must presuppose itself. In spite of this iterated presupposition, however, in Kant's view a thinking self-reference is not impossible, since the ego, each time it is presupposed, is in analytical identity with the categorical moments in which it thinks of itself. Kant here has in mind the critique of metaphysics that pretends to know the substantiality of the soul. If the pure ego thinks itself to be substantial, simple, numerical one, and so forth, it does not comprehend itself in ontological determinations but merely in the kinds of logical unity of its own thinking. Since it is not an existing individual, but general thinking established as the principle of logic, it conceives in thinking of this pure mental content a spontaneous intellectual activity that is united in itself and conformable to logical unity and more specifically conformable to the kinds of logical unity that are thought in the categories. The pure thinking ego that is thinking of this thinking does think of itself. According to the Kantian theory, there is no problem to be found in the possibility of such a self-reference. Apart from the problem, however, of the development of the forms of judgments and of the categories out of the logical unity in general, it remains an open question how, within subjectivity, the content of it is to be constituted. By content is meant the mental or intentional object in which the pure ego is thinking of itself.

If the ego not only has thoughts but also has knowledge of itself, it must be presented to itself likewise in different intuitions that are always sensible for us. The thinking of the ego then is understood as a special psychical act that has to meet the general requirements of thinking as such but that is performed by a subject the existence of which is determinable in time. Kant discusses here Descartes's highest certainty according to which the ego during the performance of thinking is unshakably certain of its own existence.[20] This certainty is not accepted by Kant, neither in the form of an intuitive knowledge nor in the form of a syllogism. Furthermore, the existence of the ego, as Kant's critical doctrine shows, is not knowable as a simple substance from which immortality could be deduced. In his own theory, Kant splits up the highest Cartesian certainty into a pure "I think" comprehended as a principle of logic without any knowledge of existence, on the one hand, and a psychical, not yet determined certainty or a still undetermined "perception" ("*Wahrnehmung*") of actual performances of thinking by which the ego acquires a certainty of its own existence determinable in time, on the other hand. This temporal existence of the ego will be determined and concretely known by time determinations that are enriched by empirical content in intuition. So, for instance, a year in the life of an ego and its phases are determined by the climatically and planetarily characterized course of a year in general and its special consequences in which the manifold of space intuition is included. It is to be added that for concrete self-knowledge of an empirical ego, understood as an individual person, self-conceiving as well as action within the intersubjectivity of the spatiotemporal life-world are required. Kant, however, states only the general conditions of empirical self-knowledge and of the relation between the ideal determinations of the pure ego and the real ones of the concrete empirical self-consciousness.

Despite many open questions, Kant makes the Cartesian "Ego cogito" the subject of an original and to a certain extent well-developed theory. He substantially improves the exposition of the thinking ego and also changes the sense of it in his critical philosophy. For the first time, Kant raises in this context central problems in the theory of subjectivity. He determines the systematic place of the exposition of pure subjectivity considered as a principle of logic. And even with regard to content the debate on the spontaneity of self-consciousness and on its self-reference is marked by this systematic conception. The circumstance that Kant in his theory does not or does not sufficiently resolve many questions, for instance, the questions concerning the constitution of self-reference or concerning the relation of the self-consciousness to the constitution of objects or its relation to the empirical self, on the one hand, is based on the novelty and unusualness of his investigations. On the other hand, these questions do not pertain necessarily to the theory of objective knowledge and its limits, the explanation of which is the proper task of the first "Critique," and thus naturally receive less than complete treatment. But just those problems are developed by idealistic theories of subjectivity, which, however, radically alter the Kantian epistemological foundation.

II

These problems with the theory of pure subjectivity are further developed and brought to a special solution in idealism and especially in Hegelian idealism. Hegel maintains the Kantian view of pure self-consciousness as self-referential thinking. Fichte and, following him, Schelling also treat these problems; they conclude, indeed, that the self-representation of the pure ego is an intellectual intuition. No judgment is made here on whether these theories withstand the critical arguments that led Kant to abandon a comparable theory of intellectual self-intuition that he had had formulated and accepted earlier. However, they fall into systematic difficulties because they try to develop the immediate self-intuition of the pure ego and the constitution of objects within a separately established transcendental idealism; this idealism is thought to be a foundation for logic. In this account, logical determinations and laws are already presupposed as valid in the deduction and justification of them. Here arises a circle that, even when discovered, as it was by Fichte, remains vicious. Those difficulties can be avoided if pure subjectivity is explained not in a theory that precedes logic, but within logic itself, where it is conceived as a principle. This conception is connected with the view that for the pure ego no self-intuition is available, only self-thinking. In that sense, we can say that Kant outlined this conception and that Hegel carried it out by means of a modification and a speculative interpretation.[21]

Hegel's critique of Kant is judged by interpreters who often are indebted to Hegel. Contemporaneous critiques of *Phenomenology* reproach Hegel for having established a new system without having sufficiently refuted the Kantian one. But Hegel scholars, for instance, Rosenkranz, then adopt Hegel's standpoint in their own interpretations of Kant.[22] The Neohegelian Kroner calls attention to the neglect of Hegelian philosophy in Neokantianism, but he understands the Kantian theory of apperception and of the synthesis a priori as a conception of the metaphysics of subjectivity. This theory is in his Hegelian view further developed in the idealism of Fichte and Schelling and is completed only by Hegel in a speculative idealism. The explanation of Kroner has a number of successors. So Marcuse and Günther accept the view that Hegel alone completes and perfects the idealistic philosophy. Marcuse starts from Dilthey's and Heidegger's philosophy and tries to show that the conception of vivid motion is the foundation of Hegel's critique of Kant. Günther points out that in his critique of knowledge Kant leaves traditional logic with its clear separation of subject and object as it is but that Hegel in his new metaphysical logic overcomes this separation dialectically. Rather closely connected with this Hegelian renaissance is Hyppolite's favorable explanation of Hegel's critique of Kant, especially as it is found in "Glauben und Wissen."

A series of recent investigations differ from this sort of interpretation. Hegel's interpretation of Kant is paralleled by the Heideggerian one by Henrich and van der Meulen, according to which both Hegel and Heidegger stress the idea of the original center of the self interpreting apperception and imagination.[23] Van der Meulen's position is a metaphysical one, but Henrich's is critical in the Kantian sense in regard to the knowability of a basic power of the subject. Standing a certain critical distance from Hegel but starting from Marxian presuppositions, Merker interprets Hegel's Jena critique of Kant, namely, Hegel's speculative understanding of the antinomies and his speculative conception of pure apperception. Görland also regards critical deviations from Hegel's philosophy as necessary; and she endeavors to prove historically that Hegel, especially in the *Phenomenology*, emphasizes a Kantian theory of self-consciousness, a theory that was already interpreted and altered by Fichte. For Maluschke, Hegel's critique of Kant, particularly of his conceptions of apperception and imagination, can only be understood if Hegelian speculative premises are presupposed. But there are, of course, recent interpreters of the relation between Hegel and Kant who take Hegel's side of the disagreement. For example, we might mention Griffiss,[24] for whom Hegel surmounts the finitude of pure self-consciousness so that a logic, which is dialectical as a whole, is possible; and J. E. Smith, who, although he does not accept several objections of Hegel to Kant, advocates the idea that the Hegelian metaphysics of reason overcomes Kant's theory. In a comparable manner, Petry holds that Hegel's critique of Kant's inconsistencies concerning the distinction and the relation between the logical and the psychological ego is valid. Rotenstreich finds in Kant's own fundamental motives still more evidence, but he agrees with Hegel's view in general. He delineates Hegel's criticism of Kant's argument against the substantial character of the thinking ego and also Hegel's sublation of the substance in the subject that is, conceived as self-referential spirit, the basis of ethical and religious life.[25] Favoring Hegel's theory in a similar way, Lugarini and Verra give an interpretation of the Hegelian critique of Kant; but they also notice that Kant's position is somewhat modified in Hegel's interpretation. Lugarini shows the development of the critique of Kant in Hegel's thought and highlights the speculative motives that Hegel sees in Kant's doctrine, for instance, regarding apperception. Verra analyzes Hegel's interpretation and critique of the Kantian concepts of imagination and of intuitive understanding in the context of the intellectual climate of 1800, and he distinguishes Goethe's interpretation of intuitive understanding from the Hegelian one. There is also an interpretation, given by myself, of Hegel's critique of Kant with special regard to the problem of self-consciousness; this attempt is connected with a Kantian critique of metaphysics but brings to prominence the exemplary character of Hegel's theory of subjectivity.

Hegel's approval and critique as well as his interpretation, which is fundamental for this controversy, of the Kantian theory of pure apperception will be explained. It will be shown that Hegel's discussion of the Kantian theory is carried out not in an immanent way but on the basis of Hegel's own premises and that, however, some problems of subjectivity that Kant raised but did not solve are further developed and speculatively resolved by Hegel. Also, critical-idealistic alternatives that are opposed to those speculative solutions will be taken into consideration.

First, in "Glauben und Wissen" (1802) the Kantian theory of apperception is reviewed by Hegel in detail and independently. Hegel in substance continues to adhere to the special arguments he urges here in his later critique of the philosophy of Kant, although his own systematic premises yet will change.

It is decisive for Hegel's critique of Kant that the possibility of scientific metaphysics, which Kant examines critically, is accepted without question. From the beginning of his Jena period (1801), he outlines a science of metaphysics, including complete knowledge of the absolute by pure reason. Therefore, Kant's theorems and proofs that refute such a view and lead to the limitations of our knowledge in the eyes of Hegel appear to be indecisive, inconsequential, and invalid. From this the Hegelian interpretation and change of the question of how synthetic judgments a priori are possible can be understood.[26] In his opinion, the idea of the *absolute identity* of contrary determinations is pointed to by those judgments in which subject and predicate, particular and universal, and even being and thought are united, provided that distinctions between them are maintained. Their principle, the absolute identity, in such judgments, which Hegel conceives as a partition, as an original division (*"Ur-teilung"* in acceptance of Hölderlin's etymology) and thus as the sphere of the finite consciousness, is present only in a state of predominant difference. Properly speaking, according to Hegel, the absolute identity as such is contained in the synthetic unity of apperception in its speculative sense. Although Kant distinguishes the meaning of "synthetic" in synthetic judgments and in the synthetic unity of apperception because the latter is a principle of analytic judgments, too, Hegel conflates them and substitutes a very different one, i.e., the absolute identity. Also, apperception in Hegel's theory is a principle of judgment, not, however, in a logical but in a metaphysical sense; it is the absolute identity, which by dividing itself in itself produces the opposites of consciousness. Hegel understands the Kantian transcendental deduction of the categories as a proof of the absolute identity of subject and object by which their principle, pure apperception, is imprinted. Also, for him, it is identity of thought and intuition that, only by the disjunction and dividing action of reflection, are separated into the one-sided determinations of the empty ego or understanding, on the one hand, and of the given sensible intuitions, on the other. On Hegel's view, Kant falls back on the concept of the separating reflection in his systematic constructions and thus does not retain the original speculative comprehension of the principle of absolute identity, which he outlines in the concept of pure apperception. The same arguments, according to Hegel's explanation in "Glauben und Wissen," apply to other fundamental Kantian concepts as, for instance, to the transcendental imagination or to the intuitive understanding; each of them is interpreted by Hegel as the original center or the identity of extremes and is considered as the content proper of knowledge by reason. Accordingly, Hegel denies the unsystematic doctrine of faculties and its idea of a "sack full of faculties"[27] established in the eighteenth century and extended by Kant and demands a systematic development of faculties and performances out of one principle just as before him Fichte and Schelling did in their programs of a systematic history of self-consciousness.

The conception of knowledge of the absolute comprehended as the absolute identity, which is the premise of Hegel's interpretation and critique of Kant, follows in this period of Hegel's thought a Spinozistic theory of a single, all embracing substance.[28] Pure self-consciousness as such and distinguished from absolute identity is for Hegel only one-sided and finite; it must be sunk in its truth, in absolute substance. So his disagreement with Kant is most strikingly seen in Hegel's systematic program of an idealistic metaphysics of substance.

Later on, Hegel abandons that metaphysics of substance in favor of a theory of absolute subjectivity. So the fundamental systematic premises of his critique of Kant had to change. The new view is basic to the *Phenomenology* of 1807. There, explanation of particular patterns of consciousness implies a critique of Kant, which must be omitted here, for in the first place Hegel "idealizes" the philosophy of Kant in those patterns of consciousness and confounds it with the philosophy of Fichte, which he believes to be a consistent realization of the Kantian one. In the second place, only appearances of spirit are exhibited and shown to be untrue by concepts that are not part of Hegel's own doctrine of true knowledge but belong to the sphere of the appearance of spirit and to the transition from one mode of appearance to the following one, which likewise proves to be untrue. In this exposition, indeed, speculative-logical arguments are employed by Hegel that in part are incompatible with the Kantian theory. Therefore, the proper domain for the discussion between Hegel and Kant is the logic of truth.

Hegel, also in the *Science of Logic*, considers the synthetic unity of apperception as speculative, absolute identity; but this identity no longer has the anonymous meaning of an absolute substantial unity for him. Now it is an essential part of pure *subjectivity* in a speculative-logical sense, i.e., of the concept of self-thinking.[29] Hegel does not mean here a traditional discursive concept, which is only as a content of understanding an analytic unity of multifarious matters, but the concrete universal, which procures for itself in its own thinking its different, particular determinations and which thus is thinking of itself. In outlining this thought, Hegel refers to the Kantian concept of the synthetic unity of apperception that is for him the concept itself as concrete universal. He accepts and appropriates central Kantian ideas that belong to that synthetic unity, that is, pure synthesis and its unity, simplicity in itself, intellectual spontaneity, and self-reference. So he adopts and promotes the Kantian theory of pure acts of thinking and of their fundamental condition, the thinking pure ego. Hegel's objection, however, that Kant falls into a "psychological idealism," is unwarranted because these pure acts, as has been shown, are no psychical events or facts.[30] Furthermore, Hegel conceives the Kantian proof that the intellectual synthesis in accordance with logical unity constitutes objectivity is from the first an explanation of self-objectification of pure subjectivity that is self-referential thinking. Hence, the *object* for Hegel is not, as it is for Kant, a universal, lawful unity that is brought about in the synthesized manifold of intuitions, but the "objective unity," which specifically is "the identity of the Ego with itself,"[31] that is, what is thought and known in pure self-thinking. So Hegel understands the transcendental deduction of the categories as a demonstration of the possibility and reality of intellectual self-knowledge of the pure subject. This view is consistent neither with Kant's purpose in offering the proof nor with Kant's doctrine of the dependence of human knowledge on sensible intuitions. Intellectual self-reference, according to Kant, is, as has been explained, only pure self-*thinking* that can be performed merely on the basis of representations given in the inner sense and that is not already self-knowledge.

At the same time, however, Hegel raises a problem in his interpretation that Kant has left unresolved, the problem of the connection between intellectual self-reference and constitution of objectivity. This connection is to be clarified in a theory of subjectivity. Whereas Kant expressly distinguishes in his latest reflections between the object that is the content that the pure ego thinks in self-thinking, on the one hand, and the knowable object given in intuitions, on the other hand, the specific character of Hegel's speculative-idealistic theory of the constitution of objectivity is to be found in the conception of the identity of the two of them. So Hegel develops in a speculative-idealistic way a problem that belongs essentially to a theory of subjectivity.

The pure ego, which is self-objectifying and thereby self-knowing, according to Hegel, is not dependent on a given manifold of representations; on the contrary, it *produces* the manifold as a content of its thinking and self-knowledge. In Hegel's view, this manifold consists first in the determinations that belong to the pure concept or to the pure subject itself. The idea of a pure subject that produces its own manifold may be made clearer by considering its background, which is the Hegelian speculative doctrine of the sublation of the *substance* in the *subject*.[32] Following Spinoza, Hegel introduces the single and universal substance as a category, and this proves to be pure actual activity and absolute power in the creation and destruction of its own determinations. But this activity and power as such are present in a simple and unchecked way. According to Hegel, they are merely a positively subsisting identity that lacks negation. The sublation of this one-sidedness and thereby of the substance is to be achieved by the development of a negativity that must be immanent in the identity of the all-embracing substance and that consequently cannot refer to other things but only to itself. So the actual activity becomes an intellectual spontaneity that is distinguished in itself by that negative self-reference and that thus produces different determinations of itself while, however, at the same time retaining its self-identity. In this way, the self-thinking of the pure subject or of the concept considering itself in its own determinations is brought about.[33] It contains the substance that traditionally is the primary being in a sublated mode in itself; it is the substance that has become subject.

Since Kant cannot assign to his doctrine of pure apperception that metaphysical sense and the metaphysically founded thesis of the production of the manifold, his philosophy is criticized by Hegel as a theory of mere understanding that separates the ego from the manifold of intuitions. In Hegel's view, Kant has not reflected on the circumstance that the proof of the finitude of knowledge is attained only by finite knowledge and, therefore, cannot require absolute truth. Kant, however, is alive to the difference between the knowledge of objects and the transcendental reflection on possibilities and limits of such a knowledge, for the theory of the limitation of knowledge is a reflective one and is not a knowledge of objective appearances, still less a knowledge of things in themselves, i.e., of absolute truth as Hegel insinuates it in his objection.

The pure subjectivity, conceived as a pure concept in Hegel's theory, is thus the foundation of its own determinations produced by itself. So Hegel reproaches Kant for having not derived the different logical forms and categories from the unity of "I think," which, therefore, becomes a void identity.[34] In fact, Kant did not explain this derivation in his published works; he did, however, outline it in reflections and letters but still not in a fashion that fits the Hegelian scheme of generation. On the other hand, in Hegel's view the Kantian account of the relation between the thinking self-reference of the ego and the categories is insufficient, Kant speaks of an "inconvenience" and of a "circle" in self-representation by categories. Hegel violently criticizes these formulations, since he believes that Kant holds that the circle is a "fallacy" and that he, therefore, tries to abstract from the thinking self-reference in the "I think." Certainly, Hegel considers the connection between those Kantian statements and the critique of the metaphysics of the soul regarded as a substance. But in Hegel's opinion Kant here is only criticizing an abstract theory that is traditional metaphysics that establishes virtually abstract relational determinations as ontological predicates of the soul, by his own theory that is even more abstract. According to it, the ego is the mere subject of thoughts and cannot be determined by predicates at all. The Kantian explanation that the ego cannot be known by pure thinking because it lacks the manifold of intuitions is conceived by Hegel quite without scrutinizing Kant's own reasons for it, as a separation of the subject from the object and as a retention of the subject in mere abstraction even without thinking self-reference. So, in Hegel's eyes, in Kant's theory the concrete nature of the concept and of the pure ego is absent altogether, for it is to be defined by thinking self-reference, i.e., by intellectual self-objectification, which includes a distinction of the ego in itself, and by self-identification of the ego with itself in those separate moments. So the ego spontaneously produces a plurality of its own determinations in which it knows itself. This self-objectification and self-reference that is a polemical formulation of Kant's view, to be sure, is for Hegel the "circle." In Kant's view, the circle understood as a circle in a metaphysical proof makes impossible, as has been shown, any progress of knowledge but does not make pure self-thinking impossible. The ego, which is a logical unity in general in the categories, qua kind of logical unity, thinks of itself. For Hegel, however, the "circle" signifies just the concrete thinking self-reference of the pure ego, which, in the plurality of its own determinations, knows itself as its object and comprehends itself as concept or concrete universal. This "circle," the self-objectification and self-knowledge of the ego, is to be distinguished from the circle as Kant explains it and cannot, on pain of being judged frivolous by classical logic, be regarded as a circle in a proof. A systematic exposition shows that it is not such a logical circle.

In fact, Hegel avoids the logical circle as well as the infinite regress in his own doctrine of the constitution of thinking and knowing self-reference of the pure ego. The immediate unity of the concept or subject in itself does not arise for Hegel from the concept already unfolded but from a development of simple determinations of being and of determinations of relation, specifically of the substance becoming in itself a negative and self-referential entity. His conception of the further development of this immediate self-reference into mediated self-thinking is indicated in the context of his discussion of Kant. The concept is "the absolute relation to itself . . . which as a dividing judgment makes itself its own object . . . ."[35] "Judgment" here means original division of the unity of the concept into separated conceptual determinations as well as the logical function of statements that differentiates itself systematically into diverse functions. The content of a judgment with respect to the roles of "subject" and "predicate" is important in speculative logic; it is determined a priori, since it consists in diverse conceptual determinations, for instance, "The individual is universal." Because these determinations in judgment are other for one another and because each of them represents the concept itself, the concept here is "object" for itself; i.e., it contrasts with itself in a judgment, being an independent otherness in itself and for itself. So conceptual self-reference, which at first was only immediate, is developed by its self-objectification in a judgment.[36] Since the identity of the concept that is divided into its diverse determinations in a judgment is only expressed by a simple copula that is empty of conceptual meaning, the concept or the pure subject comprehends itself sufficiently only in a copula enriched by the concept itself. This act of comprehension takes place, according to Hegel, in a syllogism[37] in which the conclusion is mediated by a concept or two different conceptual determinations are connected by a third mediating one. If the middle term is no longer a third determination separated from the other two but represents their original unity and thus a concrete universal, as Hegel teaches, then it is the objectivity by which the pure subjectivity knows itself, or it is the developed subjectivity itself as the known content of its self-knowing. Whether Hegel succeeds in carrying out this program convincingly may be left an open question. But in this way he does avoid the logical circle in a proof, because the subjectivity from which the argument starts is the immediate and undeveloped unity of the concept, and this is not iterated in the speculative syllogism. Similarly, he also avoids the infinite iteration or regress, since the developed self-thinking ego is not presupposed in the mediated intellectual self-reference achieved in the syllogism. There are only more simple moments or constitutive principles, i.e., the spontaneity of thinking in general, the self-division, and the production of a conceptual unity of the separated determinations of the concept. Therefore, the developed self-referential ego does not precede the developed thinking self-reference. The same argument is valid for the avoidance of a circle in the definition of self-representation, which circle is only a different formulation of the infinite regress objection. Such a circle in the definition, according to which, in the determination of the self-representation of the ego, the ego, or its conceptual equivalents, is presupposed, is likewise avoided by the speculative-logical development of subjectivity.[38]

In spite of Hegel's rather violent critique of Kant, they both unanimously accept the fundamental systematic importance of pure apperception or pure subjectivity in a specific sense. They both think it is the *principle of logic*, the meaning and the relevance of which for the systematic explanation of logical determinations come to evidence within this logic itself. So the difficulties do not arise into which Fichte and Schelling fall trying to explain the principle of subjectivity as prelogical and as foundation of the logic in a separate theory of transcendental idealism. In Kant, the pure apperception is the principle of the forms of judgment and, furthermore, of formal logic; it is also the principle, aside from that of the pure sensible intuition, of transcendental logic in its positive part, that is, in the part that is fundamental to knowledge. In Hegel, however, the pure subjectivity comprehended as the concept is a sufficient principle of a systematic explanation of speculative subjective logic, specifically of the forms and contents a priori of conceptual determinations, of judgments and syllogisms, for this manifold of determinations and relations is constituted by subjectivity that in thinking of them thinks of itself. But this self-constitution is completed only in an exposition of an adequate concept that is for Hegel in the idea. So pure subjectivity conceived as the foundation of a systematic explanation of logical determinations in its complex structure is itself developed in the course of subjective logic obtaining more and more pregnant determinations. It is for Hegel, however, not only the principle of the subjective, but also the principle of the entire logic. The previous categories of objective logic, i.e., the simple determinations of being and the determinations of relation, are only less complex elements of constitution from which the more complex concept of thinking self-reference and of the pure subject arises. So speculative logic as such becomes even in its ontological meaning a theory first of pure and then finally of absolute subjectivity.

Pure subjectivity for Hegel as well as for Kant is systematically the principle of logic. But the meaning of logic and the relation between subjectivity and special logical determinations is comprehended by each of them in a different way. Hegel likewise accepts as necessary the Kantian assumption of pure acts of thinking and of a reflection of the thinking subject upon them or of the self-reference of the pure ego. His critique of the Kantian theory of pure apperception, as has been shown, is mainly not immanent; it starts from speculative premises in which scientific metaphysics is accepted, the possibility of which was exactly Kant's burning question. It uncovers, however, gaps in the Kantian theory that Hegel fills in with his own logic, for instance, the systematic development of logical determinations out of the principle of subjectivity or the connection of thinking self-reference with the constitution of objects, understood as self-objectification of the pure ego. Furthermore, in his interpretation of the Kantian problem of the circular proof for pure intellectual self-knowledge, Hegel effectively weakens the objection of an infinite iteration and regress that otherwise would make self-representation incomprehensible. Kant, after having abandoned his earlier, more pretentious conception of self-knowledge as intellectual self-intuition, sticks to the possibility of self-thinking; but Hegel's theory is developed further in its arguments against that objection. Moreover, the objections raised to the substantiality of the Cartesian "Ego cogito" are not valid for the Kantian but also not valid for the Hegelian theory, for even in Hegel's view the self-thinking of the concept is not substantiality, but freedom. The Hegelian speculative logic is indeed metaphysics; more exactly, it is an ontology and an ontotheology of the absolute subjectivity. Therefore, in diverging from the Kantian conception, for instance, the pure acts of thinking in which the subjectivity determines itself, Hegel's account takes on ontological meaning. It may be doubted whether this metaphysics, as opposed to the Kantian critique of metaphysics, can be maintained.[39] But some fundamental insights of Hegel into systematic requirements of a theory of subjectivity are independent of his metaphysics, for instance, the idea of a pure, self-thinking subjectivity as the principle of logic and of its rules and categories, the systematic explanation of logical determinations in general based on subjectivity as their principle, and the exposition of the genesis of its self-objectification and self-identification and with that the avoidance of an infinite iteration by the constitution of pure subjectivity out of more simple elements and as the result of this development. But it must be guaranteed that the logical rules and categories are valid a priori, that their being thought and that thus the ideal but not real pure acts of thinking necessarily are assumed. Finally, it must be guaranteed that these acts are based on self-thinking, pure subjectivity understood as their ideal principle. In view of the prevelance and, in some quarters, dominance of empiricism in contemporary philosophy, the idea that such a conception, which encompasses both the conditions of scientific thought and of scientific experience, is neither impossible nor meaningless might be recommended for fundamental serious consideration.

Notes

Acknowledgment: For important and friendly help in the English version of this paper and for philosophical suggestions, I thank Prof. M. G. Yoes of the University of Houston and the University of Siegen (West Germany) in 1981/1982.

1. Cf. E. Mach, *Die Analyse der Empfindungen und das Verhältnis des Physischen zum Psychischen*, 6th ed. (Jena: Fischer, 1911), 18ff; see for the following E. Husserl, *Logische Untersuchungen* (Halle: Niemeyer, 1900/1901), Vol. 2, pp. 325-42; W. James, *The Principles of Psychology* (New York: Henry Holt and Company, 1890), Vol. 1, 329ff.; W. James, "Does Consciousness Exist?" in *Essays in Radical Empiricism*, 2nd ed. (New York: Longmans, Green and Company, 1922), 1ff.

2. Cf. B. Russell, *The Analysis of Mind*, 10th ed. (London: Allen and Unwin, 1971), 9ff.; B. Russell, *An Outline of Philosophy*, 8th ed. (London: Allen and Unwin, 1961), 218ff. See for the following J. Chr. Lichtenberg, *Aphorismen*, ed. A. Leitzmann, Vol. 5 (Berlin: Behr, 1908), p. 128; Vol. 3 (Berlin: Behr, 1906), 7ff.; G. Ryle, *The Concept of Mind* (first published 1949; London: Penguin Books, 1968), 186ff.

3. Cf., for instance, N. Hartmann, *Der Aufbau der realen Welt*, 2nd ed. (Meisenheim a.G.: Hain, 1949), 5ff., 512ff.; see for the following M. Heidegger's discussion of the philosophy of Hegel: "Die ontotheologische Verfassung der Metaphysik," in *Identität und Differenz*, 4th ed. (Pfullingen: Neske, 1957), pp. 31-67; see furthermore for the Marxian critique, for instance, Th. W. Adorno, *Zur Metakritik der Erkenntnistheorie* (Stuttgart: Kohlhammer, 1956), 196ff.

4. Cf. D. Henrich, *Fichtes ursprüngliche Einsicht* (Frankfort/M.: Klostermann, 1967). Cf. Plotinos, *Enneades*, II, 9, 1, 55ff.

5. Cf., for instance, H. Cohen, *Kants Theorie der Erfahrung*, 3rd ed. (Berlin: Cassirer, 1918), 393ff.; H. Heimsoeth, "Persönlichkeitsbewußtsein und Ding an sich in der Kantischen Philosophie" (first published in 1924), in *Studien zur Philosophie I. Kants, Kant-Studien*, supplementary Vol. 71 (Cologne: Universitäts-Verlag, 1956), pp. 227-57; M. Heidegger, *Kant und das Problem der Metaphysik*, 2nd ed. (Frankfort/M.: Klostermann, 1951), 76ff., 134ff., 171ff.; and Heidegger, *Gesamtausgabe*, Vol. 25 (Frankfort/M.: Klostermann, 1977), 386ff.; H. J. Paton, *Kant's Metaphysic of Experience*, 5th ed. (first published in 1936; London and New York: Allen and Unwin and Humanities Press, 1970), Vol. 1, 396ff., 503ff.; H. J. de Vleeschauwer, *La Déduction transcendantale dans l'oeuvre de Kant*, 3 vols. (Antwerp: De Sikkel, 1934-1937); J. Ebbinghaus, *Kantinterpretation und Kantkritik* (first 1924), in *Gesammelte Aufsätze, Vorträge und Reden* (Darmstadt: Wiss. Buchgesellschaft, 1968), pp. 1-23; K. Reich, *Die Vollständigkeit der kantischen Urteilstafel* (first 1932; 2nd ed. Berlin: Schoetz, 1948), 25ff.; P. F. Strawson, *The Bounds of Sense* (first 1966, 3rd ed., London: Methuen, 1973), 93ff.; J. Bennett, *Kant's Analytic* (first 1966, 2nd ed., Cambridge: Cambridge University Press, 1975), 100ff.; M. Hossenfelder, *Kants Konstitutionstheorie und die transzendentale Deduktion* (Berlin and New York: de Gruyter, 1978), 96ff.; D. P. Dryer, *Kant's Solution for Verification in Metaphysics* (London: Allen and Unwin, 1966), 117ff.; D. Henrich, *Identität und Objektivität: Eine Untersuchung über Kants transzendentale Deduktion* (Heidelberg: Winter, 1976), pp. 54-112. For further

interpretations, cf. the general review of V. Gerhardt and F. Kaulbach, *Kant* (Darmstadt: Wiss. Buchgesellschaft, 1979).

6. Cf. *Critique of Pure Reason* B 129ff. (§15); cf. the commentary on this passage by Paton, *Kant's Metaphysic of Experience*, Vol. 1, 503ff.; cf. also D. Henrich, *Identität und Objektivität*, 55ff. See furthermore here and for the following K. Düsing, *Hegel und die Geschichte der Philosophie*, "Ontologie und Dialektik in Antike und Neuzeit," Chapter 3, Section II on Kant (Darmstadt: Wiss. Buchgesellschaft, 1983 [in press]).

7. For Kant, *"Einheit des Selbstbewußtseins"* often has two meanings: "unity," understood as a whole of various representations united in itself, and "identity," conceived as sameness in the manifold of representations. Here both of them are meant. See the explanations below about Kant's own analogous distinction between synthetic and analytic unity of apperception.

8. See, for these connections, Heimsoeth, *Persönlichkeitsbewußtsein und Ding an sich in der Kantischen Philosophie*, and I. Heidemann, "Spontaneität und Zeitlichkeit: Ein Problem der Kritik der reinen Vernunft," *Kant-Studien*, supplementary Vol. 75 (Cologne: Universitäts-Verlag, 1958), p. 185ff.; recently, N. Rotenstreich, *Theory and Practice in Kant and Hegel* (to be published in the proceedings of the Stuttgart Hegel-Conference, 1981).

9. Cf. for this thought D. P. Dryer, *Kant's Solution for Verification in Metaphysics*, p. 121. See for the following *Critique of Pure Reason* B 158 ". . . that I think myself . . ." (". . . daß ich mich denke . . ."), further B 135.

10. Cf. *Critique of Pure Reason* B 133ff. Paton notices this passage in his commentary; but he does not discuss the specific problem that lies in the relation between these determinations; cf. *Kant's Metaphysic of Experience*, Vol. 1, pp. 513ff. But cf. L. Lugarini, *La logica transcendentale kantiana* (Milan-Messina: Principato, 1950), pp. 183ff., and K. Düsing, "Das Problem der Subjektivität in Hegels Logik: Systematische und entwicklungsgeschichtliche Untersuchungen zum Prinzip des Idealismus und zur Dialektik," *Hegel-Studien*, supplementary Vol. 15 (Bonn: Bouvier, 1976), pp. 237ff.

11. Cf. *Critique of Pure Reason*, B 137ff.

12. That *"Objekt"* for Kant very often has the meaning of regular unity or of law in general is also to be drawn from his characterization of the moral law as an "objective" practical law. Although he does not distinguish *"Gegenstand"* and *"Objekt"* terminologically, the moral law could not be designed as *"gegenständlich."*

13. Although Kant has not explained a systematic deduction of the forms of judgment in his published works, he has designed it in reflections and letters; cf. K. Reich, *Die Vollständigkeit der kantischen Urteilstafel*.

14. I. Kant, *Vorlesungen über die Metaphysik*, ed. by C. H. L. Poelitz (Erfurt, 1821; reprint, Darmstadt: Wiss. Buchgesellschaft, 1964), p. 133: ". . . der einzige Fall, wo wir die Substanz unmittelbar anschauen können." Cf. *Kant's gesammelte Schriften*, ed. by the Prussian Academy of Sciences, Vol. XXVIII/1, 266. See for those thoughts H. Heimsoeth, *Persönlichkeitsbewußtsein und Ding an sich* . . . , pp. 232ff.

15. *Kant's gesammelte Schriften*, XVII, 470 (reflection 4234): ". . . daß sie [die Seele] eine unmittelbare Anschauung seiner [!] selbst durch die absolute Einheit *Ich* sei, welcher der singularis der Handlungen des Denkens ist." For the following cf. II, 337.

16. *Kant's gesammelte Schriften*, XVII, 465 (reflection 4225): "Das Ich ist eine unerklärliche Vorstellung. Sie ist eine Anschauung, die unwandelbar ist"; XVII, 509 (reflection 4336): ". . . einen Begriff . . . durch unser intellektuelles inneres Anschauen (nicht den inneren Sinn) unserer Tätigkeit, welche durch motiva intellectualia bewegt werden kann." Cf. also Kant's formulation: "Anschauung der Selbsttätigkeit zu möglichen Wirkungen" (XVII, 509, reflection 4334).

17. A remnant of the earlier conception apparently is to be found in the formulation of the *Critique of Pure Reason* in the solution of the third antinomy (B 574): "The human being . . . knows itself by mere apperception too" ("Der Mensch . . . erkennt sich selbst auch durch bloße Apperzeption").

18. *Kant's gesammelte Schriften*, XXII, 77: "Der erste Akt des Vorstellungsvermögens ist das Bewußtsein meiner selbst, welches ein bloß logischer Akt ist, der aller übrigen Vorstellung zum Grunde liegt, wodurch das Subjekt sich selbst zum Objekte macht"; cf. also *op. cit.*, pp. 89, 98.

19. Cf. *Critique of Reason* B 422 and 404. Passages of such a kind have become the starting point of various discussions and theories. Hegel criticizes Kant vehemently, as will be shown. In Neokantianism, Cohen, Natorp, or Rickert revert to those passages in order to develop their own theories. Natorp especially thinks such a circle makes the conception of self-objectification and self-reference of the ego impossible. He establishes his own theory, which starts from the inconceivability of the spontaneous ego. Kant's thesis of the circular metaphysical proof is changed here into the assertion that the definition of the self-referential ego is circular. In my opinion, this is a far-reaching misinterpretation that is followed by recent German expositions. A critical comment on Kant's explanation is to be found in J. Bennett, *Kant's Dialectic* (Cambridge: Cambridge University Press, 1974), pp. 69ff.

20. Cf. *Critique of Pure Reason* B 422ff. note. Cf., for instance, the critical interpretation in J. Bennett, *Kant's Dialectic*, pp. 66ff.; cf. also P. F. Strawson, *The Bounds of Sense*, pp. 162ff.

21. For these theses see K. Düsing, "Das Problem der Subjektivität," pp. 120ff., also 141ff. and 20ff., 336ff.

22. Cf. K. Rosenkranz, *Geschichte der Kant'schen Philosophie* (Leipzig: Voss, 1840), especially pp. 10ff., 489. For the first critiques, cf. W. Bonsiepen, "Erste zeitgenössische Rezensionen der Phänomenologie des Geistes," *Hegel-Studien* 14 (1979), pp. 9ff., cf. especially pp. 25, 27ff. Concerning the following cf. R. Kroner, *Von Kant bis Hegel*, 2 vols., (first published 1921/1924, 2nd ed., Tübingen: Mohr-Siebeck, 1961); H. Marcuse, *Hegels Ontologie und die Grundlegung einer Theorie der Geschichtlichkeit* (Frankfort/M.: Klostermann, 1932), especially pp. 18ff., 24ff., 132ff., 183ff.; G. Günther, *Grundzüge einer neuen Theorie des Denkens in Hegels Logik* (first published 1933, 2nd ed., Hamburg: Meiner, 1978), especially pp. 40ff., 104ff., 108ff., 147ff.; J. Hyppolite, "La Critique hégélienne de la réflexion kantienne," *Kant-Studien* 45 (1953/1954), pp. 83ff.

23. Cf. D. Henrich, "Über die Einheit der Subjektivität," *Philosophische Rundschau* 3 (1955), pp. 28-69; J. van der Meulen, *Hegel: Die Gebrochene Mitte* (Hamburg: Meiner, 1958), especially pp. 218ff., also 31ff., 168ff. Concerning the following, cf. N. Merker, *Le Origini della logica hegeliana* (Milan: Feltrinelli, 1961), especially pp. 218ff.; I. Görland, *Die Kantkritik des jungen Hegel* (Frankfurt/M.: Klostermann, 1966); see also my review in *Hegel-Studien* 5 (1969), pp. 298ff.; G. Maluschke, "Kritik und absolute Methode in Hegels Dialektik," *Hegel-Studien*, supplementary Vol. 13 (Bonn: Bouvier, 1974), especially pp. 82ff.

24. Cf. J. E. Griffiss, "The Kantian Background of Hegel's Logic," *The New Scholasticism* 43 (1969), pp. 509-29; see for the following J. E. Smith, "Hegel's Critique of Kant," in *Hegel and the History of Philosophy*, J. J. O'Malley, K. W. Algozin, and F. G. Weiss, eds., (The Hague: Nijhoff, 1974), pp. 109-28 (first published 1973); G. W. F. Hegel, *The Berlin Phenomenology*, ed. and trans. with an introduction and explanatory notes, M. J. Petry (Dordrecht/Boston: Reidel, 1981), especially pp. XXff., XXXVIIff., XLIXff.

25. Cf. N. Rotenstreich, *From Substance to Subject: Studies in Hegel* (The Hague: Nijhoff, 1974); cf. also N. Rotenstreich, "On Spirit: An Interpretation of Hegel," *Hegel-Studien* 15 (1980), pp. 199-240. With regard to the following, cf. L. Lugarini, "La 'Confutazione' hegeliana della filosofia critica," *Hegel interprete di Kant*, ed. V. Verra (Naples: Prismi, 1981), pp. 13-66; V. Verra, "Immaginazione trascendentale e intelletto intuitivo," *op. cit.*, pp. 67-89. See also K. Düsing, "Das Problem der Subjektivität," pp. 109ff., 233ff., and with a review of the literature K. Düsing, *Hegel und die Geschichte der Philosophie*.

26. Cf. here and in the following Hegel's discussion of the Kantian philosophy in "Glauben und Wissen," *Gesammelte Werke*, Vol. 4 (Hamburg: Meiner, 1968), pp. 326ff.

27. *Gesammelte Werke*, Vol. 4, p. 237, cf. p. 329. Hegel maintains this critique later on, cf. for instance, *Encyclopedia*, 3rd ed. (Heidelberg: Winter, 1830), § 445 note.

28. For Hegel's metaphysics of Spinozistic substance in his early Jena period established in

common with Schelling, cf. K. Düsing, "Idealistische Substanzmetaphysik: Probleme der Systementwicklung bei Schelling und Hegel in Jena," *Hegel in Jena, Hegel-Studien*, supplementary Vol. 20 (Bonn: Bouvier, 1980), pp. 25-44.

29. Cf. *Gesammelte Werke*, Vol. 12, pp 17ff. Concerning the difference between the traditional and the Hegelian doctrine of concept, cf., for instance, G. R. G. Mure, *A Study of Hegel's Logic* (first published 1950, Oxford: Oxford University Press, 1967), pp. 159ff.

30. Cf. *Gesammelte Werke*, Vol. 12, pp. 22ff.; cf. Vol. 4, p. 332.

31. *Gesammelte Werke*, Vol. 12, p. 18 ("welche objektive Einheit die Einheit des Ich mit sich selbst ist").

32. Cf. especially *Gesammelte Werke*, Vol. 11, pp. 394ff.; Vol. 12, pp. 11ff. Cf. about this problem in general N. Rotenstreich, *From Substance to Subject* and specifically concerning the Hegelian argumentation also K. Düsing, "Das Problem der Subjektivität," pp. 228ff., and K. Düsing, "Idealistische Substanzmetaphysik," pp. 41ff. Walsh demonstrates in a similar context that Hegel does not accept the Kantian dualism of the sources of knowledge; cf. W. H. Walsh, "Subjective and Objective Idealism," (to be published in the proceedings of the Hegel conference in Stuttgart, 1981).

33. This sketch may comprise the leading idea of Hegel in a longer series of arguments in which the categories are developed out of the substance via causality and reciprocity into the concept itself. Whether the special Hegelian argument concerning the deduction of thinking, which is self-thinking and therefore self-distinguishing and self-identifying, from categories of relation in the objective logic can be convincing perhaps should be left open.

34. For this idealistic standard objection, see, for instance, Hegel, *Gesammelte Werke*, Vol. 12, pp. 44, 205, *Encyclopedia* (3rd ed.), §42 note; cf. besides that above note 13. Concerning the following cf. *Gesammelte Werke*, Vol. 12, pp. 193ff.; see also above note 19; furthermore cf. K. Cramer, "'Erlebnis': Thesen zu Hegels Theorie des Selbstbewußtseins mit Rücksicht auf die Aporien eines Grundbegriffs nachhegelscher Philosophie," *Stuttgarter Hegel-Tage 1970, Hegel-Studien*, supplementary Vol. 11 (Bonn: Bouvier, 1974), especially pp. 592ff. With regard to the problem of the circle in general and specifically in Fichte, cf. D. Henrich, *Fichtes ursprüngliche Einsicht* (Frankfort/M.: Klostermann, 1967).

35. *Gesammelte Werke*, Vol. 12, p. 194 (. . . ist "die absolute Beziehung auf sich selbst . . . , welche als trennendes Urteil sich zum Gegenstande macht . . ."). With regard to the following, cf. the more detailed explanation by K. Düsing, "Das Problem der Subjektivität," pp. 251ff., 266ff.

36. In regard to the relation between logical judgments and categories, Hegel does not follow the Aristotelian and Kantian ontological view that the fundamental kinds of being or of being an object are characterized by logical modes of judgments. Rather, his theory of the development of ontologically basic determinations is connected, if anything, with the ontology of the late Plato. Cf. for the Platonic theory, e.g., F. M. Cornford, *Plato's Theory of Knowledge* (first published 1935, London: Routledge and Kegan Paul, 1973), pp. 274ff.

37. Cf. also Hegel's determination in his Jena manuscript of 1805/1806 that the contrary moments, singularity and universality, are mediated in the syllogism and connected; "copula is Ego" ("Copula ist Ich"); the ego, which unites these contrary determinations in itself, is the true middle term. (See *Gesammelte Werke*, Vol. 8, p. 197.)

38. For this objection, as well as for the argument from infinite iteration, the assertion is decisive that the ego, for its self-representation, again and again is presupposed as being self-referential. This is thought to be valid also for the attempt to define the self-representing ego. But it remains unclear in the circle argument whether only a nominal definition is thought to be impossible – this view can be contested by an employment of equivalents of self-representation – or whether a real definition of the self-referential ego is held to be impossible. In this case, its real essence must be unknowable, whereas its thinking self-reference certainly can be thought. Because of these doubtful factors in this argument, the infinite iteration argument is more exact.

39. Concerning this problem, see K. Düsing, "Das Problem der Subjektivität."

Schopenhauers Transzendentalismus

RUDOLF MALTER

"Den Geist löscht nicht aus." 1 Thess. 5, 19

Pamphlete, die die Schuld an unheilvollen politischen Entwicklungen einem Philosophen oder einer philosophischen Richtung anlasten wollen, können am ehesten mit Zustimmung rechnen, wenn sie die Stichworte ins Spiel bringen, unter denen jener Philosoph oder jene Richtung im populären philosophischen Bewusstsein gegenwärtig sind. Als Georg Lukács in die Ahnenreihe derer, die durch Vernunftzerstörung den "Weg Deutschlands zu Hitler auf dem Gebiet der Philosophie"[1] ebneten, auch Arthur Schopenhauer aufnahm, wusste er sehr wohl, wie gut der Denker ins eingefahrene Assoziationsschema "Irrationalismus" passte. Für Schopenhauer als den irrationalistischen Vater eines Grossteils späterer Irrationalisten — für diesen Schopenhauer brauchte Lukács nicht einmal mehr eine Schein-Rechtfertigung: allzu lange schon hatte sich — in seltener Eintracht — in volkstümlichen wie in wissenschaftlichen Darstellungen der Philosophiegeschichte des 19. Jahrhunderts der Schopenhauer gebildet, der dem nach philosophischen Hitlerahnen suchenden Lukács gerade recht war.

Wenn der "Irrationalist" Schopenhauer in Wahrheit ein Schopenhauer eines Vorurteils ist, so ist er selber als Autor nicht schuldlos an der Verzerrung des Bildes, die ihm zu Unrecht widerfuhr. *Ein* Lehrstück unter mehreren interpretativ so zu isolieren, dass es so aussieht, als sei dieses schon die ganze Lehre — dies freilich steht ausserhalb des Verfügungsbereiches des Lehrenden; *ein* Lehrstück unter mehreren anderen (und vielleicht sogar wichtigeren) so betonen, dass im nicht sehr aufmerksam lesenden Rezipienten der Eindruck entstehen muss, dieser so betonte Teil sei das Ganze — dies fällt unter die Verantwortung des Autors, wenn er es ist, der in so einseitiger Weise *einen* Aspekt der eigenen Lehre akzentuiert. Es ist bekannt, welchen Aspekt des eigenen Systems Schopenhauer in besonders auffälliger Form nach dem

433

Erscheinen der ersten Auflage der "Welt als Wille und Vorstellung" (allerdings auch schon genauso in diesem Werk) herausgestrichen hat: die Akzidentalität und Instrumentalität des Erkennens vor dem Hintergrund der Wesenhaftigkeit und Aseität des gestaltlos-eigenschaftslosen Willens. Wille und Intellekt, so lautet das so sehr von Schopenhauer betonte Lehrstück, sind prinzipiell verschieden, nicht nur in ihrer Funktion als Vermögen des Gemüts, sondern in ihrer metaphysischen Rangordnung. Der Wille ist das *Wesen* schlechthin, die *Bedeutung*, der *Inhalt* der Welt, der Intellekt aber "bloss" eine unter vielen Objektivationen des Willens (wenn auch die vorzüglichste). Streicht man dann noch interpretativ die zentrale Rolle der Lehre von der Erlösung durch Erkenntnis, so hat man—mit teilweiser Stützung auf Schopenhauer selbst—die gängige Ortsbestimmung des Schopenhauerschen Denkens in ganzen: nach der Herrschaft der Vernunft (begründet durch Descartes, befestigt durch Leibniz und Kant, hypertrophiert durch Hegel) drängen—laut jener gängigen Ortsbestimmung—die zunächst noch versteckten antiidealistisch-irrationalistischen Tendenzen in die Lücke, die durch den Zerfall des Hegelianismus entstanden war; jetzt also sei die Zeit reif geworden für die Proklamation der Irrationalität des Wesens der Welt und für ihren Propheten Arthur Schopenhauer.

Hätte Schopenhauer in seinem wahrhaft irrationalen Hegelhass sich selber nicht so dezidiert als der Sieger über den Vernunftabsolutisten Hegel erhoben, wäre es nicht so leicht geworden, ihn pauschal zum Hauptverantwortlichen für eine tatsächlich zu jener Zeit einsetzende irrationalistische Entwicklung zu machen, deren verhängnisvollen Folgen erst eigentlich im 20. Jahrhundert zutage traten. Lukács hat darin recht, dass eine solche Entwicklung mit solchen Folgen im deutschen Geistesleben des 19. Jahrhunderts begann. Er verunstaltet aber die reale philosophische Situation, von der er ausgeht, wenn er Schopenhauers Philosophieren in diese die Vernunft zynisch instrumentalisierende und die Philosophie selber ruinierende irrationalistische Bewegung einreiht.

Wohin aber gehört Schopenhauer, wenn nicht zu den Zerstörern der Vernunft? Welches ist die ihm eigene Denkart? Und wo ist der wirkliche denkgeschichtliche Ort seines Systems? Die These, die im folgenden in grossen Linien entwickelt werden soll (ohne dass hierbei auf die wichtigen Detailfragen eingegangen werden könnte),[2] lautet: Schopenhauer lehrt eine Willensmetaphysik, die untrennbar verknüpft ist mit einem Transzendentalismus, der auf der Seite der Lehre von der "Welt als Vorstellung" das Erscheinungshafte begründet, auf der Seite der Lehre von der "Welt als Wille" aber selber ein konstitutiver Teil dieser Seite von Schopenhauers Systems ist. Denkgeschichtlich heisst dies: Schopenhauer gehört entschieden mehr in die Tradition transzendental-idealistischen Denkens als in die des Irrationalismus. Dass das Lehrstück von der Sekundärfunktion des Intellekts (wider die objektive Intention des Systems im ganzen) einem für irrationalistische Ideologeme empfangsbereiten Zeitalter zum willkommenen Argumentationsinstrument werden konnte—dies lag zwar auch an Schopenhauers Akzentsetzung, primär aber an den Ideologen, die zu aller Zeit grosse Gedanken atomisieren, um sie ihren Zwecken gefügig zu machen.

I. DIE ERSTE STUFE DES TRANSZENDENTALISMUS BEI SCHOPENHAUER: TRANSZENDENTALISMUS DER ERSCHEINUNG

1. Von der Faktizität der Welt zur "Welt als Vorstellung"

Wenn (in Fortführung der cartesischen und kantischen Tradition) unter Transzendentalismus diejenige Konzeption des Verhältnisses von Sein und Wissen zu verstehen ist, nach welcher Sein als Sein je eröffnet ist durch Wissen und somit ein ursprünglich-notwendiger bedingend-ermöglichender Bezug des Wissens zum Sein besteht, so ist das erste Buch des Schopenhauerschen Hauptwerkes ein klassisches Stück Transzendentalphilosophie. Das erste Buch der "Welt als Wille und Vorstellung" thematisiert nämlich die ursprüngliche Eröffnung des Seins ("Welt") durch das Wissen ("Vorstellung"); es bringt also den ursprünglich-notwendigen Bezug des Seins zum Wissen und die bedingend-ermöglichende Vorgängigkeit des Wissens innerhalb der untrennbaren Wissen-Sein-Korrelation zur Sprache. "Die Welt ist meine Vorstellung" — dieser erste Satz des Hauptwerkes,[3] der für alle erkennenden Individuen gilt und vom Menschen allein "in das reflektirte abstrakte Bewusstseyn"[4] gebracht werden kann (und dessen Eingetretensein den Zustand der "philosophische[n] Besonnenheit"[5] ausmacht) drückt den *Transzendentalismus der ersten Stufe* aus. Er besagt: wenn überhaupt etwas ist ("Welt"), dann ist es *für* das Wissen ein "etwas." "Sein" heisst auch für Schopenhauer — wie für Berkeley, den er als Kronzeugen zitiert "Vorgestelltwerden." Hat demnach der Mensch die "philosophische Besonnenheit" erreicht, dann wird ihm "deutlich und gewiss, dass er keine Sonne kennt und keine Erde; sondern immer nur ein Auge, das eine Sonne sieht, eine Hand, die eine Erde fühlt; dass die Welt, welche ihn umgiebt, nur als Vorstellung daist, d.h. durchweg nur in Beziehung auf ein Anderes, das Vorstellende, welches er selbst ist."[6] Der Satz von dem Vorgestelltsein der Welt durch das individuelle Subjekt ist für Schopenhauer "eine Wahrheit," die schlechthin "a priori ausgesprochen werden kann,"[7] denn "sie ist die Aussage derjenigen Form aller möglichen und erdenklichen Erfahrung, welche allgemeiner, als alle andern, als Zeit, Raum und Kausalität ist."[8] Die Aussage, "Sein" heisse je "Vorgestelltsein" durch ein Vorstellendes, geht den Aussagen bedingend-ermöglichend voraus, welche die Bestimmtheit des Seins in seinem Vorgestelltsein bezeichnen. Dieser ursprünglichste transzendentale (d.i. den notwendigen bedingend-ermöglichenden Bezug des Wissens zum Sein betreffende) Satz ist auch ursprünglicher als die fundamentalen Bestimmtheiten, auf welche alle weiteren Bestimmtheiten vorgestellten Seins zurückzuführen sind (nämlich die schon genannten Formen "Zeit, Raum, Kausalität"), "denn alle diese setzen jene eben schon voraus,"[9] nämlich die Form des Vorgestelltseins überhaupt. Die Urbestimmtheiten alles vorgestellten Seins, die von Schopenhauer als Gestaltungen des Satzes vom Grund gefasst werden, und von denen jede jeweils "eine besonders Klasse von Vorstellungen"[10] ausmacht, haben selbst wiederum eine sie an Ursprünglichkeit übersteigende "gemeinsame Form" — diejenige, "unter welcher allein irgend eine Vorstellung, welcher Art sie auch sei, abstrakt oder intuitiv, rein oder empirisch, nur überhaupt möglich und denkbar ist."[11]

Da das Philosophieren auch ein Vorstellen ist, kann es selbst gar nicht anders als mit der Feststellung beginnen, dass Sein je vorgestelltes Sein ist. *Hinter* diese Feststellung, die als eine unausweichliche Einsicht dem Nachdenken sich aufdrängt, kann daher nicht zurückgegangen werden, weil das Nachdenken selber Vorstellen ist. Es ist daher sinnlos und falsch, dem Erkennen, das immer Etwas-Erkennen ist, eine andere vorgängige Bedingung seiner Möglichkeit als eben diese Bezogenheit des Etwas auf das Erkennen vorzuschalten. Das Je-vorgestellt-sein der Welt ist also unableitbar; das Nachdenken selber über die Möglichkeit einer dem Je-vorgestellt-sein zugrunde-liegenden ursprünglicheren Form setzt das Je-vorgestellt-sein schon voraus und erweist sich so als eine "unerweisliche" Wahrheit (um einen terminus technicus der an Leibniz anknüpfenden wolffianischen Schulphilosophie zu gebrauchen). Schopen-hauer sagt: "Keine Wahrheit ist also gewisser, von allen andern unabhängiger und eines Beweises weniger bedürftig, als diese, dass Alles, was für die Erkenntniss daist, also diese ganze Welt, nur Objekt in Beziehung auf das Subjekt ist, Anschauung des Anschauenden, mit Einem Wort, Vorstellung."[12]

Wenn wir diese "Wahrheit" als die erste Stufe des Schopenhauerschen Transzen-dentalismus bezeichnet haben, dann ist zur Verhütung eines Missverständnisses folgendes zu beachten: die Wendung "*erste* Stufe des Transzendentalismus" besagt nicht nur, dass bei der Betrachtung des Erkennens mit der Faktizität des notwendigen bedingend-ermöglichenden Bezugs des Erkennens (des "Vorstellens") auf das Sein ("die Welt") begonnen werden muss, sondern auch: es muss überhaupt mit der Betrachtung des *Erkennens* (und nicht: des *Seins*), d.h. mit der Betrachtung des Betrachtens begonnen werden, wenn von einem "fundamentum inconcussum" aus philosophiert werden soll. Philosophie ist eo ipso Transzendentalphilosophie —in-sofern sie den Anspruch erhebt, ohne eine andere Voraussetzung zu beginnen, als die es ist, die das philosophierende Denken in seiner Eigenschaften als Vorstellungs-vollzug darstellt.

Aber: die Unabdingbarkeit und Evidenz des transzendentalistischen Anfangs allen Nachdenkens über die "Welt" schliesst für Schopenhauer nicht aus, dass *in-nerhalb* des absoluten Horizonts der Selbstreflexion des je sich vorfindenden Vorstel-lens die Einsicht aufgeht, dass dieser für das Vorstellen unüberschreitbare (weil ja das Vorstellen selbst ausmachende) Horizont *qualitativ* einen Mangel aufweist, der innerhalb seiner Grenzen, aber nicht durch ihn, d.h. durch das Vorstellen selber behoben werden kann. Der Transzendentalismus geht bloss auf den Bezug der Vorstellung zur Welt (in dem angezeigten bedingend-ermöglichenden Sinne); er betrifft die ursprünglichste *Form*, in welcher die Welt da ist.

Wenn Schopenhauer in direktem Anschluss an die Erörterung der Vorgestellt-heit der Welt von dem "inneren Widerstreben" spricht, "mit welchem er [gemeint: "Jeder"] die Welt als seine blosse Vorstellung annimmt,"[13] so drückt sich für ihn in diesem Widerstreben das Gefühl für jenen Mangel aus, der gespürt wird, wenn die Welt nur ihrer *Form* nach betrachtet wird. Der Transzendentalismus ist notwendig, aber er ist nicht schon das Ganze der Betrachtung der Welt, denn er lässt die Frage nach dem *Inhalt* des Vorgestellten offen. Dies ist die "Einseitigkeit" der im ersten Buch des Hauptwerkes vorgenommenen Betrachtung Welt-Betrachtung: "Also nur von der angegebenen Seite, nur sofern sie Vorstellung ist, betrachten wir die Welt in diesem ersten Buche. Dass jedoch diese Betrachtung, ihrer Wahrheit unbeschadet, eine einseitige, folglich durch irgend eine willkürliche Abstraktion hervorgerufen, ist, kündigt Jedem das innere Widerstreben an, mit welchem er die Welt als seine blosse Vorstellung annimmt; welcher Annahme er sich andererseits doch nimmermehr entziehn kann. Die Einseitigkeit dieser Betrachtung aber wird das folgende Buch ergänzen, durch eine Wahrheit, welche nicht so unmittelbar gewiss ist, wie die, von der wir hier ausgehn; sondern zu welcher nur tiefere Forschung, schwierigere Abstraktion, Trennung des Verschiedenen und Vereinigung dès Identischen führen kann, – durch eine Wahrheit, welche sehr ernst und Jedem, wo nicht furchtbar, doch bedenklich seyn muss, nämlich diese, dass eben auch er sagen kann und sagen muss; 'Die Welt ist mein Wille.'"[14]

2. Vom Transzendentalismus der Erscheinung zur Metaphysik des Willens

Die durch die transzendentalistische (d.i. "die Seite der Erkennbarkeit"[15] der Welt betreffende) Betrachtung nicht mehr zu erreichende Wahrheit, die in der Willensmetaphysik des zweiten Buches des Hauptwerkes entwickelt wird, bietet sich, wie Schopenhauer selber sagt, offenbar nicht in der Evidenz an, wie dies bei der "ersten," der transzendentalen Wahrheit der Fall ist. Sie bietet sich vor allem aber nicht als die "erste" Wahrheit an – und doch ist sie, insofern sie den *Inhalt* ("Bedeutung," "Wesen," "Was") der Welt betrifft, ursprünglicher als die Wahrheit "Die Welt ist meine Vorstellung." Ursprünglicher als diese Wahrheit ist die Aussage über den Willenscharakter der Welt deswegen, weil der Wille es ist, ohne den die "Welt als Vorstellung" die völlig inhaltslose wäre, ja – wie Schopenhauer im zweiten Buche zu zeigen versucht – überhaupt nicht wäre ohne das materiale Weltprinzip "Wille": der Wille ist das Kantische "Ding an sich," die Vorstellung aber ist "Erscheinung." Der Transzendentalismus, der von der Vorgestelltheit der Welt spricht, ist *Transzendentalismus der Erscheinung*:[16] dass die Welt meine Vorstellung ist, heisst – auf ihre Bedeutung hin betrachtet – sie ist Erscheinung, kein Wesenhaftes, sie ist *Form*, nicht *Inhalt*.

In unmittelbarer Evidenz freilich bietet sich diese Einsicht, dass die Welt in ihrem Wesen Wille ist, und dass daher alles Vorgestellte, auf seine Bedeutung hin betrachtet, nichts Primäres, sondern *Erscheinung* dieses Ersten und Wesenhaften ist, offenbar nicht an. Die Faktizität von "Welt" wird in der "philosophischen Besonnenheit" als identisch mit der Vorstellungshafigkeit von "Welt" (in abstracto) erkannt. Die Welt als Wille (und von da aus: die vorstellungshafte Welt als Erscheinung) ist in der faktischen Evidenz der vorstellungsartig gegebenen Welt ausgespart. Von ihr kündet die Vorstellung nichts an. Wie aber soll dann, wenn der Transzendentalismus gilt, ohne Selbstwiderspruch vom "Wesen," dem "Ansich" der Welt (dem gegenüber die vorgestellte Welt nur Erscheinung ist und der Transzendentalismus sich bloss auf dieses Erscheinen bezieht) gesprochen werden? Muss man nicht doch wieder das Vorstellen bemühen, um das an sich Nichtvorstellungshafte offenbarmachen zu können?

Hier stossen wir auf die *erste Hauptschwierigkeit*, die sich bei der Erörterung von Schopenhauers Transzendentalismus ergibt. Wenn die Rede von dem Ansich der

Welt nicht der Rede von der Vorstellungshftigkeit der Welt widersprechen soll, so kann dies nur dann der Fall sein, wenn es ein "Offenbarsein," ein "Bekanntsein" gibt, das zumindest kein "eigentliches," vollständiges Vorstellen ist, sondern bloss Elemente von diesem enthält. Das heisst: wenn das Ansich der Welt, der Wille, in irgendeiner Weise offenbar werden soll (und nur dann ist ja die Rede von ihm sinnvoll), so kann dies weder im eigentlichen Sinne durch *Erkenntnis* (Vorstellen im vollständigen Sinne) erfolgen, noch aber so, dass die durch den Transzendentalismus festgelegte absolute Grenze des Vorstellens überschritten wird—höhere Eingebungen oder mystische Erleuchtungen sind bei Schopenhauer ohnehin nicht gefragt. In irgendeiner Weise muss sich also das Offenbarwerden des Wesens der Welt im Horizont des Vorstellens ereignen, nämlich als ein Vorgang im *Subjekt* (ohne welches eine Rede von einem Offenbarwerden sinnlos wird), zugleich aber muss es sich dergestalt ereignen, dass die Weise, in welcher das Subjekt das Objekt im strikten Sinne erkennt, geändert ist. Das Subjekt, das selber nicht unter dem Satz vom Grund steht (und so grundlos ist wie dieser),[17] erkennt das Objekt jeweils unter den Gestaltungen des Satzes vom Grund—Zeit, Raum, Kausalität (welche selber wiederum ableitbar ist aus den beiden anderen Formen).[18] Von einer Erkenntnis im eigentlichen und vollständigen Sinn kann nur die Rede sein, wenn sie *Anschauen* ist (also durch Zeit *und* Raum) bestimmt ist. Wenn das Offenbarwerden des Wesens der Welt erfolgen soll, so kann es sich daher nicht eigenlich mehr um eine Anschauung handeln. Dies expliziert Schopenhauer auf negative (A) und auf positive Weise (B).

(A) Vorstellend, d.i. anschauend, sich zur Welt verhalten besagt: die Welt unter Raum, Zeit, Kausalität auffassen; da diese "Formen" aber nur *ein* Prinzip, ausdrücken, nämlich den Satz vom Grund, steht die angeschaute Welt unter der strengen Notwendigkeit von Grund und Folge. Das anschauliche ("intuitive") und das ihm nachgeordnete begriffliche ("abstrakte") Erkennen der Welt, speziell das in den Wissenschaften vollzogene Erkennen, hat daher immer nur "das Verhältniss der Erscheinungen der Welt zu einander, gemäss dem Satze vom Grunde und am Leitfaden des durch ihn allein geltenden und bedeutenden Warum"[19] aufzuzeigen. Schopenhauer nennt dies die "Erklärung" der Welt.[20] Sie reduziert nach dem Vorgesagten alle Phänomene, die sich anschaulich darbieten oder rein begrifflicher Natur sind, auf *Relationen*, letztlich auf die oberste Form aller Relationalität, auf den Satz vom Grund, der ja nichts anderes ausdrückt als "die gesetzmässige Verbindung einer Vorstellung mit einer anderen."[21] Die "Erklärung" der Welt—im Sinne des Erforschens der vorgestellten Welt—führt daher niemals aus der Grund-Folge-Kette (in ihrer vierfachen Gestaltung) hinaus. Am deutlichsten zeigt sich diese Restriktion der "Erklärung" der Welt auf dem Gebiete der Natur, wo neben der Gestaltenbeschreibung ("Morphologie") die Aetiologie die eigentliche Methode ist, nämlich die Nachweisung der Art, "wie eine bestimmte Veränderung nothwendig eine andere, bestimmte, bedingt und herbeiführt."[22] Von der Aetiologie erwarten zu wollen, sie bringe eine abschliessende Ursache, gar einen ersten Weltgrund, hiesse ihr Prinzip, den Satz vom Grund, welcher Unabschliessbarkeit impliziert, verkennen. Aber nicht nur unabschliessbar ist die durch den Satz vom Grund bestimmte Welt, sie hat auch, insofern sie als *nur* unter dieser ihrer Bestimmtheit angesehen wird, keinen *Inhalt* und keine

Bedeutung—sie ist ein blosses Beziehungsgefüge, und der Aetiologe, der sich methodisch ja ausschliesslich auf den Satz vom Grund stützt, kann nur immer Aussagen über die Welt in ihrer relationalen Gefügtheit, nie aber Aussagen über das *Was* und den *Sinn* der Welt machen. Ihm lösen sich ständig Qualitäten bei genauerer Forschung in Relationen auf. Wer daher von der Aetiologie eine positive Auskunft über das *Was* dessen erwartet, über welches diese Forschung Aussagen macht, befragt den falschen Adressaten. Besteht, wie Schopenhauer behauptet, das eigentliche Erkenntnisinteresse im Wissen des *Was* der Welt (und nicht ihres blossen—vorstellungshaften—*Wie*), dann befriedigt die Aetiologie, welche per definitionem immer auf die "Verhaeltnisse" geht, dieses Erkenntnisinteresse nicht. "Also auch die Aetiologie kann uns nimmermehr über jene Erscheinungen, welche wir nur als unsere Vorstellungen kennen, den erwünschten, uns hierüber hinausführenden Aufschluss geben. Denn nach allen Erklärungen, stehn sie noch als blosse Vorstellungen, deren Bedeutung wir nicht verstehn, völlig fremd vor uns. Die ursächliche Verknüpfung gibt bloss die Regel und relative Ordnung ihres Eintritts in Raum und Zeit an, lehrt uns aber das, was also eintritt, nicht näher kennen."[23]

Gleichwohl zeigt die Aetiologie, wie bereits in dieser Textpassage anklingt, auf negative Weise etwas hinsichtlich der Frage an, ob die Welt "noch etwas Anderes"[24] sei als Vorstellung "und was sodann dieses sei"[25]; sie zeigt negativ an, "dass dieses Nachgefragte etwas von der Vorstellung völlig und seinem ganzen Wesen nach Grundverschiedenes seyn muss, dem daher auch ihre Formen und Gesetze völlig fremd seyn müssen."[26] Die negative Anzeige dessen, zu dem man positiv aetiologisch nicht kommen kann, findet Schopenhauer in einer Erfahrung, die jeder Naturforscher an einer bestimmten Stelle seines (durch und durch aetiologischen) Forschens macht: er stösst—sowohl in der unbelebten als auch in der belebten Natur—auf Kräfte, die er selber nicht wieder auf andere Kräfte (als auf ihre Ursachen) zurückführen kann. Der Naturforscher trifft, ohne dass er einer weiteren Methode als der aetiologischen Methode sich bedienen würde, auf das "Unbegreifliche."[27] Nur der Metaphysiker— in ihm selber oder in einer anderen Person—kann ihm dieses Unbegreifliche in der "Welt als Vorstellung" begreiflich machen: durch ein Nichtvorstellungshaftes, das dem vorstellungshaften Weltbetrachten in Gestalt unbegreiflicher Kräfte entgegentritt. Woher aber nimmt der Metaphysiker die positive Deutung dieses vorstellungshaft Unbegreiflichen?

(B) Die Antwort ist das Zentralthema des zweiten Buchs des Schopenhauerschen Hauptwerkes. Anschauender Verstand und reflektierende Vernunft, beide zuständig (in je verschiedener Weise) für die aetiologische Forschung, haben es mit der Relationalität der Welt zu tun. Der erkennende Mensch braucht gleichwohl nicht über sich selbst hinauszugehen, wenn er nach der Kompetenz des Menschen hinsichtlich des Offenbarwerdens des *Inhalts* der Welt fragt. Er selbst, der nach dem Inhalt Fragende, *ist* der Schlüssel, der jenes Offenbarwerden ermöglicht.[28] Freilich nicht insofern er sich im eigentlichen und vollständigen Sinne erkennend zur Welt verhält, ist ihm "das Wort des Rätsels" gegeben, sondern insofern als er, in seiner Eigenschaft als Subjekt des Erkennens, je leiblich-individuell existiert. Der Mensch braucht sich bloss auf diese seine individuelle Leiblichkeit zu besinnen, um unmittelbar einzusehen, dass "einen Leib haben" und "Wille sein" eines und dasselbe sind. Diese Einsicht wird nicht im eigentlichen Sinne erkennend gewonnen; denn für die Erkenntnis ist der eigene Leib ein "Objekt unter Objekten"[29] die von Schopenhauer gemeinte Einsicht in die qualitative Identität von Leib- und Wille-sein ist eine unmittelbar-erlebnismässige Einsicht, die nur uneigentlich eine Erkenntnis heissen darf. Sie ist also, wenn man sie über überhaupt "Erkenntnis" nennen darf, streng zu unterscheiden von der objekthaften Leiberkenntnis. Nur dem unmittelbaren Sich-selbst-erleben als Leib, d.i. dem Selbstbewusstsein, nicht dem sich auf Anderes als auf das Selbst beziehenden Bewusstein, wird die Willensbeschaffenheit aller Leibvorgänge offenbar:

> Dem Subjekt des Erkennens, welches durch seine Identität mit dem Leibe als Individuum auftritt, ist dieser Leib auf zwei ganz verschiedene Weisen gegeben: ein Mal als Vorstellung in verständiger Anschauung, als Objekt unter Objekten, und den Gesetzen dieser unterworfen; sodann aber auch zugleich auf eine ganz andere Weise, nämlich als jenes Jedem unmittelbar Bekannte, welches das Wort *Wille* bezeichnet. Jeder wahre Akt seines Willens ist sofort und unausbleiblich auch eine Bewegung seines Leibes: er kann den Akt nicht wirklich wollen, ohne zugleich wahrzunehmen, dass er als Bewegung des Leibes erscheint. Der Willensakt und die Aktion des Leibes sind nicht zwei objektiv erkannte verschiedene Zustände, die das Band der Kausalität verknüpft, stehn nicht im Verhältniss der Ursache und Wirkung: sondern sie sind Eines und das Selbe, nur auf zwei gänzlich verschiedene Weisen gegeben: ein Mal ganz unmittelbar und ein Mal in der Anschauung für Verstand.[30]

Entscheidend für Schopenhauers Reflexion ist der Umstand, dass der Unterschied zwischen Willensakt und Leibvorgang kein qualitativer, d.i. die *Bedeutung* betreffender, Unterschied ist. Der Unterschied ist *metaphysischer* Art: die Seinsart des Leibes unterscheidet sich von der Seinsart des Willens dadurch, dass der Leib auf *sichtbare* Weise dasjenige ist, was der Wille *an sich* selbst ist; seine Sonderstellung unter allen anderen Seienden hat der Leib darin, dass er die unmittelbare Sichtbarkeit, d.i. die von dem individuellen Subjekt, das auch Subjekt des Erkennens ist, ohne Bezug auf einen äusseren Gegenstand erlebte Erscheinung des Willens ist: Der Leib ist die "*Objektität des Willens*"[31] — mein Leib ist mein sichtbar gewordener Wille.

Welcher Art ist näherhin diese Identitätsgewissheit, von der schon gesagt wurde, sie sei nicht objektiver Art, d.h. sie bestehe nicht in eigentlicher, durch Zeit, Raum, Kausalität bestimmter Objekthabe? Die erste Hauptschwierigkeit des Schopenhauerschen Transzendentalismus, von der wir sprachen, zeigt hier ihren spezifischen Problemaspekt: es ist die Behauptung, Willensaktion und Leibvorgang seien qualitativ identisch und könnten in dieser ihrer Identität unmittelbar eingesehen werden. Schopenhauer bringt auch den nachvollzugsbereiten Leser in eine prekäre Situation: da sich unmittelbares Bewusstsein seiner Unmittelbarkeit wegen nicht mitteillen oder gar beweisen lässt, muss der je Angesprochene an seiner eigenen Person überprüfen, ob die These des Philosophen stimmt.[32] Wie aber, wenn jene Identitätseinsicht sich nicht einstellt? Da die Schopenhauersche Metaphysik des Willens, d.i. das Herzstück seiner gesamten Philosophie, von jener Identitätseinsicht abhängt,

hängt alles davon ab, ob diese haltbar ist oder nicht. Schopenhauer versucht seine These insofern allgemein plausibel zu machen, als er den Unmittelbarkeitscharakter jener Einsicht (die rein *empirisch* ist) zumindest analog vorstellungshaft-erkenntnisartig zu interpretieren versucht. Er bezeichnet das Offenbarwerden des Willens im Leibe also "eine Erkenntniss ganz eigener Art";[33] sie ist nicht Erkenntnis wie alle andere Erkenntnis, welche jeweils Beziehung der Vorstellung auf eine andere Vorstellung ist; was ihn überhaupt dazu ermutigt, bei der Identitätseinsicht von "Erkenntnis" zu sprechen, ist allein der Umstand, dass hier eine *Beziehung* zwischen zwei Formal-Verschiedenen vorliegt, die aber materialiter identisch sind. Die Identitätseinsicht stellt sich daher zwar *urteilsartig* dar, meint aber kein Urteil im üblichen objektiv-vorstellungsartigen Sinn, sondern ein "Verhältniss, welches eine anschauliche Vorstellung, der Leib, zu dem hat, was gar nicht Vorstellung ist, sondern ein von dieser toto genere Verschiedenes: Wille."[34] Wer fragt, wie eine solche Beziehung zwischen Vorstellung und Nichtvorstellungshaftem möglich ist, darf nicht mit einer Antwort rechnen, die über den Hinweis auf das eigene Selbstbewusstsein, also auf das unmittelbare Sich-selbst-als-Leib-erleben, hinausginge. Die Leiberfahrung, die Schopenhauer im Auge hat, ist die empirische Basis seiner Metaphysik — es ist dasjenige, was in Schopenhauers Sicht die Auszeichnung des eigenen Systems vor allen bisherigen Systemen der Philosophie ausmacht: waren die Metaphysiker vor ihm transzendente Metaphysiker, so nimmt er für sich in Anspruch, die erste *immanente* Metaphysik aufgestellt zu haben[35] — immanent darin, dass sie den Zugang des Menschen zum Sinn des Seins (des "Wesens der Welt") weder in höhere Offenbarung noch in raffinierte Begriffsspekulation setzt, vielmehr jedem (seiner selbst bewussten) Individuum allein schon aufgrund der eigenen Leiblichkeit die Möglichkeit gibt, das Rätsel der Welt unmittelbar erlebend aufzulösen. Aber diese Auszeichnung — das hat Schopenhauer sicher gespürt — ist auch die Achillesferse des Systems. Die urteilsartige Formulierung der Identitätseinsicht ist eine nachträgliche, erkenntnisanaloge Fassung eines unmittelbaren Bewusstseins, das eo ipso als solches präintuitiver und präreflexiver Art ist.[36] Die — hinsichtlich ihres Wertes — ambivalente Sonderstellung der urteilsartig formulierten unmittelbaren Identitätseinsicht kommt bei Schopenhauer darin zum Ausdruck, dass er diese Einsicht nicht unter die Genera der "Wahrheiten" einordnen kann, die er aufgrund der vierfachen Gestaltung des Satzes vom Grund, also geltend für die "Welt als Vorstellung," aufgestellt hat. Schopenhauer sieht darin freilich nicht die Ambivalenz der eigenen Position zum Vorschein kommen, er sieht vielmehr in der Unmöglichkeit, die urteilsartig formulierte Identitätseinsicht den vier Wahrheitsgenera einordnen und doch diese Einsicht als eine *Wahrheit* bezeichnen zu können, die besondere Bedeutsamkeit dieser Wahrheit: "Ich möchte . . . diese Wahrheit vor allen andern auszeichnen und sie κατ' εξοχην *philosophische Wahrheit* nennen."[37] Der urteilsartige Ausdruck dieser Wahrheit, also das, was sie formal als Wahreit konstituiert, lässt sich (da diese Wahrheit in materialer Hinsicht ja eine unmittelbare Einsicht meint) in verschiedenen Wendungen formulieren, "und sagen: mein Leib und mein Wille sind Einesi — oder was ich als anschauliche Vorstellung meinen Leib nenne, nenne ich, sofern ich desselben auf eine ganz verschiedene, keiner andern zu vergleichende Weise mir bewusst bin, meinen Willen; — oder, mein Leib ist die *Objektität* meines Willens;—oder, abgesehn davon, dass mein Leib meine Vorstellung ist, ist er nur noch mein Wille; u.s.w."[38]

Wie die verschiedenen Formulierungen zeigen, enthält die "philosophische Wahrheit" für Schopenhauer einen Doppelaspekt: (a) die *washafte* Identität (Bedeutungsselbigkeit) von Wille und Leib, (b) den *wiehaften* Unterschied und eine Beziehung zwischen Wille und Leib. Die *washafte* Identität ist jedem Menschen, insofern er ein leibliches, seiner selbst bewusstes Wesen ist, unmittelbar zugänglich im Selbstbewusstsein.[39] Das zeigen ganz konkret die Lust-und Schmerzempfindungen: sie sind nach Schopenhauer noch keine Vorstellungen, "sondern unmittelbare Affektionen des Willens, in seiner Erscheinung, dem Leibe."[40] Es gibt also leiblich-erlebnishaft ein unmittelbares Offenbarwerden von *Wille*.

Der *wiehafte* (urteilsartige) Ausdruck für dieses Offenbarwerden des Willenscharakters meiner Leibvorgänge bringt diese ursprünglich-erlebnishafte (und daher noch nicht eigentlich vorstellungshafte) Identität von Leib und Wille unter die Urteilsbeiziehung; wir *reden* (als Philosophen) also von Wille und Leib unter der Form des Vorstellens. Heisst das aber gerade nicht, die eine Seite der Bezogenen, die nicht vorstellungsartig ist, selber vorstellungsartig machen, also von Wille und Leib so zu reden, als seien beide Vorstellungen? Die Relationierung von Wille und Leib soll dies aber gerade vermeiden. Die "philosophische Wahrheit" schlechthin soll ja gerade ausdrücken, dass die qualitative Identität von Wille und Leib eine Relation impliziert, und zwar insofern, als das individuelle Subjekt, das diese qualitative Identität je unmittelbar erlebt (im Selbstbewusstsein), zugleich auch als Subjekt des Erkennens (das mit jenem unmittelbar erlebenden Subjekt identisch ist) diese seine qualitative Identität als Wille und Leib ausdrückt: für das Subjekt des Erkennens, das mit dem Subjekt, welches die Identität Leib/Wille erlebt, identisch ist, stellt der eigene Leib sich nicht als ein qualitativ anderes dar als der mit dem Leib identisch *erlebte* Wille. Denn: das individuelle Subjekt erkennt in seinem Leibe den Willen, es setzt sich darin nichts anderes gegenüber, es drückt in dieser Erkenntnis nur aus, dass es selbst als individuelles erkennendes Subjekt, als Leib, seinem Wesen nach Wille ist. Die vom erkennenden Subjekt aufgestellte urteilsartige Beziehung Wille-Leib ist eben deshalb kein vorstellungsartiges (d.h. kein eigentliches) Urteil, weil in dieser Beziehung nicht Vorstellung mit Vorstellung, Objekt mit Objekt, sondern qualitativ Identisches verbunden wird.

Dass es überhaupt möglich ist, dass die beiden als identisch erlebten Momente Wille und Leib auch in eine urteilsartige Beziehung gebracht werden, ergibt sich aus einem nicht weiter ableitbaren Faktum—aus der Identität von Subjekt des Wollens und des Erkennens im Menschen. Von der Erkenntnisseite aus erfolgt die Deutung der eigentümlichen Beziehung zwischen Wille und Leib. Schopenhauer bedient sich bei dieser Deutung der Kantischen Unterscheidung, "Ding an sich"—"Erscheinung." Kraft dieser Unterscheidung wird es ihm möglich, die qualitative Selbigkeit von Wille und Leib zugleich als eine fundamentale Differenz zu denken. Der Leib ist die *Erscheinung* des Willens, welcher das positive Ding an sich ist (von dem Kant nur im "negativen Verstande" reden konnte). Die Auszeichnung des Leibes vor allen anderen Erscheinungen besteht—dank der Identität von Subjekt des Wollens und Subjekt des

Erkennens — darin, dass er die primäre und ursprünglichste "Objektität" des Willens ist; er ist so fundamental, dass Schopenhauer von ihm sagt: ". . . [den] Willen ohne meinen Leib kann ich demnach eigentlich nicht vorstellen."[41] Und weiterhin gilt, dass der Leib, indem er die ursprünglichste Objektität des Willens ist, die also selber nicht wieder durch etwas anderes vermittelt ist, das Vermittelnde aller anderen Erscheinungen des Willens ist und so das Bindeglied darstellt zwischen der Welt als Wille und der Welt als Vorstellung. Der Transzendentalismus der Erscheinung ist metaphysisch fundiert; der *Leib* eröffnet die Bedeutung dessen, was im Transzendentalismus der Erscheinung schon vorausgesetzt ist, ohne von ihm, der sich nur auf die blosse Form des Erscheinens (Vorstellens) bezieht, berührt zu werden. Auch wenn sich die Bedeutung der Welt, die im Leiberfahren aufgeht, urteilsartig ausdrücken lässt und also — wie Schopenhauer zumindest behauptet — zur blossen Form, der Vorstellung, in eine Beziehung treten kann, so beruht die *Möglichkeit* dieser Beziehung *nicht* auf einer eigentlichen und vollständigen Erkenntnis, sondern auf einem ursprünglichen Identitätsbewusstsein, das ganz und gar empirisch ist.

II. DIE ZWEITE STUFE DES TRANSZENDENTALISMUS BEI SCHOPENHAUER: TRANSZENDENTALISMUS DES WESENS

1. Von der Metaphysik des Willens zum Transzendentalismus des Wesens

Mit der Einführung der unmittelbaren Leiberfahrung, die zur Metaphysik des Willens führt,[42] ist der Transzendenalismus der Erscheinung überschritten, ohne dass seine Geltung im geringsten angefochten wäre. Die Metaphysik des Willens antwortet nach Schopenhauers Konzeption auf eine Frage, die der Transzendentalismus der Erscheinung im Gefolge hat, die er aber nicht beantworten kann. Der Transzendentalismus der Erscheinung betrifft nur die Vorstellung in ihrer Vorstellungshaftigkeit, das heisst aber: er gibt die Notwendigkeit des Vorgestelltseins von Welt an, wenn Welt ist. Was indes diese je notwendig auf ein bedingend-ermöglichendes Subjekt bezogene Welt ist — dies lässt der Transzendentalismus der Erscheinung offen. Die Metaphysik des Willens erlaubt es erst, das Was der Welt zu wissen und von diesem Wissen aus zu sagen, dass die erste Stufe des Transzendentalismus, indem sie es mit der Vorstellung zu tun hat, es mit der Erscheinung eines Anderen, auf die er sich nicht bezieht, zu tun hat. Der Transzendentalismus der Erscheinung geht somit auf die "eine Hälfte' der Welt," die Metaphysik des Willes auf die andere. Aber hat es dann noch Sinn von einer "ersten Stufe" des Transzendentalismus zu sprechen? Wäre es nicht richtiger, den Transzendentalismus der Erscheinung als die erste Hälfte des Systems, die Metaphysik des Willens als die zweite Hälfte anzusehen?

In der Tat scheint diese Sicht des Schopenhauerschen Gesamtsystems allein schon vom Titel des Werkes her sich anzubieten. Denn: (1) aufgrund der Faktizität des Vorstellens bei der Welthabe muss das Denken, das über die Welt etwas aussagt, transzendentalistisch beginnen — zunächst und vor allem anderen ist die Welt meine Vorstellung, (2) die Unmöglichkeit, bloss aufgrund transzendentalistischer Weltbetrachtung zum Inhalt und zur Bedeutung der Welt zu gelangen, treibt das Nachdenken über diese Betrachtung hinaus; das transzendentalistisch nicht Auffindbare liefert die Metaphysik des Willens im Ausgang von der Feststellung, dass das erkennende Subjekt, insofern sein Erkennen durch den Leib vermittelt ist, identisch ist mit dem Subjekt des Wollens—der Mensch also seinem *Wesen* nach durch und durch Wille ist. "Die Welt ist mein Wille." Obwohl in der Ordnung der Betrachtung die transzendentalistische Reflexion der willensmetaphysischen Reflexion vorausgeht, bringt die Willensmetaphysik, da sie ja vom *Wesen*, der Transzendentalismus aber von der Erscheinung dieses Wesens handelt, eine Fundierung des Transzendentalismus. Diese Fundierung beginnt bereits (wie wir schon anzeigten) dort, wo das Kantische Unterscheidungspaar "Ding an sich/Erscheinung" auf den Willen einerseits (Ding an sich), auf die Erscheinung andererseits (Leib) angewendet wird. Diese Fundierung hätte, ohne dass dadurch die Ergänzung der Betrachtung des *Wie* der Welt (Welt als Vorstellung) durch die Betrachtung des *Was* der Welt (Welt als Wille) gestört worden wäre, auch unterbleiben können. Schopenhauers Absicht geht aber gerade auf die *fundierende* Verbindung zwischen Transzendentalismus und Metaphysik des Willens, und zwar dergestalt, dass dasjenige, wovon der Transzendentalismus ausgeht: *dass* die Welt primär als Vorstellung gegeben ist (Faktizität der Vorgestelltheit der Welt), nicht mehr als blosses unbegreifliches *Dass* gewusst wird, sondern in seiner Willensursprünglichkeit offenbar gemacht wird. Vom Transzendentalismus aus gesehen kann über das *Dass* der Vorgestelltheit der Welt nicht hinausgegangen werden; die Tatsache nämlich, *dass* die Welt meine Vorstellung ist, ist bereits *ein* zum Transzendentalismus gehörendes Moment; auf seiner Basis wird dann—und dies ist das Kernstück des Schopenhauerschen Transzendentalismus—die Vorgestelltheit der Welt als Bedingung der Möglichkeit von Welthaben expliziert. Wenn nun aber im Rahmen der Willensmetaphysik von einer Fundierung des Transzendentalismus gesprochen wird, dann ist gemeint, dass jene Faktizität der Vorgestelltheit, also die Basis des Transzendentalismus, eine Sinndeutung erhält, die uns sagt, dass sie nur ist, weil der Wille auf einer bestimmten Stufe zur Vorstellung geworden ist. Die Willensmetaphysik führt nach Schopenhauer also insofern über den Transzendenalismus hinaus, als sie—mit dem Offenbarmachen des *Was* der Welt—auch offenbar macht, dass die Vorstellung eine Äusserung dieses Wesens ist, eine Objektivation des Willens, ja seine höchste und abschliessende Objektivation, nämlich diejenige, auf die hin der Wille im ganzen strebt: auf seine Selbsterkenntnis.

Schopenhauer hat seine Philosophie als die Explikation dieses *einen* Gedankens interpretiert—die Welt ist die Selbsterkenntnis des Willens.[43] Die Selbsterkenntnis—dies lehrt die Metaphysik des Willens (2. Buch)—vollendet sich dort, wo die Vorstellung auftritt. Für den Transzendentalismus ist die Vorstellung bloss da, sie ist Faktum; für die Metaphysik des Willens aber ist auch ihr—dem Transzendentalismus verborgen bleibender—Sinn offenbar: auch das Vorstellen und das ihm zugeordnete Vermögen, der Intellekt (zusamt der auf ihn sich stützenden Vernunft), gehen aus dem Verwirklichungsprozess des Willens (Objektivation des Willens) hervor. Das Vorstellen steht so im vorhinein ganz im Dienst des Willens, der ja nur sich selber in allem, worin er sich objektiviert, will, und sonst nichts; auch das Sich-selbst-erkennen-wollen, welches das Streben des Willens im ganzen ausmacht, zielt nicht auf eine Autarkisierung des

Erkennens, sondern auf das Sich-selbst-wollen. Schopenhauer meint diese totale funktionale Abhängigkeit des Vorstellens und Erkennens vom Willen, wenn er die Akzidentalität und die Instrumentalität des Intellekts so sehr betont. Aus der Perspektive der Willensmetaphysik spielt der Intellekt somit zwar eine Sonderrolle unter den vielen Objektivationen des Willens, aber prinzipiell ist auch er ein Mittel, dessen der Wille sich zu seinem Wollen bedient; das Erkennen taucht in der Reihe der stufenförmigen Objektivation des Willens "spät," ja insofern er nicht nur tierisches (anschauender Verstand), sondern menschliches Erkennen (reflektierende Vernunft) ist, auf der obersten Stufe auf, aber das hindert nichts an der Tatsache, dass das Erkennen ebenso wie die anderen Objektivationen in der unbelebten und in der belebten Natur unselbständige Äusserungen des allein selbständigen unbeschränkt freien, in seinen Objektivationen souveränen Willens sind. Der Transzendentalismus wird durch die Willensmetaphysik zu einem (zwar unverändert in sich fortgeltenden) sekundären Lehrstück des Systems. Die Sekundärfunktion des Intellekts im Ganzen der Willensobjektivation ist auf jeden Fall das zentralere Lehrstück. Schopenauer scheut nicht davor zurück, objektivistisch den Ursprung des Vorstellens zu beschreiben; auch das Vorstellen ist, objektivistisch betrachtet, einzuordnen in den evolutionären Stufengang der naturhaften Willensobjektivation:

So sehn wir denn hier, auf der untersten Stufe, den Willen sich darstellen als einen blinden Drang, ein finsteres, dumpfes Treiben, fern von aller umittelbaren Erkennbarkeit. Es ist die einfachste und schwächste Art seiner Objektivation. Als solcher blinder Drang und erkenntnissloses Streben erscheint er aber noch in der ganzen unorganischen Natur, in allen den ursprünglichen Kräften, welche aufzusuchen und ihre Gesetze kennen zu lernen, Physik und Chemie beschäftigt sind, und jede von welchen sich uns in Millionen ganz gleichartiger und gesetzmässiger, keine Spur von individuellem Charakter ankündigender Erscheinungen darstellt, sondern bloss vervielfältigt durch Zeit and Raum, d.i. durch das *principium individuationis*, wie ein Bild durch die Facetten eines Glases vervielfältigt wird.

Von Stufe zu Stufe sich deutlicher objektivirend, wirkt dennoch auch im Pflanzenreich, wo nicht mehr eigentliche Ursachen, sondern Reize das Band seiner Erscheinungen sind, der Wille doch noch völlig erkenntnisslos, als finstere treibende Kraft, und so endlich auch noch im vegetativen Theil der thierischen Erscheinung, in der Hervorbringung und Ausbildung jedes Thieres und in der Unterhaltung der innern Oekonomie desselben, wo immer nur noch blosse Reize seine Erscheinung nothwendig bestimmen. Die immer höher stehenden Stufen der Objektität des Willens führen endlich zu dem Punkt, wo das Individuum, welches die Idee darstellt, nicht mehr durch blosse Bewegung auf Reize seine zu assimilirende Nahrung erhalten konnte; weil solcher Reiz abgewartet werden muss, hier aber die Nahrung eine specieller bestimmte ist, und bei der immer mehr angewachsenen Mannigfaltigkeit der Erscheinungen das Gedränge und Gewirre so gross geworden ist, das sie einander stören, und der Zufall, von dem das durch blosse Reize bewegte Individuum seine Nahrung erwarten muss, zu ungünstig seyn würde. Die Nahrung muss daher aufgesucht, ausgewählt werden, von dem Punkt an, wo das Thier dem Ei oder Mutterleibe, in welchem es erkenntnisslos vegetirte, sich entwunden hat. Dadurch wird hier die Bewegung auf Motive und wegen dieser die Erkenntniss nothwendig, welche also eintritt als ein auf dieser Stufe der Objektivation des Willens erfordertes Hülfsmittel, $\mu\eta\chi\alpha\nu\eta$, zur Erhaltung des Individuums und Fortpflanzung des Geschlechts. Sie tritt hervor, repräsentirt durch das Gehirn oder ein grösseres Ganglion, eben wie jede andere Bestrebung oder Bestimmung des sich objektivirenden Willens durch ein Organ repräsentirt ist, d.h. für die Vorstellung sich als ein Organ darstellt. — Allein mit diesem Hülfsmittel, dieser $\mu\eta\chi\alpha\nu\eta$, steht nun, mit einem Schlage, die *Welt als Vorstellung* da, mit allen ihren Formen, Objekt und Subjekt, Zeit, Raum, Vielheit und Kausalität. Die Welt zeigt jetzt die zweite Seite. Bisher bloss *Wille*, ist sie nun zugleich *Vorstellung*, Objekt des erkennenden Subjekts. Der Wille, der bis hieher im Dunkeln, höchst sicher und unfehlbar, seinen Trieb verfolgte, hat sich auf dieser Stufe ein Licht angezündet, als ein Mittel, welches nothwendig wurde, zur Aufhebung des Nachtheils, der aus dem Gedränge und der komplicirten Beschaffenheit seiner Erscheinungen eben den vollendetsten erwachsen würde. Die bisherige unfehlbare Sicherheit und Gesetzmässigkeit, mit welcher er in der unorganischen und bloss vegetativen Natur wirkte, beruhte darauf, dass er allein in seinem ursprünglichen Wesen, als blinder Drang, Wille, thätig war, ohne Beihülfe, aber auch ohne Störung von einer zweiten ganz andern Welt, der Welt als Vorstellung, welche zwar nur das Abbild seines eigenen Wesens, aber doch ganz anderer Natur ist und jetzt eingreift in den Zusammenhang seiner Erscheinungen.[44]

Die objektivistische Art, in welcher Schopenhauer hier über die Sekundärfunktion des Intellekts und der "Welt als Vorstellung" im ganzen redet — so, als könne der Willensmetaphysiker den Transzendentalismus überspringen und gleichsam "von aussen" das Vorstellen betrachten (wie Schopenhauer dies mit besonderem Nachdruck in seiner Schrift "Über den Willen in der Natur" tut) — eben diese von ihm zum ausdrücklichen Lehrstück erhobene "objektive Ansicht des Intellekts" ist *die zweite Hauptschwierigkeit,* auf die man stösst, wenn man Schopenhauers Transzendentalismus zu durchdenken versucht; die Schwierigkeit kommt, wie die erste Hauptschwierigkeit, durch die Verbindung des Transzendentalismus mit der Willensmetaphysik zustande. Wieso kann das Vorstellen, das der Horizont aller Aussagen über die Welt ist, selber so vorgestellt werden, als sei es ein Objekt unter Objekten, genauer: eine Objektivation unter Objektivationen? Woher nimmt sich die Willensmetaphysik das Recht zu einem solchen höheren Standpunkt und zum Überspringen des im ersten Buch gelehrten Transzendentalismus? Wird nun nicht gerade (was im ersten Buch streng untersagt wurde) das Subjekt des Erkennens nicht auch zum Objekt — insofern nämlich, als die im weitesten Sinne als Vorstellung verstandene Welt, als Subjekt-Objekt-Korrelation, nun selber en globe zu einem Objektiven, d.i. zu einer Objektivation des Willens wird? In der Tat scheint die Willensmetaphysik mit ihrer Lehre von der Sekundärfunktion des Vorstellens und der objektivistischen Sicht des Erkennens den

Transzendentalismus in Frage zu stellen, ja noch mehr: sie scheint sogar einen entschiedenen Irrationalismus zu lehren.

Dass dies aber nicht der Fall ist, zeigen die beiden weiteren Bücher des Hauptwerkes. In ihnen nimmt Schopenhauer den Irrationalismus, der der Willensmetaphysik des zweiten Buches und vor allem der Naturphilosophie in dem Werk "Über den Willen in der Natur" tatsächlich eignet,[45] indirekt wieder zurück, zumindest relativiert er ihn durch die Lehre von der Erlösung durch Erkenntnis in einem Masse, dass es—aufs Ganze der Schopenhauerschen Lehre gesehen—ungerechtfertigt erscheint, die zweifelsohne in ihr vorhandenen irrationalistischen Züge zur Totalsignatur des Systems zu machen. Die beiden letzten Bücher des Hauptwerkes lehren nämlich einen Transzendentalismus, der ursprünglicher und eigentlicher ist als der Transzendentalismus der Erscheinung, dem wir eben deswegen das Prädikat "erste Stufe" zusprechen konnten, weil es jenseits der Willensmetaphysik (auf ihrer Grundlage freilich) noch einen anderen Transzendentalismus gibt, der die durch die Willensmetaphysik instrumentalisierte und akzidentalisierte Funktion des Erkennens gegen den Willen selbst gekehrt sein lässt und diesen seiner Herrschaft über den Menschen beraubt.

Dies gilt es abschliessend in Hauptlinien zu zeigen.

2. Die Gleichursprünglichkeit von Metaphysik des Willens und Transzendentalismus des Wesens

Das erste Buch des Hauptwerkes trägt den Untertitel "Die Vorstellung unterworfen dem Satze vom Grunde: das Objekt der Erfahrung und Wissenschaft." Das Vorstellung-sein, dessen Unabdingbarkeitscharakter beim Welthaben im Transzendentalismus der ersten Stufe gewährleistet ist, wird—laut zitiertem Untertitel—dahingehend betrachtet, dass es dem Satz vom Grund unterworfen ist. Der Satz vom Grund (der selber grundlos ist) ist die Bedingung dafür, dass die vorgestellte Welt einen notwendigen, nämlich einen Grund-Folge-Zusammenhang aufweist und dass sie, je nach den vier verschiedenen Gestaltungen des Satzes vom Grund, in je verschiedener Weise Gegenstand der alltäglichen und der wissenschaftlichen Erfahrung ist.

Die Willensmetaphysik des zweiten Buches führt dann zur Einsicht, dass diese unter dem Satz vom Grund stehende "Welt als Vorstellung" insgesamt Objektivation des Willens ist und dass die "Welt als Vorstellung" *eine* der Stufen jener Objektivation ausmacht, Akzidenz also des in sich erkenntnislosen Willens ist. Aus der Perspektive der Willensmetaphysik wurde der Transzendentalismus der ersten Stufe als "Transzendentalismus der Erscheinung" bezeichnet: das Vorgestelltsein von Welt, als Bedingung der Möglichkeit von Welt, steht unter dem durchgängigen Prinzip der Erscheinung, dem Satz vom Grund, von welchem das Ding an sich, der Wille als solcher, frei ist.

Dass allerdings die "Welt als Vorstellung" dem Satz vom Grund unterworfen ist, gilt nach dem ersten Buch ausdrücklich nur für das *Objekt* der Erkenntnis ("Vorstellung" im engeren Wortsinne). Das erkennende Subjekt, das strukturell mit dem Objekt gleichursprünglich ist, fällt dort aus der Determination durch den Satz vom

Grund heraus (wogegen die Willensmetaphysik des zweiten Buches und vor allem die Naturphilosophie der Schrift "Über den Willen in der Natur" die Tendenz enthalten, die gesamte "Welt als Vorstellung," Subjekt sowohl als Objekt, objektivistisch zur Erscheinung zu machen und sie darin *beide* dem Satz vom Grund zu unterwerfen). Da das Subjekt, "der Träger der Welt, die durchgängige, stets vorausgesetzte Bedingung alles Erscheinenden, alles Objekts"[46] ist, als solcher Träger aber dem Satz vom Grund entzogen ist, nimmt das Subjekt im "Transzendentalismus der Erscheinung" die eigentlich transzendentale Funktion ein: das Subjekt ist Bedingung der Möglichkeit von Objekt. Insofern das Subjekt in dieser seiner bedingend-ermöglichenden Funktion jeweils das Subjekt für das durch den Satz vom Grund bestimmte Objekt ist, steht es zusammen mit dem Objekt, für welches jeweils Subjekt ist, in der Dienstbarkeit des Willens, in welcher (nach dem zweiten Buch) die Erkenntnis im ganzen steht. Da aber nun gleichwohl "Subjekt-sein" prinzipiell (trotz gegenläufiger Tendenzen im 2. Buch) die Qualität der Unabhängigkeit von Objektbestimmtheiten meint,[47] steht auf der Seite des Subjekts prinzipiell die Möglichkeit offen, diese Unabhängigkeit zu verwirklichen.

Es muss betont werden, dass es sich bei dieser Unabhängigkeit um eine *Möglichkeit* handelt, die zumeist nicht realisiert ist, d.h. zunächst und zumeist—im alltäglichen Leben der Menschen—dient das Erkennen, obwohl es aufgrund der prinzipiellen Autarkie des Subjekts auch *autark* sein könnte, den Interessen des Willens. Die von Schopenhauer immer so sehr betonte Instrumentalität des Erkennens will nicht nur metaphysisch den Rang des Erkennens (im Vergleich mit dem Rang des Willens) kennzeichnen, sie soll auch eine Beschreibung der *tatsächlichen* Situation liefern, in der die Menschen—Glück suchend, Leid fliehend—sich des Verstandes und der Vernunft bedienen, um ihre mannigfaltigen insgesamt der eigenen Glückseligkeit gewidmeten Tätigkeiten zu dem Ziel zu bringen, das ihnen—ohne dass sie dies wüssten—der in sich blinde Wille gesetzt hat: zu sein, um zu vergehen.

Dass indes auch die (auf der Subjektseite des Erkennens gelegene) Möglichkeit der Freiheit von der Dienstbarkeit des Willens in die Wirklichkeit umgesetzt wird, beweist sich für Schopenhauer in zwei Fakten: im Faktum der ästhetischen Kontemplation (3. Buch) und im Faktum der weltentsagenden Heiligkeit (4. Buch). Schon im 2. Buch, wo ja gerade die Dienstbarkeit des Erkennens für den Willen erörtert wird, deutet Schopenhauer auf diese Möglichkeit der Befreiung des Erkennens und auf die faktische Verwirklichung dieser Möglichkeit hin:

Die Erkenntniss überhaupt, vernünftige sowohl als bloss anschauliche, geht also ursprünglich aus dem Willen selbst hervor, gehört zum Wesen der höhern Stufen seiner Objektivation, als eine blosse μηχανη, ein Mittel zur Erhaltung des Individuums und der Art, so gut wie jedes Organ des Leibes. Ursprünglich also zum Dienste des Willens, zur Vollbringung seiner Zwecke bestimmt, bleibt sie ihm auch fast durchgängig gänzlich dienstbar: so in allen Thieren und in beinahe allen Menschen. Jedoch werden wir im dritten Buche sehn, wir in einzelnen Menschen die Erkenntniss sich dieser Dienstbarkeit entziehn, ihr Joch abwerfen und frei von allen Zwecken des Wollens rein für sich bestehn kann, als blosser klarer Spiegel der Welt, woraus die Kunst hervorgeht; endlich im vierten Buch, wir durch diese Art der Erkenntniss, wenn sie auf den Willen zurückwirkt, die Selbstaufhebung desselben eintreten kann, d.i. die Resignation, welche das letzte Ziel, ja, das innerste Wesen aller Tugend und Heiligkeit, und die Erlösung von der Welt ist.[48]

An dieser Stelle bereits zeigt Schopenhauer an, dass er alles andere im Sinn hat als jenen theoretischen und lebenspraktischen Irrationalismus, für den man gerade ihn so häufig verantwortlich macht. Das Wesen der Welt, d.i. der in sich in der Tat irrationale Wille, wird von Schopenhauer nicht so angesehen, wie ihn der echte Irrationalist ansieht; dieser strebt auf Vereinigung mit dem ungeistigen oder noch vor-geistigen Wesen der Welt und sagt gerade aller Erkenntnis ab. Schopenhauer verabscheut aber das Ungeistige und lehrt, wie der Mensch sich von diesem Ungeistigen, das den Wesenskern der Welt ausmacht, befreien kann. Was an seiner Erlösungskonzeption irritiert – was aber indes genau Schopenhauers Intention ausmacht, ist der Umstand, dass die Soteriologie, die im 3. und 4. Buch des Hauptwerkes vorgetragen wird, eine *Erlösung vom Wesen der Welt* anzielt. Die Irritation, die diese Konzeption hervorruft, ist kulturgeschichtlich bedingt: die jüdisch-christliche Soteriologie lehrt (in diesem Punkt gleichförmig über alle dogmatischen Modifikationen hinweg) als Ziel der Erlösung die Teilhabe an dem wahren Wesen aller Dinge, sei es, dass diese Teilhabe in die visio beatifica (in das auf das Glauben folgende Schauen) oder in ein mystisches Vereinigungserleben gesetzt wird. Demgegenüber lehrt Schopenhauer, abweichend von dieser auch noch in säkularisierten Formen im Abendland allüberall präsenten Tradition, als Ziel der Erlösung die *Abkehr* vom Wesen der Welt, welches er wiederum, auch hier gänzlich abweichend von der jüdisch-christlichen Tradition und asiatischer Religiosität folgend, mit dem schlechthin Geistlos-Willenshaften identitfiziert. Dass diese Abkehr durch Erkenntnis erfolgt – das freilich ist bestes Erbe abendländischer Tradition: wenn es überhaupt einen absoluten Wert gibt, dann ist dies offensichtlich der *Geist*; die Soteriologie Schopenhauers predigt unablässig das pfingstliche Ereignis. Der Geist, nicht der Wille, bringt uns das Heil.

Auf diese Funktion des Erkennens aufmerksam zu machen und die Bedingung der Möglichkeit dieser Funktion aufzudecken, ist die These dieser unserer Studie. Sie will mit Nachdruck herausstellen, dass der irrationale Wille, der sich aus seiner unverfügbaren Freiheit heraus in der Erkenntnis ein Instrument geschaffen hat (wir wiesen auf die Aporetik dieses Lehrstücks schon hin), durch diese seine eigene Erscheinung entmächtigt wird; das Wesen wird durch die eigene Erscheinung besiegt; Kronos, so könnte man metaphorisch-mythologisch sagen, unterliegt um des Heiles der Menschen willen seinem Sohn Zeus. Fast jedoch erweckt diese Erhebung des Erkennens zum erlösenden Prinzip den Eindruck, als wolle Schopenhauer nach der Einsicht in das Wesen der Welt seine Zuflucht in dem suchen, was für die idealistische Weltsicht selber schon das Wesen der Welt ausmacht, und als komme er über einen Umweg dort an, wo der christlich inspirierte metaphysische Idealismus immer schon ist. Mag dieser Eindruck etwas Richtiges enthalten, so ist zumindest auf die Unabdingbarkeit des "Umweges" hinzuweisen – und in dieser Unabdingbarkeit besteht die unüberbrückbare Kluft zu allem Idealismus. Was ihn zu dem Umwege, der freilich nur ein solcher ist, wenn man die idealistische Geistmetaphysik zum Massstab macht) nötigt, ist dasselbe, was ihn zwingt, das Wesen der Welt in den blinden geistlosen Willen zu setzen: die in der Tat unbestreitbare Erfahrung, dass das Leben durch und durch Leiden ist und dass alles Leiden vom Wollen stammt. Wenn das Leiden die Grundbefindlichkeit unserer Existenz ist, so kann das *Was* dieser Existenz nicht kausal reduziert werden auf einen allgütigen Schöpfer und die Erlösung nicht in der Rückkehr zum Wesen bestehen, sondern in der Abwenddung von ihm.

Die durch Erkenntnis geleistete Abwendung vom Wesen der Welt erfolgt, wie es in der zitierten Textstelle schon andeutet wurde, doppelt: zum einen ästhetisch-kontemplativ und augenblickshaft, zum anderen ethisch-resignativ und endgültig. In beiden Fällen geschieht eine Befreiung des Subjekts des Erkennens von der Dienstbarkeit des Willens, d.h. das Subjekt verwirklicht seine ureigenste Möglichkeit, es kommt in dieser Befreiung zu dem, was es an sich ist: "ewiges Weltauge," ungetrübt durch die dem Objekt ureigenen Formen des Satzes vom Grund.

Die uns interessierende Hauptfrage lautet hier: Wie ist die Loslösung des erkennenden Subjekts von der Willensherrschaft überhaupt möglich? Was ermöglicht es dem Subjekt, das gewöhnlich gar nicht ewiges Weltauge, blanker Spiegel, ungetrübter Blick ist, die vom Satz des Grundes beherrschte Welt der Vorstellung zu verlassen? Geschieht ein plötzliches Wunder—ein Nichtvorhergesehenes und eigentlich auch Unbeabsichtigtes, vor allem: etwas mit der Systemkonzeption Schopenhauers Unvereinbares?

Auch wenn das 3. und 4. Buch ihren ganzen Nachdruck auf die Beschreibung der beiden Wege zur Erlösung legen und explizit nicht eigentlich von der Bedingung der Möglichkeit der Erlösung durch Erkenntnis reden, so enthalten sie doch Aussagen genug, die eine Rekonstruktion dieser Bedingung der Möglichkeit der Erlösung durch Erkenntnis erlauben. Wir treffen in diesen beiden Büchern auf einen neuen Transzendentalismus; er betrifft aber nicht mehr die Bedingung der Möglichkeit erscheinungshaften (d.h. unter dem Satz vom Grund stehenden) Vorstellens. Es handelt sich hier vielmehr um eine zweite Stufe des Transzendentalismus: um denjenigen Transzendentalismus, in welchem es sich um das durch den Satz vom Grund *nicht* bestimmte Sichtbargewordensein des Willens handelt, also um die Bedingung der Möglichkeit nicht mehr erscheinungshaften, sondern *reinen* oder *wesen*haften Erkennens. Daher kann man diesen Transzendentalismus den *Transzendentalismus des Wesens* nennen.

Der Transzendentalismus des Wesens besagt: der Wille ist im vorhinein schon zur Vorstellung geworden, die nicht unter dem Satz des Grundes steht. Es gibt eine zeit-, raum-, kausalitätslose Objektität des Willens. Sie stellt sich dar in der *Idee*, genauer gesagt: die ursprüngliche Objektität des Willens haben wir in den (platonischen) *Ideen* vor uns. Schopenhauer führt sie ohne eigentliche Begründung bereits in der Naturphilosophie des 2. Buches in sein System ein[49]—zwecks Erklärung der anschaulich gegebenen Stufenordnung der Objektivation des Willens. Auf das Problem einer Deduktion der Ideen bei Schopenhauer kann hier nur hingewiesen werden: dass es gerade die gegebenen und keine anderen Ideen sind, die allem Objektivieren des Willens die Regel geben, wird sich wohl nur empirisch ausmachen lassen. Wie

Schopenhauer freilich darauf kommt, *überhaupt* Ideen anzunehmen, hat er im 3. Buch des Hauptwerks erläutert und implizit mit dieser Erläuterung auch den Transzendentalismus des Wesens ins Spiel gebracht: die Ideen sind transzendental notwendig.

Die platonischen Ideen sind selber *nicht* das Wesen als Wesen. Sie gehören, wie schon der Untertitel des 3. Buches anzeigt, der Seite der Vorstellung an. Die in ihnen gemeinten Vorstellungen sind auch nicht Vorstellungen im Sinn der ersten Stufe des Transzendentalismus.

Was also ist die Idee? Sie ist "die Vorstellung, unabhängig vom Satze des Grundes."[50] Wie aber kann es solch eine Vorstellung geben, wenn der Satz vom Grunde das durchgängige Prinzip des vorstellungshaft erscheinenden Willens ist?[51] Diese Frage stellt sich unter der Voraussetzung, dass man—bloss dem Transzendentalismus der Erscheinung folgend—nicht beachtet, dass noch ursprünglicher als der Satz vom Grund die Form aller Vorstellung ist, die nichts weiter enthält als das Gegenübergetretensein von Subjekt und Objekt. Das Objekt, bloss als formales Moment, d.h. als Korrelat des Subjekts betrachtet, ohne die Bestimmtheit, durch die es vereinzelt auftritt (Satz vom Grund), haben wir in der Idee vor uns. Der Wille hat sich selbst sichtbar gemacht, ohne dass seine Sichtbarkeit mehr wäre als blosse Sichtbarkeit, "Objektität." Das aber heisst, dass der Wille, das Ding an sich, weder ineins fällt mit der Idee, die jene Objektität ist, noch aber dass der Inhalt, der in der Idee sichtbar wird, vom Willen selber verschieden wäre. Wille und Idee sind materialiter dasselbe, formaliter sind sie verschieden, aber wiederum nicht so verschieden wie der Wille verschieden ist von den individuellen Objekten, in denen er sich vorstellungshaft erscheinend auch objektiviert. Da der Wille in der Idee sich dergestalt sichtbar wird, dass er sich nur durch diese seine Sichtbarkeit von sich selbst (als an sich gestaltlos-unsichtbarem Wesen der Welt) unterscheidet, sonst aber genau mit der Idee—dem Inhalt nach—selbig und nicht durch die Einzelnheit der Erscheinung bestimmt ist, die aus dem Satz des Grundes kommt, nennt Schopenhauer die Idee die "adäquate Objektität" des Willens, wogegen er die durch den Satz des Grundes determinierte, je einzelne Erscheinung ausdrücklich der "inadäquaten Objektität" des Willens zuschreibt.[52]

Daraus ersieht man, dass Schopenhauers Ideenkonzeption selber wiederum metaphysisch fundiert ist: der Wille, behauptet Schopenhauer, kann sich adäquat und inadäquat objektivieren. Diese Behauptung stellt *die dritte Hauptschwierigkeit* des Systems dar. Sie bleibt auch unaufgelöst und interpretativ unauflösbar, wenn man die festgefügte Stufenordnung der Natur (in der von Schopenhauer gelehrten Art) leugnet. Teilt man demgegenüber die Auffassung Schopenhauers, dass die Natur eine festgefügte Stufenordnung ihrer Gebilde enthält, und dass die Individuen sich je nach dieser Stufenordnung klassifizieren lassen (wobei jedes Individuum einer Stufe die Gestalt der ganzen Stufe verwirklicht, wie z.B. der einzelne Mensch die Stufe Mensch repräsentiert), dann gewinnt die zunächst rein thetische und willkürlich erscheinende Unterscheidung zwischen einer adäquaten und einer inadäquaten "Objektität des Willens eine gewisse Plausibilität (wenn auch nicht Beweischarakter). Die je unabweisbar faktisch auftretenden Individuen verweisen auf festgelegte

Formen, durch die sie konstituiert werden, die sie aber nur unvollkommen ausfüllen (so z.B. der einzelne Mensch Sokrates die Menschheit im ganzen); diese ihre "Inadäquatheit" zu den ihnen zugrundeliegenden, sie selbst konstituierenden Form verweist wiederum auf die Existenz dieser Form ausserhalb der Welt der Individualität, d.h. der durch Zeit, Raum und Kausalität geprägten Welt. Schopenhauers Platonismus ist also in gewissem Sinne *realistisch* zu nennen, denn er behauptet die Existenz zeitlos-raumlos-kausalitätsloser Sinngebilde, der Ideen, in denen der Wille, ohne Störung durch die Individuation, eine ihn genau abbildende und ihm genau entsprechende ("adäquate") Objektität hat.

Ding an sich und Idee fallen, wie schon bemerkt, also nicht zusammen, sie sind sich aber so nahe, dass die Idee das getreue, uneingeschränkte Abbild des Willens unabhängig von aller Bestimmtheit der Objektität durch den Satz vom Grund ist. Vorgestelltsein und Grundlosigkeit kommen also in der Idee widerspruchslos überein. Wie man sich dies zu denken hat, versucht Schopenhauer dadurch zu erläutern, dass er die Idee als ein Zwischenwesen zwischen dem Willen, dem Ding an sich, und seiner individuellen Erscheinung konzipiert. Von ihr unterscheidet sich die Idee durch ihre Unbetroffenheit von der Grund-Determination, also durch die Adäquatheit, mit der der Wille von der Idee abgebildet wird; von dem Willen unterscheidet sie sich durch ihren Vorstellungscharakter. In §32 des Hauptwerkes heisst es:

> Die Platonische Idee . . . ist nothwendig Objekt, ein Erkanntes, eine Vorstellung, und eben dadurch, aber auch nur dadurch, vom Ding an sich verschieden. Sie hat bloss die untergeordneten Formen der Erscheinung, welche alle wir unter dem Satz vom Grunde begreifen, abgelegt, oder vielmehr ist noch nicht in sie eingegangen; aber die erste und allgemeinste Form hat sie beibehalten, die der Vorstellung überhaupt, des Objektseyns für ein Subjekt. Die dieser untergeordneten Formen (deren allgemeiner Ausdruck der Satz vom Grunde ist) sind es, welche die Idee zu einzelnen und vergänglichen Individuen vervielfältigen, deren Zahl, Beziehung auf die Idee, völlig gleichgültig ist. Der Staz vom Grund ist also wieder die Form, in welche die Idee eingeht, indem sie in die Erkenntniss des Subjekts als Individuums fällt. Das einzelne, in Gemässheit des Satzes vom Grunde erscheinende Ding ist also nur eine mittelbare Objektivation des Dinges an sich (welches der Wille ist), zwischen welchem und ihm noch die Idee steht, als die alleinige unmittelbare Objektität des Willens, in dem sie keine andere dem Erkennen als solchem eigene Form angenommen hat, als die der Vorstellung überhaupt, d.i. des Objektseyns für ein Subjekt. Daher ist auch sie allein die möglichst *adäquate Objektität* des Willens oder Dinges an sich, ist selbst das ganze Ding an sich, nur unter der Form der Vorstellung.[53]

Der Transzendentalismus des Wesens ist in dieser Konzeption des Verhältnisses von Wille und Idee enthalten. Das Subjekt und das Objekt sind hier nicht mehr zwei qualitativ Getrennte (wie es dort der Fall ist, wo das je individuelle Subjekt das je individuelle Objekt erkennt), sie sind nur vorstellungshaft-formal geschieden; die Idee ist "das ganze Ding an sich"[54] (hinsichtlich des Was); der Wille ist also von der

Idee dadurch geschieden, dass er an sich nicht Vorstellung ist, die Idee aber sein Vorstellungsgewordensein ausdrückt. Das aber besagt, dass der zeitlose, raumlose, eigenschaftslose Wille ursprünglich schon *Subjekt* ist, indem er — unabhängig von der Determination des Satzes vom Grund — sich selbst als Objekt ("Idee") gegenüber getreten ist. Der Wille hat sich immer schon erkannt, auch unabhängig von der unter dem Satz vom Grund stehenden Objektivation. Dass die unter dem Satz vom Grund stehende Welt überhaupt die Selbsterkenntnis des Willens sein kann, hat zur Voraussetzung, dass der Wille sich schon ausserhalb aller Zeit je zur Vorstellung geworden ist. Er ist nicht im nachhinein der sich selbst erkennende Wille, er kann vielmehr die Welt nur deswegen als seine eigene Manifestation erkennen, weil die erscheinende Welt unter der Ordnung erscheint, unter der der Wille sich von Ewigkeit her selber anschaut. Der Transzendentalismus des Wesens besagt also, dass das Wesen selber schon je erkannt ist: von sich selbst ist es erkannt; dieses Sich-selbst-erkannt-haben (unabhängig vom Satz des Grundes — "adäquate Objektität") ist die Bedingung der Mölichkeit für das Vorgestelltsein der Welt unter dem Satz des Grundes ("inadäquate Objektität"), d.i. für die Welt der Individuen. Die "adäquate Objektität" des Willens ist es auch, die die Bedingung der Möglichkeit für die zwiefache Befreiung von der Willensherrschaft ist. Der Transzendentalismus des Wesens ist somit auch für die Soteriologie Schopenhauers die Voraussetzung: Erlösung geschieht durch Erkenntnis; das ist aber nur möglich, wenn der Wille schon (unabhängig von derjenigen Objektivation, die unter dem Satz vom Grund steht) Selbsterkenntnis ist. Macht man hiermit aber Schopenhauer nicht zum Idealisten Schellingschen oder Hegelschen Typs? Stellt die von Schopenhauer immer so sehr betonte Akzidentalität des Erkennens nicht im Widerspruch zu dieser Interpretation? Wird der Wille nicht selbst zu einem Geistigen — das Wesen selber zur Idee?

Schopenhauer hat sich vor diesen Einwürfen selber zu schützen versucht: wenn auch der Wille in der Idee seine adäquate Objektität hat und das *Was* der Idee unabhängig von aller Individuation unter der Form der Erkenntnis auftritt, so ist dieses *Was als Was* doch nicht der Geist, sondern der in seiner Washeit absolut geistlose Wille. Dass der Wille in der Idee zur adäquaten Selbsterkenntnis gekommen ist, heisst nur: der an sich, seiner *Bedeutung* ("Was") nach geistlose Wille hat die *Form* der Vorstellung angenommen, ohne aber dabei sein "Was" in die Form selber zu verwandeln.

An dieser Stelle wird *die vierte Hauptschwierigkeit* des Schopenhauerschen Systems und zugleich seine *fundamentalste* These sichtbar: das System wird vermittels des Begriffspaares Form-Inhalt (Wie-Was) (Vorstellung-Wille) erbaut; auf der Geltung dieser Unterscheidung beruht es; seine Spezifik erhält es bei der Ausführung dadurch, dass gelehrt wird, der Inhalt sei zwar immer nur — adäquat oder inadäquat — als Form existent (doppelter Transzendentalismus), er sei aber gleichwohl absolut autark und unauflösbar in die Form. Der Wille bleibt Wille, auch wenn er je schon Idee ist und durch sie die individuelle Welt der Vorstellung ermöglicht. Der Wille bleibt trotz des Transzendentalismus des Wesens das Absolut-Andere zur Idee.

Die Beachtung dieses fundamentalen Dualismus verhindert sowohl den Irrtum, Schopenhauer verwandle unter der Hand die Willensmetaphysik in eine Geistmetaphysik; sie verhindert aber auch — und darauf kam es uns hier vor allem an — die

Auffassung, die Willensmetaphysik sei eine schlechthinnige Absage an die Rationalität. Wie auch sollte ein Denker Irrationalist sein, der – auf der Grundlage eines doppelten Transzendentalismus – die Erlösung in die Erkenntnis setzt und gerade nicht, wie der echte Irrationalist, in die Vereinigung mit dem irrationalen Weltgrund?

Der Preis freilich, unter dem sich Schopenhauer durch die Skylla der Geist-metaphysik und die Charybdis des Irrationalismus hindurchzwängt, sind die *Haupt-schwierigkeiten*, auf die wir hingewiesen haben, um Ansatzpunkte für ein weiteres Nachdenken über die Aktualisierbarkeit des Schopenhauerschen Systems zu bezeichn-en. Unbestreitbar dürfte aber jetzt schon sein, dass die Philosophie Schopenhauers, transzendentalistisch verstanden, der Reflexion auf das Verhältnis von Wissen und Sein insofern eine ideale Ausgangsposition bietet, als es den unglaubwürdig geworde-nen absoluten Idealismus (der in theoretische Ungereimtheiten führt) ebenso zu ver-meiden sucht wie den Irrationalismus, vor dessen Zerstörungsmacht – so Schopen-hauers grosse Einsicht – uns nur *Erkenntnis* rettet.

Anmerkungen

1. Georg Lukács: *Die Zerstörung der Vernunft*. Bd. I: *Irrationalismus zwischen den Revolutionen*. Neuwied 1973 (= Sammlung Luchterhand, Bd. 133), S.10. – Zu Schopenhauer vgl. S.172ff.

2. Es werden nur die Hauptschwierigkeiten bei Schopenhauer bezeichnet, d.s. diejenigen, die den inneren Fortgang des Systems in Frage stellen. Auf eine Auseinandersetzung mit der Sekundärliteratur muss aus Platzgründen verzichtet werden. Wir verweisen aber nachdrücklich auf Arthur Hübschers Schopenhauer-Bibliographie (Stuttgart 1981, vor allem Nr. 1192ff.). Die Werke Sch. s werden zitiert nach der kritischen Werkausgabe: Arthur Schopenhauer. *Sämtliche Werke*. Hrsgg. v. Arthur Hübscher. 7 Bde. Wiesbaden, 3. Aufl., 1972. Abkürzungen: W I = Die Welt als Wille und Vorstellung, 1. Bd. (= Werke Bd. 2); W II = Die Welt als Wille und Vorstellung, 2. Bd. (= Werke Bd. 3).

3. W I, S.3.
4. W I, S.3.
5. W I, S.3.
6. W I, S.3.
7. W I, S.3.
8. W I, S.3.
9. W I, S.3.
10. W I, S.3. Vgl. Schopenhauer Schrift über den Satz vom Grund (die 1. Aufl. in Bd. 7; die 2. Aufl. in Bd. 1 der Werke, ed. Hübscher.)
11. W I, S.3.
12. W I, S.3-4.
13. W I, S.5.
14. W I, S.4-5.
15. W I, S.5.
16. Vgl. W I, S.130ff.
17. Vgl. W I, S.96.
18. Vgl. W I, S.9ff.
19. W I, S.95.
20. Vgl. W I, S.115.
21. W I, S.114; zum Problem der Auflösung der Form vgl. W I, 142ff.
22. W I, S.115.
23. W I, S.117.

24. W I, S.118.

25. W I, S.118.

26. W I, S.118.

27. Vgl. W I, 113ff.; vgl. besonders auch die §§24 u. 27 von W I; vgl. auch die Schrift "Über den Willen in der Natur" (Werke, ed. Hübscher, Bd. 4, S.1ff., S.27ff.; vgl. auch W II, 190ff.).

28. Vgl. für das Folgende den §18 von W I (S.118ff.).

29. W I, S.118.

30. W I, S.119; vgl. auch W II, S.213ff.

31. W I, S.120.

32. Ausgespart bleiben muss hier das Problem der Übertragung des Willenscharakters des individuellen Menschen auf alle Menschen (vgl. W I, §19) und auf die Natur im ganzen (vgl. W I, §§21ff.).

33. W I, S.122.

34. W I, S.122.

35. Vgl. u. a. Arthur Schopenhauer: Gesammelte Briefe. Hrsg. v. Arthur Hübscher. Bonn 1978, S.291. Vgl. auch W II, Kap.17.

36. Im Unterschied zur anschaulichen Erkenntnis steht diese "Erkenntnis" *nur* unter der Form der Zeit; vgl. W I, S.121. Vgl. auch W II, Kap.18.

37. W I, S.122.

38. W I, S.122f.

39. Vgl. die "Preisschrift über die Freiheit des Willens" (Werke, ed. Hübscher, Bd. 4, S.9ff.); vgl. auch W II, Kap.18 u. 19.

40. W I, S.120.

41. W I, S.121.

42. Vgl. W I, §19 und die §§21-29. Vgl. Anm. 32.

43. Vgl. W I, §71, vor allem S.485.

44. W I, 178f.

45. Vgl. Über den Willen in der Natur, Werke Bd. 4, S.2ff., 19ff., 42ff., 47ff., 51ff., 54ff., 72ff., 86-94.

46. W I, S.5.

47. Vgl. W I, §2 (S.5ff.).

48. W I, S.181f.

49. Vgl. W I, §26 (S.159ff.).

50. W I, S.197.

51. Vgl. für das Folgende W I, §32 (S.205ff.).

52. Vgl. W I, S.206.

53. W I, S.206.

54. W I, S.206.

Schopenhauer on the Will in Nature

D. W. HAMLYN

I t is probably well known that Schopenhauer maintained that motives are causes seen from within. He meant by that, not merely what many modern philosophers would accept, whether rightly or wrongly—that to explain actions by reference to motives is to explain them by reference to a kind of cause. He meant also that what one is aware of when one is aware of the motivation for one's actions is just the same sort of thing that one is aware of in the operation of causality in the world in general. For that reason, our inner awareness of what one may call 'will' is itself an awareness of what governs phenomena in general.

I say "governs," but it is necessary to make an important qualification with regard to that. For the actual *course* of phenomena, what follows what and what is due to what are for him a matter of the principle of sufficient reason, which can take four forms, as is spelled out in his *The Fourfold Root of the Principles of Sufficient Reason.*[1] Of these the two that need concern us at present are the principle of sufficient reason of becoming and the principle of acting. Of these the first amounts to the principle that every phenomenon is related to other phemonena as cause and/or effect; the principle that is involved is that of causality. The second amounts to the principle that every action, considered as phenomenon, as something that is an object of knowledge or consciousness, is due to phenomena that constitute the motives of that action; the principle that is involved is that of motivation. There is nothing in that, considered by itself, however, to suggest any identification of the two principles or of the phenomena with which the principles are concerned; there is nothing to suggest the identification of causality and motivation or even to suggest the thought that they are two species of the same genus. It is true that Schopenhauer insists that the principle of sufficient reason has a single, if fourfold, root; but that does not in itself entail that the four forms of the principle are to be in any sense identified or thought of as species of a genus.

Again, when Schopenhauer discusses causality, he frequently says (e.g., *FR*

20, p. 70) that there are three kinds of cause. There is that which applies in the "inorganic kingdom," where Newton's Third Law that action and reaction are equal and opposite holds good; there is that which applies in connection with organic life, where causes function as stimuli without the necessary reciprocity implied in Newton's Third Law; and there is that which applies in connection with conscious beings, where, as objects of consciousness, causes feature as motives. If that may suggest that motives (which, be it noted, must always be conscious) are related to causes as they figure in the "inorganic kingdom" as species of a single genus (though even that needs further argument), it does not suggest the legitimacy of any attempt to identify the two. That is to say that it does not suggest that in being aware of the motives for our actions we are aware of just the same thing, considered in functional terms, as we see operating in the world at large.

Yet, the claim that motives constitute causality seen from within does imply that or something like it. What it presupposes, on Schopenhauer's view, is that phenomena, considered as events in time, are always related to each other in, to use his own words (FR 16, pp. 41-42) "a law-like connection," and that the appearance of the connection and that alone is a matter of how the phenomena present themselves to us. If they are presented directly to consciousness, if they have in that sense an immediacy, then the connection appears as one of motivation; if they are presented more indirectly and do not have the same immediacy, then the connection appears as one of causality in the sense that is applicable to organic or inorganic phenomena (there being a further distinction between these two). Hence, the difference in the appearance is simply a matter of the immediacy or otherwise of the phenomena to consciousness.

Philosophers who hold that reasons for action can be construed as the causes of those actions might, on the face of it, be taken to hold essentially the same thesis. Donald Davidson, for example, maintained in "Actions, Reasons and Causes"[2] that the primary reason for an action is its cause, even if the causal law that lies behind that must be construed as one that holds under some other description than one involving beliefs and desires—a physical description. That could be said to amount to the thesis that the lawlike connection involved in the relation of actions to their reasons is one of essentially the same kind as that found among physical phenomena generally, although in the case of action and its reasons the cause is available to us in a way and under a description that is not applicable to physical phenomena generally.[3] Such views as that seem to imply a monism in the sense that all events constitute or at any rate are supervenient upon one kind of thing.

Among contemporary philosophers it is materialism that is dominant, so that it is assumed that it is material things that basically exist. That is hardly true of Schopenhauer. He was certainly passionately opposed to the cruder materialism of his time. That, however, was because he was an idealist and thought that the phenomena of which I have been speaking were representations (Vorstellungen). There is for that reason a sense in which the monism, to the extent that it exists, goes in his case in the opposite direction to that of the modern monisms of which I have been speaking; it is always representations that are connected according to the principle or principles in question. If motives are for that reason mind dependent, so are all phenomena, even if there are, as we have noted, differences in the degree of mind dependency. Since, however, Schopenhauer was a *transcendental* idealist and thus held that what is transcendentally ideal is also empirically real, it might be held legitimate, if one wished to slough off the idealism, simply to take him as saying that the one kind of thing that exists is comprised by phenomena, without presuming the mind dependence of these. Phenomena are whatever is empirically real.

For that to be plausible in relation to Schopenhauer, however, it would be necessary to interpret him as saying also that motives are empirically real in this sense. Schopenhauer does, of course, speak of them as representations, but he does that because, in accordance with his idealism, he counts as representation anything that is an object of consciousness or knowledge. He thus includes under the heading of 'representation' not just those things for which we can speak of perception in a genuine sense but also any form of modification of consciousness, including sensations.[4] Although motives are not exactly sensations, they involve states of consciousness. They exist only as objects of a certain sort of inner consciousness and have no being apart from that. Hence, they are not just run-of-the-mill representations. They have a special status, and, as I will emphasize later, it is a status that presupposes volition, also. It follows that, if motives are causes seen from within in the strong sense that in having them we are aware of just the same thing as functions as a cause in nature in general, we need a stronger consideration in support of the view than the bare suggestion that they, like everything else, are phenomena. What could such a consideration be?

Some of the considerations that Schopenhauer brings to bear in considering the "will in nature" have to do with evidence of teleology in nature. Even when it is appropriate to invoke teleology to explain natural processes, however, it would not be right from that consideration alone to infer that something parallel to motives is also applicable. For there is a gap between the kind of purposiveness involved in volition where motives come into the picture and the goal directedness that may be found in nature. It is indeed, in my opinion, arguable that purposive behavior need not be goal directed in the sense that the pattern of behavior need not be obviously construable as convergent on to some end product as the goal.[5] For such reasons, it is not feasible to suggest that one can find in nature clear evidence of the kind of purpose that in the case of action makes it appropriate to appeal to motives in explanation of such action. Nor, in fact, does Schopenhauer think otherwise. In that sense, he is not arguing from what holds good of us to what holds good of nature generally.

It would be wrong to interpret Schopenhauer as saying that nature is simply what is human writ large. It is indeed sometimes said that, in fact, his argument goes in the opposite direction. Human beings, qua bodily and qua having brains, are part of nature and are subject to the same principles as apply to nature at large. While, however, it is true that Schopenhauer attaches a great importance to the body and to the brain,[6] it also remains true that he thinks that causality as a genus works differently and is subject to different laws in the three parts of nature that he distinguishes — inorganic nature, the organic kingdom, and human action. Hence, it is not the case that for him human action is understandable in terms of causality of the same kinds as holds good of the body qua physiological. On the other hand, he certainly thinks that the causes that are seen from within in the case of action and its motives are the same as those that are seen in those parts of nature where teleology is *not* in point, let alone those parts where it is.

Why then does teleology have any special relevance to the issue? To ask that question is in effect to ask about the form of Schopenhauer's argument. I have suggested elsewhere[7] that it is a form of what Gilbert Harman has called an "inference to the best explanation." If it is that, I suggest that a consideration of it may be illuminating, not merely in connection with Schopenhauer's views about the world and the nature of reality but also in relation to the cogency of that particular form of argument. Schopenhauer's *The Will in Nature* was written explicitly to record an attempt to investigate the extent to which the identification of the nature of reality with the will has a reflection in nature. One might well ask why it should be supposed to have any such reflection. It is, of course, a cardinal point of Kant's doctrine of the distinction between the noumenal and the phenomenal that the noumenal has no evident connection with the phenomenal. That is to say that the noumenal does not reveal itself in the phenomenal; things-in-themselves are quite unknowable through any empirical means, however much they may be a presupposition of freedom and moral thought generally. It might, of course, be said that Schopenhauer was already deserting that whole conception, itself an essential part of transcendental idealism, in supposing that he could arrive at an identification of the thing-in-itself. But Schopenhauer did not suppose that that identification was one that could be arrived at through an appeal to empirical experience. Hence, in that respect he did not go against the Kantian doctrine.

That is to say that his great discovery, as he deemed it to be, that the thing-in-itself is the will does not go against the stream of transcendental idealism in claiming an empirical ground for that identification. On the other hand, he does not say, with Kant, that it is only in our consciousness of freedom that we have any grounds for appeal to the noumenal, however much he agrees that the only real freedom is transcendental. The first step in his argument is to claim that there is something of which we do *in a sense* have experience, or at any rate to which experience is relevant, namely, ourselves as agents — the fact of agency — which cannot be identified with anything phenomenal. I have discussed the details of that argument both in my *Schopenhauer* and in the paper "Schopenhauer on Action and the Will," and I will not repeat here my observations on this part of the general argument. Nevertheless, what I have said in claiming that access to the noumenal lies in Schopenhauer's view in some kind of experience, even if one that is different from experience of the phenomenal in the straightforward sense, may require some justification.

One way of attempting to provide that justification might be to suggest that Schopenhauer had a wider conception of experience than Kant did and that that was the reason why he "discovered" something that Kant failed to see. The trouble with that suggestion is that there are ways in which Schopenhauer's conception of experience is narrower than Kant's. Although Schopenhauer claimed to provide an account of the understanding that was truer to the word so translated than Kant's account—the understanding being always intuitive rather than discursive—this had the result that he could have nothing of Kant's theory of the interrelationship between untuitions and concepts or of the idea that experience is basically a function of judgment in bringing intuitions under concepts. Hence, his conception of experience cannot be one according to which experience is enriched by our conceptual understanding.

Nevertheless, it can justifiably be maintained that Schopenhauer gave closer attention to our awareness of ourselves as agents than Kant did. He also thought that that awareness had a connection with experience. I say that because it is a central point of Schopenhauer's account of these matters that awareness of the will arises only in the context of bodily action and is therefore inseparable from knowledge of the body, which comes, of course, from experience. If Schopenhauer had been faced with Wittgenstein's question about what is left over from my raising my arm when my arm arises, he might well have said that what is left out is the will and what that entails. But he would have sympathized with the question, for he would have seen in the idea of the *raising* of one's arm the crucial point at issue. The raising of one's arm is a bodily action and therefore involves the arm rising—something that might be seen by others as due to certain causes. It is, nevertheless, an *action*, an expression of the will, and the agent for that reason must see what happens as due to motives.

It has been suggested to me by Christopher Janaway[8] that Schopenhauer would not have said what I have claimed that he would. He would have said that there is *nothing* that is left out; the difference between the raising of the arm and the arm rising is merely a matter of two points of view, that of the agent and that of the spectator. But for that to be true it does matter *how* my arm rises. If it is caused to rise by, say, being pulled upward by strings, I should not see *those* causes from within as motives, for there are in that case no motives. On the other hand, if I intentionally move my arm, then what I see as the motives for doing so will, on Schopenhauer's view, be what others see as causes. It is not the case simply that something counts as a motive only when it produces an action. As Schopenhauer says in the *Essay on the Freedom of the Will*,[9] a motive is the content of a volition, and he goes on to speak of them as thoughts. That a motive has a content at all implies something cognitive and, therefore, in Schopenhauer's view involves the intellect. But it can be the content of a volition at all only if the will also is involved, and involved in a way that it is not involved in phenomena generally.

It is far from clear that in the end Schopenhauer has a coherent account to offer of what all this involves. He says that the way in which the will and the intellect come together in the agent is a miracle par excellence. It is natural, therefore, that he should at this point have recourse to metaphors and analogies. (I have in mind the image of the will as a strong, blind man carrying the intellect as a sighted but lame man on his shoulders [*WR* II 19, p. 209][10] and the image of the relationship of the will to the conscious, knowing ego as being like that of a concave mirror to the image in its focus [*WR* II 22, p. 278].) For this reason, too, he says that "the I is not *intimate* with itself through and through" (*WR* II 18, pp. 196-97), and he goes on to say in the same place that an act of will, in the sense of a willed action, is "only the nearest and clearest *phenomenon* of the thing-in-itself." It must, of course, be *phenomenon* if it is to be an object of experience in any sense, and, given Schopenhauer's view that the will expresses itself most directly in bodily action, one's awareness of that must involve experience, the experience of the bodily. It is as though in that awareness one gets a glimpse of reality but one still tinged with appearance.

The point is that the awareness of agency that is involved when one is aware of oneself engaged in some willed bodily action is, as experience, an experience that is unique. It is like no other experience, and on that Schopenhauer is undoubtedly right. The awareness involved is that which more recent philosophers have groped after in speaking of knowledge without observation or practical knowledge. Neither of those descriptions really brings out exactly what is involved, although the former makes clear the noninferential character of the knowledge and the latter its intimate association with action. At all events, as Schopenhauer sees it, knowledge of agency is not itself an empirical experience, although it is inseparable from that. It is that latter fact that perhaps makes it reasonable to speak of the knowledge of the will as a form of experience. If it is not exactly that, it is certainly *not without* a form of experience.

So far, one might see Schopenhauer as groping after a truth about what the awareness of oneself as acting consists in. The knowledge of which I have spoken must, however, be such as to be knowledge of an object if there are to be any grounds for thinking that the "experience" in question can provide access to reality as thing-in-itself. That is to say that we need assurance that in having the "experience" one has knowledge *of* something, or rather *of some thing*. Otherwise, one might be inclined to say that all that is involved in willed action is that what is done is done knowingly — and, although that is certainly true and important, it is not enough to give us knowledge of *some thing*. As I have tried to show elsewhere,[11] what the argument in fact justifies is only the conclusion that the knowledge in question is not entirely phenomenal and that, given the terms of reference, may again be accepted as right, for knowledge of agency is not knowledge of phenomenon in the way that knowledge of the movement of our limbs may be if we experience their movement as brought about by some cause. At the same time, it is, as I have tried to emphasize, not possible to have that knowledge of agency without knowledge through experience of such phenomena and their causes as motives. It is a further matter whether that is enough to justify the claim that in knowledge of agency we have knowledge of a nonphenomenal *thing*, to be called for that reason "will"; and examination shows that it is not enough. It is a plausible suggestion that Schopenhauer would not have thought that knowledge of *that* was provided in agency unless he thought, given his acceptance of transcendental idealism, that there was a thing-in-itself to be discovered. Given that, it would have been natural for him to think also that in the nonphenomenal knowledge that knowledge of agency seems to involve we are given knowledge of the thing-in-itself. Although perhaps natural, however, that thought is not justified; all that remains acceptable is that knowledge of agency is not a form of experiential knowledge or not that alone.

It is "not that alone" because, as we have seen, Schopenhauer holds that the nonphenomenal knowledge is inseparable from a form of phenomenal knowledge, in that agency, properly speaking, manifests itself to us only in bodily action, and in so acting we must be experientially aware of certain bodily events and their causes. Since, however, those bodily events occur in the context of agency and action and since for that reason they are not just bodily *events*, what we are experientially aware of as their cause is not physiological events but motives. There is no room in the Schopenhauerian view of action, therefore, for any identification of motives simply with causes of bodily movements, for motives are causes seen from within only where there is *action*. Indeed, as we will see, there is a sense in which, if there is to be any identification between motives and causes of movement, it is the other way round in that any sequence of events that involves causality is thereby an expression of the will. In Schopenhauerian terms, access to that will, or at any rate the most direct access to it, comes at the point at which there is "the nearest and clearest *phenome-non* of the thing-in-itself"; there is no access to it at all where there is no such phenomenon. As I said earlier, if one gets at this point a glimpse of reality, it is one still tinged with appearance.

Schopenhauer does not hold that the relation between the will and its expression is a causal one. Causal relations hold only between phenomena, according to the principle of sufficient reason. One cannot hold, if one is to be true to Schopenhauer's theory, that agency is to be explained in terms of causation, not even what is now sometimes called agent causation, according to which the agent brings about causally in acting that certain states obtain. For Schopenhauer, "agent-causation" would be just another, misleading, name for agency itself, that is to say, for willing. It has, in fact, nothing to do with causation, since it does not involve a relation between two phenomena. That, however, is not incompatible with the view that, although agency is not itself causal, it depends on causality for its efficacy. That indeed is what Schopenhauer holds when he claims that actions are always subject to motives, which are causes seen from within. But, if agency depends for its efficacy on causality in that way, the particular kind of causality involved in action—motivation—could not take place unless there were agency. (It might also be noted that the motivation must also be conscious, although that might be taken to follow a fortiori from the fact that motives are *phenomena*. If the transcendental idealism with its special construal of phenomena is sloughed off, the need to think of motives as essentially conscious may go with it.)

Schopenhauer's next thought is, I believe, that something like the above may be generally true—not true merely of actions and motives but true of phenomena generally, even if in the case of other phenomena causality does not work in quite the same way (i.e., even if the form of the causal laws involved is not the same, as I indicated earlier was Schopenhauer's belief). That is to say that in the case of action and motives one merely has a more direct access to what also holds good elsewhere in a way that does not make possible direct access to it. In effect, that means that all applications of the principle of sufficient reason to phenomena need a basis or support that makes that application possible. The basis or support in question is not causal, although it does provide a certain kind of rationale for connections between phenomena that are of lawlike form.

One can say, as I have said elsewhere,[12] that if this were true it would mean that, although the form taken by things and their connections in general is a function of the principle of sufficient reason, what there is is to be seen as an expression of the will as thing-in-itself. It is so because that is what is willed. It is indeed that which enables Schopenhauer to say, "The world is precisely as it is, because the will, whose phenomenon is the world, is such a will as it is, because it wills in such a way" (WR I 60, p. 331), or, in one of his more telling sentences, "As the will is so is the world" (WR I 63, pp. 351-52). If that is so, however, why does Schopenhauer, in considering the "will in nature," put so much weight upon teleology, and what has it to do with inference to the best explanation?

Given what I have said earlier, the answer to the first part of that question ought now to be apparent. Different forms of causality within phenomena are related to the will in a way that is analogous to the way in which motivation is related to agency as it manifests itself in us. Because those other forms of causality relate to phenomena that are not "in us," however, the access to them is not so direct. Ontologically it is always the same, one might say, but epistemologically there are differences in the degree to which the nature of phenomena may be evident to us. Schopenhauer is claiming that with teleological phenomena that inner nature—that they are expressions of a will—is more evident than with other phenomena such as those in the "inorganic realm" (although even here the evidence of a force provides some indication of the same kind of thing). Differences in degree of evidentness do not, however, affect the facts; the world is in general the expression of a will. Or so Schopenhauer thinks and so he argues.

This is an inference to the best explanation; Schopenhauer is in effect saying to us, "If you are puzzled as to why the world is as it is, look at in this way. . . . Does it not now make sense?" Not by any means everyone has thought or would think that it does make sense in the way that Schopenhauer makes out. For present purposes, however, what is important is that the argument would have no force at all, other than as a mere speculation, if it were not for the initial insight into what is involved in agency and motivation. I said earlier that there was a sense in which, far from its being the case that there is any room in the Schopenhauerian view of action for any identification of motives simply with causes of bodily movements, it is the other way round. What I meant by that is that in Schopenhauer's view the truth about the causes of bodily movement is that they work like motives only not so obviously and in a way that makes the form of the law involved different. They work like motives in that they would not work at all if there were not something like agency at the back of them. It is in that context that they ought, strictly speaking, to be seen. The key to that conception, however, is provided by what is supposed to be evident in the case of motives and not so evident elsewhere. Nevertheless, it is a key at all only if it is really true that what is evident in the case of motives is something about causation. That would not be sufficient for the use of the key in other contexts, in the way that is implied by what Schopenhauer has to say about the will in nature, but it is certainly necessary. I do not think that anyone would be persuaded by what Schopenhauer has to say about the will in nature unless they had the key provided by the story about agency and motives, whether or not they are persuaded when they have that key.

That is one of the cardinal points about an inference to the best explanation—one needs some principle for the selection of possible explanations, and that is what I have been calling the "key." A second point is that the "key" must really function in an explanatory way in its own domain, and that means also that there must be at least some analogy between the case or cases to which the "key" is directly applicable and those to which it is subsequently applied. It is in effect a matter of: "The key opens this door; perhaps it will open that one. And, if it does that at all, is it not likely that the explanation of the lock that it opens in the one case is the same as that of the one that it opens in the other?" The argument thus depends on analogies and is as good as those analogies, although it does not depend on the analogies having been definitely discovered to obtain. The argument invites us to contemplate as the best explanation of the phenomena something that works in other cases to which, it is suggested, the phenomena in question have some analogy.

What Schopenhauer suggests is that the facts of teleology provide an obvious analogy with what holds good in the case of agency—the suggestion of purpose, etc. That, in turn, suggests that a similar though less obvious analogy holds with cases where, although there is no explicit teleology, there is reason to speak of force. There is much to doubt about such analogies, and it cannot be said that the cogency of the argument as presented is very great. As I indicated earlier, there is really not much analogy between purposiveness and goal directedness considered simply as phenomena. The convergence of a sequence of movements on to a goal may *suggest* something like single-mindedness, and it may be that which has so often led people to see in goal directedness evidence of purpose. But purpose does not always imply single-mindedness. Nor is it obvious that the attainment of a purpose is achieved in all cases by the kind of means that it seems appropriate to invoke in the case of so-called goal-directed mechanisms. It is indeed arguable that we speak of 'goal directedness' rather than, say, 'convergence on to an end product', only because of a certain anthropomorphism. To go on to infer an analogy would be to beg the question by presupposing the point at issue. If the analogies here are not strong, they are weaker still between purposiveness and the manifestation of a force. If all that is the case, then, while the "grand hypothesis" of the will remains as hypothesis possible (for *could* it not be the case that a possible way of regarding natural phenomena is to regard them as the expression of a will?), it is not one that has any particular cogency or that provides us with any particular reason to accept it, however fascinating it may be to contemplate, as a possibility.

To finish, however, I would like to go back to the "key" and make one other comment on the relation of Schopenhauer's views about agency and motivation to the view that motives might be identified with causes of bodily movement. Davidson says in the Introduction to his *Essays on Action and Events* (p. xiii) that subsequent thinking and doubts have led him to qualify certain of the views expressed in "Actions, Reasons and Causes." Part of those qualifications stem from the fact that the existence of a motive and of a causal connection between it and the action is not sufficient to show that the action is done from that motive, that it is intentionally so done. That is a point that has lately come to be discussed under the heading of "deviant causal chains." A further point that has influenced Davidson is the existence of what he calls pure intentions. For that reason he says that of the three things that G. E. M. Anscombe[13] claimed as marking off the field of intention—acting intentionally, acting from an intention, and intending—he now gives more importance than he did to the last. I think, however, that he ought also to give more importance to the first, since, as I indicated in "Schopenhauer on Action and the Will," one lesson that we ought to learn from Schopenhauer is that intention is not something that can be reduced to acting from reason but that acting from reason presupposes the prior notion of intention. The implication of what I have said here is that we ought also to pay attention to Schopenhauer's "Wittgensteinian" claim that the will expresses itself only in action. In other words, we ought to take seriously the thought that the most important of the Anscombian trio is intentional action or acting intentionally.

That is so, Schopenhauer implies, because it is only in the context of intentional action that one becomes aware of what agency really means and also of the fact that agency and the conformity of action to motives as causes mutually presuppose each other. That mutual presupposition indicates that it is here that there is the meeting place of two things that it is very difficult to reconcile, let alone to reduce to each other—human agency and the subjection to causes that the expression of agency in bodily action entails. Present-day materialists would like to reduce the former to the latter, and, as Schopenhauer saw clearly, that is impossible. He did not himself propose the reduction of the latter to the former. It is indeed difficult to think of anyone who would think that a plausible line to take. He did, however, think that the paradox or mystery par excellence that is there in bodily action with its combination of agency and conformity to causes was the secret that explained the universe in general. If he were right, it would mean that there was an equal mystery in how there could be a universe at all, for what goes unexplained in Schopenhauer's scheme of things is why the will should will a world in which things are subject to causes at all—or, to put the matter the other way round, why the world that we have, subject to causes in the way that it is, should be, not so much the expression of a will at all, but subject to the kind of will that Schopenhauer says it is. For on his view the will is blind, lacking any intrinsic connection with the intellect. If that remains a mystery, it is at least an interesting exercise to consider what cogency there might be thought to exist in an argument that sees an analogy between nature and certain aspects of human beings, rather than, as current prejudices see as more attractive, the other way round.

Notes

1. Translated by E. F. J. Payne (La Salle, Ill.: Open Court, 1974). I will refer to it henceforward as *FR*.

2. *Journal of Philosophy*, Vol. 60 (1963), pp. 685-700, reprinted in his *Essays on Action and Events* (Oxford: Clarendon Press, 1980), pp. 3-19.

3. I have in "Schopenhauer on Action and the Will" (in *Idealism: Past and Present*, Royal Institute of Philosophy Lectures 13, 1979/1980, *Philosophy* Supplement 1982), suggested that there is a lesson to be learned from Schopenhauer that has application to the difficulties that Davidson subsequently detected in his account.

4. See my *Schopenhauer* (London: Routledge and Kegan Paul, 1980), pp. 19-20, 55-56.

5. See my critical notice of Charles Taylor's *Explanation of Behaviour* in *Mind*, Vol. 76 (1967), esp. pp. 132-33.

6. This is to an extent that has, in the latter case, made him subject to the accusation that his thought constitutes a sad falling off in that respect from that of Kant. See, for example, Maurice Mandelbaum, "The Physiological Orientation of Schopenhauer's Epistemology" in *Schopenhauer: His Philosophical Achievement*, ed. M. Fox (Brighton: Harvester, 1980).

7. In "Why Are There Phenomena?" in a *Festschrift* for Arthur Hübscher, *Zeit der Ernte*, ed. W. Schirmacher (Stuttgart: Frommann-Holzboog, 1982).

8. I am grateful to Christopher Janaway for his comments on an earlier draft of this paper.

9. Translated by Konstantin Kolenda (Indianapolis and New York: Bobbs-Merrill, 1960), p. 14.

10. *WR* = *The World as Will and Representation*, trans. E. F. J. Payne (Indian Hills, Colo.: Falcon's Wing Press, 1958; paperback edition, New York: Dover, 1969).

11. *Schopenhauer*, pp. 92ff; "Schopenhauer on Action and Will," pp. 134-35.

12. In "Why Are There Phenomena?"

13. *Intention* (Oxford: Blackwell, 1957).

Mill on Necessary Truth

CHARLES LANDESMAN

I

Mill's basic strategy in defending a radical empiricist theory of knowledge against the a priori or rationalist theory is to admit that there are analytic truths, to deny that their existence represents a challenge to empiricism, and then to offer an inductivist account of mathematical truth. His approach contrasts with that of the later logical positivists, who agreed with the rationalists that the truths of number theory are indeed necessary but thought that this concession could be rendered harmless by explicating necessity in terms of analyticity. It also contrasts with that of the currently fashionable holistic empiricism that rejects the analytic-synthetic contrast as inexplicable, the notion of necessity as hopelessly obscure, and attempts to explain our alledged knowledge of necessity by reference to a proposition's degree of importance or centrality in our conceptual scheme.

The problem with holism is that the attempt to dispense with logical necessity renders the bearing of experience on theoretical change inexplicable. If, for example, the truth of "This A is not B" does not necessitate the falsehood of "All A is B," then no observation reported by "This A is not B" could be recalcitrant, that is, no such observation could require us to modify our theories.[1] The concept of logical necessity is presupposed by any empiricist program that undertakes to show that experience constrains and influences the content of our theories. The problem with the logical positivist program is that any conception of analytic truth broad enough to constitute the basis of number-theoretic truth classifies as analytic many propositions that rationalists would classify as synthetic a priori. In the end, the disagreement between traditional rationalism and positivism turns out to be more verbal than real. So Mill's approach seems to be the only plausible line to adopt against rationalism. Let us see how well it works.

II

Mill distinguishes verbal from real or instructive truths. A verbal truth is a proposition of universal affirmative subject-predicate form "in which the predicate connotes the whole or part of what the subject connotes, but nothing besides" (I, 6, 2).[2] He notes that this distinction "corresponds to that which is drawn by Kant and other metaphysicians between what they term *analytic* and *synthetic* judgments" (I, 6, 4*n*). According to Mill, the existence of verbal truth does not represent any challenge to empiricism because such truths do not forrmulate any matters of fact but only express the meanings of names. Mill suggests that they express linguistic conventions and "are not, strictly speaking, susceptible of truth or falsity, but only of conformity or disconformity to usage or convention" (I, 6, 1).

When Mill attempts to explain the notion of connotation used in his account of verbal truth, he says: "We may predicate of a name which connotes a variety of attributes, another name which connotes only one of these attributes, or some smaller number of them all. . . . A proposition of this sort . . . conveys no information to any one who previously understood the whole meaning of the terms" (I, 6, 2). He thus introduces attributes as a type of entity connoted by general names. Now Mill rejects the sort of Platonist ontology according to which abstract entities such as classes or attributes are "regarded as a peculiar kind of substances, having an objective existence distinct from the individual objects classed under them" (II, 2, 2). He also rejects nominalist accounts of naming that would dispense with attributes altogether. And, in a long note directed against Spencer's theory of universals, Mill rejects the view that attributes are abstract particulars, that they are as particular as the things that exemplify them. The theory of abstract particulars cannot explain the fact that there are general names in language. "A name would have no general meaning if *man* connoted one thing when predicated of John, and another though closely resembling thing when predicated of William" (II, 2, 4*n*). Attributes are truly general entities; two distinct particulars can exemplify the very same attribute; attributes, for Mill, are points of resemblance or common features of objects given in sensation (II, 2, 4*n*; II, 3, 6).

Mill's rationale for insisting that some names have connotation as well as denotation is that "whenever the names given to objects convey any information, that is, whenever they have properly any meaning, the meaning resides not in what they *denote*, but in what they *connote*" (I, 2, 5). In many cases, names are not merely arbitrary labels applied to things but convey genuine information available to anyone who knows their meaning. The information conveyed consists of imputations of attributes or properties to the thing named. So nominalism as well as a purely extensionalist account of meaning cannot explain the informativeness of our verbal predications. And Platonism goes too far by supposing that the attributes imputed exist independently of the things to which they are imputed.

Mill's account of why verbal propositions fail to be factual is inconsistent with his account of their meaning. A verbal or analytic truth does indeed convey a matter of fact, namely, a fact that consists of the inclusion of one attribute (that connoted by the predicate) in another (that connoted by the subject). Attribute inclusions or exclusions are as good candidates for the status of being matters of fact as anything else. After all, for Mill, attributes are real beings that exist independently of language. They bear relations to one another just as do particulars. And language can be used to formulate these relations just as it formulates relations among particulars.

Mill's denial of factual content to analytic truths was probably influenced by his confusion of an analytic proposition such as (1) "All men are living beings" with a statement of meaning such as (2) "The word 'man' connotes living being." That he was so confused is evidenced by his occasional identification of analytic truths with definitions (I, 6, 2) that probably misled him into classifying them as verbal propositions. Whereas the only information that (2) conveys is about the meaning of a word, (1) is true in virtue of the inclusion of one attribute in another and says nothing whatever about the meaning of any word. Of course, in order to know that (1) expresses a truth and which truth it expresses, one must know what its constituent words mean. But that is true of any sentence that expresses a truth. And in order to know that what (1) expresses is indeed a truth, it is not sufficient to know what its constituent words mean in the sense of knowing what attributes they connote. One must also know that one attribute is included in another. One may be able to identify two distinct entities without realizing that one is included in the other. That realization, that insight into a relationships among attributes is an essential component in our knowledge of analytic truth. So, once one admits that there are analytic truths, as I think one must, the purity of one's empiricism has been sullied, for one has thereby conceded, first, that there exist abstract objects not reducible to sense given particulars and, second, that we have a faculty or capacity — call it intellectual intuition — of grasping relationships among such objects, relationships whose necessity is not given or discriminable in sense-perception.

III

Mill asks: "Why are mathematics by almost all philosophers . . . considered to be independent of the evidence of experience and observation, and characterized as systems of Necessary Truth?" (II, 5, 1). The philosophers, thinks Mill, are mistaken because "this character of necessity ascribed to the truths of mathematics and even . . . the peculiar certainty attributed to them is an illusion" (ibid.). Here Mill agrees with many contemporary philosophers about the illusory character of mathematical necessity. Mill and many contemporaries agree that the necessity often ascribed to the truths of logic and mathematics is really something else that is mistakenly interpreted as necessity.

For Mill, a geometrical axiom such as (L) "Two straight lines cannot enclose a space" is an inductively confirmed approximate truth: "it receives constant confirmation in almost every instant of our lives, since we cannot look at any two straight lines which intersect one another without seeing that from that point they continue to diverge more and more. Experimental proof crowds in upon us in such endless profusion" (II, 5, 4). It has, therefore, a greater degree of certainty than the truths of the physical sciences. We need not impute any a priori origin to our knowledge of (L) because its high degree of certainty is explicable in inductivist terms. The illusion of the philosophers thus consists of mistaking this high degree of empirically grounded certainty for something else entirely, which they call "necessity," and of inventing a fictitious a priori basis for our alleged knowledge of necessary truth.

One of Russell's main arguments against empiricist accounts of mathematical knowledge such as Mill's hinges upon a different view of mathematical certainty. Russell writes:

> The general propositions of mathematics . . . can obviously be known with certainty by consideration of a single instance, and gain nothing by enumeration of other cases in which they have been found to be true. Thus our knowledge of the general propositions of mathematics (and the same applies to logic) must be accounted for otherwise than our (merely probable) knowledge of empirical generalizations. . . .[3]

The issue between Mill and Russell hinges upon differing explanations of the high degree of confidence we have in the truth of some mathematical propositions. It is not the mere fact that we have such a high degree of confidence that marks off the mathematical from the nonmathematical. One may feel quite sure of the truth of propositions whose contingency is not in question, such as statements describing what one was doing one minute ago, and so on. The question is whether our high degree of confidence, assuming that it is not a mere prejudice, can be justified on empiricist grounds. Mill thinks so because "experimental proof crowds in upon us in such endless profusion," whereas for Russell the endless profusion is unnecessary and irrelevant because one instance will do.

IV

Mill has stacked the cards in his favor by using an example, (L), for which it is plausible to say that there is a profusion of empirical evidence. Let us then choose another example that does not fit his preconceptions as well: (C) "A cube has 12 edges." Most people go through their whole lives without counting the edges of a cube or even wondering how many there are. When I ask people how many edges there are, they usually do not know and have to make an effort to find out. What they most often do is to form a visual image of a cube and then rotate it in their "mind's eye" in various directions, counting the edges and being careful not to count any edge twice. Very often, people make mistakes or are not sure of their answer even when it is correct. Mental verification is a fallible process and does not yield the unshakable certainty often attributed to it by advocates of the a priori theory. The mind's eye is an imperfect instrument. But we may check our answer, count the edges several times, and find ourselves in agreement with others so that after a time we may feel quite sure that we know the right answer. Russell was just a bit too optimistic in insisting that a single instance would suffice. But Mill was mistaken in thinking that an endless profusion of confirmations is required to achieve the high degree of confidence that actually obtains.

According to Whewell's version of the a priori theory that Mill criticizes, a proposition such as (L) or (C) is seen to be true simply by thinking about it. The faculty of verifying propositions a priori is called intellectual intuition. A priori knowledge is achieved in an exercise of this faculty by means of which we directly apprehend the truth of certain propositions without having to rely upon inductive confirmations. Such propositions are thought to be necessary rather than contingent.

Can anything be said about those processes of thought in which we exercise our faculty of intellectual intuition? According to Mill's interpretation of the a priori theory, they are alleged to possess two characteristics. First, "Intuition is 'imaginary looking;' but experience must be real looking: if we see a property of straight lines to be true by merely fancying ourselves to be looking at them, the ground of our belief cannot be the senses, or experience; it must be something mental" (II, 5, 5). This description fits the cube case. We imagine a cube; we do not have to count the edges of real physical cubes. Second, according to the a priori theory, a necessary truth is one whose negation is inconceivable (II, 5, 6). We try to imagine what it would be like for (L) or (C) to be false and fail to produce even an imaginary instance. With a contingent proposition, on the other hand, we can always imagine to ourselves what it would be like for it to be false. We can also apply this test to the cube case. We try to construct in our imagination an object that is both cubical and has either more or less than twelve edges, and we never succeed. According to the a priori theory, this is a reason for thinking that (C) is a necessary truth.

Mill's argument against the inconceivability of the negation test for necessary truth is that whether or not something is inconceivable depends not on its alleged necessity but on the habits and associations established by experience (II, 5, 6). The profusion of instances that continuously confirms (L) also causes us to be unable to imagine what it would be like for (L) to be false. But Mill's response to the a priori theory depends on the particular example he has chosen. Since there is no profusion of confirmatory instances for (C), there is no opportunity for the requisite associations to be established, and so his argument fails.

If there are necessary truths, then the inconceivability test is a good method for identifying them. A necessary truth is one that is true in all possible worlds. Whenever we imagine or conceive a state of affairs, we are imagining a fragment of all those worlds in which the state of affairs obtains. If a supposed state of affairs is inconceivable to us, this is a reason, though not a conclusive reason, for thinking that there is no possible world in which it obtains and that, therefore, its negation is a necessary truth. The test is not conclusive because our failure to imagine or to conceive a state of affairs may be a failure of our skills or ingenuity rather than an indication of the presence of necessity. Our confidence in the presence of necessity may be increased by the failure of other members of the community of inquirers to conceive an instance of the proposition's negation. The a priori theory, following Descartes's example, has been too individualistic. Just as we have learned that scientific empirical investigation presupposes agreement within the relevant community of inquirers, we need to realize that a priori verification also is something that goes on within a community and that the results of the individual investigator need to be checked and corrected through the endeavors of others.

V

Let us now consider Mill's argument against the a priori theory's view that intellectual intuition is a case of imaginary looking. Mill insists that the reason we trust the verification in imagination is that the mental image is an exact replica of, and thus adequately represents, real objects. "The conclusion, therefore, is still an induction from observation. And we should not be authorized to substitute observation of the image in our mind for observation of the reality if we had not learnt by long continued experience that the properties of the reality are faithfully represented in the image" (II, 5, 5). For Mill, mental verification is basically an exercise of memory (II, 5, 5n). For example, we remember what a cube is like, having seen plenty of them in the past. We can trust our visual images of cubes to embody accurately the basic facts about cubes because we trust our memory. So the mental verification of (C) simply makes use of remembered instances. No intellectual intuition need be posited to account for what goes on.

Mill is perfectly correct in stating that quite often mental verification is merely an exercise of memory. There are cases in which it is still based on memory even though it yields new information. Mill gives a good example.

> A person . . . if asked which of two blue flowers was of the darker tinge, though he might never have compared the two, or even looked at them together, might be able to give a confident answer on the faith of his distinct recollection of the colours; that is, he might examine his mental pictures, and find there a property of the outward objects (II, 5, 5n).

But this is a case in which we discover a particular fact by recollecting specific experiences that include this fact by implication.

But, when we verify a universal truth such as (C) by examining our mental pictures, we have quite a different situation. Remember that the case we are considering is one in which an individual, trying to determine how many edges a cube has, had never counted them previously. So he is not recollecting a fact he has previously learned. And, even if the cube he imagines is one that he has previously seen so the fact that *it* has twelve edges is carried along by his memory, his conclusion is still that all cubes, observed and unobserved, actual and merely conceivable, have twelve edges. No information that just happens to accompany the remembered particular cube can provide an inductive justification of such a conclusion. After all, there is no end to the actual and possible cubes. So a mental glance at a memory image can hardly provide, if interpreted as an induction, a basis for accepting (C).

In addition, reliance upon a mental image is not necessary. After all, we could just as well count the edges of a real cube. And there are alleged necessary truths that cannot be represented by images because they are too complex or because they refer to entities that are not of the picturable sort. So any theory about how we come to know (C) by imaginary looking that is part of a general account of a priori knowledge must be compatible with the fact that imaginary looking is not indispensable.

So Mill's theory fails because it cannot account for our knowledge of (C). Can the a priori theory do any better? I think it can. What convinces us that any cube has twelve edges upon inspecting one or more imagined cubes is that sooner or later we realize that the fact that this cube has the property or attribute of having twelve edges depends solely on its being cubical and on nothing else. We also realize that this dependency is not one that *might* fail to hold in other cases but that does hold by virtue of the fact that the property of being cubical entails the property of having twelve edges. Because of this property entailment, we are entitled to conclude that any cube, actual or possible, must have twelve edges. Our knowledge of what obtains in every possible world (in which cubes exist) is founded upon an insight into an entailment relation among properties, an insight that is elicited by imaginary looking. Such an insight could also be elicited by looking at a real cube instead. And in some cases it could emerge just by thinking about properties, without the use of images at all.

So the a priori theory can be defended against Mill's arguments, provided we can establish that there are abstract objects such as attributes or properties; that various relations such as inclusion, exclusion, and entailment obtain among them; and that we are able by thought aided, in some cases, by imagination to gain an insight into such relations. Now Mill, as we have seen, has accepted some of these conditions. Against nominalism, he defends the existence of properties. He concedes that we can gain insight into relations of inclusion among attributes by virtue of the implications of his account of analytic truth. So he is only one short step away from the a priori theory that he found so erroneous. There is a lesson to be learned from this episode. A philosopher who wishes to provide a consistent version of radical empiricism needs to keep careful accounts on his ontological commitments. Apparently innocent moves can cause him to lose the game.

Notes

1. Jerrod J. Katz, *Language and Other Abstract Objects* (Totawa, N.J.: Rowman and Littlefield, 1981), p. 210.

2. All references are to the eighth edition of John Stuart Mill's *A System of Logic* (New York: Longmans, Green and Company, 1952). The reference (I, 6, 2) is to Book I, Chapter 6, numbered section 2.

3. Bertrand Russell, *The Problems of Philosophy* (Oxford: Oxford University Press, 1951), p. 84.

Making Sense of the *Tractatus*

MORRIS WEITZ

The great problem round which everything that I write turns is this: Is there an order in the world *a priori*, and if so what does it consist in? (*Notebooks*, 1.6.15; p. 53e.)

In 6.54 Wittgenstein sums up his reading of the *Tractatus*:

My propositions serve as elucidations in the following way: anyone who understands me eventually recognizes them as nonsensical [*unsinnig*], when he has used them—as steps—to climb up beyond them. (He must, so to speak, throw away the ladder after he has climbed up it.)

Commentators have expressed dismay or disgust at the self-defeating, even self-contradictory character of the *Tractatus*. Some, however, have tried to salvage the nonsense of the *Tractatus* by interpreting its avowal as useful or illuminating nonsense or as not really being nonsense at all. Black, for example, sees much of the avowed nonsense as legitimate philosophical extension of the meaning of certain fundamental terms that culminates in a proposed new way of looking at the world. Kenny, on the other hand, accepts the illegitimacy of these nonsensical propositions but applauds them as useful because they are instructive in the way that they break down.

Wittgenstein's assessment of what he says in the *Tractatus* promises (secular) salvation—seeing "the world aright" (6.54)—not a salvaging of his propositions. But even he does not do full justice to the nonsense he proclaims. In 6.53 he restricts nonsense to the failure "to give a meaning to certain signs in his [the metaphysician's] propositions." Yet, the full text reveals a nonsense that includes violating the syntax of certain signs (3.33; 3.331ff. on Russell's Theory of Types); failing to understand the logic of our language (4.003); trying to say what can only be shown (4.1212; 4.115); trying to show what can only be said (4.1212); trying to show what cannot be shown or said; trying to say what cannot be said or shown (4.1212); and confusing a formal with a proper concept (4.126).

There is also the nonsense of a failure to give a meaning to certain signs, a failure that Wittgenstein shares with those philosophers whom he condemns, a glaring instance of which is Wittgenstein's "*The limits of my language* mean the limits of my world" (5.6). Where, one must ask, does Wittgenstein give a meaning to "my" in the *Tractatus*?

Or, what are we to make of this piece of nonsense, in the Preface, and not even acknowledged by Wittgenstein as nonsense, unless we read it as a piece of irony; that there are thoughts expressed in the text and that "the *truth* of the thoughts . . . seems to me unassailable and definitive"? As the text reveals, this is an empty claim, true only in the Boolean sense, since by his own definition of "thought" (4) there are *no* thoughts in the *Tractatus*. The only thoughts there are in the sciences, not in philosophy, neither Wittgenstein's nor anyone else's.

In 6.54 Wittgenstein talks about "my propositions," but, since he characterizes "proposition" as a logical picture that must be either true or false, there is no place for "my propositions," with the consequence that there can be no elucidation of them either: "My propositions" is as empty as "thoughts" in the *Tractatus*.

The *Tractatus*, then, as it stands, is not only self-defeating or self-contradictory, it is also incoherent with its thoughts that are not thoughts, its propositions that are not propositions. The work, therefore, is unamenable to any attempt at salvage. With the exception of logical tautologies and mathematical equations, both characterized by Wittgenstein not as nonsense but as without sense (*sinnlos*) and things that can be shown but not said (also *sinnlos*), the *Tractatus* is totally nonsensical (*unsinnig*).

The ubiquity of the nonsense in the *Tractatus* can be reinforced by the two fundamental distinctions—of sense versus nonsense and of saying versus showing— that Wittgenstein introduces in the *Tractatus*. Both, as important as they are to Wittgenstein, are nonsense in the deepest sense of incoherent, for Wittgenstein's sense rests on nonsense, his showing on saying, and saying, being nonsense, cannot contrast with the showing. That which is with sense (*Sinn, sinnvoll*) presupposes that which is nonsense (*unsinnig*), namely, those putatively sensible (*sinnig*) propositions that turn out to be nonsensical (*unsinnig*). Wittgenstein's two basic dichotomies that he needs to distinguish sayable science from unsayable metaphysics and showable metaphysics from sayable science are both incoherent. If this is correct, the *Tractatus* is not a salvageable failure but an unmitigated, irredeemable (even if admittedly brilliant) failure.

In the *Tractatus* propositions or thoughts have sense (*Sinn*), names have meaning (*Bedeutung*). All true propositions or thoughts, it is claimed, belong to science (4.11). To say something about the world that is true or false is to project a proposition onto a propositional sign. Propositions are names in concatenation. These names, with their meanings, presuppose that there are objects that the names name or mean. Thus, the sense of a proposition, as a true or false sayable about the world, presupposes that there are objects, and all talk about objects is nonsense (4.1272). It follows from this that a necessary condition of sense is the nonsense of a world of objects.

The concept of sense (*Sinn*) presupposes that there are objects (also concatenated, in states of affairs or atomic facts), which presupposition is an avowed piece of nonsense. If, then, sense is unintelligible without this piece of nonsense, the distinction between sense and nonsense is radically incoherent. Nothing can have a sense or be sensible (*sinnvoll*) unless there are names that combine in a certain manner, and nothing can be a name without its naming its object: Nothing can be sensible unless it rests on the nonsensical.

Wittgenstein admits that "there are objects" is nonsensical: The claim confuses a formal with a proper concept (4.1272). What he does not affirm is that since it is nonsensical, the whole enterprise of saying — uttering propositions or having thoughts — is in inescapable jeopardy. From which it follows that the whole of science that, as we are told, is the sum total of the sayable or sensible (4.11) is as nonsensical as the metaphysics it is supposed to contrast.

The notion of sense is as fundamental as anything in the *Tractatus*. That sense makes no sense without the ontological nonsense of simple, unalterable objects renders the *Tractatus* incoherent, not merely self-defeating or self-contradictory.

That there are these objects makes it possible that there are atomic facts or states of affairs and corresponding elementary propositions about them. If "there are objects" is nonsense, the whole notion of the world or of reality, along with our thinking and talking about it, is also nonsense.

What, now, of Wittgenstein's distinction between saying and showing? His letter to Russell (dated 19 August 1919) says and shows just how fundamental the distinction was to Wittgenstein:

> Now I'm afraid you haven't really got hold of my main contention, to which the whole business of logical propositions is only corollary. The main point is the theory of what can be expressed [*gesagt*] by propositions — i.e., by language (and, what comes to the same, what can be *thought*) and what cannot be expressed by propositions, but only shown [*gezeight*]); which, I believe, is the cardinal problem of philosophy . . . .

This distinction between saying and showing, however, rests on saying, and, because saying involves nonsense, the distinction collapses. Suppose, however, that saying is not incoherent, can we then draw a fundamental distinction between saying and showing? What, then, is showing? Is *it* incoherent?

For Wittgenstein, in the *Tractatus*, showing must have a reference, namely, *what* is shown; but, unlike names that must have a meaning and unlike propositions that must have sense, showing is without sense (*sinnlos*).

Is anything or everything that can be shown but not said the same as that which is without sense? What, to begin with, is only shown? In the full text of the *Tractatus*, the following are offered as what can be shown but not said: that a proposition has sense (4.022); that "*a*" is a name (3.221); that there are objects (4.1211); that a name shows that it signifies an object (4.126) (what, one wonders, does this do to "there are objects" is nonsense, 4.1272?); that *ab* — that *a* is to the left of *b* — is a logical picture (3.1432); that -(*p.-p*) is a tautology (6.1201); that $2 + 2 = 4$ is a mathematical equation (6.241); that there are elementary propositions (4.221); that all propositions are elementary or truth-functions of elementary propositions (5); that solipsism is true (5.62); that the sense of the world is out of the world (6.41); that there is the mystical (6.44, 6.45, 6.522); that "the world is independent of my will" (6.373); that tautologies reveal the logical properties of language and the world (6.12); that there are logical constants and that they are not representatives of the logic of facts (4.0312); that in *"fa" "a"* occurs in the sense of *"fa"* (4.1211); that there is no causal nexus (5.1361); that identity of two things or of one thing is nonsense (5.5301); that there are nets for the propositions of science (6.341); that there is the limit (5.5561); that philosophy shows but cannot say that what can be shown cannot be said and, by contraposition, that what can be said cannot be shown (4.111ff.); that a proposition is not a name (3.144); that *ab* is a logical picture (3.1432); that there is a difference between a sign and a symbol (3.22); and, in Wittgenstein's own words, "A picture cannot, however, depict its pictorial form; it displays it" (2.172); "Propositions *show* the logical form of reality" (4.121); "Propositions show what they say: tautologies and contradictions show that they say nothing" (4.461); "The possibility of inference from *(x).fx* to *fa* shows that the symbol *(x).fx* itself has generality in it"; "An operation manifests itself in a variable; it shows how we can get from one form of proposition to another" (5.24); ". . . . 'A believes that *p*', '*A* has the thought *p*', and '*A* says *p*' are of the form ' "*p*" says *p*': and this does not involve a correlation of a fact with an object but rather the correlation of facts by means of the correlation of their objects" (5.542); "This shows too that there is no such thing as the soul. . . . Indeed a composite soul would no longer be a soul" (5.5421); "The limit . . . makes itself manifest in the totality of elementary propositions" (5.5561); ". . . What the solipsist *means* is quite correct; only it cannot be *said*, but makes itself manifest" (5.62); "The world is *my* world: this is manifest in the fact that the limits of *language* (of that language which alone I understand) mean the limits of *my* world" (5.62); "The fact that the propositions of logic are tautologies *shows* the formal—logical—properties of language and the world" (6.12); "Every tautology itself shows that it is a tautology" (6.127); "The logic of the world, which is shown in tautologies by the propositions of logic, is shown in equations by mathematics" (6.22); "If there were a law of causality, it might be put in the following way: There are laws of nature. But of course that cannot be said: it makes itself manifest" (6.36); "There are, indeed, things that cannot be put into words. They *make themselves manifest*. They are what is mystical" (6.522).

Showing, as these examples show, whatever else it is, is a most varied lot. Wittgenstein's best case, I think, is that of a tautology: we show, e.g., that $-(p.-p)$ is a tautology by showing a row of T's in its truth table. Here we have a criterion for showing—a row of T's.

This tautology also is *sinnlos* in the explicit sense of lacking a true-false polarity, which is a requirement for propositions or thoughts. $-(p.-p)$ is, nevertheless, a proposition that Wittgenstein says is without sense but not nonsense (4.4611).

Are all of his examples of showing like $-(p.-p)$? Are they all *sinnlos*? What for example, counts as a manifestation of the mystical in the way that a row of T's counts as a manifestation or showing of the tautological character of *-(p.-p)*? All Wittgenstein offers here is that there is a world that we feel is a limited whole: "it is not *how* things are in the world that is mystical but *that* it exists" (6.44); "Feeling the world as a limited whole — it is this that is mystical" (6.45). The mystical thus shows itself and is *sinnlos*, but the criteria here are very different from the objective criterion of the showing of a tautology.

Consider another example. How is it shown that there is no causal nexus, that the belief in such a nexus is superstition (5.1361)? How can one show a universal negative? How could it be shown that "there is a causal nexus" is false? It seems to me that what is to count for the absence of a causal nexus could equally count for the presence of such a nexus.

Showing, then, as Wittgenstein's examples show, is not an exact concept; on the contrary, it is ambiguous, vague, and indeterminate, indeed, a violation of Wittgenstein's own commitment to the exactitude of sense (3.23ff.). Is showing also incoherent? Can we or something show or manifest itself without saying?

One contender is the proposition that "*shows* its sense . . . how things stand if it is true. And it *says* that they do so stand" (4.002). Is this remark a counterexample to 4.1212: "What *can* be shown, *cannot* be said"? I think not, for Wittgenstein is not saying that a proposition says as it shows; rather, he is saying that a proposition shows but does not say its sense; and at the same time it says what cannot be shown, that things stand in a certain way. A proposition, then, shows and says, but what it shows cannot be said and what it says cannot be shown. Wittgenstein's remark would be incoherent only if he said that the sense of a proposition says or what a proposition says includes its sense.

What we need, therefore, is an example in which showing rests on, depends on, presupposes, or implies saying in order to show the incoherence of showing. Does showing imply saying as, if I am right, sense presupposes nonsense? Take causality again: Can we show that there is no causal nexus (or even that there is) without saying it? If "there is no causal nexus" is *sinnlos*, not *unsinnig*, how can it be shown without saying it? It cannot. What is shown when it is shown that there is no causal nexus is that "there is no causal nexus" is true, its denial false. But this has to be said in order to show it. Otherwise, how could one ascertain what is being shown? Showing, then, in this case, is distinguishable from saying, but one cannot show it unless one can first say it.

Without going into further examples, what Wittgenstein shows but does not say is that in many cases of showing a necessary condition for showing is saying. And, because saying is incoherent, the distinction between saying and showing is also incoherent. Even though one could show, however difficult it would be, that there is no causal nexus (or that there is), one could not show it without saying it. The distinction between saying and showing vanishes: One needs to be able to say it in order to be able to show it. Showing, thus, implies saying even though saying does not imply showing.

Sense, then, presupposes nonsense; and showing, at least in some cases of showing, implies saying. Thus, both crucial distinctions are incoherent. Moreover, that showing requires saying and that saying presupposes nonsense render the distinction between saying and showing incoherent in what we might call "weakly" incoherent. But the distinction is also "strongly" incoherent in that showing in many cases requires saying as a necessary condition of identifying the particular showing and of discriminating among different kinds of showing.

All of the *Tractatus*, then, is either without sense or nonsense. It contains nothing with sense. *Sinn* and *sinnvoll* — that which is sensible or with sense — are confined to the language of science alone. Thus, the two dichotomies of sense versus nonsense and saying versus showing that Wittgenstein uses both destructively and constructively to distinguish science from logic, mathematics, metaphysics, ethics, aesthetics, and natural theology, because they are incoherent, render incoherent the sense of science since its sense rests on saying.

Is the *Tractatus* full of nonsense, without sense, and incoherent? Or does it have sense as the sciences have sense? The answer to both questions is negative. Is there, then, some other sense that it has that is not the attributed sense of science? If the *Tractatus* is to be read and understood as a nonfailure, the answer must be affirmative, in which case the *Tractatus* needs no apology or defense of its avowedly self-defeating character.

Where does one start — in the *Tractatus* — to make sense of it? As revealing a place as any is Wittgenstein's remarks on the nature and language of science (6.32-6.341). There Wittgenstein introduces his distinction between the propositions of science and the forms of representation or the nets (conceptual frameworks) imposed upon these propositions. The propositions are true or false, the forms or nets through which these propositions are filtered and formulated are not propositions, not true or false. Hence, they are not logical pictures, thoughts, or a subset of facts, as propositions are. What, then, are they? Wittgenstein says they are not a priori beliefs ". . . but rather *a priori knowledge* of the possibility of a logical form" (6.33). They "are *a priori* insights about the forms in which the propositions of science can be cast" (6.34). "Newtonian mechanics, for example, imposes a unifed form on the description of the world" (6.341). Moreover, these forms or nets are options. Science can choose among different nets, where the criteria of choice are aesthetic, not their truth or falsity.

Wittgenstein's remarks on science — questionable as they are about the propositional character of science in which he offers no clue as to the nonpropositional character of much of the language of science, no indication of how that language, reducible to elementary propositions about atomic facts, can capture either the generality or the lawlike character of much of scientific discourse — are, nevertheless, important to the sense of the *Tractatus* because, according to Wittgenstein, the laws of science are about the nets and not what the nets describe (6.35). A net, therefore, is neither true or false nor a proposition. Is it, then, with sense, without sense, or nonsense? I think it is none of these. Does it, too, show itself or manifest itself as Wittgenstein's examples of showing do? It does not. The text, instead, strongly suggests that talk about a net is not propositional, true or false; nor is it without sense. And it is not nonsense in any of the ways in which nonsense is presented in the

Tractatus. The laws of science, then, are not like the laws of logic or of mathematics or even like the general propositions of science.

Net-talk, it strongly appears, is language that is immune from Wittgenstein's dichotomies of sense versus nonsense and saying versus showing. The status of net-talk, Wittgenstein allows us to aver, is sensible even thought it does not share in the *Sinn* of propositions as true or false logical pictures or in the *sinnlos* character of logic, mathematics, some metaphysics, ethics, etc.

If net-talk has sense even though it is not propositional, why cannot the putatively ontological remarks of the ones and twos of the *Tractatus* also have sense without their being propositional, true or false logical pictures? Then ontological remarks are like remarks about the nets of science, *not* in their optionality, but in their having sense without their being propositions as true or false logical pictures. If net-talk is immune from Wittgenstein's two dichotomies, why cannot the talk about simple, unalterable objects and states of affairs or atomic facts also be immune from these dichotomies? They can be and, in my opinion, they are. The reason why this similarity of net-talk and ontology-talk has been missed by the major commentators of the *Tractatus* is that they have unanimously taken the ontological remarks to be inferences or derivations or transcendental deductions from Wittgenstein's conception of language and logic. However we interpret the ones and twos, it is, I submit, an exegetical scandal that they are unanimously construed as dependent upon Wittgenstein's conception of language and logic. That the ones and twos come first, in spite of the (supposedly) true fact that most of them were written after the threes, fours, etc., is a fact about the text of the *Tractatus* that cannot easily be interpreted as dependent upon the later sections of the *Tractatus.*

There is no textual evidence, unless we allow ourselves to be misled by the *Notebooks,* that the ones and some of the twos, even if written after the threes, etc., are derivations, inferences, or deductions from the threes, etc. Indeed, the textual numerical reading is, I think, logically right: The ones and twos do not depend on the threes through sixes; rather, Wittgenstein's conception of language depends on the ones and early twos. The early textual parts of the *Tractatus,* then, are presuppositions of, not inferences from, the later textual parts.

If we persist in reading Wittgenstein's remarks on simple objects or states of affairs as inferences from his conception of language, we inevitably end up with Wittgenstein's assessment of these remarks as nonsense, as nonsensical as the premises from which these remarks are derived.

The putatively ontological remarks of the ones and twos, like the net-talk of the sixes, are not propositional in Wittgenstein's stringent sense of logical pictures of facts. That there are objects and atomic facts in which these objects are necessary constituents is Wittgenstein's setting forth the necessary conditions for there being a language at all. These necessary conditions are metaphysical—statements about what there must be in order for there to be a language—and not ontological statements about what there is in the world: "how the world is."

If we read the ones and much of the twos as ontological, they are not immune from Wittgenstein's destructive use of his two dichotomies. But, if we read them as metaphysical, they are immune from them, as immune as is his net-talk. It is my contention that Wittgenstein's introductory talk about the world, reality, fact, and object offers the overall conditions of language and of his dichotomies of sense versus nonsense and saying versus showing; and, therefore, they are, as necessary conditions of sense or nonsense, not themselves subject to their being sense or nonsense, saying or showing.

The reason the ones and twos come first in the *Tractatus* is thus logically absolutely right. They offer necessary conditions of the intelligibility of discourse and of sense rather than a set of ontological statements that are deduced from language, subject to sense or nonsense. As necessary conditions of intelligible discourse, including the sense versus nonsense or the saying versus showing of certain propositions, they are governing rules for the logical syntax of the language of science.

If I am right that Wittgenstein's metaphysics is the articulation of the necessary conditions of language and not ontological assertions about the world that are derived from his theory of language and logic, then Wittgenstein is, I think, the first philosopher since Plato to recognize and to apply the crucial difference between metaphysics and ontology. For on my understanding of Plato's Theory of Forms, that there are forms is not an ontological doctrine about what there is but a metaphysical doctrine about what there must be if there is to be anything, whether there is anything or not. In a similar vein, Wittgenstein affirms in the ones and twos a set of necessary conditions for there being a language, whether there is a language or not.

Both Plato and Wittgenstein implicitly ask: What must there be in order for there to be anything, even if there were nothing. It is Aristotle, not Plato, who shifts philosophy from the metaphysical to the ontological, a shift that is not reversed on my reading of the history of philosophy—not even by Kant—until the *Tractatus*, unless we find in Chapter 9 of Russell's *Problems of Philosophy* the same platonic argument for universals that they must be if there is to be anything, not simply that there are universals that subsist and that are intuited in conception. So far as Kant is concerned, it seems to me that he did not raise Plato's or Wittgenstein's question. Instead, he asked: What must there be in order for there to be the world we have? I do not think it ever occurred to him to raise the question of that is a priori, whether there is anything or not.

Wittgenstein, to return to the *Tractatus*, seeks in the ones and twos the necessary conditions for the intelligibility of discourse, not for the essences of things. Moreover, it is this necessary condition—this metaphysical presupposition of the intelligibility of discourse—that Wittgenstein implicitly accepts in the *Tractatus* and explicitly rejects in the *Investigations*. It is not the ontological remarks about the essences in the *Tractatus* that are countered by the antiontological remarks in the *Investigations*, for Wittgenstein does not attack essences in the *Investigations*, he attacks the metaphysical presupposition that there must be essences and, in particular, an essence of language. On this reading of Wittgenstein's two main works, the attributed concern for the necessary conditions of the intelligibility of discourse seriously challenges those attempts of commentators of Wittgenstein's development to find a unity in these two major books, for these two books divide sharply on the necessity of the overall condition of intelligent discourse.

The *Tractatus*, therefore, on my reading of the ones and twos, is not self-defeating, self-contradictory, or incoherent. These charges vanish when the talk about objects and facts is seen for what it is in the text—presuppositions, not ontological propositions. These presuppositions of sense and nonsense, saying and showing, cannot themselves be any of them: The presuppositions cannot be subject to the very distinctions they guarantee.

My reading of the putatively ontological claims of the ones and twos as metaphysical rather than as ontological is not an attempt to salvage the *Tractatus* but to make sense of the text, which supports my reading: the fact that they do come first in the text and that they are like Wittgenstein's remarks about the nets of science, at least in the latter's not being either with sense or without, either sayable or showable. But there is a price to pay, already demanded by the syntactical and semantical status of net-talk versus empirical science-talk: as a priori, the presuppositions regarding objects and facts, though they are not orthodox, Tractarian true or false logical pictures, as propositions and thoughts are, force an extension of Wittgenstein's conception of language. Even though these presuppositions are not with or without sense, or nonsense, or sayable or showable, they are, as necessary conditions of intelligible discourse, substantive, nontautological, *a priori assertions* about what there must be. And, as assertions, they are true or false, and, because they are necessary conditions, they are necessarily true. A place must be found for them in the *Tractatus*. That place is, I think, in the logical syntax for *any* language and not in the logical syntax of the only language of science.

The *Tractatus*, thus, is more than a clarification of the language of science. It includes also the formulation of the logical syntax of such a language. Russell is almost right in his interpretation of Wittgenstein's conception of language as ideal, except that what he says is ideal applies to the logical syntax governing *any* language, not to the actual language of science. The *Tractatus*, thus, is, among other things, an ideal logical syntax for any language; it is not simply the logical syntax of the ideal language of science.

It is true, I think, that Wittgenstein starts in the *Tractatus* with the language of logic, mathematics, science, and philosophy. He asks, what syntax or rules must such a language have in order for it to be a language? Part of his answer is that it must be able to say. It must be capable of being true or false. It must allow for the creation of new sentences or propositions. It must be precise, exact, allow no indeterminacy. And it must be able to attach itself to the world.

What, then, are the conditions of such a language? (1) There must be simple, unalterable objects in order to guarantee the meanings of the names of this language. (2) There must be facts or states of affairs to ensure sentences in this language and to ensure a correspondence between this language and the world, such that some propositions are true, others are false, and no proposition is neither. (3) There must be negative facts to ensure the truth or falsity of negative propositions and their correspondence to reality. (4) Every term in this language must be precise—a univocal sign for a univocal symbol—otherwise, analysis would be incomplete. There are undoubtedly other conditions in the *Tractatus* for something's being a language that I have missed, but Wittgenstein seems not to think that one of these conditions must be that it allows for tensed statements or statements about dispositions or modalities.

It is the major thesis of this paper that much of the putative or avowed nonsense, especially in the ones and twos, affirmed as nonsense by Wittgenstein and by his commentators, is nonsense only if it is construed as ontology that is inferred, derived, or deduced from his views on language. But it is not nonsense if it is construed, as Wittgenstein's net-talk requires, as neither sense or nonsense, saying or showing, nor without sense. That there are objects, that they are simple and unalterable, that they combine into states of affairs or atomic facts, each independent of the others, are necessary conditions of the language of science as well as conditions of the two dichotomies and, as such, are not subject to any of the rubrics of sense, nonsense, saying, showing, or without sense.

The sense of the *Tractatus*, then, divides at least into the a priori metaphysical truths about the necessary conditions of any language—the ideal syntax of any language; the logical syntax of the language of science; the logical syntax of the language of logic and mathematics; the implicates of the logical syntax of any language or of the language of science, of logic, or of mathematics; and the implicates of the logical syntax of the language of science.

Let me now try to substantiate this wholesale claim by looking closely at some of the remarks in the *Tractatus*. My aim is not to present another commentary—we have enough of them—but to center on the remarks that seem (at least to me) to be crucial to the truth or falsity of my thesis about the sense and intelligibility of (almost all of) the *Tractatus*.

Consider the ones that, being brief, I quote in full.

1   The world is all that is the case.

1.1   The world is the totality of facts, not of things.

1.11   The world is determined by the facts, and by their being *all* the facts.

1.12   For the totality of facts determines what is the case, and also whatever is not the case.

1.13   The facts in logical space are the world.

1.2   The world divides into facts.

1.21   Each item can be the case or not the case while everything else remains the same.

These remarks are neither metaphysical statements about what there must be in order for there to be a world and a language about it nor ontological statements about what there is. Instead, with the exception of 1, which is a pure, if grand, linguistic tautology, on a par with Dewey's (Tom, not John) "The future lies before us," they are implicates of the (ideal) logical syntax of any language. They are indeed deductions or derivations or inferences but from the overall necessary conditions for there being a language; they are not inferences from the language or logical syntax of the language of science. Hence, they are not nonsense but as a priori as the premise from which they are derived: that there must be states of affairs or atomic facts. Given that there must be simple objects combined in states of affairs or atomic facts in order for there to be a language at all, the primacy of facts rather than of things, the independence of states of affairs or atomic facts from each other, the identification of the world with these states of affairs or atomic facts are each of them *consequences* of the metaphysical necessary condition of language. They are thus conceptual statements about the ideal syntax of any language, not statements about an ideal language of science or ontological statements about the essence of facts.

The twos begin with a further implicate of the necessary condition that there must be facts.

2   What is the case—a fact—is the existence of states of affairs.

2.01   A state of affairs (a state of things) is a combination of objects (things).

2.011   It is essential to things that they should be possible constituents of states of affairs.

These propositions spell out further what a fact is: it is a combination of objects in which these objects necessarily are possible constituents of facts. There must be objects as a necessary condition of there being facts, even though the actual combinations of these objects are contingent. This condition guarantees that the sentences about the world consist of combinations of names that, as sentences, are independent of one another. That there are facts and that there are objects, again, are not ontological remarks but metaphysical statements about the necessary conditions of there being a world and a language about it. There must be facts that consist of objects. The actual facts that there are are contingent, but the fact that there are facts and their constituent objects is necessary. There may be nothing, but, if there is something, it must comprise facts and their objects. Thus:

2.012   In logic nothing is accidental: if a thing *can* occur in a state of affairs, the possibility of the state of affairs must be written into the thing itself.

Propositions 2.0121 through 2.014 spell out the independence of objects from their actual combinations and their dependence on the states of affairs of which they are constituents. Proposition 2.014 sums up the relation between objects and facts:

2.014   Objects contain the possibility of all situations.

2.02   Objects are simple.

Proposition 2.02 affirms the simplicity of objects, but it presupposes that there are objects. It, too, then, is an implicate of the claim that there must be objects if there is to be a world and a language about it.

2.0201 Every statement about complexes can be resolved into a statement about their constituents and into the propositions that describe the complexes completely.

2.021   If the world had no substance, then whether a proposition had sense would depend on whether another proposition was true.

2.0212   In that case we could not sketch out any picture of the world (true or false.

Propositions 2.0201, 2.021, and 2.0212 clinch my view that there must be facts composed of simple objects if there is to be a world and a language about it. If there were no facts or constituent simple objects, there could be no true or false talk about the world.

This is reinforced by:

2.026   There must be objects, if the world is to have an unalterable form.

If there were no objects, there could be no world and talk about it.

2.0271   Objects are what is unalterable, and subsistent; their configuration is what is changing and unstable.

2.04   The totality of existing states of affairs is the world.

Here are more implicates of there being facts and objects:

2.0272   The configuration of objects produces states of affairs.

2.03   In a state of affairs objects fit into one another like the links of a chain.

2.031   In a state of affairs objects stand in a determinate relation to one another.

2.033   Its form is the possibility of its structure.

2.034   The structure of a fact consists of the structures of states of affairs.

2.04   The totality of existing states of affairs is the world.

Propositions 2.05 through 2.063 introduce negative facts and reality. Here, again, we have a series of implicates or inferences from the metaphysical claims that there must be facts and their objects if there is to be a world and a language about it, only the implicates here have to do with the nonexistence of states of affairs. Every existing state of affairs determines which state does not exist. These nonexistent states of affairs, also independent of each other, needed for the intelligibility of negative propositions, together with existing states of affairs, needed for the intelligibility of positive propositions, constitute reality. The world is all of these positive and negative facts; that is the same as reality.

2.063   The sum-total of reality is the world.

Proposition 2.1 is the first empirical claim in the *Tractatus*: "We picture facts to ourselves." Proposition 2.1 is not ontological, metaphysical, or a statement in the sciences. Is it with sense, without sense, or nonsense? Is it an attempt to say what can only be shown or an attempt to show what can only be said? None of these seems appropriate. Proposition 2.1 looks like an empirical proposition; yet, it is not like the empirical propositions of science. For Wittgenstein, it should be a piece of nonsense, since it is not a logical picture of anything, trying as it does to say what can only be shown—by the fact that we picture facts to ourselves. But how can it be nonsense or without sense? It seems a straightforward empirical claim about us. If it is, 2.1 has sense without its being a logical picture: It is thus Wittgenstein's narrow conception of proposition that has to give way. Something can be true (or false) even if it is not a proposition as a logical picture. Moreover, 2.1 does not seem to be implied by any necessary condition of there being a world and a language about it. Or is 2.1 the implicit claim that we must picture facts to ourselves in order to have a language about the world? But we do not need to picture facts as we do need to postulate objects and facts in order to render intelligible our world and language.

Can 2.1 be false? It is too difficult to determine from 2.1 through 2.225 whether 2.1 could be false. Wittgenstein seems to imply that 2.1 is a truth, contingent, not necessary. It is a fact that we picture facts to ourselves; it is not a necessary condition of talking about the world that we picture facts. In which case, one wonders what 2.1 is doing in the *Tractatus*. And, since it is doing a great deal (connecting up language with reality), it must have some legitimate status; yet, *sinnvoll*, *sinnig*, *sinnlos*, or (important) *Unsinn* seems out of keeping with 2.1, for 2.1 presents itself as empirical, a posteriori, not a priori. Still, one feels that 2.1 should be a priori if it is to be integral to the Tractarian view of language about the world.

Whatever the difficulties of getting clear about the status of the simple 2.1, 2.12 through 2.225 are, I think, *explications* of 2.1.

2.12   A picture is a model of reality.

2.131   In a picture the elements of the picture are the representatives of objects.

2.14   What constitutes a picture is that its elements are related to one another in a determinate way.

2.141   A picture is a fact.

2.15   The fact that the elements of a picture are related to one another in a determinate way represents that things are related to one another in the same way.

        Let us call this connexion of its elements the structure of the picture, and let us call the possibility of this structure the pictorial form of the picture.

2.151   Pictorial form is the possibility that things are related to one another in the same way as the elements of the picture.

2.1511   *That* is how a picture is attached to reality; it reaches right out to it.

2.1512   It is laid against reality like a ruler.

2.15121   Only the end-points of the graduating lines actually *touch* the object that is to be measured.

2.1513   So a picture, conceived in this way, also includes the pictorial relation-ship, which makes it into a picture.

2.1514   The pictorial relationship consists of the correlations of the picture's elements with things.

2.1515   These correlations are, as it were, the feelers of the picture's elements, with which the picture touches reality.

2.16   If a fact is to be a picture, it must have something in common with what it depicts.

2.161   There must be something identical in a picture and what it depicts, to enable the one to be a picture of the other at all.

2.17   What a picture must have in common with reality, in order to be able to depict it—correctly or incorrectly—in the way it does, is its pic-torial form.

2.171   A picture can depict any reality whose form it has. A spatial picture can depict anything spatial, a coloured one anything coloured, etc.

2.172   A picture cannot, however, depict its pictorial form: it displays it.

2.173   A picture represents its subject from a position outside it. (Its stand-point is its representational form.) That is why a picture represents its subject correctly or incorrectly.

2.174   A picture cannot, however, place itself outside its representational form.

2.18   What any picture, of whatever form, must have in common with reali-ty, in order to be able to depict it—correctly or incorrectly—in any way at all, is logical form, i.e. the form of reality.

2.181   A picture whose pictorial form is logical form is called a logical picture.

2.182   Every picture is *at the same time* a logical one. (On the other hand, not every picture is, for example, a spatial one.)

2.19   Logical pictures can depict the world.

2.2   A picture has logico-pictorial form in common with what it depicts.

2.201   A picture depicts reality by representing a possibility of existence and non-existence of states of affairs.

2.202   A picture represents a possible situation in logical space.

2.203   A picture contains the possibility of the situation that it represents.

2.21   A picture agrees with reality or fails to agree; it is correct or incorrect, true or false.

2.22   What a picture represents it represents independently of its truth or falsity, by means of its pictorial form.

2.221   What a picture represents is its sense.

2.222   The agreement or disagreement of its sense with reality constitutes its truth or falsity.

2.223   In order to tell whether a picture is true or false we must compare it with reality.

2.224   It is impossible to tell from the picture alone whether it is true or false.

2.225   There are no pictures that are true *a priori*.

Propositions 2.12 through 2.225 characterize pictures. Are all of these propositions true or false, empirical or a priori, or are they conceptual exfoliations of the picture? Do they say something about pictures, or do they show it? I find the answer as difficult as the determination of 2.1. They do not seem to be implicates of pictures as necessary vehicles for talking about the world, and yet they do seem to be implicates of what it is to be a picture. They are nonsensical only if "we picture facts to ourselves" is nonsense, which I do not think it is for Wittgenstein. But whether they are *sinnlos* or *sinnig*, I do not know, and Wittgenstein does not tell us. They look as though they had sense, but how can they, given Wittgenstein's definition of sense? So, again, sense must encompass more than propositions as logical pictures of facts. All that seems clear is that a necessary condition for *x* being a picture is that there are facts and objects, even though a picture as a fact is not a consequence of the necessary condition. Nor is it the premise of an inference to facts and objects. Wittgenstein's picture theory of language presupposes facts and objects; facts and objects are not inferences from the picture theory.

The threes begin with a definition of a thought:

3   A logical picture of facts is thought.

Is 3 true or false? A priori or a posteriori? Proposition or nonsense? Thought or not? Is this one of Wittgenstein's propositions that we use and then throw away after we see it as nonsense? Is thought a formal or a proper concept? What about "there are throughts," "there are four thoughts"?

Proposition 3.001 affirms that states of affairs—facts—are necessary conditions for what is thinkable.

3.001   "A state of affairs is thinkable"—this means that we can picture it to ourselves.

3.01   The totality of true thoughts is a picture of the world.

Propositions 3.02 through 3.0321 affirm that thought cannot be illogical. Each is a conceptual necessity.

3.04   If a thought were correct *a priori*, it would be a thought whose possibility ensured its truth.

3.05   *A priori* knowledge that a thought was true would be possible only if its truth were recognizable from the thought itself (without anything to compare it with).

Propositions 3.04 and 3.05 seem to imply that there are no a priori thoughts, since the latter would be logical pictures that did not picture. If, then, there are a a priori thoughts, and I think Wittgenstein thinks there are, they cannot be logical pictures of facts or objects but must be true as a necessary condition of the intelligibility of fact and object.

Proposition 3.1 introduces the term "proposition": "In a proposition a thought finds an expression that can be perceived by the senses." This means that:

3.11   We use the perceptible sign of a proposition (spoken or written, etc.) as a projection of a possible situation.

The method of projection is to think out the sense of the proposition.

Proposition 3.12 stipulates that we express thoughts with propositional signs. A proposition, thus, is a propositional sign projected onto the world; a proposition is this projection but not what is projected. A propositional sign is a fact, like a logical picture.

3.142   Only facts can express a sense, a set of names cannot.

3.1431   The essence of a propositional sign is very clearly seen if we imagine one composed of spatial objects (such as tables, chairs, and books) instead of written signs.

Then the spatial arrangement of these things will express the sense of the proposition.

The elements of the propositional sign correspond to the objects of the thought. These elements are simple signs.

3.202   The simple signs employed in propositions are called names.

3.203   A name means an object. The object is its meaning.

3.221   Objects can only be *named*. Signs are their representatives. I can only speak *about* them: I cannot *put them into words*. Propositions can only say *how* things are, not *what* they are.

3.23   The requirement that simple signs be possible is the requirement that sense be determinate.

I take this to mean that names and propositions require that there are simple objects combined into atomic facts. If this condition is absent, sense is indeterminate, therefore, nonsense.

3.25   A proposition has one and only one complete analysis.

3.251   What a proposition expresses it expresses in a determinate manner, which can be set out clearly: a proposition is articulated.

3.3   Only propositions have sense; only in the nexus of a proposition does a name have meaning.

Wittgenstein sums up 3.12 through 3.41:

3.5   A propositional sign, applied and thought out, is a thought.

Proposition 4 offers another definition of thought: "A thought is a proposition with a sense."

4.001   The totality of propositions is language.

We now have an identity of logical pictures of fact with thoughts, propositions, and language. Wittgenstein has so ordered things that our language about the world consists of thoughts that are propositions as logical pictures of facts. As stringent as his identification is, it is founded on the conditions of the object, fact, and exactitude. That there are propositions, thoughts, logical pictures, and language presupposes that there simple objects and atomic facts. These latter guarantee the characterizations and analyses of logical picture, thought, proposition, and language; they are not inferences from logical picture, etc. They are needed to get language off the ground and hence cannot be derived from Wittgenstein's picture theory of language. Much of the threes, then, is logical syntax of the language of science—the only language there is. This logical syntax is not nonsense; rather, it is a set of propositions that have sense as they depend on the ideal syntax of any language.

The fours deal with language, traditional philosophy, what Wittgenstein takes philosophy to be, the rule of projection, propositions as pictures, truth and falsity, the logical constants, showing and saying, formal and proper concepts, variables, elementary propositions, names, truth-possibilities, tautologies and contradictions, and the general propositional form, among other topics. My major concern is whether any of the fours are with sense, without sense, or nonsense.

Propositions 4 and 4.001, which define proposition and language, seem more like stipulations than they do like logical pictures: They are not *sinnlos*. Are they *sinnig*? Not according to Wittgenstein's stringent notion of *sinnig* or *Sinn*. Yet, they are not *unsinnig* either. They function, as I have suggested, as part of a whole identification: A logical picture is a fact; thought is a logical picture, thought is a proposition with a sense; language is the totality of propositions, thoughts, logical pictures. Here is philosophy as stipulation, not as clarification.

Traditional philosophy consists for the most part as nonsensical questions and answers that arise from failure to understand the logic of our language. It is to be replaced by a clarification of thoughts or propositions.

4.113   Philosophy settles controverseries about the limits of natural science.

4.114   It must set limits to what can be thought; and in doing so, what cannot be thought.

4.115   It will signify what cannot be said, by presenting clearly what can be said.

Are Wittgenstein's description of traditional philosophy and his diagnosis of its failure correct? If they are, his observations must be true. How can they be true on his conception of a true proposition?

Even if Wittgenstein replaces traditional philosophy by clarification and clarification is an activity, not a body of doctrine, 4.113 through 4.115 are, nevertheless, propositions, normative or descriptive. Are they nonsense, without sense or, as they serve in the *Tractatus*, with sense? Once again, Wittgenstein's conception of sense is bursting at the seams.

What, now, about the rule of projection?

4.014   A gramophone record, the musical idea, the written notes, and the sound-waves, all stand to one another in the same internal relation of depicting that holds between language and the world.

4.0141   There is a general rule by means of which the musician can obtain the symphony from the score, and which makes it possible to derive the symphony from the groove on the gramophone record, and, using the first rule, to derive the score again. . . . And that rule is the law of projection which projects the symphony into the language of musical notation. It is the rule for translating this language into the language of gramophone records.

Propositions 4.014 and 4.0141 are impeccable. But the problem is the same: These remarks are correct, so they are true; so they cannot be nonsense. Are they scientific propositions, or are they philosophical propositions about the logical syntax of the language of music and, by implication, of the language of science?

Propositions about the logical syntax of a language are not the same as propositions about the logical syntax of any language. Even so, both are legitimate, although neither are propositions as logical pictures of facts. Ideal logical syntax and the actual logical syntax of the language of science ought to make us wary as we approach Wittgenstein on his conception of a proposition.

4.021   A proposition is a picture of reality; for if I understand a proposition, I know the situation that it represents. And I understand the proposition without having had its sense explained to me.

4.022   A proposition *shows* its sense.

           A proposition *shows* how things stand *if* it is true. And it *says that* they do so stand.

4.023   A proposition must restrict reality to two alternatives: yes or no.

           In order to do that, it must describe reality completely.

           A proposition is a description of a state of affairs.

4.024   To understand a proposition means to know what is the case if it is true.

4.04   In a proposition there must be exactly as many distinguishable parts as in the situation that it represents.

           The two must possess the same logical (mathematical) multiplicity.

4.06   A proposition can be true or false only in virtue of being a picture of reality.

4.064   Every proposition must *already* have a sense: it cannot be given a sense by affirmation. Indeed its sense is just what is affirmed.

4.1   Propositions represent the existence and non-existence of states of affairs.

4.11   The totality of true propositions is the whole of natural science (or the whole corpus of the natural sciences).

4.12   Propositions can represent the whole of reality, but they cannot represent what they must have in common with reality in order to be able to represent it — logical form.

Each of these propositions from 4.021 through 4.12 is said. They raise the question, who is saying them: the traditional philosopher, Wittgenstein the philosopher, Wittgenstein as natural scientist or linguist, Wittgenstein as nonsensemonger, or what? If any or all of them are true, how can they be unless propositions about the logical syntax of our language comprise a number of descriptive and normative truths about language and specifically the propositions that constitute it? It is my contention that it is Wittgenstein the philosopher who asserts these propositions, which are (mostly) about the logical syntax of the language of science.

Again, who is speaking when Wittgenstein distinguishes between a formal and a proper concept?

4.126   When something falls under a formal concept as one of its objects, this cannot be expressed by means of a proposition. Instead it is shown in the very sign for this object.

4.1271 Every variable is the sign for a formal concept.

4.1272 Thus the variable name '*x*' is the proper sign for the pseudo-concept *object*.

Wherever the word 'object' ('thing', etc.) is correctly used, it is expressed in conceptual notation by a variable name. . . .

Wherever it is used in a different way, that is as a proper concept-word, nonsensical pseudo-propositions are the result.

Object, complex, fact, function, number (what about thought?) are all formal concepts. When used otherwise, nonsense results.

Here, too, I think, if we are to preserve the distinction between formal and proper concept, these remarks must be taken to be propositions, not pseudo-propositions, about the logical syntax of our language. Thus, that one function of philosophy is to formulate and clarify the logical syntax of our language, under the criteria of the ideal logical syntax of any language, is inviolate. These are truths and must be taken to be such by Wittgenstein the philosopher and must not be dismissed as nonsense (as they are in 6.54). They have *Sinn*, so sense is larger than Wittgenstein's articulation of it. In any case, these remarks about formal and proper concepts cannot be construed as inferential ontological claims about the world.

What about elementary propositions? Wittgenstein introduces these in the following propositions.

4.21   The simplest kind of proposition, an elementary proposition, asserts the existence of a state of affairs.

4.211   It is a sign of a proposition's being elementary that there can be no elementary proposition contradicting it.

4.22   An elementary proposition consists of names. It is a nexus, a concatenation, of names.

4.221   It is obvious that the analysis of propositions must bring us to elementary propositions that consist of names in immediate combination.

That elementary propositions are intelligible only if they are buttressed by simple objects and states of affairs or atomic facts, which are the necessary condition of their being elementary, is given in:

4.2211   Even if the world is infinitely complex, so that every fact consists of infinitely many states of affairs and every state of affairs is composed of infinitely many objects, there would still have to be objects and states of affairs.

Both elementary propositions and states of affairs have 2^n possibilities of truth and falsity for the first and possibilities of existence and nonexistence for the second (4.27-4.28).

Truth-possibilities can be expressed by a truth table (4.31).

These truth-possibilities of the elementary propositions are the conditions of the truth and falsity of propositions (4.41).

For n elementary propositions there are 2^{2^n} possible groups of truth-conditions (4.45).

4.46   Among the possible groups of truth-conditions there are two extreme cases.

In one of these cases the proposition is true for all the truth-possibilities of the elementary propositions. We say that the truth-conditions are *tautological*.

In the second case the proposition is false for all the truth-possibilities: the truth-conditions are *contradictory*.

In the first case we call the proposition a tautology; in the second, a contradiction.

4.461   Propositions show what they say: tautologies and contradictions show that they say nothing.

4.4611 Tautologies and contradictions are not, however, nonsensical. They are part of the symbolism, just as '0' is part of the symbolism of arithmetic.

4.462 Tautologies and contradictions are not pictures of reality.

4.466 Tautology and contradiction are the limiting cases — indeed the disintegration — of the combination of signs.

These propositions about tautologies and contradictions are also about truth-conditions and truth-possibilities. The tautologies and contradictions are *sinnlos*. What about the claim that they *are sinnlos*? Is it *sinnlos*? Does Wittgenstein show that tautology and contradiction show what they say — nothing? Or does Wittgenstein state that tautology and contradiction show what they say — nothing? It seems to me that he states it as well as shows it. The characterization of logical tautologies and contradictions is true, where other characterizations, for example, the Platonic, are false. Wittgenstein, then, has described the logical syntax of the language of logic. A necessary condition for his having done this is that there are elementary propositions that correspond to the existence and nonexistence of states of affairs. Logic mirrors reality all right, but reality is not an inference from logic; it is a presupposition of logic, of its tautologies and contradictions. Logic may be able to take care of itself, but it could not if there were no conditions of its truth or falsity, where these conditions revolve around simple objects and states of affairs or atomic facts.

The fives begin with:

5 A proposition is a truth-function of elementary propositions.

Much of the fives is an explication of 5 and, through 5, an explication of its implications. Given p and q, for example, we can specify sixteen combinations of them, ranging from tautology to contradiction (5.101). Wittgenstein introduces the concept of truth grounds of a proposition:

5.101 I will give the name *truth-grounds* of a proposition to those truth-possibilities of its truth-arguments that make it true.

He then clarifies the notion of a proposition that follows from another proposition.

5.11 If all the truth-grounds that are common to a number of propositions are at the same time truth-grounds of a certain proposition, then we say that the truth of that proposition follows from the truth of the others.

5.12 In particular, the truth of a proposition 'p' follows from the truth of another proposition 'q' if all the truth-grounds of the latter are truth-grounds of the former.

5.122 If p follows from q, the sense of 'p' is contained in the sense of 'q'.

5.124 A proposition affirms every proposition that follows from it.

Further, there are no separate laws of inference.

5.132   If p follows from q, I can make an inference from q to p, deduce p from q.

5.133   All deductions are made *a priori*.

Inferences hold not between elementary propositions but only between non-elementary propositions, and not between facts.

5.135   There is no possible way of making an inference from the existence of one situation to the existence of another, entirely different situation.

5.136   There is no causal nexus to justify such an inference.

5.1361   We *cannot* infer the events of the future from those of the present.

Belief in the causal nexus is *superstition*.

5.1362   The freedom of the will consists in the impossibility of knowing actions that will lie in the future.

These propositions, 5.132 through 5.1362, raise the question of the range of inference. Wittgenstein says inference is present only in the relation between non-elementary propositions, not in any relation among facts. That it is present among these propositions is, I think, a straightforward bit on the logical syntax of the language of logic. But what of absence of inference from facts? What kinds of claims are those that deny a causal nexus that would justify inference from one fact to another? Are they ontological claims, or are they, too, part of the logical syntax of the language of logic? Are they inferences from the inferential relation between q and p? None of these seems right. "There is no causal nexus" and "the belief in a causal nexus is superstition" seem to be putatively true claims. How can they be when they are not logical pictures of facts? Once again, Wittgenstein's view of proposition and language is too narrow to encompass what he wants to say. Perhaps the ontological disclaimer of a causal nexus is an inference from Wittgenstein's metaphysics regarding the independence of states of affairs from each other, in which case 5.136 follows from 2.061: "States of affairs are independent of one another." If so, we have another striking case of a proposition, in this example, the denial of a causal nexus, being an inference from a metaphysical claim, that states of affairs are independent of one another. It follows that we do not infer from our language to the world; rather, we infer from the world to our language.

The second important topic of the fives is that of probability. Here is Wittgenstein's definition:

5.15   If T_r is the number of the truth-grounds of a proposition 'r', and if T_{rs} is the number of the truth-grounds of a proposition 's' that are at the same time truth-grounds of 'r', then we call the ratio $T_{rs}:T_r$ the degree of *probability* that the proposition 'r' gives to the proposition 's'.

This definition makes probability a relation among propositions, not a character of a single proposition.

5.153   In itself, a proposition is neither probable nor improbable. Either an event occurs or it does not: there is no middle way.

Wittgenstein's conception of probability is more than a stipulation, as can be seen from his implied rejection of at least one theory, that probability is a feature of single propositions. What, then, is the status of his claim about probability: Is it with sense, without sense, or senseless? It purports to be a truth about probability, but it cannot be such on Wittgenstein's notion of propositional truth. Is his definition of probability also founded on an ideal syntax of any language, or is it perhaps a report on the logical syntax of the language of science? It does not seem to rest on the metaphysical conditions for there being a language, namely, objects and facts. So, if it is informative, as it surely must be for Wittgenstein, his definition is another bit on the logical syntax of the language of science. His remarks on probability are very much like his remarks on the logical constants: There are no special objects peculiar to either (5.1511).

What pertains to the concept of probability holds, I think, for Wittgenstein's next topic in the fives, the notion of an operation. Wittgenstein characterizes it by laying down, once again, the logical syntax, this time, of "operation." Here, there is nothing metaphysical or ontological. All that is involved is that our language allows certain deductions. How is it done? By operation, Wittgenstein says.

5.23   The operation is what has to be done to the one proposition in order to make the other out of it.

This remark, and the others attending it (5.21-5.41), are all observations on the logical syntax of our language, especially as this syntax pertains to the structure of internal relations among different propositions (5.2). Wittgenstein, this time as Tractarian philosopher, explicates one of the rules that generate propositions from other propositions in our present language.

Proposition 5.32 offers another bit of the logical syntax of our actual (not ideal) language:

5.32   All truth-functions are results of successive applications to elementary propositions of a finite number of truth-operations.

Related to Wittgenstein's remarks on operation is his rejection of any hierarchy of propositions in logic.

5.454   In logic there is no co-ordinate status, and there can be no classification.

In logic there can be no distinction between the general and the specific.

Nor can there be in logic anything self-evident (5.4731).

The general proposition form $[\bar{p}, \bar{\xi}, N\,(\bar{\xi})]$ is the essence of a proposition (5.471).

This gives us:

5.4711   To give the essence of a proposition means to give the essence of all description, and thus the essence of the world.

What is the essence of the world?—that it satisfies the necessary conditions of any world: simple objects combined in atomic facts or states of affairs. What is the essence of all description?—that it consists of a complete list of true elementary propositions (4.26). What is the essence of a proposition?—that it is a logical picture of a fact, a set of names with a sense. Thus, the essence of the world determines the essence of all description, including the essence of the proposition; not the other way round, that the essence of the proposition determines the essence of description, which determines the essence of the world.

Another topic of the fives is identity. Here, too, Wittgenstein rejects one theory of identity and promotes another.

5.53   Identity of object I express by identity of sign, and not by using a sign for identity. Difference of objects I express by difference of signs.

This, too, I believe, is a bit of logical syntax of our language. It purports to be a truth about identity and at the same time the rejection of others' falsehoods about identity. But it is a putative truth about that part of language that employs "identity"; it is not a truth about the world, except that the sign of identity shows that it functions like the logical constants and probability in their having no correspondence in the world.

The final topic of the fives that throws light on the question I have been raising about the status of the remarks in the *Tractatus* is that of limits: the limits of language and of the world and its relation to solipsism and realism.

Wittgenstein begins with 5.6: "*The limits of my language* mean the limits of my world." As I pointed out earlier, the claim as it stands violates Wittgenstein's strictures about fixing a meaning to introduced signs and reveals his failure to do this with "my." But, now, suppose we do fix the meaning of "my," what kind of claim is 5.6? Is it deduced from the logical syntax of the language of science, from the ideal syntax of any language, or from the identity of language with the totality of thoughts or propositions as logical pictures of facts? None of these possibilities seems to fit. Perhaps 5.6 is an implicate from the metaphysical presuppositions of the ones and twos about objects and states of affairs: the limits of the world; i.e., all the objects and states of affairs that there are mean all the names and elementary propositions that there are. But this will not work either because these limits are also beyond my experiences, even if they may not be beyond my comprehension of such a world of concatenated objects.

Wittgenstein seems to provide an answer in 5.61: "We cannot think what we cannot think; so what we cannot think we cannot *say* either." The limits of what I can say are the limits of what I can think. But what I can think must be what I can think, not the limits of my world, unless these limits are the same as my thoughts. Thus, 5.6 remains inexplicable. It is not nonsense or with sense, and it does not appear to be without sense either. If it is not a stipulation, as I think it is not, what kind of proposition is it? It claims to be a truth about my language and my world. But how to legitimize this claim, even as a claim, not as a true or false claim, baffles one. Nothing seems to work. It is neither a priori nor a posteriori, neither sayable nor showable. And yet he uses it to explicate solipsism.

5.62   This remark provides the key to the problem, how much truth there is in solipsism.

For what the solipsist *means* is quite correct; only it cannot be *said*, but it makes itself manifest.

The world is *my* world: this is manifest in the fact that the limits of *language* (of that language which alone I understand) mean the limits of *my* world.

This gives us "the world is *my* world" as *sinnlos*, but it does not yield "the limits of that language which alone I understand mean the limits of *my* world" as *sinnlos*. Is solipsism, then, the view that the world and my world are the same or the view that the limits of my world are the same as the limits of that language that I alone understand? I cannot find Wittgenstein's answer.

But, of course, there is no answer because 5.62 is absurd, and not for reasons given in the *Investigations* against such a "private" language, but for two reasons given in the *Tractatus*. (1) Language is taken to be the totality of propositions (4.001) and the totality of true propositions is the whole or natural science; it is egregious, if not downright absurd, to identify this only language with a language that I alone understand. (2) Even if the limits of my language mean the limits of my thoughts, propositions, logical pictures, it cannot mean, on Wittgenstein's own definition of logical pictures, the limits of my world, since my world includes what the logical pictures are pictures *of* and that cannot be part of my logical picture, my language. Proposition 5.62 remains the worst, perhaps the one real, piece of nonsense in the *Tractatus*. It is, therefore, incredible that so many readers have found 5.62 profound when it is so obscure and, I think, truly incoherent within the boundaries of the *Tractatus*.

5.621   The world and life are one.

Can this be taken seriously? For Wittgenstein, it is nonsense unless it is without sense. It certainly is not with sense (*sinnvoll*, *sinnig*). In fact, it is another putatively true (or false) claim, even though it is not a logical picture. But it is questionably false if it is construed as an ontological assertion.

5.63   I am my world. (The microcosm.)

This seems harmless as, indeed, does:

5.632   The subject does not belong to the world: rather, it is a limit of the world.

Whether either is true or not is another question. But at least 5.63 and 5.632 are with sense in a way that 5.6 is not. The next proposition asks:

5.633   Where *in* the world is a metaphysical subject to be found?

Wittgenstein answers nowhere, which implies, for him, that solipsism coincides with realism.

5.64   The self of solipsism shrinks to a point without extension, and there remains the reality co-ordinated with it.

What is of interest here is Wittgenstein's denial of the self as a findable entity. His argument is Hume's, except that for Hume this was an empirical discovery, which it cannot be for Wittgenstein unless the philosopher can proclaim the discovery of certain facts. And Wittgenstein should not end the fives as he does:

5.641   The philosophical self . . . is the metaphysical subject, the limit of the world—not a part of it.

The sixes begin with:

6   The general form of a truth-function is $[\bar{p}, \bar{\xi}\, N\,(\bar{\xi})]$. This is the general form of a proposition.

6.001   What this says is just that every proposition is a result of successive applications to elementary propositions of the operation $N\,(\bar{\xi})$.

In the sixes, Wittgenstein returns to his characterization of the propositions of logic.

6.1   The propositions of logic are tautologies.

6.113   It is the peculiar mark of logical propositions that one can recognize that they are true from the symbol alone, and this fact contains in itself the whole philosophy of logic.

6.12   The fact that the propositions of logic are tautologies *shows* the formal—logical—properties of language and the world.

6.121   The propositions of logic demonstrate the logical properties of propositions by combining them so as to form propositions that say nothing.

6.1222   Not only must a proposition of logic be irrefutable by any possible experience, but it must also be unconfirmable by any possible experience.

6.124   The propositions of logic describe the scaffolding of the world, or rather they represent it. They have no 'subject-matter'. They presuppose that names have meaning and elementary propositions sense; and that is their connexion with the world. It is clear that something about the world must be indicated by the fact that certain combinations of symbols—whose essence involves the possession of a determinate character—are tautologies. This contains the decisive point. We have said that some things are arbitrary in the symbols that we use and that some things are not. In logic it is only the latter that express: but that means that logic is not a field in which *we* express what we wish with the help of signs, but rather one in which the nature of the natural and inevitable signs speaks for itself. If we know the logical syntax of any sign-language, then we have already been given all the propositions of logic.

Wittgenstein concludes his account of the propositions of logic:

6.13   Logic is not a body of doctrine, but a mirror-image of the world.

Logic is transcendental.

Mathematics consist of pseudopropositions, as a series of equations, none of which expresses a thought (6.2-6.21).

6.22   The logic of the world, which is shown in tautologies by the propositions of logic, is shown in equations by mathematics.

Proposition 6.31 introduces Wittgenstein's philosophy of science.

6.31   The so-called law of induction cannot possibly be a law of logic, since it is obviously a proposition with sense. —Nor, therefore, can it be an *a priori* law.

6.32   The law of causality is not a law but the form of a law.

6.33   We do not have an *a priori belief* in a law of conservation, but rather *a priori knowledge* of the possibility of a logical form.

6.34   All such propositions . . . are *a priori* insights about the forms in which the propositions of science can be cast.

6.341   Newtonian mechanics, for example, imposes a unified form on the description of the world. Let us imagine a white surface with irregular black spots on it. We can then say that whatever kind of picture these make, I can always approximate as closely as I wish to the description of it by covering the surface with a sufficiently fine square mesh, and then saying of every square whether it is black or white. In this way I shall have imposed a unified form on the description of the surface. The form is optional, since I could have achieved the same results by using a net with a triangular or hexagonal mesh. . . . The different nets correspond to different systems for describing the world.

6.343   Mechanics is an attempt to construct according to a single plan all the *true* propositions that we need for the description of the world.

6.35   Laws like the principle of sufficient reason, etc. are about the net and not about what the net describes.

6.36   If there were a law of causality, it might be put in the following way: There are laws of nature.

But of course that cannot be said: it makes itself manifest.

Let us pause and reflect on the sixes discussed thus far. Wittgenstein's discussions of logical and mathematical propositions or pseudopropositions are, I think, integral parts of the logic syntax of the language of logic and mathematics. His discussion of the propositions of science as either net-talk or nature-talk leaves us with great difficulties, especially about his univocal description of the propositions of science. Are all of them logical pictures of facts, reducible to elementary propositions about objects and their presence in states of affairs, where there is no difference between empirical and nomological generalization? Are all the laws of science univocally describable as nets imposed upon the empirical propositions of science? I have already asked whether these remarks about the net are with sense, without sense, or nonsense? Wittgenstein suggests that talk about the nets is without sense (*sinnlos*). Nets show or manifest themselves. Do nets show themselves in their axiomatic nature or in their application to the specific propositions of science? The laws of science may be read as a priori axioms, but that they impose on actual descriptions of the world does not render them *sinnlos*, at least in the way that logical tautologies are rendered *sinnlos*—by a row of T's in the truth table of the respective tautology. There may be laws about science, capturable in Wittgenstein's talk about the net or nets of science, but there must be laws in science if there is to be science at all. Wittgenstein's relegation of talk of laws in science as talk about the nets, not about the world, hardly does justice to the richness and diversity of the nature and language of the sciences themselves.

6.373 says: "The world is independent of my will." As empirical as this looks, it is not an empirical or even an ontological remark but a consequence of his view that the only necessity is logical.

It also follows from his view about necessity that the presence of two colors at the same place in the visual field is impossible—logically impossible. From which it further follows for him that propositions about colors cannot be elementary since the logical product of two elementary propositions can be neither a tautology nor a contradiction.

6.41   The sense of the world must lie outside the world. In the world everything is as it is, and everything happens as it does happen: *in* it no value exists—and if it did, it would have no value.

There are, then, no propositions of ethics. Further, ethics, being transcendental, cannot be put into words. Wittgenstein embroiders this theme of what is in as against what is outside the world and sums up:

6.4312   The solution of the riddle of life in space and time lies *outside* space and time.

6.52   We feel that even when *all possible* scientific questions have been answered, the problems of life remain completely untouched. Of course there are then no questions left, and this itself is the answer.

6.521   The solution of the problem of life is seen in the vanishing of the problem.

Wittgenstein concludes with his statement of the correct method in philosophy: to distinguish between science and philosophy and to identify science with what can be said and *some* metaphysics with what can only be shown. The rest of metaphysics is the nonsense of introducing terms or signs without fixing their meanings (6.53). His own propositions are also nonsense to be thrown away after we have used them, with the result that we will then "see the world aright."

7   What we cannot speak about we must consign to silence.

In spite of the nonsense of enjoining us to climb a ladder with no horizontal rungs and no vertical side pieces and aside from the injustice Wittgenstein practices on his own diversity of nonsense presented in the *Tractatus*, there is actually very little nonsense in the *Tractatus*. There is nothing nonsensical about the metaphysical assumptions that serve as the necessary conditions of the very intelligibility of language and the world: that there are simple objects and states of affairs. Nor are the implicates from these presuppositions nonsense. Indeed, both, as I have tried to show, are a priori substantial, nontautological truths of the highest, most fundamental order. Moreover, his clarification of the logical syntax of the language of logic and of mathematics is not nonsense. Nor is his philosophy of science, especially his talk about the a priori, optional nets of science. And, of course, his stipulation cannot be nonsense since they involve the fixing of the meanings of certain terms.

The only glaring piece of nonsense in the *Tractatus* is, I believe and have tried to argue, his remarks on the limits of "my" language meaning the limits of "my" world.

On the whole, then, the *Tractatus* is a grand amalgam of the ideal syntax of any language; the logical syntax of the language of logic, mathematics, and science; what can be shown but not said, which is without sense but not nonsense. The basic thrust of the book is metaphysical, not ontological or even logical. It is the search for the conditions of the intelligibility of discourse; it is not even remotely the search for the essences of things that can be inferred from the language of science, logic, or mathematics. Logic, as Wittgenstein says, may mirror the world, but the world reflects the metaphysical necessary conditions, not the language, of the world. What makes the *Tractatus* the great book it is is its overarching metaphysics—its concern for what there must be if there is to be anything, even if there were nothing. This thesis retains its perennial plausibility in a way that Wittgenstein's theories of logic, mathematics, science, and language itself do not. It may very well be that the central problem of philosophy—what Ryle used to characterize as what is proprietary to philosophy—is this metaphysical one. To have posed it, as most philosophers have not, is his grandest achievement in the *Tractatus* and will ensure its originality and importance when all his theories of language and the nature and language of logic, mathematics, and science and even traditional philosophy have been rightly forgotten.

Old Analyses of the Physical World and New Philosophies of Language

RICHARD FUMERTON

INTRODUCTION

In this paper I wish to reexamine two historically prominent analyses of the physical world in the light of recent developments in philosophy of language, developments that suggest a new metaphilosophical conception of the nature of philosophical analysis. The two analyses of the physical world that I will discuss are the causal theory and phenomenalism. Although there are all kinds of variations on each approach, the two views have been traditionally thought of as diametrically opposed. Phenomenalism is now almost universally held in disrepute. But I will argue that unless one accepts certain contemporary views in philosophy of language, the most plausible version of the causal theory is as vulnerable as phenomenalism to the argument widely viewed as laying phenomenalism to rest. Because I believe the new philosophy of language is radically mistaken and further believe that either the causal theory or phenomenalism is correct, my ultimate aim is to persuade these longtime foes that they have a vested interest in finding a common solution to a common problem.

The paper is organized as follows. In Part I, I will offer a preliminary sketch of a causal theory of the external world. After raising the metaphilosophical problem of distinguishing philosophical analysis from scientific analysis, I suggest one classical conception of what philosophers are doing in offering a causal theory of the external world and sketch what I think is the most plausible version of a causal theory within that framework. In Part II, I consider and reject the new views in philosophy of language that would allow one an alternative conception of what the causal theorist was doing in providing his or her theory, and I emphasize one important consequence of rejecting the new philosophy of language for the causal theorist. In Part III, I sketch phenomenalism and the argument that has historically been taken to be most decisive as an objection to phenomenalism and go on to show how the argument is equally telling against the causal theory.

PART I

The causal theorist sometimes roughly characterizes his or her view as simply the view that in veridical perception physical objects are the causes of our sensations. One historically prominent variant of the view was representation realism. The representative realist held that in veridical perception our sensations in some sense *represent* the physical objects that are their cause. Most representative realists have been sense-datum theorists and have held that the representation consists in some kind of correspondence between the properties exemplified by sense data and properties exemplified by the physical objects that are their cause. They have held, for example, that in veridical perception of a red, round ball there would be a sense datum that was round and the roundness of the sense datum would in some sense represent the roundness of that ball, the presence of which caused the red, round sense datum. This sort of representation presumably would consist in the sense datum and the physical object sharing the same or similar properties. (Since many of the early representative realists accepted a primary/secondary quality distinction, the *redness* of the sense datum would not be said to represent the redness of the object in the same way that the shape of the sense datum would represent the shape of the ball.) I will discuss representative realism in more detail shortly. I mention it here primarily to emphasize that it is just one version of a causal theory of physical objects. As we will see, there are others.

Historically, both proponents and critics of the causal theory of physical objects have often discussed the analysis without having made clear their metaphilosophical conception of analysis. In suggesting that physical objects are the causes of our sensations or that in veridical perception the physical object that we take to be there is an important link in a causal chain that results in a sensation, the causal theorist is, on one interpretation, making a claim with which almost no philosopher would disagree. Anyone who is not a radical skeptic with respect to the existence of physical objects believes that when you seem to see a table that sensation is usually caused, at least in part, by the presence of a table. The *phenomenalist* who explicitly rejects the causal theory is going to end up agreeing that tables are sometimes the partial cause of sensations of tables.

The causal theorist is concerned with answering such questions as (1) what are physical objects? and (2) what is involved in veridical perception of a physical object? The most obvious answer to the second question, outside of a philosophical context, is probably an answer that identifies the intricate causal chain that proceeds from a physical object to the stimulation of various sense organs and culminates in either neural or mental activity (depending on whether the dualist or the identity theorist is right). The most natural answer to the first question, outside of a philosophical context, is one that would take you from molecular and atomic structure to the nethermost regions of the microworld and the more exotic universe of electrons, protons, quarks, and the like. These are obviously perfectly appropriate answers to questions (1) and (2); yet they are answers that, even in these days of naturalistic philosophy, are likely to disappoint most philosophers who take seriously the classical problems of perception. But, if the traditional causal theorist was not interested in providing scientific answers to these questions, we must find another interpretation of what it is he or she was doing.

One of the ways some twentieth-century analytic philosophers have tried to distinguish metaphysical questions from scientific questions is to construe metaphysical questions as questions concerned with the meanings of certain statements. The philosopher who takes this approach would immediately suggest a more perspicuous reformulation of questions (1) and (2): (1a) what is the meaning of statements asserting the existence of physical objects? and (2a) what is the meaning of a statement asserting of a subject that he or she actually (veridically) perceives a physical object? Such a metaphilosophical interpretation of what philosophers were doing (perhaps only implicitly since this metaphilosophical view was rarely explicitly accepted) fits rather nicely the writings of at least some historically prominent causal theorists. Descartes, for example, clearly endorsed the causal theory of objects as an adequate analysis of our conception of veridical perception, even when he purported to be skeptical with respect to the existence of physical objects and veridical perception.

If the causal theorist is construed as offering a meaning analysis, then a more accurate, though still very rough, characterization of his or her position would be that statements asserting the existence of physical objects are analytically equivalent to statements asserting the existence of certain causes of sensations. The proposition that there is a table before me now, for example, is to be understood as equivalent in meaning to a proposition asserting the existence of an object causally responsible for the occurrence of certain sensations. Similarly, the representative realist must also be construed as making a claim about the *meaning* of statements asserting the existence of physical objects. The representative realist understands a statement asserting the existence of the table in terms of a statement asserting the existence of an object causing and *represented by* certain sensations. When we distinguish causal theories as meaning claims from causal theories as empirical claims, the causal theories become, of course, much more controversial. Let me try to develop within this metaphilosophical conception of analysis what I take to be the most plausible version of a causal theory of objects, and let me begin by making an important distinction.

The reader may have already noted that I have used the relatively unfamiliar locution "causal theory of objects" in place of the more well known locution "causal theory of perception." The two philosophical views are quite independent despite the fact that they can easily be and often have been confused. As I use the expression, a causal theory of perception is a view about the correct analysis of veridical perception. If philosophical analysis is meaning analysis, it is a view about the meaning of statements having the form, S perceives X (where "X" is a name, an indefinite or a definite description that is such that, if it denotes, it denotes a physical object). *Roughly* stated, a causal theory of perception holds that S perceives X iff S has a sensation that is caused (in part) by the presence of X. In attempts to rule out certain sorts of deviant causal chains the analysis invariably becomes more complex.

Note that the causal theory of perception leaves completely *open* the correct analysis of the proposition that there is a table in front of me. Again, a *phenomenalist*, despite the fact that he or she is often represented as diametrically opposed to the causal theory of perception, can quite consistently embrace the causal theory of perception as an analysis of propositions asserting the occurrence of veridical perception and at the same time embrace a phenomenalistic analysis of propositions asserting the existence of physical objects.

If philosophical analysis is meaning analysis, then a causal theory of physical objects, in contrast to a causal theory of perception, is a view about the meaning of statements asserting the existence of physical objects. *Roughly* stated, a causal theory of physical objects holds that statements asserting the existence of physical objects are analytically equivalent to statements asserting the existence of certain causes of sensations. Thus, a crude causal theory of physical objects might hold that the statement that there is a table before me now is equivalent to the statement that there exists before me now that which under certain conditions produces the sensations of seeming to see, feel, etc., a table. The filling out of the "certain conditons" clause gives one different versions of a causal theory of physical objects. In what follows I will be concerned only with causal theories of physical objects.

I indicated earlier that representative realism was just one version of a causal theory of objects, and this will be true however one construes the nature of philosophical analysis. Before I discuss an alternative to thinking of philosophical analysis as meaning analysis, I want to suggest some respects in which representative realism might be one of the more implausible versions of a causal theory of objects. There are three main objections that might be raised against representative realism. One is epistemological in character; the other two question the very intelligibility of the theory.

One historically prominent criticism of a causal theory of physical objects is that such a theory inevitably leads to skepticism. Berkeley is probably the best example of a philosopher who made such a claim, and, because Berkeley took as absurd the suggestion that we do not know the world around us, he rejected the causal theory of physical objects. Berkeley considered a number of different causal theories of objects and claimed with respect to all that, even if they were intelligible, they would lead to skepticism. It is obvious, however, that, whatever problems there are in finding justification for beliefs about the physical world on a causal theory of objects, these problems would be exacerbated on that version of a causal theory that is representative realism. To oversimplify somewhat, the more properties one requires the cause of certain sensations to have in order to be a physical object veridically perceived, the harder it is to justify one's belief that there are physical objects. To justify *his or her* belief in the existence of a table, the representative realist not only must establish that there exists that which has the power to produce certain sensations, he or she must also establish that the cause of these sensations is represented by them. But how would one even go about justifying one's belief that the cause of a certain sensation exemplifies the same properties as the sensation (or some element in the sensation) when all one is ever directly acquainted with are the contents of one's sensations. As Hume argued so eloquently, we are certainly not going to establish the claim through enumerative induction.[1] Since the British empiricists and the radical positivists who came after seemed at least to accept implicitly the view that the only legitimate kind of nondeductive reasoning is inductive reasoning, many reached the conclusion that representative realism leads inevitably to skepticism.

I think one must hesitate before accepting the above argument. First, it is not all that obvious that skepticism is false, and, besides, it is probably foolish to reject an analysis of the physical world on the grounds that induction is the only legitimate nondeductive reasoning; and induction will not get you knowledge of the representative realist's physical objects. *If* induction is the only source of nondeductive inference, I doubt we are going to have justification for believing anything beyond the content of our present sensation, *whatever* analysis we accept of physical objects. Specifically, it seems obvious that induction will never get one knowledge of the past. This would be a particularly unpleasant development for the philosopher who sanctions only inductive and deductive inference, for knowledge of the past is presumably necessary to get the premises from which one can inductively infer conclusions. In short, if induction is the only legitimate sort of nondeductive reasoning, we will never be able to use it. In any event, I think it is a mistake to press epistemological objections to representative realism, for the arguments that question the intelligibility of the view have more force.

The first argument I have in mind is very much a product of the twentieth century, and, unfortunately, it is an argument I cannot discuss in any detail because it rests on a rejection of the sense-datum theory, a theory I cannot do justice to in the space available here. The representative realist defines physical objects in terms of those causes of sensation that exemplify at least some of the same properties as the objects (sense data) with which we are directly acquainted. If we reject the sense-datum theory, however, we will not have the mental analogues of physical objects to share properties with physical objects. To embrace representative realism with an adverbial or appearing theory of sensation, one would have to hold either that minds exemplify the defining properties of physical objects (such properties as color, extension, etc.), or one would have to weaken the concept of representation. The first alternative seems to me unintelligible, and the second only slightly more plausible. Representation, for example, could be defined in terms of a one-to-one correspondence or an isomorphism between the features of ways of being appeared to and their causes. But, if this is to result in a view significantly different from classical representative realism, the concept of isomorphism must become so weak that it is hard to see how it places much, if any, restriction on what cause of sensation can count as a physical object. The above objection to representative realism is, of course, no stronger than arguments against the sense-datum theory, but, even if one were to accept the existence of mind-dependent sense data, it is not clear that one can make sense of classical representative realism, for there is a much older objection questioning the intelligibility of the view.

The representative realist claims that physical objects are the causes of sense data and exemplify at least some of the same properties as sense data. But which properties? Is the shape of the physical object represented by the shape of a visual sense datum or the "shape" of a tactile sense datum. And, indeed, as Berkeley argued, even if we restrict our attention to one mode of sensing, which of the many shapes of the indefinitely many sense data produced by a physical object is the shape the physical object must have.[2] The representative realists were sensitive to such problems, and that is why so many rejected the idea that the secondary qualities (colors, smells, tastes, etc.) of objects are represented in the same way that the primary qualities are. But again, as Berkeley argued so convincingly, the so-called primary qualities exemplified by sense data are no less subject to perceptual relativity than are the secondary qualities. Our reasons for rejecting straightforward representation between the former and the properties of physical objects are reasons for rejecting straightforward representation between the latter and the properties of physical objects.

The representative realist, the critic maintains, was in the grips of a powerful but ultimately misleading metaphor. The mind was a tabula rasa upon which the objects of the physical world left their imprint. The metaphor was, however, just that, a metaphor. There are simply too many qualitatively different "prints" left on the tabula rasa to allow for a nonarbitrary definition of a physical object as that which is represented by any one of the prints. And, if representation consists in exemplifying the same properties, it is contradictory to suppose that the many different "prints" all represent the same property of a physical object. I think this objection to representative realism is telling, and in what follows I will focus on those versions of a causal theory of physical objects that attempt to define physical objects as the causes of certain sensations without making reference to the nonrelational properties of such causes. One of the earliest statements of such a view was put forth by Hylas in the course of his steady retreat from representative realism.[3] Before trying to make more precise a version of such a view, however, I wish to consider that alternative conception of philosophical analysis to which I alluded in my introduction, a conception of philosophical analysis that would allow us to interpret what the classical causal theorists were doing in a quite different way.

PART II

Since Kripke's "Naming and Necessity,"[4] many philosophers appear to have forsaken meaning for reference. Crudely, put, the idea is that for many terms there is no more to the meaning of an expression than its referent. One can end up referring in one of three ways. In a few very rare cases, when one's access to the thing in question is immediate, one can, so to speak, fix the label directly on the thing. This use of a name would seem to correspond closely to Russell's conception of a logically proper name. Such privileged access to a thing is the exception, and it is important to realize that it is there only as long as the object is. As soon as we become separated from our referent in space or time, our access will presumably become indirect. How is "indirect" reference achieved? Well, one can "fix the reference" of ordinary proper names and names of so-called natural kinds using definite descriptions, where the referents of the respective terms are the individuals and "kinds" denoted by the definite descriptions. Or, one's use of proper names or common nouns can have a certain causal origin, where the referents of the respective terms are the individuals or "kinds" that figure in some important way in these causal origins. On either of these last two ways of coming to refer, one could clearly be using the respective terms to refer without knowing to what one is referring. One can use the definite description "the cause of sensation S" to fix the reference of "heat,"[5] for example, without having the slightest idea what is the cause of sensation S. Similarly, one's use of the expression "electron" can have a certain causal origin that determines its referent—a natural kind—without one's having the slightest idea what that causal origin is. This view rather naturally suggests an alternative to the conception of philosophical analysis as meaning analysis. Specifically, it suggests the view that in at least some cases the only kind of philosophical "analysis" one can perform is the attempt (a) to discover the referents of certain fundamental expressions and (b) to describe as clearly as possible the nature of these referents.[6]

A proponent of the above theory of language, who also took seriously the view that our access to the physical world is *indirect*, obviously would be tempted to claim that the expressions we use to talk about the physical world get their life through reference-fixing definite descriptions involving causal claims and the relevant causal chains initiated through the use of such reference-fixing definite descriptions. More specifically, just as Kripke suggested that we could understand "heat" as an expression introduced through the reference-fixing description "the cause of sensation S," so he could hold that "table" was introduced in the language in terms of some set of reference-fixing definite descriptions, for example, "the kind of thing that causes my seeming to see and feel a table." There is a sense in which such a view could be called a causal theory of physical objects, but the proponent of the view will stress that he or she is not claiming that talk about tables is equivalent in *meaning* to talk about the causes of certain sensations. Definite descriptions purporting to denote the causes of certain sensations give our talk about the physical world life. It is through a connection to such definite descriptions that we can understand talk about the physical world, but we do not view these definite descriptions as *synonymous* with the expression whose "life" in a language is parasitic upon them.

It would be "nice" if this new philosophy of language were plausible, for it would make the task of the philosopher grappling with the traditional metaphysical problems of perception so much easier. The advantages of having the concept of "reference fixing" are in many ways like the advantages of having the older Wittgensteinian concept of a nondefining criterion. In both cases, one can make claims about conventional "connections" between expressions and avoid having to worry about counterexamples that rest on claims about what can or cannot be conceived. A proponent of a causal theory of objects would no longer be committed to finding necessary and sufficient conditions for the truth of statements about the physical world. The most he would have to do is come up with some definite descriptions that could plausibly be construed as explicitly or implicitly fixing the reference of physical object terms and perhaps sketch some causal chains that account for the meaningful use of such expressions by people who do not have at their disposal relevant reference-fixing descriptions. Given the concept of fixing reference these philosophers have, one would not even need to suppose that different people who "speak the same language" use the same definite descriptions in "fixing the reference" of terms referring to physical objects. According to these philosophers, I might fix the reference of "table" by using the definite description "the kind of thing that is causing the visual sensation I'm having now" and you might fix the reference of "table" by using the definite description "the kind of thing that is causing the tactile sensation I had yesterday morning at ten o'clock" and henceforth, by virtue of the common denotation of our reference-fixing definite descriptions, we can "mean" the same thing by table.

The new philosophers of language, then, present us with an alternative to the metaphilosophical conception of philosophical analysis as meaning analysis. It would, I think, be foolish to ask which conception of philosophical analysis the historically prominent causal theorists endorsed. Seventeenth- and eighteenth-century philosophers obviously are not going to have had any explicit views on twentieth-century controversies. The most we can reasonably do is determine which conception of what they were doing the classical causal theorists ought to have endorsed.

Despite the fact that the concept of fixing reference could work many wonders as far as dissolving traditional philosophical problems of perception, there is, I am convinced, one rather important difficulty facing the new philosophers of language. Put simply, the difficulty is that the critical concept of fixing reference is unintelligible. There is no difference between giving an expression the meaning of a definite description and using a definite description to fix the reference of an expression. To support this claim I appeal to a thought experiment. For simplicity, I will focus on the idea of fixing the reference of a name referring to an individual, but my remarks will apply mutatis mutandis to the idea of fixing the reference of terms referring to kinds of things. (It is the latter that would be required to carry out the task of understanding physical object terms as terms whose reference is fixed by definite descriptions purporting to denote the causes of certain sensations.)

Imagine the following situation. Two philosophers, R and K, come up to you and each tells you he is about to introduce a new term into the language. R tells you that he is going to use the term "Alpha" and give it the *meaning* of "the tallest man in America at t" (where t is the name of some particular time), and K tells you that he is going to use the term "Alpha*" and is going to fix its reference by using that same definite description. K warns R that, in general, it is a mistake to think of a name as having the same meaning as a definite description, but R assures K that, be that as it may, *he* wants "Alpha" to have the same meaning as the definite description "the tallest man in America at t." Without in a sense knowing about whom they are talking, K and R proceed to make statements using the expressions they have introduced.

Now, if there is a distinction between giving "Alpha*" the meaning of "the tallest man in America at t" and fixing its reference by using that description, I presume it is a difference that ought to *make* a difference. There ought to be *some* statement that K can make using "Alpha*" that will have different truth conditions (or that will at least strike us as asserting something different or conveying different information) than the corresponding statement that R makes substituting "Alpha" for "Alpha*." But what could such a statement be?

R says to me, "Alpha is taller than you are," and K says, "Alpha* is taller than you are," and I suppose I understand both of them, but only because I understand both of them as asserting precisely the same thing, namely, that the tallest man in America at t is taller than I am. I will view their statements as conveying the same information about the world and as having precisely the same truth conditions. Note that I am not here concerned with the causal theory of reference per se, only that aspect of it connected with the introduction of a term by reference fixing. Consequently, in performing this thought experiment, I want you to consider those who can only use the term because they have fixed its reference by using a definite description (i.e., ignoring those who may succeed in referring because their use of the term is causally connected to the use of the term by others who *have* fixed its reference). It seems clear to me that as long as we confine our attention to purely extensional contexts it will be hopeless to try to illustrate the difference between giving a name the meaning of a definite description and fixing its reference by using a definite description.

The same applies to intentional complexes. K believes that Alpha* is taller than I am, and R believes that Alpha is taller than I am. Surely, *what* they believe is precisely the same thing; there is but one intentional object of their respective beliefs. In what sense could K believe that Alpha* is taller than I am but not believe that the tallest man in America at t is taller than I am (or vice versa). If we were present at the reference-fixing ceremony for "Alpha*" and we heard the man who fixed the reference of "Alpha*" using the definite description "the tallest man in America at t" announce that he believed that Alpha* probably worked in a circus but did not believe that the tallest man in America at t worked in a circus, we would be confused in precisely the same way that we would be confused if a man told us that by "P" he just meant "Q" and went on to affirm P while he denied Q.

But perhaps we should not have expected either extensional or intentional contexts to reveal the distinction, for it is primarily in modal contexts that the new philosophers of language try to illustrate the difference.

In considering the use of "Alpha" and "Alpha*" in modal contexts, it is crucial that we distinguish between de dicto and de re modality. That there is a distinction I take to be uncontroversial, though it is an open question as to whether either sort of modality can be analyzed in terms of the other. Consider the following two statements:

(1a)   The bachelor next door might have been married by now (had he, for example, been more pleasant to his girlfriend.

(1b)   It might be that the bachelor next door is married.

Now, despite the fact that there are serious difficulties involved in providing a philosophical analysis of (1a), there are contexts in which it would strike most of us as a relatively unproblematic and obviously true assertion. Roughly, it asserts of an individual who is identified by means of a certain property that he need not have, might not have had that property. Statement (1a) is a statement of de re possibility. Statement (1b) would strike us as contradictory. We would assume that the person making the statement either misunderstood the meaning of "bachelor" or was trying, in an inappropriate way, to say what (1a) says. Statement (1b) is a statement of de dicto possibility. It asserts (falsely) of a given proposition that it might be true. I do not, of course, intend to analyze either de dicto or de re necessity here. It is enough for my present purposes that we acknowledge that there are statements of necessity and possibility de re and that (1a) in most contexts would strike us as a relatively unproblematic example of a true statement of de re possibility.

Let us now examine the respective uses of "Alpha" and "Alpha*" in statements of de re possibility, for I think that those who embrace the concept of fixing reference mistakenly think that it is in such context that they can make clear the distinction between giving a name that meaning of a definite description and fixing its reference by using a definite description. Consider the following statements.

R says:

(2a)   Alpha might not have been the tallest man in America at *t*, if his older and bigger brother hadn't died at the age of three.

K says:

(2b)   Alpha* might not have been the tallest man in America at *t* if his older and bigger brother hadn't died at the age of three.

Now, (2a) might strike one as involving a contradiction if "Alpha" just means the same as "the tallest man in America at *t*," but it clearly involves a contradiction only if one perversely understands it as asserting a de dicto rather than a de re possibility. There is nothing odd or unusual (let alone contradictory) about the statement you get by substituting for "Alpha" in (2a) "the tallest man in America at *t*":

(2a*) The tallest man in America at *t* might not have been the tallest man in America at *t* if his older and bigger brother hadn't died at the age of three.

The new philosopher of language often suggests that it is a sign of a *name* that it is used as a *rigid designator*, by which he or she means that a name can be used to talk about an individual in all possible worlds (in less flamboyant terminology, in any counterfactual situation). But, if this view is meant to imply that a definite description (or expression equivalent in meaning to a definite description) cannot be used as a rigid designator, i.e., cannot be used to refer to an individual in all counterfactual situations, the view is false. One can use a definite description, "the *F*," to pick out an individual and to assert counterfactually of him or her that, had certain conditions obtained, he or she would not have been *F*. That is just what the definite descriptions in (1a) and (2a*) do.[7]

One cannot, therefore, explain the difference between giving a name the meaning of a definite description and fixing the reference of a name by using a definite description by pointing out that (2a) and (2b) have different truth conditions. Where (2a) is a statement of de re possibility, it can be viewed as unproblematically true. What about statements of de dicto necessity? Consider the following.

(3a)   Necessarily, Alpha (if he exists) is the tallest man in America at *t*.

(3b) Necessarily, Alpha* (if he exists) is the tallest man in America at t.

I suppose that one who thinks that the notion of fixing reference is intelligible may argue that (3a) is true while (3b) is false. But I cannot think of what would justify such an assertion. As I have already suggested in connection with intentional contexts, if someone introduces the expression "Alpha*" and tells me that he or she is using it to pick out the tallest man in America (whoever that may be) and then tells me that it might not be the case that Alpha* is the tallest man in America, I would be completely at a loss as to how to understand his or her use of the expression "Alpha*."

In trying to give sense to the concept of fixing reference, one might appeal to modal contexts in yet another way. The proposition that Alpha* is F, one might argue, would be about the same individual in all possible worlds, whereas the proposition that Alpha is F would be about different individuals in different possible worlds. This suggestion seems no less question begging than the above, however. Everything rests on our criteria for identifying propositions through possible worlds. If K introduces "Alpha*" in this world in the way I described, when Jones is the tallest man, "Alpha*" will pick out Jones. If in $P2$ K introduces "Alpha*" *in the same way* when Smith is the tallest man, "Alpha*" will pick out Smith. Kripke and company would deny that the statement "Alpha*" is F" in this world expresses the same proposition as the statement "Alpha* is F" in $P2$, but one would find this denial plausible only if one were antecedently convinced that there exists a referential magic wand capable of transforming an unknown individual into a constituent of the thought expressed by a given statement.

The expression "fixing reference" is a technical philosophical expression that must be given meaning. Finding out what it is not supposed to mean is not finding out what it does mean. I very much fear that a rather large number of philosophers are allowing an expression that has no sense to come into their philosophical vocabulary. If you think that there is a difference between fixing the reference of an expression by using a definite description and giving a name the meaning of a definite description, then you should be prepared to give an example of a statement in which substitution of "Alpha" for "Alpha*" would alter the truth-value or at least the sense of the statement. There are no such examples.

I conclude that a proponent of a causal theory of physical objects has no alternative to the admittedly painful task of trying to find analytical equivalence between statements asserting the existence of physical objects and statements asserting the existence of the causes of certain sorts of sensations. We would be doing the classical causal theorists a disservice if we reconstructed their views as presupposing the incoherent notion of fixing reference.

There is one extremely important consequence of rejecting reference-fixing definite descriptions as that which enables us to talk meaningfully about the physical world. If one is committed to a program of *defining* physical objects as the causes of sensations, one obviously cannot include in the definition reference to anyone's *actual* sensations. Such a view would be as absurd as the crudest form of idealism. No part of what we mean by asserting the existence of a physical object can be captured by a statement asserting the existence of a cause of someone's actual sensations, for that would make the occurrence of those sensations a logically necessary condition for the existence of the physical object. The very concept of a physical object is that of an object whose existence is logically independent of the existence of conscious beings and their sensations. (The reference fixers, of course, *could* use definite descriptions that refer to actual sensations in order to fix the reference of physical object terms, for they are not committed to finding synonymy.)

If the causal theorist cannot define physical objects as the causes of certain actual sensations, in which direction should he or she move? Subjunctive conditionals beckon, and, despite all the dangers, I believe the causal theorist has no alternative than to move in that direction. If one is to reduce talk about the physical world to talk about the existence of things causally connected to sensations or patterns of sensations, it must be in terms of statements that assert the existence of that which *would* under certain conditions produce certain sensations or patterns of sensations.

The fact that the causal theorist must turn to subjunctive conditionals in providing his or her analysis of physical object statements is interesting, for there is, of course, another historically important analysis of physical object propositions famous for its reliance on subjunctive conditionals. I refer, of course, to classical phenomenalism. The wary philosopher should already be alert to the possibility that objections raised against phenomenalism (often by causal theorists) might eventually come back to haunt the causal theorist. In fact, I think this is just what happens.

PART III

By classical phenomenalism I mean the view according to which propositions asserting the existence of physical objects are analytically equivalent to propositions that assert that a subject would have certain sequences of sensations were he or she to have certain others. Berkeley occasionally hinted at the view, but the first consistent presentation of it was John Stuart Mill's.[8]

With the benefit of hindsight, I think we can see classical phenomenalism as an inevitable outgrowth of the evolution in philosophical thought initiated by the skeptical concerns Descartes expressed in the early *Meditations*. Convinced (usually by some version of the argument from illusion or hallucination) that the only way to justify a belief in the existence of physical objects (thought of as enduring, mind-independent entities) is to infer their existence from the occurrence of fleeting and subjective experience and further convinced that only deduction or induction is available as a means of bridging the gap between knowledge of sensation and knowledge of the physical world, some radical empiricists and early positivists presented phenomenalism as the only alternative to a radical skepticism. If propositions about the physical world are equivalent in meaning to assertions about what sensation or sequence of sensations a subject would have were he or she to have certain others, then the truth or falsity of such propositions would be mind independent in the way in which the truth or falsity of propositions about the physical world is mind independent; but, at the same time, to the empiricist's great relief, it looks as though such propositions could be established inductively. Subjunctives that assert connections holding between sensations can presumably be justified without having to correlate anything but sensations.

The idea behind phenomenalism was, in the abstract, enormously attractive for many philosophers, but difficulties arose in the attempt to make it more concrete. Philosophers, understandably, grew impatient with vague sketches of the general form a phenomenalistic analysis should take and wanted specific examples of conditionals that could adequately capture the meaning of some ordinary assertion about the physical world. As soon as the phenomenalist tried to give even one example of a conditional that constitutes a partial analysis of the meaning of a proposition about the physical world, the door was open to the argument from perceptual relativity. The argument was so devastating that singlehandedly it almost cleared the philosophical community of phenomenalists.

Many philosophers have endorsed the argument from perceptual relativity, but the first, clearest, and most concise version of it was presented by R. M. Chisholm.[9] Chisholm offers, in effect, a strategy for attacking any phenomenalistic analysis. The first move in the strategy is to force the phenomenalist into giving at least one example of an alleged analytic consequence (expressed in phenomenal language) of a proposition asserting the existence of some physical object. When one gets the example, one simply describes a hypothetical situation in which, though the physical object proposition is true, its alleged analytic consequence would obviously be false. If the physical object proposition really did entail the experiential proposition, then there could be no hypothetical situation in which the one is true and the other false, and so we would have constructed a reductio of the proposed analysis. C. I. Lewis, for example, claims[10] that the proposition that there is a doorknob in front of me and to the left (P) entails the proposition that, if I should seem to see such a doorknob in front of me and to the left and if I should seem to be initiating a certain grasping motion, then in all probability the feeling of contacting a doorknob would follow (R). Chisholm argues that P does not entail R, for there is another proposition Q (the proposition that I am unable to move my limbs and my hands but am subject to delusions such that I think I am moving them; I often seem to myself to be initiating a certain grasping motion, but, when I do, I never have the feeling of contacting anything), which is obviously consistent with P and which when conjoined with P entails not-R. When we understand why the argument works in this case, we should realize that all phenomenalistic analyses are equally vulnerable to this kind of objection.

How will we generalize a description of the problem facing a phenomenalist? The problem is, I think, intimately connected with the nature of contingent subjunctive conditionals. The vast majority of contingent subjunctive conditionals we assert are not such that their antecedents are nomologically *sufficient* for their consequents.[11] When we assert a contingent subjunctive conditional, we usually presuppose a *context*, and the most we are claiming is that there exists some set of conditions X (we may have very little idea what X is) such that the antecedent of our conditional together with X leads nomologically or logically to the consequent. The subjunctive conditionals the phenomenalist wants to employ in his or her analysis all seem to be context dependent in just the above way. It would, no doubt, be true to assert *in some contexts* that, if I were to seem to see a table and seem to reach out and touch it, then I would seem to feel it—indeed, such a conditional is presumably usually true when I am standing in front of a table under relatively normal conditions. The antecedent of this conditional, however, is obviously not nomologically sufficient for its consequent. If the conditional is true, it is true because there exists some set of conditions X such that the antecedent together with the statement of these conditions leads nomologically to the consequent. We all take at least some of these conditions, however, to be *independent of the existence of the table*. Thus, we assume that X involves reference to the internal and external conditions of perception, conditions that are neither logically nor causally connected to the existence of the table. It is for this reason that one can imagine *contexts* in which the conditional would be false even though the proposition asserting the existence of the table would be true. Since the truth of phenomenal statements will always depend on contexts logically independent of the physical object proposition the phenomenalist is trying to analyze, his or her project is doomed to failure.[12]

In an effort to escape this argument, the phenomenalist might try to "protect" the conditionals he or she employs in his or her analysis with a "normal conditions" clause added to the antecedents. When I believe that there is a doorknob in front of me now, part of what I believe is that, if I were to seem to reach out and touch it *and the causally relevant conditions of perception are normal*, then I would seem to feel it. One might argue that this analysis would survive Chisholm's counterexample, for the hypothetical situation he describes is not one in which the causally relevant conditions are normal.

At this point, however, the nonphenomenalist is obviously going to complain that the phenomenalist has violated his or her own criterion for an adequate phenomenalistic theory by referring to something beyond the experientially given. He or she will claim that the normal conditions referred to in the antecedent of the subjunctive conditional can only be facts about the physical world (the internal and external conditions surrounding perception). The phenomenalist, the critic continues, must be prepared to substitute for "normal conditions of perception" an adequate phenomenalistic analysis (presumably, more conditionals describing the sensations a subject would have were he or she to have others) of the conditions that are in fact normal. This he or she will never be able to do, for each conditional or conjunction of conditionals that is designed to eliminate some distorting condition of perception will fail to do so precisely because it itself is susceptible to additional distorting conditions.

The argument from perceptual relativity certainly seems to reveal a serious problem facing the classical phenomenalist. It is important to realize, however, that it is a problem that also faces the causal theorist who tries to define physical objects solely in terms of their nomological relations to sensations. I have already argued that the causal theorist cannot *define* a physical object as the cause of any actual sensation, for that is incompatible with our concept of a physical object as logically independent of the existence of conscious beings. The only alternative I could suggest was to turn to subjunctive conditionals. To say that there is a red, round physical object in front of me now might be to say that there exists that which *would* under certain conditions produce certain sensations, for example, the visual sensation of seeming to see something red and round. But let us examine this suggestion more carefully. Two questions immediately arise, one more obvious than the other. The obvious question concerns the interpretation of the "under certain conditions" clause. The less obvious question involves difficulties relating to the fact that the concept of cause fails to uniquely denote some one of many different causally relevant conditions. Let me consider the latter problem first.

We, in fact, believe that sensations are the end product of a very long and enormously complex causal chain. Most often we assume that a table is one critical link in the causal chain that results in my seeming to see a table, but it is no more critical than the change that takes place in the retina of the eye or the changes that take place in certain regions of the brain. Indeed, if our commonsense beliefs are correct, the table is in one sense less critical than the occurrence of certain brain states in producing the sensation of seeming to see a table, for one can produce the sensation without a table but cannot produce it without the relevant brain state.

If the causal theorist defines the red, round object simply as that which would produce under certain conditions a sensation of seeming to see something red and round, it seems that, in the hypothetical situation that reflects our actual beliefs, the image on the retina or the brain state each has as good a claim to being the table as anything farther removed in the causal chain leading to the occurrence of the sensation.

The obvious way out of this difficulty is to define the red, round object in such a way as to "triangulate" in on that which would be the *common* link in a number of different causal chains leading to the occurrence of different sensations. Thus although we cannot define the red, round object as the thing that would cause under certain conditions my seeming to see something red and round, we might be able to define the red, round object as the thing that would under certain conditions cause a sensation of seeming to see something red and round and would under certain conditions produce a sensation of seeming to feel something red and round. The concept of a physical object is the concept of that which would be the common link in a number of different causal chains leading to the occurrence of a number of different sensations. So far, so good. But we must now address the first of the questions referred to above, the question concerning the interpretation of the all-important "under certain conditions" clause.

The causal theorist we are considering here is committed to a program of *defining* propositions that assert the existence of physical objects in terms of propositions that assert the existence of "possible" causes of sensation. The causal theorist, consequently, can no more *replace* the "under certain conditions" clause with a description of internal and external *physical* conditions of perception than can the phenomenalist. Yet, *without* the protecting clause the causal theorist is even more vulnerable to the argument from perceptual relativity than is the phenomenalist. The round object cannot be defined simply as that which would result in certain visual sensations, for we can trivially conceive of it being the case (we all believe that it often is the case) that there is a round object there even though it would not produce a sensation of seeming to see a round object—there might be no one there to see it, it might be too dark, the person who is there might be blind, and so on. To make it less obvious that he or she is vulnerable to this objection, the causal theorist might borrow a leaf from the phenomenalist's book. We cannot, of course, define a round object simply as that which would produce a sensation of seeming to see a round object. We must, instead, understand the physical object as that which would produce certain sensations, provided that there was a subject having certain other sensations. The round object can be understood, for example, as that which would produce a tactile sensation of feeling something round if there were a subject who had the visual sensation of seeming to see something round and had the visual and kinesthetic sensations of seeming to initiate a certain grasping motion. Such a move might raise the plausibility of the causal theory to the level of classical phenomenalism, but it would, of course, fare no *better* than classical phenomenalism against the argument from perceptual relativity. The concept of a round physical object is at best the concept of that which would produce a certain tactile experience following the appropriate visual and kinesthetic sensations *under certain conditons*. And the causal theorist, like the phenomenalist, is prohibited from describing these conditions by using physical object language on pain of circularity.

It is important to realize, I think, that, even if considerations of circularity did not prohibit replacing the "under certain conditions" clause required by both the phenomenalist and the causal theorist with an exhaustive description of the causally relevant internal and external conditions of perception, it obviously would be a mistake to do so. The ordinary concept of a physical object clearly should not be defined even in part by reference to physiological conditions of perception, many of which are just now being discovered and most of which have never even been thought of by ordinary people. The vast majority of us know next to nothing about the operation of light waves, sense organs, and neural processes. In asserting the existence of a table, we are surely not asserting anything about what would occur if light waves were reflecting off the surface of an object striking optic nerves and producing alpha waves in the brain. Most of the people of this world have never even heard of light or alpha waves but have the same concept of a table that we have.

If I am right, phenomenalism and the causal theory are equally in need of a solution to problems generated by perceptual relativity. And this really should not be that surprising, for from the very start the two views had more in common than many philosophers seem to realize. Both views, after all, are committed to understanding talk about the physical world by relating it to what can be given in experience. On both views, it is predicate expressions referring to the qualitative character of sensations that carry the burden of the cognitive content of a physical object proposition, that distinguish the analysis of one physical object proposition from another. And, indeed, on both views, the concept of nomological connection plays a critical role. The causal theorist, of course, makes overt reference to causation, and the phenomenalist's contingent subjunctive conditionals make implicit reference to nomological connections.

I suspect that we face a new age of causal theorists armed with a new philosophy of language. There is, I think, considerable irony in the fact that, without the protection of a mistaken view of language, the new causal theorists must cope with the very objection that most everyone has taken to be decisive against phenomenalim.

Notes

1. *A Treatise of Human Nature*, ed. L. A. Selby-Bigge (London: Oxford University Press, 1967), Book I, Part IV, Sec. II, p. 212.

2. See Berkeley's *Three Dialogues between Hylas and Philonous* (Indianapolis: Bobbs-Merrill, 1954), p. 60.

3. *Op. cit.*, p. 60.

4. "Naming and Necessity" in D. Davidson and C. Hartman, eds., *Semantics of Natural Languages* (Dordrecht: D. Reidel, 1972).

5. Kripke gives this example in "Naming and Necessity."

6. Some would take (b) to be the task of discovering the essential properties of these referents.

7. In "Kripke on Proper Names," Peter A. Finch, Theodore E. Uehling, Jr., and Howard K. Wettstein, eds., *Midwest Studies in Philosophy*, Vol. II, *Studies in the Philosophy of Language* (Morris: University of Minnesota, Morris, 1977), pp. 64-69; B. A. Brody makes the same point in rejecting an argument Kripke appears to give against Russell's theory of ordinary names.

8. *An Examination of Sir William Hamilton's Philosophy* (London, 1865), Chapter 11.

9. "The Problem of Empiricism" in R. Swartz, ed., *Perceiving, Sensing and Knowing* (Garden City, N.Y.: Doubleday, 1965).

10. In *An Analysis of Knowledge and Valuation* (LaSalle, Ill.: Open Court, 1962), p. 240.

11. Although it sounds a little odd, it is convenient to speak of the antecedent (a linguistic item) of a conditional being, or not-being, nomologically sufficient for its consequent. I will say that one linguistic item P is nomologically sufficient for another Q if there is a law of nature L such that $(P$ and $L)$ entails Q (when P alone does not).

12. This is, I believe, Sellar's diagnosis of the failure of phenomenalism in "Phenomenalism," *Science, Perception and Reality* (London: Routledge and Kegan Paul, 1963), p. 81.

Moral Crisis and the History of Ethics

J. B. SCHNEEWIND

The history of philosophy is not usually seen, in English-speaking circles, as a major tool for the resolution of philosophical problems. It is admitted to be useful for understanding classical authors. But it is not seen as offering direct aid in deciding whether their views are true or false. Still less is historical study taken to be a necessary step in analyzing current social and political problems. This commonplace stance is one of many challenged in Alasdair MacIntyre's original and wide-ranging book, *After Virtue*.[1] He believes that the history of moral philosophy is indispensable for understanding and criticizing any ethical theory, including those now current. He also holds that ethical theories mirror or articulate the actual moral structure of society and that problems in moral philosophy are inseparable from problems in moral life. Consequently, he thinks that the history of ethics must be understood if we are to improve the condition of society.

These are large claims. Their interest is increased by the extreme position MacIntyre takes about the theories and problems of our times. He sees current Anglophone ethics as obsessed with moralities of rule or principle and hopelessly mired in varieties of emotivism. These facts, he argues, reflect the extensive and deeply rooted moral malaise of our culture. Modern liberalism, and the individualism that infects both it and contemporary Marxism, are illnesses that have now become unendurable (AV viii). None of the current political approaches offers any hope. To find a cure for our ailment, we must first diagnose it properly. The diagnosis will show that we must abandon the views that dominate modern analytical ethics. We must return to a morality centered on the virtues and to the corresponding Aristotelian tradition of moral philosophy. At the end of his book, MacIntyre suggests, darkly, that our only hope is to work our way back to smaller, more unified kinds of community than we now have, in which lives structured by such a morality will be possible.

In backing these claims MacIntyre attributes a central role to historical argument. The main support for the virtue-centered theory elaborated in the latter half of the book is that it alone offers a proper way out of our present unhappy condition, and MacIntyre says that it is historical analysis that both reveals the nature of our present situation and shows us what the alternatives are. I do not believe that MacIntyre's positive theory can provide solutions to the problems he sees.[2] But in this paper I will examine only the line of reasoning through which he hopes to persuade us that we must accept that theory. I first examine it as a straightforward historical argument. I sketch a different way of looking at the history of modern ethics and indicate that it suggests a different analysis of our current moral situation than MacIntyre's. I then try to bring out some assumptions underlying MacIntyre's approach and to show that there is reason to doubt that his historical argument is what really carries the weight of his position.

I

MacIntyre tells us that both the language and the practice of morality in our times are in a state of "grave disorder" (AV 2) and that we cannot understand their condition unless we see the essential steps in the history that led to it. Two features distinctive of modern morality show that it is chaotic. One is the occurrence of numerous debates over important moral issues. The examples MacIntyre gives are controversies over what constitutes a just war, whether abortion is permissible, and the extent to which it is right to limit freedom to increase equality of opportunity. What is distinctive is not the extensiveness of the debate about these issues. It is that the arguments cannot be settled. A perfectly valid case can be made to support either side of any issue, but each case depends on premises the other side does not accept. And "the rival premises are such that we possess no rational way of weighing the claims of one as against the other." Hence, MacIntyre thinks, it is appropriate to say that the premises are "incommensurable." The second distinctive feature of our morality is that, while it is articulated in language that claims impersonal objectivity, its terms are, in fact, used manipulatively for private purposes. This reflects our inability to provide "unassailable criteria" for our selection of even our own moral premises (AV 8-9; cf. 38). And it leads MacIntyre to say that emotivism, although false as a theory of the meaning of moral language, is true of the way in which objective-sounding moral terms are actually used in our culture (AV 17). Thinkers of the emotivist persuasion—MacIntyre includes Hare, Sartre, and Nietzsche along with Stevenson—tell us that morality must always rest on arbitrarily chosen principles, and modern analytic philosophers have been quite unable to show that this is false. But both emotivists and their critics suffer from a crippling lack of historical perspective. This prevents them from seeing that, while emotivism is supported by our culture in a striking way, not every culture would have been accurately articulated by it. There was a time, MacIntyre holds, when authoritative rational justification for morality could be given and when its objective language provided genuine impersonal standpoints for judgment. Now, it seems, this is not so. History must tell us how we got from then to now.

The crucial events took place during a period that MacIntyre locates roughly between 1630 and 1850. It was then that "the project of an independent rational justification of morality" became and remained central not only to philosophy but "to Northern European culture" as well (AV 38). The end of the period is marked by Kierkegaard's decisive revelation that the project had failed. Kierkegaard shows us that no reason can be given for preferring the moral life to the aesthetic life: if one adopts either, one does so by making an arbitrary choice. But morality presents itself to us as that which claims our allegiance regardless of personal choice. So its authority cannot be explained by saying we just choose to be moral (AV 39-41). Kierkegaard was responding, MacIntyre says, to Kant, who was too sensitive to the distinctive claim of morality to try to found it on mere choice. Rejecting revealed religion and the pursuit of happiness as also unsuitable to ground morality, Kant tried to show that it springs from reason alone. It was the complete failure of his effort to show how the contents of morality can be derived from such a base that forced Kierkegaard into his position (AV 42-45). And Kant, in turn, was responding to the challenge posed by Hume and Diderot. They tried to "found morality on the passions" (AV 47) and failed, as Kant saw. All four of these thinkers held a common view of the substance of morality, which they shared with their culture. Hence, the collapse of their efforts shows that "the project of providing a rational vindication of morality had decisively failed; and from henceforward the morality of our predecessor culture—and subsequently of our own—lacked any public, shared rationale or justification" (AV 48).

We are not to suppose that this failure was a mere accident, that cleverer thinkers might have done a better job. The problem is intractable. It springs from the Enlightenment rejection of Aristotelianism in all its shapes. Briefly put, MacIntyre's analysis goes like this: On Aristotle's view, we humans have a *telos*, or goal, built into our nature. "Human" is therefore a function word, like "hammer." Function words pick out both physically identifiable characteristics of that to which they refer and criteria for the goodness of function of that sort of thing. Thus, the notion of "hammer" and that of "good hammer" are interdependent. And both the criteria identifying hammers physically and the criteria identifying their good functioning are, MacIntyre says, factual.

> Hence any argument which moves from premises which assert that the appropriate criteria are satisfied to a conclusion which asserts that 'this is a good such and such', where 'such and such' picks out an item specified by a functional concept, will be a valid argument which moves from factual premises to an evaluative conclusion (AV 55).

Thus, in a culture, such as the Christian culture of the West, which accepts a fundamentally Aristotelian framework of thought, rational vindications of morality are available. Morality is to be understood in terms of three notions: "untutored human nature, man-as-he-could-be-if-he-realised-his-telos, and the moral precepts which enabled him to pass from one state to the other." Moral injunctions in a Christian culture say both what God ordains and what will lead to realizing the individual end. Since "the whole point of ethics . . . is to enable man to pass from his present state to his true end," the function of moral judgments is simply "to correct, improve, and educate" human nature (AV 52). And they do this while stating what is factually the case.

Now, the project of giving a rational basis to morality, as the Enlightenment understood it, arose because the teleological concept of human nature was dropped, along with the rest of Aristotle. The problem then was to find a new way of connecting the moral rules with human nature. But for two reasons this had become impossible. First, the moral injunctions inherited from the past were meant to be *at odds* with human nature as it initially is, so dropping the notion that human nature is meant to be something else leaves a code of rules radically unsuited for a human nature understood in no such way. Second, these now "incoherent fragments" cannot be given the kind of grounding they once had. Abandon the idea of essential human functions, MacIntyre says, and "it begins to appear implausible to treat moral judgments as factual statements." And if, as Enlightenment thinkers did, one gives up the idea that morality is a matter of God's commands or laws, the problem is made much worse. Hume's famous discovery of the impossibility of drawing a legitimate inference from factual premises to a conclusion about what ought to be done is not, as it is commonly thought to be, the uncovering of a timeless law of logic. It merely reveals the problem that emerged for the Enlightenment due to the abandonment of teleological and religious beliefs and the "impoverished moral vocabulary" that was the upshot (AV 55-56).

This "transition into modernity," MacIntyre says, "was a transition both in theory and in practice, and a single transition at that" (AV 58). The breakdown of the Enlightenment project in philosophical ethics gives expression to the collapse of the moral framework and so begins to explain the condition of morality in our own culture. Our interminable disputes arise because we cannot make rational sense of the "series of fragmented survivals from an older past" that constitutes our morality. Where an Aristotelian theory could relate rules and ends perfectly well, we cannot. The deontological aspect of morality is for us merely "the ghost of conceptions of divine law which are quite alien to the metaphysics of modernity." The teleological aspect is no better than a remnant of the abandoned Aristotelian belief in a human nature with a given end. Bentham, who saw the need for a new account of the teleological side of morality, failed to help the situation, because the way he tried to solve the problem—by appeal to the greatest happiness—involved a "notion without any clear content at all" (AV 62). The intuitionism that arose in opposition to utilitarianism as an effort to explain the deontological side of morality was actually the move that led to emotivism. For intuitionism in its practice, as opposed to its rhetoric, is in fact emotivist (AV 14-17, 63). And recent neo-Kantian attempts to ground morality must also be accounted complete failures, as witness the hopelessness of Gewirth's central argument (AV 64-65). Once we realize, however, that modern morality is nothing but an "incoherent conceptual scheme which we have inherited" (AV 66) we will not be surprised that "the problems of understanding and assigning an intelligible status to moral judgments . . . prove inhospitable to philosophical solutions" (AV 104-5). An anthropologist, not a philosopher, is the sort of expert who might make the condition of morality in our culture comprehensible (AV 106).

MacIntyre concludes the first, diagnostic, part of his book with the claim that Nietzsche, more clearly and devastatingly than anyone else, revealed the incoherence of our morality. By showing that none of the accepted moral stances of Europe had any rational justification at all, he made it finally impossible to ignore the actual manipulative purposes served by high-sounding enunciations of principle. He went further: he claimed that no morality could have any justification. And here, MacIntyre believes, Nietzsche "illegitimately generalised from the condition of moral judgment in his own day to the nature of morality as such" (AV 107). He therefore posed the question that MacIntyre thinks we must now face. If Aristotelianism in ethics is rejected, as it was by the Enlightenment, then it seems as though we are compelled to accept Nietzsche's conclusion. So the "key question" is: "can Aristotle's ethics, or something very like it, after all be vindicated?" (AV 111). Instead of following MacIntyre in his construction of an affirmative answer to this question, I turn to an assessment of the diagnosis that, as he thinks, makes it necessary.

II

MacIntyre's sketch —it is, of course, meant to be no more—of the history of the collapse of morality is brilliantly conceived. It succeeds in making us see how we could understand our own culture as the natural concomitant of the conceptual shift involved in the rejection of Aristotelianism. It thus reinforces the descriptive diagnosis of our current condition with which MacIntyre begins. And that description, in turn, provides a focal point for a narrative that leads us to see it as an almost unavoidable outcome. If we are to assess MacIntyre's argument, we must separate his narrative of the past from his description of the present and examine them separately. How convincing, then, is his diagnosis of our current condition? As far as I can see, there are two lines of thought supporting MacIntyre's view, and neither of them seems compelling.

The first seems to be implicit in his repeated charge that the presence of interminable debates over moral issues shows that our morality is in grave disorder.[3] I suppose the idea here is the familiar Wittgensteinian one, that, if a language-bound practice like morality is to be in order, there must be agreement not only in definitions but also in judgments. But MacIntyre does not tell us in detail about how much disagreement can exist within a practice that is in good working order, though he suggests that a great deal can (AV 242). He does not advert to the extensive areas of agreement evident within ordinary morality. And, perhaps most strikingly for one with so historical an orientation, he never tries to compare the amount of disagreement in our culture with amounts in earlier times. I should have supposed, for example, that sixteenth-century debates about religious toleration and those about the duty to obey magistrates who ordered citizens to act against their consciences must have been, in MacIntyre's sense, interminable. But the morality of the sixteenth century, on his time scheme, is still "in order." So this line of argument, if MacIntyre means to suggest it at all, does not go very far.

The same is true for the more purely sociological discussions. That MacIntyre gives us an insightful and chilling version of one aspect of contemporary life no one can deny. His portrayals of the therapist, the aesthete, and the manager and his attacks on pretensions to social expertise speak to much of what is most worrisome in our times. But this is not followed by sociological data purporting to reveal the extent of the rot. For all that MacIntyre says, there might still be extensive areas of our common life—not merely of the life of surviving "premodern" groups—in which the uses of moral language remain in accord with the impersonal and objective meanings that he allows moral terms to possess. Would we, in fact, still have a common life or a common culture at all if this were not so? But if society has not wholly disintegrated, then the manipulative use of moral language can be explained as the natural and normal parasite on its nonmanipulative use; and the core areas of agreement can provide a model for the kind of settlement we hope to achieve where we currently disagree. There have, after all, been theories of morality—perhaps interpretable, in MacIntyrean fashion, as sociologies—that incorporate the facts of controversy and unsettleable differences of deep commitment into a vision of an ongoing moral community. MacIntyre mentions Berlin's version of this position but does not take it seriously enough to criticize it. The argument from contemporary behavioral patterns, like the argument from interminable debates, is thus inconclusive. The burden must be carried by MacIntyre's history.

III

What MacIntyre presents in his history of ethics is a study of the internal logic of its development rather than a narrative of its events. I have no objection to this way of viewing the past of moral philosophy. But I think that a different inner logic was at work in it. To break the powerful hold of MacIntyre's outline, I will indicate, very briefly indeed, the story I think is preferable.

It is a commonplace of intellectual history that the thought of the seventeenth and eighteenth centuries must be understood against the background of a deep, but deeply challenged, belief in God. God is purposeful, just, and good as well as omnipotent. He made the universe for a purpose, and every part in it has a purpose as well—a special function or role, a special contribution toward achieving the purpose of the whole. The *telos* He built into human nature is simply an instance of a general fact about created beings. It points out the special role we are to play in the cosmos. Natural laws structure this role for all created beings: inanimate objects have their laws, the lower animate beings have theirs, and we have ours—in a special way, because we alone in the world we know are guided through *consciousness* of our laws. Since God is just, He does not require us to do what we cannot do. So we must be able to know what we are to do, and we must be able to do it. Hence, every human has adequate instruction about the role that, qua human, he or she is to play in the cosmos. The laws of nature are written in our hearts or in our consciences. We may need special help in seeing how to apply them in complicated circumstances, but they provide a framework for common human life because we know that other humans have the same laws written in their hearts.

Now, given this general background, it is clear that the task for the moral philosopher or the theologian will not be one of the justification or vindication of morality. It will rather be one of explanation. The moral philosopher, in this period, is not sharply distinguished from the natural philosopher. Both seek the laws God built into his universe, and both show them to us, thereby revealing the order behind the apparent disorder of the world as we first see it. The laws are there and are recognized by everyone or will be once they are clearly articulated. The question of vindicating or justifying them has not arisen. Such a question arises only when there is a challenge to one's claim or a sheer absence of any conviction one way or another about it. That simply was not the situation facing the moralists of the period that concerns us. There was—as MacIntyre himself points out several times—consensus on what morality required, a consensus including Hume and Diderot (and Hobbes can be listed here, too). So the moral philosopher could explain what the laws of morality are—could, for instance, argue about whether they all reduce to one or whether several basic laws must be assumed—and could explain how it is that all of us receive adequate guidance from them—perhaps by knowing them, perhaps through feeling—but all of this is in aid of helping us to understand a moral world about whose existence we have no doubts.

A second important point arises from the fact that for the culture of our period the world is supervised by the Christian God. The religious understanding of morality leaves a place for the individual's search for earthly happiness and an even more central one for the personal quest for salvation, which is what the Aristotelian *telos* is transmuted into under Christianity. But it also requires that we see the individual as linked through divinely ordained laws to other individuals, and to other kinds of beings, in a vast collaborative venture. MacIntyre says that the Aristotelian scheme of morality—humans as they are, being guided by rules to what they are to be—is "complicated and added to but not essentially altered when it is placed within a framework of theistic beliefs" (AV 51). My own view is rather that the longstanding incorporation of the older teleological tradition into the Christian framework is a matter of central importance. For a grasp of the logic of the relations of rules and ends in the special kind of collaborative endeavor Christianity sees us engaged in is indispensible for an understanding of the development of the moral philosophy of the period. I will try to explain this briefly, using the notion of cooperation to bring out the essential points. This notion is not fully appropriate for every stage of the history that concerns us, but it will do here as a rough first approximation.

Cooperation involves the division of labor. To divide up work is to accept the idea that each agent in a common venture has a special job or station. Performing the duties of that station is the agent's primary responsibility. It is only the joint or appropriately successive performance by all the agents of their duties that will produce the good at which the cooperative endeavor aims. Thus, no agent has a task properly described as producing the good. Consequently, in a well-run venture, no one has any business going beyond the assigned duties of his or her station. Those duties have at least a prima facie absolute deontic status just because of their functioning within a complex teleological enterprise. In ordinary cooperative ventures it is, of course, easy to see reasons for overriding the prima facie absolute status of one's duties. I may doubt the wisdom of the assignment of duties; I may see that someone else is failing to do a job without which mine would be pointless or harmful; I may note an opportunity to save everyone a lot of trouble by taking advantage of an unpredictable lucky break. In all such cases, of course, I must fully understand the good we are all trying to bring about and know a fair amount about how everyone else's contribution fits in. Otherwise, I would not be in a position to reason directly from my understanding of the goal to a decision about the means.

Now, in the strongest form in which we understand God's governance of the world, individual humans are never in the position I have just described. We do not understand God's glory, the goal of cosmic cooperation; we cannot challenge the wisdom, or the fairness, of His assignment of duties; we know that His providence and His omnipotence will make up for any failings by any of the imperfect agents we see; and in any case we have no idea of what the other parts of the universe are really meant to be doing or of how they contribute to the goal. Hence, for us our duties must always have an absolute deontic status, although—as Butler points out— God may well be utilitarian and may understand the laws of morality in that sense. If we weaken some of these assumptions about God and His governance, we can see a tension develop between deontology and teleology. Suppose the aim of the enterprise is human happiness, rather than cosmic displays of God's glory: then we can begin to understand the goal. Suppose God no longer intervenes in particular cases in the world: then we cannot be sure He will make up for failures by our fellows; then each of us has some degree of responsibility to see to it that the end is indeed brought about by doing our duty. The absolute deontic status is gone; we are required, morally, to judge to some extent by results. Thus, the inner logic of a cooperative venture carries us toward utilitarianism as an explanation. But there is a countervailing pull toward "intuitionism," that is, toward reassertion of the absolute deontic status of moral demands, for it is essential in this special cooperative venture—since it is a just one, given its Creator—that everyone be equally able to be aware of what is demanded. If morality demands that each agent figure out what is for the best in each case, it is extremely difficult to see how this can be maintained. But on the assumption that intuitive truths are equally available to everyone, or that moral feelings are, we can maintain the justice of the cooperative venture by arguing that everyone is aware of dictates that are deontically absolute.

I think this dynamic helps us understand many of the actual positions of eighteenth-century moralists, and it carries us to further developments as well. God's role may be taken over by Nature (as MacIntyre notes, AV 217) if we think that Nature has so constructed us that our sentiments will coordinate our actions toward a common good and that our own happiness will be found in the course of so acting. But if Nature, too, becomes unavailable to play this role, the problems of morality begin to take on a new shape. For if we live in a neutral universe, not in a just world, we can have no rational assurance that our moral sentiments or our intuitive convictions will lead us to coordinate our actions with those of others to a common end: our duties, even if somehow separately possessing a cognitive warrant, may not have a rational point. And we cannot be sure, even if this problem is resolved, that acting on moral directives will also be for our own good, as in the just world we could be assured it had to be. It is at this point, with the emergence of the very different views of Kant and Bentham—and not, as MacIntyre seems to think, earlier—that the rational justification of morality becomes an important issue. With it there emerges also the problem posed by the rationality of concern for one's own good in its distinctively modern form. The reason is the same in both cases. At this point it becomes clear that the way things go in the moral world is up to us. It is all our responsibility, and we must be able to justify whatever we do.

IV

The aim of MacIntyre's narrative is to lend support to his diagnosis of our present moral condition as one of disorder and confusion. Today's chaos is yesterday's order, wrecked by the loss of its foundation, the fixed human *telos*. To make sense of moral life, history shows, we must find a way to restore that base. Otherwise, the rules of morality will continue to seem arbitrary, the debates go on forever, moral discourse merely mask personal aims in impersonal language. In opposition to this, I have suggested that we should not accept MacIntyre's portrayal of morality as being, prior to the collapse, centered solely on directing agents to their naturally determined individual good. Morality was seen to have another function as well, that of coordinating efforts toward a good that could only come about through cooperation. So, the disappearance of the fixed-*telos* view of human nature did not leave behind it a morality whose substance was totally at odds with the nature of the agents whose actions it was to guide. As Hobbes makes evident, cooperation is as much a necessity for persons viewed mechanistically as for persons viewed teleologically. The nature of the good they must cooperate to produce may differ, but in either case it is indispensable.[4] And the existing morality, since it had functioned to guide cooperation when framed in teleological terms, could continue to guide it even when framed quite differently.

Thus, the continuity, of which MacIntyre makes so much, between the content of the older, "Aristotelian," morality and its Enlightenment descendant is no surprise, still less evidence of radical incoherence. What the continuity shows is that the vitality of the morality itself is greater than that of what MacIntyre views as its foundations. People cannot avoid living together and therefore cannot avoid having a morality. When an old common understanding of it ceases to be viable and supportive, there is a need to replace it with a new one, which will do better at helping people continue the effort to sustain a just moral world. Changes in science and religious belief may have eroded the old understanding, and the new one may have to accommodate new criteria of what is generally acceptable to reasonable people, but morality itself sets some of the criteria. It does not merely respond to those established by scientific practice. To ignore this is to fall victim to one of the deeper prejudices of contemporary analytic philosophy, that of seeing morality as always the dependent variable in the history of thought. MacIntyre seems, surprisingly, to have constructed his history on this basis. But the facts to which he has drawn attention suggest that it is not obvious that moralities are abandoned because what we now locate as their foundations have been.

If we examine our present situation and its dynamics in this light, it will not look quite the way it does from MacIntyre's historical perspective. A number of issues might illustrate this. I will touch briefly on a few, beginning with a point about the language of morality.

If morality provides the framework for just cooperation, we need not see its language as being in the grave disorder that MacIntyre portrays. The distinction between impersonal and personal appeals to others and the idea that morality involves reasonable objective standards make sense in terms of the belief that those to whom we are speaking share with us the wish to sustain a moral community. Our very use of moral language is to be taken as an indication that we draw a distinction between aims, ideals, interests, and desires that can be publicly accommodated within such a community and those that cannot. We do not need to have a fixed human *telos* or an authoritative divinity to make sense of this distinction or to see that there continues to be a point in making it. Of course, some people will use the language of morality for private (or class-based) manipulative purposes. But history does not give us any reason to suppose that the language itself has lost its function and is therefore in disorder.

The "interminable" current debates about different views of justice, abortion, war, and so on, which MacIntyre takes as further evidence of moral disintegration, also look different in the perspective of a more adequate history than his. If deliberate cooperation is to be possible, the cooperating agents must be able to rely on one another. This requires, among other things, that each be able to be sure that others have both appropriate instructions about what to do and appropriate motivation to do it. In a neutral universe, there is only one way in which we can be sure that others have the appropriate moral instructions—which must be the same for everyone. That is by relying on received opinion, the positive morality of one's community. But to be sure that everyone has a stake in the cooperative venture, and so is motivated to try to continue it, that venture must represent everyone's concerns fairly. In a neutral universe, there is no a priori reason to suppose that commonsense morality does so. In fact, in particular areas we have good reason to suppose that it does not. The problem facing modern morality in this respect can, therefore, be described as that of sustaining a common core of received opinion while reforming it so as to make it responsive to the deepest concerns of all who are to live according to it. The moral community must respond to hitherto unrecognized interests of persons who are already members but some of whose aspirations have in the past been flouted, suppressed, or rejected as immoral. And it must look toward increased interaction with other moral communities with vastly different historical backgrounds, working out common modalities with them. It may be argued that both of these difficulties are greater now than they have been at any time in the past, though one should perhaps be suspicious of a claim of this kind, which seems to be made by every generation. But at any rate we need not look at these "interminable debates" as showing that the fabric of morality is in tatters. We can see them, rather, as testing the extent to which different concerns can be publicly accommodated within a single moral community.

As I indicated earlier, debates of this kind have been a recurrent feature of the history of morality. Their upshot is not to destroy it but to alter received opinion so as to include within it new sets of understandings concerning some vexed area of life, such as lending money at interest or divorce or voting. We cannot know a priori what interests or principled commitments or ideals people will try to incorporate publicly into our common life, and so we cannot know a priori what tests a sense of moral community will have to sustain. We can be sure that we will bring our existing understandings to current debates, and we will naturally try to make them explicit by stating them as rules or principles. Explicit articulations make sense where unspoken consensus seems to have reached its limits. An appeal to principle is a way of seeing whether that consensus can be projected into a novel area of controversy. Statements of rules and principles thus have a social function in this sort of context, one quite different from that often envisaged by moral philosophers but important nonetheless. If the deontic and teleological aspects of morality are not MacIntyrean fragments left alone of a temple once complete, neither are they simply contenders for the dignity of being the epistemological starting points of moral knowledge. They are, as we would expect from our historical perspective, inevitable functional elements in what we view as a complex cooperative enterprise. Debate about them is a way of discussing the stresses that arise when the justness of some feature of the enterprise is challenged or when it is questioned whether its point is adequate. It is not simply a futile endeavor by all the king's philosophers to put Humpty-Dumpty together again.

V

I have argued that MacIntyre does not present compelling reason based on current data to accept his portrayal of our culture as in a state of moral collapse and that a historical narrative more adequate than his would not lead to that conclusion either. If this is correct, then we are not forced to choose between an unacceptable Nietzschean nihilism and MacIntyre's revised Aristotelianism. But MacIntyre holds that "arguments in philosophy rarely take the form of proof, and the most successful arguments on topics central to philosophy never do" (AV 241). He insists from the beginning that his view will necessarily seem implausible and that presently accepted philosophical stances will not enable us to find truly basic "disorders of moral thought and practice" (AV 2-5). My criticisms thus far may seem, therefore, to have failed to touch the nerve of his position. They look like just one more reassertion of precisely that modernist stance that MacIntyre is attempting not to refute but to undermine. To come to grips with this we must examine the nature of his own enterprise.

The key is to be found in MacIntyre's notion of an epistemological crisis.[5] Such a crisis arises, he says, when a new discovery casts doubt not just on a particular belief or a set of beliefs but on a whole conceptual scheme, including "criteria of truth, intelligibility, and rationality" (EC 455). For example, one might face such a crisis on learning that one's spouse does not and never did love one. Then, one's whole past would have to be reinterpreted, because one would be faced with "alternative and rival schemata which yield mutually incompatible accounts" of what happened (EC 454).

The crisis is resolved only when the agent can construct a new narrative of the past, one that "enables the agent to understand *both* how he or she could intelligibly have held his or her original beliefs *and* how he or she could have been so drastically misled by them" (EC 455). MacIntyre uses this idea to illuminate "epistemological progress" generally (EC 456) and in particular to cover scientific revolutions. Galileo's work, he says, shows how a new, more adequate theory enables us to understand older theories that we now see to be inadequate, for only after Galileo could we distinguish real counterexamples to medieval theories from mere anomalies justifiably handled by "ad hoc explanatory devices." Nor is it an accident that a successful theory enables us to do this. "The criterion of a successful theory," MacIntyre asserts, "is that it enables us to understand its predecessors in a newly intelligible way" (EC 460). MacIntyre's aim is to combine a modified Kuhnian view of scientific revolution with a narrativist perspective to show that scientific reason is "subordinate to, and intelligible only in terms of, historical reason. And," he adds, "if this is true of the natural sciences, *a fortiori* it will be true also of the social sciences" (EC 464; cf. 467). This general idea, I believe, guides MacIntyre's study of morality. Society is in a moral crisis — the practical equivalent of an epistemological crisis — and only historical understanding, arising ultimately from a new theory, will enable us to see where we are and where to go.

This brings together a number of features of MacIntyre's position. It gives a broader base to his insistence on the importance of narrative history for understanding moral problems.[6] It explains why he stresses understanding different societies through their stories (e.g., AV 201), for he also holds that what ends up as science begins in the "myths or fairy stories which are essential to a well-ordered childhood" (EC 456). It puts in its rightful central place MacIntyre's concern with deep shifts in the entire framework of morality, rather than disagreements within a shared scheme (e.g., AV 161-62). It helps us to understand his very strong view on the unity of theory and practice in morality. And it enables us to see why MacIntyre is so willing to say that his diagnosis of our times is one that is necessarily implausible, masked by the present structure of the academic disciplines (AV 4). For he says that the structure of an epistemological crisis and that of a paranoid frame of mind are not wholly dissimilar (EC 462-63).

There is some difficulty in mounting direct arguments against a critique of our culture and its philosophy that has this structure, and I do not propose to embark on criticism of MacIntyre's general theory of epistemological crisis. Still, there are two kinds of consideration that might tell against the paradigm charge that MacIntyre is recommending. The first uses a test that MacIntyre himself proposes for the superiority of one theory or paradigm over another. We have, in fact, already traversed this ground, since the test he proposes is historical. It is, he says, rational to accept a later theory or paradigm and reject an earlier one if from the standpoint of the later, "the acceptance, the life-story, and the rejection of the previous theory or paradigm can be recounted in more intelligible historical narrative than previously" (EC 467). My historical sketch was meant to raise doubts that MacIntyre's history, inspired by a virtue-centered theory, is more intelligible, or better, than one not so inspired. The second kind of consideration has to do with the coherence of MacIntyre's execution of his project. The key question here is what it takes, on his view, for morality to be "in order." I am not at all sure that I have found the answer to this question. Several possibilities are suggested by the text.

Because of the stress on the significance of disagreement in showing that we are in a moral crisis, we naturally think first that MacIntyre would consider a morality "in order" only if it contained a method for obtaining rational agreement on any moral question that might arise. This would make him an ally of Kant and Bentham at their most extreme. But he criticizes Aristotle for not allowing for tragic conflict within morality and makes ample room for it in his own theory (AV 153, 183). Moreover, he insists that "there are bound to be occasions on which no formula is available in advance" to give clear guidance (AV 143). So, this cannot be what he requires for a morality to be "in order." The next plausible candidate for the criterion of order is the existence of a rational justification or vindication of the basic principles of morals. MacIntyre presents the failure of Enlightenment philosophers to come up with such a justification as the central episode in our culture's sorry descent into moral crisis, and he repeatedly tells us that it is the absence of such a justification that makes us all into emotivists in practice (AV 38, 111). But it would be puzzling if this were MacIntyre's criterion, for, in his own neo-Aristotelian theory, he does not offer anything readily recognizable as such a justification. He finds rock bottom in a functional vocabulary whose terms moral agents use to think of their own deepest personal identity. These terms, he says, are inherited from the community in which one is born and educated. As his own historical study of the virtues makes clear, such terms change through time and vary from community to community. It is, therefore, hard to see how they can have any purely rational justification or vindication.[7]

We may, nonetheless, have a clue here to MacIntyre's implicit criterion. He may think that morality is "in order" only if it somehow rests on a shared vocabulary that simply cannot be put in doubt. (He tells us that even Descartes was unable to doubt what he inherited in the languages he used [EC 458].) If we must use an inherited, shared vocabulary for self-description and if, as MacIntyre tries to make out, the terms of that vocabulary are functional, then we will have that shared, unquestioned framework for evaluations that is so sadly lacking from contemporary culture. This idea of what MacIntyre thinks it takes for morality to be "in order" fits in well with his denunciations of emotivist selves with "no necessary social content" or identity (AV 30). It also enables us to make sense of the otherwise baffling claim that Diderot, Hume, Kant, Kierkegaard, Bentham, and Gewirth all tried to work out some one thing called a foundation for morality, which MacIntyre himself has alone found. What, after all would come even close to describing all of the endeavors referred to in that assertion if not the statement that they are all quests for something indubitable?

If this, or anything like it, is MacIntyre's root thought about what it would take for morality to be "in order," then two observations are called for. First, there is a striking discrepancy between MacIntyre's treatment of morality and his treatment of science. He tells us that in science we must think that the theory we presently accept is a closer approximation to the truth than earlier views, but we need not think that we have now gotten to a final truth. Satisfactory and workable acceptance of a scientific theory is compatible with admitting both that we might be mistaken and that future radical changes might be necessary (EC 464-67). In short, no unquestionable vocabulary or principle is required for science to be "in order." Morality is required to meet a sterner test. It is because it currently fails to do so that MacIntyre tells us we have no rational vindication for it and are emotivist in practice. But, if we are to see science as having moved away from any need for unalterable foundations and unquestionable vocabularies, why should we not see morality as making a similar transition? If we did so, we could interpret meta-ethics generally as part of the experimentation involved in learning to live cooperatively in a world in which we cannot have certainties of the kind our predecessor culture had. Philosophical emotivism might be seen historically as having arisen from exaggeration of the contrast between morality and science, from noting an absence of unshakable foundations in morality while believing them to be present in science. MacIntyre's criterion would require us to exaggerate the difference in the other direction. But it is unclear why we should insist on this difference at all.

Second, MacIntyre does not put his criterion for morality's being "in order" in any historical perspective. He is prepared to be historicist to the extent of relativizing the truth of some basic ideas about the status of morality to the moralities embedded in different cultures. He has given us a historical account of the rise of the demand for a rational vindication of morality as it affected our predecessor culture and affects our own. But his account does not cover certain vital features of that demand: that it was from the start apparently a demand for an indubitably certain foundation and that it became a demand for a principle capable of supporting a comprehensive method for decision making. He himself seems to have abandoned the latter of these demands while retaining the former. As I have frequently said, he uses this demand as the basis for his critical diagnosis of our culture. But he has given us no historical account that might justify the demand by showing that the conditions that once made it appropriate still obtain. And, if, as I have argued, a more comprehensive picture of the history of ethics than his does not lead to his diagnosis, than he must admit, I think, either that his diagnosis is badly off the mark or that history is quite irrelevant to it.[8]

Notes

1. *After Virtue* (Notre Dame, Ind.: University of Notre Dame Press, 1981). All page references to this book will be given in the text, indicated by the letters AV.

2. I argue this in "Virtue, Narrative, and Community: MacIntyre and Morality," *Journal of Philosophy* Vol. LXXIX (1982).

3. "The most striking feature of contemporary moral utterance is that so much of it is used to express moral disagreements" (AV 6). Indeed; and the most striking fact about modern science is that so much of it is concerned with problems we have not solved. Science is there to solve problems; morality, to resolve disagreements. Outside the classroom, why should we expect to dwell on what is settled?

4. MacIntyre thinks that the "notion of the political community as a common project is alien to the modern liberal individualist world" (AV 146). This is a more complex issue than MacIntyre allows. The persistence in our schools of courses in civics and American history suggests

that we still think it essential to educate our children to understand the special values of our form of democratic society, even if we think of the political community in a libertarian, minimalist way as being no more than the communally guaranteed safe arena for pursuit of private good. This does not make us into a Greek city-state. It does give us some shared values.

5. For this I draw on his "Epistemological Crises, Dramatic Narrative, and the Philosophy of Science," *The Monist*, Vol. 60 (1977), pp. 453-72. Page references are given in the text indicated by the letters EC.

6. It is worth noting that MacIntyre develops an additional theory of the role of narrative in knowledge and understanding in the latter part of his book. It is used to provide a foundation for part of his view of virtue. See especially Chapter 15 of *After Virtue*.

7. MacIntyre promises us a new theory of practical rationality (AV 242). Perhaps when we have it, this difficulty will vanish.

8. Versions of this paper have been read at Harvard, the New York Philosophy Club, and the Washington Area Philosophy Club. I am grateful to members of those audiences, and to Prof. Richard Flathman of Johns Hopkins University, for helpful comments and criticism.

Contributors

Notes on Contributors

Robert Merrihew Adams is Professor of Philosophy at the University of California, Los Angeles. He has published articles in metaphysics, ethics, and the philosophy of religion, as well as in the history of early modern philosophy.

Richard E. Aquila is Professor of Philosophy at The University of Tennessee. He is author of *Intentionality: A Study of Mental Acts* and *Representational Mind: A Study of Kant's Theory of Knowledge*. He has published numerous articles in major philosophical journals.

Margaret Atherton is an Assistant Professor at the University of Wisconsin-Milwaukee. She has written papers in the philosophy of mind and the history of philosophy, including several about Locke.

Jonathan Bennett teaches philosophy at Syracuse University. His most recent completed works in the field of early modern philosophy are (with Peter Remnant) a translation and edition of Leibniz's *New Essays on Human Understanding* and a book entitled *Spinoza's Ethics* (forthcoming).

Willis Doney is Professor of Philosophy at Dartmouth College. His interests focus on the theory of knowledge and the history of philosophy in the seventeenth and eighteenth centuries, and his publications include articles on Descartes, Spinoza, Malebranche, Locke, and Berkeley.

Klaus Düsing is Professor of Philosophy at the University of Siegen (West Germany). He is author of German books about Kant's teleology, Hegel's logic, Hegel and the history of philosophy, and he has published articles on Kant, Hegel, ancient philosophy, and modern phenomenology. He is coeditor of Volume VI of the new critical Hegel edition.

Paul Feyerabend holds appointments at the University of California, Berkeley, and the Federal Institute of Technology in Zürich. He has held previous appointments at Bristol, London, Berlin, New Haven, and Auckland.

Richard Fumerton is Associate Professor of Philosophy at the University of Iowa. He has published papers in epistemology, metaphysics, philosophy of science, and ethics.

Daniel Garber is Associate Professor of Philosophy at the University of Chicago. His recent work includes studies in seventeenth- and eighteenth-century philosophy and science and in contemporary philosophy of science. Under preparation is an annotated edition of Part II of Berkeley's *Principles of Human Knowledge*.

Moltke Gram is Professor of Philosophy at the University of Iowa. His publications include *Kant, Ontology and the A priori; The Ontological Turn; Interpreting Kant; Kant: Disputed Questions;* and *Direct Realism: A Study of Perception*. He has also published numerous articles and monographs in metaphysics and the history of modern philosophy.

S. D. Guttenplan is Lecturer in Philosophy at Birkbeck College, University of London, and assistant editor of *Mind*.

D. W. Hamlyn is Professor of Philosophy of Birkbeck College, University of London, and Editor of *Mind*. He is a past president of the Aristotelian Society and author of several books, one of which is *Schopenhauer*.

Eli Hirsch is Professor of Philosophy at Long Island University, Brooklyn. He is the author of *The Concept of Identity*.

Philip Kitcher is Associate Professor of Philosophy at the University of Vermont. He is the author of *Abusing Science: The Case against Creationism* and *The Nature of Mathematical Knowledge*. He has published articles on topics in the philosophy of mathematics, the philosophy of science, and Kant.

Charles Landesman is Professor and Chairman of the Department of Philosophy of Hunter College of the City University of New York. His publications include *Discourse and Its Presuppositions*.

Peter Machamer is Professor and Chairman of the Department of History and Philosophy of Science at the University of Pittsburgh. He has done work on a number of topics dealing with sixteenth- and seventeenth-century philosophy and science.

Rudolf Malter is Professor of Philosophy at Johannes Gutenberg-Universität in Mainz (West Germany). He is first vice-president of the Schopenhauer-Gesellschaft. He has written articles on Kant and the history of Kantianism, Schopenhauer, Luther and the philosophy of the Reformation, and on subjects in aesthetics, metaphysics, and epistemology.

Ruth Mattern teaches the history of modern philosophy and the philosophy of medicine at Rice University, where she is Associate Professor. She has published articles on Locke, Descartes, and Spinoza.

Arthur Melnick is Associate Professor of Philosophy at the University of Illinois. He is the author of *Kant's Analogies of Experience* and is presently completing a book titled *Kant's Theory of Space, Time and Thought.*

Peter H. Nidditch, late Professor of Philosophy at the University of Sheffield, was the general editor of the Clarendon Edition of the Works of John Locke. His recent publications include "Preface to the Grammar of Postulates" and critical editions of Draft A and Draft B of Locke's *Essay.*

Francis Jeffrey Pelletier is Associate Professor of Philosophy and Computing Science at the University of Alberta and an executive editor of the *Canadian Journal of Philosophy.*

J. B. Schneewind is Chairman of the Department of Philosophy at Johns Hopkins University and works primarily in the history of moral philosophy. His major book is *Sidgwick's Ethics and Victorian Moral Philosophy.* He is currently studying the period from Montaigne to Kant.

R. C. Sleigh, Jr., is currently a member of the School of Historical Studies at the Institute for Advanced Study in Princeton. He has authored articles on intensionality and epistemic logic and, more recently, articles on Leibniz.

Morris Weitz, late Richard Koret Professor of Philosophy at Brandeis University, was the author of many articles on aesthetics and the philosophy of language. His last book was *The Opening Mind: A Philosophical Study of Humanistic Concepts.*

T. E. Wilkerson is Lecturer in Philosophy at Nottingham University. He is the author of *Minds, Brains and People, Kant's Critique of Pure Reason: A Commentary for Students* and many articles on a wide range of topics.

Margaret D. Wilson is Professor of Philosophy at Princeton University. She is the author of *Descartes*, as well as numerous articles on seventeenth- and eighteenth-century philosophy, and is editor of *The Essential Descartes.*

Peter A. French is Lennox Distinguished Professor of Philosophy and chairman of the philosophy department at Trinity University in San Antonio, Texas. He has served as research professor in the Center for the Study of Values at the University of Delaware and is the author of *The Scope of Morality* and several other books in philosophy. **Theodore E. Uehling, Jr.**, is professor of philosophy at the University of Minnesota, Morris. He is the author of *The Notion of Form in Kant's Critique of Aesthetic Judgment* and articles on the philosophy of Kant. **Howard K. Wettstein** is visiting associate professor of philosophy at Stanford University and associate professor of philosophy at the University of Minnesota, Morris.